ARTHUR M. WEIMER, Ph.D., University of Chicago, M.A.I., S.R.A., is Professor of Real Estate and Land Economics, Savings and Loan Professor of Business Administration, and Special Assistant to the President at Indiana University. He was for many years Dean of the School of Business at that institution. Dr. Weimer is President of Business and Real Estate Trends, Inc., and is a director of several companies and organizations. He serves as consulting economist for the U. S. Savings and Loan League, and is a past president of the American Finance Association and the American Association of Collegiate Schools of Business.

HOMER HOYT, J.D., Ph.D. University of Chicago, M.A.I., is President of Homer Hoyt Associates, consulting real estate economists. Dr. Hoyt previously taught economics at the Universities of North Carolina and Missouri, Columbia University, and Massachusetts Institute of Technology. A Member of the Supreme Court Bar, Dr. Hoyt has served as Principal Housing Economist of the Federal Housing Administration. His firm has conducted economic, market, and appraisal surveys for many nationally known real estate projects.

GEORGE F. BLOOM, D.B.A., Indiana University, M.A.I., S.R.A, is Professor of Real Estate and Real Estate Director at Indiana University. He has been active in the development of educational programs for the American Institute of Real Estate Appraisers and the Society of Real Estate Appraisers. He helped develop the Indiana State Approved Real Estate Salesmen's Course, and was founding president of the American Real Estate and Urban Economics Association. Dr. Bloom is Director of Real Estate Education of the Foundation for Economic and Business Studies, and Director of the Indiana Realtors Institute.

# REAL ESTATE

**ARTHUR M. WEIMER**
INDIANA UNIVERSITY

**HOMER HOYT**
HOMER HOYT ASSOCIATES

**GEORGE F. BLOOM**
INDIANA UNIVERSITY

## SIXTH EDITION

THE RONALD PRESS COMPANY · NEW YORK

Library of Congress Catalog Card Number: 78–190214
PRINTED IN THE UNITED STATES OF AMERICA

# Preface

In preparing the Sixth Edition the authors have tried to build upon and strengthen those features that have made this book a widely used introduction to the field of real estate.

Thus this volume continues to offer a decision-oriented approach to the subject, starting with basic concepts that provide a foundation for subsequent analytical discussions of trends and problems. Consideration is given to the physical, legal, and economic aspects of real estate, governmental and business conditions, regional and local economic trends, real estate markets, location factors, and appraising methods. The student is introduced to practical problems of decision making and implementing in the areas of real estate production, marketing, and financing. The final chapters provide an overview of several kinds of properties and problems including housing, urban trends, commercial and industrial real estate, farms, forests, recreational land and international real estate trends.

Emphasis is placed on the special characteristics of real estate decisions in comparison to decisions in other business areas—particularly those factors related to income production at fixed sites. Throughout, an effort has been made to show the relationships between the real estate business and other areas of business administration, between real estate resources and other types of resources, and between the social, economic, political and environmental problems of the real estate sector and the American economy as a whole.

The book has a forward-looking orientation. Past experience and current knowledge are presented in a manner calculated to help in the solution of future problems. The "why" rather than the "how to" approach is stressed, although a number of typical applications of general concepts are presented in the cases and study projects, which are placed at the end of each chapter. Revised and updated review questions are provided for all cases and projects.

Some of those who have used previous editions have provided suggestions for improving the book's effectiveness. For these the authors are particularly grateful. As a result of such suggestions certain consolidations of subject matter have been made, along with a slight change in the order of presentation.

ARTHUR M. WEIMER
HOMER HOYT
GEORGE F. BLOOM

February, 1972

# Acknowledgments

It is not possible to recognize all of the assistance that has been provided for the various editions of this book. We are much indebted to former students, colleagues and friends in business, government and the academic community.

We are indebted especially to the following faculty members of Indiana University: Troy J. Cauley, D. Lyle Dieterle, Edward E. Edwards, J. C. Halterman, Charles M. Hewitt, Edward J. Kuntz, John D. Long, Harold F. Lusk, E. W. Martin, Jr., John F. Mee, Robert R. Milroy, S. F. Otteson, Mrs. D. Jeanne Patterson, W. George Pinnell, John H. Porter, Donald H. Sauer, Howard L. Timms, Robert C. Turner, and L. L. Waters. The current classes in Indiana University's Graduate Program in Real Estate and Land Economics helped in reviewing the materials for the Sixth Edition as well as various of the new study projects and cases.

We appreciate especially the suggestions provided by Fred E. Case of the University of California, Los Angeles; James E. Gillies of York University; E. Norman Bailey, University of Iowa; and Robert O. Harvey of the University of Connecticut.

Assistance with the current edition or with earlier editions was also provided by Lyle C. Bryant, Washington, D. C.; Norman Strunk, U. S. Savings and Loan League; Arthur E. Warner, University of Tennessee; Earl L. Butz, Secretary of Agriculture; Robert C. Suter and Ed Lott of Purdue University; Maurice Seldin, American University; Gail E. Mullin, Kent State University; Ernest M. Fisher, formerly of Columbia University; Richard U. Ratcliff, University of British Columbia; James R. Price, George E. Price, David Price, William J. McCullough, and Frank Flynn of the National Homes Corporation; David W. Thompson, Peat, Marwick, Mitchell and Company; and a number of others, including: L. Durward

v

Badgley, Frederick M. Babcock, Paul I. Cripe, Albert E. Dickens, Carl F. Distelhorst, Curt C. Mack, and Herman O. Walther.

Editorial and research assistance was provided by Richard L. Haney, Jr., and Richard May. We are especially grateful to those who helped to prepare the book for publication, including Mrs. Pat Hall, who carried the major share of the work, Mrs. Charlotte Pitcher and Mrs. Doris Horn.

A.M.W.<br>H.H.<br>G.F.B.

# Contents

## Part II.   ANALYSIS FOR REAL ESTATE DECISIONS

Outlook, Current Business Activity  ·  **Business Fluctuations:** Secular Trend, Seasonal Fluctuations, Cycles  ·  **Future Spending Patterns:** Consumers, Business, Government, Foreign Spending and Receipts  ·  **Gross National Product Method:** GNP Definition, Personal Consumption, Gross Private Domestic Investment, Export of Goods and Services, Government Purchases of Goods and Services, Total Output, National Income, Flow of Income  ·  **Flow of Funds:** Sources and Uses, Flow of Funds Accounts, Uses of Accounts  ·  **Other Methods of Analysis:** National Wealth Statistics, Input-Output Tables, Regional Studies  ·  **Industry Analysis:** Sales Data, Durables and Nondurables, Industry Cycles and Trends

Land Use, Social and Political Competition, Attitudes and Preferences, Physical Factors, Planning and Renewal, Anticipating Changes · **Urban Growth and Change:** Stages, Methods of Expansion, Topography, Land Use Patterns, Concentric Circles, Wider Dispersion · **Sector Theory— Residential Neighborhoods:** Outward Movement, Multiple Nuclei, Individuality of Regions · **Business Districts:** Central Districts, Outlying Centers, Shopping Centers · **Industrial Districts:** Bands and Clusters, Influence of Land Values · **Methods of Analyzing Land Use:** Time Interval Maps, Land Use Changes · **Future Metropolitan Patterns:** Dispersed Sheet, Galaxy, Core City, Urban Star, Ring, Diversity of Future Patterns, Toward Ecumenopolis?

Quantity Survey, Effective Age, Depreciation Tables, Depreciation Techniques, Land Value, Plottage Value, Valuation for Tax Assessment · **Correlation:** Judgment of Appraisers, Use of Data, General Rules for Data, Appraisal Report, Main Parts of Appraisal Report

## Part III.  REAL ESTATE DECISION AREAS

## APPENDIXES

# INTRODUCTION

We present a general overview of the field of real estate administration in the first chapter. A case study, "The Ambitious Student," points up some of the topics covered.

The second chapter discusses the subjects of real estate decisions and decision makers, comparing various decision problems in the real estate field with those in other areas of business. An interesting study project, which reviews the careers of several real estate entrepreneurs, helps to illustrate the discussions in Chapter 2.

Since the physical characteristics of real properties and their environment are of great importance, these topics are considered in the third chapter. A study project at the end of the chapter presents a review of major architectural styles.

Real estate is not simply a matter of land and buildings, but of property rights in these physical things; thus, the legal aspects are reviewed briefly in the fourth chapter.

The final chapter of the Introduction considers the major economic characteristics of real estate. Both the physical and legal characteristics of real property have an important bearing on their economic worth, which depends basically on their income-producing capacity. Income may be derived from the direct use of the property as in the case of a home owner or a business occupying its own building, or income may take the form of monetary returns.

Real estate income must be produced at a fixed site. The economic units are relatively large and they have a long life. Local factors play a major role in markets which are characterized by relatively fixed supplies. Governmental factors play an important role in the utilization of private properties.

# 1

# The Field of Real Estate Administration

## IMPORTANCE OF REAL ESTATE DECISIONS

Each of us uses real estate every day. Real estate provides shelter, protection, comfort, convenience, privacy and other things. Real estate may be a factory, a home, a store, a drive-in hamburger shop, a motel or a golf course. Business firms need a place of business—a store, office, plant, or other parcel of real estate—in order to carry on operations. Farms and ranches, of course, rely heavily on real estate. Govenmental, educational, religious and cultural institutions all make use of real estate. We live in homes of many types. Our real estate resources—the homes, factories, office buildings, stores, shopping centers, farms, rights of way, roads, streets, parks, recreational areas, and other kinds—represent more than half of our national wealth.

Obviously, the decisions made with respect to resources of this magnitude have an important effect on the well-being of our people, the success or failure of business firms, and the general prosperity of the country. Effective utilization of real estate resources requires good decisions on the part of owners and users, whether they are home owners or the managers of business firms, those engaged in the real estate business, or the officials of government agencies and quasi-public institutions.

### Improving Real Estate Decisions

Decisions made by business executives, government officials, or private citizens determine the amount and kind of real estate resources we have and the effectiveness with which they are used. Thus, we may begin our discussion by suggesting that a major objective of studying this field is that of improving decisions relating to real estate resources.

For example, a business manager faced with a decision regarding the choice of a site for a new plant needs an understanding of real estate resources and the forces that affect them. As a minimum, he needs enough knowledge to make use of the assistance of specialists in the field. Similarly, a government official who must decide on an appropriate tax rate for real property needs at least a basic familiarity with this field. A private citizen trying to decide whether to buy or build a home or to continue to rent housing facilities will be aided greatly by a knowledge of this area of study. The owner or manager of a firm in the real estate business, of course, needs a command of this field of knowledge.

## Implementing Decisions

We are concerned, however, not only with the improvement of decisions relating to real estate but also with the *implementation* of such decisions. Thus, we are interested in the processes of putting decisions into effect, of "getting things done" that decisions indicate should be done —or stated in another way, the administrative or management process. Hence, we might state the general objective of our study of this subject as the improvement of decision-making and implementation in the real estate field, both with respect to the utilization of real estate resources and the operation of real estate enterprises.

## Study Objectives

Your interest in this subject may arise from several sources. As a user, an owner, or potential owner of real estate, or as an investor in real property or securities based on real estate, you will need information about its uses and capacity to produce income. As an owner, manager, or employee of a business firm, or of a governmental or institutional agency, you will find a knowledge of this subject highly useful. If you are now connected with the real estate business or intend to engage in it, you have a particular interest in the study of this subject. As a voter, you are concerned with such problems as property taxation, land planning, zoning, environmental controls, slum clearance, housing programs, and the general efficiency with which we make use of our real estate resources.

## Future Needs

As we have suggested above, a major objective of studying this field is that of improving decisions relating to real estate resources. Such decisions may have major significance for our future prosperity and well-

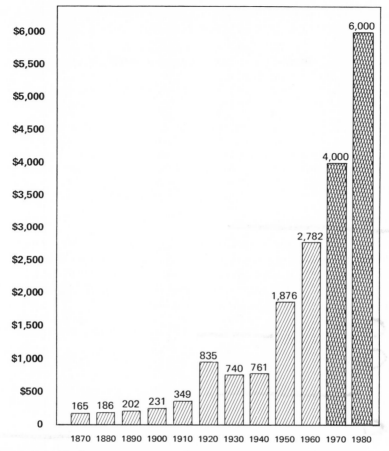

**Fig. 1–1.** Market economy growth—per capita gross national product in current U. S. dollars. (Source: Statistical Abstract of the U. S.; projections by economic analysis and study, Chamber of Commerce of the United States.)

being. Recent projections indicate that prospects for economic development to the year 2000 are highly favorable. By that time, there may be some 300 million people in this country (compared to 204 million in 1970); the labor force will increase somewhat more rapidly than total population because of age composition; the gross national product (the total output of goods and services) may advance from the trillion dollar level in the early 1970's to over $2 trillion by 2000 (in 1970 dollars). Disposable personal income for the average family may advance from somewhat over $7,000 to around $10,000 by 1980 to perhaps $15,000 by the year 2000 (in constant dollars). Perry Prentice has made a dramatic statement regarding growth potential in this field:

> Week after week, year after year, each average week from now to 1999 urban America will need to build the equivalent of another brand new city with nearly 70,000 population!
> I don't just mean that every week, week after week, year after year, we will need to build enough more homes to house 70,000 more people. We will also need to build, week after week, enough more stores for 70,000 more people to shop in, enough more places of business for 70,000 more people to work in, enough more recreation facilities for 70,000 more people to play in and at the same time, week after week, year after year, we will need to add all the new streets, new schools, new colleges, new hospitals, new water supply systems, new sewage and sewage disposal systems, new transit facilities, new police and fire facilities, etc., etc., etc., needed for a city of 70,000 people.[1]

## Decisions and Future Trends

Decisions affecting the utilization of real estate resources will play a major role in making many future developments possible. Reaching sound decisions in the real estate area will not be a simple matter because of a number of important current trends, which undoubtedly, will continue. Consider, for example, the following:

1. There will be more people, and they will require proportionally more resources for their support.
2. Housing will be one of our more difficult problems, in part because of the greater number of people, but also because people will demand better housing; for example, the two-house family will become more commonplace as larger blocks of leisure time become available.
3. People will be increasingly concerned with the quality of life, for example, problems of environmental pollution will come in for greater attention.
4. People will continue to move about a good deal, and the population is likely to be increasingly mobile.
5. The rate of technological and scientific change will continue to accelerate. The "knowledge explosion" will mean higher rates of obsolescence for many real properties.
6. The scientific and technological revolution may help us to find solutions to congestion and pollution, including sanitation and waste disposal, air purification, better and more reliable water supplies, and related problems.
7. Although we have solved some of our longer-distance transportation problems, shorter-distance and local transportation continue to present some very difficult challenges. It may be that travel

[1] Perry Prentice, Speech to National Association of Real Estate Boards, 1970, by permission.

requirements can be reduced by improved communications facilities such as the wider use of closed-circuit television, interconnecting computer centers, phonovision and similar developments.

8. Some people will continue to move to suburban areas, to new towns and developments and away from central cities. Other people will continue to desire the excitement and stimulation that is often associated with some of the more highly concentrated and older parts of our cities.

9. Business firms will move about even more than in the past in search of desirable locations. At one time, factories and stores concentrated in or near city centers; recent years have seen the decentralization of such installations to suburban and rural areas. These trends are likely to continue, but many new developments may also emerge.

10. Increasing attention may be given to problems of the local area and region. Problems of local government will be given more attention. The impact of local taxes on real estate resources is likely to be especially heavy.

11. There are likely to be increasing demands for land planning and zoning regulations related to environmental control. The problems of imposing regulations and still making provision for enough flexibility so as not to inhibit growth and development are difficult ones indeed.

We could add to this recital of important factors likely to affect our lives and to complicate the problems of the real estate decision-maker. Interesting and dramatic as the events of recent years have been, the future promises to be even more challenging and demanding, particularly for those with interests in the dynamic field of real estate decision-making and implementing.

## METHODS OF STUDY

Real estate provides some unusual study opportunities in terms of the properties as well as the people engaged in this field of activity. Real estate markets are unique. And real estate involves many types of papers and documents.

### Study of Properties

The study of the real estate field provides an unusual form of "laboratory work." The house or apartment building in which you live, a store, a farm, a vacant lot or any other piece of real property with which you are familiar can serve as an excellent starting point for your study of this subject. You can use it as your own special laboratory for analyzing the various materials you will be studying, especially those that pertain to real properties and to the forces that affect the decisions of people regarding them. This should become your "study property."

Your home neighborhood and the town or city in which your study property is located may also be considered as a part of your laboratory. Decisions in regard to every parcel of real estate are affected by its surroundings, since it is a *share* in the community of which it forms a part. By carefully training your powers of observation, you can learn a great deal about the effects of economic, political, and social forces on the uses to which people put different types of real estate, on the trends of real estate values, and on business and personal decisions.

### Study of People

Another interesting method of studying this subject is through discussions with people who are in one or another branch of the real estate business or who dabble in real estate investments. Find out what their experiences indicate as the most important things to learn about real estate. Discuss career opportunities in real estate or related fields. Ask about current conditions in the real estate market and about potential market changes. Inquire about trends of land uses and the development of new subdivisions, shopping centers, and industrial locations. Find out about real estate investment possibilities. Study major transportation changes and especially projected new developments. Consider changes in the central city including urban renewal projects. Look into tax changes, zoning regulations, building codes, community controls, and related developments.

### Study of Markets

Market forces, both national and local, have important effects on real estate. Such forces, of course, are the results of billions of decisions made by millions of people. Local market factors are especially important in their influence on residential real estate. Each local real estate market has its own unique characteristics. Even a small operator in the real estate field, whose interests may be centered in a single area, can often be of great help to you in gaining an understanding of local market conditions and trends.

### Study of Documents

In addition, people who are actively engaged in business—especially those in real estate practice—will supply you with examples of the many forms and documents that are involved in real estate transactions. Sales agreements, listing agreements, deeds, leases, sales contracts, mortgages, and many other documents are in constant use.  It is often easier to learn about these from actual cases and situations than from merely reading descriptions of them in books.

## Study Techniques

Development of your ability to read, write, and speak properly, and to handle basic mathematics should be one of the important results of work in this field.  Clear and precise writing is an essential tool for everyone engaged in business.  The development of proficiency in writing and clarity of expression is a process that should go on throughout life.

## Franklin's Methods

Of interest in this connection is Benjamin Franklin's description of the process by which he taught himself to write clearly:

About this time I met with an odd volume of the Spectator.  I had never before seen any of them.  I bought it, read it over and was much delighted with it.  I thought the writing excellent, and wished if possible to imitate it. With that view I took some of the papers, and making short hints of the sentiments in each sentence, laid them by a few days, and then without looking at the book tried to complete the papers again, by expressing each hinted sentiment at length and as fully as it had been expressed before in any suitable words that should occur to me.  Then I compared my Spectator with an original, discovered some of my faults, and corrected them.  I also sometimes jumbled my collection of hints and confusion, and after some weeks endeavored to reduce them into the best order, before I began to form the full sentences and complete the subject.  This was to teach me method in the arrangement of the thoughts.  By comparing my work with the original, I discovered many faults and corrected them; but I sometimes had the pleasure to fancy, that in particulars of small consequence, I had been fortunate enough to improve the method or the language, and this encouraged me to think that I might in time come to be a tolerable English writer, of which I was extremely ambitious.

## Reading, Listening, Calculating

In recent years considerable attention has been given to increasing the speed of reading and the rate of comprehending written materials.  By constant practice, you can improve greatly your capacity to read.

Another ability that is valuable in the field of real estate, as it is in many other areas, is that of listening.  Many of us fail to learn because we are not good listeners.  Many a promising business transaction has failed to develop because one or another of the parties involved failed to listen carefully enough to make possible a real understanding or a meeting of minds.  Listening requires attention and concentration.  It also requires constant practice.

The real estate field, like other business fields, deals to a considerable extent with figures, financial statements, and accounting reports of various types. Thus, your ability to use basic mathematics, accounting, and statistics should be developed in the course of studying this subject. You should become familiar with the work of the computer, since its role is expanding rapidly in the business world.

## Creative Thinking

One of the important abilities you should acquire through your study of this subject or others is that of producing ideas. Sometimes it is called creative thinking. Professor John F. Mee has summarized the steps in this process as follows: first, selection and definition of the problem; second, exploration and preparation; third, the development of partial solutions or hypotheses; fourth, the stage of incubating ideas, mulling over the problem, or engaging in "unconscious cerebration"; fifth, illumination or the appearance of the idea; and last, verification and application of the idea.[2] He also suggested the possibilities of "causative thinking," which is the development of an image of a desired future situation or event and then thinking back from it to identify the steps necessary to bring it about.

Since all business progress, including that in the real estate field, depends greatly on new methods, techniques, and products, and since ideas are the basis of new developments, you will find it advantageous to improve your ability to think creatively and to stimulate your imagination and ingenuity. The creative thinking process is to a large extent an adaptation of the scientific method. Both inductive and deductive processes are involved, the former including the collection and analysis of pertinent information in order to arrive at a general summary or theory or principle, the latter including the process of reasoning from a general principle or theory to a specific situation or problem.

Creative thinking is especially important in the real estate field. For example, it may provide the basis for developing a new subdivision, a way of financing a challenging project, or a method of selling a property that has been on the market for a long time.

## Prediction Methods

A knowledge of methods of prediction should prove to be useful. A number of methods of prediction may be distinguished. For example, we may make use of *persistence prediction*—that is, we may assume the

---

[2] John F. Mee, "The Creative Thinking Process," *Indiana Business Review*, Vol. XXXI, pp. 4–9. See also, Arthur Koestler, *The Act of Creation* (New York: The Macmillan Co., 1964), chap. x.

continuation of conditions that currently exist. In predicting changes in the real estate market, we may assume that tomorrow will be like today—that is, that current conditions will persist unless there are good reasons for believing otherwise. If conditions have been generally stable, persistence prediction often works very well; when conditions are unstable, other types of prediction usually are preferable. If change has been occurring in a given direction—for example, if prices are generally advancing—we may make use of such a *trend* as the basis of prediction. Of if the market is moving upward and downward, predictions of the *cycle* type may be useful.

Another method that is often used is *associate prediction.* This is based on an assumed or established relationship between two sets of events—for example, an increase in real estate market activity may precede a rise in real estate prices, or a lowering of interest rates may be followed by an increase in the volume of building.

Predictions may also be made on the basis of *analogy.* A mathematical model of a real estate market may be considered as analogous to the market. An analogy may be drawn between the reactions of a sample of people in the housing market and the entire market.

## Publications

Students of real estate must also know how to find and use the major types of published information that are available. You should learn how to use the library and should familiarize yourself with the more important services published, such as Standard & Poor's, Moody's, Prentice-Hall Real Estate Service, and others. Increasingly, reference materials are organized in such a manner as to permit the use of the computer in speeding up the processes of identifying and retrieving significant information.

Real estate transactions do not take place in a separate division of the business world but are a part of the total economic system. Consequently, you should cultivate the habit of reading current newspapers and magazines. The *Wall Street Journal,* the *New York Times* (especially the Sunday edition), and one or another of the weekly news magazines, such as *U. S. News and World Report, Newsweek,* or *Time* will be helpful. *Business Week* provides a good weekly summary of business developments, *Nation's Business* and *Fortune* are also good current publications to follow. *The Survey of Current Business* published by the Department of Commerce, the Federal Reserve *Bulletin,* the Federal Home Loan Bank Board *Journal,* and *Economic Indicators* published by the President's Council of Economic Advisers present summaries of business conditions. For regional and local information, the publications of Federal Reserve District Banks, Federal Home Loan Banks and various university bureaus of business research are valuable.

## APPROACHES TO THE SUBJECT

The study of real estate may be approached from several directions. For example, we may emphasize general concepts rather than practices. We may stress the administrative point of view or that of the land or urban economist. We may pay particular attention to those activities related directly to the real estate business or pursue a broader approach with emphasis on the relationships between real estate, business administration and the society as a whole.

### Administrative Viewpoint

In these discussions we will be concerned primarily with the administrative point of view. We will stress concepts rather than practices and procedures. We will emphasize the processes of decision-making and implementation, and their relationships to the efficient utilization of real estate resources in the achievement of desired results. Although we follow an administrative approach, we recognize that the processes of managing and administering real estate resources and activities take place in our total economic, political, and social environment.

### Other Approaches

Other approaches to the study of this subject may also be followed. For example, an engineering and architectural approach would emphasize the physical factors involved in real estate resources, the character of the land, its size, shape, and other physical qualities, the character and quality of buildings and other improvements, the design, style, and functional arrangements relating to the property as a whole. A legal approach would stress the property rights involved in real estate ownership and use. An economic approach to the study of this subject would emphasize cost and benefit relationships, income-producing characteristics, and the interrelationships between real estate and other resources.

Although other approaches to the study of real estate administration might be followed, we believe that decision-making and implementing provide both a stimulating and a practical approach to the study of this subject.

### Why vs. How

We emphasize the "why" rather than the "how" or "how to" aspect of the subject. This is not intended to minimize the importance of current practices in the business world or in the real estate field. Many current practices will be covered. It is well to recognize, however, that many business practices change in response to altered conditions, increased knowledge, legislative enactments, or for other reasons.

We are concerned with general concepts based on experience, that is, with hypotheses, theories, principles, and laws. Experience may be personal or it may involve the experience of others. The degree of relative validity varies from hypotheses, which are very tentative generalizations, to laws, which are accepted universally. Principles are usually thought of as generalizations from experience that have sufficient validity to be everywhere acceptable but which do not have the status of laws. In the social sciences, and we consider the study of business as a part of this area, we seldom are sufficiently sure of our generalizations to classify them as laws.

Thus, we shall try to develop our abilities to understand the "why" rather than the "how" aspects of the real estate field. If you are able to acquire an understanding of the major forces that affect decisions in regard to real properties and the real estate business, and if you know the principles that explain changes in property incomes or in business practices, then you should be able to develop the necessary know-how to meet specific problems situations as they arise. In the short run, a how-to-do-things approach might be more valuable. In the longer run, however a broader approach based on general concepts undoubtedly will be the more practical, since it provides a basis for continuing growth and development.

## Economy

The field of real estate administration draws heavily on the fields of economics, management and administration. Many of the basic concepts of these fields are used in real estate. For example, there is the concept of *economy*. This term can have no real meaning unless it is considered in connection with a *stated objective*. Economy, like efficiency, is a relative term. Usually we think of economy in terms of savings, or in terms of return per dollar of investment. *Efficiency*, in the language of management or of economics, is usually considered as reflecting a relationship between input and output of energy, materials, or manpower. It is obvious that neither term can have any meaning unless there is a stated objective to measure against.

Economy, then, in its most general sense, means getting as much as possible of what one wants (in terms of objectives) by the use of the means which are available.

## Economics

Specifically, economics as a branch of organized study deals with the principles and concepts which help to explain the allocation of resources in the attainment of desired ends or objectives. General economics deals with the problems of the community or society as a whole. *Macroeconomics* deals with such problems as total output, income, employment, and other aggregate measures of economic change. *Microeconomics* relates to various components of the economy such as business firms or other units. Managerial economics deals with the effective organization and allocation of the resources of the business firm in the attainment of its objectives. *Land economics*, which traditionally has been the branch of general economics most nearly related to our subject, deals with the utilization of land resources in the attainment of selected objectives.

## Urban Economics

Recently the area of urban economics has been given increasing attention. The area tends to be broader than land economics since it views the urban community as an integral part of the national economy but stresses the particular sets of problems related to specific local communities. On the other hand, it is narrower than land economics since it deals with urban communities only. Primarily urban economics deals with the effective use of urban resources in achieving community objectives. Students of business administration are becoming increasingly aware of the impact of urban economic problems on business policies and, in turn, of the effect of business policies on the urban economy. Problems of air and water pollution are cases in point as are problems of congestion.

## Analysis and Action

The basic interests of the economist and of the manager or administrator have a number of similarities. Both are concerned with the effective utilization of resources in the attainment of desired objectives. Typically the economist serves in an advisory capacity, while the manager is a man of action whose job is to get things done. Thus, the administrative approach differs from that of the land economist or urban economist primarily in that administration involves *action*. It includes analysis, as well as investigation and prediction; the work of the economist will also include such activities. But administration or management is concerned ultimately with action, that is, with the use of ways and means to achieve desired results.

Administration or management may be described in terms of processes or major activities such as establishing objectives, setting up plans to achieve them, organizing resources and controlling operations. Leadership, decision making, decision implementing and related activities are all involved in these functions.

## Real Estate Administration

Real estate administration, then, like the processes of administration or management in other fields, includes decision-making and implementation in the use of resources to achieve desired objectives. In terms of objectives, our interest centers in those of property owners and users (including individuals, families, business firms, or governmental or institutional agencies), the objectives of those engaged in the real estate business, and the ends or goals of our society as a whole as well as their relationship to private objectives.

We are interested in *resources*—primarily in these discussions with real estate resources—but also in the relationships between real estate and other types of resources. We emphasize the fact that real estate resources, like others, have no significance except in terms of people. We pay special attention to the distinguishing characteristics of real estate resources and to those factors which have a major impact on decisions regarding the use of real estate resources in the attainment of objectives. Of primary importance in this connection is the *capacity of real estate to produce income at fixed locations*. We are concerned not only with income production but income in excess of costs and in proper relationship to the risks that are assumed.

We consider in our discussions the general *environmental factors* that influence the decisions of property owners, users, developers, investors, and marketers. Thus, we are concerned with location factors, the physical environment, market forces, general business conditions, political trends, the legal framework, and governmental regulations and programs.

## REAL ESTATE OBJECTIVES

As we have indicated, administration is concerned with the use of resources to achieve objectives. In the real estate field we have two principal sets of objectives: those of property owners and users, and those of the people engaged in the real estate business. To a sginificant degree these two sets of objectives tend to coincide. Each of these two sets of objectives must also bear an appropriate relationship to the objectives of our society as a whole. While we have a system which largely permits each of us and each business firm to pursue individually determined objectives, the community or society as a whole will not long allow the pursuit of private objectives that are detrimental to the public interest. We have found that in our system of democracy and competition it is possible for us, within rather broad limits, to pursue individually determined objectives and still serve the best interests of the community as a whole. Ours is a society in which we agree to disagree.

### Objectives of Real Estate Enterprises

Various types of business enterprises operate in the real estate field. These include not only real estate brokerage and property management firms, which popularly are referred to as "the real estate business," but land development and building companies and financial institutions as well. In addition, we may include various specialists such as appraisers, engineers, architects, real property lawyers, market analysts, and others.

Business firms in the real estate field will pursue objectives that are similar to those of business firms in other areas. Typically, business firms pursue such objectives as survival, growth, and the attainment of recognition or a prestige position. In order to do these things, they must make a profit. Some firms attempt to maximize profits, others to gain a "reasonable" or some other level of profit. Their specific objectives may vary widely; but, as we shall see, it is virtually impossible to manage a business firm in the real estate or in any other field without a clear understanding of the objectives that are being pursued.

### Objectives of Owners and Users

Similarly, the owners or users of real estate resources may pursue a wide variety of objectives. Many will try to maximize profits. Some will hope to achieve maximum monetary returns over the long run, others in the short run. Some will try to maximize satisfactions from the direct use of real properties. In some cases objectives may be stated in terms of using real properties in connection with other resources to achieve a maximum total result, as in the case of a business firm using real estate and other resources in producing and marketing goods and services.

### Highest and Best Use

To an important degree in the field of real estate, as in many other fields, the interests of the community as a whole are closely related to the activities of private real estate owners, users, dealers, managers, and investors. Despite differences in the reasons behind their decisions and actions, both the community as a whole and practical men of affairs in their private capacities demand the development of each parcel of real estate to its *highest and best use.* This is a convenient concept, and the term is used often in the real estate business. One should recognize, however, that it involves some logical pitfalls and must be used with care. In general it means the utilization of a property to its greatest economic advantage. The term has been defined in terms of *greatest net income, highest land value,* and *largest return in money or amenities* over a period of time.

In addition to economic factors, social and political considerations have a bearing on the meaning of "highest and best use." The term would have different meanings in a society organized under a dictatorship than in one organized on democratic principles. Even in our own society, the highest and best use of a property may change with shifting consumer preferences, improved techniques and equipment, or for other reasons. The market reflects changes in buyer preferences and production methods. Changing attitudes and techniques are also reflected in zoning laws, building codes, and other regulations governing the development and use of real property. For example, problems of air and water pollution reflect changing conditions.

### Maximizing vs. Satisficing

Sometimes it is argued that business firms tend to "satisfice" rather than maximize returns. Typically the economist thinks in terms of maximizing, that is getting the most out of the use of given resources. This may be true of business executives; in some cases, however, they may aim at goals that are less than the maximum. They may be satisfied with "good enough" performance rather than the best. Thus we should recognize that some owners, managers, and users of real property will try to maximize net income or maximize income over the long run but that others may "satisfice" or pursue other objectives. The objectives that are established, of course, will serve as important guidelines for decisions related to programs of property use and development.

### Social and Business Objectives

In our society, the owners of real property and those who own or manage various types of real estate firms are allowed to pursue their objectives within the general framework of our legal, governmental, and institutional arrangements. We allow this type of operation because we have found that in our competitive and democratic type of society the owners of real estate resources or real estate enterprises tend to serve the long term interests of our society as a whole by pursuing their own best interests. This is not always the case, of course. For example, it is necessary to impose limits on the decisions of property owners through zoning laws to prevent the development of inharmonious land uses. Within certain limits, however, we rely on competition to regulate business activities for us and to assure buyers and users of good value per dollar of cost. Similarly, democratic political processes assure a fairly direct response to the programs of the owners and managers of properties or firms, either supporting them or not supporting them if they do not conform to the standards which the voting public expects of them.

A method of illustrating the relationships between the objectives of property owners, business owners, or managers on the one hand, and those of society on the other, is provided by an example from another field. We maintain a free press in this country and within very broad limits allow it freedom of expression. The objective of this arrangement is to disseminate the truth. This objective is achieved, not by requiring that all publications print nothing but the truth, but by allowing them (within the limits of the law of libel and other broad regulations) to print what they please. In this way we come very close to achieving our objective of disseminating the truth by means of freedom of expression and publication.

### Private Objectives

Much the same thing may be said about the real estate field. By allowing owners of property to pursue their own objectives, to maximize income or to develop properties to what they consider to be the highest and best use of such properties, general community as well as purely private objectives are served. In most cases such objectives are served better than if more direct and specific controls are set on the ownership, use, development, financing, or marketing of private real properties.

Similarly, by allowing the owners of real estate enterprises to pursue their own objectives—maximizing profits, surviving in the face of competition, achieving growth, or attaining prestige positions—they serve also to help further general social objectives. For example, if a savings bank, in order to increase earnings, charges interest rates on its mortgages that are higher than those of its competitors, it will lose business and hence income. Competition will force it to lower its rates. Thus, competition is a higher effective method of social control. It brings about a blending of private and public objectives.

## REAL ESTATE RESOURCES

Real estate resources include land and buildings plus property rights in these physical objects. These property rights represent income or income potentials. These rights have value to the people who own, use, produce, finance, or market them.

Real estate resources may be considered in terms of their physical, legal, or economic characteristics. From a physical standpoint, a piece of real property is made up of land and buildings or other improvements. It is a part of the total physical environment. In turn, it creates an environment for those who use it. From a legal point of view, a real property represents certain legal rights in land and buildings or other improvements. From an economic or business standpoint, the land and buildings and the property rights they represent have significance primarily because of their ability to serve the needs of people—that is, to produce income either in terms of monetary returns or in terms of direct use, thereby providing convenience, shelter, protection, privacy, or other property services.

### Types of Real Estate Resources

Real estate resources include residential properties of many types: single-family houses, doubles, duplexes, three and four dwelling-unit structures, and apartments such as walk-ups, elevator or high-rise buildings, garden apartments, and others. The general classification of business properties covers both commercial and industrial properties. Commercial properties include stores, office buildings, shops, places of amusement, and the like. Industrial properties include both light and heavy manufacturing installations and various types of warehouses and related properties. In addition, we may distinguish farms and other rural real estate, government and institutional real estate, and special-purpose properties.

### Valuation of Resources

We all recognize that the value of real estate resources may change rapidly. This is also true of other resources. Unfortunately, there are no market quotations in the real estate field comparable to the daily reports of the major securities exchanges. Such reports, of course, are important to many business decision makers. Real estate decision makers, however, often find it necessary to ask that estimates of value or appraisals be made on various properties which are under consideration. Unlike stocks which are homogeneous and represent interchangeable shares in the equities of companies, each property is unique. No two locations on the earth's surface are exactly alike. Relatively few properties are sold and bought in a given business day. In some communities relatively few properties are bought and sold in a period as long as a month. Since it is often necessary to call on real estate appraisers to make estimates of real estate values they play an important role in this field.

## Localization of Income

Real estate resources produce income at fixed sites. As has often been said the three major matters of importance in real estate are (1) location, (2) location, and (3) location. This is hardly an overstatement since fixity of location is a major characteristic of real estate resources and since each property must produce property services and hence income either through direct use or through monetary returns at a fixed site. Although each piece of real property is a fixed point on the earth's surface, it is part of a highly dynamic framework. This framework includes the economic, political, social and physical environment. The property is influenced by international, national, regional and local trends all of which have an influence on its capacity to produce income at its fixed location.

## Real Estate Parcels as Shares

Each parcel of real estate may be thought of as a share in our total national wealth. General economic trends will have a bearing on the predictions and decisions of people in regard to the ability of real estate to produce income. Each piece of real estate is a share in the community in which it is located. The income potential of a piece of urban real estate is dependent on the economic strength of the city and the character of its district or neighborhood. Similarly, the economic future of any piece of property is dependent to a large degree on market forces; typically, it is affected more by local market conditions than is almost any other type of goods or services. Analyses of such forces and predictions based on these analyses play a major role in programs for carrying out decisions related to property ownership and use.

## SUMMARY

We will be concerned primarily with the improvement of decision-making and implementation in the real estate field. We stress the concepts that help us to understand the effective use of real estate resources in achieving desired objectives. This means that we emphasize the administrative point of view.

This process includes both decision-making and implementation. Decisions and programs of action are influenced by the objectives to be achieved, the resources available, and the general environment or climate within which the decisions are made and the programs are carried out. In our discussions, we pay special attention to the objectives of those in the real estate business, and the interrelationships between their objectives and those of our society as a whole.

In order to give you a general introduction to the discussion in this book, the following outline may be helpful.

In Chapter 2 our attention centers on real estate decisions and decision makers. Chapters 3, 4, and 5 consider various physical, legal, and economic characteristics of real estate. These five chapters constitute the introductory section of the book.

Part II covers various analytical tools and decision guides related to real estate resources including governmental and political trends, business conditions and industry trends, regional and local economic analyses, real estate market analysis, and location factors including city structure and land use patterns as well as neighborhoods and districts. These factors are related to appraisal methods in the final discussions of this section.

Part III centers on the major real estate decision areas: production, including subdividing, land development and building operations; marketing, which involves brokerage, promotion and property management; and finance, covering financing methods and instruments, financial institutions and agencies, and the processes of mortgage lending.

In Part IV we consider a variety of special properties and decision problems, including housing, commercial and industrial properties, and farms and other rural real estate. International real estate trends are reviewed and analyzed. Implications of future trends for real estate resources and for the improvement of real estate administration are discussed in the final chapter.

## QUESTIONS FOR STUDY

1. What are *your* objectives in studying real estate?
2. Identify some of the major problems faced by real estate decision-makers in a growing economy with a prosperous future.
3. What is the administrative approach to real estate and how does it differ from other approaches?
4. Compare the approaches to the study of urban economics and land economics to that of real estate administration.
5. Describe various prediction methods. When should they or should they not be used?
6. What are the typical objectives of a real estate enterprise? How are they determined? How do private and public objectives blend?
7. What are the major real estate resources? What is unique about them? What problems are encountered in valuing them?
8. What are the major economic services provided by real estate resources?

9. Why is the study of income so important in the fields of economics and business administration? In what ways is the study of real estate a study of income production at fixed sites?
10. Why is the study of real estate administration concerned with the legal and physical as well as the economic characteristics of real properties?

## SUGGESTED READINGS

Brown, Robert Kevin. *Essentials of Real Estate*. Englewood Cliffs, N.J.: Prentice-Hall, Inc., 1970. Chap. 1.
David, Philip. *Urban Land Development*. Homewood, Ill.: Richard D. Irwin, Inc., 1970. Introduction.
Landsberg, Hans H., Leonard L. Fischman, and Joseph L. Fisher. *Resources in America's Future*. Baltimore: The Johns Hopkins Press, 1963. Pp. 3–68.
Unger, Maurice A. *Real Estate* (4th ed.). Cincinnati: South-Western Publishing Co., 1969. Chap. 1.
Weimer, Arthur M. *Introduction to Business: A Management Approach* (4th ed.). Homewood, Ill.: Richard D. Irwin, Inc., 1970. Chaps. 1, 2.

Note: It is suggested that you become familiar with a number of general references and current publications, including the following: census reports, especially the *Census of Housing, House and Home, Land Economics, The Appraisal Journal, The Real Estate Appraiser, The Survey of Current Business, The Federal Reserve Bulletin, Economic Indicators, Business Horizons,* and *The Harvard Business Review.*

You might also write your local district Federal Reserve Bank and ask to be included on the mailing list for their monthly economic bulletin. These reports may be followed as a guide to regional and local economic trends.

## CASE 1–1

### The Ambitious Student

One of your student friends, John Robinson, a senior who was recently married, knows you are studying real estate and asks you to advise him in regard to his housing. You point out that you are in the very early stages of your study of this field. He takes the position that some knowledge is better than no knowledge and proceeds to present his problem.

John and his wife have been living in a small furnished efficiency apartment. The rent is $135 per month and they are renting on a month to month basis. They have about $4,500 available as a result of savings and wedding gifts. He says he knows that a lot of people make money in real estate so why shouldn't they buy a house, live in it for a year and then sell it for more than they paid for it or at least for as much as they paid and get free rent. Or he asks, why not buy a rooming house? His wife could look after it and he would have some time available to help her. Or why not buy a small apartment house—say a four-unit apartment?

You point out that you have already been convinced that there is no assurance of a specific property going up in value even though the general trends have been in that direction. You also suggest that much would depend on what may be available since this is a fairly small university town and the real estate market is not very extensive.

John reports that they recently met a young real estate broker who has several properties for sale. One is an old residence built in the later 1920's and fairly near the campus. It is owned by a retired faculty member who wants to move to a warmer climate. It has two bedrooms, living room, large kitchen, dining alcove, one bath and a half basement. There is an old one car detached garage at the back of the lot.

The lot has a frontage of 50 feet and a depth of 150 feet. It is on the west side of a paved street. The house measures 34 feet by 30 feet. Plastering is in fair condition; however, the bathroom should be replastered at an early date. The grounds are well maintained. There are several good sized shade trees. The legal description of the property is lot number 76 in Eroica's section 10, township 12 north, range 9 west, City of Eroica, Sunrise County, State of Illinois (known as 1776 North Upton Street).

Properties in this area are 40 years or more old. There is a small shopping center about four blocks away. The property is readily accessible to schools. It is priced at $19,750, but the owner would be willing to sell on a 12 year contract at 10 per cent interest with $3,500 down. The monthly payments would total $194.32 not including taxes and insurance. Repairs are estimated at $1,500 although part of this—perhaps one-third to one-half—could be accomplished on a do-it-yourself basis. Taxes are estimated at $378 and insurance at $92.

Upon inquiry you find that this house has been on the market for almost two years and you tell your friend that he may not be able to get his money out quickly if he takes a job elsewhere upon graduation. If he had to forfeit his contract, he would be paying a high rate of rent.

About this time you happen to notice an ad in the real estate section of the local paper describing a rooming house that is for sale and you call your friend's attention to this possibility as well.

The rooming house is located on South Seventh Street very near the campus. The offering price for the eleven bedroom structure is $57,500. The original portion of the house is approximately 60 years old, with a five year old addition in the rear. The gross annual rentals, with 100 per cent occupancy, total $11,280. The entire house has been rented for the next summer and fall.

The building had originally been the home of the Kingery family, whose heirs had sold it in 1961 for $16,900. The new owner, a Mrs. Barringer, was housemother for a local sorority. She utilized her experience in turning the South Seventh Street property into a rooming house for university students. In 1964, she added the new wing to the structure, nearly doubling the capacity. In 1966, desiring to move out of Illinois, Mrs. Barringer sold the property to the present owner, Robert Werneke, for $37,500 on a land contract. Mr. Werneke, because of ill health, wants to sell the property. Initially, he listed it for $59,500.

During the years Werneke owned the property, the following improvements were made: three new gas furnaces installed, exterior painted every other year, interior panelled and carpeted, much of the older furniture replaced, storm windows and screens replaced, structure checked for and protected against termites.

Werneke's problem in selling his property apparently stemmed from two factors. First, he wanted his cash at the time of sale and secondly, there was not a great deal of demand for older rooming houses such as the South Seventh Street property.

Werneke has indicated that he might sell on a land contract if he knew the buyer and if the down payment were sufficient. For a cash sale Werneke would probably accept an offer in the low $50,000 range because the property has been on the market for so long.

Figures supplied by Werneke, using some of his own estimates are:

| | | |
|---|---:|---:|
| Rent Schedule Income | | $11,280 |
| Less 10% vacancy | | 1,128 |
| Gross Rent Income | | $10,152 |
| Expenses: | | |
| Insurance | $ 315 | |
| Taxes | 900 | |
| Utilities | 1,382 | |
| Management | 500 | |
| Maintenance Reserve | 500 | $ 3,597 |
| Net income before depreciation | | $ 6,555 |

Assuming he could buy the property for $50,000, with the owner taking a second mortgage for $10,000 at 10 per cent, you computed his financing requirements as follows:

| | | |
|---|---:|---|
| Equity (down payment) | $ 5,000 | |
| Mortgage 8%–20 yrs. | 35,000 | (70% of price, assuming property is appraised at price level) |
| 2nd mortgage from owner | | |
| at 10%–10 yrs. | 10,000 | |
| Total Price | $50,000 | |

You pointed out to John that obtaining a $35,000 mortgage from a local financial institution would depend on whether the property would be appraised for $50,000 or more. You suggested that the capitalized value of the net income on the basis of 10 per cent in perpetuity would be $65,555. On a more modest 13 per cent basis, which might be more typical for this type of property, its capitalized value would be only $50,427.

### Questions

1. Make John a list of the advantages and disadvantages of each of his alternatives.
2. If he buys the rooming house, what are some ways he can make up the difference between the $5,000 down payment and his $4,500?
3. What difference might a $65,000 or $50,000 appraisal of the rooming house have on the mortgage arrangements?
4. What is your recommendation to John?

# 2

# Real Estate Decisions
# and Decision Makers

This chapter considers the special characteristics of real estate decisions and compares them to various other business and personal decisions. The major decision makers in the field are discussed briefly; the real estate business is reviewed along with the general framework and climate within which it operates.

## DECISION MAKING

Decisions related to real estate resources are similar in most respects to those made in relation to other resources or other areas of business. Some decisions are made on a logical and rational basis, others are the result of hunches, intuition, inspiration or snap judgments. Decisions in the real estate field, however, are likely to be influenced by several sets of unique factors: (1) income from real estate resources must be produced at fixed locations; (2) long term commitments usually are required; (3) real estate transactions typically involve relatively large amounts of money, and (4) private, public and quasi-public interests are heavily interrelated; for example, streets and utilities are necessary to allow a private real property to perform its functions and taxes, laws and regulations play an important role in the making of private decisions. In addition it should be noted (5) that the real estate market differs from other markets because of the relative inflexibility of supply in the short run.

## Decision Techniques

In recent years as business decisions have tended to become more rational in character, scientific methods have been used increasingly along with operations research and management science to aid decision makers. We will not undertake to discuss these topics except to suggest that they provide highly sophisticated ways of making use of information in arriving at rational decisions. When information is not available, imagination, inspiration, judgment, or so-called "heuristic" thinking, often are used.

Even though the scientific method is used increasingly, it would be a mistake to draw too close an analogy between the scientific method and rational decision making processes. The scientist is seldom concerned with taking action. His objectives are to discover knowledge rather than to take action on the basis of it. The decision maker in business, whether in the real estate area or others, is trying to find programs which will lead to successful results. The decision maker may rely on models which are set up to help him. He may be able to develop various "decision rules." He may make use of the computer and other highly sophisticated equipment. He may employ mathematical techniques such as linear programming, game theory and others. He often draws on information from the physical sciences and engineering, lawyers, statisticians, mathematicians, accountants and specialists in many other fields.

Often in the process of determining which decisions may be possible, a good deal of bargaining and negotiation are required. Compromises may be necessary.

In a final analysis, however, judgments must be made about an uncertain future. Decisions are forward looking. They require that estimates be made about the future. Regardless of rational approaches or sophisticated techniques, we should recognize that the future can seldom be anticipated with great accuracy. Indeed it is this uncertainty that challenges all of us, and especially those who have major decision making responsibility.

## Stages in Decisions

Although they are not easy to separate, most decisions tend to go through a series of stages which may include the following:

1. Identification of the problem and the objectives to be achieved.
2. Establishment and analysis of practical alternatives.
3. Evaluation of the alternatives and choice of the one preferred.
4. Carrying the decision into action.
5. Reviewing results of the decision and making corrections and adjustments.

## Limitations on Decisions

In the real estate field as well as in others, the decisions of those who control finance, such as the executives of financial institutions, those who regulate activities such as government officials or those who control special resources such as labor leaders often have a major impact on decisions.

Along with all of us, major decision makers face many factors that are uncontrollable such as the weather, fires or other unpredictable occurrences. The term "state of nature" helps to define this area.

Those who make decisions can never be sure how competitors will act or react. Often "competitive strategies" are developed but they are limited by the strategies of competitors or the anticipated strategies of competitors.

Decisions will also be influenced by the values that are applied in given situations. For example, if the ultimate goal is to maximize return on investment, this may vary if one property or a number of properties are involved. Thus, it may be desirable to take a lesser return on one property in order to gain a better return on a block of properties. This is sometimes referred to as "suboptimizing."

## Programs of Action

Business executives in general as well as those in the real estate field make decisions and also implement them. They are both "deciders" and "doers." It is almost impossible to separate these two roles.

In the modern corporation efforts are made to relieve the executive who carries major responsibilities of routine decisions. Thus, he is able to give primary attention to major decisions and to the more difficult programs required for carrying them out. The process of making decisions, putting them into action, and then re-evaluating them goes on continuously. It may be viewed as a "closed loop" with decisions, actions, feedback, review and correction of the original decision or its continuation going on almost constantly.

One decision sets the stage for another or requires that still another be made. An action program often opens the way for new decisions and in turn for new programs. A review of the results of past decisions may indicate that new decisions are necessary and that new programs must be developed.

As has been pointed out:

We have a tendency to think of a decision as final. This is true in a literal sense, but we should recognize that we reappraise and review most decisions and frequently modify them, change them entirely, or supplant them by new decisions.

Business decisions are reviewed and reappraised almost continuously. For example, a manager may decide to lease space for his store. Even before he occupies the location, however, he may have found another one that offers many additional advantages. He may then sublease the first location and occupy the new one. Often decisions are modified or changed, or canceled out. In some cases, of course, it may be impossible to change a previous decision, even if the manager wishes to do so. In the illustration above, for example, the manager might have found it impossible to take the new location if he has been unable to sublease the first one. Even in this case, however, he may occupy the first location for a time and later be able to make a shift.[1]

### Management Process

In order to implement a decision it is necessary to develop *plans* for carrying the desired action into effect. Choices must be made between alternative plans. The plan selected in turn must be put into effect and this usually requires that various resources including land and buildings along with manpower, materials, money and other things be *organized* so that the effort can be made with reasonable changes of success. In order to assure that an organized effort will be most likely to succeed, *controls* are established to evaluate the results and to modify the organized effort as required. These stages of planning, organizing and controlling activities often are referred to as "the management process." It includes a continuing series of decision making and decision implementing activities, all of which get mixed up together.

## DECISION MAKERS—OWNERS AND USERS

Nearly everyone participates to some extent in real estate decisions, since each of us uses real estate in some way every day. Some have only minor decisions to make such as deciding whether to rent a motel room for the night or buy a share of stock in a real estate enterprise. Others have major decisions to make often involving many properties and large amounts of money. We may think of the primary decision makers in the real estate field as those who own real estate resources. In some cases owners are also users of properties; in other cases, ownership and use are separated. Users may exert major decision making authority or occupy a minor role, depending on the situation.

Those who engage in various aspects of the real estate business are involved in a variety of decision making activities. These decision makers include those who develop and subdivide, build, market or finance real estate resources and operations.

---

[1] Arthur M. Weimer, *Introduction to Business: A Management Approach* (4th ed.; Homewood, Ill.: Richard D. Irwin, Inc., 1970), p. 248.

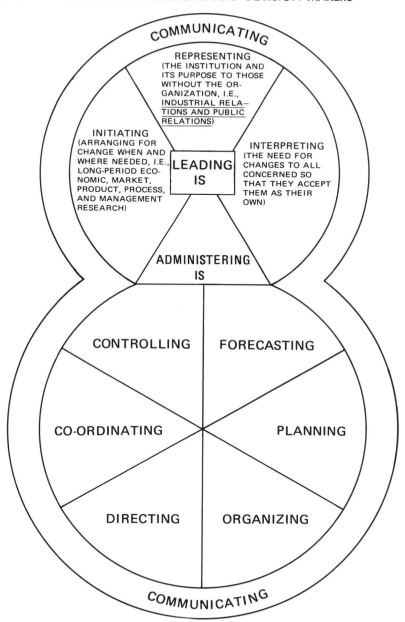

**Fig. 2–1.** The functions of leadership. (Source: Ernest Dale and Lyndall F. Urwick, *Staff in Organization* [New York: McGraw-Hill Book Co., 1960], p. 20. Used by permission.)

## Owners

Ownership has a wide range of meanings. In some cases the owner may have relatively little decision making authority. Typically, however, ownership provides a major basis for controlling decisions. When ownership and use are combined, decisions are based both on the authority of the owner and his experience as a user of the property. When ownership and use are separated the ultimate decisions are made by the owner but he is likely to be influenced considerably by the recommendations of the user of the property. In some cases, the user may be able to specify very definitely the conditions under which he will make use of it and hence have a major influence on the owner's decisions. This is often the case when a long-term lease is being negotiated or when the user plans to improve the property in order to use it in some specific manner.

## Real Estate Ownership

The ownership of real estate in this country is widely dispersed. Indeed, the opportunity to acquire ownership interests in real property was one of the main attractions for those who first settled in this country. Around two-thirds of our homes are owned by those who occupy them. Many people have a variety of investments in real estate. A high percentage of our farms are owned by those who operate them; a substantial number are owned by retired farmers. Many business firms own their places of business. Thus, there is relatively little concentration of real estate ownership in this country although there are some localities where old families, larger corporations or major institutions control much real property. Inheritance taxes have brought about the breaking up of some holdings that might have resulted in large concentrations of ownership. Competition from other types of investments also has had an effect.

Owners of real estate exercise their rights to control property within certain broad limits imposed by government, notably those resulting from taxation, eminent domain and the police power. (We will consider this topic at greater length in Chapter 4.) Governments at all levels also are important owners of real estate. Such ownership includes areas devoted to roads, streets, parks, national and state forests, conservation areas, military reservations, government office buildings, schools and many others. The uses to which publicly owned real estate is put may have important influences on the ways in which private property is used.

The people in the real estate business may or may not be owners of real property. Some of them invest in properties on a long-term basis; others buy and sell properties in the hope of short-term gains.

### Users of Real Estate

In terms of their decision making importance we may distinguish between (1) owner-users, and (2) nonowner users or those who typically lease properties for varying periods of time. The second group may be divided between (a) those who have widespread decision-making authority, such as those who use property under long term leases or under leases which grant substantial powers to determine the ways in which property may be used and improved, and (b) those who use property under short term leases or other limited arrangements—for example, a student who rents a room for a term, a newly married couple renting a small apartment for a month or two, or a business firm renting a storeroom on a temporary basis.

Those who lease property under arrangements which allow wide decision making latitude stand in much the same relationship to real estate as owners. Either directly or indirectly such users of property have a great influence on decisions. To some degree all users of real estate exercise some influence on owners through competition.

Buildings are constructed, modernized, equipped, repaired and maintained in ways that will attract users. Sometimes users may spell out the specifications for development very precisely, as in the case of sale and lease back arrangements. A large chain store corporation may buy a desirable location and sell it to a local investor provided he agrees to improve it in a specified manner and lease it back to the corporation under stated conditions.

## DECISION MAKERS—THE REAL ESTATE BUSINESS

The real estate business includes a wide variety of enterprises. Many real estate brokerage firms are small operations. The office with one broker and a secretary is not unusual. Some brokerage firms attain fairly large size and offer complete real estate services. Building and development firms range from small to very large scale organizations. Investors may range from small to very large, including many types of financial institutions. Many people own and manage a few rental properties or lend money on the security of a home or two. Quite a number hold vacant land for future use. Banks, savings and loan associations and insurance companies invest billions of dollars in real estate each year.

Of growing importance in the real estate field are the real estate departments of business firms. Many of our larger corporations now engage in extensive real estate operations in addition to those required for their own company purposes.

## Functions of the Real Estate Business

Real estate enterprises exist because they perform useful functions for all of us, functions that people are willing to pay for. We may divide the principal functions of the real estate business into three divisions: production (subdividing, developing and building) marketing, and financing. We use the terms developing and building to describe the processes of preparing land for use, constructing buildings and other improvements and making the completed properties available for use. Marketing includes the processes of putting real properties and property services into the hands of consumers. Brokerage and property management constitute the two main subdivisions of the marketing function. This function also includes promotion, advertising and public relations activities. Financing provides for the channeling of a portion of the savings of the country into the production and use of real estate resources. Because of their long life, these resources require special types of financing arrangements. In addition there are various specialized functions which facilitate the work of the real estate field. These include those who engage in land planning, architecture and engineering, appraising and analysis, market research, real estate law, and others.

## Production

As producers of real estate resources, land developers and subdividers by their decisions as to how a tract of land will be laid out and subdivided, the types of streets, sewers, and other facilities that will be provided and by related decisions tend to exercise a controlling influence on future decisions regarding the properties located there. Future owners and users may be able to make decisions only within a fairly limited range of possibilities. The builder plays an important role in real estate decisions in terms of both original construction and subsequent modernization and repair programs. A builder who does high quality work, for example, prevents the occurrence of many problems that may cause difficulties for both original and future owners and users.

Land development and building firms may be combined or conducted on a more specialized basis. Combined arrangements are of growing importance. Operations may range from a small builder who constructs a few houses a year to the developer of an entire new town. Some of our larger corporations are now engaging in a broad range of development and building operations including Alcoa, Chrysler, Gulf Oil and others.

## Marketing

Real estate brokers, by providing information for prospective buyers and sellers and by making available as wide a variety of choices as possible, also influence a broad range of decisions in the real estate field. They may also assist in making financial arrangements and thus exert additional influence on decisions.

Some brokerage offices specialize in the selling of particular kinds of property such as residential, commercial, industrial, recreational or farm properties. Others cover a broad range of activities. Brokers are usually paid on a commission basis. They list properties for sale, promote sales, arrange for the closing of transactions and carry on related activities.

Property managers may influence the decisions of both owners and users of properties by recommending programs of development, improvement and effective use. A property manager is more than a lease broker although many start in this way. Usually a property manager acts for the owner in all matters pertaining to a property including the leasing of space, collecting rents, selection of tenants, maintenance of the building and grounds and related activities. He is usually paid on a commission basis, five percent of rentals collected being a typical arrangement. A property manager may specialize in the management of specific types of properties. Larger management firms, however, usually manage many types.

Those who engage in public relations, promotion and advertising efforts often help to attract investments into the real estate field and to stimulate the sale and rental of properties.

## Financing

Those who engage in financing either as individuals or as executives of financial institutions play an important role in real estate decision making. Typically the equity or owner's investment represents a small percentage of total property value; the remainder usually is provided by borrowed funds. Sometimes the lender becomes a part owner—he takes a "piece of the action." In other cases he remains a lender only. Of major importance in this area are commercial and savings banks, savings and loan associations, insurance companies, and mortgage bankers and brokers. In recent years real estate investment trusts, pension funds and other larger pools of capital have been playing an expanding role in this area.

Real estate financing usually is long term in character and is accomplished by the use of mortgages or similar legal arrangements which provide for the pledging of greater or lesser degrees of interest in a real property as security for loans. Sometimes leases are used as a means of financing as in the case of sale and leaseback arrangements. Construction loans are generally made for short term periods during the building period but often are merged with long term financing.

### Special Functions

The many specialists who assist the various parts of the real estate business typically operate in an advisory capacity rather than as primary decision makers. This is generally true of real property lawyers, architects, engineers, land planners, appraisers, counselors, analysts of various types and others. In general they advise the owners and users of property or those who develop and build, market or finance real properties. These functions may be performed by individuals, professional firms, small businesses or multinational corporations and major financial institutions. By providing expert information and counsel specialists help to improve the efforts of real estate decision makers.

### Appraising

Of the various specialists, the appraiser occupies a unique position in the real estate field. Because the market for real estate is not highly organized, it is often necessary to estimate the value of properties for various purposes. Appraisals or estimates of value serve as one of the major sources of information for business, personal, governmental and institutional decisions pertaining to real property. Such estimates are often made by professional appraisers although others may at times undertake to do this. Because of the complexity of the appraisal process, laws and regulations which require appraisals, and the policies of major financial institutions and corporations, more and more appraisals are being done by specialists. Such organizations as the American Institute of Real Estate Appraisers and the Society of Real Estate Appraisers have helped to develop training programs and standards of practice in this field.

### Entrepreneurs

The entrepreneurial function in real estate is performed to a greater or lesser extent by all of the individuals and firms that participate in this field. Sometimes those who act as individual entrepreneurs are referred to as "operators." They may buy land and hold it until it is ripe for development, promote projects of various types, buy and sell property, change property from a lower to a higher use or engage in other activities. Often brokers may operate on their own as well as for others;

sometimes builders take an equity in their projects; even specialists may on occasion participate with the equity owner or take "a piece of the action" rather than the usual fee.

## Organizations

As in other fields, activities may be carried on by individuals, partnerships, corporations or under other arrangements such as trusts and syndicates. In an individual proprietorship a single person serves as owner and operator. He may manage activities himself or hire others to do this or perform other services for him. No legal formalities are needed except as may be required in the real estate field for brokerage or salesmen's licenses. In a partnership two or more persons are owners and may operate with varying degrees of formality. They are both individually and jointly responsible for all acts of the firm. Of special importance in real estate are limited partnerships; under this arrangement, the general partner or partners have overall responsibility, the limited partners are only responsible to the extent of their investments. The corporate form is widely used; financial institutions almost always are set up as corporations.

## Corporations

A corporation is a legal entity created by state or federal charter for the purpose of carrying on specifically authorized activities. There are corporations for profit and also those not for profit, the latter usually being established for educational, research, religious, or similar purposes. There may also be government corporations of various types.

In corporations organized for profit, the owners are the stockholders. Bonds may be issued to creditors. Bondholders have no ownership interest, although they may become owners in case of reorganization. Convertible bonds or debentures may lead to stock ownership. The owners of a corporation enjoy limited liability for the obligations of the firm— that is, liability is limited to their stock interests. Individual proprietors are personally liable for the obligations of their firms. Partners are liable for all of the obligations of the firm unless special limitations are established, and this type of arrangement depends on the statutes of the states where the partnerships are set up.

Since a corporation is a legal entity, it is taxed directly and its owners are also taxed on dividends received from the corporation (except in some small corporations whose owners may elect to be taxed as partners). This is not true of individual proprietorships and partnerships. Financial institutions are required to obtain federal or state charters in order to engage in business.

Usually no special licenses or other permissions are required to engage in land development or building activities. But, while the firm as such is not licensed, permissions usually must be secured to subdivide and improve land, especially when zoning laws are in operation; and building permits typically are required before construction can be undertaken.

### Other Forms

We should note that a specific piece of real property may form the basis for an enterprise established in any of the above forms. For example, the ownership of a store building might be set up as a corporation, and this property could be purchased by buying a majority of the shares of the corporation.

Some real estate ventures are undertaken as syndicates. Usually this is done for a specific operation such as carrying out a major contract or developing a large tract of land. Syndicates may be made up of individuals or of several firms. The organization of a syndicate depends on the arrangements made to govern the interests of the syndicate members at the time it is established.

Trusts are often established for various purposes in the real estate field. An owner of property may establish a trust for his heirs. Title to the property is transferred to a trustee who administers the property in accordance with the trust agreement. The trust form may be used by owners of land to pool their interests with a trustee developing it; a shopping center may be set up as a trust.

## THE FRAMEWORK OF THE REAL ESTATE BUSINESS

The three functions of developing, financing, and marketing real estate must be performed regardless of how a society is organized. For example, in a dictatorship one huge government agency might perform all of them. Those in charge of such an agency would decide how much subdividing and building should take place, how the properties should be financed, who should be allowed to buy or rent them, and for how much. The government officials would be paid salaries rather than commissions, fees, rents, interest, or profits.

### Private Sector

In an enterprise system these functions are organized through the market. Through competitive bidding, each person, within the limits of his economic resources, by buying or not buying, or by buying more or less, or by selling or not selling, or by selling more or less, helps to make the decisions which govern the development, financing, marketing, and use of real estate resources. Government, of course, has the responsibility for making market competition work and for supplementing it when necessary.

A large portion of the real estate business is carried on by private enterprises such as brokerage firms, management organizations, subdividing, development and building companies, financial institutions, and individual entrepreneurs on a full- or part-time basis. In addition, however, federal, state, and local governments participate in varying degrees in real estate administration.

### Public Sector

Government agencies, for example, establish the rules of the game within which the private firms and individuals operate. Government defines and protects property, organizes and enforces a system of private contracts (in effect a system of "private law"), provides protection for private owners in the occupancy and use of their property, and regulates the uses to which property may be put. Government also taxes property, provides various subsidies, conducts research, collects and disseminates information, provides counsel, facilitates the financing of property ownership and use, lends money, insures and guarantees mortgages, and also develops, leases, owns, and operates certain real properties. In addition, government may regulate the practices of those engaged in the real estate business by licensing laws and similar devices.

The relationships between business and government appear to be growing more and more complex. This is particularly true in the real estate field. No commodity except narcotics is more definitely regulated and controlled than real estate. In part this is because the concept of real property ownership is itself a creation of the law. Also, the close relationship between public and private property in the real estate field helps to account for this situation. Accessibility alone virtually requires the use of public and private real estate in combination. In addition, the use of one property is likely to have significant effects on the use and hence the value of real estate located adjacent to it or nearby. The "neighboring effect" is of major importance.

Obviously the effectiveness with which government agencies are administered has a special bearing on the utilization of real properties. This is important on the federal and state levels, but in the case of real estate, especially important on the local level. Local government agencies may on occasion be hampered by limitations of funds or personnel, but they are tending to respond to the increasingly demanding requirements of the modern business community.

### Quasi-Public Agencies

Another set of agencies of major importance in the real estate field includes trade associations, nonprofit organizations, mutual benefit societies, and a number of similar quasi-public institutions. These agencies carry on a number of activities such as providing information, advice, and assistance to member firms, lobbying and other legislative activities. In addition, labor unions play a significant role, especially in the construction industry.

It is not easy to present a diagram showing the relationship between these heterogeneous groups of private enterprises, government agencies, and quasi-public organizations; but the accompanying chart may be helpful (see Fig. 2–2). This chart stresses the fact that when we think of the real estate business or of real estate administration, we must think of all of these agencies, rather than only of one or another type.

### Government Agencies

Federal, state, and local agencies of government carry on a wide variety of activities that have a bearing on real estate administration. Some of the practices of the individuals and firms engaged in the real estate business are regulated—for example, by licensing laws. Some government agencies provide information and counsel. There are also some activities that are designed to stimulate or retard private activity.

The federal government does not regulate the real estate business specifically, other than to apply to it the regulations which are imposed on all business practices. Thus, antitrust laws and those regulating monopolistic practices apply in this area, as in others. Many of the informational activities of such federal agencies as the Department of Housing and Urban Development, Bureau of the Census, Department of Commerce, Bureau of Labor Statistics, Department of Agriculture, and others are of importance to those engaged in real estate business.

Probably the influence of the federal government on the real estate business is felt principally through real estate finance. The work of the Federal Housing Administration, the Federal Home Loan Bank System, the Veterans' Administration and the Federal and Government National Mortgage Associations has been of major importance.

### License Laws

State governments have special influences on real estate administration and practice through license laws.[2] The first real estate license law was enacted in California in 1917 but was declared unconstitutional. Another

---

[2] See "Real Estate License Laws" in Appendix B of this book.

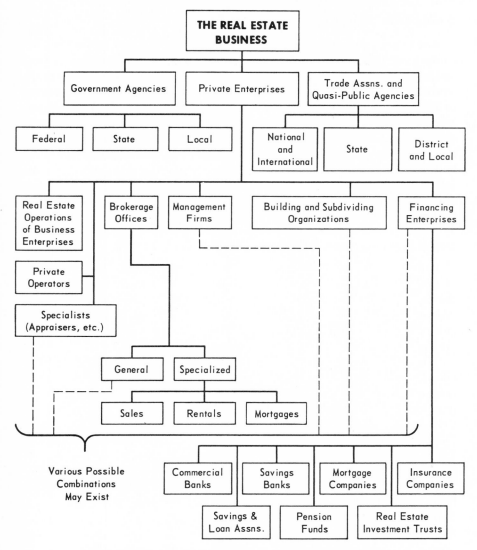

**Fig. 2–2.**  General outline of the real estate business.

act was passed in 1919 which met constitutionality requirements, and Michigan enacted a similar law in the same year.

All of the 50 states have regulatory laws in effect, plus the District of Columbia, the Territory of the Virgin Islands and Guam. Five provinces in Canada also have effective license law legislation. Many of these laws were patterned after a model law which was prepared in 1914 by N. W. MacChesney, who was then general counsel for the National Association of Real Estate Boards.

A license law makes provision for regulating the practices of real estate brokers and real estate salesmen in the interests of the public. Typically, such laws require that each person desiring to carry on brokerage or other marketing activities in the real estate field secure a license, and that only persons with stated qualifications may obtain licenses. Usually the people licensed are divided into two classes, brokers and salesmen, with supervision being exercised directly over the brokers, who are responsible for the salesmen working for them. Provisions are made for machinery to administer and enforce the licensing laws, and for the revocation of licenses and imposition of penalties if the laws are broken.

License laws for their areas regulate the entrance of architects and engineers into their respective fields and thus have an effect on the real estate business. In addition, some state governments require that contractors and workmen in the plumbing and electrical trades be licensed.

In order for a new applicant to secure a broker's or salesman's license he normally is called upon to (1) secure the endorsement of a certain number of responsible citizens (usually two) who vouch for his reputation, (2) meet certain minimum educational requirements, (3) pay a nominal fee, and (4) in some cases post a bond. Examinations are required in all states. These regulations are generally administered by a real estate commission. Standards for admission to the business have tended to be made more rigorous in most of the states.

There appears to be general agreement that license laws have helped to improve the personnel of the real estate brokerage business, that fraudulent practices have been reduced, and that the confidence of the public in real estate brokers and salesmen has been increased. It is probable that these license laws have helped to stimulate educational activity in the real estate field and that greater uniformity of practices among different regions has resulted.

### Local Regulations

Although there are many variations, local governments seldom regulate the real estate business directly but exercise profound influence on it by their tax policies, zoning and planning regulations, building codes, and related controls. Of special importance are building regulations, building permit requirements, regulations affecting the safety and health standards of buildings, changes in transportation systems and regulations, urban renewal programs, housing projects, and the like.

## Trade Associations

A number of trade associations are of importance in the real estate field. The National Association of Real Estate Boards and its affiliates, a nationwide organization, has branches in each state and in many cities. It includes such institutes, societies, and councils as the following: American Institute of Real Estate Appraisers, Institute of Farm Brokers, Institute of Real Estate Management, National Institute of Real Estate Brokers, American Society of Real Estate Counselors, Secretaries Council, Society of Industrial Realtors, International Real Estate Federation, States' Council and Women's Council.

The National Association of Home Builders, The Society of Real Estate Appraisers, the National Association of Building Owners and Managers, and the Home Manufacturers' Institute are important organizations in this field. In finance, a number of organizations carry on work of importance to real estate, including the American Bankers Association, U. S. Savings and Loan League, National Association of Mutual Savings Banks, Life Insurance Association of America, and Mortgage Bankers Association. Others might also be mentioned.

Most of these organizations strive to serve their members by representing them before the public, collecting and disseminating information, carrying on educational activities, undertaking such lobbying and legislative activities as appear to be in the interests of their members, and conducting numerous related types of work. Of special importance are their attempts to raise the standards of business practice in their areas by educational programs, recognitions of various kinds, and restriction of membership to qualified personnel.

Organizations that play a leading role in educational activities include the American Savings and Loan Institute, the American Institute of Banking, the American Institute of Real Estate Appraisers, the Society of Real Estate Appraisers, the American Real Estate and Urban Economics Association, and others.

## Realtor

The efforts of the National Association of Real Estate Boards to establish and maintain certain minimum standards of practice are deserving of special mention. In 1916 this organization adopted the term *Realtor* as "a distinctive name to be applied solely to persons who are members of a constituent board of, and as such having membership in, the National Association of Real Estate Boards." This name may be used only by those who are affiliated with the Association. To the extent that members follow high standards of practice, this term acquires value in distinguishing them from other persons engaged in the real estate business.

### Code of Ethics

In order to guarantee high standards of practice, the National Association of Real Estate Boards adopted in 1924 an official code of ethics. Every local organization which becomes affiliated with the Association is required to adopt and enforce this code. Its principal objectives are to regulate relationships between those in the real estate business and the public, and also to regulate relationships of brokers with other brokers, with owners, with operators, and with others in the real estate field. (See Appendix C.)

### Is Real Estate a Profession?

Many people engaged in the real estate business believe that they are doing work of a professional type and that they should be accorded recognition as members of a profession or professions. Such recognition in a final sense depends on the general attitudes and standards of the public rather than on published rules, codes, or distinctive names. To date, those in the various divisions of real estate business have not been considered by the public at large to be members of a profession. This does not suggest that those in business activities in these areas occupy any lower position in the public mind than do those in medicine, law, or the ministry. It is a different position, to be sure, since the public in general appears to think of work related to real estate in terms of business rather than in professional terms. Whether this public estimate is correct or not may be determined by considering some of the basic criteria of a profession.

A professional person is an expert in an area that is of major importance to the public such as health, legal guidance, or education. The patient or client stands in a dependent role and cannot be expected to protect himself. Usually the members of a profession are products of a specialized educational and training program. They develop standards of practice and impose these on members of the profession. The services of a profession are largely rendered in person and are provided to a considerable extent on the basis of need rather than economic gain. Thus small rather than large scale operations are the rule.

If we accept this general description of the requirements of a profession, only a limited number of those in the various branches of real estate qualify on all counts. The appraisers come close to meeting many of these requirements and are developing into a truly professional group. Architecture is already recognized as a profession. Land planners and market analysts also are moving in the direction of professional status. Some of the other branches of the real estate business, however, may move in the direction of the professions more slowly. Brokerage, management, financing, developing, and related activities are likely to develop into areas of larger- rather than smaller-scale activity by virtue of the increasing needs for more economical production, marketing and financing of properties, and property services.

## SUMMARY

Decisions related to real estate resources are similar to other business decisions but are influenced by such unique factors as income production at fixed locations, long-term commitments, large commitments, close interrelationships of public and private interests and the special characteristics of real estate markets. Real estate decision makers are both "deciders" and "doers." They make decisions and implement them, hence are concerned with the management processes of planning, organizing and controlling operations.

Principal decision makers are owners and users. The real estate business may be involved in primary or supporting decision making activities. The major functions of the real estate business include production, marketing, financing and specialized functions such as appraising, engineering, architecture, real estate law and various analytical efforts. Some of those engaged in the real estate business may function as entrepreneurs or operators on their own; many others from individuals to major corporations may engage in a wide range of entrepreneurial activities.

The real estate business operates within a framework of private enterprises which operate within a system of competition that is directed by laws and regulations on federal, state and local levels. Many public and quasi-public agencies operate in this field. Of special importance are a variety of trade associations and similar organizations. Commissions which administer license laws play an important role. The term "Realtor" designates someone who has met the qualifications established by the National Association of Real Estate Boards which enforces a code of ethics to which members subscribe.

## QUESTIONS FOR STUDY

1. How do real estate decisions differ from other types? How do different circumstances result in different approaches to decisions?

2. Explain the statement that managers and administrators are both deciders and doers.

3. What are the two classes of real estate decision makers? How do their goals differ?

4. What are the main steps in making a decision?
5. Discuss the functions of the real estate business. Which organizations generally perform these functions?
6. How does the federal government influence real estate decisions?
7. How does competition act as a method of control in the real estate field?
8. How do the private and public sectors interact in the real estate area?
9. How are financing institutions likely to exercise influence on real estate decisions?
10. List the principal local governmental regulations that influence the activities of land developers and builders. Which regulations apply most directly to brokers?
11. Explain the functions of real estate license laws. Do you favor such laws? Why or why not?
12. How might license laws, building codes, and other regulations adversely affect the allocation of real estate resources?
13. Which specialists in the real estate field are most likely to obtain professional status?
14. Who can designate himself as a Realtor?

## SUGGESTED READINGS

SAMUELSON, PAUL A. *Economics: An Introductory Analysis* (8th ed.). New York: McGraw-Hill Book Co., Inc., 1970. Chaps. 1, 5.

WEIMER, ARTHUR M. *Introduction to Business: A Management Approach* (4th ed.). Homewood, Ill.: Richard D. Irwin, Inc., 1970. Chaps. 10–12.

————. "Real Estate Decisions are Different," *Harvard Business Review* (November–December, 1966).

## STUDY PROJECT 2–1

### Entrepreneurial Biographies *

A recent class of MBA students in real estate and land economics was given the opportunity to study the business biographies of eight men who had enjoyed outstanding success in this field. Success was defined rather broadly as outstanding achievement in any part of the real estate area and ranged over a wide variety of activities.

The men whose business biographies were studied in the order of their meetings with the class are as follows:

Max Karl, President, Mortgage Guaranty Insurance Corporation, Milwaukee, Wisconsin
John C. Hart, President, John C. Hart and Associates, Indianapolis, Indiana
Guthrie May, President, Guthrie May and Company, Evansville, Indiana
Homer Hoyt, President, Homer Hoyt Associates, Washington, D.C.

* Arthur M. Weimer.

Thomas F. Seay, Chairman of the Board, Seay & Thomas, Inc., Chicago, Illinois

James C. Downs, Chairman of the Board, Real Estate Research Corporation, Chicago, Illinois

A. D. Theobald, Chairman of the Board, First Federal Savings and Loan Association of Peoria, Illinois

Philip M. Klutznick, Chairman of the Board, Urban Investment and Development Corporation, Chicago, Illinois

It should be noted that these were not typical "organization men." Many of them had been involved in establishing their own enterprises. Some of them had worked for corporations or government agencies for varying periods. Several had spent some time in the military service. Some had served in professional capacities. For the most part, however, these were entrepreneurial types. They were selected in the hope that the class would be able to learn about entrepreneurship, especially in the real estate field, by direct association with entrepreneurs. In addition the class had the benefit of discussions of entrepreneurship which were led by:

Edward E. Edwards, Fred T. Greene Professor of Finance, Indiana University

Stephen Slipher, Staff Vice President and Legislative Director, U. S. Savings and Loan League, Washington, D. C.

Joseph R. Ewers, President, Federal Home Loan Bank of Indianapolis; Associate Professor of Business Administration, Indiana University

These three men brought the academic, governmental and trade association areas into the class discussions.

**Not Defeated.** Throughout these business biographies runs a constant theme of unwillingness to accept defeat. These people refused to acknowledge failure even when it seemed very close. They had a strong determination to succeed. To a man they were proof of Marshal Foch's famous statement: "No one is defeated who will not admit that he is defeated."

One of the outstanding illustrations of this was provided by Mr. Karl during the period when he was establishing the Mortgage Guaranty Insurance Corporation. In order to gain a national position quickly he had decided to appoint a nationally recognized board of driectors and this plan had been approved by those selected. Just a few days prior to the planned announcement of the new board, several members of the proposed board called Mr. Karl to indicate that they had decided not to go ahead with this plan.

Mr. Karl refused to accept this decision without making further effort. He inquired as to the basis for their position and upon learning that it resulted from the suggestion of one of their principal advisers, he asked who this man was, made a heroic effort to see him and to convince him of the validity of the new enterprise. In this he was successful. The new board was established according to plan and the Mortgage Guaranty Insurance Corporation as a result attained a national position in a relatively short time.

Mr. Downs started publishing his Real Estate Market Letter without any subscribers. He sent this to people he thought might have an interest in it.

Even though recognition was a long time in coming, he persisted in this effort until the Letter came to be recognized as an important source of information. In turn it opened for him various other avenues to success.

Early in his career Mr. Klutznick was trying to assist a "clean up" administration in Omaha. The city desperately needed work projects. Every effort to secure federal grants proved to be frustrating since they required matching funds and Omaha had no funds available. Mr. Klutznick, who was serving as Assistant Corporation Counsel to the City of Omaha, found in the new public housing program funds which could be made available on a non-matching basis. This, however, required the designation of certain areas as slum areas and the city government was reluctant to do this. After further efforts, however, the required procedures were adopted and a public housing program was developed in Omaha, the first west of the Mississippi River. This in turn brought Mr. Klutznick to the attention of those administering the public housing program and started him on a career in the housing field which included both extensive governmental and private activities.

Mr. Seay suffered setbacks early in his career as a result of the depression of the 1930's. He lost almost all of his savings which had been invested in real estate ventures. He persisted, however, and subsequently was able to rebuild his savings and his career. As he has said, "The 30's were the real proving ground for all of us who loved this business and were determined to stick it out."

Mr. Hoyt had a similar experience losing nearly all his holdings in the Chicago real estate depression of the late 1920's and early 1930's. This experience, however, caused him to try to find out why developments had occurred as they did and to determine whether Chicago real estate values might be revived. As a result he wrote his famous *100 Years of Land Values in Chicago* which was accepted as a doctoral dissertation at the University of Chicago. Thus he was able to finish a Ph.D. program he had started some years before. This in turn launched him into a highly successful career, first with the Federal Housing Administration and then as a real estate consultant and investor.

After World War II when he returned from military service, Mr. Theobald found that a commitment to head an organization where he had been second in command would not be honored. He had no immediate alternative but to return. He persisted in his desire to be in a top leadership position and in a few months found an opportunity to take such a position.

Mr. May persisted with his new home building organization in the face of labor union problems. He often undertook ventures which his advisers and others believed could only lead to failure. Often when a venture looked bad in its early stages, he stayed with it, often committing further resources to it.

Mr. Hart refused to give in to disadvantages arising from the uneven enforcement of governmental regulations. He entered politics himself in order to correct some of the difficulties he encountered. He was almost as successful in politics and government as in business.

**Innovative Approaches.** The second major conclusion may be stated this way: Each business biography reflected a highly innovative type of person. These men were not limited by traditional approaches to problems nor to traditional solutions. When established methods and procedures failed, they invented new methods and procedures. When resources of the usual type were not available, they substituted others. They all had imagination and in varying degrees had creative ability.

The ability to innovate and indeed to invent new approaches to problems has already been illustrated in part in the preceding discussions. For example, Mr. Karl substituted a well-known national board for more traditional ways of developing a national market. He did not have the resources to launch a widespread promotional campaign but his national board in effect provided this for him. In turn the reputation of his new board served as a substitute for a lack of capital since the confidence which people in the mortgage business placed in these men was the equivalent of a substantial investment which could only be built over a period of time.

Mr. Hoyt adapted the techniques of the historian and statistician to the analysis of the real estate market. He designed ways of handling voluminous amounts of data prior to the days of the computer. He used maps in novel ways to summarize information. He patterned his investments after his sector theory of city growth, which was a new explanation of city growth and structure. Thus he combined business and academic innovations. He adapted the theory of international trade to economic base analysis for the appraisal of local economic conditions. This in turn contributed to many of his analytical studies as a real estate consultant.

Mr. Theobald used a community orientation as the basis for promoting the First Federal Savings and Loan Association of Peoria. He identified the growth of the association with the growth of the community. This gave him an unusual and attractive approach to the development of this savings and loan association.

Mr. Seay adapted the syndication idea to many real estate ventures, often in unusual ways. He frequently used salesmanship as a substitute for capital, arranging partnerships and joint ventures which would enable him to substitute his work and efforts for monetary investments. He learned early in his career that the best way to increase real estate value is to transfer a property from a lower to a higher use. Thus, he was imaginative in changing run-down hotels to apartments and office buildings, loft buildings to office uses, farm land to industrial parks and in similar ways to create higher values. The ability to see increased potential in real properties was a major factor in his success.

Mr. Downs recognized early the possibilities in Florida real estate and the real estate in Hawaii. He saw the potential impact of the jet airplane on vacations at a very early stage. He was able to recognize early the potential in the prefabricated housing field and to capitalize on it. To get the required land he substituted a high price offer and longer term financing for a lower price plus a large down payment and shorter term financing.

**Enjoyment of Life and Work.** In general these entrepreneurs enjoyed life and work. Most of them were healthy and had an abundance of energy. They seemed to be too busy and too interested in their work to let any minor disruptions bother them. They were careful about their living habits and guarded their health, recognizing the need to feel well in order to perform well.

Mr. Downs, for example, learned from an early employer that minor illness should be no excuse to be absent from work. He found that one must feel good in order to do good work. So he has been careful about his health. This seems to be generally true of people of this type.

Almost all of these men liked their work. They enjoyed work almost to the extent of not being interested in hobbies or sports or other forms of relaxation. Few were much interested in vacations, which tended to represent interruptions in an otherwise pleasant existence.

Builders like Guthrie May and John Hart often spend their week ends looking over their properties. Almost all of these men enjoy the process of looking at new developments or looking for new opportunities while supposedly relaxing on week ends. Mr. Theobald likes to spend some of his leisure time checking on new developments which are being financed by his association.

It would be easy to multiply illustrations of the extent to which these men enjoyed their work almost to the exclusion of other things. In many cases when they did find other interests they translated these into work opportunities. For example, Mr. May's interest in boating led to his purchase of several barges on the Ohio River. Mr. Klutznick's enjoyment of rural life led to the development of substantial farming interests. Mr. Downs' early desire to live in the country led not only to the purchase of land but to the establishment of a prefabricated house dealership and to the development of a substantial subdivision.

None of the men expressed much interest in retirement. Mr. Klutznick said he had retired over and over again from the government service but there is little doubt that he will remain active as long as possible. Much the same thing is true of the others.

**Independent and Tough Minded.** These men were independent in thought, outlook, and attitude. They did not easily accept the opinion of others. They liked to do their own thinking based on facts insofar as possible.

These were not organization men. Mr. Hoyt worked for brief periods for AT&T and for the federal government. He reported almost complete frustration in both types of assignments. He was not entirely happy when serving as a member of several university faculties. He seemed to operate best as a completely independent consultant and investor.

Mr. May often employed consultants and market analysts but did not necessarily follow their recommendations. Against the advice of various of his associates and bankers he moved into a major shopping center development after it appeared to be a virtually hopeless project and brought it to completion.

Mr. Hart undertook developments which other builders had turned down. He often cooperated with National Homes in their developments but on occasion moved contrary to their plans.

Mr. Downs bought real estate bonds when they were selling for a few cents on the dollar against the advice of many, thus matching his judgment against that of others. He persisted in publishing his Real Estate Market Letter even though there seemed to be little demand for it. Ultimately it proved to be highly successful.

Both Mr. Seay and Mr. Hoyt might have been knocked out by the depression had they not had a strong belief in their own capabilities and in their eventual success.

Mr. Downs undertook his first independent real estate management venture in a field where others were facing failure. His self assurance undoubtedly was a major factor in his early success as a consultant.

Few of these entrepreneurs felt comfortable working for someone else. Many might be classified as "loners." All were highly independent in their beliefs and thoughts. They relied on other people but never in a final sense.

As a corollary to this, they all had great confidence in their own abilities. Not only were they unwilling to accept defeat as has been suggested, they believed in their capacity to succeed, even to the extent of being sure that success could not be denied them.

**Learning from Experience.**    These men knew how to learn from their experiences. They made mistakes but seldom made the same mistakes twice.

Mr. Theobald recognized that he had been operating primarily as second in command prior to World War II when he was Vice President of the U. S. Savings and Loan League and the American Savings and Loan Institute. During World War II he served on the staff of Tex Thornton who developed the famous "whiz kids" group which ultimately went to work for Ford. Theobald decided against going with this group on the ground that he would probably continue to be a second in command for a long time; he wanted to run his own operation soon. He sought another outlet for his energy and ability and soon found this in the First Federal Savings and Loan Association of Peoria.

Mr. Hoyt lost heavily because of a lack of liquidity during the depression; thereafter he was careful to adjust his land commitments to his cash flow so as not to lose property because of a lack of cash. Also he avoided other types of investments than land, largely holding only cash or its equivalent and land.

As has been suggested Mr. Seay learned early the value of syndication and built a variety of adaptations and opportunities on this device.

Mr. Klutznick recognized that the kind of experience he had gained in public housing could be adapted to private developments and on this basis undertook the ventures that brought about the Park Forest Development and subsequently others.

Mr. May recognized that the command and leadership experience he had gained in World War II would enable him to operate his own business and thus he started a prefabricated housing business as a National Homes dealer rather than returning to his former job. Later he saw that experience in the housing field could be adapted to other fields.

Mr. Hart recognized that his work as an accountant for a building organization had provided him with the experience necessary to establish his own building organization. Later he saw that successful operations in the single family home field could be adapted to apartment houses and commercial ventures. His accounting experience pointed the way to tax shelters in the real estate field.

Mr. Downs recognized that property management provided an open avenue to successful real estate investment. He learned that experience in real estate investments could be useful in developing other successful investments.

**Forward Looking.** To a man these entrepreneurs were forward looking. They had the capacity to anticipate future developments and while they could not always clearly see the shape of things to come they operated on a forward looking basis.

Mr. Hoyt's early recognition of the importance of the shopping center movement and its potential in terms of the emerging patterns of city growth is one of the best illustrations of this.

Mr. Theobald concluded that there would be no major depression and that the real estate market would expand substantially after World War II and this formed the basis for his successful operations.

Mr. May's ability to see the potential in prefabrication not only in his own town but in other cities was a major factor in his success. Ability to anticipate areas of growth along with problem areas served him in good stead.

Mr. Downs' recognition of the Florida and Hawaiian developments is a case in point as were Mr. Hart's abilities to see the potential in the northwest Indianapolis area.

All of these men had the capacity to plan. This ranged from planning day to day activities to long range planning. Many of these men liked to get to work early and plan their day before the office force assembled. Mr. Klutznick started this practice at an early stage and continues to follow it. Mr. Seay tends to plan more in terms of blocks of time rather than specific dates but is constantly aware of the directions in which he is planning to move.

Mr. Hoyt writes constantly of the future trying to probe potential developments at least to the year 2000.

Mr. Theobald is a continuous planner and he encourages planning on the part of his subordinates. He holds special planning sessions of his staff typically away from the office so that they can jointly try to anticipate problems and potential developments. In this, incidentally, he hit on an interesting device for gaining recognition for his people by taking them to outstanding places such as well known resorts. This not only appealed to the men, it also gave their wives special recognition among their friends at home.

This forward looking attitude seems to be one of the characteristics of all these men. They try to anticipate potential developments. They look ahead, rather than backward although they use past experience as a guide to the future.

**Summary.** The real estate entrepreneurs covered by these discussions represented a wide diversity of experiences and types of people. Even so, there were many similarities in their careers and points of view. These men have been stubborn in their unwillingness to accept defeat. They have been innovative in their approaches to problems, seldom relying on standard or traditional methods. Typically they have enjoyed life largely through their work. These men have been highly independent in thought and action, almost to the point of being "loners" in some cases. With great confidence in themselves and their abilities they have often undertaken highly risky projects. They knew how to learn from experience and have used this knowledge in new projects. They have been forward looking in outlook and attitude.

### Questions

1. What common characteristics do these entrepreneurs possess?
2. Do these characteristics imply a "secret of success"?
3. What are the main differences between these entrepreneurs?
4. Which entrepreneur impressed you the most?  Why?

# 3

# Real Estate Resources and Their Physical Environment

## ENVIRONMENTAL PROBLEMS

Real estate resources make up a significant part of our physical environment. Land is a basic resource; how it is used has a major effect on the air, the water and our general physical surroundings. Careful and systematic cultivation of the soil prevents erosion and keeps streams, rivers and other bodies of water reasonably free of soil runoff. Appropriate methods for dealing with human and industrial waste prevent both water and air pollution. Congestion often leads to environmental problems. Heavy industry may contribute to the pollution of air and water unless appropriate standards can be observed that can meet the economic requirements of production processes.

### Government Regulations

Government regulations may influence the quality of our environment not only by the standards imposed as to disposal of wastes and related factors but also by zoning laws, building codes, traffic patterns and standards, density and related requirements. General plans for the development of an area including the highway network, location of water and sewer mains, location and type of waste disposal systems, the placement of parks, schools and other public facilities and many related factors all have major effects on the physical environment. Plans and programs of development which avoid congestion and which make it easy for private citizens and enterprises to avoid contributing to environmental problems can mean much for long term developments. In addition, the relative attractiveness of public buildings and other installations may determine the general quality of an entire area.

### Land Development

Plans for the development of land can affect not only the general attractiveness of an area but also the efficiency with which it can be used and the extent to which it maintains and improves the physical environment or adds to problems of pollution. Land planners and engineers thus have a heavy responsibility for our environment. Those who develop land and build structures also play a big role in determining the quality of the physical environment. Careful workmanship, effective use of materials, appropriate combinations of land, buildings and other improvements can do much to avoid environmental problems. Installation of good quality waste disposal systems, underground installation of electric wires and utilities and general care in the development of an area are all important.

## APPROACHES TO REAL PROPERTY

One of the first things a real estate salesman learns is the importance of selecting the proper route to a property when showing it to a prospective buyer. He knows that the same property approached from different routes often produces very different impressions. Similarly, the decisions that people make in regard to real properties are influenced greatly by the way they approach them and think about them.

### Physical Approach

In Chapter 1 we suggested that you select a "study property." If we were to approach this property by one of the avenues leading to it, we would probably view it first as a physical entity, as land and buildings. This is the point of view of most people when they first think about real property. The land may be considered in terms of its size, type, topography and relief characteristics, the condition of the soil and subsoil, and accessibility to streets, roads, utilities, and various conveniences. The building may be viewed from the standpoint of its size, type, design, condition, structural soundness, the floor plan, the mechanical conveniences available, the relationship of the building to the lot, its orientation, and similar matters.

### Legal Approach

If our approach to the property were by another "street" or point of view, however, we would look at it as a lawyer does and see it chiefly in terms of legal rights and obligations. To a lawyer the physical land and buildings have significance only to the extent that they represent *property rights*. These rights are evidenced by a great many types of legal documents and records. Many of these documents are recorded at the courthouse in the office of the local registrar of deeds or in the offices of similar officials. The property may be identified in a plat book. The owner or his attorney will have an *abstract of title*, which contains a detailed history of the transactions which have had a bearing on the title to the property. Thus, property rights, although intangible, have a certain appearance of reality to many people because they are represented by many types of written documents and official-looking pieces of paper. The legal characteristics of real estate are considered at greater length in the next Chapter.

### Economic Approach

If we approached your study property from still another "street" or point of view, we would look at it through the eyes of the business manager, investor, property user or owner, appraiser, or real estate broker. In this case, we would consider the physical land and buildings, of course, and we would also consider the property rights which the land and buildings represented. But we would view the property first and foremost as an economic resource, as a *vehicle of productivity*, as a means of providing protection, shelter, conveniences, privacy, and other services. In short, we would think of the property in terms of its *income-producing ability* in terms of the dollars and cents which it may yield an owner over the period of its productive life, in terms of its contribution to the production and marketing activities of a business firm, or in terms of the direct satisfactions which an owner might derive from occupying it. This is the point of view with which we shall be chiefly concerned in our study of real estate decisions, resources, and operations. Our reason for stressing this point of view is the belief that factors relating to the income-producing ability of real properties are of primary importance in influencing the decisions of property owners and users. Income producing ability is a reflection of a property's economic characteristics as well as its relationship to the physical, economic and legal environment.

### Importance of Income

For our purposes, the land and buildings on the one hand and the property rights they represent on the other have significance chiefly through the direct satisfaction or the monetary income that may be derived from them. For example, good construction is important mainly because it is related to the ability of a property to produce money or real income. A sound relationship between the property and its environment will add to its income-producing ability. Similarly, property rights have significance chiefly as they facilitate or interfere with sound programs of property use.

Nevertheless, it will be necessary to study the physical characteristics of real property. Our main purpose in this connection will be to study the *income characteristics* of the physical land and buildings, their relationship to the physical environment, and to learn that portion of the language of the architect, engineer, developer, or builder which is essential to an understanding of the subject.

One of our primary purposes in considering the work of the architect and engineer as well as that of the lawyer is to learn to recognize those situations in which we should call on such specialists for advice. To paraphrase an old axiom: "He who is his own lawyer, architect or engineer has a fool for a client."

## Characteristics and Classes of Land

In the early literature of economics, land was considered to be one of the three basic factors of production: land, labor and capital. Land included everything furnished by nature, labor all human services, and capital all artificial or produced goods used in the production process.

There are serious questions about differentiating between land and capital as suggested by this classification. Natural agencies, for example, and especially as used in production are quite different from their original natural condition. Many costs have been incurred in order to make them useful. Indeed, such costs may on the average approximate the value of the natural agencies, thus suggesting that they are little different from most capital goods.

For our purposes we consider land in a physical sense as including the earth's surface; under some conditions we may also include the minerals below the surface and the air above the surface. Mineral and air rights are related to surface land through our system of land ownership but important qualifications often must be made in specific situations. A broad classification of land uses is suggested in Table 3–1.

## Building Classification

Buildings may be classified by type of use or in other ways. From the standpoint of type of use we may divide buildings as follows: farms and other rural buildings, residential, commercial and industrial, governmental, institutional and other types. The vast majority of our buildings, of course, are located in urban areas but farm and other rural uses also account for many.

Farm buildings include farm residences as well as barns, silos, granaries and other types. There are many nonfarm rural residences as well as a variety of country stores, small factories, recreational structures, and other kinds of buildings. In some cases large factories now locate in rural areas

**TABLE 3–1.  Land Use**

| | 1960 | Medium Projections 1980 | 2000 |
|---|---|---|---|
| | (million acres) | | |
| Cropland, including pasture [1] | 447 | 443 | 476 |
| Grazing land [1] | 700 | 700 | 700 |
| Farmland, non-producing | 45 | 45 | 45 |
| Commercial forest land [2] | 484 | 484 | 484 |
| Recreation (excluding reservoir areas and city parks) | 44 | 76 | 134 |
| Urban (including city parks) | 21 | 32 | 45 |
| Transportation | 26 | 28 | 30 |
| Wildlife refuge | 15 | 18 | 20 |
| Reservoirs | 12 | 15 | 20 |
| Total specified [2] | 1,794 | 1,841 | 1,954 |
| Other land (residential) | 110 | 63 | −50 |
| Total land area | 1,904 | 1,904 | 1,904 |

SOURCE: Hans H. Landsberg, Leonard L. Fischman, and Joseph L. Fisher, *Resources in America's Future* (Baltimore: The Johns Hopkins Press, 1963), p. 24.

[1] All adjustments for feeding requirements are made in cropland, with grazing land held constant.

[2] Does not provide for increased acreage to meet projected commercial forest demand. Requirements to close the projected gap in 2000 might run as high as 300 million acres to be put into forest use at this time.

and some fairly large shopping centers may be found in rural areas near the intersections of major highways.

Residential buildings may be divided by number of dwellings. Single-family, two to four-family dwellings and apartment houses with five or more units constitute the main classifications by number of dwellings. Apartments may be further subdivided by walk-up and elevator as well as by garden and high-rise types.

Industrial structures usually are classified as heavy manufacturing, light manufacturing and warehouses. Sometimes they are classified by types of products being manufactured.

Commercial structures include all types of stores, office buildings, hotels and motels, recreational and service establishments. Sometimes commercial classifications are limited to structures used for wholesale and retail purposes with separate classifications for office buildings, service establishments and the like.

Governmental structures include all types of buildings owned or oper-ated by national, state or local governments. Institutional buildings in-clude those owned or operated by educational, research or religious or-ganizations, foundations or other types. In some cases public utility build-ings are separated from others or they may be combined with others.

## Physical Factors Affecting Income

A listing of all physical factors that affect the income-producing ability of land and the buildings and other improvements on it would be an almost impossible task. We will direct our attention primarily to the following in this discussion: (1) land in terms of location, size and shape, topog-raphy, condition of soil and subsoil and various physical factors in the property's environment; (2) buildings, including type of buildings in re-lation to the land, orientation, quality and durability, depreciation, types of construction, functional plan, style and attractiveness and conformity to surroundings; and (3) other improvements.

## LAND

Of the various physical factors related to land we will pay primary at-tention to those listed above. Because of the importance of land surveys we will consider this topic briefly as well.

### Location

Although fertility is the principal factor in determining the income pro-duced by agricultural land, the location or *situs* of urban land is of primary importance in determining its income-producing ability. Since no two points on the earth's surface are exactly alike, every piece of urban real estate is unique; it differs in some respect from others. In some cases the differences may be slight, in others of major importance. Each parcel of urban real estate is a part of a neighborhood or district; it is part of a city and region. To understand even a few of the important features of the relationships between location and income we will need to consider eco-nomic trends, industry potentials, city growth and structure, and the char-acter of specific residential neighborhoods and commercial and industrial districts.

Location often means access or lack of access to various utilities and conveniences. Even the pioneer farmer had to have a road or a right of way over which he could carry his produce to market and bring back nec-essary provisions. The importance of accessibility tends to increase as our communities become more complex.

A farm may be diminished in value if it is split in two by an express highway to which it does not have access. Land at express highway intersections has a high value for motels, shopping centers, and industries.

The value of a parcel of land is related directly to the ease or difficulty of access to roads and streets, transportation facilities, water and gas mains, sewers, and electrical and telephone lines. Similarly, such services as mail delivery, police and fire protection, and garbage, trash, and snow removal are significant.

Distances to schools, shopping centers, places of employment, churches, community centers, parks, and playgrounds are of special importance in considering the value characteristics of land used for residential purposes. Nearness to main arteries of pedestrian traffic and to parking areas are of major importance in the case of business sites. Nearness to transportation lines often is important to industrial sites. Increasingly, accessibility has meant ease of access by automobile or truck transportation. Both shopping centers and industrial parks illustrate this trend.

### Size and Shape of the Land

Urban lot sizes are usually measured in square feet or the number of feet of frontage on the street and depth in feet. Farms and other rural real estate are measured in terms of acres (43,560 square feet) or sections (a square mile—640 acres). Size and shape affect the productivity of a parcel of ground. Obviously, a lot with only 30 feet of frontage cannot be used as the site for a tall office building or a large department store.

Size is an important factor in determining use, and use in turn has a very direct bearing on income-producing ability. Size also determines effectiveness of use; the trend toward larger farms as agriculture has become more highly mechanized is a case in point. Value, of course, is not directly proportional to size. Up to a point, additions to the size of a parcel of land tend to increase its income-producing ability and hence its value; thereafter, such additions tend to be of diminishing importance. *Plottage* is the term used to describe the extent to which value is increased when two or more plots are combined.

The shape of the land parcel may determine the possible uses to which it may be put and hence affect its income-producing ability. While lots of irregular shape may often be used to advantage for residential purposes, regularity is usually desirable for business, industrial, or agricultural uses. Many developers of new residential areas plan lots of irregular shape, adapting them to curvilinear streets, cul de-sacs, and park areas. This practice contrasts with the gridiron pattern formerly followed in subdivision planning. The gridiron pattern often resulted in odd shaped lots when diagonal streets were involved.

The relationship between frontage and depth is important for many types of urban real estate. Few lots of less than 50 or 60 feet in width are considered adequate for residential development. Lots used for business and industrial purposes vary greatly in width and depth, depending on the specific uses to which they are put.

## Planned Unit Development

Efforts to improve the efficiency of land use have resulted in the concept of "planned unit development." This involves the careful study of the interrelations between the various functions that are to be performed by a unit of land in order to get the maximum utilization of the land available. For example, instead of developing an area with single-family homes, garden-type apartments may be used but arranged in such a way that adequate privacy may be provided and provision made for recreational and related land uses. As a result more efficient land utilization will result.

## Topography

A study of topography includes a consideration of contour and slope, the direction and steepness of slope, and such things as gullies, streams, knolls, and ravines. These factors may have a determining influence on the uses which may be made of the land. Lots with steep slopes, for example, are not easily adapted to business, industrial, or agricultural uses. They may allow for attractive residential developments, although the cost of a house built on a sloping lot is usually greater than that of one constructed on a level lot. Note Figure 3–1 in this connection. Topography has an important bearing on drainage, on erosion, on the ease or difficulty of constructing streets or roads, and on landscaping problems.

In addition to the topography of a specific land parcel, it is usually necessary to consider the topography of adjoining land, since drainage and related problems may be involved. Gently rolling land is usually considered desirable in residential neighborhoods and for farming operations, while level or nearly level land is more desirable in business and industrial areas.

It is well to give special attention to streams or bodies of water on or near a piece of land. The possibility of flooding is always an important consideration, and stagnant water may invite hordes of mosquitoes. Some streams are polluted or are in danger of it.

As a general guide to the study of the contour of a tract of land, consider on the one hand those factors which will be advantageous to its income-producing ability and on the other those things which will be detrimental. For example, drainage problems often require expensive tiling operations; steep lots may require the building of retaining walls.

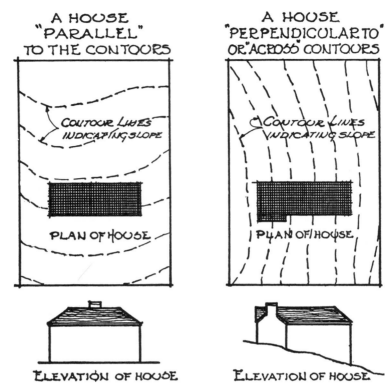

**Fig. 3–1.** Construction parallel and perpendicular to contours.

### Condition of the Soil and Subsoil

The condition of the soil and subsoil is of basic importance in determining the income-producing ability of farms. It also has a bearing on city lots. In some cities expensive piles must be driven to provide a bearing surface for any buildings of major size because of the unstable nature of the soil. If rock formations are encountered at a point only a few feet from the surface, it becomes expensive to excavate and to install water mains and sewer lines. In such cases special provision must usually be made for drainage as well. For buildings of moderate size, subsoils of clay, gravel, and coarse sand are usually the most desirable.

In rural nonfarm areas near cities but beyond sewer mains, percolation tests are important in determining whether the soils will absorb sewage.

The condition of the topsoil is of lesser importance in the case of lots used for business and industrial purposes, since they are usually covered over with concrete or asphalt. For residential and agricultural uses, however, the condition of the topsoil is of major importance. Surface rock, some types of clay, muck land, and quicksand often create special problems.

## Physical Environmental Factors

The condition of the physical environment has an important bearing on the income producing potential of real estate. For example, polluted streams, lakes and ocean front as well as smog and other undesirable atmospheric conditions can affect large areas of land and hinder its development. Favorable or unfavorable weather conditions such as extreme cold or heat, hurricanes, heavy snowstorms, fog and the like may have a bearing on various areas. Industrial wastes, trash dumps, open sewers, certain types of sewage disposal plants and a variety of other environmental factors may have adverse effects. On the other hand, desirable environmental conditions can have a favorable effect on an area and on the properties located there.

## Surveys

In connection with most land development activities, or in connection with mortgage financing, surveys by licensed surveyors or engineers are often required. Such surveys usually show (1) exact dimensions and (2) boundaries in relation to streets or roads; they may show (3) levels of land by contour lines, (4) position of trees, rock formations, and so on, and (5) location of sewer, water, gas and electric lines. The purpose of the survey usually determines the items covered. See Figure 3–2, for example.

## BUILDINGS

Except for parking lots and a few other uses, it is necessary to construct a building in order to earn income from urban land. Thus buildings should be thought of as the means by which the earning power of urban land is released. Considered in another way, the services of buildings and other improvements on urban land may be thought of as similar in some degree to the crops which are produced on farm land. Buildings are also important to farming operations but play a lesser role than they do in urban land uses.

In this section we will consider some of the physical characteristics which increase or diminish the income-producing ability of buildings and consequently have a bearing on value. Land value arises from residual income remaining after expenses of operating the building, real estate taxes, and interest and depreciation on the cost of the building are deducted from

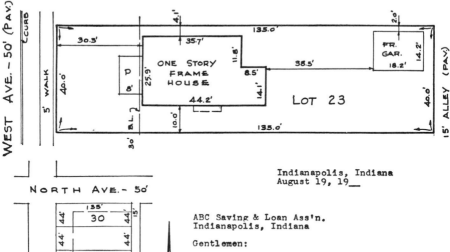

**PAUL I. CRIPE, INC.**
150 E. MARKET STREET
INDIANAPOLIS 4, INDIANA
MELROSE 6-5411

CIVIL ENGINEERING
LAND SURVEYING

SUBDIVISION DESIGN
BUILDING DESIGN

Indianapolis, Indiana
August 19, 19__

ABC Saving & Loan Ass'n.
Indianapolis, Indiana

Gentlemen:

I, the undersigned, hereby certify that the above plat represents a survey made by me on the 19th day of August, 19__ on the following described real estate to-wit:

Lot 23 in John Doe's Subdivision to the City of Indianapolis, as per plat thereof, recorded in Plat Book 19, page 30, in the office of the Recorder of Marion County, Indiana.

Based thereon, I further certify that the buildings situated on the above described real estate are located within the boundaries of said premises. I have shown on said plat the distances from the sides and fronts of the buildings to points on the side lines and front line of the lot. I further certify that the buildings on the adjoining property do not encroach on the lot or real estate in question.

The property is improved with a one story frame dwelling, occupied by John Jones, and located at 2735 North West Avenue, Indianapolis, Indiana.

This survey is for Mortgage purposes and does not purport to be sufficient for the location of corner stakes and the establishment of lot lines.

**Fig. 3–2.** Surveyor's plat of a city lot for mortgage purposes. (Courtesy Paul I. Cripe, Inc.)

gross income. If the wrong type of building is constructed, the value of the land may be destroyed.

We should note that while a lot and a building together form a single income-producing unit, the building can be replaced while the land cannot. In the case of especially well-located lots, the land is one of the paramount supports of the value of the entire property. In other cases it is of lesser importance. In some cases land can be "made," as in Miami or Chicago, where watercovered areas have been filled in or there are cases where steep hills have been graded down.

### Type of Building in Relation to Land

As we have pointed out, it is desirable from both private and public standpoints for each piece of real estate to be put to its highest and best use. One of the important considerations in developing a property to its highest and best use is a balanced relationship between land, buildings, and other improvements. The income-producing ability of a property may be greater or less than required to pay a return on the investment. This difference is often referred to by appraisers as *improved value.*

For example, a building costing $500,000 to construct may be placed on a lot priced at $100,000. Faulty planning and improper improvement may result in a value based on anticipated returns of only $400,000. On the other hand, a proper combination of land and buildings based on careful planning by the architect, plus cleverness, imagination, and risk-taking by the promoter, may produce an income that will support a value of $800,000.

Some buildings represent an *overimprovement*—that is, a larger expenditure than can be supported by the site. Others represent an *underimprovement,* an investment that is not great enough to bring out the full income-producing potential of the site.

### Orientation

The position of the structure on the land and its general relationship to its surroundings are usually referred to as its orientation. In solidly built business streets, of course, there is little latitude for special arrangements. Even in such cases, however, position on the street, easy access for customers, accessibility to delivery trucks, relationship to adjacent buildings, and the like are important factors in a property's income-producing ability. In the North, locations on the street facing the sun may command a premium; in the South the opposite is often true. An industrial building must be placed advantageously with respect to the movement of materials and workers into and out of the plant.

Orientation is a major problem in the case of residential buildings, particularly single-family homes. A house placed on the lot in such a way as to bring out the greatest potentialities of the entire property will be more valuable than an identical house located to lesser advantage. In addition, proper orientation to the sun, prevailing winds, and attractive and unattractive views are major considerations. Attention is often given to solar orientation in order to take greatest advantage of the sun's heat in the winter and protection from it in the summer. Also, houses should be located to advantage with respect to the local environment including lot lines, setback lines, and other houses in the area.

## Quality and Durability

The quality of workmanship and materials in a building have an important effect on its durability. If properly constructed a building will resist both the elements and usage over a long period of time and without incurring excessive maintenance costs. The durability of a building has a direct relationship to its life cycle—that is, to the period during which it can produce an income adequate to justify the investment involved. While the physical life of a building is usually longer than its economic life, there tends to be some relationship between physical life and the period during which satisfactory returns can be earned. These returns, of course, may be either in the form of monetary income or, in the case of an owner-occupied home, in direct usage.

It may be said in general that physical decay has not been a major factor in bringing the useful or economic lives of buildings to an end. Generally, buildings are demolished in order to make room for a higher land use. Indeed, the rate of obsolescence of buildings appears to be higher than it was several decades ago. Rapid changes in the structure of cities, especially under the impact of heavy automobile traffic, have brought swift changes in land values and in the economic usefulness of many buildings. Competition of outlying areas is affecting land uses in central business districts.

## Depreciation

As we have indicated, the income-producing ability of a building tends to decline and its value to diminish with the passage of time if other things remain equal. This process is called *depreciation*.

The American Institute of Real Estate Appraisers has pointed out that depreciation may be due to deterioration resulting from wear and tear and the action of the elements and to obsolescence which may be functional or economic. Functional obsolescence results from poor planning, design, or equipment and related factors "evidenced by conditions within the property"; economic obsolescence results from changes "external to the property," such as neighborhood changes, shifts in market preference, technological advance, and the like. [1]

## Types of Construction

The four main types of construction used in this country are wood frame, wall-bearing masonry, reinforced concrete frame, and steel frame. Another classification provides for two basic types of construction: skeleton frame and wall bearing. The former makes use of columns to transmit loads to the foundation; the latter uses the walls for this purpose.

Wooden frame construction, whether covered by weatherboarding or veneered with brick or stone, is the type most frequently used in building medium-priced houses (see Fig. 3–3). It is cheaper than other types, it can be built rapidly, and it is easy to insulate against heat or cold. Its chief disadvantage is susceptibility to fire. However, firestops, fireproof materials for insulation, aluminum coating, and flameproofed lumber help to reduce this hazard.

In masonry construction the exterior walls are of brick, stone, or concrete block. A brick wall may be of solid construction, or it may be built somewhat thicker than a solid wall to allow for an air space between the outer and inner courses of brick. Often brick or stone is backed up with hollow terra-cotta tile or cement blocks. Stucco on hollow terra-cotta tile is a better construction than stucco on wood, which is liable to shrink and crack the stucco. Masonry houses in the lower-price ranges usually have interior partitions and floor joists of wood. Steel joists may be used in more expensive types. Masonry structures tend to be more fire-resistant than frame types, and maintenance costs are typically lower. On the other hand, such structures are more expensive to build.

Concrete structures may have walls and floors of monolithic construction which are poured into place at the site, may be assembled from concrete block and precast joists and slabs, or may be constructed by a combination of these methods. The chief advantages of concrete buildings are their permanency, fireproof construction, and low maintenance costs.

Steel-frame structures are similar in principle to wooden-frame buildings. Studs, joists, and rafters made of steel are used, eliminating shrinkage; when noncombustible insulating material and exterior covering are used, the structure will resist fire. Coverings may be of any of the usual building materials desired.

---

[1] See *The Appraisal of Real Estate* (5th ed.; Chicago: The American Institute of Real Estate Appraisers, 1967), pp. 199–204; also the Institute's *Appraisal Terminology and Handbook*, 1962, p. 52. See also Richard U. Ratcliff, *Modern Real Estate Valuation* (Madison, Wis.: The Democrat Press, 1965), pp. 58–64.

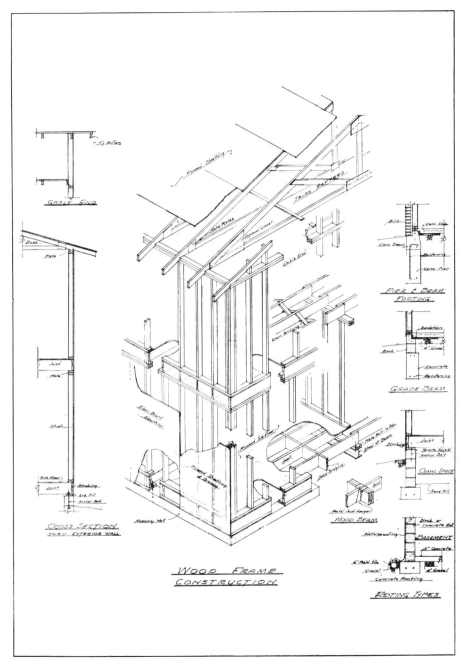

**Fig. 3–3.** Wood frame construction. (Courtesy Paul I. Cripe, Inc.)

**Functional Plan**

Buildings are designed for many purposes, ranging from the functions of specialized industrial structures to those of small single-family residences. All of them provide protection against the elements, such as temperature extremes, rain, and snow. Nearly all provide some degree of comfort and convenience.

The development of an adequate functional plan for a building is largely the work of the architect and engineer. Careful design of spans, proper distribution of weight, adequate openings for doors and windows, correct width of corridors, suitable combinations of materials, and related factors are all involved. In recent years even low- and medium-priced single-family homes have been studied in terms of functions to be performed and the most effective arrangements of the exterior and interior of the structures for the performance of these functions. The functional plan of special-purpose buildings must reflect the specific use for which the structure is intended. General-purpose buildings aim at simple arrangements with a maximum of flexibility of the use of interior space.

Constant improvement in design is one of the important causes of obsolescence in existing buildings. The efficiency of one-story manufacturing plants with continuous assembly lines, for example, has rendered many multistory industrial plants obsolete.

Of special importance to the functional adequacy of modern buildings is the mechanical equipment that is used. The cost of such equipment is now a major item, even in the construction of a small house. The adequacy, condition, durability, and operating economy of such equipment has an important bearing on operating costs and hence on the income-producing capacity of a building. For residences the most important types of equipment are plumbing and sewage disposal, heating and air conditioning, and electric light and power. Elevators are of major importance in many office, apartment, and store buildings. Indeed, the elevator was essential to the development of modern skyscrapers. Escalators are being used to an increasing extent. Industrial plants contain a wide variety of specialized equipment of many types.

**Style and Attractiveness**

The appeal of a building to prospective users and investors is an important element in its ability to produce future income. The factors that make up appeal are difficult to identify. We know that architects and engineers often are able to impart to a building an appeal that is over and above that arising from utilitarian and economic considerations alone. Often this appeal continues over many years. In such cases the building relates well to its environment. Style in a building is usually considered to be one of the factors that provide long-range appeal to users and investors. In this connection Condit says:

> . . . the word "style" is much abused. Yet its connotation is such that the critic and the historian of art can hardly avoid it. In architecture it represents or stands for those essential characteristics of construction, form, ornament, and detail which are common to all the important structures of any particular period in history. But it also stands for those technical and aesthetic qualities of the artistic product which grow directly, logically, and organically out of the conditions of human existence and out of the aspirations and powers of human beings. We rightly feel that the buildings of a certain style—if it is a genuine style—reflect in their form the realities of man's experience and the attempt to master and give emotional expression to those realities. These buildings are constituent facts of man's history, and their revelation is a part of truth itself.[2]

There may, of course, be wide variations in the tastes and cultural standards of prospective users and investors. These tastes will vary from time to time and from region to region. In general, however, experience indicates that buildings which are constructed according to the dictates of good taste are more stable in value over long periods of time than others. For example, houses constructed in accordance with sound architectural standards are not subject to the wide fluctuations in price which arise from the unsettling influences of fads and the temporary popularity of a particular style. The mark of good taste is simplicity. This is manifest in simple masses, simple roof lines, and restrained and well-chosen detail. Good taste and good architecture depend on simplicity. Beauty is not created by gingerbread and other incongruous and superfluous features and ornaments, but by good proportions and the proper use of materials.

Simplicity, balance, proper proportions, and quality of materials and workmanship, all considered in relation to the functions of the building, are the primary considerations in judging its attractiveness. It should be noted, however, that there are no absolute standards and that real estate value rests on what potential buyers, users, or investors *think* is attractive as well as on what may be considered attractive by experts.

## Architectural Styles

Architectural styles vary widely. Most architects try to select the style which will express most adequately the use of the building. Recent trends have moved away from the limiting influences of some of the traditional styles, with greater emphasis on functional design. In the case of houses, for example, it is possible to list a number of styles which may be seen in

---

[2] Reprinted from *The Rise of the Skyscraper* by Carl W. Condit by permission of the University of Chicago Press, p. 1. Copyright 1952 by the University of Chicago.

our towns and cities every day, but in general many liberties have been taken with the prototypes of these styles so that no hard-and-fast classifications can be made.

We often refer to "English," "Spanish," "French," "colonial," or "modern" houses, and to such special types as "Cape Cod," "ranch house," "Dutch colonial," "Southern colonial," and the like. All of these architectural styles are found with many modifications and variations, but many houses of real distinction cannot be classified by style. Indeed, the trend has been away from the so called traditional style and toward the modern or contemporary style. This trend is even more pronounced for business and industrial buildings.

Consider the following statement:

> . . . architecture is not just a way of packaging a rather large product to attract potential impulse-buyers. Architecture is a system of organization, a way of putting things together.
>
> And architecture—unlike "styling" or "packaging"—possesses another quality that is of the greatest importance to any client or consumer: it only starts to live after the job is done. A box of Kleenex tissue is through once it has been designed, manufactured, sold and used up. The cycle is short, simple, direct. But a good building is a living organism—it starts to do things of its own accord once it has been born. "We shape our buildings," Winston Churchill has said, "and, afterwards, our buildings shape us." [3]

### Conformity

The degree to which buildings are compatible with their physical environment has a bearing on their value. It should be noted that factors of this type must be judged in terms of the environment in which the building is found. Conformity may affect the marketability of a property and hence its value.

## OTHER IMPROVEMENTS

In addition to the main buildings, any other improvements which form a part of a property have a relationship to its value. These other improvements may include (1) accessory buildings, such as garages; (2) walks, driveways, and parking areas; (3) protective barriers; (4) terraces; (5) service areas; (6) retaining walls; (7) landscaping, including lawns, trees, shrubbery, and gardens; (8) fences; and (9) other types.

We shall not attempt to undertake a detailed discussion of these items. Their types, extent, and quality are points to consider when studying the relationship of "other improvements" to the earning power of a property and their impact on real estate decisions.

[3] Peter Blake, "Modern Architecture: Its Many Faces," *The Architectural Forum* (March, 1958), pp. 77–78.

## SUMMARY

We usually think of real properties as distinct physical units composed of land and buildings. As such, they possess many physical characteristics which may influence real estate decision-makers. This is because physical characteristics affect income-producing ability, either directly or indirectly. The quality of the total physical environment has a bearing on income.

No two parts of the earth's surface are exactly alike, hence location is an important factor in determining the income-producing ability of real estate. For agricultural land, fertility varies from one location to another. In the case of urban real estate, some locations are more accessible than others, or have more favorable surroundings.

Although the value of a parcel of real estate is not directly proportional to its size, the size and shape of real properties are among the factors which help to determine value. Additions to the size of a piece of real property tend to increase its income-producing ability and hence its value up to a point. A large parcel of land may have, for some purposes, greater value than the sum of the values of the smaller land parcels of which it is composed. This is known as plottage value. The shape of the land parcels, as well as their size, often determines the possible uses for the properties, and thus influences their income-producing ability.

Other physical characteristics such as topography, soil and subsoil conditions, and accessibility to transportation and utilities may limit or determine land uses, and hence land values. The income-producing ability of a parcel of real etstate also is influenced by the buildings upon it and their quality of construction, their style and attractiveness, size, orientation, and conformity with the surrounding area.

## QUESTIONS FOR STUDY

1. How do government regulations affect the physical environment of real estate?

2. What are the three approaches to the study of real property? How do they differ?

3. Develop a clasification of existing land uses in the community in which your study property is located.

4. Make a list of the physical factors affecting income-producing ability of real estate that would be most important if you were in charge of selecting a site for: (a) a television repair shop, (b) a new drive-in restaurant, (c) a golf course, (d) a new post office for your community.

5. What are the distinguishing characteristics of the principal types of construction?

6. If you were planning to build your own home, which factors would you consider most important in determining its orientation?

7. Give some specific examples of overimprovement and underimprovement of real properties.

8. Mr. Carey owns a vacant lot adjacent to his grocery store. This vacant lot has a frontage of 25 feet. Adjoining it is another vacant lot of equal size owned by Mr. Gibson, whose dry cleaning establishment is located on the next lot. Mr. Anderson offers Carey $5,000 for his lot, but says that if Carey can secure Gibson's vacant lot, he will pay $13,500 for the two lots. Can you explain why Anderson would offer more than twice as much for the two lots as he would give for one of them alone?

9. What is meant by "depreciation"? What is its effect on the income-producing ability of a building?

10. In planning your own home, would you prefer to buy and build on a level lot or a sloping lot? How might the value of the house be a factor in the choice of lots?

11. "We travel together, passengers on a little spaceship; dependent on its vulnerable reserve of air and soil; all committed for our safety to its security and peace; preserved from annihilation only by the care, the work and the love we give to our craft." (Adlai Stevenson) Do you think the Stevenson quotation has special significance? Why? How does this quotation apply to the use of real estate resources?

## SUGGESTED READINGS

AMERICAN INSTITUTE OF REAL ESTATE APPRAISERS. *The Appraisal of Real Estate* (5th ed.). Chicago: The Institute, 1967. Chaps. 9–11.

FALKNER, P. G. "Understanding Basic Principles and Terms of Building Construction," *The Appraisal Journal* (January, 1964.)

## STUDY PROJECT 3–1

### Architectural Styles and Functional Utility *

**Architectural Types.** Most of the homes in this country are based on certain definite architectural types. (See following pages.) There are thousands of good and bad hybrid combinations which have evolved out of these recognized types. Perhaps the most universal classification is the colonial group— the New England colonial, the Cape Cod, the Dutch colonial, the colonial of the Middle Atlantic colonies, and the Southern colonial. Since the English were predominate in the first settlements along the Atlantic coast, it was natural that the Georgian architecture of 18th century England should have directly influenced the colonial types in New England and the Middle Atlantic colonies which have become the basis of a purely American type.

Other architectural designs not pictured here but often encountered are the Mediterranean house, the Moorish house, and the Queen Anne. The first is closely related to the Italian type, having a tile roof, brightly colored canvas

---

* American Institute of Real Estate Appraisers. *The Appraisal of Real Estate* (5th ed.); Chicago: The Institute, 1967), pp. 171–82.

awnings shading decks and terraces, vast expanses of unadorned wall spaces, and massed forms created by circular stair towers. The Moorish house with its unusual minarets and pointed arches is unmistakable. The Queen Anne houses are identified by the baroque ornamentation which characterized the architecture developed during the reign of Queen Anne.

### Questions

1. Which architectural types are most common in your area?
2. What are the major similarities and differences between the Cape Cod, Dutch and Southern Colonial styles?
3. What are major differences between the four "English" styles?
4. What are the outstanding characteristics of the California Ranch, International Modern, and Contemporary styles? Can these be related to any of the more traditional styles?
5. Would an unusual architectural style have a bearing on property's sales appeal? Why or why not?
6. Do most of the houses in your neighborhood comply with the traditional architectural types pictured? If not, what are the variations and do they affect the marketability of the houses?

*Contemporary.* A new type of modern which can and does take many forms. It is designed to promote better living with close relationship to the outdoors and the site. It is designed to incorporate new construction methods, new materials, and new uses of old materials. Characteristics are overhangs over large windows, open planning, horizontal lines, and simple details. These houses may be one or two stories or split-levels to suit site conditions. Roofs may be flat, shed, gabled, or various combinations thereof.

*New England Colonial.* These are comfortable, homelike dwellings which are the result of a distinct type developed by New England carpenters attempting to imitate in wood some of the classic motifs of the Georgian houses of brick and stone which were so prevalent in their former homeland. They are generally of clapboard exterior, painted white, with shingle roof. They are characterized by excellent proportions in which openings are often treated with mouldings of refined detail.

*Cape Cod.* This comes down to us from our earliest colonial days, and is a development of the one-story cottage. Generally, the main cornice line is at the second-story level, with a sloping roof, and sometimes with rooms on the second floor. Dormer windows are used. There is a detailed entrance feature with pilasters and cornices. These houses are most nearly correct when built of frame with clapboard or shingle walls, painted white. In some sections, however, stone is used for the first story, or even brick.

*Dutch Colonial.* This style is recognizable at once by the double slope of its gambrel roof. Exterior walls may be either masonry or frame. Usually the entrance doorway is elaborately decorated and porches are at the side. It is well adapted for flat sites but is difficult to handle on a steep slope.

*Modern Colonial.* This type is descended from the more formal early colonial homes of wealthier families in the Middle Atlantic states. There are usually two full stories, sometimes with dormers to give light to a third floor space. Windows are divided into small panes. Simplicity and balance is the keynote. Woodwork is painted white or cream, with shutters usually in green.

*Southern Colonial.* Very similar to colonial and Georgian types, but usually distinguished by the use of two-story columns forming a porch which may be across the long facade or at the side.

*Georgian Colonial.* The most formal of the colonial types. Balanced openings and chimneys predominate. Ceilings are usually higher than in the other colonial designs. Wings usually drop to follow the contour of the ground and are kept simple in detail. Porches, at front or side, are rather elaborate.

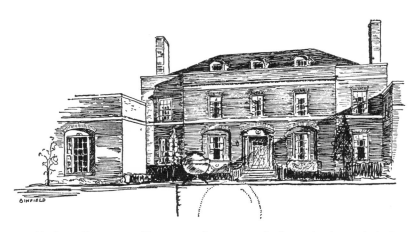

*Modern Georgian.* These stately, symmetrical, perfectly scaled Georgian houses are modern counterparts of the houses built in England during the reign of the four Georges. Extremely conventional in character, they require formal, park-like grounds for a setting.

*Pennsylvania Farmhouse Colonial.* A regional variation of the colonial, especially adapted for flat ground. It is informal in character, with the main section and its higher roof line dominating the design. The exterior stone walls are sometimes whitewashed and covered with plaster. Details are simple. Roof is either slate or wood shingle.

*English Half-Timbered (Elizabethan).* These are rustic, informal, picturesque English houses with interesting exterior treatment and ornamentation of half-timber effects, carved wood, stone, and brick. In the original Elizabethan type, the exposed timbers on the exterior constituted the structural frame of the building. Between the half-timbering there is usually plaster. Roof slopes are quite steep and project at the ends with barges rather than cornices.

*Modern English.* Called "modern" to distinguish it from the other English types described, this has many of the marks of the earlier English styles, including the steep roof slopes with variegated and graduated slate or red tile, but with no cornices or eaves. Windows are mostly casements, wood or metal. It is especially suitable for sloping ground, the informal relation of rooms and spaces adding to the exterior effect.

*English Tudor.* This style as transposed to this country is especially suitable for larger homes where formality is desired. The design is characterized by verticality with exterior walls usually of stone or brick laid in formal pattern. Window and door trim are generally of dressed or cut stone. Windows are usually casements, and the roof is of slate spaced wide and thick to give the effect of a stone roof.

*English Cotswold.* This is an adaptation of an English country or farm house characterized by informality relieved by sills, mullions, porches, and chimneys of stone dressed by a hammer. Details are generally fairly heavy. Windows are metal casements. The roof should be of variegated slate with irregular shapes, graduated from large sizes at the eaves to small at the ridge.

*Spanish.* The Spanish in Florida and in their migrations through Mexico to the Southwest brought their sprawling type of home that gives protection from hot summer suns by its heavy tile roof and walls of adobe or stucco. With its enclosed patio it is designed for outdoor living.

*French Provincial.* Of the various French styles the most easily recognized is the small formal house, perfectly balanced, with high-pitched roof, capturing the spirit of the country estates of France.

*Norman French.* If the site is large enough, this is a popular design, characterized by its round tower, generally used for the main stairway. Exterior walls are mostly of stone with both brick and dressed stone used at the openings, for the cornice, and for chimneys. Half-timbering is sometimes used as a relief.

*French Farmhouse.* An informal type using stone, painted brick, or stucco and varying considerably in adaptation and design. The example shown here has painted brick or plaster exterior walls with wood or stone around openings, and with half-timbering used as an accent. Roof slopes are steep and the roof is generally very informal in treatment.

*Italian.* Typical Italian details include completely framed windows and openings, circular heads over exterior openings, high windows and doors, and the red "S" shaped clay tile on the roof. Exterior surfaces may be masonry or plaster.

*Monterey.* The two-story Monterey house is adapted from a style prevalent in the early Spanish era in California. It is characatrized usually by a balcony across the entire front of the building.

*California Ranch.* These are modern ranch-type bungalows which sprawl out over their lot, providing the utmost in livability, light, and air.

*International Modern.* This style was derived from the early European modern trend. It is characterized by flat roofs and unadorned plain walls with geometric patterns of light and shade. Windows are large with corner window groups commonly used.

# 4

# Legal Aspects of Real Estate

## IMPORTANCE OF LEGAL FACTORS

The variety of regulations, laws, and governmental policies that have an impact on real estate is so great as almost to defy comprehensive classification and analysis. You might try, for example, to prepare a list of all the regulations affecting your "study property."

Real estate is more closely regulated as to ownership and use than any other commodity, with the possible exception of narcotics. (See Study Project 5–1 at the end of Chapter 5.) This is due to the fact that private property rights in real estate are created, guaranteed, and enforced by government. Also this situation may be explained by the tremendous impact of the utilization of one piece of real property on another and the importance of real estate resources in our total environment.

### Ownership

The ownership of real property is regulated by the laws governing titles and title transfers. Such regulation of ownership is in part the result of the gradual evolution of the common law and in part the product of legislative and administrative processes. Ownership is never "complete," since the exercise by government of the rights of taxation, eminent domain or the police power may modify various private ownership interests substantially.

**Income Production**

Influence of legal and governmental aspects on the income-producing ability of real property is profound. It ranges all the way from the definition and protection of ownership rights and the enforcement of contracts to the maintenance of full or nearly full employment conditions in our economy. Real estate is affected by all levels of government from the federal government to local townships, municipalities, and school districts. We should recognize that a major portion of the income from real estate each year is used for the payment of property and income taxes. Even so, we must also recognize that real property rights could not exist without government and that real properties would have much lower values without the opportunity to enjoy the protections and services of modern governmental organizations.

Not only governmental regulations and policies, but private agreements and regulations may also have important influences on real estate decisions and on the income-producing potential of real properties. We may think of all of the private agreements and contracts that involve real estate as constituting a system of private laws. In addition, such specific arrangements as deed restrictions or agreements of property owners' associations may have important influences on real estate decisions.

**Competition**

Decisions relating to the uses of various real properties, the contracts and agreements of owners, users, investors, and others, the rate of development of properties, and the rationing of available space are all influenced by market competition. Indeed, competition is the principal method of regulating real estate resources in this country. Through competitively determined prices and rents, decisions are made regarding what will be produced, how much, and for whom. Competition, of course, is governed by numerous laws, regulations, and informal controls that make it possible for the market to function. Competition does not work automatically; indeed, there never was such a thing as completely unregulated competition, and there never could be, especially in our complex kind of economic system.

Real estate market competition is limited by special types of regulations, including laws affecting the transfer and financing of properties, zoning and land planning laws, building codes, subsidies, taxes, price and rent regulations in some cases, government ownership, and other types of regulative methods.

## Law and Real Estate Decisions

The value of a parcel of real estate may be divided among many interests, depending on the property rights represented by the land, buildings, and other improvements. A property may represent a wide variety of interests or *estates*. It may be owned by Mr. and Mrs. X, leased to Mr. Y, who in turn has subleased it to Mr. Z, who occupies it. Mr. A may hold a mortgage secured by the property, Mr. B may have the right to a path across it, and Mr. C the right to install utility lines on it. The degree, quantity, nature and extent of interest which a person has in real property is that person's estate in the real property. Basically, the value of such rights depends on economic forces. In some cases the legal arrangements may limit decisions and programs regarding the utilization of the property and thus affect its value adversely. In other cases, legal arrangements may implement a sound program of property use.

The legal arrangements connected with property ownership, use, or transfer involve almost countless legal documents. The title, possession, or use of real property is usually evidenced by some written instrument. However, occupancy is notice to everyone of rights claimed in real property, and the rights of the occupant must always be ascertained.

Our interest in the legal aspects of real estate—in the papers and documents—arise from their effect on decisions of individuals and on business and public officials. These decisions often turn on the economic implications of the legal arrangements which may be involved.

## Use of Specialists

Those in the real estate business need to be familiar with the legal concepts and practices involved in real property ownership, use, investment, transfer, and financing. However, it is *not* their function to serve as substitutes for lawyers. Real estate entrepreneurs, brokers, and specialists have a place in the business community primarily because of their knowledge of *economic* forces and the application of such forces to specific business activities. They should know enough about real estate law to determine when situations require that competent lawyers be consulted. Such legal counsel is readily available.

There are relatively few people outside the real estate business who may be consulted in regard to the economic and business aspects of this field. It is in this area, therefore, that the real estate broker, manager, developer, appraiser, or mortgage lender tends to become a "professional" or expert in his own right. Hence, it is on the administrative and economic rather than on the legal and engineering phases of the subject of real estate that we concentrate our attention.

## PROPERTY

Property may be defined in a nontechnical manner as the exclusive right to exercise control over economic goods. This right may be exercised by one or more persons, corporations, associations, or by the community at large.

### Real vs. Personal Property

Property objects may be tangible or intangible. Even though they are intangible, they generally are described as *things*. Things may be divided into "things real" and "things personal." The land and all things permanently attached to it are considered to be realty, and all other things are personalty. The line of demarcation between the two is sometimes very hard to determine in practical situations, however.

Land is considered by the common law to have an indefinite extent upward as well as downward, so that the word *land* includes not only the fact of the earth but everything under it or over it. A strict interpretation of the concept of property as including the surface of the land plus an indefinite extent upward would make air traffic impossible. Consequently the right to space above 1,000 feet in congested areas and 500 feet elsewhere is considered as similar to rights on a navigable stream. *Air rights* have been purchased above railroad tracks to provide space for buildings, as in the case of the Daily News Building, the Merchandise Mart, and the Prudential Office Building in Chicago and the Pan Am Building in New York.

### Classes of Property

Between public property on the one hand and private property on the other, certain additional classes of property may be distinguished. One class is *common property*, which provides for the ownership of an undivided unit of land by a number of people who hold their interests by virtue of their ownership of adjoining private tracts. The New England common of an earlier period is an illustration of such an arrangement, as are the common areas in "planned unit developments."

### Requirements for Private Property

The essential requirements for private property are (1) an owner, (2) a property object, which must be a thing of economic value, and (3) an organized government to protect and enforce property rights. Private property is essentially a matter of human relationships, a combination of rights and responsibilities which are recognized and sanctioned by the community.

## RESERVATIONS ON PRIVATE PROPERTY

The exercise of the exclusive right of private property is subject to at least three reservations by the state. These reservations arise from eminent domain, taxation, and the police power. We should note also that private property for which there is no owner reverts to the state in accordance with the doctrine of *escheat*. Private property may also be limited by non-state type restrictions such as deed restrictions described later in this chapter.

### Eminent Domain

Eminent domain is the right of the sovereign government to take private property for public use. In effect it is the right to compel a sale by the owner, since compensation is always paid. The private owner has no choice in deciding whether to sell or not to sell. He must sell if his property is *condemned* for public use. Eminent domain may be exercised by the federal government, by the various states, and by municipalities, or by semipublic corporations whose existence is regarded as essential to the welfare of the public.

Before this right is exercised, attempts are made, in practice, to purchase directly from the owners such properties as are required. This avoids the formal processes of condemnation, which often are costly. However, if the owner of any parcel demands a "holdup" price, condemnation proceedings are instituted. The price is then fixed by the court, usually after hearing the testimony of expert appraisers. In the exercise of the power of eminent domain the government is not restricted to the property which is to be used directly for the public project involved. *Excess condemnation is* sometimes permitted by courts if this appears to be in the best interests of the public.

### Public Ownership

Historically, we have been committed to the policy of encouraging private ownership of both urban and rural land. However, when public parks, schools, office buildings, army, navy, and air force installations, forest preserves, and the like are considered our governments control a considerable amount of real property. In recent years special attention has centered on public ownership often through the exercise of eminent domain, to cope with such problems as slum clearance, urban renewal, soil erosion, conservation and environmental control.

When real estate is owned by government, several purposes may be served. For example, such properties may provide the basis for research and experimentation, or they may serve such purposes as income redistribution as in the case of providing improved housing for lower-income groups. Conservation of natural resources is often cited as a justification for public ownership. Control of the national environment may require public ownership. Problems of water pollution may justify public ownership in some cases. Even so, we continue in general to encourage the private ownership of real property. A large majority of our families are home owners; most of our farms are owned by those who operate them; and a large percentage of our business firms own the land used for their installations.

## Property Taxation

Taxation means the right to payments from citizens for the maintenance of the state. Property taxation means that the state may collect payments from a property owner based on some relationship to the property, usually its value. If such payments are not made, the property may be sold by the state to satisfy the claim for taxes. Taxes may be thought of as interest payments on a mortgage that never matures and never can be paid off.

The extent of the tax burden varies between properties but in some cases represents as much as a third or more of annual gross rent. Because land ownership was a fair indication of ability to pay taxes during the early years of our country's history, property taxation came to be used widely by state and local governments. The federal government cannot impose direct taxes on real property. However, the federal income tax has an important bearing on many real estate transactions and in some cases may exercise a determining influence on decisions regarding the purchase, sale, leasing, or financing of real property. Although state and local governments now make use of other forms of taxation in addition to the property tax, a heavy share of the tax burden which such governments, notably local governments, impose is borne by real estate.

The relationships between governments and individual property owners arising from taxes have created numerous problems. Taxes are important to the politician as well as to the owner or user of the property or the investor in the property. As a result, our tax structure is complex, often illogical, and in many instances unfair to real property owners, users, or investors.

## Types of Property Taxes

Taxes on real estate are of two principal types: (1) general property taxes imposed by states or municipalities and (2) those imposed by such special taxing authorities as sanitary districts or school districts. In addition, special assessments may be levied against a property owner to cover all or part of the cost incurred for paving streets, building sidewalks, or making other improvements directly affecting his property.

## Tax Liens and Penalties

Taxes and assessments are liens on property, ranking above all others; and in some cases they become personal claims against the owner as well. As we have indicated, the state is a persistent tax collector. If taxes are not paid when due, interest and penalties may be added. If payment is still not made, the taxing authority may either (1) sell the property and collect the tax out of the proceeds, returning the balance to the owner, or (2) sell the tax lien. Redemption periods are provided in many states. Thus, if a sale is made, the purchaser receives a "tax title," which ripens into full ownership if the property is not redeemed.

If tax liens are sold, the taxing authority is, in effect, selling its claim to another. In such cases, the purchaser pays the tax and looks to the owner of the property for reimbursement. In effect, the purchaser of a tax lien becomes the holder of a mortgage which is superior to all other claims against the property. If payment is not made within a stated period, varying greatly from place to place, the certificate matures and proceedings are carried out similar to those of foreclosure.

## Tax Capitalization

One of the serious difficulties with our taxation policies affecting real estate is that they have tended to ignore the effects of taxes on different members of the community and on the uses to which properties are put. For example, when a tax of any sort is imposed on a piece of real estate, unless it receives benefits from government activity financed by the tax corresponding in value to the amount of such payments, the tax (or that portion of it which exceeds the accompanying benefits) will be *capitalized,* which means that the owner of a property at the time a tax is imposed pays it for all time, under the conditions outlined above. In other words, if taxes on a piece of real estate are increased without corresponding benefit, its sale value is decreased by an amount equal to the *capitalized value of all future tax payments.* This is true because the prospective buyer will consider the amount of the tax in determining how much he will pay—deducting a sufficient amount to allow for taxes. Thus, the present owner of the real estate pays the increased tax once and for all.

It is obvious that increases in real estate taxes which are not accompanied by corresponding benefits result in gross injustices to present property owners. It is equally obvious that removal of property taxes that have once been capitalized after a parcel of real estate has changed hands many times results in wholly undeserved windfalls to those who purchased properties after such taxes were imposed.

## Police Power

The *police power* involves all regulations necessary to safeguard the public health, morals, and safety and to promote the general welfare.

The police power, in its broadest sense, includes all legislation and almost every function of civil government. . . . It is not subject to definite limitations, but is coextensive with the necessities of the case and the safeguards of public interest. . . . It embraces regulations designed to promote public convenience or the general prosperity or welfare, as well as those specifically intended to promote the public safety or the public health.[1]

In exercising the police power the state does not become the owner of property and it is not obliged to compensate private owners. From the standpoint of real property the most important use of the police power is found in zoning laws. These laws have far-reaching effects on the uses of real estate, as do building codes and related regulations.

## Land Planning and Zoning

Land planning and zoning, among the important examples of the exercise of the police power, are largely products of the present century, although some regulations of this type go back to ancient times. In this country several cities were planned at the time they were established, the most notable being Washington, D.C., under the L'Enfant Plan. In recent years the growth of both urban and environmental problems in many of our cities brought further development of land planning and zoning activities.

Land planning involves over-all programs for development concerned chiefly with public or semipublic land uses such as roads, streets, parks, and related matters; it invades private property rights only in incidental ways. Zoning is a device for carrying out the plan with respect to land use and specifically limits the rights of private individuals, since it involves the regulation by districts under the police power of such matters as the height, the bulk, and the use of buildings as well as the use of land. Density of land use and hence of population may also be regulated. City, county, metropolitan area, state, and regional planning may all be involved.

[1] Sligh *v.* Kirkwood, 237 U.S. 52 (1914).

## Building Codes

Another illustration of the exercise of the police power is provided by building codes. Such codes are in force in most American cities. Regulations of this type are justified on the grounds of safety and health. Hence, the quality and strength of materials are usually regulated and controls leading toward fire prevention and sanitation are imposed. Regulations may determine the ratio between the height and thickness of walls, the spacing of girders, and allowable stresses. Sanitary and health regulations necessitate control over plumbing, vents, ventilation, room height, and similar matters.

Although building codes provide many protections for citizens, they have been subject to numerous criticisms. In some cases they are unduly complicated; sometimes they afford certain types of protection for local firms or unions; often they "make work" for certain trades; frequently they fail to recognize new materials or practices and thus retard progress in the building industry. Despite problems, however, progress is being made in these areas.

## CLASSES OF ESTATES

Since it is possible to hold varying degrees of interest in land, lawyers have seen fit to divide these interests or estates into classes. The classification schemes commonly employed view these interests from one or a combination of the following: (1) quantity of interest, (2) *time* of enjoyment, and (3) *number* and *connection* of the interested parties.

## Quantity of Interest

From the standpoint of quantity of interest, estates have been divided into those of *freehold* and those *not of freehold*. (See Fig. 4–1.) The concept of freehold has had a long historical development. It originally was synonymous with *possession*, but later came to be a more inclusive right than possession and was distinguished from it. Originally nonfreehold estates were considered as little more than contracts, although this concept was broadened with the passage of time. Since feudal society required that someone always hold a freehold interest, the legal doctrine developed that "seisin (possession by virtue of feudal investiture) of land can never be in abeyance." Hence, with minor exceptions, there is always a freehold interest underlying an estate less than freehold. While this distinction between estates of freehold and those not of freehold is historical rather than logical, it helps to clarify the various types of interest which may exist. Freehold estates include the *fee simple, fee tail,* other qualified estates, and the *estate for life.* Nonfreehold estates include estates for years, from year to year, and at will and at sufferance, or those commonly called *leasehold* estates. In this country a leasehold is now generally held to be personal property.[2]

## Fee Simple Estate

An estate in fee simple may be defined as the highest type of ownership in real estate known to law. The owner is entitled to the enjoyment of all the rights of the property. The terms *fee, fee simple* and *fee simple absolute* may be considered equivalent.

A fee simple estate carries with it the right to use or not use the property in any way the owner wishes. He may sell it, give it away, will it to his heirs or others, or trade it for other property. Furthermore, he may use his property in any way which will not interfere with the rights of other property owners within the limits established by the state, which were discussed above.

## Fee Tail Estate

A fee tail or limited estate restricts the alienation of the property in that it must pass to descendants of the owner. Originally this device was used to insure the passing of land in a direct ancestral line. When liberalizing tendencies caused modifications of this condition, statutes were enacted which restored the limitation. Later changes provided that fee tail estates could be created which could be transformed into fee simple interests by appropriate court action. The fee tail estate has been abolished by legislative enactment in a number of our states.

## Estates for Life

Estates for life or life estates are freehold estates in land and are limited in duration to the life of the owner, or to the life or lives of some other person or persons. Estates of this type cannot be transmitted by inheritance. Termination of a life estate depends on a future, uncertain event.

Thus, an estate so long as a specified person lives or during widowhood may be classified as a life estate. The life tenant may occupy the property or rent it to another and thus enjoy the income from it.

Estates for life are limited in time and involve a less complete form of ownership than the fee simple estate. Estates for life may be created either by act of the parties (conventional) or by operation of the law

[2] See Robert Kratovil, *Real Estate Law* (5th ed.; Englewood Cliffs, N.J.: Prentice-Hall, Inc., 1969), p. 37.

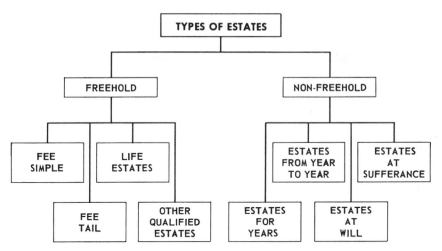

**Fig. 4–1.** Types of estates.

(legal). Of the former, there are estates granted by one party for his life, or estates granted for the duration of the life of another. In the first case the estate ends at the death of the grantee, and in the second, at the death of the party named.[3] Life estates created by operation of the law include *curtesy* and *dower*. Curtesy is the life estate of the husband in the real estate owned by his wife, while dower is the life estate of the wife in the real property owned by her husband. These estates are no longer recognized in some states. A number of western states recognize the arrangement of *community property*. This provides that in the absence of a will the surviving husband or wife will receive half the estate and the heirs of the deceased the other half.

The right of homestead entitles the head of a family to an interest in his owned residence which is exempt from the claims of creditors. It is often referred to as homestead exemption. Statutes set limits to the amount of the exemption and usually require the filing of a written declaration of homestead. This type of interest has been created by statute, not through the common law.

### Nonfreehold Estates—Leasehold Estates

The estates which are "less than freehold" include *estates from year to year, estates at will,* and *estates by sufferance.* These interests are commonly called *leasehold estates,* or rights of tenants as distinguished

[3] This estate is technically called *estate d'autre vie.*

from those of a freeholder. An estate from year to year is a contract for a definite period of time—the period may be short or long. Estates at will are similar, but the duration of the lease depends on the will of both, as either party may terminate it. In the case of an estate by sufferance, the term of a lease for a definite period has expired and the tenant continues to hold over without special permission. However, *periodic tenancy* is sometimes involved in similar situations; for example, leases which run from year to year and month to month are assumed to be renewed if the owner accepts payment after the expiration of the lease and if appropriate notice of its expiration has not been given. It is necessary to differentiate between these types of tenancy and a tenancy for one year or for one month.

### Estates Classified as to Time of Enjoyment

Estates may also be classified as to time of enjoyment. As we have pointed out above, one may either be in immediate possession of an estate or expect to secure possession at some future date. The latter type of estates include *reversions* and *remainders.*

A revesion is the residue of an estate left with the grantor which entitles him to possession after the end of another estate. For example, if Mr. X leases his property to Mr. Y for ten years, Mr. X has the reversion.

A remainder is the right of a person to interests which mature at the end of another estate. For example, if Mr. G. I. Jones grants a life estate to Mr. I. G. Brown and thereafter to Mr. I. M. Smythe in fee, Mr. Smythe holds a remainder. If such an estate passed to Mr. Smythe only if he paid some obligation or fulfilled some other requirement, he would hold a *contingent remainder.* It should be noted, however, that a remainder must not be postponed for too great a period of time or it will be void because of the "rule against perpetuities." Usually this limits the postponement of estates to the lives of people who are living at the time the conditions are established.

### Estates Classified as to Number and Connection of Owners

Classification of ownership by number and connection of interested parties results in two main groups of estates: *joint estates,* or what might be called co-owners, and *estates in severalty.* The latter are estates held by single owners, the former by more than one. In cases where more than one owner is involved, a number of possible arrangements may exist, the chief of which are *tenancies in common* and *joint tenancies.* If two or more persons own separate estates in the same property, each holding a distinct interest which may be sold or transmitted in any way, a tenancy in common exists. However, if two or more persons hold ownership in the same degree, acquired by purchase or grants, but not as separate shares, a joint tenancy exists. Joint tenancy is also distinguished by the doctrine of survivorship; that is, if one of the joint tenants dies, his interest passes to the survivor or survivors. While a joint tenant cannot will his share of such an estate, he may convey it while living. In such cases, however, a tenancy in common exists after such a grant. Any of the joint tenants may occupy the property without paying rent to the others, but if the property is leased to strangers, the rents are divided between the joint tenants. While the common law tended to favor joint tenancies, the present tendency is to favor the tenancy in common. In Oregon, for example, joint tenancies have been abolished by statute.

Another type of estate is tenancy by entirety. Since husband and wife are considered one person under the common law, each becomes the owner of the entire property when they take title to it together, and upon the death of either spouse the survivor is sole owner. Special statutes in the various states now fix interests of this type.

## Business Ownership

In case real estate is transferred to a partnership, the individual persons composing the partnership become the owners of the property. Hence, when a business operates as a partnership, it is usually found expedient to acquire real estate under a business name or in the name of one or more of the individual partners. Under such an arrangement the partners are the equitable owners. Since a corporation is a separate legal entity, it may own real estate in much the same manner as an individual if given this power directly or by implication in its charter or certificate of incorporation.

## The Condominium

A recent innovation in real estate ownership, the condominium, presents another problem in property description. The condominium has been described as follows:

. . . the legal term for real property ownership providing fee simple ownership of an individual apartment or other enclosed space in a building; at the same time, it provides for common ownership by the individual unit owners of such areas as halls, elevators, and recreational facilities related to the building. . . . Traditionally, under Anglo-American law a fee simple title to land has meant the ownership of a certain area of the earth's surface that could be appropriately described. Generally, ownership of the airspace above this area, as well as the right to exploit whatever lay beneath, has attached to the ownership of the surface. However, separate conveyance of subsurface mineral rights has been well recognized. Not so commonly recognized has been the right of the owner to convey title to the airspace above the surface he owns in fee simple. The condominium makes possible the individual ownership, alienation, and mortgaging of a portion of the airspace occupied by an apartment—for example, one situated fifteen stories above the ground.[4]

## CORPOREAL AND INCORPOREAL RIGHTS

In addition to the types of estates which may be held by the occupant of a property or *corporeal rights,* there may be certain nonpossessory interests in real estate, or rights held by those who are not entitled to actual occupation. The latter interests are called *incorporeal rights* and include (1) those rights which may ultimately develop into complete possessory or corporeal interests and (2) those which may not. Reversions and remainders, which have already been described, may be classified in the first group. In the second group of incorporeal rights in property, the most important are *easements* and *right of way.* Both include the right to make a limited use of land without taking anything from it or having possession, such as the right to pass over another's property. Sometimes these interests are classified as rights in another's property and include (in addition to easements and rents) profits and covenants running with the land, such rights as mortgages, statutory liens, and equitable charges or liens.

### Liens

A lien is the legal right of a creditor to have a debt or charge paid or satisfied out of the property belonging to the debtor. Liens may be divided into specific and general classes, the former including mortgages, local taxes and assessments, and mechanics' liens, while the latter includes judgments, estate taxes, and the like.

*Mechanics' liens* protect those who furnish materials and labor for the improvement of a property by giving them a claim against it. Such liens are governed by statute and vary widely among the states. Typically such a lien affects only the property that is benefited by the materials and labor involved. Usually such liens are enforceable by foreclosure.

### Tax and Special Assessment Liens

Taxes, of course, are liens on real property when levied against it, and the property may be sold to satisfy the claim. Special assessments, which generally arise when all or a part of the cost of public improvements is charged against the property which is benefited, may be collected in the

---

[4] Robert R. Milroy, "The Condominium," *Business Horizons* (Spring, 1964), p. 51.

same way.  In addition, there are ways for federal or state governments to obtain a lien on a delinquent taxpayer's property even though the tax was not levied on the property.  For example, the federal government may have unpaid income taxes made a lien.

## Mortgages

While at common law a mortgage amounted to a conveyance of an estate to the mortgagee or lender, the conveyance to become void when the terms of the mortgage agreement were fulfilled, today the mortgage is considered more in the nature of a lien upon a property to insure the repayment of a loan or the performance of an act.  In many states a mortgage is restricted, by statute, to a lien.  If the loan is not repaid, the mortgagee may take the necessary legal steps involved in foreclosure in order to recover his claim.

## Judgments

When judgments involve money awards, they become liens on the property of the debtor, and his property may be sold to satisfy the claim. Estate taxes or inheritance taxes are a lien on the property of an estate, and such property may be sold to satisfy the tax if it is not paid.

## TITLE TO REAL ESTATE

While one may hold a wide variety of interests in real property, he must be able to prove ownership.  Such proof or evidence of ownership is called *title*.

At one time the fact of possession was considered evidence of title, just as the possession of most personal property is considered evidence of ownership today.  Because of the complexity of the interests which may exist in real property, written evidence of ownership became essential. False statements or errors of memory created so many problems that the Statute of Frauds was enacted in England in 1677.  It provided that all agreements affecting the title to real estate must be in writing to be enforcible.  The party refusing to perform the contract can be held if he signed the written memorandum, whether or not the other party signed. Similar requirements were established in each of our states.

## Public Records

Not only was written evidence needed, but permanent public records were found to be essential to systematic recording of real property ownership and of the transactions involving such ownership.  The "recording acts" have met this requirement. In each of our states there is provision for the recording of transactions affecting real property.

The registry laws do not make recording compulsory. They merely provide that recording of an instrument informs all who deal in real property of the transaction and that, unless an instrument is recorded, a prospective purchaser without actual notice of its existence is protected against it.

Such records have been set up for two purposes: (1) to preserve evidence of all instruments affecting title, and (2) to provide any person with notice of their existence and content. If the records are complete, it is possible to determine all claims against a property and all transactions affecting it. If any questions exist regarding outstanding claims, the title is termed "cloudy" or "defective" and is not "clear." In such cases the property is not readily marketable, since "a good and merchantable title" cannot be given.

## Types of Records

Various records must be kept in order to preserve adequate information about the status of title. These include deed books, mortgage books, plat books, and other records which preserve information about judgments, tax liens, attachments, mechanics' liens, wills, estate administration, divorce, marriage, bankruptcy special assessments and similar matters. In addition, restrictions on the use of real estate established by zoning laws or deed restrictions also affect the status of titles to real property.

## Place of Recording

Recording must be made in the county in which the land is located. If a property lies in two or more counties, the instruments pertaining to it must be recorded in each. A land records office is usually located in each county or similar subdivision in the state, and the officer in whose charge such records are placed ordinarily is called the *recorder* or *registrar of deeds,* although in some states the clerk of the county or the county clerk keeps such records, and in others the auditor does this work.

## Abstract of Title

The history of the title to a property may be traced by a study of those instruments in the public records which have affected it. Such a study is referred to as a *search of title.* It is usually made by abstracters or lawyers who prepare an *abstract of title* or an *abstract*, which contains a summary of the documents having a bearing on the history of the title to property. From this information it is possible for a competent lawyer to tell whether the title is *clear* or *defective*. He renders an *opinion of title*. This opinion may indicate that the title is clear or that certain matters must be cleared up before a purchaser can afford to take title to the property. The mere fact that an abstract is available is no assurance of good quality of title.

## Title Insurance

Because of the many factors which may affect the title to a piece of real property and the countless risks which a purchaser may assume, title insurance companies have been established. In return for a premium such companies will guarantee that the title to property is clear, or that it is clear except for defects which are noted. Title insurance has been found to facilitate real estate transactions, since title insurance companies usually can act with greater speed in checking titles than individual lawyers and abstracters. Typically, such companies employ highly skilled personnel. Because of the care with which the work is done, and the fact that risks are spread over many properties, it is possible to carry out transactions which might otherwise be blocked because of minor defects in title. Title insurance does not guarantee title but will pay for damages resulting from defects in title.

## The Torrens System

A system of land title registration by which the state guarantees title has developed from the work by Sir Robert Torrens in Australia during the middle of the last century. This system is in use in a number of our states. In a sense it does publicly what title insurance companies do on a private basis.

This system of land title registration provides for the establishment of title in an owner once and for all when he makes application to a duly elected or appointed *registrar*. The registrar institutes court proceedings in order that any claims against the property may be made. If none is made or such as are made are settled, the title is decreed to rest with the applicant, a decree is entered in a book of registry, and a certificate of ownership is issued to the owner or owners.

The owner pays a fee which becomes part of a revolving fund and may be used to repay those who may have been cut off from their interests by the proceedings.

## Acquiring Title to Real Estate

Property in real estate may be acquired in various ways, the most important of which are (1) by public grant, (2) by devise or descent, (3) by adverse possession, and (4) by private grant.

Title by public grant means that the federal government or a state issues a patent or grant to a private party. Much of the land originally held by the United States government was transferred to private ownership in this way.

Since one of the more important rights of property is the right to will it to survivors, a property owner may make a will. If the will is valid, he may dispose of his property as he wishes. Title secured in this way is called title by devise. After the death of the devisor the will is *probated*—that is, presented to a court for action. The property then passes automatically to those designated by the will if no one contests its validity. The right to convey property by will is subject to statutory limits which vary from state to state.

If a property owner dies intestate—that is, without making a valid will—the distribution of his property is governed by the statutes of the state in which the real property is located. Title acquired in this manner is said to be title by descent. Title may also be acquired by adverse possession, that is, by occupying and using the property openly as if ownership actually existed for a specified number of years (varying from state to state.) Under modern conditions this is an unusual way to acquire real property.

## Private Grant Deeds

The sale of property by one person to another is usually referred to as a *private grant*, and in such cases title is passed by the use of a *deed*.[5]

The principal requirements essential to the validity of a deed have been outlined by Kratovil as follows:

The validity and legal effect of a deed are matters governed by the law of the state where the land is located, and the requirements vary somewhat from state to state. Generally, however, and subject to the exceptions hereinafter mentioned, the essential elements of a deed are a competent grantor, a grantee, recital of consideration, words of conveyance, adequate description of the land, signature and seal of grantor, and a delivery of the completed instrument to the grantee. In addition, a deed may contain warranties of title, recitals showing mortgages and other encumbrances, a date, witnesses, an acknowledg-

[5] Kratovil, *op. cit.*, p. 115.

ment, and revenue stamps. Delivery is usually followed by filing or recording of the deed in the proper public office.[6]

The types of deeds which are used most frequently are the *warranty deed*, in which the seller warrants that the title to the property is "good and merchantable," and the *quitclaim deed*, in which the seller transfers only such title as he may possess. The grant deed is often used and may be classed between the warranty and quitclaim types. Also, there are various types of officers' deeds, such as the deeds given by sheriffs or other officials. In addition, there are trustees' deeds, executors' or administrators' deeds, conservators' or guardians' deeds, and related types. Since the most important is the warranty deed, you are urged to study Figure 4–2 with some care.

### Deed Restrictions

In addition to such public controls of private property use as may result from zoning regulations, building codes and similar public programs, appropriate provisions may be inserted into the deeds by which properties are transferred which will further restrict property uses. Through deed restrictions private owners can limit the uses to which property may be put, establish building restrictions, regulate land coverage, and control property in other ways. Such restrictions may be special, applying to only one property, or general, relating to an entire area.

Because of the attitudes of the courts arising from the long struggle to liberate land from feudal ties, there is a tendency to look with disfavor on restrictions that unduly limit the use and free transfer of real property. Thus, in cases of doubt the courts tend to favor the freer rather than the more limited use of property.

Deed restrictions may be enforced by the seller, or may provide that the restrictions run with the land and be jointly enforcible by seller and owner. In case of covenants running with the land, the usual remedy is a suit in equity to enjoin violations. Where restrictions are conditions upon which the deed is given, a reverter clause may provide that the property will revert to the seller if violations are claimed and can be proved.

## DESCRIPTION OF PROPERTY

In order for real estate to be described in a sufficiently clear manner so that it can be located without question, several methods have been developed.

[6] *Ibid.*, p. 51.

**CONSULT YOUR LAWYER BEFORE SIGNING THIS INSTRUMENT—THIS INSTRUMENT SHOULD BE USED BY LAWYERS ONLY.**

**THIS INDENTURE,** made the   1st   day of   May     , nineteen hundred and

**BETWEEN**   WILLIAM J. JONES, residing at 115 Lenox Hill Avenue, in the City, County, and State of New York

party of the first part, and   JOHNATHAN WHITE, residing at 711 Front Street, in the City, County, and State of New York

party of the second part,

**WITNESSETH,** that the party of the first part, in consideration of ten dollars and other valuable consideration paid by the party of the second part, does hereby grant and release unto the party of the second part, the heirs or successors and assigns of the party of the second part forever,

**ALL** that certain plot, piece or parcel of land, with the buildings and improvements thereon erected, situate, lying and being in the Village of Lyons, in the County of Wayne, State of New York, and bounded and described as follows:

BEGINNING at a point on the southerly side of One hundred and seventh Avenue (Wayne Avenue) distant forty feet westerly from the corner formed by the intersection of said southerly side of One hundred and seventh Avenue with the westerly side of One hundred and thirty-fifth Street (Clinton Avenue) running thence southerly parallel with One hundred and thirty-fifth Street one hundred feet; thence westerly parallel with One hundred and seventh Avenue forty feet; thence northerly parallel with One hundred and thirty-fifth Street one hundred feet to said southerly side of One hundred and seventh Avenue and thence easterly along said southerly side of One hundred and seventh Avenue, forty feet to the point or place of beginning.

SUBJECT to covenants, restrictions and reservations contained in former instruments of record and to encumbrances of record.

TOGETHER with all right, title and interest, if any, of the party of the first part in and to any streets and roads abutting the above described premises to the center lines thereof; TOGETHER with the appurtenances and all the estate and rights of the party of the first part in and to said premises; TO HAVE AND TO HOLD the premises herein granted unto the party of the second part, the heirs or successors and assigns of the party of the second part forever.

AND the party of the first part, in compliance with Section 13 of the Lien Law, covenants that the party of the first part will receive the consideration for this conveyance and will hold the right to receive such consideration as a trust fund to be applied first for the purpose of paying the cost of the improvement and will apply the same first to the payment of the cost of the improvement before using any part of the total of the same for any other purpose.

AND the party of the first part covenants as follows: that said party of the first part is seized of the said premises in fee simple, and has good right to convey the same; that the party of the second part shall quietly enjoy the said premises; that the said premises are free from incumbrances, except as aforesaid; that the party of the first part will execute or procure any further necessary assurance of the title to said premises; and that said party of the first part will forever warrant the title to said premises.

The word "party" shall be construed as if it read "parties" whenever the sense of this indenture so requires.

**IN WITNESS WHEREOF,** the party of the first part has duly executed this deed the day and year first above written.

IN PRESENCE OF:

*Wm. K. Murray*          *William J. Jones* _____ (Seal)

**Fig. 4–2a.** Warranty deed. (Courtesy The Title Guarantee Company, New York.)

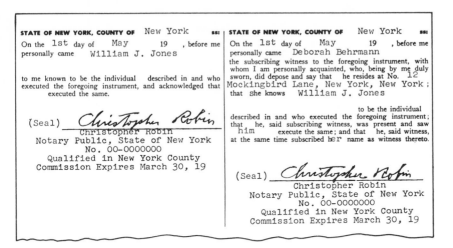

**Fig. 4–2b.**    Warranty deed—reverse.

## Quadrangular Survey

Except for the thirteen original colonies, much of the land in this country was surveyed before it was opened for sale to the public. The township six miles square formed the basic unit of measuremnet. Townships are identified by surveying lines running east and west, called *parallels,* and north and south, called *meridians.* North and south rows of townships are called *ranges,* and east and west rows are referred to as *tiers.* Within each township, sections are identified by numbers in accordance with the method illustrated in the accompanying diagram. Farms are ordinarily identified with respect to their location in sections and townships. (See Fig. 4–3.)

## Subdivision

When land is platted by a subdivider and a copy of the plat is made a matter of public record, the lots involved may be identified by block and number.

While the description of a property by the street and number of a house may be adequate for general purposes, a more detailed description is necessary when property actually changes hands. Indeed, it is usually considered advisable to have a careful survey made prior to undertaking purchase, mortgage lending, leasing, or improvement.

## Metes and Bounds

In those parts of the country which were not surveyed prior to being opened to sale to private individuals, the system of "metes and bounds" is used. The term *metes* refers to measures, and *bounds* to direction. For example, at a designated starting point, it is possible to indicate certain distances in various directions and return to the original starting point, thereby describing adequately a tract of land. The key to the success of such description is the adequacy of the description of the original starting point. Some difficulty is encountered, for example, if bodies of water, trees, and other natural formations are chosen as starting points. In such cases the destruction of a tree or a *monument* will invalidate the property description. For the purposes of land description, such things as bodies of water or trees are referred to as *natural monuments,* and fences, houses, or walls as *artificial monuments.* In case of conflict, monuments control over metes and bounds.

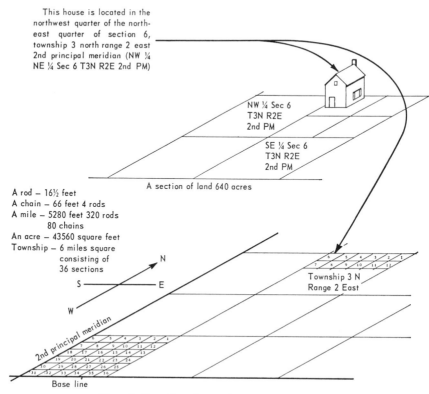

**Fig. 4–3.**  Quadrangular survey system.

Since there are possibilities for error, descriptions by metes and bounds usually contain the words "more or less," which give some protection in case a new survey does not coincide exactly with the original. These terms are usually interpreted by the courts within the limits of a reasonable standard.

## REAL ESTATE CONTRACTS

Almost all transactions involving the sale, purchase, or exchange of real estate result in the drawing of a contract. Such contracts in the real estate business may be of a number of types, including purchase and sale contracts, listing contracts, land contracts, and others.

The regulations governing contracts pertaining to real estate are similar to those governing contracts in general. The contract must be made by persons who are legally competent. There must be an offer and an acceptance. There must be a valid consideration. Each party must be obliged to do something. The object for which the contract is drawn must be legal.

In addition, however, contracts which involve real estate transactions must be in writing and must be signed by the parties who are to be bound by them. Real estate contracts differ in this regard from other types of contracts. This difference grows out of the provisions of the Statute of Frauds referred to above.

### Contracts for Sale

Contracts for the sale of real estate are usually drawn in accordance with forms which are approved by a local real estate board or similar group. Typically, such contracts provide for a property description, a financial statement, a closing date and place, and signatures. In addition, such contracts should contain an exact statement of the kind of deed involved and an agreement regarding the evidence of title which the seller will furnish. It should be noted that real estate contracts are "specifically enforcible." The courts may force either party to a real estate contract to carry out an agreement exactly. However, this decision is discretionary with the court. If specific performance is not requested, the contract may be rescinded with adjustments in the monetary arrangements. Also, one party may sue the other for breach of contract and damages.

### Land Contracts and Related Arrangements

Land contract, or contract for deed, is the term used to identify a purchase and sale contract which provides for the payment of the purchase price in installments over a period of time. Sometimes similar arrangements are made under a *lease with option to purchase.* Such leases allow the tenants to purchase the property at a specified price within a stated period with the understanding that all or part of the rent paid will apply toward this purchase price.

### Listing Contracts

There are four general types of listing arrangements: (1) *open listing,* in which the seller may list his property for sale with a number of brokers; (2) the *exclusive agency,* in which the seller gives one broker an exclusive agency, but reserves the right to sell the property himself; (3) the *exclusive right-to-sell contract,* which gives the broker the sole right to dispose of the property for a given period and if the owner sells the property himself he still must pay the broker his commission, and (4) *multiple listing,* a system in which a number of brokers have an agreement by which any one of them may sell property for which another member of the group has an exclusive right-to-sell contract. Under such an arrangement, there is provision for dividing the commissions involved. All of these contractual arrangements are best explained on the basis of when a commission is earned and by whom. In the open listing, whichever broker completes the transaction earns the commission. Of course, the owner pays no commission if he sells it himself.

In the exclusive agency, either the owner or the one listing broker may sell the property. If the owner sells the property, no commission is paid. The broker only is paid a commission if he negotiated the transaction. Under the exclusive-right-to-sell contract, the listing broker qualifies for the commission regardless of who makes the sale.

## LEASES

Leases are agreements entered into by an owner or lessor with a tenant or lessee in which the possession of the property is granted to the tenant, usually for a specified period of time, in return for a stated rental.

Leases may be oral or written. In some states, leases for periods of more than one year must be in writing to be valid, while in some states oral leases are valid for as long as three years.

Property may be leased for a long period of time. There are leases that run for as long as 999 years. *Ground leases* are sometimes drawn up to run for long periods and allow the tenant to construct buildings or other improvements on the property.

### Standard Forms

Because of the importance of the provisions of a lease, many real estate boards have drawn up standard lease forms, as have many business firms when the rental of property is an important part of their activities.  In a transaction of considerable financial importance or involving any unusual rights of either lessor or lessee, it is advisable to have a competent real estate lawyer prepare the lease.

### Types of Rents

Rents may be fixed for a flat rate, or related in some way such as *gross or net sales to the amount of business* handled by the tenant.  Sometimes there is provision for a *graded* or *step-up lease.*  In such cases, the rent is established at one level for a given period and then advances for another period.  A reappraisal is sometimes required in such cases.  As has been pointed out above, some leases contain an option to purchase.

### Termination

Leases are terminated either by expiration, by mutual agreement, by a breach of the provisions of the lease, or in other ways.  Some leases are for an indefinite period and operate from month to month.  Leases are important to the business of property management, and the details of lease agreements will be described in Chapter 16.

## UNIFORM COMMERCIAL CODE

The Uniform Commercial Code has now been adopted in many of our states.  Although not closely related to real estate law, there are a number of situations where it may be applicable.  For example, such things would be included as a security interest in annual crops, fixtures, or goods before they become fixtures.  There are many difficult problems involved as to the applicability of the code or traditional real estate law and they are too specialized for our consideration here.  We should recognize the growing importance of the Uniform Commercial Code, however, and its current and potential significance for various real estate decisions.

## SUMMARY

Real estate is one of the most heavily regulated sectors of our economy, being subject to the direct or indirect regulations of federal, state, and local units of government.  Private ownership of real estate resources is never complete, as this ownership may be modified by the governmental powers of taxation, eminent domain, or the police power.  The exercise of these powers may therefore be a key factor in private decision-making.

Real estate administration is conducted in an atmosphere of institutional arrangements and procedures which have developed within the legal system.  Many legal details and legal documents are involved in the establishment of ownership or the transfer of ownership of real estate. Legal arrangements in some cases limit the utilization of property and thus reduce its income-producing ability; in other instances legal arrangements may promote sound property uses and enhance the value of real estate.

Property involves the right to exercise control over economic goods, including real estate resources. Various interests, or estates, in real property may exist and may be classified according to the quantity of interest, the time of enjoyment, or the number of interested parties. Also of importance are nonpossessory interests such as easements and rents.

The prudent individual or business manager will seek competent legal assistance in handling the detailed legal procedures involved in real estate transactions.

## QUESTIONS FOR STUDY

1. Prepare a list of the various laws and regulations that have an effect on your study property and indicate their importance.
2. How could you establish proof of ownership of your study property?
3. Explain why organized government is necessary to the existence of private property.  What is meant by eminent domain?
4. Why do we rely on real estate taxes so exclusively? What are the principal types of real estate taxes?  How significant are real estate taxes in the total tax receipts of state and local governments?
5. Explain the use of a tax lien.
6. Can a real estate tax be imposed upon all future owners of a specific property?  Explain your answer.
7. What are the principal uses of the police power in regulating real estate?
8. Could an interest in real property exist that did not include either ownership or possession of the property?  Discuss.
9. It is sometimes said that private property is a matter of human relationships.  Explain.
10. Distinguish between "title" and "deed."
11. What is an abstract?
12. What is the purpose of title insurance?
13. What is the difference between a quitclaim deed and a warranty deed?
14. What are the principal methods of property description?
15. How are land contracts affected by the Statute of Frauds?
16. Mr. Adams owns a building in which you intend to open a hardware store. He offers to negotiate with you either a flat-rate lease or a percentage lease. Indicate reasons why you might prefer one type of lease over the other.

## SUGGESTED READINGS

KRATOVIL, ROBERT. *Real Estate Law* (5th ed.). Englewood Cliffs, N.J.: Prentice-Hall, Inc., 1969. Chaps. vi–ix.

LUSK, HAROLD F., CHARLES M. HEWITT, JOHN D. DONNELL, and JAMES A. BARNES. *Business Law: Principles and Cases* (Second Uniform Commercial Code Edition). Homewood, Ill.: Richard D. Irwin, Inc., 1970. Chap. 30.

## CASE 4–1

### Wall v. Ayrshire Corporation *
### Tex. Civ. App. 352, S.W. 2d 496 (1961)

This was an action by N. R. Wall (plaintiff) against Ayrshire Corporation (defendant) to recover a judgment for commissions claimed to be due on a real estate brokerage contract. Judgment for Ayrshire Corporation and Wall appealed. Judgment affirmed.

Ayshire Corporation purchased a 215-acre tract of unimproved land which it planned to subdivide and plot into city lots. On February 1, 1946, Wall entered into a contract with Ayrshire Corporation (Ayrshire) under the terms of which he was given the exclusive sales agency to sell the lots into which the property should thereafter be subdivided. Wall was to receive a 5 per cent commission on the sale price of all lots plotted and sold. In 1957 Ayrshire gave Wall notice of the termination of the contract. Wall sued to recover commissions on lots and acreage sold after the termination of the contract.

BELL, CHIEF JUSTICE. Wall's position is that Ayrshire could not unilaterally terminate the contract because he had made extensive expenditures of money in connection with promotion of the subdivision and he should be given a reasonable opportunity to accomplish the purpose of the agency. Additionally he says the agency is one coupled with an interest.

We are unable to agree with Wall. The agency fixed no time for its termination. It was of indefinite duration. The general rule is where an agency to sell real estate, or a brokerage contract, which this is, is of indefinite duration, it not being for a fixed time, it may be terminated at the will of the principal. We are unable to see that any different rules are aplicable where the contract involves sales of lots in a subdivision. We deem the authorities cited by Wall factually distinguishable from the case before us.

We are not confronted with a situation where the agent may have made substantial expenditures and is given no reasonable opportunity to perform, and we do not pass upon an agent's right in such situation.

Neither was the agency one coupled with an interest. To be an agency coupled with an interest the agent must have a present interest in the property upon which the power is to operate. It does not suffice that the agent have an interest in the proceeds to be derived from the sale of the property. There must be a beneficial interest in the thing itself.

---

* Harold F. Luck, *Business Law: Principles and Cases* (Uniform Commercial Code Edition; Homewood, Ill.: Richard D. Irwin, Inc., 1966), pp. 440–41.

Our holding that Ayrshire Corporation has effectually terminated the contract will also prevent Wall from any recovery of a commission for the unsold part of said 215 acres should it ever be sold.

## Questions

1. Which type of listing contract did Wall have with Ayrshire? What are the important provisions of such a contract?
2. Do you feel the decision of the court was correct? Why or why not?

## CASE 4–2

### Brown v. Southall Realty Co.*
### 237 A.2d 834 (Ct. App. D. C. 1968)

This was an action brought by Southall Realty (plaintiff) to evict Mrs. Brown (defendant) for nonpayment of rent. Mrs. Brown contended that no rent was due under the lease because it was an illegal contract. The trial court held for the landlord, Southall Realty. Judgment reversed on appeal, holding that no rent was owed by the tenant.

QUINN, JUDGE. The evidence developed, at the trial, revealed that prior to the signing of the lease agreement, Southall was on notice that certain Housing Code violations existed on the premises in question. An inspector for the District of Columbia Housing Division of the Department of Licenses and Inspections testified that the violations, an obstructed commode, a broken railing and insufficient ceiling height in the basement, existed at least some months prior to the lease agreement and had not been abated at the time of trial. He also stated that the basement violations prohibited the use of the entire basement as a dwelling place. Counsel for Southall Realty at the trial below elicited an admission from Brown that "he told the defendant after the lease had been signed that the back room of the basement was habitable despite the Housing Code Violations."

This evidence having been established and uncontroverted, Mrs. Brown contends that the lease should have been declared unenforceable because it was entered into in contravention to the District of Columbia Housing Regulations, and knowingly so.

Section 2304 of the District of Columbia Housing Regulations reads as follows:

No persons shall rent or offer to rent any habitation, or the furnishings thereof, unless such habitation and its furnishings are in a clean, safe and sanitary condition in repair, and free from rodents or vermin.

* Harold F. Lusk, Charles M. Hewitt, John D. Donnell, and James A. Barnes, *Business Law: Principles and Cases* (Second Uniform Commercial Code Edition: Homewood, Ill.: Richard D. Irwin, Inc., 1970), pp. 687–89.

Section 2501 of these same Regulations, states:

> Every premises accommodating one or more habitations shall be maintained and kept in repair so as to provide decent living accommodations for the occupants. This part of the Code contemplates more than mere basic repairs, and maintenance to keep out the elements; its purpose is to include repairs and maintenance designed to make a premises or neighborhood healthy and safe.

It appears that the violations known by appellee to be existing on the leasehold at the time of the signing of the lease agreement were of a nature to make the "habitation" unsafe and unsanitary. Neither had the premises been maintained or repaired to the degree contemplated by the regulations, i.e., "designed to make a premises . . . healthy and safe." The lease contract was, therefore, entered into in violation of the Housing Regulations requiring that they be safe and sanitary and that they be properly maintained.

In the case of *Hartman v. Lubar*, the court stated that:

> the general rule is that an illegal contract, made in violation of the statutory prohibition designed for police or regulatory purposes, is void and confers no right upon the wrongdoer.
>     . . . To this general rule, however, the courts have found exceptions. For the exception, resort must be had to the intent of the legislature, as well as the subject matter of the legislation.

A reading of Sections 2304 and 2501 infers that the Commissioners of the District of Columbia, in promulgating these Housing Regulations, were endeavoring to regulate the rental of housing in the District and to insure for the prospective tenants that these rental units would be "habitable" and maintained as such. . . . To uphold the validity of this lease agreement, in light of the defects known to be existing on the leasehold prior to the agreement (i.e., obstructed commode, broken railing, and insufficient ceiling height in the basement), would be to flout the evident purposes for which Sections 2304 and 2501 were enacted. The more reasonable view is, therefore, that where such conditions exist on a leasehold prior to an agreement to lease, the letting of such premises constitutes a violation of Section 2304 and 2501 of the Housing Regulations, and that these Sections do indeed "imply a prohibition" so as "to render the prohibited act void."

The result reached in this case is not typical of the attitude many courts would presently take. It is, however, becoming an increasingly common result in large cities where courts and legislative bodies are attempting to deal with "slum" housing.

## Questions

1. Are Sections 2304 and 2501 of the District Columbia Housing Regulations typical of current housing regulations?
2. Do you think regulations of this type will become more widespread?
3. Do you agree with the decision? Why or why not?

## CASE 4–3

### Heislet v. Heislet *
### 10 Utah 2nd 126, 349 P.2d 175 (1960)

This was action by Annie Ray Heislet (plaintiff) against Nadine Heislet (defendant) to quiet title to certain real property. Judgment for Nadine Heislet and Annie Heislet appealed. Judgment affirmed.

Annie Heislet acquired, through conveyance and inheritance, a five-ninths interest in a house and lot. Nadine Heislet acquired a four-ninths interest by inheritance. Annie and Nadine owned the property as tenants in common. In 1945, Annie and her husband moved into the house, and during the years they lived there they improved it by constructing a fruit and furnace room, a utility room and stairway to the basement, by remodeling the bathroom and kitchen, rewiring the electrical system, painting the inside and outside of the house and blacktopping the back yard at a cost of $4,075. They paid the taxes on the property. Although Nadine knew that the improvements were made, she was not asked nor did she offer to contribute for them or for taxes.

After Annie's husband died in 1951, she continued to live in the property until 1958 when she sold it for $10,500. Annie and her husband, during the time they had possession of the property, rented it to third persons for a period of 17 months and collected and used the rent money collected. The court found that the fair rental value of the property during this period was $75 per month. Annie claims ownership of the property by adverse possession. Nadine claims that she is the owner of four-ninths of the property and asks an accounting for the rents collected and the rental value of the house during the time Annie occupied it. Annie in turn claims the right to contribution for the improvements made.

WADE, JUSTICE. Annie contends that the court erred in failing to find that her possession of the property was adverse to Nadine. The court found that at no time prior to the commencement of this action did Annie inform Nadine that she claimed to be the owner, nor did Nadine seek possession of the property involved herein. In *Clotworthy v. Clyde* this Court quoted with approval the test laid down by this Court in *McCready v. Fredericksen* to the effect that in order for a tenant to adverse his contenant he must "bring it home" to his cotenant and by the most open and notorious acts show to the world that "his possession is intended to exclude, and does exclude, the rights of his cotenant."

Since the court found that Annie's possession was not adverse to her cotenants this Court will not disturb such finding unless it was clearly against the weight of the evidence or unless the court has misapplied the principles of law or equality. The mere fact that Annie paid the taxes would not be such an act as would unequivocally inform her cotenants that she was claim-

---

* Harold F. Lusk, *Business Law: Principles and Cases* (Uniform Commercial Code Edition; Homewood, Ill.: Richard D. Irwin, Inc., 1966), pp. 730–33.

ing adversely because as we pointed out in *McCready v. Fredericksen,* unless the interest of each tenant is assessed separately it is the duty of one tenant as much as the other to pay all of the taxes and when he does so it is for the benefit of all and the only right he has is for contribution. The further fact that extensive improvements were made while Annie was living on the property also are not inconsistent with cotenancy. As this court stated in *Sperry v. Tolley:*

> It is likewise true that the repairs and improvements made in the dwellings, buildings and fences are acts normally consistent with a tenancy in common and not adverse to it.

In the instant case the repairs and improvements were such as a person in possession would make for one's own convenience and satisfaction and would not necessarily show an intent to oust cotenants of their rights or rebut the presumption that they were made for the benefit of all the cotenants. This being so this Court will not disturb the District Court's finding that Annie's possession was not adverse to her cotenants.

Nadine has cross-appealed, contending that the court erred in deducting from her interests in the property her proportionate shares of the moneys expended by Annie and her husband for taxes and improvements and not offsetting against these expenditures the reasonable rental value of the property for the number of years in which they had sole possession of it. In *Utah Oil Refining Co. v. Leigh* we approved the doctrine that

> . . . a tenant in common is not chargeable with rents by his cotenant for taking exclusive and sole possession of part of the property, as long as he does not take and hold more than his just proportion.

However, even though Nadine is not entitled to her proportionate share of the reasonable rental value of the premises because she was not ousted or excluded from possession of her portions had she desired to take such possession, the question of whether Annie is entitled to contribution from her for improvements made is a difficult one. As stated in 14 Am. Jur., Cotenancy, 49, commencing on page 115:

> While contrary doctrines have been enunciated and the question is conceded to be one of great difficulty, it appears to be generally agreed that a cotenant who has made improvements upon the common property without the assent of his cotenants is not ordinarily entitled to contribution and cannot, as a matter of right, charge them with the value or costs thereof or maintain any action that would result in a personal judgment against them. . . . Compensation for improvements is allowed, however, where the other cotenants have stood by and permitted him to proceed to his detriment.

> •   •   •   •   •   •   •   •   •   •   •   •   •   •   •   •   •
> It follows that in passing on a claim for contribution arising out of the erection of improvements, all the circumstances of the case should be taken into consideration. Where it appears that the cotenant making the improvements has acted in good faith, without any design to injure or to

exclude his cotenants . . . the court may allow him the amount which represents the increase in the value of the estate.

·  ·  ·  ·  ·  ·  ·  ·  ·  ·  ·  ·  ·  ·  ·  ·  ·  ·  ·  ·  ·  ·  ·  ·  ·  ·

Although there is authority to the contrary, the great weight of authority holds that compensation may be awarded where the improving tenant acted in the bona fide belief that he was the sole owner of the property.

Taking into consideration the fact that there is no evidence that Annie did not act in good faith and in the further belief that she was the sole owner of the premises when the improvements were made, the circumstances are not such as to make the District Court's decision inequitable that Nadine in the furtherance of justice should contribute her proportionate share for the improvements.

## Questions

1. What are the distinguishing characteristics of the type of co-tenancy Annie and Nadine shared?
2. Was adverse possession indicated in this case? Why or why not?
3. Do you feel Annie Ray Heislet should be compensated for improvements to the property? Why or why not?

# 5

# Economic Characteristics of Real Estate

## INCOME PRODUCTION AT FIXED LOCATIONS

As we have pointed out, decisions relating to real estate turn largely on the analysis of income and estimates of income-producing potentials at fixed locations. Such incomes may be in the form of monetary returns or may result from the direct use of a property. But the services produced by a property can be provided only at a given site, for all real estate is *fixed in location*. The land is immovable, and the cost of moving buildings and other improvements is so great that such projects are seldom undertaken.

All types of economic activity and decisions related to them are concerned with income—that is, the production of returns in excess of costs. Indeed, *income* has often been referred to as *the fundamental fact of economic life*. In real estate we are concerned with income and more particularly with the *localization* of income. In nearly all other types of business it is possible for the commodity or service involved to follow the market, to move to the point where the greatest income-producing potential exists. In the real estate field this is not true. The market must be induced to come to the property. Once a property has been developed, its future is dependent entirely upon its ability to command a market for its services at its specific location.

115

## Unique Properties

Because of fixity of location, every parcel of real estate differs from every other one. It is a unique point on a changing economic framework. Not even a vacant lot is identical in every respect with an adjoining vacant lot. Physical structures differ with respect to condition, style of architecture, materials of construction, and in many other ways. Real properties also differ from each other with respect to distances from transportation lines, from places of employment, from civic and social centers, from other sections of the area, and from other parts of the country or the world. Decisions related to city properties are affected greatly by the "urban plant" which serves them, the system of streets, sewers, water mains, utilities, parks, playgrounds, schools and the like. The extent of crime in a locality, adequacy of police and fire protection and the general protection of the area all influence real estate decisions. Similarly, decisions related to rural properties are influenced by the availability and cost of public or quasi-public facilities and services. All are affected by the general physical environment and this varies greatly from locality to locality.

## Neighboring Influences

Because of fixity of location, real estate resources can never escape from developments of an economic, social, political or physical character which may affect them favorably or adversely. Thus neighboring influences are strong. If the street on which your home is located develops into a high-speed traffic artery, you cannot as a practical matter move even the house to a quieter or safer street. Nor can you move a house or any other piece of real estate away from unfavorable conditions in the physical environment such as smog or polluted waterways. Conversely, you cannot help but reap the benefits of any developments which reflect favorably on the city or the district or neighborhood in which your property is located. The influence of factors of this type on real estate expectations and decisions is considered at greater length in Chapters 10 and 11.

Although fertility, topography, soil conditions, annual precipitation, length of the growing season, and temperature extremes form the principal basis of the income-producing capacity of farm land, location or *situs,* as we have pointed out take priority in the case of urban land. As a specific area on the earth's surface, a land parcel is almost indestructible. Its usefulness and income-producing ability and hence its value can be reduced or eliminated. The desirability of location changes as conditions change. The fertility of farm land may decline with use. Thus, even if the land remains in a physical sense, it may lose all or nearly all of its economic value.

## Limited Markets

Because of the fixity of location of real estate, the real estate market tends to be more limited in extent than are the markets for most other commodities. The market for owner-occupied homes typically is limited in geographic extent to a single city and often to a certain section of that city. The market for commercial and industrial real estate, however, is somewhat broader and may be thought of as at least regional in extent. Farm lands typically are bought and sold throughout a county or other relatively limited area. The market for a property varies somewhat with the point of view from which it is considered. Thus a New York investor might buy an apartment house in Chicago. The people who rented the apartments, however, would in almost all instances be Chicagoans.

## Legal Implications

Fixity of location is the principal basis for the legal distinction between real and personal property as we saw in our discussions in the preceding chapter. Also, fixity of location makes it possible to establish definite boundaries and to describe the property for legal and business purposes.

## OTHER BASIC REAL ESTATE CHARACTERISTICS

In addition to the fixity of location, real estate has several other basic characteristics which have a major impact on real estate decisions. These are long life and long term implications of decisions, the relatively large economic units involved and the heavy interdependence of public and private property.

## Long Life of Real Properties

Decisions relating to real properties are influenced greatly by the long life of these resources. Income expected ten years hence is worth less today than current income. This is because we discount the future due to the many uncertainties and risks that lie ahead and because of the waiting involved. As a site for buildings and other improvements, land is relatively permanent. Buildings and other improvements on the land have a longer life than that of most other commodities. Hence, investments in real estate tend to be fixed for long periods of time. It is not easy to change urban land from one use to another. If an apartment house is built on a lot, it usually remains there for many years, even if the market at times is depressed to the point where the owner cannot earn a satisfactory return on his investment.

Although agricultural land can be shifted from the production of one crop to another from year to year, crop rotation and other considerations may place limitations on land use.

### Long Term Implications of Decisions

Some decisions in regard to the purchase, sale, or leasing of real estate are made for short-run purposes. They may be made for purposes of speculation, to provide space for temporary periods such as staying at a motel overnight, or to protect a position previously taken. Most such decisions, however, are made for longer-term periods. Even the leasing of a dwelling unit usually covers a period of a year, often longer; most commercial leases are for a term of years. Purchases are usually made with a long-term program of property use or development in mind. Some speculative purchases, of course, are long term in character. Thus, the long-term nature of most real estate decisions is an important factor in understanding programs of property use and the operation of real estate markets.

### Real Properties as Large Economic Units

The fact that real properties are relatively large economic units is one of the reasons for the existence of the real estate business. Brokers are needed to bring together buyers and sellers—investors in and users of various properties or property services. Property managers are essential to the operation of large buildings or blocks of properties. Since special financial arrangements usually are necessary in real estate transactions because of the large amounts of land involved, an elaborate system of financing has developed.

### Interdependence of Private and Public Property

Rarely can a piece of real estate be used except in conjunction with some public land, and the interdependence of private and public land tends to increase as the community becomes more complex in structure and organization. In order to have access to private land, there usually must be either a public road or street or an easement providing a right-of-way over another private property. Since private arrangements of the latter type are usually difficult to make, we normally depend on public streets and roads for access to our properties. The proportion of the land area given over to public streets, alleys, parks, and similar uses increases as cities grow in size and complexity.

In addition to the problems of access to real properties, provision must be made for water, drainage, and disposal of sewage; for electricity, gas, telephones, and other utilities and conveniences; and for police and fire protection. Indeed, one of our problems in the future may center on channeling enough capital into public projects and properties to support private real estate resources. Problems of law and order, for example, may require substantially larger expenditures for police and fire protection.

## REAL ESTATE VALUE

Economists tell us that real estate, like other commodities, is valuable in proportion to its utility and scarcity. As an interesting case in point, consider the houses in one of the old western ghost towns. Many of these towns were established originally at points where new mineral deposits were discovered. People flocked there in the hope of amassing wealth. Real estate values, of course, rose rapidly. When the mineral deposits were exhausted, people moved on, leaving ghost towns to mark their earlier hopes. As a consequence, the real estate there became worthless because it no longer served a useful purpose and was available in greater quantities than the demands for it.

As a general rule people will demand what is important to them; what is important, however, tends to change from generation to generation. The modern supermarket might have faced early bankruptcy a few decades ago. The fertile prairies of Illinois were less valuable to the early settlers than to those who were able in more recent years to use improved machinery and technology. The value of a home cannot be measured entirely by what it will bring in the market; it may have a high subjective value to the family living in it even though its market value may be relatively low. By contrast the value of an office building will depend almost entirely on the rents it can command in the market.

Thus the value of real estate, like the value of other things depends on its relative utility and scarcity. But the measure of utility and scarcity will vary with the times, the people, the community and the technology that are involved. The term value needs to be considered in relation to community and individual standards, resources and objectives.

### Value and Price

To the nation as a whole, value is a matter of the comparative importance to its citizens of the different things, including real estate, that are essential to its welfare according to its standards, but that do not exist in sufficient quantities to meet the demands for them. To the individual citizen, concerned primarily with his own stake in the community, the value of a parcel of real estate depends fundamentally on how much of other things or the services of other things or persons he can get in exchange for a piece of real estate or the services which it renders. In practice, the relative importance of real estate is reflected in prices, which are values translated into monetary terms, such as dollars, pounds or whatever monetary unit is commonly used. Because the market for real estate is not highly organized, the prices paid for real properties may not coincide with their values at any specific time. Price and value will tend to be identical under conditions of perfect or near-perfect market competition. In such cases the full play of all forces having a bearing on the market results in prices which reflect with reasonable accuracy the values of the commodities that are traded.

### Value and Cost

Costs must be borne in order to bring goods and services into the market. Costs are almost always necessary in order to produce income. Because of costs, goods and services tend to be scarce relative to the demands for them. In the case of real estate, the costs of new developments usually are large; costs must be borne in order to acquire a lot and hold it until it is ripe for development and the costs of a building and other improvements usually are substantial. An owner or developer will not incur costs unless he thinks that incomes produced will be warranted by the required costs. Thus, when prices or rents are high relative to costs, people will tend to build; when low no construction will take place. Thus, costs affect values and prices as they affect supply. Over the long run costs and values tend to coincide, but at any given time costs may be well above or below values as reflected in selling prices or rents.

The fact that $40,000 was spent to buy a lot and build a house does not necessarily mean that the value of the property is $40,000. The expenditure would certainly be considered as one element by an appraiser in making a valuation. Such costs are important at the time they are incurred; once incurred production costs are passive factors.

### "Value is a Word of Many Meanings"

The foregoing discussion emphasizes the validity of Justice Brandeis' remark, "Value is a word of many meanings." There is much confusion about value because the term has been interpreted in many ways, especially in the real estate field. For example, economists tend to identify value with market price, provided the price is set under genuinely competitive conditions. Appraisers tend to define value in terms of "warranted selling price," or the price that a willing buyer would offer and a willing seller would accept, neither acting under compulsion. The "most probable selling price" of a property has sometimes been stressed.

Appraisers help to resolve some of the difficulty by raising the question: "Value for what purpose?" The same property may at the same time have different values for different purposes. It may have one value in terms of a quick sale, another for longer exposure to the market, still others for mortgage lending purposes, tax purposes and insurance purposes. Thus, a property does not have "one true value" as has sometimes been contended. Its value will vary with purposes and with the conditions that prevail at the time. It is imperative in discussing real estate values to clearly identify the kind of value.

## Value and Income

As we indicated above, income is the fundamental fact of economic life. Thus, it is important for us to think in terms of the income producing ability of real properties in trying to determine their value. Real properties must produce income at fixed locations. This income may be received through the direct use of the property's services as in the case of an owner-occupied home or a merchant using a store building which he owns. In other cases incomes may be in the form of monetary returns—a landlord collecting rents or an investor receiving dividends on his property investment. Real properties produce income over relatively long periods of time, as we have pointed out. Future income is worth less than present income. We discount the future; a dollar a year hence is worth 94 cents now at an interest rate of six percent. The risks involved over future time may be great and we also allow for these in evaluating future income. Thus, the present value of anticipated future income produced at a specific site may well be considered the most logical definition of real estate value.

Present value is indicated by the process of capitalization, that is by reflecting future income in current worth. Thus, we may think of the property as its earning expectancy. As Frederick M. Babcock pointed out in his classical study of valuation, ". . . *the property is the earning expectancy*, and the capitalized figure—the total value—is a *derived* fact depending upon the future income stream in some manner." [1] This earning expectancy can be bought for a present amount. The size of this present amount will vary with the expected size and duration of the future income stream and the rate at which it is capitalized. Thus, if an investment is expected to earn an average of a thousand dollars per year in perpetuity

---

[1] By permission from *The Valuation of Real Estate* by Frederick M. Babcock, p. 129, N.Y.: McGraw-Hill Book Co., 1932. (Italics added.)

and if investors were requiring a ten per cent return, its value could be put at $10,000 (dividing $1,000 by .10).

If the future income stream could be predicted with accuracy and if a sufficiently broad market for real estate existed, there would be less difficulty in determining real estate values. In reality, valuations are affected by differences of opinion regarding future trends, the relative inefficiency of real estate markets, variations in the availability and cost of money and related things. The future income stream will be influenced by governmental and political trends, general and local business conditions, market forces, and location factors. Consideration will be given to these topics in the next part of the book.

## SUPPLY OF REAL ESTATE

The supply of real estate available at any given time may be considered from two standpoints: (1) the *properties* themselves, and (2) the *property services* provided by these real estate resources.

### Supply of Properties

The properties include all types of real estate: residential, commercial, industrial, agricultural, institutional, public, and special-purpose properties. They include the land, buildings, and other improvements as well as the legal rights represented by these physical resources. In this use of the word "properties" we are thinking in terms of an inventory of real estate—by numbers, type, size, uses and locations.

### Supply of Property Services

In a sense real properties may be thought of as "factories" producing services—shelter, protection, privacy, comforts, conveniences, and other services. For example, a hotel may be thought of as a producer of the various services it provides its guests. Once a property is improved, property services must be utilized or they will be wasted through depreciation and obsolescence. In this respect, property services may be compared to labor: the loss of a day of a worker's time is an irrevocable loss, just as is the case with the loss of a day of property utilization.

### Utilization Arrangements

Various arrangements may be made for the utilization of the available supply of real properties. An entire property may be purchased for a lump sum. This sum will represent the present value of the services the property is expected to render over the period of its productive life. Usually some borrowing is involved in such purchases because of the relatively large sums typically required. Or a property may be leased, with rental payments being made for the property services as used on the basis of fixed amounts per month or per year, or on percentages of gross or net earnings, or on some other basis.

## Supply of Real Estate Inflexible

Because of the long life of real properties, the supply of real estate resources at any given time is relatively fixed.[2] These resources may be used more or less intensively, of course, and consequently the supply of *property services* is somewhat more flexible than the supply of *properties*. Even in terms of property services, supply is relatively fixed, however, since there are fairly narrow limits within which the property services from a given property can be expanded through more intensive use. Also, even though a property is not used, it tends to affect current market conditions by virtue of its being a part of the available supply.

## Slow Additions to Supply

The present supply of real properties has been accumulating over many years. The amount added in any one year represents a very small percentage of the total. If 2,000,000 nonfarm housing units are started in a year this represents only a little more than three per cent of the total nonfarm housing supply.

The supply of commercial and industrial properties also is not expanded rapidly year by year. We have actually reduced the acreage under cultivation for agricultural purposes in recent years, although we have increased, of course, the intensity of use and expanded productivity through improved methods and machines.

When new construction declines to low points because of sluggish market conditions, the total supply of real estate is not reduced to any marked extent. The additions may be small but seldom are less than demolitions or losses from fire and other hazards.

## Deterioration of Properties

Structures deteriorate with use and the passage of time. By 1980, for example, the remainder of the 20,264,000 dwellings built before 1920 will be at least 60 years old. Some of these will remain in good condition, but

---

[2] See Edward E. Edwards, "Real Estate Economics: A Return to Fundamentals," Study Project 5–1 at the end of this chapter; also, Paul A. Samuelson, *Economics: An Introductory Analysis* (8th ed.; New York: McGraw-Hill Book Co., Inc., 1970), Chap. 4.

many will tend to deteriorate rapidly. Many of our present dwelling units
have to be replaced every year.

### Fixed Supply Means Demand Controls

Since the supply of properties and even of property services is relatively
fixed, *demand* is the most important factor in determining market prices
and rents during short-run periods of a year or two. When demand exceeds supply at current prices and rents, there is a tendency for prices and
rents to move upward and to continue to advance for a prolonged period,
since it takes a long time to add substantially to the supply available.
When demand falls below supply at prevailing prices and rents, the market slows up and prices and rents fall and continue to decline for a long
time.

Because of the relative inflexibility of supply and the informal nature of
real estate markets, there probably never was a time when the markets were
in balance. Tendencies toward balanced relationships between supply,
demand, and price, however, do exist, and it is the identification of these
tendencies that is of greatest importance in analyzing real estate markets,
as we shall see in Chapter 9.

## DEMAND FOR REAL ESTATE

The demand for real estate is based on a wide variety of considerations.
It reflects the standards, attitudes, and objectives of individuals, families,
business firms, government officials and others. It indicates preference for
real estate relative to other goods and services. In the case of commercial
and industrial real estate, demand is a reflection of company policies based
on estimates of the potential income-producing capacity of real property
in relation to cost, including construction costs and operation expenses, and
in relation to potential return from other resources. Industrial firms demand more real estate when the market for their products is brisk and
market potentials are good. Commercial properties are in heavy demand
when profit prospects are favorable. As a result of the adoption of long-
range planning programs by many business firms, there is more of a tendency to buy real estate well in advance of current or short-term needs.

### Impact of Incomes

The demand for residential real estate is largely a reflection of consumer incomes. To a large degree the demand for residential real estate
is similar to the demand for luxury goods. Minimum requirements for
shelter could be met with very small expenditures. The demand for housing, however, is much more than a demand for shelter. It may include

prestige factors; it may reflect the desire to attain the comforts and conveniences that are provided by modern living accommodations. The demand for residential real estate increases as consumer incomes rise. This increase may be both for more space and for space of higher quality. Conversely, demand drops sharply when incomes go down.

## Demand and Credit

To the extent that residential real estate partakes of the nature of a luxury, and for a large majority of dwellings this is the case, it is in competition with other luxury goods for the consumer's income. But more than the consumer's income is involved. Credit is a major factor in the demand for commercial and industrial real estate. The demand for farm real estate is largely a reflection of both farm incomes and the credit position of farmers and investors in farm real estate.

Since real properties typically represent relatively large economic units, few buyers are able to pay for their properties as they are purchased. Credit usually plays a major part in such transactions. The amount that a prospective buyer is prepared to bid for a piece of real estate depends to a marked degree on the amount he can borrow. This is true of most home buyers and to a considerable degree of the buyers of commercial, industrial, and farm real estate as well. Except for loans arranged through friends, associates, or relatives, how much can be borrowed on a specific property depends on the attitudes and policies of the managers of lending institutions. Typically, financial institutions consider such factors as the following in deciding how much of a loan can be made to finance a specific transaction: (1) the borrower's income and income prospects, (2) the present and potential value of the property, (3) the purchasing power risk and the interest rate risk, (4) the relative attractiveness of other forms of investment, and (5) the legal restrictions surrounding financing arrangements.

## Lending Policies

The policies of lending institutions are affected by market conditions. For example, their lending policies may tend to exaggerate the effect of incomes and income prospects on the demand for real estate. When incomes are high and income prospects are favorable, lending institutions tend to be optimistic about both the borrower's income and the value of the property. When incomes are declining and markets are sluggish, the policies of lending institutions tend to be very conservative.

The relative attractiveness of other forms of investments is an important factor in determining the availability of credit for real estate transactions. The availability of funds and the interest rate that must be paid are determined in part by conditions and events entirely outside the real estate market, such as the yield on government and corporate bonds and other investments. Relative attractiveness involves more than yield. There may be a preference for liquidity of investments, as is usually true during depression periods. At such times the funds available for real estate financing may dry up, even though high yields are offered, because investors place a heavy premium on liquidity.

Inflation tends to reduce the funds available for real estate investment since it leads to high interest rates. The real estate market does not compete effectively for funds under such conditions.

### Government Influences

The lending policies of real estate financing institutions are closely regulated by state governments and the federal government. The importance of the federal government in this field has grown with the insurance of deposits and savings accounts, the insurance and guarantee of mortgages, and the increasing role of the Treasury and Federal Reserve in the money markets. The roles of the Federal Home Loan Bank System, The Federal National Mortgage Association and the Government National Mortgage Association have expanded in recent years.

Thus at any given time the demand for real estate depends to a considerable extent on the willingness of financial institutions to finance property purchases. This is particularly true of residential real estate, but has considerable validity in the case of commercial, industrial, and farm property as well. The willingness of these institutions to make loans and the terms on which they may be made often are influenced substantially by the monetary and credit policies of the federal government.

### Population and Real Estate Demand

If a rising population is accompanied by favorable income prospects, the demand for real properties and property services tends to be high. But an increase in population will not bring a rise in the demand for real estate if incomes are falling, unless there should be a sudden shift in the preference of buyers for real estate relative to other goods and services. Thus, the primary factors in real estate demand are considered to be incomes and the terms and availability of financing. However, population trends and movements may be clues to real estate demand when considered in relation to income trends.

The age distribution of the population is an important factor to consider as well as the trend of total population growth. If there are a large number of people of marriageable age, as will be the case for some years, demand for residential real estate will tend to be strong—assuming that income and financing conditions are favorable. As children reach school age, interest in single-family homes tends to rise. The trend toward fewer children per family in recent years undoubtedly shifted the demand from larger to smaller dwelling units. With a larger number of people in higher age groups and with the expansion of pension funds, both public and private, there is a growing market for small, efficiently designed town houses and apartments for retired persons and couples. There is also increased interest in locations in warmer climates.

Cities with growing populations usually have more active real estate markets than those with stable or declining populations. But there must be income-producing opportunities in a city to induce people to move there. Except for resort areas or "dormitory towns," people are attached to cities by good income prospects.

## MARKET COMPETITION

The basic force in markets is competition, and this is the key to understanding how markets work. Through competition, prices and rents (as well as interest rates) are set and the market performs its functions of allocating space, determining rates of development of properties, and determining land uses.

### Informal Market

If the owner of a parcel of real estate wishes to sell it, he offers it in the real estate market. If a prospective buyer wishes to purchase or lease real property, he "enters the market" and attempts to secure the property or property services that will meet his requirements. This market has no single geographical focus, but operates through scattered transactions of owners, brokers, and users of real estate resources or services. There is no organized exchange where real estate transactions take place, as in the case of the large security or commodity markets. "The market" is a highly informal series of negotiations ranging all the way from direct sales of properties by owners to complicated transactions in which numerous brokers and their principals participate.

### Nature of Exchange

The market process arises from the *mutually beneficial nature of exchange*. If the owner of a house sells it for $20,000, he must want the money more than the house. On the other hand, the buyer must want the house more than the $20,000. Unless these conditions were present no sale or purchase would be made. Both buyer and seller expect to benefit from the transaction at the time it is made. Later on, of course, changing

conditions may prove that one of the parties to the transaction was benefited to a greater extent than the other. At the time of the agreement,
however, both expected to benefit.

We should recognize that markets are made up of people, and more
specifically, of people with economic capacity, that is, with available funds
or the ability to command credit. The decisions of people are behind
whatever happens in markets. Thus, when we refer to "market forces" we
are really thinking of various actions that are being taken as a result of
decisions made by people in connection with their personal, business, or
governmental activities.

### Resource Allocation

Competition for various kinds of space is a major factor in the setting
of prices (and rents) and in establishing price relationships. This process
largely determines how real estate resources are allocated among those
who demand them, and it influences the rate of adding to and subtracting
from the available supply.

### Scope of the Market

Because of the fixed location of real properties we usually tend to think
of the real estate market as being local in character, typically including
only one city or community. While stores, factory buildings, homes, and
farms cannot be moved from one locality to another, there are wide variations in the scope of the market for different kinds of properties or property
services. Typically the market for owner-occupied homes is a local one.
It is confined to the people living in the community or moving to that
specific area. The market for resort property, however, may be widespread, since such dwellings are usually occupied for only a portion of the
year and purchasers or tenants may come from any part of the country or
the world. Income from property can be compared on a regional, national
and often on an international basis. Thus, the market for investment properties of nearly all types tends to be regional and in some instances is national and international in scope. An investor in Chicago might buy a
farm in Kansas. A New York investor might purchase an apartment house
in Los Angeles.

The market for commercial and industrial property tends to be regional
or national rather than local in scope. Large industries like General Electric, Ford, and U. S. Steel buy, sell, and lease real estate on a national and
international basis. Chain store organizations analyze the population and
purchasing power of numerous trade areas throughout the country, determine new store locations, the volume needed to support stores of various
sizes, and the population and income required to achieve such volume.

Sales volumes of existing stores, of course, provide a valuable guide in making such estimates.

Unimproved urban sites or vacant suburban tracts are sold in a series of local markets. Since their value depends on estimates of their future use and income, prices often advance quickly on favorable news. The market tends to be a "thin" one and a few sales may send prices up rapidly.

## BASIC MARKET PRINCIPLES

A market is a set of arrangements for bringing together buyers and sellers. The market process is commonly symbolized by specialized trading rooms where major dealers assemble daily for making transactions and where the transactions are all promptly reported to the public. However, it is only in connection with a few highly standardized and heavily traded items like wheat, cotton, copper, and the securities of large corporations that highly organized exchanges are found. Such highly organized exchanges are often used as illustrations of the general economic theory of markets. This is partly because they are dramatic, but mainly because the geographic concentration of transactions and the comparative freedom from other complications make it fairly easy, in connection with them, to visualize the basic principles that operate in all kinds of competitive markets. In other words, in the great exchanges, actual operations resemble very closely the competitive model of economic theory. It should be understood, however, that other markets, including the real estate market, follow the same model, though not so closely.

### Fundamental Concepts

The most fundamental of the general principles of market operation relates to the tendency, in a given market as of a given time, toward uniformity of prices for like commodities. Other basic principles of general market operations are these:

1. When demand exceeds supply at the current price, price tends to advance. When supply exceeds demand at the current price, price tends to decline.
2. An advance in price tends to reduce demand and to increase supply. A decline in price tends to stimulate demand and to decrease supply.
3. Price tends to move to the level at which demand and supply are in balance.
4. An increase in demand, or a decrease in supply, will tend to raise price at least temporarily; a decrease in demand, or an increase in supply, will tend to lower price at least temporarily.

In markets where specialized trading rooms are characteristic, these tendencies are easier to observe, but their operation can be detected no less certainly in markets like that for real estate which are characterized by other means for getting buyers and sellers together. This is the case, for example, in the over-the-counter securities market, where major dealers, despite their separation, get together by telephone and wire services.

The departures from the model outlined above are considerably greater in the real estate market, where the complications include lack of standardization as well as separation of buyers and sellers. However, even in the real estate market the basic principles of market operation outlined above are in evidence.

By and large, pieces of property approximately comparable in size, quality, and desirability tend to rent or sell for about the same prices at a given time in a given locality. Also, the rents and sales prices of properties of different sizes, qualities, or degrees of desirability tend to reflect more or less accurately these differences. While the processes by which adjustments take place do not operate as smoothly or as quickly as in the organized exchanges, they do regulate changes affecting real estate; and in a very fundamental sense they help to govern the uses of these resources.

### Criteria of an Effective Market

In our preceding discussion we stressed the point that the real estate market corresponds in a general way to the theoretical model of market competition. It is equally important to understand how the real estate market departs from this model. In this connection we need to ask what are the criteria of a good or effective market. Competition can operate more easily if the goods involved are durable and capable of bearing long carriage, if they can be standardized, graded, and bought and sold from samples. Furthermore, a market requires good organization, preferably as a central exchange which is easily accessible to all and where offers to buy and sell can be cleared with a minimum of difficulty.

The more complete the knowledge which buyers and sellers possess of all forces bearing on the market, the more effective market competition becomes. Finally, buyers and sellers must be free from compulsion (as, for example, where some single group dominates the market) if competition is to be effective.

### Competitive Market Model

In the model of a competitive market, sellers and buyers are numerous and they are seen as bidding against each other until a price is set at which the market is cleared. The action of any single buyer or seller in this model has only an infinitesimal effect on the market as a whole; but the interactions of all operators taken together create changes in supply, demand, and price. All that any individual buyer can do is to buy or not buy, or buy greater or smaller quantities, as prices change. All that an individual seller can do is to sell or not sell, or sell more or less. If he is a producer, he can produce or not produce, or vary the amount of his production. The quanties supplied will thus be changed and this will affect price.

### Real Estate Market Comparisons

The real estate market ranks comparatively low in effectiveness among various types of modern markets and contrasts in several ways with the model of a competitive market we outlined above. In the market for agricultural staples like wheat, for example, the conditions mentioned above as essential for a good market are approached rather closely; but they are found only to a limited extent in the real estate market. In general, real properties cannot be graded or bought and sold from samples. Also, dealings in the real estate market take place in terms of an assortment of legal rights which vary in details from case to case. In addition, every transfer of real property involves many papers, documents, and legal formalities.

In the case of some real estate markets, for example, the market for vacant and unimproved land, a single buyer may exercise a significant effect. This is due to the relative "thinness" of the market. A comparable situation is that of stocks traded in limited volume on the over-the-counter securities market.

## FUNCTIONS PERFORMED BY THE MARKET

Real estate market operations contribute to the performance of at least three important functions which are essential to satisfactory business and community life. Consideration of these functions is helpful in gaining an understanding of market operations.

First, adjustments must be made to sudden changes in the requirements for space. Thus, rapid changes in the needs for space may result from such things as the establishment (or disestablishment) within a community of a private business or of a governmental agency. When changes in space requirements occur on short notice, as they usually do, it is obviously impossible to expand or contract the supply of buildings simultaneously. When such changes occur only on a temporary basis, expansion or contraction would not be desirable even if it were possible. Hence, the situation calls for apportioning existing quarters in as satisfactory a manner as is possible among all of those who need to use them.

Second, unless changes in land or building requirements are only temporary, the situation calls for expanding or contracting the space available in order to meet the changed conditions. Otherwise the people in the community would be subjected to prolonged inconvenience and economic loss.

A third function which has to be performed relates to land use determination and has as its objective the creation of a proper balance in the development of a community by arranging to have each parcel of land devoted to its most important use in relation to other parcels in the area. The efficiency of a city as an economic and social unit depends largely on the adequacy with which this function is performed in the light of the needs of the community as a whole.

In periods of national emergency, of course, the market allocation of real estate resources may be superseded by laws and regulations. For example, rent controls may be established and building materials may be rationed. As a result, the competitive market forces became largely inoperative and the allocation of real estate resources is undertaken by government authorities.

### Short-Run Market Changes

Suppose City A, U.S.A., with a population of around 30,000 families, or about 100,000 people, is selected as the location for a new industry. As a result, suppose that approximately 1,000 families move to City A within a few months. Requirements for both business space and living quarters would expand suddenly. The situation would be complicated by the fact that the success of this industry may not be assured and investors may be unwilling to take the risk of adding new permanent housing facilities. Adjustments would be worked out, however, through market competition.

If a similar situation occurred in City B, located in a controlled society that did not rely on market competition, the processes of adjustment would be quite different. In both cases, it is apparent that the situation would call for a considerable amount of doubling up or crowding together of the prior residents to make room for the newcomers. In City B, this process would be attacked directly by administrative methods. The space would be catalogued and rationed out on some predetermined basis to those who had demands for it. In City A, similar results would be achieved through market competition. Rental levels would move upward to the point where the required adjustments would be made. Many families would be compelled to move to smaller quarters or to double up as rents advanced, thus making space available.

### Illustration of Short-Run Changes

The various sets of conditions and the adjustments which would take place is illustrated diagrammatically in Figure 5–1. Curve $D_1$ represents

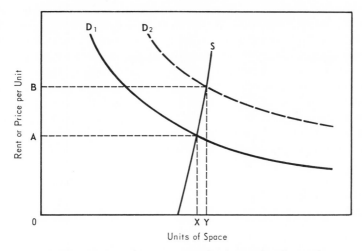

**Fig. 5–1.**  Short-run supply-demand relationships.

the character of the requirements (or demand) for residential space as of some moment of time prior to the coming of the new industry. It simply shows the amount of space and other house services that would have been required by the citizenry at all possible levels of rent per unit [3] within the range of rents shown. The dotted curve $D_2$ shows the new character of requirements for residential space as of some moment of time after the coming of the new industry.[4] Both curves imply that any given group of people under specified conditions would use less space as a result of rent increases.

Curve S reflects the amount of space that would be made available for various purposes within a fairly short period of time (a month or so) at different levels of rent. It will be noted that the curve has practically no elasticity; in other words, under the condition shown, very little increase in the amount of space and property services available could be expected as a result of an increase in the level of rents.

---

[3] In drawing a diagram of the sort presented here, which seeks to describe certain features of the market situation for an entire city, one is obliged to reduce all existing and potential building space to comparable units. Definition of such a unit in physical terms is almost impossible, but some such concept must be used in this connection. This diagram is based on *a priori* considerations and not on direct statistical data. For illustrative purposes, however, it should be helpful.

[4] It is important to note that curves $D_1$ and $D_2$ both represent sets of demand conditions *as of a moment of time.* As new families moved to the city and as incomes of families already there increased, a steady day-to-day movement to the right of the actual demand curve undoubtedly took place.

If this diagram were drawn to reflect accurately the actual demand and supply conditions in City A at the time, it would indicate the direction toward which average rents would tend to move under each of the two sets of demand conditions stated. Under the conditions existing prior to the advent of the new industry, the rent per unit would tend toward the OA figure; under the conditions reflected by the $D_2$ curve, rents would tend toward the OB level.[5] At any time, of course, average rents might actually be higher or lower than those points—but, should rents be higher, there would tend to be a higher percentage of vacancies; likewise, if rents were ever to fall lower, demands for space would increase and rents would be raised.[6]

### Demand Controls Short Run

From the illustration it is apparent that when we are interested in knowing what will happen during some short period of time, such as a few months, as a result of a given change in the real estate market, demand forces are the determining factors, since supplies are relatively fixed. Consequently, any short-run analysis of the real estate market requires that demand considerations be given greatest attention. Over longer-run periods this is not the case, as the following discussion will show.

### Longer-Run Changes

The second function which the real estate market performs is that of adjusting the available supplies of space to changes in requirements which are expected to be permanent. If a new industry moved into a city, there would be a tendency for rents to move upward, as we noted above. Now, if it became apparent after a year or two that this industry would succeed and remain prosperous for some time, this would provide grounds for expecting the level of rents to continue to a high plane and would give some assurance of higher than average profits to anyone who wished to construct new residential or office buildings in the city.

It is reasonable to expect that considerable building activity would result. The rapidity of the response would depend largely on how much the rent per unit in that city exceeded that in other cities. If the rent differential were large, adjustment would presumably be made in a shorter time than if the differential were smaller. (If diagrams are helpful, the supply curve in Fig. 5–1 would be drawn with a less sharply upward slope.)

[5] In the conventional language of economics, OA and OB, under the supply conditions represented by curve S, represent the equilibrium prices for the demand conditions represented by curves $D_1$ and $D_2$ respectively. They are the prices which, under the conditions specified, will just clear the market.

[6] For a more complete discussion of demand, supply, and price relationships, see Paul A. Samuelson, op. cit., chaps. 20–22.

Variations in the rate at which additional space is made available in a given real estate market depend not only upon variations in the rate of return on capital invested in real properties but also upon variations in the length of time allowed for adjustments to work themselves out. Differences in the rate at which supply may be increased in adjustment periods of different length reflect the fact that as soon as the rate of building in a given market exceeds the normal capacity of local builders and suppliers of materials, increases in that rate are possibly only if greater remuneration is offered for those necessary services. Overtime must be compensated, allowances must be made for lower efficiency of operations, and laborers and tradesmen must be attracted from other cities.

Periods of active building often result in excessive supplies of space. Builders may continue to develop new properties even after demand has started to decline. The vacancy rate then increases and a considerable time may be required for readjustments to be made due to the long life of real properties.

### Land Use Determination

In considering the ways in which market forces performed their first two functions, we must not overlook the fact that market competition is one form of social control. Frequently, some government action is necessary to harness the forces of competition, especially in the form of contract enforcement, the maintenance of order, and the limitation of forces tending toward monopoly. In the performance of its third main function, that of land use determination, the community must rely to a much greater extent on governmental action to direct and regulate the operation of competitive forces than in the case of the rental market.

If we take for granted a particular pattern covering the layout of streets, public transportation routes, boarding points, and the like, it can be said that rents and market prices obtainable for various tracts of land provide the most serviceable indexes of their relative importance to the community as a whole. Within this sphere, market competition, which tends to force land into the uses from which the greatest returns can be secured, affords the most workable device for deciding the alternative uses to which these land resources may be put. We should note that returns cannot necessarily be computed in dollars. In some cases esthetic considerations or sentimental attachments may be major factors in decisions related to land use. Such decisions, however, will also tend to be reflected in the market. While some other qualifications are necessary, such as those arising from a given type of income distribution, it may be said that the use which can pay the most for a given site is the use which will be most advantageous for the community as a whole.

This, of course, is not the whole story. We have assumed a *given pattern* for the street, transportation and utility system. Had the basic plan been laid out on another basis or had the main transportation and utility lines been located elsewhere, altogether different parcels of land would have commanded the highest prices and rents.

### Modifying Factors

Also, it may not pay to demolish an existing structure and build another until the present building is in a late period of its economic life. Tax depreciation factors may play a major part in a decision to demolish or not to demolish a structure. In addition, some land uses are very detrimental to adjoining properties. For example, a warehouse located in a residential area might bring great returns on the tract upon which it was built, but it might reduce the value of many neighboring properties. The net result might represent a loss in the total property values of the area.

The net loss in a property's value from the development of a particular parcel of land in a manner that is out of harmony with the character of the area in which it is located is likely to reflect a diminution in the economic welfare of the entire community. The effects are felt even beyond adjacent tracts of land, since the people who previously were the land users (and any potential users under the prior conditions) are now forced to seek new areas, which in all probability are less desirable than was the original district before the adverse development occurred. Furthermore, the very existence within an area of uncertainties as to whether such adverse developments may occur tends to exert a restraining influence on new investment and to make necessary a higher prospect of return before developments can be expected. For business risks of this type there can be no economic justification, either for private enterprise or for the community at large.

### Need for Planning and Zoning

These observations suggest the conclusion that the potentialities of individualistic competition in connection with land use determination can be realized to the fullest extent only if government or private groups act to minimize the dangers and risks arising from the manner in which particular owners may use their properties. This provides the economic justification for zoning, land planning, and private restrictions on land use. Zoning can be economically beneficial or detrimental to a community depending on the extent to which it substitutes certainty for economically unnecessary and unproductive uncertainty. Zoning plans obviously tend to lose their economic justification if they fail to lay down definite policies expressed in rules simple enough so that they can be generally understood. In other words, uncertainties of all sorts should be minimized—political and governmental as well as other types—and the area left for administrative discretion narrowed as much as possible.

Zoning may result in an uneconomic arrangement of land uses if more land is zoned for industrial or commercial uses than is required. If zoning authorities make use of market surveys, they may be able to adapt the regulations to the needs of the market. It would be desirable to do this without opening the door to unlimited "spot" zoning.[7]

## SUMMARY

Income is the fundamental fact of economic life. Real properties must produce income at fixed locations. Such properties have relatively long life, come in large economic units and there are significant interrelationships between public and private property. Real estate value reflects the relative utility and scarcity of real properties or their services. Value may be related to market price under conditions of effective competition, warranted selling price, most probable selling price or to the present value of future income. Value tends to vary with purpose, especially in the real estate field.

The supply of real properties available at any given time is relatively fixed. However, because of possible changes in intensity of use of real properties, the supply of property services tends to be more elastic than the supply of properties themselves.

With supply relatively inelastic, demand factors are the most important determinats of prices and rents in any short-run period. The expected profitability of investment in real estate as compared with investments in other resources is a key determinant of demand for commercial and industrial real estate. For residential real estate, consumer incomes are a major demand factor. Because of the high unit values of real properties, the terms and availability of credit also play a crucial part in determining the demand for real estate. Population trends and movements do not constitute a demand for real estate unless income and

[7] Although it is not appropriate to discuss in detail here the relation of competitive forces to the problem of the social control of real estate, we should note that an important relationship exists between them. For example, in the case of the third market function which is discussed above, it should be noted that most programs for planning set the balanced and economical development of cities as their major goal. Of course, this goal can be achieved only by getting individual parcels of land assigned to their proper places in a comprehensive and generally satisfactory pattern. From what has been said, it should be apparent that the real estate market contains powerful forces which can be made to do a major part of this work if they are understood and skillfully harnessed.

financing prospects are favorable, but population factors may provide clues to future real estate demand when considered in relation to incomes.

Real estate markets perform the major functions of rationing space in the short run, adjusting supplies over the longer run, and land use determination.

## QUESTIONS FOR STUDY

1. In which respects can it be said that the supply of property services is more flexible than the supply of properties?
2. Indicate the ways in which fixity of location affects the income-producing capacity of real properties.
3. Give illustrations of changing social or political conditions that may affect the value of real properties.
4. What types of real estate (residential, commercial, industrial, agricultural, etc.) have the broadest market? Which have the most localized market?
5. Why is credit an important factor in the demand for real estate? Which factors determine the availability of credit for potential purchasers of real properties?
6. In which ways does the value of private properties depend upon the existence of public properties?
7. What is the relationship between demand and value? Price and value? Cost and value? Income and value?
8. What is the value of a property that earns $1,000 per year at a capitalization rate of 10%? At a capitalization rate of 8%?
9. Herbert Smith has a choice between two properties. The asking price of each is $100,000. Property A earns a net cash flow of $10,000 per annum and property B earns a net cash flow of $12,000. However, because of increased risk, Smith must project a capitalization rate of 15% for property B, whereas a 10% rate seems appropriate for property A. What is the value of each to him?
10. Why are demand factors more important than supply factors in determining real estate prices and rents in any short-run period?
11. Describe the effect of a growing population on the demand for real estate. How may age distribution be an influence?
12. Which demographic variables other than population size and age distribution affect the real estate market? How?
13. Why is the market for owner-occupied homes more highly localized than the market for commercial or industrial property?
14. Explain this statement: "competition represents a type of social control, not the absence of control."
15. List and explain the functions performed by real estate markets.
16. How does the real estate market differ from other types of markets?
17. How does the market serve as a rationer of space?

18. Compare and contrast the allocation of space under competitive market conditions and under administrative regulations.
19. How does the market determine which additions will be made to the supply of real properties or of property services? How does the market determine the amount of such additions?
20. How is zoning justified in an economic sense?

## SUGGESTED READINGS

HOYT, HOMER. *Dynamic Factors in Land Values,* Technical Bulletin No. 37. Washington, D.C.: Urban Land Institute, March, 1965. Reprinted in *According to Hoyt* (2nd ed.). Washington, D.C., 1970; pp. 513–527.

REYNOLDS, LLOYD G. *Economics: A General Introduction.* Homewood, Ill.: Richard D. Irwin, Inc., 1969. Chaps. iv–v.

SAMUELSON, PAUL A. *Economics: An Introductory Analysis* (8th ed.). New York: McGraw-Hill Book Co., Inc., 1970. Chap. 4.

## STUDY PROJECT 5–1

### A Return to Fundamentals

This study project is intended to stimulate some reflective thinking about the economic characteristics of real estate.

#### Real Estate Economics: A Return to Fundamentals *

Real estate prices behave quite differently in the market place than do prices of other economic goods. Why is this so? Can the differences be explained in terms of economic principles? Will an understanding of economic principles help to explain price behavior in the past? Will such an understanding help to predict future real estate prices?

A study of the behavior of prices for single family homes leads to the conclusion that real estate prices can be explained and predicted in terms of five economic principles, which are as follows:

1. The supply of real estate is relatively fixed.
2. The demand for real estate is dependent in the first instance on income.
3. Effective demand is dependent largely on the availability and terms of financing.
4. The real estate market is a local, disorganized one.
5. The influence of government is very great.

These economic principles are well known and are not the discovery of the author. Perhaps, because they are so well known, they are frequently overlooked. This article, which deals with these five simple concepts only, may be considered a return to fundamentals in real estate economics.

* Edward E. Edwards, "Real Estate Economics: A Return to Fundamentals," *The Appraisal Journal* (April, 1949).

**Supply of Real Estate Relatively Fixed.** This first principle hardly needs to be proved. Our present supply of real estate includes structures that have been built over a long period of years. The new structures added in any one year occasionally exceed in number the old structures that are torn down, but only in a building boom do they add as much as two or three per cent to the existing supply. When new construction ceases, the supply declines slowly, since neither government nor private enterprise can afford wholesale destruction of accumulated capital investment in real property.

Because the supply is relatively fixed, demand is the most important factor in determining price. When demand exceeds supply, as at the present time, real estate prices rise and continue to rise for quite some time, since there is little chance that the supply will catch up. Conversely, when demand falls below the existing supply, real estate prices fall and continue to fall or remain at low levels for a prolonged period.

The inflexibility on the supply side probably is such that there never is a time when supply and demand are equated. By the time an inadequate supply has caught up with a heavy demand, the demand has already shifted downward. On the low side, supply is never reduced to a depression-low demand, and the real estate market must wait until demand has again moved upward.

**Demand for Real Estate Dependent in First Instance on Income.** Real estate, as it is known in this country, is not a necessity of life, but a luxury. The amount of real estate actually needed for the bare necessity of shelter is very small. This is especially true when real estate is measured in terms of dollar value rather than in dwelling units. The demand for dollars' worth of real estate, therefore, behaves very much like the dollar demand for any other luxury good.

What are the characteristics of the demand for luxury goods, particularly real estate? First, the demand for real estate increases sharply with increased personal incomes. In this connection, it must be remembered that the increase in demand is an increase in the dollars offered for real estate. This is not necessarily an increase in the number of houses demanded; in fact, it is more likely to be an increase in the dollars that the prospective buyer will put in a single house. An increase in total demand therefore may be accompanied by a decrease in demand for certain properties.

Second, the demand for real estate decreases sharply with falling off of personal incomes.

Third, the maintenance of demand, or the increasing of demand, except in periods of rising incomes, requires aggressive selling to meet competition of other luxury goods.

By putting the first two principles together, the conclusion may be reached that the most important factors in determining the price of real estate are the level of personal incomes and the competition of other luxury goods for those incomes. If the subject of real estate economics had to be reduced to a single theorem this would be it. The idea that real estate values over the long run must equal cost of construction is of little use in explaining the real estate market. Real estate prices practically never equal cost of construction; they are either higher or lower.

**Effective Demand Dependent Largely on Availability and Terms of Financing.**
Most buyers of real estate enter the market with some money of their own
and as much or more of some financial institution's money. The amount that
they are prepared to bid for real estate is therefore largely dependent on the
amount that they can borrow.

While it is true that most mortgage lenders apply some standards which
relate the amount of the loan to the income of the borrower, these standards
change from time to time. Unfortunately, the changing standards tend to
accentuate differences in personal income levels rather than to equalize them.
For example, lending institutions generally have been more liberal in periods
of prosperity when the level of personal incomes is high than during depressions when the level of personal incomes is low.

The amount of funds which a financial institution will place in the hands
of a prospective buyer of real estate is dependent not only on the borrower's
income but also on the institution's judgment as to the appraised value of the
property. Here again the judgment of the lending institution frequently rises
and falls with the level of personal incomes. The result is that the action of the
financial institutions tends to exaggerate the effect of changes in personal incomes on real estate prices.

There are, of course, many factors other than the level of personal incomes
and appraised values which affect the amount of funds available for the financing of real estate. One very important factor is the relative attractiveness of
other forms of investment. Mortgagors must compete in an open-money market
for their funds. The availability of funds and the interest rate that must be paid
are determined at least in part by conditions and events entirely outside the
real estate market.

The relative attractiveness of an investment is not solely a matter of yield.
All too frequently, in the past, this country has had periods when the investor
would much prefer money in the bank or in his safety deposit box to any income
producing investment. This has resulted in a drying up of mortgage funds,
hence a virtual elimination of the demand for real estate.

The influence of the financial institutions on demand for real estate is especially significant in view of the fact that the lending policies of so many financial
institutions are regulated or influenced by federal government action. The
insurance and guarantee of particular types of loans has a profound influence
on the demand for real estate. The influence of the federal government on real
estate prices is so important that it has been listed separately as one of the five
factors necessary to explain real estate prices.

**Real Estate Market a Local, Disorganized One.**    Real estate cannot be moved
from one market to another, nor can demand be shifted from a market in tight
supply to one having a surplus of properties. A vacant house in Indianapolis
cannot be moved to Detroit, nor can a Detroit family solve its housing problem
by moving to Indianapolis. Even within a single city separate markets exist
for houses in different neighborhoods and for houses of different sizes and
prices. For any given piece of property there are very few potential purchasers; for any prospective purchaser there are very few properties that will
satisfy his wants.

As a result, the so-called real estate market is in reality a large number of separate markets. One market may be enjoying a real estate boom while another is in a real estate depression. Comparable properties sell at widely differing prices, and there is no national market of investors and speculators to equalize prices as there is in securities and commodities.

Even within a single real estate market the equalization of prices is difficult if not impossible because of the cumbersome, slow, costly, and risky procedures involved in real estate transfer. Compared with a well organized securities or commodity market, real estate market can only be described as highly disorganized.

**Influence of Government Very Great.** No other economic goods with the exception of narcotics is so greatly affected by government as is real estate. Perhaps this is inevitable in view of the fact that real estate after all is not a commodity but merely a bundle of rights created by government.

Until comparatively modern times only the state and local governments had much interest in real estate. In recent years, the federal government has moved rapidly into this field and its influence upon real estate prices is now of prime importance.

Real estate prices are affected by two more or less separate and distinct types of federal action. The federal government is now dedicated to the proposition that it must maintain a high level of personal incomes in this country. To the extent that the federal government's actions in this direction are successful, the demand for real estate is stimulated and a continuing strong demand is more or less assured.

But the federal government is not limiting its influence to the indirect effects of its full employment policies. It supervises the lending policies of many mortgage lending institutions. It guarantees and insures mortgage loans, it controls rents, it expedites the construction of new housing units, and at times it encourages public housing.

The actions of the federal government are not always consistent. The insurance of mortgage loans developed as a means of stimulating new construction during a depression, yet guaranty and insurance of mortgage loans continue during a period when there is full employment and runaway inflation is threatened. Rent control continues when there is a shortage of supply, and rationing is needed. Inconsistencies such as these are likely to continue. Perhaps politics is more important than economics, and no one should explain real estate prices except in political terms.

**Summary.** This discussion of real estate prices perhaps can be summarized in the form of a prediction of future real estate prices. Such a summary might read as follows:

*The present real estate boom will not end because of new construction; it may end because of reduced demand. A reduced demand for real estate may come from a reduction in the national income, from a reduction in the proportion of personal incomes that people are willing to spend for housing in competition with other luxury goods, or from further tightening of real estate financing. No matter what happens, real estate prices will behave differently in each real estate market. Finally, the federal government, both directly in the field of real estate and indirectly in monetary and fiscal policy, will be a major influence.*

*On the assumption that the federal government will seek to maintain or increase the present level of personal incomes and to continue easy financing of home ownership, the prediction might be made that real estate prices will continue high on the national average, but that weak spots may develop in individual markets with changing local demands for real estate and widely varying increases in supply from new construction.*

## Questions

1. If demand for real estate advances, how will rents and prices be affected? Why?
2. If personal incomes of consumers were to double, would you expect expenditures on residential real estate to double? Explain.
3. How do financing terms influence the effective demand for real estate?
4. What are the chief characteristics of the real estate market? Why does the market for real estate differ from the market for automobiles?
5. Explain the impact of the federal government on real estate values.
6. Explain the statement ". . . real estate after all is not a commodity but merely a bundle of rights created by government."

# II

# ANALYSIS FOR
# REAL ESTATE DECISIONS

This part of the book deals with various types of analysis that may be used to aid the real estate decision maker.

Chapters 6, 7, and 8 deal with governmental, political, economic and business trends on a national and regional basis, particularly as they affect the real estate sector. Chapter 6 includes a study project which presents a brief review of federal housing programs. The study projects for Chapter 7 deal with potential business developments in the 1970's. Chapter 8 which considers local and regional economic trends includes a case study of a mythical community named Bel Aire and also presents as a study project a discussion of the Kentucky input-output study.

Chapter 9 considers the general subject of real estate market analysis and includes discussions of the major features of a market analysis with suggestions for applying these to different types of markets. Two study projects are included. The first deals with the housing market of College Town, and the second a market survey for Chester Grove Shopping Center.

Chapters 10 and 11 consider location analysis, the former discussing various patterns of land use and the latter, neighborhoods and districts. Chapter 10 presents a study project by Dr. Hoyt which outlines potential shopping center changes during the rest of the century. Also a short project describing a computerized game for use in city planning is presented. Chapter 11, dealing with neighborhoods and districts, includes two brief case studies; one requires a house-buying decision relating to neighborhood factors, and the other a department store's location. This chapter also provides as a study project a short article by Professor Birch on "The Future of American Cities—and Suburbs," and another project which presents excerpts from an article by Professor Harriss on pollution with special reference to real estate.

Part II ends with a discussion of appraising methods. Chapter 12 concentrates on the income approach, Chapter 13 on the market and cost approaches. Chapter 12 includes a short case which calls attention to some valuation principles. At the end of Chapter 13 a fairly complete appraisal report is presented for student analysis and discussion.

# 6

# Governmental and Political Trends

## TREND ANALYSIS

It is far from easy to analyze governmental and political trends and to determine their potential impact on real estate incomes, values, and decisions. Nevertheless, such analyses must be undertaken by real estate decision-makers. Every governmental and political development has a potential effect on real property. Those who make decisions regarding the purchase, sale, development, use, management, or financing of real estate find it necessary to try to anticipate political and governmental trends, to estimate their potential impact on real property in general as well as on particular properties, and to arrive at decisions on the basis of such anticipations and estimates. The generation of income at fixed sites is influenced greatly by potential developments in the governmental and political sector.

### Information Sources

Although information about governmental and political affairs is available in every newspaper, magazine, and radio or television broadcast, it is hard to select the key information, weight its implications and determine its significance. Some assistance is available to the decision-maker. For example, there are a number of trade associations operating in the real estate field and in related fields as we noted in Chapter 2. Often they can provide pertinent information since they follow developments in

Washington and in state capitols with considerable care. On the local level, real estate boards, chambers of commerce, and other business and citizens organizations may be helpful. Sometimes lawyers can provide assistance in analyzing proposed legislative changes and in assessing their chances for enactment. It is often possible to secure help from one's congressman, senators, or legislative representatives in state or local government.

In some cases, various types of "public opinion polls" give indications of public attitudes and points of view although there are variations in their reliability. In addition, the real estate decision maker usually follows opinion closely in his own circle of acquaintances.

## Research Efforts

Various federal, state and local governmental agencies as well as educational and private foundations and other organizations carry on a broad range of research activities in the real estate field. Of special importance is the Bureau of the Census and especially the Census of Housing. The National Bureau of Standards and the Forests Products Laboratory carry on continuing research. The Department of Housing and Urban Development and the Federal Home Loan Bank system are important sources of research reports in the technical, market and financial areas. Many states provide information about a variety of subjects in the real estate area. Local government agencies often sponsor studies and publish a wide variety of information. Various university divisions and bureaus of business and economic research also are sources of real estate, housing and urban economics research reports and related information.

## Evaluation of Information

Each of us can learn something from the evaluation of research reports, headlines, news stories, and editorials. This is not always easy to do. As has been pointed out:

Often government officials or politicians issue statements that are designed to "smoke out the opposition" or to "send up a trial balloon" to test public reaction or to lay out a claim to an area in which there is likely to be new legislation. The business manager soon develops a healthy skepticism in regard to current news reports. He tries to understand what is back of them, what the motives of government officials or politicians may be, and what kinds of results may be anticipated. He attempts to think in terms of who exercises the real power in political and legislative campaigns. Often the actions of elected representatives or public officials are taken with one eye on those who control important blocks of votes or who provide substantial financial support for political campaigns. In short, *things are not always as they seem* to be in this interesting sector of our business environment.[1]

## Special Interests and Attitudes

We should note also that while the bulk of regulations and controls are proposed or set up to serve the public interest, there are numerous cases where special interest groups are trying to secure an advantage. An example may be found in some of the building regulations which favor local builders and workers as against competition from other cities or localities.

As has been suggested above, things are not always what they seem to be in the governmental or political field. Governmental machinery often offers opportunities for closely knit groups to exert their influence and secure competitive advantages over other groups that are not situated in as fortunate a position. Such advantages usually last until the other groups become sufficiently organized to exert presures for their own purposes. In most federal, state, and local governments these processes are going on more or less constantly. Their extent and nature is often difficult to determine without access to the kind of information that usually is *not* found in the official pronouncements.

The analysis of governmental and political (or other) trends varies somewhat with the point of view of the analyst and decision maker. For example, the viewpoint of the private investor differs from that of the public official. The federal government official's outlook will differ from that of the local official. The point of view of a company executive differs from that of the home owner. As we have indicated, the viewpoints of buyers and sellers, borrowers and lenders, and owner-users and nonowner-users may differ widely. We need to remind ourselves from time to time of the variety of points of view from which real estate decision makers may consider their problems and their decisions.

## Long vs. Short Run

We should recognize also the variations that may arise between a short-term and longer-term outlook. Although real estate decision makers are primarily concerned with the latter, they dare not ignore the former. The real estate decision maker may be able to identify long-term governmental and political trends. We will consider several of these in the following discussion. He usually will find it helpful to follow our periodic elections on local, state, and national levels with care. In addition, he needs to be alert to the possibilities of sudden shifts in governmental

---

[1] Arthur M. Weimer. *Introduction to Businesss: A Management Approach* (4th ed.; Homewood, Ill.: Richard D. Irwin, Inc., 1970), p. 116.

or political conditions such as may result from an unexpected emergency. Usually, opinions and attitudes change slowly but now and then sudden shifts occur. If they can be anticipated, of course, chances for sound decisions are greatly improved.

### Types of Regulations

It is often helpful to think in terms of the various types of regulations that may have a bearing on real estate. Although we tend to emphasize public regulations and controls, we should recognize also that various private regulations may be important. For example, deed restrictions are very important as are policies, programs, and regulations imposed by groups such as labor unions, property owners' associations, business associations, and others.

The various types of regulations and programs that affect real estate may also be divided according to whether they are of the *coercive* or *inducive* types. Coercive regulations typically are of the "thou shalt" or "thou shalt not" types, with penalties imposed for failure to comply. Inducive regulations accomplish their objectives by offering rewards for compliance or by providing information on the basis of which individuals will tend to make decisions that are in line with the public interest. Subsidies are generally of this type, as are the information-giving services of federal, state, and local governments, trade associations, universities, business firms, and private individuals.

Regulations may also be classified as to whether they are imposed on properties or on the real estate business. For example, many informal controls such as custom, accepted procedures, status, personal relationships, and the like affect businessmen and business practices.

Regulations may also be classified as to whether they supplement or supplant competition. Either type may have favorable or unfavorable implications for real estate. Special circumstances may at times require careful evaluation.

## TYPICAL AREAS FOR ANALYSIS

It would be impossible to set forth all of the governmental and political areas that will be of concern to the real estate decision maker. Consequently, we outline here some of the areas that are likely to hold substantial interest for those operating in this field. We have tried to select more or less typical areas but recognize that others could well have been included and some of those covered here might have been omitted. We will review briefly various of the current issues and trends related to the role of private property, public ownership, modification of competition, subsidies both direct and indirect, government contracts, inflation and deflation, war and peace, economic stability, conservation and renewal, environmental priorities, quality of life and equality versus excellence.

### Role of Private Property

We should note that the rights and responsibilities that go with the ownership of real estate vary somewhat from generation to generation, even when no formal changes are made in our laws. General attitudes toward such rights and responsibilities reflect the economic, political, and social standards of the community. Thus, real estate is a part of the general *institutional* framework of our society. It is affected by customs, standards, mores, folklore, traditions, and generally accepted ways of doing things. It is often difficult to explain how various institutions or accepted ways of doing things came about or when or how they will change. But it is important to recognize their existence.

While trends in many parts of the world have been in the direction of limiting or reducing the private ownership of real property, this has not generally been the case in the United States. Property rights have usually been protected and encouraged, although public opinion appears to be moving more in the direction of justifying private property in terms of efficiency of use and opportunity of widespread participation in the economic system rather than in terms of guaranteeing the exclusive right of ownership as a special privilege.

A growing percentage of the income derived from real estate, however, has been drained off in recent years for general community purposes through property and income taxes. The important consideration from the standpoint of analyzing income is to determine whether investments in real estate are being penalized or are likely to be penalized in the future relative to other types of investments as a result of taxes.

### Public Ownership

Despite generally favorable attitudes toward private property in real estate both historically and currently, we have always had a great deal of public ownership of such resources. The public domain, of course, was very large during the pioneer period of American history. Much of this domain was transferred to private ownership through a variety of land acts culminating with the Homestead Act at the time of the Civil War. Various changes were made subsequently to meet the needs of the Far West.

Even though much land was transferred to private ownership, much continued or was placed under public control, including our great national parks, forest preserves, highway rights-of-way, conservation areas, and many other types of land uses. Also, it has often been necessary to take land back from private ownership either through direct purchase or condemnation proceedings to provide for superhighways, wider streets, sites for schools or school expansion, flood control, urban renewal programs, recreational programs, and other types of requirements.

There is little doubt that programs of this type will continue and may expand. In some cases this will mean an expansion of public ownership, although in some programs provision is made for resale of various properties to private owners. Of special interest, for example, are provisions for allowing low-income families who live in public housing facilities to become home owners.

### Modification of Competition

The regulations imposed during periods of stress often have set important limits to competition in real estate markets. Of major importance are rent controls. Such controls supplant competition in important segments of our housing markets and shift the use and development of many real properties.

Public-housing programs may bring the government into competition with private owners of rental properties. To the extent that such programs serve groups which are unable to compete effectively in housing markets, however, they do not change greatly the competitive situation. Renewal and redevelopment programs hold possibilities both for facilitating and restraining competition depending on market conditions.

In addition, government assists some portions of the real estate field to compete more effectively; for example, the insurance of mortgages by the Federal Housing Administration and the guaranteeing of mortgages by the Veterans' Administration.

### Subsidies

As our society grows more complex, the number and types of subsidies appear to increase. Subsidies may take a number of forms. The most important type used by local governments is the device of tax exemption. In many instances smaller cities and towns offer tax exemptions to industrial establishments in order to induce them to locate in such places. Churches, schools, government properties, and various others ordinarily are exempted from taxation. In some cases exemptions are allowed in varying amounts to home owners whose properties are mortgaged. Home owners are allowed to deduct interest payments on a mortgage when computing their federal income taxes. Real estate investors in various housing projects are accorded special depreciation allowances in computing their federal income taxes. Interest rate and rental subsidies have grown in importance especially for lower and moderate income families. If subsidization is to be employed at all, outright grants are preferable to tax exemptions. Subsidies which are open and aboveboard may be desirable or undesirable, depending on the objectives of the specific grant. It is relatively easy, however, to count the cost involved.

Subsidies in the real estate field are of many types, the most important being those resulting from the activities of the federal government. To some extent, the activities of the Federal Housing Administration and the Mortgage Guarantee division of the Veterans' Administration may subsidize various real estate activities. However, losses to date have been negligible in connection with these activities; and in addition, improved methods and practices resulting from the work of those agencies may well justify any subsidies involved.

There are cases of one government subsidizing another. The payments of the federal government toward urban renewal projects developed by local governments illustrate these practices. In these cases, subsidies, government ownership, and tax exemption may all be involved. It is probable that the number and type of subsidies will continue to expand and to create special problems and uncertainties for real estate decision makers.

### Indirect Subsidies

Some subsidies operate in an indirect manner. For example, a tariff that protects the products of a locally produced industry may be an indirect subsidy to the property owners in that area. Similarly, federal payments under a crop control program may be of special benefit to the real estate in a particular locality.

As Thompson points out:

The purpose of evaluating the impact of national economic policies on the local economy is not only to prepare the urban area to correctly perceive its own interests so that it may pursue them intelligently—lobby rationally—but also to smooth local adjustments to national policy changes not of the community's own making or liking. Specifically, a clear conception of the vulnerability of the local economy to foreign imports may not enable the community to halt a reduction in the protective tariff, but this knowledge may well alert the community to the coming change and suggest alternative avenues of adjustment.[2]

[2] By permission from *A Preface to Urban Economics,* by Wilbur R. Thompson, p. 83. Copyright, 1965, The Johns Hopkins Press, Baltimore, Md.

### Government Contracts

One of the important ways that federal or state programs may affect a particular locality and the real estate of the area is through the letting of contracts for the construction of important government installations or the purchase of products. The installations of the National Aeronautics and Space Administration in the southern part of this country illustrate the impact of the expansion and reduction of government programs on local areas. The establishment on the one hand and the closing on the other of various military installations is another case in point.

Similarly, the letting of contracts for the production of major items of military or space hardware has had an important effect on economic activity in various localities. The cancellation of contracts tends to have depressing effects on the locality involved. The awarding of a contract to one firm as against others may benefit the property owners of one locality relative to those in the other areas that did not get the contract.

### Economic Stability

The general concept that it is the responsibility of the federal government to prevent extreme fluctuations in economic activity is rather generally accepted by the American people. Although greater emphasis may be given to stabilizing the value of the dollar, full employment appears likely to continue as a major policy objective. Maintenance of employment and incomes helps to strengthen the market for all types of properties.

In addition, the insurance of bank deposits and accounts in savings and loan associations helps to avert serious financial stringencies. Insured and guaranteed mortgages along with secondary mortgage markets provide financial institutions with some assurance of liquidity. Improvements in the credit and banking systems, farm price support programs, unemployment insurance, and other related programs help to ease the effects of recessions.

Prior to World War II the declines in real estate prices, rents, and volume of activity were much greater than the average declines for other commodities. Thus, modification of the swings of the business cycle, such as occurred in recent recessions, tended to benefit real estate. Even so, the use of monetary and credit policies to control the economy has from time to time created special problems for the real estate sector. It is not a good competitor for funds when interest rates are high and funds are scarce.

### Inflation and Deflation

Historical trends in this country have been in the direction of gradual inflation. Downward adjustments in prices, of course, have occurred from time to time especially prior to World War II. But after each downward swing, prices typically have advanced to levels higher than previously.

This long-run tendency has been of great importance to real estate ownership and investments. Except for poorly located or improperly designed properties or those which were the victims of changes in the internal structure of land uses in our cities, the dollar investments in real estate over the years have tended to be maintained. The major problem has been the ability of owners and investors to hold on during depression periods.

An interesting case in point is the experience of the Home Owners Loan Corporation. Although over a million mortgages were financed during the depression of the early 1930's, by the time the Corporation was liquidated in 1952 it had been able to operate without loss and turned over nearly 14 million dollars to the Treasury.

On the basis of past trends it appears that gradual inflation will continue over future years, interrupted from time to time by recession periods. Gradual inflation tends to benefit equity investors in real property and is to the disadvantage of those who invest in mortgage loans or bonds. Rapid inflation may not prove to be advantageous to real estate investors, however, since rent controls or other restrictions may be introduced under such conditions. It would be a mistake, also, to assume that long-term inflation is inevitable. For example, it may be possible to stimulate higher levels of saving. Technological progress, new products, better management, and improved production and marketing methods may prevent significant price increases. Or prices may advance but "dollar's worths," that is, the quality as well as the amount of goods and services may advance even faster.

## War and Peace

International relations and defense programs are likely to have important effects on real estate decisions and on the income-producing ability of real properties in the foreseeable future. The unsettled condition of world affairs, the varying temperatures of cold to hot wars, and the many related uncertainties undoubtedly mean that the defense and related industries will continue to have an important place in the American economy. They may become a smaller percentage of the total GNP but undoubtedly will continue to be large in absolute terms. Much will depend on the degree of international stability or lack of stability that emerges in the years ahead. Factors of this type will complicate the making of decisions related to the long-term commitments involved in real estate ownership, management, and investment.

## Conservation and Renewal

As a nation, we have placed relatively less emphasis on private and public programs for conservation, reclamation, and renewal of real estate resources than have many older countries. We have generally been more interested in the development of new properties than in conserving or renewing old ones. Cutover timberland, eroded agricultural land, and the deteriorated condition of some of the "near-in" areas of our cities all reflect the pioneer tendency to abandon worn-out land or structures and to develop new resources.

We should recognize, of course, that there are some nonrenewable resources. For example, a natural recreational area may not be subject to renewal. The same thing is true of such resources as coal, petroleum and natural gas. Renewable resources are subject to replacement either through natural processes or through human decisions and programs. Basic soil fertility may be destroyed but is also subject to renewal.

## Environmental Priorities

In recent years, however, increasing attention has been given to the conservation of national resources and to the preservation of the physical environment. Relatively more attention has been given to programs of flood control, soil conseration, reforestation, urban renewal, and related activities than previously. Programs in these areas are gaining more recognition by government agencies at all levels as well as by private investors and developers.

Concern about the physical environment has required that special consideration be given to environmental factors in connection with industrial developments. Urban congestion has brought a variety of problems of air and water pollution as have various industrial processes. Residential developments are being planned with increasing attention being given to such factors as the preservation of natural advantages, provision of adequate waste disposal systems and related factors.

## Quality of Life

Although we continue to be interested in economic growth and expanding opportunities we have become increasingly concerned with the quality of life. Problems of the environment have come in for widespread attention. Social costs of economic growth are being assessed with increasing care.

Government programs for subsidizing research, disseminating information, and for related activities have general widespread support. Programs undertaken in the interest of small business firms and farms are popular and help to guarantee a widespread distribution of economic opportunity. Continued support of our public school system, extending through universities, is one of the best guarantees that young people of ability will have a chance to rise on independent terms.

Security against illness, unemployment and old age has come in for increased attention. Concern with the quality of life and security could impose limits on economic development if carried to extremes. Real estate decision makers, of course, must carefully assess the significance of trends of development in these areas.

## Equality vs. Excellence

Our society has the difficult task of pursuing both equality and excellence, even though these are in some degree incompatible objectives. Even in the pioneer community on the American frontier we believed that "all men are created equal," but still insisted, "let the best man win!"

Today we expect outstanding performance of scientists, managers, and government officials at the same time that we put restraints on them in the interest of equality. Standards of employment continue to move upward and there is greater intensity of competition both at home and abroad. We often take pride in some of our more exclusive residential developments but we are making efforts to include a wider distribution of income levels in our neighborhoods than formerly. We need the incentives that come from some exclusiveness, but cannot afford to allow this to emphasize inequality to a marked degree. This is particularly true if exclusiveness can lead to a stratified society. Gardner says:

> No democracy can function effectively until it has gone a long way toward dissolving systems of hereditary stratification. This is presumably true of any democracy, but overwhelmingly true of the urbanized, industrial democracy with which we are familiar. On the other hand, no democracy can give itself over to extreme emphasis on individual performance and still remain a democracy—or to extreme equalitarianism and still retain its vitality.[3]

At the present time tendencies toward increased equality may be noted in the real estate field as efforts are being made to provide broader access to markets and to eliminate discrimination between color, religion or income with respect to housing. This creates some uncertainties for real estate investors but should lead to a more democratic society.

## REAL PROPERTY TAXATION

Of all the ways in which government programs and political trends affect real estate decisions none is more important than taxation. It has aptly been said that the power to tax is the power to destroy. Real property cannot be concealed. Hence, it seldom can escape from taxation.

[3] John W. Gardner, *Excellence* (New York: Harper & Row, Publishers, 1961), pp. 28–29.

In addition taxes tend to be capitalized. As a result, any change in the tax burden of a real property has a direct effect on its value. An increase in the taxes on a residence of $100 would at a 10 per cent rate mean a loss of value of $1,000 unless benefits resulting from the tax increase in proportion to it.

## Trends in Taxation

Historically, we relied heavily on the property tax as a source of revenue for state and local governments. It continues as a prime support of local government programs and services; however, the property tax has been supplemented by other types, notably income and sales taxes. It may be that we are reaching the limits of taxes on real property for several reasons. First, the tax burdens themselves are already high; second, a substantial majority of homes are now owned by their occupants, a situation that contrasts with that of two or three decades ago; and third, other sources of revenue are proving to be productive.

It is doubtful, however, that property tax reductions are likely to occur. In part this is due to the tax capitalization process which would mean that owners at the time of the reduction would reap a major windfall. In addition, it would be politically unpopular in some quarters to reduce such taxes. (As property ownership becomes more widespread, this situation may change.) About all owners and prospective owners of real property may hope for in the near term is the approximate freezing of tax burdens at or near present levels.

## Uniformity in Taxation

Problems related to uniformity in taxation point up some of· the difficulties faced by real estate decision makers. The real estate tax burden is considered to be equitably apportioned between real property owners if all property is valued uniformly at the ·same proportion of value. If a property which sold for $15,000 is assessed for $6,000, and another that sold for $10,000 is assessed for $4,000, both owners pay their fair share of the tax burden, because each property is assessed at 40 per cent of its value and the owner of the $15,000 house pays 50 per cent more than the owner of the $10,000 house. It would be unfair, however, if both houses were assessed at $4,000, because the owner of the more expensive house would be paying less than his fair share in taxes.

The tax levy is determined by making a budget of all expected local government expenses. All of the real and personal property is then valued for tax purposes. If the total budget of local government costs for the ensuing year is estimated at $4,500,000, and it is estimated that only 90 per cent will be collected, the amount of the levy will be $5,000,-

000. If the total assessed value of all the real and personal property in the local government jurisdiction is $200,000,000, then the tax rate will be $2.50 per $100 of assessed value. A house and lot assessed for $10,000 would then pay $250 in taxes. This assessment of $200,000,000 may be less than half of the actual market value of the property in the jurisdiction based on recent sales. However, if all the assessed values in the jurisdiction are doubled or raised from $200,000,000 to $400,000,000, the actual taxes paid by any specific property would not be affected if the increase were uniform. The budget of $5,000,000 should remain the same. The tax rate to raise this amount from a $400,000,000 tax roll would be only $1.25, or half the former tax rate. The taxes on a house on which the assessment was raised from $10,000 to $20,000 at a tax rate now reduced to $1.25 per $100 of assessed value would be $250, the same as before.

## Low vs. High Assessments

Whether assessments are relatively high or low does not automatically affect their uniformity or their equity in distributing the tax burden. However, it is believed that an extremely low level of assessment encourages lack of uniformity. An owner whose property is worth $10,000 and is assessed for $6,000, has a just cause for complaint if the average level of assessment is only 20 per cent of value; but if he complains, he is often asked whether he would sell his property for the assessed value and his complaint is dismissed. An extremely low assessment also limits the bonding power of the municipality. Sometimes, as in New York, there is a constitutional limit on the tax rate. This tends to cause high assessments which are above market value in depressions.

## State and Local Uniformity Problems

Where the state levies taxes on local real estate, it is to the self-interest of counties and cities to assess their properties at low valuations so that they will pay a lower share of state taxes. To overcome this, the state tax commission of some states may make its own appraisal and may order the local assessments raised by a factor that is supposed to equalize assessments throughout the state. Uniformity of assessment between all type of property in cities is difficult to achieve because of political considerations. Single-family homes, since they contain the most voters, are usually undervalued in comparison with apartments and commercial or industrial properties.

There are frequently many different local taxing districts which overlap. There are school districts, sewer districts, local city governments, park districts, mosquito abatement districts, and others. Each district may impose taxes upon real and personal property to cover its costs. The tax on any specific property is a composite of local city taxes, county taxes, school district taxes, park district taxes, and others. All the taxes may be collected by one government authority and distributed to the others; or sometimes taxes must be paid separately to different authorities, such as the city and the board of education.

The need for reassessment of all the real estate in a given jurisdiction does not arise from the fact that real estate values change, but that they do not change uniformly. Some districts decline in desirability but they may still retain old levels of assessed values. Other new districts may have increased rapidly in value and are underassessed.

### Relative Tax Burden

As we have pointed out, differences in tax burdens and in relative tax burdens often have a major impact on real estate decisions. There is a great difference in local tax burdens, not only between cities in different regions of the country, but even between local communities in the same metropolitan area. Such differences may be accentuated in the future since they are due to the following factors.

1. The number of surplus-producing properties such as stores, factories, vacant land, and high-priced homes compared with the number of low-valued single-family homes which typically do not pay enough in real estate taxes to cover their share of local government costs. One community in a metropolitan area may have the regional shopping center and most of the high-priced homes. Its taxes will be relatively low compared with surrounding communities.

2. The quality and quantity of local government services. In some suburban communities taxes are low because no sewer or water systems are provided and there is inadequate police and fire protection. Highways are provided by the state without local government cost. Taxes are high in some central cities not only because of the cost of sewers, water mains, and street, but also because of heavy payments for social services.

3. The amount of tax-exempt property. A large amount of tax-exempt property throws heavier burdens on other property.

4. Homestead exemption. In Florida, homestead exemption gives extremely low taxes to low-value homes.

5. The amount of subsidies, or grants-in-aid, or allocations of state revenues received from state income taxes, liquor license taxes, or gasoline taxes, or federal government aid for education, highways, or other purposes.

6. The amount of taxes collected locally from sources other than real estate, such as license fees, fines, local sales taxes, and so forth.

7. The amount of surplus received from local government-owned utilities, such as water and in some cases electricity. When a city-owned utility incurs a deficit, such as the New York City subway, it adds to the taxes paid by real estate.
8. Differences in wage and salary scales paid teachers, policemen, and other municipal employees.
9. The efficiency of local governments. The number of municipal employees required to perform equal services varies in different cities.
10. The amount of the local government debt and the interest and principal payments.
11. The compactness of the city. Compact cities require less cost for sewers, water mains, highways, and police and fire protection than diffuse cities in which vacant blocks intervene between settled areas.
12. The amount of taxes levied and collected on such personal property as furniture, livestock, automobiles, stocks, bonds, bank deposits, and so on.
13. The number of overlapping jurisdictions.

## APPROACHES TO URBAN AND HOUSING PROBLEMS

We have undertaken a wide variety of programs to try to cope with the growing complexity of our urban and housing problems. (See Study Project 6–1, "A Brief History of Federal Housing Programs," at the end of this chapter.) The Chicago World's Fair of 1893 gave an early impetus to city planning and related programs. The reinstitution of the L'Enfant plan for Washington in 1900 added widespread interest in this area. Concern about the slum problems of New York had brought a tenement house law as early as 1867 with a substantial revision in 1901. The first comprehensive zoning law, covering both land use and the height and bulk of buildings, was enacted in New York in 1916. In the same year traffic studies brought electrically operated traffic lights to Detroit. The federal government constructed some housing during World War I.

It took the depression of the early 1930's, however, to bring a major federal approach to many of our urban and housing problems. Efforts were made to encourage housing and to improve slum conditions which in turn were expected to expand employment opportunities. These efforts included a system of federal mortgage insurance through the Federal Housing Administration, the improvement of housing finance through the establishment of the Federal Home Loan Bank System, early programs in public housing and slum clearance and related efforts. Following World War II came the establishment of broad programs of urban renewal. More recent years have seen the expansion of these earlier programs plus the addition of new ones especially after the establishment of the Department of Housing and Urban Development in 1965.

## Housing Finance

On the federal level, government probably has influenced real estate and housing decisions through programs of finance to a greater extent than in any other way. The general governmental functions related to the regulation of currency, credit, and financial institutions have an impact on the real estate sector through the work of the Department of the Treasury, Comptroller of the Currency, the Federal Reserve, the Federal Deposit Insurance Corporation and related agencies. Because of the heavy impact of federal economic stabilization policies on housing, monetary and credit policies have had a special significance for the real estate field.

A number of specialized agencies operate more directly in the area of real estate finance including the Federal Home Loan Bank System and the Federal Savings and Loan Insurance Corporation, the Department of Housing and Urban Development, usually referred to as HUD, which includes the Federal Housing Administration, Government National Mortgage Association and other agencies. The mortgage guarantee programs of the Veterans' Administration have played an important role in real estate finance. Also of importance are the programs of the Federal National Mortgage Association, a semiprivate agency which helps to provide a secondary mortgage market. We will have more to say about these agencies in our more detailed discussions of real estate finance. We should note, however, that future governmental and political trends are likely to be influenced greatly by programs in the financial field.

Currently the programs of greatest importance in this area include mortgage insurance and guarantees, secondary mortgage market operations, diect federal lending in some situations, the financing of cooperative programs in cooperation with local governments especially in public housing, the insurance of savings accounts, and the regulation of financial institutions that have a strong interest in real estate and housing.

The priorities enjoyed by these programs, of course, change from time to time. For example, federal mortgage insurance and guarantees appear to be somewhat less important than a decade ago with the emergence of systems of private mortgage insurance. Concern about inflation has brought attention to the problems of providing some type of protection against interest rate and purchasing power risk. Such risks were hardly recognized a decade ago. Today they are of greater concern than the more traditional areas of borrower, property, legal and administrative risks usually associated with mortgage lending.

## Urban Renewal

Of special importance have been a variety of urban renewal programs, including efforts in the areas of land acquisition, replanning, demolition or rehabilitation and resale.[4] Bringing structures that are substandard or in a deteriorating condition up to acceptable standards and efforts at conservation and upgrading are parts of the renewal process. Modernization and repair efforts are sometimes included. In some cases complete rebuilding of areas has been undertaken either in cooperation with private developers or with provision of housing and other structures by direct federal or local government investment. For example, a number of major firms have undertaken the redevelopment of land after it has been assembled and cleared by governmental or quasigovernmental authorities. These include Mellon and Alcoa, various Rockefeller interests, Chrysler, and others. Various universities, hospitals, and other institutions have taken increasing interest in urban renewal efforts.

## New Towns and Model Cities

Recent developments of "new towns" on a private basis such as Columbia and Reston have brought provision for federal assistance in this area. In addition the socalled "model cities" program and other related activities have been undertaken to provide for large scale efforts to improve urban living conditions.

## Public Housing

Federal, state and local efforts of a variety of types have been undertaken to provide housing directly by government investment and management. Many early projects were entirely the responsibility of the federal government. More recently federal and local government cooperation has been the rule in the public housing area. In some cases public housing projects have helped to rehabilitate deteriorating areas and have enjoyed considerable success; in others such projects have turned into "urban jugles" and appear to have generated worse problems than existed before efforts at improvement were made. Recent efforts to allow occupants of public housing projects to become owners of their dwelling units appear to hold considerable promise.[5]

---

[4] See the President's Task Force on Urban Renewal, *Urban Renewal: One Tool Among Many* (Washington, D.C.: U.S. Government Printing Office, 1970), p. 2.

[5] See report of the President's Task Force on Low Income Housing, *Toward Better Housing for Low Income Families* (Washington, D.C.: U.S. Government Printing Office, 1970).

### Interest and Rent Supplements

The early 1960's saw the beginnings of below market interest rate subsidies. These programs were expanded to include both interest and rent supplements later. Of special importance were Sections 235 and 236 of the Housing Act of 1968. These programs were expanded in the early 1970's. In general provision is made for subsidies of rents which exceed 25 per cent of a tenant's income; in the home ownership programs subsidies are provided above 20 per cent of a buyer's income.

### Multiple Approaches

The early 1970's saw expansion of efforts in urban renewal, public housing, housing finance, model cities and other areas. "Operation Breakthrough" undertook to stimulate innovation in housing, especially in housing technology. Increasing efforts were made in neighborhood development and in the provision of community facilities that would improve urban life, as well as in the field of local transportation.

### Zoning Regulations

On the local level of government, zoning and building regulations have a continuing influence on real estate decision makers.

The zoning of land uses appears to be expanding. Now a commonplace practice in most municipalities, zoning has been expanding in use throughout the country. Increasingly zoning is carried out on a countywide basis and to entire metropolitan areas in some cases. Successful zoning laws and planning regulations typically conform to the general pattern of city growth and do not run contrary to such patterns. Some flexibility, of course, is usually needed since none can be entirely sure of long-range land use needs.

We should recognize that zoning sets limits on competition and in effect establishes certain noncompeting areas as between types of land use. This is done because of the recognition that some land uses are incompatible and that orderly development cannot be relied upon to result from open market competition. Typically residential districts are designated and divisions may be made as between single-family and multifamily dwelling house areas; commercial areas are marked out as are industrial areas. One type of land use is not permitted to invade another.

Virtual monopolies may be granted and substantial gains may be had by getting certain land rezoned. In some cases zoning is used to serve the purposes of a special group. For example, "snob zoning," which typically requires three to five acres per residence, may protect existing exclusive communities and prevent development of new areas by builders for the general market. Builders sometimes seek out communities with lenient zoning laws.

In *The Urban Condition* the current thinking about zoning and planning is summarized in this statement:

What our present legal system represents, however, is something else again: a recognition of public and indeed of national responsibility to undertake not merely improved zoning but an affirmative initiative in planning and in building, at least with regard to the physical and economic future of the cities, and perhaps their social and political future as well. That far-reaching step correlatively accepts the proposition that effective action to shape and structure our cities is beyond the power and capacity of private business acting alone, although the plan for urban planning that we are forging utilizes the energies and initiatives of private business at many points. The essence of the matter, however, is an entirely new concept: that the growth of cities should be controlled by public agencies, in this instance by a combination of national and municipal agencies, bringing the national authority directly into the precincts and neighborhoods of urban communities. The idea is not one of uniformity or centralization. In accordance with standards centrally established, and procedures which require a large measure of community initiative and participation, cities are stimulated to organize themselves and to confront and solve a series of economic, social, and aesthetic problems which most of them have been neglecting for a generation, while our urban centers fell apart. This is a process which has galvanized and released a flow of thought and action within cities, to the benefit of the city as a physical and economic entity, and as a more integrated community as well.[6]

### Building Regulations

Building codes which usually regulate quality and strength of materials, allowable stresses, and make provision for various sanitary and health considerations, have been subjected to a considerable amount of study and criticism in recent years. Often they add unduly to construction costs. They usually fail to establish performance standards but rather impose a variety of detailed regulations and bureaucratic practices. They may be used to protect local workmen and business firms and often they delay the introduction of new construction materials and methods. Changes may be slow in coming, however, since numerous local special interests typically are involved.

### SUMMARY

Real estate is among the most highly regulated of all commodities; hence governmental and political trends are important factors in real estate decisions. Information must be evaluated carefully with due re-

---

[6] Eugene and Edna Rostow, "Law, City Planning, and Social Action," in Dahl, Leonard J. (ed.), *The Urban Condition* (New York: Basic Books, Inc., 1963), pp. 363–64.

gard to the special interests and attitudes that may be present and with respect to both short and long run considerations.

Areas for analysis that typically have special interest for the real estate decision maker include the changing role of private property, the extent of public ownership, the changes and modifications occurring in competition, the availability and use of direct and indirect subsidies, government contracts, economic stability, inflation and deflation, war and peace, conservation and renewal, environmental priorities, quality of life, and the priorities given to factors favoring equality on the one hand or excellence of performance on the other.

Taxation is especially important in real estate decisions. Factors related to uniformity in taxation often are of major concern. Special problems are involved in securing uniformity in state and local taxation. The tax burden carried by a property will vary with numerous conditions and factors.

We have undertaken a variety of approaches to our urban and housing problems. Of special importance in these areas are programs of housing finance, urban renewal, new towns and model cities, public housing, interest and rent supplements, and zoning and building regulations. Multiple approaches are followed increasingly and the rate of change requires that constant attention be given to new developments in these areas.

## QUESTIONS FOR STUDY

1. Make a list of regulations designed to maintain competition in real estate markets. Do the same for regulations that have the effect of reducing or supplanting competition in real estate markets.
2. Give examples of both coercive and inducive regulations.
3. Describe the probable impact on real estate of inflation and deflation in the future.
4. How would the elimination of depressions affect real estate decisions?
5. What effect will concern for the environment have on the use of real estate resources?
6. Explain the effect of civil rights legislation on real estate. Does such legislation impose a hindrance on free market activities?
7. Explain how owners of real property would be affected by a reduction of taxes on real property.
8. Explain the procedure by which real property taxes are determined.
9. If taxes on real property are uniform, what objections might property owners have to low assessments? What disadvantage or advantage would exist for the taxing body?
10. Do you believe the federal government should make special effort in aiding home financing?
11. What programs have been undertaken by governmental and private groups to renew or improve the urban environment?

12. What is the purpose of zoning regulations?

13. Explain the purpose of building codes. Do such codes tend either to restrict or intensify competition?

## SUGGESTED READINGS

THOMPSON, WILBUR R. *A Preface to Urban Economics.* Baltimore: The Johns Hopkins Press, 1965. Chaps. vii, x.

WEIMER, ARTHUR M. *Introduction to Business: A Management Approach* (4th ed.). Homewood, Ill.: Richard D. Irwin., 1970. Chap. 5.

## STUDY PROJECT 6–1

### A Brief History of Federal Housing Programs *

**Initial Efforts.**    Congress directed its attention to housing problems as early as the 1890's when it held the first hearings on slums and blight.

The Federal Government became active in the housing field during World War I, the Federal Government built close to 30,000 units, about half of them as dormitories. Most were completed after the armistice and all were eventually sold.

**Home Finance.**    In the early thirties, Congress and the Executive Branch found themselves faced with two overwhelming problems: (1) the collapse of mortgage credit and the system of home finance which had been in use; and (2) the need to generate jobs. The Home Loan Bank System was created in 1932, and was authorized to extend loans to its member savings and loan institutions through regional Federal Home Loan Banks. In effect, the savings and loan associations were required to invest primarily in real estate mortgages and, consequently, became major factors in residential finance.

After the inauguration of President Franklin Roosevelt and the bank holiday which followed, a system of deposit insurance was set up to guarantee deposits in commercial and savings banks. A separate insurance system was eventually created for savings and loan associations. Public confidence in the banking system was greatly enhanced.

Another effective measure to support the mortgage market was the establishment in 1933 of the Home Owners Loan Corporation (HOLC) which had the power to buy mortgages threatened with foreclosure. The Corporation was able to rescue families for whom loss of home was imminent and also to provide an opportunity for mortgage lenders to convert "frozen" assets to cash, thereby shoring up the banking system and protecting depositors from the loss of their savings. Although established amid dire predictions of its financial future, the Home Owners Loan Corporation at its peak held over 15 per cent of the mortgage debt of the entire country and proved extremely effective

---

* An excerpt from The Kaiser Report, of The President's Committee on Urban Housing, *A Decent Home* (Washington, D.C.: U.S. Government Printing Office, 1968).

in its role.  By the time of its end some years after World War II, it had fully repaid the Treasury and its books showed a small profit.

**Mortgage Insurance.**  A second major effort, this time in the area of mortgage instruments, was also highly successful.  This was the National Housing Act of 1934, which established a system of mortgage insurance to be administered by the newly created Federal Housing Administration (FHA).  The motivation was primarily that of creating jobs by improving the flow of mortgage credit, but FHA eventually brought about major changes in the practices used in financing housing.

The FHA mortgage insurance programs begun in 1934 were designed to reduce the risks of mortgage lenders in order to induce them to make credit available on more liberal terms.  In return for a premium paid by the borrower, FHA insures the lender against the risk that the borrower will default.  (The lender does absorb some of the foreclosure costs.)  In case of default, FHA pays the lender the amount due on the mortgage from a fund in which the premiums are deposited.  Because of this protection, lenders were willing to lengthen the term of the mortgage and to make it "fully amortized," so that no large lump sum had to be paid at the end of the term.  In addition, lenders were willing to increase their loan-to-value ratios so that homes could be purchased with smaller down payments.  FHA mortgage insurance with its long-term loans, high loan-to-value ratios, and level of payment amortization has become a major tool for meeting the credit needs of the subsidized housing market.

Another development which also helped primarily the middle class market was the creation of secondary market facilities in which government insured mortgages could be bought and sold.  As will be noted in our description of major events of the fifties, the Federal National Mortgage Association (FNMA, commonly known as Fannie May), originally incorporated in 1938, is chartered to perform this function.

**Public Housing.**  The effort to create jobs took other forms besides the new mortgage insurance technique.  In 1933 the Public Works Administration had offered loans to nonprofit and limited dividend housing corporations for the construction of inexpensive apartments.  So little interest developed that a program of direct Federal construction of low-rent housing projects, primarily in slum areas, was initiated in 1934.  Some 60 projects were built, but the program ran into local opposition and eventually into legal obstacles.  A change in technique became politically imperative, and the Public Housing program was born with the passage of the United States Housing Act of 1937.

The salient feature of the Public Housing program is that the development, ownership, and management of projects are the responsibilities of local government bodies.  Rents in Public Housing projects are lowered significantly by a combination of Federal and local subsidies.  Thus, 1937 was a major watershed in Federal housing policy: in that year the first significant subsidy program to lower rents was established.  (Other countries acted earlier; housing subsidy programs had been established in England and Sweden by 1919.) Admission to, and continued occupancy of, Public Housing was restricted to families of relatively low income. The families of fully employed blue-collar and semi-skilled workers were intended to be eligible. The Housing Assistance Administration, which presently is responsible for handling Federal relations with local housing authorities, is the successor to the Public Housing Administration, which itself succeeded the original United States Housing Authority.

**The War and After.** World War II also brought with it the creation of the National Housing Agency. For the first time many of the numerous activities of the Federal Government having a direct concern with housing were pulled together under one roof. A second major development of the war years was the creation in 1944 of the veterans' mortgage guarantee program administered by the Veterans' Administration (VA).

This was part of the package of veterans' benefits known as the G.I. Bill of Rights. The G.I. Loan, as it became known, is in effect an extension of the FHA system. Instead of insuring mortgages, however, the Veterans' Administration guarantees the top portion of a mortgage loan without fee, enabling qualifying veterans to borrow 100 per cent of the cost of the house.

Housing production leaped from 140,000 units in 1944 to one million in 1946 to close to two million in 1950. The growing pace of post-war housing activity brought pressure on interest rates and Congressional efforts to maintain these rates at a low level. At the same time Congress liberalized the basic FHA mortgage terms by authorizing a longer mortgage life and higher loan-to-value ratios. Mortgage loans based on estimated replacement costs were allowed under the 608 Multifamily program; and because of the severe housing shortage, builders were encouraged by FHA to take advantage of the profit potential under this program.

In response to the need for greater Federal support if relatively low interest rates were to be maintained, Congress restructured the Federal National Mortgage Association in 1948 and expressly prohibited creation of the other Federally-chartered, privately funded National Mortgage Associations that had been authorized through the 1930's. FNMA was authorized to make commitments to purchase in advance and by such commitments began to support the low interest rates of VA loans.

The landmark Housing Act of 1949 authorized a Public Housing program of 135,000 units annually for six years established a separate slum clearance and urban redevelopment program, which has since evolved into Urban Renewal. It was to be the responsibility of this program to clear slums and blighted areas and (later in its growth) to provide sites for private enterprise to build new moderate-cost housing as well as for such residential, commercial, industrial, and public facilities as were most appropriate for the sites.

The best known provision of the Act of 1949 was its statement of a National Housing Policy. The most frequently quoted extract of this policy statement is that which establishes the goal of "a decent home and a suitable living environment for every American family." Other portions of this declaration of National Policy are equally important but less well known. They include the statement that "private enterprise shall be encouraged to serve as large a part of the total market as it can," and that "Governmental assistance shall be utilized where feasible to enable private enterprise to serve more of the total need."

**The 1950's.** Although Congress had authorized large appropriations for Public Housing in the Housing Act of 1949, the program was curtailed in the early 1950's. The cutback was a result of Korean conflict budget stringencies. . . . In 1950 FNMA became part of the Housing and Home Finance Agency (successor to the National Housing Agency in 1947).

The major housing legislation of the fifties was the Housing Act of 1954. It represented the first opportunity since the early 1930's for a Republican administration to have a major impact on national housing policy. Because the Act of 1954 made few major changes in the program which had been established in the two preceding decades, it was looked upon as a confirmation of the bipartisan nature of housing policy. The Act grew out of a report by the President's Advisory Committee on Government Housing Policy and Programs established by President Eisenhower in 1953. In addition to the Charter Act which created the framework of FNMA as it operated until 1968, the bill added conservation and rehabilitation programs to broaden the 1949 slum clearance and urban redevelopment program into a more comprehensive tool.

The Housing Act of 1954 also initiated the requirement that a local government develop a "workable program" for community improvement before it could be eligible for assistance under the Public Housing, Urban Renewal and later, the 221 (d) (3) programs. To be certified as having a workable program, a locality was required to develop a master plan, to adopt or to update various codes governing building, zoning, and fire standards, and to muster relocation and financial resources. Although they were not required to be in effect at once, a community had to show significant progress toward enacting the necessary local legislation and carrying it out. During the post-war years, Public Housing slowly lost many of its working class residents and came to house large concentrations of poor families, many with serious social problems.

FNMA's responsibilities were divided in 1954 into three functions, all separately funded. These were its secondary market operations, its special assistance functions, and its management and liquidation operations. The secondary market function involves the trading of FHA and VA supported mortgages originated by private institutions. "Special assistance" involves the purchase of mortgages which cannot be marketed to private lenders because of noncompetitive interest or because of lack of market experience with the program or instrument. This function became important in later subsidy programs like 221 (d) (3). The special assistance purchases are entirely funded by Government borrowing, whereas the secondary market operations use federal borrowing to support private borrowing, and for that reason can be used as an instrument of monetary policy.

The 1954 Act modified Urban Renewal to enable production of housing at reduced cost. The more liberal multi-family and single-family terms offered under the new Section 220 FHA mortgage insurance program for Urban Renewal areas were designed, in combination with provision for a land cost writedown, to attract the private sector into building middle-income housing in Urban Renewal areas.  FNMA special assistance was made available for these insured loans.

**Evolution of Subsidies in Privately Owned Buildings.**  The Housing Act of 1959 contained the first break in the pattern that restricted development and operation of subsidized projects to public owners.  The Section 202 program begun in that year authorized direct loans from the Federal Government, originally at a rate based on interest rates on outstanding Federal debt (amended in 1965 to be no higher than 3 per cent per year), to nonprofit sponsors of rental projects for the elderly and handicapped.  The major significance of the 202 program is that, by its adoption, Congress authorized direct loans at less than market rates to *nonprofit private corporations,* although only nonprofit ones.  In addition, this was the first statutory expression of the need for subsidy if the cost of shelter for those marginally above Public Housing levels was to be met.

The 221 (d) (3) Below Market Iinterest Rate (BMIR) program, established by the Housing Act of 1961, expanded opportunities for private development of subsidized housing.  The program authorized FNMA to purchase mortgage loans made to limited dividend and cooperative, as well as nonprofit, entities at low interest rates based on the average interest paid on the outstanding Federal debt.  For the first time in the history of American housing, *profit-motivated private organizations* could develop subsidized housing.  The subsidy was rather modest and indirect, being in effect a tender of the Federal borrowing power through FNMA's special assistance functions.

More important steps toward the use of subsidies in privately owned buildings were taken in the Housing Act of 1965.  By the spring of 1965, the average interest on the Federal debt had risen above 4 per cent.  The 1965 Act acknowledged the decreasing utility of the borrowing power technique used in the 221 (d) (3) and 202 programs and pegged the below market interest rate at no higher than 3 per cent.  Both programs now enjoyed direct subsidies since FNMA and ultimately the Treasury would have to make up the difference between the Federal borrowing rate and 3 per cent.

The 1965 Act also created two new subsidy techniques, one of which, Rent Supplements, became the subject of heated political controversy.  The Rent Supplement program, unlike 202 and 221 (d) (3), attempted to adjust housing subsidies to the needs of individual families, rather than simply to provide financial support of total project costs.  Tenants were required to pay at least 25 per cent of their income toward rent, and the Federal Government would make up the difference between that payment and the rental value of the units they occupied.  As with the earlier private programs, rent levels were to be controlled to prevent private owners from making undue profits.  The second new technique introduced in 1965 was the Section 23 leasing program which enabled local public housing authorities to subsidize rents in existing rental units.

The year 1965 also saw the creation of the Cabinet-level Department of Housing and Urban Development to succeed the Housing and Home Finance Agency.

Other Federal efforts in the 1960's attacked the non-physical aspects of slum problems. The Model Cities program, which attempts to coordinate Government policies, both physical and social within a defined neighborhood, was established in 1966. The various manpower programs, poverty programs, and changes in welfare policy had their own effects on housing conditions.

The Housing Act of 1968 culminated the strong movement toward use of housing subsidies in private dwellings. Its most important new feature was the Homeownership program in Section 235. This program provided modest subsidies to enable lower-income families to purchase new and, in some cases, existing homes. The Act also initiated a new rental program, Section 236, for families above the Public Housing income levels. This program is intended ultimately to replace both the 202 and 221 (d) (3) programs since it provides a larger interest subsidy equal to the excess over an interest rate of 1 per cent instead of 3 per cent and since it has the advantage of correlating the amount of subsidy with the tenant's need. Both of these new programs rely almost exclusively on private developers—profit-motivated, nonprofit, and cooperative. Both programs also rely totally on private mortgage financing supported by subsidies payable directly to the mortgage lender in contrast to the Government's purchase of the mortgage in addition to the interest subsidy.

The Act of 1968 contained many other important innovations. It made FHA mortgage insurance more easily available in declining urban areas and for families with imperfect (but defensible) credit histories. FNMA's secondary market operations were transferred to a new privately owned corporation, and a new Government National Mortgage Association was established within HUD to handle the special assistance management and liquidating functions. The National Housing Partnership proposal, which was developed by this Committee, was enacted. Urban Renewal was given a new slant by the introduction of the "neighborhood development program" which provides greater program flexibility and encourages and rewards steady annual performance.

Most important of all, the Act of 1968 authorized large appropriations for the new homeownership and rental programs, as well as Rent Supplements and Public Housing, thereby making possible the President's goal of the construction and rehabilitation of six million housing units over a 10-year period for low- and moderate-income families. An annual report to establish targets and report progress was also required. In addition, the Act extended and expanded the funding of the Model Cities, Urban Renewal, Code Enforcement, and Community Facilities programs to permit a comprehensive attack on central city programs.

The Housing and Urban Development Act of 1970 created the Council on Urban Growth (similar to the Council on Environmental Quality) to develop a national urban growth policy, and the Community Development Corporation (within HUD) to administer a new and expanded program of financial assistance for the development of new communities. The CDC is empowered to guarantee the obligations of developers for land acquisition and development— 100 per cent for public developers and up to 80 per cent for land and 90 per cent for improvements for private developers. Four types of new communities can be assisted:

1. Economically balanced new communities within metropolitan areas, which would serve as alternatives to urban sprawl.
2. Additions to existing smaller towns and cities which can be economically converted into growth centers to prevent decline and accommodate increased population.
3. Major new-town-in-town developments to help renew central cities, including the development of areas adjacent to existing cities, in order to increase their tax base.
4. Free standing new communities where there is a clear showing of economic feasibility, and which would be built primarily to accommodate expected population growth.

### Questions

1. Which of the various areas covered by federal housing legislation do you believe has been most important?
2. Which aspect of federal housing legislation is likely to be most important for the decade of the 1970's?
3. If you could prepare housing legislation which would guide developments during the remainder of the 1970's, which types of legislation would you emphasize?

## STUDY PROJECT 6–2

### Zoning Regulations (see Summary on pp. 174 and 175)

### Questions

1. What changes, if any, would you make in the Los Angeles Code for use in your own city? Be sure to explain your reasons carefully.
2. Note that in certain commercial and industrial zones that the Code permits residential uses. Do you feel that zoning codes should permit less intensive uses within a described use or should restrict the use to that specific type of use specified? Explain your answer.
3. How well can man plan the growth of an urban area?
4. As an alternative to planning and zoning, some sources prefer to let the market operate freely in the determination of land uses. Do you believe this?

# Summary of Zoning Regulations—Study Project 6-2.

| Category | Zone | Use | Height Stories | Height Feet | Front | Side | Rear | Area Per Lot | Area Per Dwelling Unit | Minimum Lot Width | Parking Space | Eagle Prismacolor Pencil Chart |
|---|---|---|---|---|---|---|---|---|---|---|---|---|
| Residential | RE | Residential Estate One-Family Dwellings Parks—Playgrounds Community Centers Truck Gardening—Horses | 2 / 3 If Shown in Height District | 28' / 45' | 25 Ft. | 3' Min. 5'-2 Stories 6'-3 Stories | 25' Max. | 11,000 Sq. Feet | 11,000 Sq. Feet | 70 Ft. | 1 Garage Per Dwelling Unit | 950 Gold |
| Residential | RS | Suburban One-Family Dwellings Parks—Playgrounds | 2 / 3 If Shown in Height District | 28' / 45' | 25 Ft. | 3' Min. 5'-2 Stories 6'-3 Stories | 25' Max. | 7,500 Sq. Feet | 7,500 Sq. Feet | 60 Ft. | 1 Garage Per Dwelling Unit | 911 Olive Green |
| Residential | R1 | One Family Dwelling RS Uses—Incidental Commercial Farming on 20,000 Square Foot Lots | 2 / 3 If Shown in Height District | 28' / 45' | 20 Ft. | 3' Min. 5'-2 Stories 6'-3 Stories | 25' Max. | 5,000 Sq. Feet | 5,000 Sq. Feet | 50 Ft. | 1 Garage Per Dwelling Unit | 916 Canary Yellow |
| Residential | R2 | Two Family Dwelling R1 Uses Two-Family Dwellings | 2 / 3 If Shown in Height District | 28' / 45' | 20 Ft. | 3' Min. 5'-2 Stories 6'-3 Stories | 25' Max. | 5,000 Sq. Feet | 2,500 Sq. Feet | 50 Ft. | 1 Garage Per Dwelling Unit | 917 Yellow Orange |
| Residential | R3 | Multiple Dwelling R2 Uses—Boarding Houses Multiple Dwellings | 3 | 45' | 15 Ft. | 3' Min. 5'-2 Stories 6'-3 Stories | 25 Ft. 15 Feet if No Accessory Bldg. in Yard | 5,000 Sq. Feet | 800 to 1,200 Sq. Feet | 50 Ft. | Varies from 1 for 1 to 1¼ for 1 | 918 Orange |
| Residential | R4 | Multiple Dwelling R3 Uses—Churches Schools—Hotels | 6 / Unlimited* if in Height District | 75' | 15 Ft. | 3' Min. 5'-2 Stories Increase 1 Ft. Thereafter 16' Max. | 25 Ft. 15' to 20' if No Accessory Bldg. in Yard | 5,000 Sq. Feet | 400 to 800 Sq. Feet | 50 Ft. | Varies from 1 for 1 to 1¼ for 1 | 943 Burnt Ochre |
| Residential | R5 | Multiple Dwelling R4 Uses—Clubs—Lodges Hospitals—Sanitariums | 13 / Unlimited* if in Height District | 150' | 15 Ft. | 3' Min. 5'-2 Stories Increase 1 Ft. Thereafter 16' Max. | 25 Ft. 15' to 20' if No Accessory Bldg. in Yard | 5,000 Sq. Feet | 200 to 400 Sq. Feet | 50 Ft. | Varies from 1 for 1 to 1¼ for 1 | 946 Dark Brown |
| Agricultural | RA | Suburban R1 Uses—Limited Agricultural Uses—Libraries—Museums Churches—Houses | 2 / 3 If Shown in Height District | 28' / 45' | 25 Ft. | 3' Min. 5'-2 Stories 6'-3 Stories | 25 Ft. | 20,000 Sq. Feet | 20,000 Sq. Feet | 70 Ft. | 1 Garage Per Dwelling Unit | 910 True Green |
| Agricultural | A2 | Agricultural RA Uses—Extensive Agricultural Uses on Five Acre Farms—Hospitals or Sanitariums | 2 / 3 If Shown in Height District | 28' / 45' | 25 Ft. | 3' Min. 25' Max. | 25 Ft. | 2 Acres | 1 Acre | Minimum Average Lot Width 150 Ft. | 1 Space Per Dwelling Unit | 912 Apple Green |
| Agricultural | A1 | Agricultural A2 Uses—All Agricultural Pursuits—Dairies on Twenty Acre Farms | 2 / 3 If Shown in Height District | 28' / 45' | 25 Ft. | 3' Min. 25' Max. | 25 Ft. | 5 Acres | 2½ Acres | Minimum Average Lot Width 300 Ft. | 1 Space Per Dwelling Unit | 909 Grass Green |
| Parking | P | Automobile Parking Property in a P Zone May Also Be in an A or R Zone. Parking Permitted in Lieu of Residential or Agricultural Uses. | | | | | | Area Per Lot and Unit | Loading Space | —None— Unless Also in an A or R-Zone | — | 967 Cold Grey Light |
| Parking | PB | Parking Building | 2 | | 0'-5' to 10' Depending | 5 Ft. | 5 Ft. if 2 Story | | | | | 936 |

| District | Uses | Height (Stories / Feet) | Front Yard (Interior) | Front Yard (Corner) / Upper-Story Setback | Side Yard | Rear Yard | Loading | Residence Setback | Parking | Color |
|---|---|---|---|---|---|---|---|---|---|---|
| **CR** | Limited Commercial<br>Most R5 Uses—Office Building<br>Banks—Business Schools<br>No Merchandise Display or Sale | 6<br>75' | 10 Ft. Interior Lot Except on Major Highway | 5' to 10' Corner Lot only Residential Uses As in R4 Zone | 25 Ft.<br>15' to 20' if no Accessory Bldg. in Yard | Same as R5 for Dwellings. Otherwise None | ➤ Where Lot Abuts Alley | 50 Ft. for Residence Use | 1 Space for Each 500 Square Feet of Floor Area | 939 Flesh |
| **C1** | Limited Commercial<br>R3 Uses—Local Retail Stores,<br>Offices or Businesses | 3 —— 45'<br>Unlimited* if in Height District | Only if Part of Block in Dwelling Zone | None Unless Lot Adjoins Dwelling Zone | 25 Ft.<br>15 Feet if No Accessory Bldg. in Yard | Same as R3 for Dwellings. None | Minimum Loading Space 400 Square Feet. | 50 Ft. for Residence Use | 1 Space For Each 500 Square Feet of Floor Area in Buildings Containing 5,000 or More Square Feet. | 929 Pink |
| **C2** | Commercial<br>C1 and R5 Uses—Retail Business<br>with Limited Manufacturing | 6 —— 75'<br>Unlimited* if in Height District | None | None for Comm'l. Bldgs. Residential Uses—Same As in R4 Zone | None for Comm'l. Bldgs. Residential Uses—Same As in R4 Zone | Same as R4 for Dwellings. Otherwise None | Additional Space Required For Buildings Containing More Than 50,000 Square Feet of Floor Area | 50 Ft. for Residence Use | Must Be Located Within 750 Feet of Building. | 922 Scarlet Red |
| **C3** | Commercial<br>Same As C2 | 13 —— 150' | None | Above Sixth Story for Comm'l. Bldgs. Residential Uses—Same As in R4 Zone | None for Comm'l. Bldgs. Residential Uses—Same As in R4 Zone | Same as R5 for Dwellings. Otherwise None | | 50 Ft. for Residence Use | | 923 Scarlet Lake |
| **C4** | Commercial<br>C 2 Uses (with Exceptions) | 13 —— 150'<br>Unlimited* if in Height District | None | None for Comm'l. Bldgs. Residential Uses—Same As in R4 Zone | None for Comm'l. Bldgs. Residential Uses—Same As in R4 Zone | Same as R5 for Dwellings. Otherwise None | | 50 Ft. for Residence Use | | 924 Crimson Red |
| **C5** | Commercial<br>C 2 Uses—Limited Floor Area<br>For Light Manufacturing | 13 —— 150'<br>Unlimited* if in Height District | None | None for Comm'l. Bldgs. Residential Uses—Same As in R4 Zone | None for Comm'l. Bldgs. Residential Uses—Same As in R4 Zone | Same as R5 for Dwellings. Otherwise None | | 50 Ft. for Residence Use | | 925 Crimson Lake |
| **CM** | Comm'l. Manufacturing<br>C 2 Uses—Wholesale Business<br>Storage Buildings<br>Limited Manufacturing | 3 —— 45'<br>Unlimited* if in Height District | None | None for Industrial or Comm'l. Bldgs. Residential Uses As in R4 Zone | None for Industrial or Comm'l. Bldgs. Residential Uses As in R4 Zone | Same as R5 for Dwellings. Otherwise None | ➤ Where Lot Abuts Alley | 50 Ft. for Residence Use | 1 Space For Each 500 Square Feet of Floor Area in Buildings Containing 5,000 or More Square Feet. | 905 Aqua-Marine |
| **M1** | Limited Industrial<br>CM Uses—Limited Industrial<br>and Manufacturing Uses | 3 —— 45'<br>Unlimited* if in Height District | None | None for Industrial or Comm'l. Bldgs. Residential Uses As in R4 Zone | None for Industrial or Comm'l. Bldgs. Residential Uses As in R4 Zone | Same as R4 for Dwellings. Otherwise None | Minimum Loading Space 400 Square Feet | 50 Ft. for Residence Use | Must Be Located Within 750 Feet of Building. | 904 Light Blue |
| **M2** | Light Industrial<br>M1 Uses—(Except No "R" Uses)<br>Additional Industrial Uses<br>Storage Yards of All Kinds | 13 —— 150'<br>Unlimited* if in Height District | None | Above Eighth Story None if in Height District | None | Note. R Zone Uses Prohibited | Additional Space Required For Buildings Containing More Than 50,000 Square Feet of Floor Area | None | | 902 Ultra-Marine |
| **M3** | Heavy Industrial<br>M2 Uses<br>Any Industrial Use—Nuisance Type<br>500 feet From Any Other Zone | 13 —— 150'<br>Unlimited* if in Height District | None | Above Eighth Story None if in Height District | None | Note. R Zone Use Prohibited | | None | | 931 Purple |

Commercial: CR, C1, C2, C3, C4, C5
Industrial: CM, M1, M2, M3

**Height District***

| No. 1 | Floor Area of Main Buildings May Not Exceed Three (3) Times the Buildable Area of the Lot. |
|---|---|
| No. 2 | Floor Area of Main Buildings May Not Exceed Six (6) Times the Buildable Area of the Lot. |
| No. 3 | Floor Area of Main Buildings May Not Exceed Ten (10) Times the Buildable Area of the Lot. |
| No. 4 | Floor Area of Main Buildings May Not Exceed Thirteen (13) Times the Buildable Area of the Lot. |

Note: All Information General · For Specific Details Check With Department of Building and Safety

City Planning Commission

[O] Oil Drilling

Supplemental Use Districts
(Established in Conjunction With Zones)

[S] Animal Slaughtering

[G] Rock and Gravel

Building Height Unlimited in the R4-R5-C1-C2 C4-C5-CM-M1-M2 and M3 Zones.

# 7

# Business Conditions

## BUSINESS CONDITIONS AND REAL ESTATE DECISIONS

The general level of business activity has an important bearing on the income-producing capacity and potential of real properties and hence on real estate decisions. The real estate sector of the economy is greatly influenced by the economy as a whole and, in turn, influences general economic conditions in varying degrees.

### Regions and Industries

Not only are general conditions likely to influence real estate decisions, but conditions in specific industries, in regions, and in particular cities and local areas also have their impact. Conditions in specific industries or regions may be more favorable than conditions in the economy as a whole. Although local economic conditions tend to parallel general economic trends, special local situations may bring substantial deviations from such trends.

For a particular industry or line of business, it is necessary to anticipate changes in competitive conditions, market preferences, government regulations, taxes, and many other related factors. Regional economic trends often are hard to forecast due to possible changes in competitive conditions and in regional economic opportunities. It is even difficult to anticipate economic trends for a particular locality. A sudden shift in government policies or the decisions of a major corporation to withdraw its programs or investments may cause marked changes in the local economic outlook.

## Widespread Decisions

Estimates of the future trends of economic activity for the economy as a whole, for an industry, for a region, or for a particular locality are far from easy to make. For the economy as a whole, estimates of future economic conditions involve predicting the decisions that will be made by some 70 million households, over 4 million farmers, and nearly 5 million business firms, as well as thousands of government officials on federal, state, or local levels. In some cases, it is necessary to anticipate the decisions of government officials in other countries, as well as the decisions of consumers, farmers, and businessmen abroad.

## Localization of Income

The real estate decision maker will have as much concern with general economic trends, regional changes, and the prospects of various industries as those interested in other major fields of business activity. In addition, he will emphasize the localization of income, as we have pointed out at various places in earlier discussions. The value of a particular piece of real estate may be influenced by anticipations as to general economic or industry trends but it will be influenced especially by anticipated changes in the stream of income flowing into a local economy. Even within a local economy the effect of local economic trends on various parcels of real estate may differ markedly.

In this chapter we consider various problems related to the analysis of general business conditions and industry trends. In the following chapter we discuss regional and local economic trends and their significance for the real estate decision maker.

## Long-Term and Short-Term Outlook

Real estate decision makers are concerned both with potential changes in the short run and in the longer term. Because of the long life of real properties, long-term trends may be somewhat more important in the real estate field than in others.

Thus, we pay special attention to projections of the longer-term future, including potential trends of development for the American economy as a whole and for some of its principal sectors to the year 2000.[1] Similarly, we are particularly interested in the long sweep of historical development. Often trends of development that have persisted for a long time

---

[1] See, for example, Hans H. Landsberg, Leonard L. Fischman, and Joseph L. Fisher, *Resources in America's Future* (Baltimore: The Johns Hopkins Press, 1963); and Raymond W. Goldsmith and Robert E. Lipsey, *Studies in the National Balance Sheet of the U. S.*, Vol. I (Princeton, N.J.: Princeton University Press, 1963).

may give keys to future potentialities. For example, a study sponsored by the Committee for Economic Development identifies principal factors in past economic growth and points to their probable future effects. It emphasizes the education of the work force and the advancement of knowledge as major factors in economic growth along with a larger work force, increased use of capital, more efficient operations, and economies of scale. The report states:

Whatever period we examine, it is clear that economic growth, occurring within the general institutional setting of a democratic, free-enterprise society, has stemmed and will stem mainly from an increased labor force, more education, more capital, the advance of knowledge, with economies of scale exercising an important, but essentially passive, re-inforcing influence.[2]

### Current Levels of Business Activity

An understanding of the current status of business activity and its relation to previous trends is essential in studying business conditions. The decision maker usually follows business activity regularly through trade journals, financial newspapers such as the *Wall Street Journal,* and general business magazines such as *Business Week.* However, he may wish to undertake a more detailed analysis. There are several general measures of business conditions, reported in current government publications, which will prove helpful.

One of the more important indicators of business activity is the level of industrial production. The Federal Reserve System makes monthly estimates of industrial production and publishes an index in the *Federal Reserve Bulletin.* This index is separated into various types of industrial activity which can be compared to each other or to the total.

Other general measures of business conditions which will prove helpful are the volume of employment and the level of personal income. Such information is published regularly in the *Survey of Current Business,* published by the Department of Commerce, the *Federal Reserve Bulletin,* and *Economic Indicators,* which we referred to in Chapter 1. Detailed data on population estimates are available in the Bureau of the Census' *Current Population Reports.*

What about business income? These same sources will provide information about corporate profits, proprietors' incomes, unincorporated business and professional income, and farm income. Information is also readily available in regard to business sales and inventories; manufacturers' sales, inventories, and orders; the number of firms in business; new firms started; and number of business failures—all of which are help-

---

[2] Edward F. Denison, *The Sources of Economic Growth in the United States and the Alternatives Before Us* (New York: Committee for Economic Development, 1962), p. 273.

ful figures when related to past levels. The *Survey of Current Business,* in addition, publishes data on retail trade, advertising, securities and security markets, and industrial activities and product lines.

## TYPES OF BUSINESS FLUCTUATIONS

In considering the relationship of current business activity to that of preceding periods, three major types of changes in business activity may be distinguished: secular trends, seasonal fluctuations, and cycles.

### Secular Trend

A secular trend results from basic underlying forces, such as population growth or technological change, which exert a more or less steady influence on general business activity or on an industry over the long run. For example, in the United States during the last six or seven decades, the total output of all goods and services (called *gross national product,* or GNP), measured in constant dollars, has increased *on the average,* by about 3 per cent a year.

Note that we said "on the average." Substantial fluctuations may, and usually do, take place around the trend line. These are the cyclical and seasonal fluctuations. It is sometimes difficult to distinguish between a fluctuation which is cyclical in character and one which represents a basic trend change.

There are various methods of identifying the trend line of a business series. Regardless of the mathematical technique employed, however, they all require the exercise of judgment. Unless we make proper allowance for the secular trend factor, erroneous conclusions may be drawn regarding business conditions and business prospects. For very short-term comparisons, however, trend can often be ignored.

### Seasonal Fluctuations

With regard to seasonal fluctuations, little need be said. These are variations caused by factors associated with the calendar year cycle: the weather, the varying lengths of months, holidays, conventional vacation periods, and so forth. Almost any measure of business activity exhibits some seasonal fluctuation. More houses are usually built in the spring and summer than in the fall and winter, and the reasons for this are obvious (at least in the northern part of the United States).

Again, there are recognized statistical techniques for identifying normal seasonal variation, and the business analyst should know what to expect in the way of seasonal variation in studying any phase of business activity. Otherwise, he may be unduly disturbed (or encouraged) by what is, in fact, only a normal seasonal fluctuation. The business analyst should be on the lookout, however, for any changes in seasonal patterns. In recent years, for example, vacation periods and plant close-downs in July have become increasingly common. Any seasonal adjustment derived from past data is likely to undercorrect for this factor.

## Cycles

Assuming that proper allowance has been made for trend and seasonal variation, the main concern of the business analyst is with cyclical fluctuations.[3] We all know that the record of American business is one of ups and downs. At times, nearly all business firms have been prosperous and nearly all employable persons have been working. At other times, nearly everyone has found business poor, jobs scarce, and unemployment high. These swings in general business activity—through prosperity, recession, recovery, and prosperity again—are business cycles.

Before we go any further, we should dispose of the notion that there is anything rhythmical about business cycles. They have varied in timing from about two to about twelve years. They vary even more in magnitude, all the way from the boom of 1929, followed by the deep depression of the early 1930's and the partial recovery of 1937, to the milder cyclical swings of 1948–49, 1953–54, 1957–58, 1960–61, and 1969–71. Unfortunately for the forecaster, each business cycle seems to be unique, and its length and amplitude are determined by a combination of forces never duplicated before and probably never to be duplicated in the future. In the past thirty years the amplitude of both business and real estate cycles has been less than previously largely because of the economic stabilizers.

## ESTIMATING FUTURE SPENDING PATTERNS

It is not safe to project a trend into the future by purely mechanical means. It is necessary to analyze the fundamental forces at work and to draw some conclusions as to whether these forces will continue to operate in the future.

In an exchange economy, the level of business activity depends to a great extent on the volume of spending. The principal spending divisions are consumers, business firms, and governments. Besides infor-

---

[3] Although a more detailed description might differentiate between major and minor cycles or between cycles and random fluctuations, we are using the term "cycle" in this general treatment of the subject to refer to the fluctuation remaining after removal of trend and seasonal factors.

mation on past and current levels of spending, some guides to the future intentions of each of these three major spending divisions are available.

## Consumer Spending

Since consumer spending currently makes up over 60 per cent of the total expenditures in our economy, this area requires special consideration when estimating future levels of business activity. The Federal Reserve has sponsored various studies of consumer buying intentions and the general financial condition of consumers. The Bureau of the Census, the Survey Research Center at the University of Michigan, and various industry groups also carry on studies of this type. These surveys are, of course, subject to the usual errors of sampling and to the risk that consumers may change their minds after the surveys have been completed.

Of special interest to us are reports on plans for home buying, current levels of home ownership, home mortgage debt, owner equities, and re-

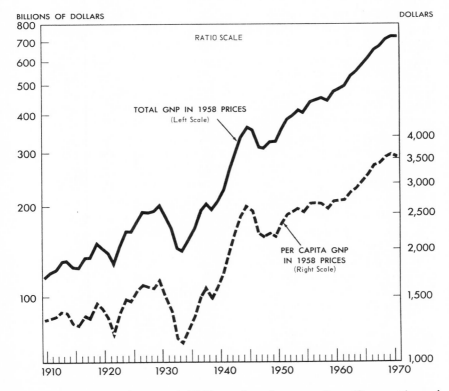

**Fig. 7–1.** Growth in real GNP, total and per capita. (Source: Annual Report, Council of Economic Advisers, 1971.)

lated information. Such information may be related to current levels of consumer income, volume of employment, and the terms and availability of financing for such items as consumers purchase.

In recent years, total consumer spending has reflected fairly consistent growth, although there have been some shifts among various types of expenditures. Even during periods of recession when unemployment rose and industrial production dropped, consumer spending held up well.

## Business Spending

Another major area for consideration is the volume of spending by business. Business spending for wages and salaries is of major importance with respect to the level of consumer incomes. Investment by business firms in plant and equipment is especially vital to anyone seeking to forecast future business conditions. Expansion of plant and equipment usually takes place when profit prospects are favorable and declines when they are not. Special programs such as tax inducements may also affect the volume of business spending.

The Department of Commerce and the Securities and Exchange Commission make a joint estimate of business plans for expenditures of this type, which is published in the financial newspapers and in the *Survey of Current Business.* McGraw-Hill Publishing Company also makes surveys of business plans for plant and equipment expenditures and reports them in *Business Week.* As in the estimates of consumer spending, of course, these estimates may be affected by any changes in plans.

In short-run analysis of business conditions, the level of inventories and inventory plans are of special importance. Low levels of inventory during periods of rapid expansion indicate the possibility of further advances in the volume of business activity. On the other hand, during a period of level or declining activity, a substantial rise in inventory levels may create instability because of pressure to reduce these levels. Information about inventories is reported regularly by the *Survey of Current Business* and also by the financial press.

It should be noted that improved methods of inventory control have enabled business managers to operate on relatively small inventories in recent years. Even so, inventories are an important factor in the short-run business outlook.

## Government Spending

The third major area of spending is that of federal, state, and local governments. Information about the expenditure plans of state and local governments is not readily available, although past levels of expenditure are reported in the *Federal Reserve Bulletin* and the *Survey of Current Business.*

The earliest indication of future federal government expenditures is the President's Budget Message, submitted to Congress early in each regular session of Congress. The business conditions analyst must subsequently follow the appropriation and tax actions of Congress to determine whether they coincide with the original request.

After Congress has acted, estimates of the timing and amount of receipts and expenditures of the federal government are reported in the financial news and in *Economic Indicators.* Funds are allocated by appropriations, but it is important to note expenditure plans, because the effect of federal government spending on business conditions depends largely on actual spending. A considerable period of time may elapse between appropriations and actual spending.

### Foreign Spending and Receipts

In addition to spending by consumers, business, and governments, spending in foreign countries, balanced against receipts, may at times be significant. Although in the United States these items do not claim the attention that they do in such countries as Holland and England, they are a factor of growing importance in estimating business trends.

## GROSS NATIONAL PRODUCT METHOD

In order to make more detailed and complete analyses of business conditions, the gross national product (GNP) method has been developed. In this procedure, the major income and expenditure (product) accounts in the nation are analyzed. The total is the sum of expenditures by the major groups outlined above. You will see summaries of the accounts regularly in the *Survey of Current Business* and in *Economic Indicators,* as well as in the Economic Report of the President and the *Annual Report* of the Council of Economic Advisers. They are useful for short- and longer-term projections and often help to estimate trends in various industries or sectors of the economy.

### GNP Definition

Gross national product is the total value of all goods and services produced in the economy in any given period, usually a year. The method used by the Department of Commerce in calculating the official GNP figures avoids double counting by counting only the total value of final products and ignoring primary and semifinished products (except to the extent these add to business inventories). Calculated in this way, GNP indicates amounts actually paid in the market and there-

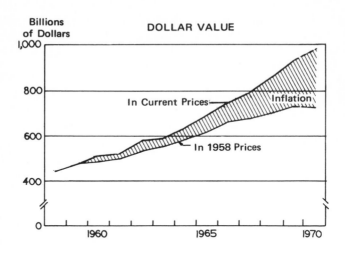

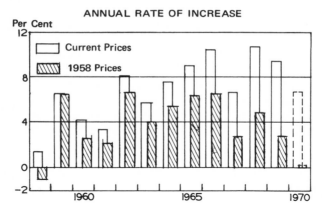

**Fig. 7–2.**  Gross national product, 1958–1970.

fore reflects price fluctuations as well as changes in physical output. (Allowances for changes in the value of the dollar are provided by the use of price deflators.) Prices not otherwise available are estimated for goods and services wherever possible and are included in the GNP calculation. This includes assigning price values to government services, the output of self-employed persons, food produced on the farm for home consumption, and the imputed rental value of owner-occupied dwellings. The items included in Table 7–1 are discussed briefly here.

**TABLE 7-1.  National Income or Expenditure, 1960 and 1970
(billions of dollars)**

|                                            | 1970  | 1960  |
|--------------------------------------------|-------|-------|
| Gross national product                     | 974.1 | 503.7 |
| Personal consumption expenditures          | 615.8 | 325.2 |
| Gross private domestic investment          | 135.3 | 74.8  |
| Net export of goods and services           | 3.6   | 4.0   |
| Government purchases of goods and services | 219.4 | 99.6  |

SOURCE: *Economic Report* of the President, and *Annual Report* of the Council of Economic Advisers, 1972.

## Personal Consumption Expenditures

Personal consumption expenditures include food, clothing, haircuts, books, football games, and so forth.  The term personal consumption expenditures excludes expenditures for capital goods—that is, things used in future production.  This causes some problems.  For example, an automobile bought for personal use is classified as a personal consumption expenditure, but it is considered a capital expenditure if bought by a company for business use.  Houses are classified as capital goods, partly because so many of them are owned, as business ventures, by someone other than the occupant, and partly because of their long life, yielding property services over many years.

## Gross Private Domestic Investment

Gross private domestic investment includes, principally, expenditures by business for new capital goods—machines, factories, stores, locomotives, and the like.  It also includes, as a plus or minus factor, net changes in business inventories.  Moreover, it includes expenditures for new housing.  An expenditure for an existing house simply reflects a shift of ownership.  Nothing is added to total output.

## Net Export of Goods and Services

Net export of goods and services includes principally the excess of domestic output sold abroad over purchases by the United States of foreign output; it also includes certain other international balance of payment items.

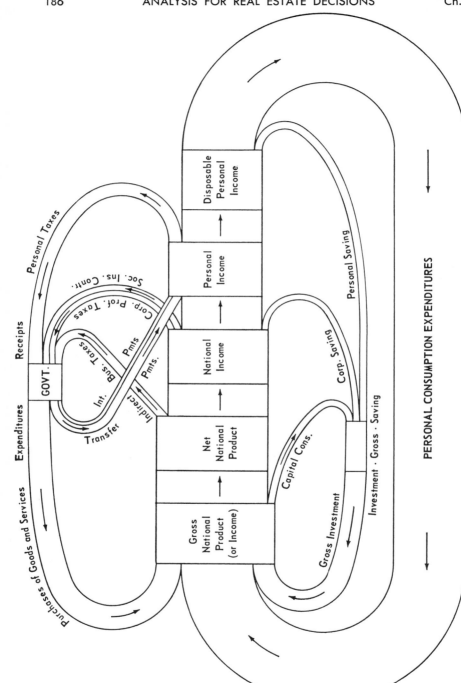

**Fig. 7–3.** The flow of money income and expenditures: the circular flow in a given time period. (Adapted from

### Government Purchases of Goods and Services

Government purchases of goods and services include all governmental units: federal, state, and local. Included are compensation of employees (including military personnel) and government purchases of goods and services from business. National defense accounts for a big share of the total. Government investment in atomic energy installations or in other properties or capital equipment is also included.

### Total Output

These general categories of expenditures, by consumers, business, and government, and of net sales abroad, together account for the total output, the gross national product (GNP), measured by what was actually paid for that output.

### National Income

National income represents the aggregate earnings of labor and property from the current production of goods and services in the nation's economy. In addition to national income, however, several other items must be included to account for the total of payments. One of these is indirect business taxes which are not received as income by any of the private factors of production. A second is capital consumption allowances, which consist chiefly of the charges made against current output for depreciation of capital goods. Adjustments are allowed to cover certain minor factors, including the statistical discrepancy between gross national income as calculated from receipts and gross national product as calculated from payments.

### Flow of Income

So far we have been concerned with a static concept; an accounting of the nation's total output in a given, finite time interval. The dynamic concept of the moving, changing flow of income through the economy is shown in Figure 7–3. The chart is intended to illustrate not what happens in any finite time period, but rather the process of change from one time interval to the next.

## FLOW OF FUNDS

Another important method of analyzing the economy and projecting future business conditions is the flow-of-funds approach, showing the relationship between GNP purchases and the nation's debt structure.

This approach was originally developed in the early 1950's and was subsequently adopted and refined by the Federal Reserve System. Quarterly data is reported each month in the *Federal Reserve Bulletin*, with a lag of about four months.

### Sources and Uses of Funds

As compared to the income-statement form taken by the GNP data, flow-of-funds data are in the form of a "sources and uses of funds" statement. Instead of the three basic sectors in GNP data (consumers, business, and government) the flow-of-funds accounts system adds a fourth sector, that of financial institutions. One further sector, "rest of world," corresponds roughly to the "net sales abroad" in GNP statements. The accounts are developed for the entire economy, complete and consistent throughout, to show the interrelationships between these four sectors in their sources and uses of funds.

### Flow of Funds Accounts

Businesses and consumers make their spending decisions in light of the availability of credit, their own liquidity positions, and their plans for saving and investing. Government policy is also affected by anticipations of the future structure of monetary assets and liabilities. Although the assets and liabilities of any one sector need not balance, debt (liabilities) must be accounted for in the system as a whole. The holdings of such debt are recorded in the flow-of-funds accounts. With the financial sector added, considerable information on the activities of financial institutions is also provided.

### Uses of Accounts

There are many potential uses of these flow-of-funds accounts. For example, current quarterly information on the flow of mortgage funds is available through the accounts, showing both lender and borrower by sector. Economists have also used these accounts in an attempt to forecast interest rates and in making short-run projections of future credit demands. Annual estimates are now available back to 1946 and quarterly data from 1952, so that historical perspective may be gained in an effort to understand present and future relationships.

## OTHER METHODS OF ANALYSIS

Efforts are being made constantly to improve the methods available for analyzing and forecasting potential changes in economic activity or to develop new approaches to these problems. In addition to gross national product and flow-of-funds, several other analytical methods are important, including "national wealth statistics," input-output tables, and balance-of-payments accounting.

## National Wealth Statistics

National wealth statistics are set up in a manner that resembles an individual firm's balance sheet but pertains to the economic system as a whole. They provide measurements of the size and composition of the weath of the entire economic system and record changes in them. The comprehensive study by Goldsmith and Lipsey referred to above is an outstanding illustration of this method of analysis.

## Input–Output Tables

Input-output tables trace the movement of goods and services between major industries of the economy. The method is attracting increasing attention. The Office of Business Economics of the U. S. Department of Commerce is increasing the amount of data that are needed for these types of analyses.[4] Balance-of-payments accounting is used chiefly in measuring the volume and composition of a nation's international transactions.

## Regional Studies

Both input-output and balance-of-trade analyses have been applied in studying regional economies. Smaller countries, with somewhat homogeneous characteristics, might be considered regions for analytical purposes. In a country the size of the United States, with varying regional characteristics, comprehensive national income accounting such as GNP has proved more useful. However, in the following chapter we will see how the input-output and balance-of-payments methods, as they develop, can be used in regional analysis. Input-output analyses have been used also in various industry studies.

## INDUSTRY ANALYSIS

Many studies that undertake to make short- or long-run projections of a particular industry start with GNP projections and relate potential industry developments to them. National markets, of course, are often related to personal or business spending plans. In some cases, a given

---

[4] Wassily W. Leontief, "The Structure of the U. S. Economy," *Scientific American* (April, 1965), pp. 25–35; see also "The Interindustry Structure of the U. S.," *Survey of Current Business* (November, 1964).

industry bears a fairly fixed relationship to one or another national measure of economic activity.

In many cases we have accumulated a substantial store of statistical information about an industry. The construction industry is a case in point. Good statistical data are available for new construction, both public and private, and for maintenance and repair activities. Estimates can be made for, say, a year ahead, or for the longer-term future. The study of *Resources in America's Future* projects principal categories of construction to 1980 and to 2000. (See Table 7–2.)

TABLE 7–2. **Medium Projections for Principal Categories of Construction, 1980 and 2000 (billion 1960 dollars)**

| Category | 1950 | 1960 | Medium projection | |
|---|---|---|---|---|
| | | | 1980 | 2000 |
| Total construction | 58.6 | 76.2 | 166.3 | 348.4 |
| New construction | 42.2 | 56.6 | 130.1 | 280.9 |
| Maintenance and repair | 16.4 | 19.6 | 36.2 | 67.5 |
| of which for residential construction | 6.2 | 7.2 | 10.8 | 14.7 |
| Residential new construction incl. additions and alterations | 19.6 | 22.6 | 54.7 | 126.4 |
| Non-residential new construction | 22.7 | 34.1 | 75.4 | 154.5 |
| Private new construction | 32.8 | 40.6 | 90.2 | 196.8 |
| Public new construction | 9.4 | 16.0 | 39.9 | 84.1 |
| Components of public new nonresidential construction: | 9.1 | 15.3 | 37.2 | 77.8 |
| Schools and hospitals | 2.3 | 3.2 | 5.0 | 7.4 |
| Highways | 2.6 | 5.5 | 16.1 | 34.6 |
| Military & industrial | .6 | 1.8 | 5.1 | 12.3 |
| All other (water, sewerage, etc.) | 3.6 | 4.8 | 11.0 | 23.5 |

SOURCE: *Resources in America's Future*, p. 113.

## Use of Sales Data

Industry studies may attempt a forecast of costs, capital requirements, competitive factors, markets, and sales. Usually short-range estimates for a single business firm or an entire industry start with the basic projection of sales, which are related to some more-general measure of economic activity such as gross national product or disposable personal income. Past relationships are studied and the principal factors likely to cause variations are identified and analyzed.

## Durables and Nondurables

The Department of Commerce has worked out relationships between disposable personal income and personal consumption expenditures for a variety of nondurable goods ands services. The demand for nondurables tends to be easier to estimate because of the frequency of purchases and the short life of these products. Contrast this, for example, with housing or with automobiles.

In the case of automobiles, demand may fluctuate widely from year to year. Hence, long-term, year-to-year, and seasonal factors all play a part in such projections. In the case of housing or closely related industries such as furniture, short-term estimates can be based largely on demand factors, since supply is relatively fixed in a period of a year of two. Demand factors are likely to relate fairly closely to incomes and the terms and availability of financing in the short run. Over longer periods, population trends, the estimated rate of household formation, income trends, and the competitive position of housing relative to other goods and services bear careful study and consideration.

## Industry Cycles and Trends

Some individual industries exhibit a cyclical movement which is more or less independent of general business cycles. However, as with general business cycles, the length and amplitude of the cycles are irregular. Some analysts claim to detect, for example, a cycle in real estate activity of roughly fifteen to twenty-five years in duration.

It is not our purpose here to outline even in a very general way the methods that are used in analyzing industry trends. Rather, we hope to indicate the importance of such studies, their relationship to the broader studies and projections of GNP and its components, and their implications in determining the values of specific parcels of real property.[5] The real estate decision maker ultimately has to deal with specific, definite, practical problems related to particular properties and their income-producing potentials. We may be able to gain further insights into some of these relationships in the following chapter.

### SUMMARY

The level of general business activity is an important determinant of income from real property. We are concerned with the localization of income. In many cases local business conditions tend to parallel general

[5] For an illustration of the use of input-output analysis in industry studies, see "Input-Output Relations of the Auto Industry," *Economic Review* (Federal Reserve Bank of Cleveland, March, 1965).

trends; in others local factors are of greater importance in determining the level of business activity. Industry trends and regional patterns of economic change also are important. Because of the impact of business conditions on real estate income, the analysis of such conditions provides a guide to decision making. Such analyses are usually based on data related to employment, income, production, and prices. Such data and related information are published in *Economic Indicators, Survey of Current Business, Federal Reserve* Bulletin, *The Economic Report* of the President and the *Annual Report* of the Council of Economic Advisers, and other government publications, and in the business and financial press.

Changes in business activity may be the reflections of seasonal, cyclical, or secular trend influences. Each of these may be analyzed.

The level of spending is an important determinant of total business activity. Consumer spending makes up the largest single element of total spending, although this in turn is dependent largely on business expenditures for wages and salaries.

The national income accounting system is an organized framework for measuring and analyzing economic activity. The most widely used measure of total activity is gross national product, which measures output in terms of expenditures on final products. Flow of funds, input-output tables, and other methods of analyzing business conditions also are in use. Industry projections often are related to GNP measures although other methods are also followed.

## QUESTIONS FOR STUDY

1. Are real estate decision makers more concerned with local or national business trends? Short- or long-term trends? Explain your answers.
2. How do general business conditions affect the income-producing ability of real properties?
3. List the main indicators of current levels of general business activity.
4. What is meant by "gross national product"? How does gross national income differ from GNP?
5. Distinguish between secular trend, seasonal fluctuations, and cycles in business activity. Explain why each of these might be important to the analysis of real estate markets.
6. Explain the importance of each of the following to the level of general business conditions: (a) spending by consumers, (b) government spending, (c) business spending for plant and equipment; business spending for inventories, (d) spending by foreign countries for U. S. goods.
7. What types of information are included in the flow-of-funds accounts?
8. Discuss the relationship between the construction industry and: (a) General business conditions, (b) local business conditions.
9. How can industry analysis be used to project long-term trends?

## SUGGESTED READINGS

DENISON, EDWARD F. *The Sources of Economic Growth in the United States and the Alternatives Before Us.* New York: Committee on Economic Development, 1962 (Supplementary Paper No. 13). Chaps. xxiii–xxv.

HOYT, HOMER. *The Urban Real Estate Cycle—Performance and Prospects,* Technical Bulletin No. 38. Washington, D.C.: Urban Land Institute, 1960. Reprinted in *According to Hoyt* (2nd ed.). Washington, D.C., 1970; pp. 537–547.

LEWIS, JOHN P., and ROBERT C. TURNER. *Business Conditions Analysis* (rev. ed.). New York: McGraw-Hill Book Co., Inc., 1966. Part IV.

See also current issues of *Economic Indicators, the Federal Reserve Bulletin, The Survey of Current Business,* the President's *Economic Report,* and Federal Reserve Bank publications.

## STUDY PROJECT 7–1

### U.S. Population Forecasts for the 1970's

Forecasts for the 1970's include estimates regarding population changes. Total population at slightly over 200 million in 1970 is expected to reach near the 230 million mark by 1980 and 240 million by 1985. The age distribution of the population is expected to change with a big gain in the young adult group in the 25–34 age bracket. Additions of 11 million in this group are anticipated. In the 18–24 year age group the gain is also substantial, being estimated at 5 million. There will be only a modest gain in the 35–44 age group, estimated at around 2 million. The 45–54 age group will actually decline by 1 million. Age groups above 54 will register substantial gains, perhaps as much as 6 million. The teen-age market will not be expanding as during the 1960's. The 14–17 age bracket, for example, will neither gain nor lose in numbers. The 5–13 bracket will show a decline of about 4 million while those under 5 years of age will register a modest gain of around 3 million.

### Questions

1. What do these anticipated population changes mean in terms of markets?
2. What are they likely to mean for the housing market? For the home furnishings market?
3. What do they mean for the market for executive talent? For the young adult job market?
4. What do these population changes imply in regard to environmental problems?

## STUDY PROJECT 7–2

### Business Expectations for the 1970's

Dean S. Ammer presents some interesting observations in his article "What Businessmen expect from the 1970's" in *Harvard Business Review* January-February 1971.

The article was based on a survey of a substantial segment of the readers of the *Harvard Business Review*. It generally concludes that although businessmen do not share the optimism reflected in a number of economic forecasts for the seventies they are nevertheless generally optimistic for the prospects of their own businesses. In combination, of course, such optimism may make the general forecast come true.

About two-thirds of those surveyed expected their sales to be better than the growth of the total economy and about one-half of them expected sales to be better than their competition. On profit margins, however, optimism was less pronounced. Only about one-third expected to register significant gains and nearly as many saw a slower growth of profit margins.

About one-half of those covered expected to reduce the labor content of their products. Internal expansion is expected to be the most important source of profit growth rather than either from acquisition or expansion abroad.

Those covered by the forecast expect the seventies generally to see more inflation and less real growth than the sixties.

### Questions

1. Do you agree that if businessmen are optimistic about their own operations, even though they may not be so optimistic for the economy as a whole, that this makes the more optimistic general forecasts come true?
2. If there is less optimism for profit margins than for sales, does this suggest a more or less competitive economy during this period?
3. Why are efforts being made to reduce the labor content of products?
4. Do you agree or disagree with the general assessments of the 1970's presented here? Explain.

# 8

# Regional and Local Economic Trends

## REGIONAL AND LOCAL INFLUENCES ON DECISIONS

As we have suggested, the real estate decision maker has a basic interest in the localization of income. Although economic activity in a region or locality may move parallel with general business conditions, there are often significant differences. For example, the Southwest and Southeast have grown substantially faster than the American economy as a whole in recent years.

### The "Little Economies"

Of major importance for most real estate decision makers is the potential direction of economic activity in a particular locality—a metropolitan area or city or local rural community. We sometimes refer to these as the "Little Economies" [1] in contrast to regional or national economies. Real estate decision makers are also interested in the outlook for smaller sections of a local economy—in the market for the type of property under consideration and in the neighborhood or district in which the property is located. Again, we recognize that there may be variations between the growth rates of local areas and various types of markets within them.

---

[1] This term was popularized by the CED (Committee for Economic Development) and used in connection with its publication the "Little Economies," problems of U. S. Area Development, 1958.

## Importance of Local Economic Analysis

Interest in local economic activity results from a variety of decision problems. The multi-plant firm has problems of locating and relocating branches. Chain store organizations are faced with decisions about alternative locations for their stores. Manufacturing companies do not always seek localities with strong growth potential; in some cases, a surplus labor supply or the availability of unused plant and equipment may be attractive. By contrast, retail organizations almost always seek locations with strong growth potential.

Investors have choices between properties located in one part of the country or another, one locality or another, even one country and another. Life insurance companies and other large mortgage lenders, for example, often conduct local economic analyses to determine where they will lend funds. They may rule out some areas, ration funds with respect to others, and concentrate in a few favored locations. The Federal Housing Administration has for a number of years carried on local economic analyses to help guide underwriting activities in various localities.

From a local standpoint, builders and land developers may be concerned with the extent and timing of their projects. Owners of land have problems of holding, selling, or moving their investments to alternate locations.

Local mortgage lenders need bases for developing both short- and longer-term lending policies; and government officials find it advisable to anticipate requirements for utilities, schools, and municipal services. Analyses and forecasts of local economic developments are helpful to these decision makers and to many others, ranging from home buyers to major investors.

## Type of Analysis Required

The type of analysis undertaken will vary with the nature and complexity of the decision problem. In some cases relatively simple analyses may be adequate. In some situations economic base analysis may serve the purposes of the decision maker. In others more elaborate types of economic analysis may be called for. This does not necessarily mean that one type is "better" than another; it may be more desirable in terms of its applicability to the specific decision problem.

## Definition of Region

A region may mean almost anything that an analyst chooses it to mean. For example, a region may be defined as a traditional geographic region such as New England or the Pacific Northwest, an area such as the

"Upper Midwest" or "Appalachia," a metropolitan area, or an area restricted by political boundaries.  We may have a definition of a region in
terms of ecology, natural resources or climate.  In some cases regions may
be defined economically as in the case of a Federal Reserve District or in
terms of its economic development interests or potential.

John R. Meyer has suggested that "all regional classification schemes
are simply variations on the homogeneity criterion and it is somewhat
misleading to suggest otherwise.  The only real question is what kind of
homogeneity is sought."  He suggests that a region may be homogeneous
with respect to jurisdiction of a specific government or administrative
agency, trade or function of the area, physical characteristics such as
geography or natural resource endowment, economic or social characteristics, or boundaries for statistical puposes.[2]

Economic theory has developed a branch which is referred to as "regional analysis," or "regional economics."  Those interested in this branch
of study, however, have not always agreed on the way in which a region
should be defined.  Because the boundaries of a region are so difficult to
specify without a reference point, each definition is meaningful primarily
in terms of the specific purpose involved.  For the purposes of real estate
decision makers, regional analysis tends to be restricted primarily to local
economies.  Since the methods of analysis typically are similar, we do not
try to distinguish here between different sizes of local economies.  We
consider "regional and local analyses" to refer mainly to local economies
and the surrounding areas, to the "Little Economies," depending on the
type of decision problem under consideration.

## APPROACHES TO LOCAL AND REGIONAL ANALYSIS

One may approach the problems of local and regional analysis from a
variety of viewpoints; our main concern here is the real estate decision
maker and consequently we tend to stress his interests which are largely
economic although not exclusively so.

### Resources

We may analyze the local economy in terms of local resources.  The
future of a mining or lumbering town, of course, depends on the supply
of its basic resources, their probable life, their competitive position, and
related conditions.[3]  We may consider the character of the labor re-

---

[2] John R. Meyer, "Regional Economics: A Survey," *American Economic Review*,
LIII, No. 1, Pt. 1 (March, 1963).
[3] Charles M. Tiebout, *The Community Economic Base Study* (New York: Committee for Economic Development, 1962), pp. 18–19.

sources in the local economy; the land resources, for example, the availability of desirable industrial sites; availability of capital and the ability to command it; and the presence of entrepreneurial, professional, technical, and related talent. In some cases such community resources as schools, utilities, governmental resources and services, and the like are also considered. These resources provide the general conditions in which growth may occur or fail to occur. Special problems may require analysis. Water pollution, smog or other environmental problems may inhibit the future development of a facility. Unfavorable tax policies, poor government administration, or unfavorable local attitudes often require consideration.

In addition to studies of major local resources, industry studies may be undertaken, particularly of the more important industries in the local economy. Sometimes inventories of the industrial assets and liabilities of a local economy may be developed and analyzed.

## Markets

We should note that it is possible to study the markets for the major resources of a local economy and thus to gain insights into its economic growth potential.[4] For example, the labor market, the land market, the capital market, or the market for special talents such as entrepreneurship, research ability or leadership may be studied with varying degrees of intensity. Information about such markets may be related to the specific problems under consideration by decision makers. For example, the efforts of various local communities to induce business firms to locate in their areas may be more rational than often is supposed if it is recognized that local community leaders may be interested primarily in the entrepreneurial, leadership, managerial, and research talent that may be gained.

## Economic Relationships

We might try to approach the regional or local economy as a subdivision of the national economy. For example, we might analyze local employment and income trends and make comparisons with national changes. Such indicators of economic activity as bank clearings, car loadings, electric power consumption, building permits and housing starts, and others may be analyzed and compared. If we tried to make use of GNP analysis, however, or other types of analyses useful on a national basis, we would soon encounter difficulties largely because local

---

[4] Wilbur R. Thompson, *A Preface to Urban Economics* (Baltimore: The Johns Hopkins Press, 1965).

and regional economies are "open" and not "closed." That is, there are no reasonably well-defined economic boundaries.

Efforts are sometimes made to use regional accounts which resemble national income accounting; input-output analysis is attempted in some cases and flow-of-funds methods may prove to be useful. Most of these methods, however, are difficult to use because of inadequate data or because of the sweeping assumptions that typically are required.

Despite some theoretical and practical inadequacies, economic base studies have proved to be highly useful for the analysis of local economies. The economic base has been defined as follows:

> The economic base of a community consists of those activities which provide the basic employment and income on which the rest of the local economy depends. An economic base study identifies the basic sources of employment and income and provides an understanding of the source and level of all employment and income in a community.[5]

Later in the chapter we will consider the main elements in economic base studies and outline briefly the major features of input-output analysis. Before considering these topics it may be helpful to review some of the principal characteristics of local economies, primarily urban economies.

## LOCATION OF ECONOMIC ACTIVITIES

The point at which a particular city will arise depends on factors which favor the establishment of activities which may give the city a competitive advantage over others. Usually topography has been the most important factor, although its effects have depended on whether military, political, social, or economic considerations were paramount.

### Priorities

In modern periods a specific city is established at a certain point and expands in importance mainly because opportunities to secure employment and income are available. The sites of many older cities were determined largely by defense factors.

Toynbee says, for example:

Thucydides, in his introduction to his history of the Atheno-Peloponnesian War of 431–404 B.C., has observed that, in the archaic age of Hellenic history, the Greek city-states were pulled in opposite directions by the conflicting requirements of trade and defence. Trade called for a location of the city as close as possible to good food-producing land and to good water transport, which in the Aegean basin, means maritime transport, since in this region

---

[5] Tiebout, *op. cit.*, p. 9.

there are no navigable rivers. On the other hand, defence calls for a location out of the reach of pirates, brigands and invading armies, which in this region, means a location on a mountain island. Manifestly accessibility and security were difficult to combine, even for Greek cities that had become rich enough to be able to afford to provide themselves with artificial defences in the shape of man-made walls.[6]

In a few cases social and religious factors have played a dominant part in determining city location. Sometimes political situations have determined the location of cities. For example, the location of Washington was the result of military and political factors. Most of our cities, however, grew up at points which gave them *economic* advantages. Economic advantages of various locations may result from one of the following factors or combinations of them:

1. Trade routes and transportation breaking points.
2. Access to raw materials.
3. Access to rich markets.
4. Power resources.
5. Climate.

## Transportation

Some cities developed at transportation breaking points—for example, where land and water routes met. In such cases the availability of harbor facilities was the dominant factor. Cities often grew up at points where one type of water transportation met another—or where land trade routes intersected; air routes have tended to follow established locations but jet air travel has changed a number of old patterns. One writer has aptly stated:

> It is when the transfer of goods is accompanied by a breaking of bulk or by a change of ownership, there being then added the complex mechanism of commercial exchange performed by importers, exporters, wholesalers, retailers, insurers, brokers, and bankers, that wealth is accumulated and localized, with consequent power to control business for local benefit.[7]

## Raw Materials

Easy access to raw materials has often determined the location of a city because of the economies resulting from being near the sources of supplies. Generally, raw materials of great bulk which are costly to move have had more influence on the location of cities than other types

---

[6] Arnold Toynbee, *Cities on the Move* (New York and London: Oxford University Press, 1970), p. 29.
[7] Richard M. Hurd, *Principles of City and Land Values* (New York: The Record & Guide, 1924), chap. ii.

of raw products. When such resources are exhausted, the towns which grow up near them decline, unless other economic opportunities develop.

## Market Dominance

Frequently, points which give easy access to rich markets form natural places for economic development. For example, the development of New York City was in part due to the fact that there was an easy route from the West through the Appalachian Mountains to the East. Similarly, Chicago's growth was based on the richness of its market area, the upper Mississippi Valley.

## Power Resources

Power resources have accounted for the rise of cities at certain specific points, the "fall line" in the East having resulted in the establishment of various cities because of the available water power. In more recent times, other types of power, particularly electricity, which can be transmitted for considerable distances, have eliminated the dependence of machinery on natural power. When methods of using atomic energy are further developed, the importance of the location of power resources may be eliminated entirely as a factor in determining city location and development.

## Climate

Climatic conditions also have been of importance in determining city location. Sometimes climate favors certain types of industry, the growth of cotton and woolen manufacture in areas with moist climates being a case in point. Space-age installations have largely gone to southern areas because of climatic factors. Climate usually has a more direct influence in determining the location of resort or amusement centers, such as Miami Beach or Honolulu.

## Combinations

In general, no single factor accounts for the location of a city at a certain point. For example, the *exact* point where a town starts may be largely accidental, since any of a number of points in the vicinity might be equally desirable. New York's original location was due to a combination of advantages. And so was its phenomenal growth. As Raymond Vernon points out:

The disposition among historians is to lay New York's rise to the Erie Canal; to the ice-free conditions of the East River, kept clear by its churning tides;

and to a comparatively unobjectionable sand bar at the mouth of New York's harbor—a sand bar more manageable than at the mouth of the Delaware. There is also a disposition to give credit to something in the fluid social structure of New York's life, an indefinable quality which even then attracted off-beat businessmen in search of their fortunes. At any rate, whether or not New York's social structure was part of the lure, its early growth was almost certainly based on a lead in foreign trade.[8]

The original site of Chicago was a swamp; but the point at which Lake Michigan and the Great Lakes system came closest to joining the Mississippi River and its tributaries was a natural trade center, originally for the fur trade and later for other types of makets. The decisive factor undoutedly was the Illinois-Michigan Canal; otherwise, development might have occurred farther south.

## Types of Cities

Cities may be classified in various ways. For our purposes it is desirable to classify them on the basis of the major employment and income sources represented. Such a classification might take the following form:

1. Industrial cities, including those involved chiefly in the manufacturing and processing of commodities.
2. Cities devoted principally to commerce, which include seaports, lake ports, river cities, and railroad terminals and junctions.
3. Political cities, including all those for which the activities of a state government or the Federal government provide the basic income source.
4. Recreational and health resorts, as well as cities in which retired people reside.
5. Educational, research and cultural centers.

Many cities, of course, include all or nearly all of these major activities, although one or two types may be predominant.

Extractive industries ordinarily do not produce the largest cities. Our largest cities typically are those with superior transportation facilities which place them in the main currents of trade. Manufacturing generally has developed in larger cities to a greater extent than in smaller places, and such expansion has in turn contributed to further growth. It should be noted, however, that some cities have grown very large without becoming great manufacturing centers. Kansas City, Denver, and Washington are cases in point. In recent years many manufacturing plants have been located in the countryside, away from major urban concentrations.

[8] Raymond Vernon, *Metropolis 1985* (Cambridge: Harvard University Press, 1960), p. 8.

## LOCAL GROWTH AND DECLINE

At an early stage in the development of economic thought Adam Smith pointed out:

The country supplies the town with the means of subsistence and the materials of manufacture. . . . We must not, however, upon this account, imagine that the gain of the town is the loss of the country. The gains of both are *mutual and reciprocal* and the division of labor is in this, as in all other cases, adjusted to all the different persons in the various occupations into which it is sub-divided.[9]

Toynbee has made the following observation:

In the long run a city's imports and exports must balance each other in terms of value. The penalty for a chronic deficit would be the eventual cutting off of supplies and a consequent reduction of the city's population—ultimately to zero. In the past, cities that have paid their way have not imported more in value than they have exported, but they have brought in more in bulk than they have thrown out. . . . Consequently, in the course of time, their surface has risen in height.[10]

### Specialization

Division of labor between town and country, region and region, industry and industry, and employment and employment continues to be a vital factor in explaining the character and direction of modern economic activity. Division of labor undoubtedly is the basis for the establishment of a local economy and the extent of its long-term growth. The economic base concept rests primarily on this principle, as we have pointed out.

### Power to Grow

After a local economy attains a certain size, however, it may be able to maintain its growth, if not to augment it, because it has the economic or political power to command further support. A pool of labor, particularly if special skills are represented, a supply of capital or the ability to induce it to come to a locality, a group of community leaders and hard-hitting entrepreneurs and politicians, highly trained professional people, experts and technicians all may help to assure ongoing economic activity and even some growth. Substantial additional growth, however, may depend on specialization and advantages in interregional trade.

[9] Adam Smith, *The Wealth of Nations* (London: George Bell & Sons, 1908), III, p. 383. [Italics added.]
[10] Arnold Toynbee, *op. cit.*, p. 4.

## Urban-Size "Ratchet"

Thompson suggests that an "urban-size ratchet" is at work, that once a locality attains a certain size and economic importance it can continue to grow and expand because of diversification, a "blending of young, mature and decadent industries," the influence of power politics, the large amount of sunk, fixed capital invested, the importance of the local market itself, and the chance that growth processes are stimulated in a city of some size—"a large urban area is more likely to give birth to new industries at critical points in its life cycle than is a small urban area." [11]

Whether the growth process is self-regenerative or the result of special factors, inside or outside the locality, remains an open question and the answer probably varies with the character of the local economy.

In a pattern which will appear many times during this account, growth fed on growth. For a time, New York's unique scheduled sailings, its "ship brokers," and its wholesalers could be matched nowhere else. . . . During the middle decades of the century, though New York's role as the national gateway continued to expand, its own heavy dependence on the sea was already beginning to shrink. The Erie Canal had opened up a new route through which New York could tap the wheatlands and forests of the Middle West. Bits and pieces of rail line were also beginning to be put in place, adding another means by which raw materials could be shipped east and manufactured products could move west to the new territories. [12]

He points out further that activities that had sprung originally from the Port became independent; wholesaling took on the handling of domestic products as well as foreign trade; in finance, maritime insurance shifted to domestic property risks, foreign banking to domestic banking. In subsequent developments one type of growth gave way to another. New York's size probably aided in making these adjustments but explanations of these processes are not easy to nail down.

## Variety of Economic Opportunities

The growth of Chicago from a hamlet of fifty people in the early 1830's to a metropolis of more than six million in a century and a third can be explained by a wide variety of economic opportunities. As one of the authors has pointed out:

The advantage of the site of Chicago as a meeting place first of lake, river, canal, and wagon transportation, and then of lake and rail carriers in turn, made it the principal distributing and manufacturing center for a valley containing the richest combination of agricultural and mineral resources of the

[11] Thompson, *op. cit.*, pp. 9–11.
[12] Vernon, *op. cit.*, p. 9.

world that was being exploited for the first time. . . . The magnitude of the population was but the measure of the strength of the economic advantages of the site of Chicago, and of the economic resources of its hinterland—the Upper Mississippi Valley.[13]

And the growth of the Chicago region has continued, although at not as rapid a rate as for some other cities, notably in the South and West.

### New Growth Sources

Growth comes not only from the expansion of present sources of income and employment but from new sources that may be developed. Thus, the capacity to attract new sources of employment and income deserves special attention. Such capacity typically will represent a combination of conditions ranging from availability of resources and markets to living conditions, quality of government, tax levels in relation to the services provided, quality of local leadership, environmental conditions, competitive factors and others. The competent real estate decision maker pays attention to the entire complex of factors that enables a locality to provide goods and services on terms that will compete with other cities and localities within a local climate and environment that is attractive and congenial.

### Factors Leading to Decline

While Chicago and New York were growing, some cities were declining in economic importance. Outstanding, of course, were certain mining and lumbering towns whose natural resources were exhausted. Some cities declined because others enjoyed an advantage in nearness to raw materials, or markets, availability of labor and capital, climate, political preference, or the drive and dedication of local leaders. Certain smaller cities lost their reasons for existence as improved transportation facilities enabled major cities to serve wider areas. Some cities were helped or hindered by governmental or administrative policies; e.g., differential freight rates and tax policies have had their effect on the growth of specific cities. In some cases the efforts of community leaders have stimulated city growth, while other cities failed of their potential because of inadequacy of local leadership.

As we suggested in the discussion above, an adequate supply of civic and social resources may help to stimulate economic growth. Thus, if a city possesses good local government, school system, hospitals and doc-

---

[13] Reprinted from *One Hundred Years of Land Values in Chicago*, by Homer Hoyt, by permission of the University of Chicago Press, pp. 279–84. Copyright 1933 by the University of Chicago.

tors, shopping facilities, and the like, new industries may be attracted to it. The lack of such facilities and services might repel business firms that are considering alternative locations for their new plants. The existence of difficult problems such as high crime rates, smog, water pollution, inadequate police and fire protection, and others often inhibit growth and development.

### "Don't Come Here to Live"

A recent development in certain urban areas is the changing attitude toward growth. The *HUD Newsletter* of April 5, 1971, reports that the Governor of Oregon is saying to visitors, "Don't come here to live." The report further states that

. . . the usual Chamber of Commerce invitation to people to settle in their community has been reversed in a number of places . . . "come and visit . . . but don't move here." In Florida . . . the President of the State Senate said last month: "Florida no longer desires to be known as the fastest growing State in the Union. We have our hands full taking care of over 6.8 million permanent residents without encouraging more." In Colorado . . . a plan to develop the "East Range" section covering Denver and the area east of the Rockies . . . has been abandoned . . . and industry will be invited to go to less-crowded areas of the State. In Massachusetts . . . the Cape Cod Planning and Economic Development Commission is concerned about the rapid increase in population and business activity. The Commission is attempting to slow up the rezoning of farm land for tourist use. The State's development director has said: "If we continue to insist on more and more roads and more and more motels on Cape Cod . . . we'll end up with wall-to-wall people." [14]

California is also attempting to slow down or halt growth in many of its more concentrated population areas. In Hawaii, the legislature is considering a five-year moratorium on rezoning agricultural land. Such new policies must be considered in the analysis of urban areas.

We turn now to a consideration of economic base analysis as one way of estimating the potential of a local economy.

### THE ECONOMIC BASE

The concept of the economic base was set forth by Werner Sombart in the 1920's and by Robert M. Haig as early as 1928.[15] Sombart pointed out

[14] U. S. Department of Housing and Urban Development, *HUD Newsletter* (April 5, 1971; Washington, D.C.: U. S. Government Printing Office; HUD-253-SP:).

[15] W. Sombart, *Der Moderne Kapitalismus, Dritter Band: Das Wirtschaftsleben im Zeitalter des Hochkapitalismus*, (2d rev. ed., 1927; 3d ptg.; Berlin: Duncker & Humblot, 1955), 413; also R. M. Haig, *Major Economic Factors in Metropolitan Growth and Arrangement*, Vol. I, *Regional Survey of New York and Environs*, Regional Plan Committee, 1928.

the difference between "Städtegründer," which may be translated as *Town Founders* or *Builders,* and "Städtefüller," which may be translated as *Town Fillers.* Frederick Nussbaum subsequently used the terms "Town Fillers" and "Town Builders." Homer Hoyt, co-author of this book, refined the concept of the economic base in a variety of reports and articles from 1936 onward and dealt with some of the essential ideas in the concept of the economic base or economic background in his *One Hundred Years of Land Values in Chicago,* published in 1933.[16] The economic base concept has been criticised, re-evaluated, and refined by a number of students of the subject.[17]

### International Trade Theory

Essentially, the economic base concept rests on international trade theory and on the multiplier effect of "export" activity. The locality or region is viewed in relation to other regions and its potential growth is considered as dependent upon "basic" sources of employment or income, that is, *those that command income from beyond its borders.* For example, manufacturing activity, since its usually leads to "exportable" products, is considered "basic" and the service trades as "nonbasic" or supporting activity. The impact of the former, however, is multiplied through the latter since basic income will support some service activity (ratios vary widely—1 to 1 or 1½ to 1 are not uncommon).

### Town Builders and Fillers

Nussbaum, as indicated above, distinguished between "town building" and "town filling" activities. He said:

The principal constituent elements of the town are those who are able by power or wealth to command a means of subsistence from elsewhere, a king who can tax, a landlord to whom dues are paid, a merchant who makes profits outside the town, a student who is supported by his parents. These are "town builders." After them come what we call the "town fillers," those who serve

[16] Homer Hoyt, *One Hundred Years of Land Values in Chicago* (Chicago: U. of Chicago Press, 1933); "Economic Background of Cities," *Journal of Land and Public Utility Economics* (May, 1941), 188–95; "The Utility of the Economic Base Method in Calculating Urban Growth," *Land Economics,* XXXVII, No. 1 (Feb., 1961).

[17] Ralph W. Pfouts (ed.), *Techniques of Urban Economic Analysis* (West Trenton, N.J.: Chandler-Davis Publishing Co., 1960); Charles M. Tiebout, "The Urban Economic Base Reconsidered," *Land Economics* (February, 1956). See also Tiebout's "The Community Economic Base Study" and Richard B. Andrews' various articles on economic base in *Land Economics* (May, 1953, to May, 1955); and Roger Leigh, "The Use of Location Quotients in Urban Economic Base Studies," *Land Economics* (May, 1970).

the needs of the "town builders": the shoemaker who makes the king's shoes, the jeweler who depends on the purchases of the merchant's wife, the landlady from whom the student rents his room.[18]

## Basic and Service Activities

Nussbaum's statement does not explain completely the variables involved but it does stress the division of labor on which a town or other local economy rests and its relationship to "outside" sources of income. The terms town "builders" and "fillers" are somewhat unfortunate since under some circumstances the "nonbasic" or "service" or "filler" types of ecoonmic activity may help to attract "basic" activities and thus play a leading rather than a supporting role in the local economy or region. In the Nussbaum quotation above, for example, the shoemaker might attract a tannery, the jeweler might be a factor in attracting a silversmith or metal working establishment, and the student might be so favorably impressed by the town that he later will set up a manufacturing plant there. Availability of outstanding service activities often helps to attract basic types of economic activities. Further, those who accumulate capital from either basic or service activity may invest it either locally or elsewhere and, if investing locally, thus further stimulate economic development.

## Division of Labor and the Multiplier Effect

In any event, the essential factors in the economic base concept are (1) division of labor in the international trade sense, plus (2) the multiplier effect of "export" activity.

The concept has been stated this way:

Translating conventional international trade theory into regional terms, the "economic base" of a region is that group of industries primarily engaged in exporting from the region under analysis to other regions. An empirical multiplier is determined by observing the historical relationship between this export activity and total economic activity in the region. This empirical multiplier is then applied to estimates of economic base to forecast total economic activity.[19]

## Outline of an Economic Base Analysis

For illustrative purposes we present here an outline of some of the major steps that may be taken in carrying out an economic base analysis of me-

[18] F. L. Nussbaum, *A History of the Economic Institutions of Modern Europe* (New York: Appleton-Century-Crofts, 1933), p. 36. By permission.
[19] Meyer, *op. cit.*

dium complexity. In summary these steps include: (1) determining the relative importance of major present and potential income sources; (2) analyzing each of the basic sources of income—manufacturing, trade, extractive industry, and other types; and (3) studying modifying influences—the size of the local market, quality of community facilities and services, governmental factors, and the general "climate" for local economic activities.

### Relative Importance of Basic Income Sources

The sources of employment and income in a local economy are many and varied, but for convenience of analysis they may be combined into the following primary groups: (1) manufacturing, (2) extractive industry, (3) wholesale and retail trade, and (4) special sources of income, such as political, educational, institutional, resort, or amusement activities. The stream of income brought into the city by people who receive pensions, rents, royalties, and interest from elsewhere should also be considered a part of the urban growth income. Few cities are supported by any one of these income sources alone; nearly all rely on a combination of various types.

Chicago, Detroit, Dayton, Hartford, Cleveland, Milwaukee, and Baltimore are predominantly industrial cities; while New Orleans, Minneapolis, Kansas City, Omaha, and Portland are predominantly commercial centers. Miami and Atlantic City are chiefly tourist resorts. Washington is supported principally by the activities of the federal government. In St. Louis, Boston, and Philadelphia there is a fairly equal division of employment and income between trade and manufacturing. In Springfield, Illinois, and in Oklahoma City there is an extraordinary diversity of support from manufacturing, extractive industry, trade, and state institutions. Ann Arbor, Michigan, is primarily an educational and research center.

The first step in determining the economic potentialities of a city is to estimate the relative importance of each of the various sources of employment and income. Information concerning total employment, as well as the number employed in each of the main types of economic activity, can be secured from such sources as the Bureau of the Census, state employment services and their local branches, and chambers of commerce. Where more detailed information is desirable, assistance may be secured from the personnel departments of principal firms, and local labor unions. Information concerning payrolls is often available from census reports, local or state taxing authorities, and similar sources.

From one or a combination of these sources, total employment can be obtained and the per cent of the total engaged in each of the major types of economic activity outlined above can be computed. Efforts should also be made to determine whether any new sources of income are likely to develop in the near future, and their relative importance.

## Analysis of Manufacturing

In forecasting the trend of manufacturing activities in a city as a source of future economic growth, each type of industry should be studied in some detail. Attention should be given to such factors as the nature of the products manufactured by each firm, the location of raw materials, principal markets, trends of demand for the products, and the competitive position of each of the major establishments. Such factors as the competence of management, the character of the labor supply, and special local advantages or disadvantages should be considered. In addition, tax burdens, regulatory practices, the attitudes of local community leaders toward each firm, and the trends of local government policies generally merit consideration. Special attention should be given to competitive advantage of the location, diversification of industry, competitive position of the firm, and cyclical fluctuations. From the standpoint of future effects on real estate values, it is important to determine whether the industries located in a city will remain, advance in importance, decline, or move to another location.

Among the factors that tie an industry to a city are large plants, heavy fixed capital investments in new and modern machinery, the availability of a large body of skilled labor, favorable transportation rates, convenient access to raw materials, proximity to markets, favorable attitudes of local community leaders, and taxes that are favorable relative to government services provided.

Unfavorable conditions also require analysis. Environmental, slum or crime problems, for example, may cause an industry to move from an area or repel industries that might otherwise move there.

There is always an element of risk if a city has great concentration of industrial activity along one specific line. If half of the workers in a city are employed in a single establishment, the whole structure of real estate values may collapse if that establishment moves away. If there are many establishments in the same industry, the risks are less; but the city may suffer because of a decrease in the demand for one of the locality's products or the rise of a competing product. In addition, single-industry towns are more likely to fall under the dominance of a relatively few businessmen or labor leaders, with the result that real estate values may suffer from shortsighted managerial policies or from prolonged strikes and industrial disturbances.

## Analyzing Income from Trade

The prospects for future employment and income from trade in any city depend chiefly on the following:

1. The extent to which the city is expanding its trade area at the expense of competing cities or losing out in competition with such cities.
2. The growth or decline of resources and purchasing power in the trading area.
3. The potential growth or decline of population in the trading area.

Diversification of types of trading activities and firms is not so important a consideration as in the case of industry, since we seldom find cities in which one or two stores serve all the needs of a trade area. Similarly, cyclical fluctuations in trading activities are not likely to be so marked as in the case of industry, although such fluctuations may occur.

## Analyzing Other Income Sources

A forecast of employments and incomes which are dependent upon mines, oil wells, or timber resources requires an analysis of the probable future life of the natural resources involved and of the extent to which these resources can be utilized at prevailing or anticipated price and cost levels. Competition of the products of such extractive industries with other products of the same type should be considered, as well as the possibility for the development of substitute products.

Financial institutions such as banks, insurance companies, and savings and loan associations may play a key role in the economic life of a community, either because income is brought into the area or because various types of economic activity are facilitated. The attitudes of financial lenders often have an important influence on local economic development.

## Government and Education

For several decades employment in governmental agencies has tended to expand. Incomes of government workers have advanced. Since the seats of governments, such as state capitals or county seats, are relatively fixed, the possibilities of changes of location of such governmental activities are remote. However, cities with a large number of federal agencies may lose or gain income as the activities of such agencies are expanded or diminished or as changes of location are made. The location and relocation of space and defense industries is an important factor in the future of a number of cities, especially in the South and West.

Educational institutions are usually fixed in location and are not likely to move to other places unless exceptional conditions arise. Normally employment in such institutions is relatively stable; during recent decades, however, there has been a marked expansion of educational activity, and this general trend has been strengthened by higher income levels and population growth. New institutions have been established in a number of places. Such developments may have a significant bearing on the future of an area both in terms of the employment and income that is generated and the increased attractiveness of the area for other activities.

**Resorts and Retirement**

Employment and incomes derived from resort and retirement activities are subject to unusual fluctuations.[20] The development of jet aircraft has changed the competitive pattern of resort areas. Such areas are affected considerably by the trend of general business conditions, since their incomes tend to decline sharply in recession periods. To the extent that a resort enjoys a prestige reputation or is endowed with exceptional natural advantages, of course, it will tend to be affected less by business recessions than will other resort centers.

In a number of towns and cities, retired people represent an important source of income. The extent and stability of such income depend on the sources from which it is drawn. As more and more people qualify for pensions or build up retirement funds, incomes of this type will play an increasingly important part in the economic fortunes of many cities, notably those in favorable climates.

**Local Conditions and Characteristics**

Conclusions tentatively reached in regard to the future growth of a city on the basis of a study of major income sources may be modified by favorable or unfavorable local governmental, environmental, or crime conditions; tax burdens in relation to public services provided; quality of the school system; adequacy of community facilities, such as hospitals and cultural and entertainment programs; quality of business, labor, and political leadership; and relative position with respect to other cities in the region or nation.

Long-run analysis may require that consideration be given to the "multiplier" process. Some of the income earned by a manufacturing firm may be invested locally, some elsewhere; of that invested locally some may stimulate local activity, some may bring about further export activity. The

---

[20] John F. Child, "Impact of the Tourist Industry on Real Estate Values," *The Appraisal Journal* (January 1970).

propensity to invest locally can be estimated by developing assumptions on the basis of local data and experience.

Careful investigations may indicate which persons or organizations exercise the greatest influence and wield the major power in the local community. If it is possible to identify them, some estimate of their conception of the future of the city may be an important factor in predicting its potential growth. As we have suggested also some growth may be locally generated. Tiebout very aptly points out:

Nothing here suggests that it is impossible for a community to grow without an expansion of exports. The world as a whole does not, as yet, export. Nevertheless, incomes have risen substantially. In like manner, an island community can increase its income even if it is isolated from the rest of the world. Increases in productivity and technological change are hallmarks of economic life. An increase in productivity of a locally oriented bakery will increase local income, even though exports do not increase. Nonetheless, this does not invalidate base theory. Base analysis, *qua* base analysis, does not focus on these changes. A base study, after all, cannot examine everything. All this means that changes in productivity, for example, can and should be introduced to modify any forecasts derived from a base study.[21]

## INPUT–OUTPUT ANALYSIS

Input-output analysis has been adapted to the study of local economies; its future promise depends on the much-needed improvement in the accuracy and availability of data.

### Major Producing Sectors

This type of analysis revolves around the establishment of a model, in the form of a matrix, which highlights the sales of the output of each major producing sector to each major consuming sector of the economy, for example, the total dollar output of manufacturing which was consumed by the construction industry, by the power industry, and even by the manufacturing industry itself.[22] This table can be constructed in any desired detail,

[21] Tiebout, "The Community Economic Base Study," p. 75.

[22] Fundamentals of input-output theory were developed by Wassily W. Leontief as early as 1936; see his "Qualitative Input and Output Relations in the Economic System of the U.S.," *Review of Economics and Statistics* (August, 1936). See also his *The Structure of American Economy, 1919–1939* (New York: Oxford University Press, 1951); and *Studies in the Structure of the American Economy* (New York: Oxford University Press, 1953). Robert Dorfman outlined the concept of input-output in his article, "The Nature and Significance of Input-Output," *Review of Economics and Statistics* (May, 1954), as follows: "To set forth the bare bones, conceive of an economy as being divided into some number of sectors, say *n*. Suppose that the level of output of each sector depends on the level of some or all of the other sectors, and on nothing else. Then the formulas relating the output of each sector to the outputs

for example, the manufacturing industry can be broken into heavy and light manufacturing, or an even finer classification such as the chemical industry, the petroleum industry, the steel industry, etc. The degree of refinement depends on (1) the industrial make up of the area in question, (2) the availability of detailed data, and (3) the potential value of added research effort to the problem under analysis.

### Relative Importance of Sectors

From an input-output table, it is possible to determine the relative importance of a particular line of economic activity to the community and its impact in sustaining other lines by its purchases. The earnings and expenditures of governments can be included as sectors of the economy as can the receipts and spending of households. As a matter of fact, these two sectors are usually estimated independently and are used as inputs to the model. To understand how an input-output matrix is developed, we might look at the oversimplified 5 × 5 matrix depicted in Table 8–1.

### Hypothetical Case

Reading across Table 8–1 yields the sales of each industry to every other industry. Thus, the entry in the second column of the second row reflects the sales of the manufacturing industry to itself. The entry in the fifth column of the second row reflects the amount the manufacturing industry sold to households. Total sales of the manufacturing industry are shown in the total gross output column.

The figures gleaned from reading down the column depict the purchases of each industry from every other industry. Thus, the entry in the first column of the second row reflects the purchases of the agricultural sector from the manufacturing sector. Since every sale is at the same time a purchase, it makes little difference on which basis the figures are gathered.

---

of other sectors will form a set of $n$ equations in $n$ variables. If, further, these formulas are linear the equations can be solved by straightforward algebra. The result will be a set of sector outputs which are mutually compatible in the sense that each sector produces the quantity called for by the functional relationships assumed at the outset. What we have just sketched is simply a mathematical formalism; Leontief's task was to develop a set of economic concepts which would lead to this kind of mathematical structure and would invest it with meaning. This is just what input-output achieves. An input-output table or matrix is a set of linear formulas connecting the levels of activity in the various segments of an economy. Input-output analysis is the economic justification and interpretation of these formulas and their consequences."

See also, John H. Cumberland, "Regional Interindustry Model for Analysis of Development Objectives" (Regional Science Assn., 1966), pp. 65–95; Jerald R. Barnard and Harold K. Charlesworth, "The Kentucky Secondary Data Approach and Its Potential," *Growth and Change* (April 1970). See Study Project 8–1.

**TABLE 8–1.  A Hypothetical Input–Output Matrix**

| Producing Sectors | Purchasing Sectors | | | | | Total Gross Output |
|---|---|---|---|---|---|---|
| | Agricul- ture | Manufac- turing | Power | Construc- tion | House- holds | |
| Agriculture | 20 | 20 | 1 | 4 | 12 | 57 |
| Manufacturing | 5 | 30 | 2 | 3 | 45 | 85 |
| Power | 1 | 3 | 2 | 1 | 3 | 10 |
| Construction | 2 | 2 | 4 | 1 | 1 | 10 |
| Households | 32 | 50 | 6 | 11 | 4 | 103 |
| Total inputs | 60 | 105 | 15 | 20 | 6 | 265 |

## Projections

In using this matrix for projective purposes, the household sector is usually considered as being exogenous to the model, that is, independent of the producing sectors, and is estimated first. The problem then resolves itself into estimating the production levels in each sector necessary to satisfy this household demand. This is accomplished by assuming that the production inputs will be combined in the same proportion in the future time period to produce a level of output as they were in the present period. Table 8–2 is a reconstruction of Table 8–1 in terms or these production coefficients which are then assumed constant.

Table 8–2 was derived by dividing each of the elements in a column by the first column total. Thus, by dividing the element in the second row of the first column (5) of Table 8–1 by the column total (60), we get 0.08. This means eight cents out of every dollar produced by the agricultural sector is consumed by the manufacturing industry. Similarly, 53 per cent of agriculture's output goes to satisfy household demands.

With an assumed household demand in some future time period, estimated by some other method and used as an input to the model—that is, spending by households is considered their "production" and hence an input—the problem reduces itself to finding the levels of production necessary to satisfy this demand—recognizing the interactions of the model. Thus, an increase in household demand for food of 20 per cent will occasion something different than a simple increase in agricultural output of $2.40 ($12.00 × 1.20 = $14.40) to $59.40. An increase in agricultural output must be accompanied by increases in manufacturing, power, and construction output. These increases in output of manufacturing, power, and construction must in turn be supported by higher production of their various inputs. These latter increases in production are called the indirect effects as contrasted to the $2.40 increase in agricultural output occasioned by the increased household demand for food which is a direct effect. The procedure resolves itself into one of successive iterations performed on a computer. The process is stopped when the indirect effects are of such magnitude that they have no appreciable effect on the level of the various outputs, that is, they are within acceptable limits.

**TABLE 8–2.  Direct Inputs per Dollar of Output**

| Producing Sectors | Purchasing Sectors | | | | |
|---|---|---|---|---|---|
| | Agricul-ture | Manufac-turing | Power | Construc-tion | House-holds |
| Agriculture | 0.33 | 0.19 | 0.07 | 0.20 | 0.18 |
| Manufacturing | 0.08 | 0.28 | 0.13 | 0.15 | 0.69 |
| Power | 0.02 | 0.03 | 0.13 | 0.05 | 0.05 |
| Construction | 0.04 | 0.02 | 0.27 | 0.05 | 0.02 |
| Households | 0.53 | 0.48 | 0.40 | 0.55 | 0.06 |
| Total | 1.00 | 1.00 | 1.00 | 1.00 | 1.00 |

**Problem of Analysis**

Inadequate data often handicap the input-output analyst. There are also theoretical limitations, for example, the model must be considered one of stationary equilibrium so that time is of no consequence. This is because inputs, in reality, must be produced before they can be used for output and therefore current production in the model is connected not to current supply of inputs, but to previous periods of supply.

A problem also results from the fact that industries do not have identical production methods. Thus, output determines input only if the various firms expand and contract proportionally. Likewise, as firms within the industry produce multiple products, the theory must assume constant product mix for industry as output expands. Furthermore, the use of production functions designating given outputs for given inputs is more naturally applied to mining, manufacturing, and utilities than it is to other sectors such as trade, finance, and the household. Estimation for the latter sectors may involve considerable approximation.

The theory also assumes that if output is given, the level of input is uniquely determined. Such a model does not take into account the possibility of input substitution; and this effect may be significant. In addi-

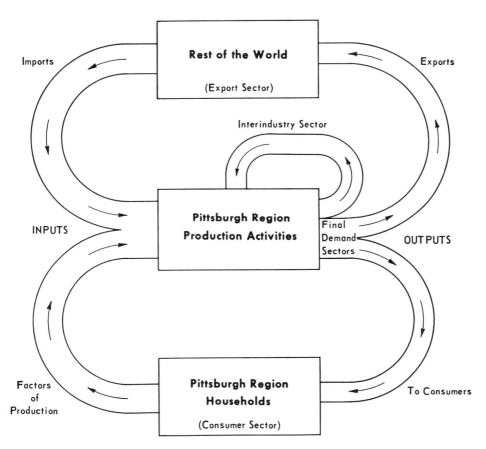

**Fig. 8–1.** Schematic flow chart of intersector relationships. (*Region with a Future,* Vol. III, p. 199; *Economic Study of the Pittsburgh Region* [Pittsburgh: University of Pittsburgh Press, 1963].)

tion, there is a problem of distinguishing between inputs used for current output and those used for investment in plant and equipment.

Many of the advantages of an input-output matrix are statistical. It enables the analyst to record in a rather concise fashion a large amount of information about a regional economy and the interrelations of its sectors. Further, it imposes a statistical discipline on data collection assuring consistency in the approach. The table itself helps to reveal where there are gaps in the data and it may be suggestive of ways to fill them.

## OTHER TECHNIQUES OF ANALYSIS

As we suggested in the introductory sections of this chapter, various other methods may also be used to facilitate the analysis of local economies, including regional accounts, balance-of-payments, flow-of-funds, location quotients, or proportionality techniques, as well as others. Each of these methods may be highly useful for particular purposes.

### Regional Accounts

The intricacy of relationships between regions complicates the development of regional accounts. As we suggested earlier, regions are "open" rather than "closed" economies. Many of our large corporations may have headquarters in one region, do a major part of their business in others or internationally, and yet make no separation on a regional basis. Domestic and international separations typically are made. Federal government receipts and payments are also hard to assign to regions.

### Balance of Payments and Flow of Funds

The Federal Reserve carries on a number of regional analyses and a variety of data have been developed on a regional basis. The various Federal Reserve districts have used regional balance-of-payment and flow-of-funds methods. Studies of the flow of goods, services, and financial payments between regions have been developed from shipping and banking data and other sources. Although often lacking in various types of data, such flow studies often provide insights into the economic life of a region.

### Location Quotients

Location quotients sometimes are helpful. In such analyses the percentage of an activity in a particular location (region, state, county) is compared with the percentage of the same activity in the nation as a whole. The Department of Commerce has been making comparisons of this type using a proportionality technique to analyze various regional changes relative to the national economy. It is planned to develop data on a county-by-county basis and to make available continuing information annually on a number of comparative bases.

To date, these studies have undertaken in a preliminary way to differentiate between "industry mix" for states and major geographic regions and to analyze what is termed the "competitive effect" in employment changes. Computations are made, first, as to what employment changes would have been if an area had grown at the same rate as the national total; second, computations are made to determine how much more or less than this amount employment would have changed because the particular industries in the area grow more or less than the national average for those industries—this being called the "industry mix" effect; and third, the difference between actual growth and normal growth for the particular "industry mix" in the area is computed to determine the "competitive" effect.[23]

## Improvement Efforts

A number of students of local and regional economies are carrying forward a variety of work to improve both the theoretical and practical approaches to analytical and forecasting efforts. For example, efforts are made to study the multiplier effect in regional economic analysis.[24] There are continuing efforts to re-evaluate and improve economic base analysis. Mathematical model building is being tried in a number of cases. The net effect of all these efforts should be to provide real estate decision makers with improved tools of analysis in the years ahead.

## SUMMARY

Regional and local economic analysis provides valuable assistance to real estate decision makers. Managers of multi-plant firms and chain store organizations can use such materials as well as investors in real estate properties, mortgage lenders, builders and land developers, and government officials. For these discussions, little effort is made to distinguish between regional and local economies since the purpose of the decision maker is largely the governing factor. Our primary concern is with the problems of the real estate decision maker and his decisions are related to factors influencing the localization of income. Natural factors and division of labor help to explain the location of economic activity along with local advantages that attract people of special competence—leaders, entrepreneurs, scientists, and the like—capital, and special facilities. These factors also help to explain expansion in one place as against another. In addition, once a certain size is reached an "urban-size ratchet" may go into operation.

The economic base method provides a useful approach to analyzing local and regional economies. It involves the application of international trade theory to local economic analysis. The relative importance of vari-

[23] Robert E. Graham, Jr., "Factors Underlying Changes in the Geographic Distribution of Income," *Survey of Current Business* (April, 1964).

[24] Richard T. Pratt, "Multiplier and Economic Base Analysis," unpublished seminar report, Indiana University. Also, "Regional Production Inputs and Regional Income Determination," *Journal of Regional Science*, Vol. 7, No. 2 (1967).

ous local income sources is determined, their future potential analyzed, and local modifying factors considered in estimating the future growth potential of a local or regional economy by means of the economic base method.

Of other methods in use, input-output analysis holds considerable promise if required data can be made more readily available. Regional accounts, balance of-payments, flow-of-funds, location quotients, or proportionality techniques are also used.

## QUESTIONS FOR STUDY

1. How can a local economic analysis help a real estate decision maker?
2. How can a region be compared to a city or urban area in terms of economic analysis?
3. How does regional analysis differ from an analysis of general (national) business conditions?
4. Discuss the economic forces that cause cities to grow.
5. What is meant by "urban-size ratchet" effect? Do you agree with this concept? Why or why not?
6. Explain how you would analyze income and employment from trade in your home town.
7. What is meant by "basic income sources" in the economic base model? What are the basic income sources for: (a) your home town? (b) the capital of your state? (c) the city in which your college or university is located?
8. What is meant by "urban service employment"? Can urban service employment contribute to city growth? Explain.
9. Why is diversification of manufacturing desirable?
10. Assume that you are to present a report on the topic "An Evaluation of Economic Base Analysis as an Aid to Decision Making." Prepare a brief outline of the main points you would want to make.
11. What are the advantages and disadvantages of the input-output method of analysis?
12. Explain the use of location quotients for analysis of a locality. What special significance might this have for the real estate decision maker?

## SUGGESTED READINGS

Hoyt, Homer. *According to Hoyt* (2nd ed.). Washington, D.C.: Hoyt, 1970. Part VIII. Pp. 548–586.

Isard, Walter. *Methods of Regional Analysis: An Introduction to Regional Science.* Cambridge: The Massachusetts Institute of Technology Press, 1960. Chaps. v, vi, viii.

Meyer, John R. "Regional Economics: A Survey," *American Economic Review,* LIII, No. 1, Part I (March, 1963).

PERLOFF, HARVEY S., and LOWDON WINGO, JR. (eds.), *Issues in Urban Economics.*
    Baltimore: The Johns Hopkins Press, 1968. "Internal and External Factors in the
    Development of Urban Economics." Pp. 43–80.
THOMPSON, WILBUR R. *A Preface to Urban Economics.* Baltimore: The Johns
    Hopkins Press, 1965. Chs. i, ii, iv.
TOYNBEE, ARNOLD. *Cities on the Move.* New York and London: Oxford University
    Press, 1970.

## CASE 8–1

### Economic Base of Bel Aire

Bel Aire is located in an agricultural and mining area of a state having no
large cities. Bel Aire is several hundred miles from a major industrial center.
Employment opportunities have diminished and there has been a reluctance on
the part of the residents to move on; hence, there is a surplus of labor in Bel
Aire.

In the past half century the rate of population growth in the town of Bel
Aire has not kept pace with that of the rest of the nation. Except for the
decade of the fifties the population has decreased in every decade since 1920.
By way of contrast, the nation as a whole has had significant population increases in the same period (see Table 1).

**TABLE 1.    Population Changes: Bel Aire and the United States**

| Year | Bel Aire | Per Cent Change | United States | Per Cent Increase |
|------|----------|-----------------|---------------|-------------------|
| 1970 | 12,000 | −4 | 200,255,000 | 10.8 |
| 1960 | 12,500 | −3.84 | 180,676,000 | 19.1 |
| 1950 | 13,000 | +23.8 | 132,122,000 | 14.8 |
| 1940 | 10,500 | −8.69 | 123,188,000 | 7.2 |

In Bel Aire at the last census the male population was 48.9 per cent of the
total. This ratio is slightly under the national average of 49.7 per cent. There
is a significant difference in age groups of the population of Bel Aire as compared with the rest of the nation. The percentage of preschool (under 5) and
school age (5 to 19) population is under the national average, whereas the
percentage of the older age groups (60 and over) is higher than the national
average.

Approximately 95 per cent of the Bel Aire population are native-born cau-
casians. The median number of school years completed is 8.5 years, which is
slightly under the national average.

Three-fourths of the labor force of Bel Aire is male.

The major sources of employment by type of industry are agriculture, retail
trade, mining, and manufacturing (see Table 2). The firms are small in size,

the largest firm employing less than 200 persons and only three firms employing more than 100 persons.

Bel Aire has an adequate urban plant.

### TABLE 2.   Employment in Bel Aire

|                                                    | 1958  | Per Cent |
|----------------------------------------------------|-------|----------|
| Total employed                                     | 4,000 | 100      |
| Agriculture                                        | 900   | 22.5     |
| Mining                                             | 600   | 15       |
| Construction                                       | 250   | 6.25     |
| Manufacturing                                      | 450   | 11.25    |
| Transportation                                     | 200   | 5        |
| Utilities                                          | 100   | 2.5      |
| Wholesale trade                                    | 50    | 1.25     |
| Retail trade                                       | 850   | 21.25    |
| Medical, educational, and professional services    | 300   | 7.5      |
| Public administration                              | 300   | 7.5      |

### Questions

1. What type of industry do you think the Chamber of Commerce should try to bring to Bel Aire? Why? How might industry be induced to locate there?
2. Assume that two manufacturing firms will locate in Bel Aire next year. One plans to employ 300 persons and the other plans to employ 200 persons. After the plants are in operation, what number of basic employees would you expect. Nonbasic employees? What would be the effect of such a development on total population?
3. What do you consider to be the long-range prospects for the marketability of real estate in Bel Aire? What are the principal factors in determining long-run marketability?

### STUDY PROJECT 8–1

#### The Kentucky Secondary Data Approach and Its Potentials *

Three types of information are needed by states or regions concerning the relationships between the private and public sectors of their economy to plan effectively for future growth or to change existing economic situations or policies. The input-output model supplies the information needs important to state and regional planning. These are: (1) measurement of the impact of changes in the volume of economic activity arising from changes in the level of activity of a particular private or public sector; (2) projections of the prob-

* Jerald R. Barnard and Harold K. Charlesworth.

able level of economic activity as a basis for making private and public investment decisions; and (3) appraisal of the effects of alternative decisions or development plans.

Increased emphasis on regional planning during the sixties has led to allocation of considerable resources for the construction of regional input-output studies. Bourque and Hansen indicated in 1967 that 54 states and regions had completed input-output studies and that 32 were in progress.[1] With costs running over $1 million for a state and as high as $300,000 for metropolitan areas, an evaluation of the methods of constructing input-output studies and the efficient allocation of research resources to these studies are pertinent.

**Kentucky Input-Output Study.**    In preparing a regional input-output study, a choice must be made between two alternative methodologies—the use of secondary data sources,[2] or the primary data approach. The former uses the national direct requirements coefficients taken from the national input-output table to estimate the state interindustry relationships.[3] The latter determines interindustry relationships from sample surveys of interindustry sales and purchases. The choice of method depends upon the degree of accuracy required at the regional level and the relative benefit to be gained from the additional cost of the primary data approach.

Five steps are involved in determining the input-output structure of a regional economy from secondary data.

First, gross output (outlay) is determined on a detailed industry basis by using the same standard industrial classifications for sectors as are used for the national data. The gross outlays for each regional industry sector are then multiplied by the matrix of U.S. direct requirements coefficients (often called the national input-output coefficients or the national technical coefficients) for each of the sectors.[4] Given below are hypothetical U.S. direct requirements coefficients in Table 1. By multiplying the total outlay by these coefficients, the hypothetical interindustry transactions table is constructed for the sectors concerned. For example, if regional agricultural output were $30 million, the interindustry transactions for agriculture from agriculture would be estimated by multiplying $30 million by .13; agriculture from manufacturing, by .23; and agriculture from services, by .20.

**TABLE 1.  Hypothetical U.S. Direct Requirements Matrix**

|  | Agriculture | Mfg. | Services |
|---|---|---|---|
| Agriculture | .13 | .16 | .08 |
| Manufacturing | .23 | .30 | .24 |
| Services | .20 | .10 | .16 |

To construct the Kentucky interindustry transactions table, estimates of output were obtained for the 99 sectors corresponding to the 1958 national input-output study. This was achieved by multiplying the Kentucky outlay for each of the 99 sectors by the U.S. direct requirements coefficient concerned. These detailed sector estimates had to be made if the study was to use the national direct requirements coefficients in estimating Kentucky interindustry transactions. This procedure resulted in a 99 x 99 Kentucky interindustry transactions table.

Second, a decision concerning the required amount of sector detail must be made. In most cases the regional study will use fewer sectors than the national study (because no state has the same number and variety of sectors as the United States); thus, a smaller transactions table is called for. In the case of Kentucky, a summation routine on the computer was used to reduce the 99 x 99 model to its present 26 x 26 size.

**TABLE 2.   Hypothetical Interindustry Transactions Table (millions of dollars)**

| | Purchasing sectors | | | | |
|---|---|---|---|---|---|
| Producing Sectors | Agriculture | Manufacturing | Services | Final demand | Total output |
| Agriculture | 4 | 8 | 2 | 16 | 30 |
| Manufacturing | 7 | 15 | 6 | 22 | 50 |
| Services | 6 | 5 | 4 | 10 | 25 |
| Final payments | 13 | 22 | 13 | 0 | 48 |
| Total outlay (Input) | 30 | 50 | 25 | 48 | 153 |

The third stage adjusts the regional transactions table developed from the national input-output coefficients to depict the regional industrial structure more accurately. One method of adjustment is to use sample surveys and collect primary data for adjusting the interindustry flows for those sectors of the economy that are known to differ from the national economy. Another method suggested by Stone is to adjust the various elements in the interindustry transactions table, relying on the subjective judgment of investigators and industrial leaders.[5] In the case of Kentucky, the subjective judgment method was followed.

The fourth step computes the regional direct requirements table.

Fifth is the computation of direct and indirect requirements matrices or the interdependency coefficients. Examples based upon Table 2 are shown in Tables 3 and 4, the latter showing the total result of the successive rounds of increased requirements generated by a change in final demand.[6]

**Problems with National Data.** The use of national production coefficients to construct regional input-output tables is essentially a disaggregation process. Boudeville points out that the secondary data approach has the virtue of coherency, although it is possibly less precise than the primary data method.[7] Moreover, it provides a set of data for the computation of the transactions table.

A regional input-output structure developed by using national production coefficients can differ from a national structure for these reasons: (1) Variations may exist between a region and the nation in the relative importance of the various sectors making up the composite sector. (2) Regional price levels may differ. (3) A larger part of the trade at the regional level may embody imports and exports. (4) Production techniques vary regionally.

For many industries, however, the type of plant is replicated in each region. Hence many national production coefficients will not differ significantly from regional coefficients, and, in any event, they can be adjusted from survey data at small additional cost.

But, not all of the first three factors may be significant upon closer observation. For example, the differences between the national and regional structure arising from the necessity to combine under a given industrial classification those industries with similar but not identical characteristics do not constitute a very significant problem if the national tables are developed on a four-digit Standard Industrial Classification (SIC) basis. The problem does arise when the coefficients for an industry are limited to a two- or three-digit SIC basis. This limitation tends to conceal a region's industrial specialization. For example, in the 1958 national input-output study, the beverage industry is represented at the three-digit level (SIC 208). In Kentucky, famous for its production of bourbon, distilled spirits (SIC 2085) make up about 35 per cent of the total output of the beverage industry. Because the inputs of the distilled spirits industry are different from those of the soft drink industry, adjustments were made to correct for the aggregation problem.[8]

For the most part, regional price differentials mainly reflect different wage levels.[9] These have a cost impact on the coecifficient matrix that can easily be taken care of, given the relative wage differentials, by a matrix multiplication routine.[10]

The treatment of imports and exports under the primary and secondary methods, however, does give rise to significant differences in input-output co-

## TABLE 3. Direct Requirements Matrix

|  | Agriculture | Manufacturing | Services |
|---|---|---|---|
| Agriculture | .13 | .16 | .08 |
| Manufacturing | .23 | .30 | .24 |
| Services | .20 | .10 | .16 |
| Final Payments | .44 | .44 | .52 |
| Total | 1.00 | 1.00 | 1.00 |

efficients and their meaning. First, the size of the region's economy is important in making any assessment of interregional export and import flows, because the larger the region's economy, the stronger the tendency toward self-sufficiency. On the other hand, for the region with a smaller economy external trade is a larger part of its total economic activity. Second, residentiary sectors such as transportation, communication, public utilities, finance, real estate, insurance, trade, and services make up a significant part of a region's economic activity and in most regional economies of any significant size tend toward self-sufficiency. A regional trade problem arises out of the conceptual differences in the basic structures of the input-output models. In the primary data method, the input-output coefficients measure the flow of trade within the region as well as between the region and other regions. By contrast, the secondary data method conceives of the input-output coefficients as technical coefficients of production rather than trade coefficients because they are derived from the national input-output table.[11]

The significance of this difference lies in the fact that under the secondary data method the flow of external trade is less than under the primary data method. For this reason, some accounting convention must be adopted to handle the problem. Under the secondary data approach, for example, a sector whose output is greater than total regional intermediate and final requirements is considered to have exported its surplus.[12] Correspondingly, a sector whose output is not sufficient to meet regional intermediate and final requirements is considered to have imported the difference.[13] This concept reduces the total trade flow because it rules out imports into the regional economy for those sectors which had surplus production and assumes that the local region uses only locally produced goods for these sectors. For example, this would have Kentuckians consuming only Kentucky-made spirits. But in spite of Kentuckians' pride in their bourbon, they do indulge in a wider variety of tastes.

By ruling out competitive imports for sectors with net exports, the secondary data method overstates the direct requirements for the regional sectors and thereby overstates regional interdependence.

**TABLE 4.   Direct and Indirect Requirements Matrix**

|             | Agriculture | Manufacturing | Services |
|-------------|:-----------:|:-------------:|:--------:|
| Agriculture   | 1.2844 | .3242  | .2149  |
| Manufacturing | .5493  | 1.6360 | .5174  |
| Services      | .3712  | .2710  | 1.3031 |

It is possible that the secondary data model can be put on the same accounting basis as the primary model, that is, on a regional trade basis. This would distinguish all imported goods by industry of origin and by industry of destination, and involves development of a supplemental transactions table which shows the flows of imported goods by sector of origin to their sector of destination. For example, in the national input-output table, the sale of livestock to the livestock sector represents the interfarm and ranch sales of feeder cattle to feedlots. Because of regional specialization, the national coefficient must be adjusted at the regional level to account for exports and imports. For the feeder *cattle-producing states,* livestock sector intrasectoral flows should be reduced, resulting in greater exports. For the *cattle-feeding states,* the intrasectoral flows should be reduced, resulting in greater imports. In this particular example, data on cattle shipments by the U. S. Department of Agriculture provide the basis for adjustment.

The data requirements to adjust the coefficients of all sectors to a regional trade basis are demanding, but both Tiebout and Boudeville suggest it may be possible to accomplish this, using secondary data sources on transportation flows.[14]  To our knowledge, no secondary data studies have attempted this for all sectors.  Instead, they have been operated under the assumption that for sectors with net exports, local requirements were met with locally produced goods.

While the secondary data model is used with this limiting assumption, the primary data study operates under the limiting assumption that trade flows are stable.  Substitution between locally produced goods and competing imports may take place in a short period of time.  Thus, the trade coefficients of the primary data method may prove to be unstable.  It is generally accepted that the technical coefficient is likely to be more stable than either of its two components—the regional trade coefficient, or the competitive import coefficient.[15]  We would urge that a study of the stability of regional trade coefficients be made.  Finally, most input-output studies have been developed on the basis of political boundaries rather than economic regions.  While this is appropriate for political planning purposes, in light of the arguments advanced regarding export-import flows, the delineation of regions without considering regional nodality and homogeneity criteria may yield unstable trade flows.

**Advantages.**    The advantages associated with the secondary data method are primarily those of time and cost.  It can produce within six months a picture of the economy that can be refined and improved as need arises.  Thus, where time and money are important economic considerations, the opportunity cost to the decision maker in business or government must be weighed in choosing which input-output method to adopt.  Some examples of the costs incurred under the two approaches are given in the cases of Kentucky, Kansas, and Texas.  The preliminary Kentucky input-output study based on secondary data cost less than $10,000; the Kansas primary data study cost over $100,000; and the projected Texas nine-region primary data study is estimated for more than $1 million.

For the small regional economy (e.g., a county or relatively small city), the cost differential between the secondary and primary method will be small.  The reason is that the secondary data method may require considerable adjustment based on currently available data to depict the unique structure of the small region.  At the other extreme is the large multi-state region, where the production processes tend to be more like the national average.  Here the cost differential turns in favor of the secondary approach.

One of the main criticisms of many regional input-output studies is that in many cases after great expenditures of time, effort, and money, they result only in the input-output transactions table, the input-output coefficient table, and the interdependency coefficient table.  While these tables provide much useful information, they require further refinement and extensions before they can be used to answer such question as the impact a certain economic policy or investment decision may have on a region's economy.  The input-output study provides the principal data for the development of analytical models from which planning information can be generated. Simulation models can be built around the input-output model. These can be used to examine impacts on the regional economy and examine alternative policies and programs. Examples include the models of Iowa and West Virginia.[16]

Given the larger budget required for a primary data input-output study, we suggest a strategy that would make use of secondary data to develop regional input-output tables and construct regional analytic economic models to measure and evaluate the impact of different regional development policies and plans. By such model building and analysis, one gains greater insight into the structure and functioning of the regional economy and a greater amount of information can be obtained per dollar of expenditure.

Another important reason favoring the secondary data method is that where comparability is important, economic structures for different regions may be compared because they have been developed from the same data base. It is impossible to make comparable and valid comparisons of the structure of different regions using the primary input-output study because each study is designed only for a specific economy and by different people. Only after primary data coefficients have been adjusted for this purpose can valid comparisons be made.

**Accuracy and Cost Requirements.** At the basis of the argument over accuracy is the question of how much accuracy is needed for effective regional decision making and planning. Indeed, if accuracy in the production of information faces the traditional production and cost functions found in economic analysis wherein improved information is produced under decreasing returns (increasing costs), then one cannot ignore the problem of attempting to determine whether the marginal cost is equal to its marginal value as a decision input.

Marschak clearly points out three essential elements in planning: information (data) production, communication, and decision making.[17] Data production is only one part of the planning process; communication and decision making are equally important elements entering into the final results. Naturally, there are costs associated not only with data production, but also with communication and decision making. The optimal choice is the combination of services with the highest value. Assuming substitution among data production, communication, and decision making, the economist should attempt to equate the marginal rate of substitution between these elements with their price ratio to determine the optimal combination. This is not, however, to argue that accuracy of information data is not important; rather it should be viewed as only one part of the total planning process.

Along these same lines, Morgenstern has suggested that all economic decisions include both quantitative and nonquantitative information: "Obviously, there must exist a point at which it is no longer meaningful to sharpen the numerically available information when the other, wholly qualitative, part is important, though a notion of its 'accuracy' or 'reliability' has not been developed."[18]

**The Application.** In specific terms, Kentucky needed an input-output study to answer the following important questions.

What is the structure of the Commonwealth's industrial sector? What industries offer the greatest and the least potential for increased employment? What particular type of tax or other revenue policy measure hinders or promotes economic development? What is the impact of federal defense expenditures on Kentucky's development possibilities, especially their effect on industry, employment, and personal income? What is the ability of heavy highways expenditures (federal interstate and state parkways) to influence economic development?

Businessmen in turn can ask pertinent questions about their own operations and about their firms' potential for expansion and more accurately estimate their markets by recognizing that each row of the input-output table is a marketing profile of an industry or a sector of industry in Kentucky. A firm can compare its market structure with those of other firms in the same industry to determine the difference between its market and the average for the industry. Also, the row will show the specific portion of the total industry sales which is sold to each of the different sectors in the input-output study. This level of detail permits the industry, the firm, or the public sector to estimate the impact of a state or federal program or the location of a new industry.

Granted the importance of answers to the above questions, why was the secondary data method chosen? The initial monetary cost to construct a regional input-output study from primary data was prohibitive as far as Kentucky was concerned. Moreover, the time required for such a study made it quite unattractive. Kentucky needed answers now—not two years from now.

We suggest that many of the questions raised in this article can only be resolved through further research. Indeed, the question of the size of the region where cost differentials between primary and secondary data methods are equal needs exploration. We believe also that more testing of regional input-output studies developed under the two approaches should be made. Finally, we urge that the U.S. Department of Commerce attempt to develop input-output studies for the 50 states, even if they cannot carry out adjustment of regional tables. This would make available to every state an input-output study that could be reviewed, adjusted, and compared with input-output studies for the other states. In this way the questions of cost, accuracy, and appropriate regional adjustment procedures might be resolved.

## Notes

1. Philip J. Bourque and Gerald Hansen, *An Inventory of Regional Input-Output Studies in the United States,* University of Washington Graduate School of Business Administration, Occasional Paper no. 17 (Seattle, 1967), p. 1.
2. J. R. Barnard and H. K. Charlesworth, *The Structure of the Kentucky Economy: An Input-Output Study* (Lexington: University of Kentucky Office of Development Services and Business Research, 1970).
3. Morris R. Goldman, Martin L. Marimont, and Beatrice N. Vaecara, "The Interindustry Structure of the United States: A Report on the 1958 Input-Output Study," *Survey of Current Business,* vol. 44 (November 1964), p. 13.
4. The multiplication process is represented in matrix form by $AX = Z$, where $A$ is the matrix of national input-output coefficients, $X$ is a diagonal matrix of

regional gross outlays by sectors, and Z is the estimated regional transactions table.

In a recent study, R. D. Peterson and R. A. Wykstra use the secondary data approach to construct an input-output table of the Idaho economy ("A Provisional Input-Output Study of Idaho's Economy," *University of Washington Business Review*, vol. 27 [1968], pp. 11–27). We take issue with their procedure whereby they first aggregated the national input-output table into a 16 x 16 matrix corresponding to their Idaho sectors and then calculated a 16 x 16 coefficient matrix. This aggregated national coefficient matrix was assumed to depict the average input mix for the Idaho sectors and was used as the first estimate of the Idaho transactions table. This table was subsequently adjusted. The point we wish to make is that the more appropriate and accurate procedure is what we have described above. Our procedure yields a regional transactions table appropriately weighted to the regional industrial mix from the national table. The approach in the Idaho study simply gives a more aggregate picture of the national industrial mix and does not make use of all the information present in the national table.

5. Richard Stone, *Input-Output and National Accounts* (Paris: Organization for European Economic Cooperation, 1961), pp. 160–63.
6. Tables 2, 3, and 4 were based on models used in an article by Jarvin Emerson, "Market Research Used in Input-Output Study," *The Kansas Industrial Extension Journal*, vol. 3 (February 1969), p. 6.
7. J. R. Boudeville, *Problems of Regional Economic Planning* (Chicago: Aldine Publishing Co., 1966), p. 88.
8. The 1963 national input-output study is developed on a 300-sector detail basis. This will considerably improve the first-round accuracy of regional tables derived from the national tables. It also will enhance the accuracy of input-output studies developed from secondary data.
9. Boudeville, *Problems of Regional Economic Planning*, p. 89.
10. Richard Stone and Alan Brown, "A Computable Model of Economic Growth," *A Programme for Growth*, part 1 (London: Chapman & Hall, Ltd., 1962), p. 70.
11. The technical coefficient of production, $a_{ij} = x_{ij}/x_j$, represents the amount of output from sector i required per unit of output of sector j. The regional trade coefficients, $tr_{ij} = xr_{ij}/xr_j$, represent the amount of output from the regional sector i required per unit of output of sector j. The technical coefficient at the regional level would be of the form, $a_{ij} = (xr_{ij} + mr_{ij})/xr_j$ where $mr_{ij}$ represents the flows of imports into the region of sector i to sector j. From the latter equation, it is clear that the trade coefficient, $tr_{ij}$, is smaller than the technical coefficient by the ratio $mr_{ij}/xr_j$. Thus, the interdependency coefficients (the inverse matrix), $1/1-a_{ij}$, derived from the technical coefficients will be larger than the interdependency coefficients derived from the trade coefficients, $1/1-tr_{ij}$.
12. This was the procedure used in the early regional input-output study of Utah: Frederick T. Moore and James W. Petersen, "Regional Analysis: An Interindustry Model of Utah," *Review of Economics and Statistics*, vol. 37 (1955), pp. 368–83.
13. Noncompetitive imports are defined as imports of goods from industries not located in the regional economy. They are entered as a separate row in the transactions table and are assumed to be imported in fixed proportion to the output of a given sector.
14. C. M. Tiebout, "Regional and Interregional Input-Output Models: An Appraisal," *Southern Economic Journal*, vol. 24 (1957), p. 145; and Boudeville, *Problems of Regional Economic Planning*, p. 90.
15. United Nations Statistical Office, Department of Economic and Social Affairs, *Problems of Input-Output Tables and Analysis* (New York, 1966), p. 51.
16. Wilbur R. Maki, Richard E. Suttor, and Jerald R. Barnard, *Simulation of Regional Product and Income with Emphasis on Iowa, 1954–1974*, Iowa State University Agricultural and Home Economics Experiment Station, Research Bulletin

no. 548 (Ames, 1966); and William H. Miernyk et al., *Simulating Regional Economic Development: An Interindustry Analysis of the West Virginia Economy* (Morgantown: West Virginia University Regional Research Institute, 1969).

17. Jacob Marschak, "Economics of Inquiry, Communicating and Deciding," *American Economic Review*, vol. 58 (1968), pp. 1–18.

18. Oskar Morgenstern, *On the Accuracy of Economic Observation* (Princeton, N.J.: Princeton University Press, 1963), p. 3.

## Questions

1. What can an input–output study do for a decision maker?
2. What are the major differences between primary and secondary data?
3. How can an input–output structure be developed from secondary data?
4. What are the advantages of the secondary data method?
5. If you were called upon to make an economic analysis of a locality, under what conditions would you make an input–output study? Explain.

# 9

# Real Estate Market Analysis

## MARKET FACTORS IN DECISIONS

Real estate decision makers have a major interest in markets and locations since such factors have important influences on the income-producing potential of real properties and hence on their value. In this chapter we are concerned with market forces and with various suggestions for their analysis. In the succeeding two chapters we consider local location factors.

Market changes and potential market changes play an important part in the decisions of real estate owners, users, investors, brokers, managers, builders, appraisers, mortgage lenders, mortgage insurers, buyers, and sellers. Government officials engaged in planning, zoning, slum clearance, new towns, the administration of taxes and public finance, building codes, or the insuring and guaranteeing of mortgages are also influenced greatly by real estate market changes and trends.

### Types of Markets

Because of the diverse nature of real estate markets and the wide variety of factors that affect them, somewhat different approaches to the analysis of residential, commercial, industrial, farm, and special-purpose real estate markets often are required. Even so, there are a number of general guides to market analysis that are applicable to each of these types of real estate markets. We consider here some of the major characteristics of real estate markets, various analytical tools that may be used, kinds of data that are helpful, and the judgmental factors that often are highly important to the real estate decision maker.

## Demand, Supply, and Price

In all types of markets, including real estate markets, the major factors involved are those related to demand, supply, and price. Note that price is emphasized in our discussions along with supply and demand. Price is viewed broadly, however, to include rent, interest rates, special charges, and the like depending on the market sector under consideration.

## THE MARKET IN OPERATION

A brief and general description of the forces operating in the real estate market, the principles explaining their relationships, and the functions which they perform may seem to imply that the competitive process brings about smooth adjustments between supply, demand, and prices. Such is not necessarily the case. Competition is the main regulative force, it is true; but the actual operation of the market is far from perfect or efficient.

### Market Influences

We pointed out some of the reasons for this condition in Chapter 5: real properties possess few of the characteristics which make it easy to carry on market dealings in them, the markets for many types of real estate are limited in extent, and there are no central exchanges to facilitate buying and selling. Furthermore, the real estate market is affected by the seasons, with spring and fall usually representing the active periods of the year. Likewise, variations in general or local business activity, the ease or difficulty of financing, and other special factors all have important effects. Government policies play a role of growing importance. The rapid industrial changes arising from scientific and technological advances are also having major effects on real estate markets.

### Buyer's and Seller's Markets

As a result, the real estate market passes through periods of varying activity. At times a seller's market exists, which means that very few properties are available and a large number of users and potential users are demanding them. At other times a buyer's market exists—that is, the buyer can fulfill his needs at low prices and on advantageous terms.

## Factors Conditioning Market Operation

The following are among the factors that condition the operation of real estate markets:

1. Each property is unique, since only one building can occupy a particular spot on the earth's surface. However, the degree of uniqueness varies. Row houses or town houses or standardized detached houses in a large homogeneous neighborhood are virtually interchangeable. In contrast, every 25 or 50 feet of land may change in value in a central business district. Also, we should note that a special-purpose building may be suitable for use by only one tenant.

2. Some properties are parts of estates or are involved in litigation, with restrictions on sale or lease so they cannot be sold or developed. Such properties, even though in desirable locations, are virtually out of the market.

3. Some owners have a sentimental attachment to their homes, farms, or other properties and refuse to to sell for prices that reflect market conditions.

4. Some properties are leased for long periods and are not available for sublease or sale.

5. Buyers are often restricted to persons living in the city or neighborhood who are in a position to take advantage of bargains or the necessities of the seller.

6. Owners living outside of a city frequently are not familiar with local developments which may increase or diminish the value of their properties.

7. Prices are affected by the terms and availability of financing.

8. Oral agreements are not binding as in stock market or grain market transactions, so that a seller or buyer may not complete a transaction even though an obligation to pay a broker's commission may be incurred.

9. Whether the seller has a good title cannot be determined quickly as in the case of stocks or merchandise, so that a period of time must elapse before the title can be passed.

10. Real estate cannot escape local taxes as is often possible in the case of personal property.

11. The value of real properties is often affected greatly by changes in local zoning laws.

12. The value of any specific property is affected by the character of the neighborhood and the economic outlook.

13. Buildings are not standardized commodities like automobiles. They may have hidden defects or exceptionally favorable features.

14. There is no machinery for selling short in real estate markets.

15. While properties may turn over rapidly in periods of advancing prices, there may be long periods of low sales volume during periods of stagnation and decline.

16. Residential real estate has been subject to rent control in times of emergency, which checked the operation of normal market forces.

17. The value of real estate will be lowered by a high crime rate in the neighborhood. Property values depend on adequate police and fire protection.

18. Property values are affected by availability and quality of water, sewer systems, utilities, and highways.

19. Air and water pollution may have highly adverse effects on real estate values.

The nature of the real estate market is thus different from other types of markets. Yet its operation can no more be called exceptional than the operation of the stock market and the board of trade, which are themselves exceptional in the unusual homogeneity and standardized character of the articles in which they deal.

## Monopoly Elements

In addition, the workings of the real estate market are sometimes modified considerably by the presence of certain elements of monopoly. For example, in many of our larger cities low income groups have been limited to certain areas and this may give property owners a certain monopoly advantage.

It should be noted, however, that higher rents or prices in such cases are secured usually by crowding the available accommodations to a greater degree than is typical of similar accommodations in the broader market. As a consequence, even badly deteriorated rental properties often produce handsome returns on the investment represented. Special efforts are sometimes made by investors in such positions to protect themselves against further competition such as might arise from new housing developments designed for the occupancy of similar groups.

In some rural areas religious or social groups form closed communities in which land purchases are restricted to the members of a particular group or sect. Thus, such markets are limited.

## Market Variations

As we indicated in earlier discussions, real estate markets can be classified according to types of properties, scope, and whether dealings are concerned with the purchase and sale of properties themselves or the rental of the services of properties for specified periods. While the rental and sale markets for properties are not mutually exclusive, both forming parts of a larger whole, the rental market is not characterized by the wide variations which occur in the buying and selling of properties themselves. In part this is due to the fact that the rental market partakes indirectly of the nature of a consumers' goods market and the sale market of a producers' goods market. Usually variations of market activities in consumers' goods are not as marked as those in producers' goods.

However, the rental market influences selling prices and the rate of building. When a seller's market exists, prices may move high enough to bring about the production of new buildings. When new structures are made available, they remain on the market for long periods of time, since they usually last for many years. If more of these are produced than can be absorbed at prices characteristic of a seller's market, a long period of time is generally required for readjustments to take place.

## Demand Pressures

An upward movement in the price of real estate services or rents and in the selling prices of real properties is normally the result of an increase in the demand for space. We have noted that in short-run periods, demand conditions are of greater importance than those of supply. The basic elements in demand are income and the terms and availability of financing. When such an increase in demand and prices occurs, the stage is set for an expansion of activity. Expansion of economic opportunities usually is necessary to attract people or to increase their incomes. Similarly, a loss of such opportunities tends to depress the real estate market.

People flock to a city from country districts, small towns, or other cities whenever new sources of income are established or old ones expanded. For example, Detroit grew rapidly after 1900 as a result of the amazing development of the automobile industry. In more recent years the Southwest and the Southeast grew rapidly as a result of the location and expansion of many industries as well as resorts and leisure time activities in those areas.

A rapid increase in the rate of population growth does not of itself cause an advance in real estate activity, for it must be accompanied by buying power on the part of the newcomers. Buying power includes consumer and business incomes, but depends also on the terms and availability of financing. Likewise, the lack of any sudden population growth does not necessarily prevent an expansion from occurring if incomes advance and financing terms are liberal.

## Inflexible Supply

Wide variations in real estate activity can be explained largely in terms of the relative inflexibility of the supply of space. While people are willing to make a smaller amount of space go around in periods of recession by doubling up, they are unwilling to live under conditions such as this when their incomes increase. Also, business firms demand more and better space when their incomes advance. Under depressed conditions new construction will be at a standstill because it will not pay to build at the low existing rents. But, as the population and business firms expand in number and rent-paying capacity, the large supply of vacant units typical of depression periods is rapidly absorbed. When the percentage of vacant units reaches a low figure, rents begin to rise. Such an advance also forces up prices and values. The net rentals advance even more sharply than gross rentals because operating costs, interest charges, taxes, maintenance, and similar expenses are relatively fixed. Hence, the rate of profit is rapidly increased, and it becomes profitable to erect new buildings.

## Market Expansion

In the early stages of expansion, construction of single-family houses predominates because many are constructed for those who have incomes sufficient to make down payments, even if the houses would not command rents sufficient to yield a normal monetary return on their cost. Similarly, business firms may expand plants or stores. As expansion progresses, however, it becomes profitable to construct apartment buildings, business blocks, industrial structures, shopping centers, and office buildings that are financed solely for pecuniary return.

As we have pointed out, net rents tend to rise more rapidly than gross rents. Costs usually do not move up as fast as rental levels. The period of construction usually begins with a period of easy credit. During such a period it may become quite easy to finance projects of various types.

As new buildings are erected, they absorb the vacant land; and a land boom results, with subdividing activity proceeding first at a slow rate and then gathering momentum if the pressure of building on land continues to increase. Large areas may be added to the supply of land available to the city. It should be noted that as outward movement from the city center occurs, the area available increases in a manner comparable to the square of the radius of a circle.

Expenditures for public improvements tend to increase at the same time that the volume of building and subdividing gains in momentum. Sometimes public improvements may be made in advance of current or immediate future needs.

## Market Contraction

Some time in the course of this period of expansion, demand begins to fall behind the rapid additions to supply which are being made available. It becomes difficult for the operators to lease or sell properties, and the sources of credit begin to tighten. The tightening of credit results in fore-closures; and unless the market continues to expand because of some increase in demand, an advance in the volume of foreclosures forecasts a period of decline. Many sectors of the real estate market may still maintain a peak level of activity. Construction of new apartments or stores may continue for some time at almost peak levels. There is as yet no marked decline in rents. Operating expenses are increasing, however, and foreclosures are likely to have an upward trend. The fact that real estate is financed more on a debt than an equity basis probably helps to intensify the variations that occur. Thus, those who finance real estate can make or break the market.

If foreclosures mount in volume as credits are tightening, the entire market is affected. It becomes impossible to sell properties without cutting prices. Land values begin to decline. Just as net rentals rose more rapidly than gross rentals in the early period of expansion, they now fall more rapidly because of the fixed charges involved. Hence, profits are wiped out and market activity falls to low levels.

The rate of recession in the real estate market will be intensified if there is a simultaneous recession in business generally. In that event incomes of tenants will drop and vacancies will increase as some families double up and others leave the city. Prospective marriages will be deferred in many cases. Business firms will reduce the space used. The result will be a rapid decline in rents. Foreclosures will increase rapidly, first on apartment and office buildings, because rents decline faster than operating expenses and owners soon find themselves unable to meet interest even on their first mortgages. Then, if a long recession ensues, the foreclosures will extend to single-family residences and owner-occupied business properties. Many owners of single-family homes will struggle to the limit of their ability to hold their homes. Others, especially those with thin equities, will give up at the first sign of recession. As a result of this process of attrition, the prices of real estate holdings are forced down.

A large volume of foreclosures is characteristic of depressed conditions in the real estate market. As a result of the foreclosure process, properties are refinanced and the financial wreckage is cleared away. Thus the stage is set for another period of expansion, which does not come automatically but which awaits some special impetus resulting in an increase in the demand for real estate resources.

## NATIONAL AND LOCAL MARKET ACTIVITY

Although activity in many real estate markets follows general national trends of business conditions, there are significant local variations. Regional differences account in part for some of these variations. The rapid expansion of the Southeast and Southwest has resulted in the acceleration of activity in the real estate markets of those regions.

Differences in the "mix" of economic activities in cities often results in local market experience that differs from general national or even regional trends. Usually cities that are largely dependent on the production of producers' goods will have wider swings in real estate market activity than those that rely largely on the production of consumers' goods. Also, cities with a diversified economic base typically enjoy greater stability of real estate market operations than those with less diversification, especially one-industry towns.

Major booms in real estate market activity are likely to come during periods of general business prosperity. Some cities, however, may experience only moderate expansion in such periods, while in others market activity may attain boom proportions. Local, regional, and industry factors largely account for the differences.

### The Cycle Controversy

There are widely divergent viewpoints as to whether there is a national cycle in real estate market activity. Some contend that such cycles can be identified, while others believe that local variations are so important as to make the concept of a national cycle meaningless.

Roy Wenzlick has been a major proponent of the concept of a national cycle; James C. Downs, Jr., and Homer Hoyt have stressed the importance of local market factors. Hoyt points out, however, that general periods of prosperity and depression tend to affect all local markets but with varying degrees of intensity and the timing of the impact of general economic changes may also vary.

There does not appear to be any regularity of such cyclical variations in real estate prices or in the volume of real estate activity as can be identified. Studies of variations in real estate activity in Chicago showed intervals between peaks of activity of 20, 16, 18, and 35 years.

It is well to note also that real estate activity varies greatly at the same time in the same urban region between different sections of the region and types of property. For example, the 1890 boom in Chicago affected chiefly the South Side near the World's Fair grounds and some central office sites; the Chicago boom of the mid-1920's was largely an outlying business center, apartment, and suburban boom.

### Reduction of Cycles

Basic changes in the American economy may reduce greatly if they do not virtually eliminate major business cycles and major real estate cycles. These changes include federal assumption of responsibility for economic conditions under the Employment Act of 1946, the guarantee of bank and savings and loan deposits, the guarantee and insurance of VA and FHA mortgages plus the widespread use of amortized mortgages, development of secondary mortgage markets through FNMA, GNMA, and FHLMC, social security, unemployment insurance, pension funds, union wage policies, widespread use of time payments and consumer credit, the strengthening of the middle-income groups and the reduction of income extremes at both the higher and lower levels, plus others. Increased knowledge about the American and world economies and the factors of major importance in determining the direction of economic activity must also be included as an important factor in dealing with major cyclical movements of economic activity, including real estate activity.

### Future Market Variations

In more recent years real estate market activity has been somewhat more stable than it was a generation ago. Variations persist as we have pointed out, but market activity typically does not change violently in short periods of time. It may be that generally improved conditions in the American economy account for this. Or other factors may have contributed to a somewhat greater degree of stability including price support and subsidy programs as well as some gradual inflation.

The Employment Act of 1946, which committed us to the pursuit of full employment, and the policies that have evolved as a result of it have been important in this connection as have the built-in stabilizers such as unemployment compensation, progressive income taxation, and old age and survivors insurance. Heavy expenditures for defense and space exploration are important modifying forces. The role of the federal government in housing, with the insurance and guarantee of mortgages, support of secondary mortgage markets, insurance of savings and checking accounts, and the development of nationwide mortgage financing systems through such programs as those of the Federal Home Loan Bank Board all have helped to provide increased stability.

Whether these and related developments will help in avoiding the extremes of booms and busts in real estate markets in the future remains to be seen. If a major business depression comes along it will undoubtedly bring substantial reductions in real estate activity of all types. Also, real estate remains vulnerable to excesses in prosperous periods.

The use of tight money and high interest rates to restrain inflation had highly adverse effects on housing markets in the tight money periods of 1966–67 and 1969–70. Housing markets may be affected in similar ways in the future unless more equitable economic stabilization policies are followed.

Much has been said and written about the long-range needs for housing, for business structures, and for other real estate as a result of the population pressures that are increasingly in evidence. As we have pointed out, however, numbers of people have little significance in terms of market demand unless the people have good incomes and the ability to command credit.

### Future Problems

There are numerous problems that may cause future difficulties, despite generally favorable prospects. Some regions and some localities will fall far below national averages in terms of the growth that appears to lie ahead. Heavy taxation of real properties, the relatively slow introduction of improved construction methods and technology, labor problems, concern with the environment, the problems of slum and downtown areas, and the competition of many new goods and services for a portion of the income produced—all may cause difficulties. Beyond these, there is the general volatility of demand for real estate resources against relatively fixed supplies in short-run periods. These conditions continue to make possible wide variations in real estate market activity. The character of efforts to control variations in economic activity are bound to have their effect on real estate as well as other markets.

## MAJOR FEATURES OF A MARKET ANALYSIS

In making an analysis of a real estate market purpose often governs the type of analysis undertaken, the coverage of various topics, and the intensity with which the analysis is carried out. The priorities assigned to the topics and the emphasis given to them will vary with specific local situations. We outline many of the topics that are usually included in a market analysis in our discussions here. In specific situations, of course, not all of these may be covered or others may be included.

### Purpose and Type of Market Analysis

As in the making of appraisals, the first step in the analysis of a real estate market is a careful definition of the problem. Why is the analysis being made? Is it to determine whether a builder should start a new project? Is an investor deciding on a major purchase or sale? Is a department store planning a new shopping center? Is a building manager trying to decide whether to raise rents? Is a mortgage lender planning to tighten financing terms? These questions and many others that might be raised suggest some of the variety of uses of market analyses.

The problems involved in making a market analysis generally will fall into two major groups: first, those pertaining to short-run objectives, and second, those pertaining to long-run objectives.[1] For example a builder may be concerned with whether he can sell the houses he builds within the next six months. An investor or a lending institution, by contrast, may be interested in the income potential and stability of properties over the next decade or two or longer. Planning commissions may be concerned with problems requiring that estimates be made for different types of land uses for as many as twenty or thirty years ahead.

Definition of purpose assists in determining whether short- or longer-run considerations should be given primary attention, the sector of the market that needs to be stressed, and the intensity with which the market must be studied. For example, if several cities are located in close proximity, all of them may be included in a market analysis. On the other hand, a specialized problem may limit the analysis to a few areas or districts. Once purpose has been defined, we may proceed with a consideration of the principal factors bearing on market conditions.

## Major Topics for Analysis

The main factors in the analysis of real estate markets may be listed as follows:

1. The general level of business activity affects real estate markets. For example, the recessions of 1948–49, 1953–54, 1957–58, 1960–61, and 1969–71 affected real estate markets of nearly all types in varying degrees.

2. The level of local business activity also requires consideration. Local business activity, of course, may deviate from general national trends because of special local factors. Usually there is some relationship between local business conditions and real estate market trends.

3. Of major importance for all types of real estate are changes in the employment and income sources of the community. Expansion of existing economic activities such as may result from new factories, new government agencies, new tourist attractions, and the like tend to increase market activity; the loss of employment and income has the opposite effect. Methods for analyzing changes of this type were outlined in the preceding chapter and are pertinent to nearly all types of real estate market analyses.

4. Financing terms and trends have a major influence on the demand for nearly all types of real estate. General and local mortgage market

---

[1] Uriel Manheim, *How To Do Housing Market Research:* Handbook for Local Home Builders Associations (Washington, D.C.: National Association of Home Builders of the United States, 1963), p. 3.

conditions form an integral part of almost every type of real estate market analysis.

5. While income and financing factors are of primary importance, population growth or decline tends to affect real estate markets. Not only are changes in the total population important, but also changes in the age distribution and composition of the population, as well as shifts of population within the market area. For example, a persistent movement to the suburbs may increase the demand for certain types of properties and bring a decline in the demand for other types, even though there are no changes in total population or in incomes.

6. Changes in the tastes and preferences of customers and potential customers may be highly important if they can be identified with reasonable accuracy.

7. The volume of building activity requires consideration, as well as construction cost levels and trends. Costs in relation to prices and rents have an important bearing on the rate at which additions will be made to the available supply. Also, the availability of improved lots and the cost of improving raw land usually require consideration.

8. Often the vacancy rate is the most important single indicator of real estate market trends. Rising vacancies usually indicate that the supply of existing space is greater than the demand for it. The rate at which vacancies are increasing or declining often provides the key to probable market changes. Closely related to vacancies in existing structures are the new structures that have not been sold or leased and remain on the market as an "overhand" for varying periods of time.

9. As we have suggested above, the interrelationship between prices, rents, and construction costs are important keys to market conditions and potential market changes. Wide differences between listing prices and final sales prices are especially significant.

10. The volume of market activity is reflected in the number of deeds recorded, the number of mortgages recorded, and the volume of foreclosures. Comparisons of present with past levels often provide good indexes of potential market changes.

11. Finally, all of the above factors must be studied in relation to each other and in relation to past developments. In this manner both short- and longer-range market trends may be identified and used as the basis for estimating future probable market changes.

## General Business Conditions

We have pointed out in several connections that local forces exercise important influences on the real estate market. This is especially true of the markets for residential real estate. We do not wish to imply, however, that general economic trends have only limited influence on local real estate markets.

In many cases local markets will follow national trends rather closely. This is usually true when the major sources of local income and employment represent a typical cross section of the American economy as a whole. In other cases local markets may deviate to some extent from national trends. This may be due to the types of employment and incomes represented or to special factors such as a rate of building that has been too rapid for local absorption, successful local efforts to bring in new industries, local financial policies that have unduly restricted building, unfavorable local government policies such as taxes, and many others.

Suggestions for analyzing general business conditions were outlined in Chapter 7. Estimates of general business trends usually precede the analysis of a specific real estate market. Then attempts are made to determine whether local conditions will follow closely or deviate significantly from general trends.

## Local Business Conditions

The real estate market of a locality will be influenced by the trend of local business conditions, which may be influenced in turn by general economic trends. Of the many factors to consider in studying local business conditions, the most important is the trend of employment and incomes, as we suggested in the preceding chapter. Such information is generally available from local chambers of commerce and from state employment services as well as from the personal office of the major local employers. Frequently local chambers of commerce publish monthly data reflecting local business trends. Some universities publish monthly summaries of business conditions. In addition the various Federal Reserve Banks make available monthly reports covering business trends for the district served and for the more important cities in the district.

Besidse showing employment and income, reports of these types frequently provide information on bank debits, department store sales, electricity production, newspaper advertising, car loadings, and similar information, as well as data on construction volume, real estate transfers, mortgages recorded, foreclosures, vacancies, and related materials more directly pertinent to the local real estate market.

While the conditions in the real estate market may at times be different from local business conditions, there is usually a close relationship between them. For example, real estate markets may be relatively inactive after a major local building boom even though other types of local business remain at high levels.

## Employment and Incomes

As we have pointed out, an analysis of local economic trends is often the starting point for the analysis of the local real estate market or some sector of that market. This was discussed in the preceding chapter. Recent changes in employment or incomes have a vital influence on all phases of local real estate market activity. Of special significance, of course, are potential developments that are likely to strengthen or diminish the demand for specific types of properties. Such potential developments must be related directly to the specific market problem that is being studied. As the discussion in Chapter 5 indicates, income appears to be the primary factor in the demand for real estate. This point cannot be stressed too strongly in market analysis. If local incomes are good and income prospects are favorable, the real estate market is likely to be active (unless there has been a great surge of building). Even though no new residents are attracted to the city, higher incomes will mean an increase in the demand for housing. Heavier spending will lead to greater demand for commercial property. Thus, demand for real estate can rise in a locality even though there has been no major increase in population. Similarly, demand will fall with a decline in incomes, even if there has been no loss of population.

It is very important in analyzing real estate markets, especially with respect to residential or shopping developments, to know what sections of the city are occupied by high, middle, or low income families. For cities of 50,000 population or over many census data are available on a census tract basis such as the average monthly rent and the average value of owner-occupied houses. These give indications of income ranges in an area.

## General Population Changes

Analyses of the local economy often provide a helpful approach to the prediction of future population trends. Past trends of population growth for census periods can be obtained from the U. S. Census of population.

The best single method of estimating the current population of most urban areas outside of central cities is to ascertain the total number of new dwelling units that have been added to the given areas since the preceding census as indicated by building permits. This total of new dwelling units may be multiplied by the average size of the family in the area in the last census to obtain the estimated additions to the population since that time. It may be preferable to secure data on the number of completed dwelling units since the preceding census from the electrical inspector's or assessor's office, but these figures on completed dwelling units are not always available and they do not differ materially from

**TABLE 9–1.    America's 50 Biggest Cities—from Final Census Reports, U. S. News and World Report, Feb. 22, 1971**

| 1970 Rank | 1970 Population | Change Since 1960 | | 1960 Rank |
|---|---|---|---|---|
| 1. New York | 7,867,760 | Up | 1.1% | 1 |
| 2. Chicago | 3,366,957 | Down | 5.2% | 2 |
| 3. Los Angeles | 2,816,061 | Up | 13.6% | 3 |
| 4. Philadelphia | 1,948,609 | Down | 2.7% | 4 |
| 5. Detroit | 1,511,482 | Down | 9.5% | 5 |
| 6. Houston | 1,232,802 | Up | 31.4% | 7 |
| 7. Baltimore | 905,759 | Down | 3.5% | 6 |
| 8. Dallas | 844,401 | Up | 24.2% | 14 |
| 9. Washington | 756,510 | Down | 1.0% | 9 |
| 10. Cleveland | 750,903 | Down | 14.3% | 8 |
| 11. Indianapolis | 744,624 | Up | 56.3% | 26 |
| 12. Milwaukee | 717,099 | Down | 3.3% | 11 |
| 13. San Francisco | 715,674 | Down | 3.3% | 12 |
| 14. San Diego | 696,769 | Up | 21.6% | 18 |
| 15. San Antonio | 654,153 | Up | 11.3% | 17 |
| 16. Boston | 641,071 | Down | 8.1% | 13 |
| 17. Memphis | 623,530 | Up | 25.3% | 22 |
| 18. St. Louis | 622,236 | Down | 17.0% | 10 |
| 19. New Orleans | 593,471 | Down | 5.4% | 15 |
| 20. Phoenix | 581,562 | Up | 32.4% | 29 |
| 21. Columbus, Ohio | 539,677 | Up | 14.5% | 28 |
| 22. Seattle | 530,831 | Down | 4.7% | 19 |
| 23. Jacksonville | 528,865 | Up | 163.1% | 61 |
| 24. Pittsburgh | 520,117 | Down | 13.9% | 16 |
| 25. Denver | 514,678 | Up | 4.2% | 23 |
| 26. Kansas City, Mo. | 507,087 | Up | 6.6% | 27 |
| 27. Atlanta | 496,973 | Up | 2.0% | 24 |
| 28. Buffalo | 462,768 | Down | 13.1% | 20 |
| 29. Cincinnati | 452,524 | Down | 10.0% | 21 |
| 30. Nashville | 447,877 | Up | 162.1% | 73 |
| 31. San Jose | 445,779 | Up | 118.3% | 57 |
| 32. Minneapolis | 434,400 | Down | 10.0% | 25 |
| 33. Fort Worth | 393,476 | Up | 10.4% | 34 |
| 34. Toledo | 383,818 | Up | 20.7% | 39 |
| 35. Portland, Oreg. | 382,619 | Up | 2.7% | 32 |
| 36. Newark | 382,417 | Down | 5.6% | 30 |
| 37. Oklahoma City | 366,481 | Up | 13.0% | 37 |
| 38. Oakland | 361,561 | Down | 1.6% | 33 |
| 39. Louisville | 361,472 | Down | 7.5% | 31 |
| 40. Long Beach | 358,633 | Up | 4.2% | 35 |
| 41. Omaha | 347,328 | Up | 15.2% | 42 |
| 42. Miami | 334,859 | Up | 14.8% | 44 |
| 43. Tulsa | 331,638 | Up | 26.7% | 50 |
| 44. Honolulu | 324,871 | Up | 10.4% | 43 |
| 45. El Paso | 322,261 | Up | 16.5% | 46 |
| 46. St. Paul | 309,980 | Down | 1.1% | 40 |
| 47. Norfolk | 307,951 | Up | 1.0% | 41 |
| 48. Birmingham | 300,910 | Down | 11.7% | 36 |
| 49. Rochester, N. Y. | 296,233 | Down | 7.0% | 38 |
| 50. Tampa | 277,767 | Up | 1.0% | 48 |

**Note:** In some cases—Jacksonville, Indianapolis and Nashville, for example —the increase in population since 1960 is at least in part the result of annexation of suburban areas.

building permit figures, since nearly all permits result in completed units. Allowance must always be made for vacancies, when the increase in population is estimated by new dwelling units. Conversions and doubling up may also be factors of importance in central cities.

The number of occupied housing units for each block in each city or urban area with a population of 50,000 or more is usually given in the United States Census of Housing. The population and number of occupied units, the median family income, and other data are usually available for each urban place of 2,500 population or more and for every county in all of the states.

Good alternative methods of estimating present population are based on the number of electric meters, since nearly every family has a meter, or on the number of water meters. The current population can be estimated by multiplying the present number of electric or water meters by the ratio of population to number of meters at time of last census.

### Special Population Information

The ratio between elementary school enrollment and population has fluctuated in recent years and varies greatly between city and suburban areas. School population is increasing more rapidly than total population in many areas, particularly in the newer suburbs, and less rapidly in older areas of cities.

Information about births and deaths for each year can be secured from city or county offices. Differences can be computed for each year, thus indicating population changes due to natural causes. Relating this to total population changes indicates net migration to or from the area. Often, local chambers of commerce or similar organizations have information of this type available. Visitation programs for new arrivals to the city may provide useful information. Also, rough estimates can be made through listings in telephone directories or numbers of gas or electric meters connected or disconnected.

While the general trend of population is important, some information should be secured about the marriage rate, since this indicates the rapidity with which new families are being established. Adjustments should be made for divorces, although a divorce does not necessarily lead to a reduction in the demand for housing. In many cases divorces lead to an increase rather than a decrease in the demand for space. Information about the number of marriage licenses and divorces can be secured from county offices.

Similarly, it is important to procure information on the extent to which doubling up or the sharing of dwellings by several families is taking place. Definite information seldom can be obtained, and estimates must be relied upon. Usually the extent of doubling up depends on general

**TABLE 9–2.**   **Population of Age Groups, Estimates 1929–1970, and Projections 1975–1985, in Thousands of Persons— Department of Commerce, Bureau of the Census**

| July 1 | Total | Age (years) | | | | | | |
|---|---|---|---|---|---|---|---|---|
| | | Under 5 | 5–15 | 16–19 | 20–24 | 25–44 | 45–64 | 65 and over |
| **Estimates:** | | | | | | | | |
| 1929 | 121,767 | 11,734 | 26,800 | 9,127 | 10,694 | 35,862 | 21,076 | 6,474 |
| 1930 | 123,077 | 11,372 | 26,983 | 9,220 | 10,915 | 36,309 | 21,573 | 6,705 |
| 1931 | 124,040 | 11,179 | 26,984 | 9,259 | 11,003 | 36,654 | 22,031 | 6,928 |
| 1932 | 124,840 | 10,903 | 26,969 | 9,284 | 11,077 | 36,988 | 22,473 | 7,147 |
| 1933 | 125,579 | 10,612 | 26,897 | 9,302 | 11,152 | 37,319 | 22,933 | 7,363 |
| 1934 | 126,374 | 10,331 | 26,796 | 9,331 | 11,238 | 37,662 | 23,435 | 7,582 |
| 1935 | 127,250 | 10,170 | 26,645 | 9,381 | 11,317 | 37,987 | 23,947 | 7,804 |
| 1936 | 128,053 | 10,044 | 26,415 | 9,461 | 11,375 | 38,288 | 24,444 | 8,027 |
| 1937 | 128,825 | 10,009 | 26,062 | 9,578 | 11,411 | 38,589 | 24,917 | 8,258 |
| 1938 | 129,825 | 10,176 | 25,631 | 9,717 | 11,453 | 38,954 | 25,387 | 8,508 |
| 1939 | 130,880 | 10,418 | 25,179 | 9,822 | 11,519 | 39,354 | 25,823 | 8,764 |
| 1940 | 132,122 | 10,579 | 24,811 | 9,895 | 11,690 | 39,868 | 26,249 | 9,031 |
| 1941 | 133,402 | 10,850 | 24,516 | 9,840 | 11,807 | 40,383 | 26,718 | 9,288 |
| 1942 | 134,860 | 11,301 | 24,231 | 9,730 | 11,955 | 40,861 | 27,196 | 9,584 |
| 1943 | 136,739 | 12,016 | 24,093 | 9,607 | 12,064 | 41,420 | 27,671 | 9,867 |
| 1944 | 138,397 | 12,524 | 23,949 | 9,561 | 12,062 | 42,016 | 28,138 | 10,147 |
| 1945 | 139,928 | 12,979 | 23,907 | 9,361 | 12,036 | 42,521 | 28,630 | 10,494 |
| 1946 | 141,389 | 13,244 | 24,103 | 9,119 | 12,004 | 43,027 | 29,064 | 10,828 |
| 1947 | 144,126 | 14,406 | 24,468 | 9,097 | 11,814 | 43,657 | 29,498 | 11,185 |
| 1948 | 146,631 | 14,919 | 25,209 | 8,952 | 11,794 | 44,288 | 29,931 | 11,538 |
| 1949 | 149,188 | 15,607 | 25,852 | 8,788 | 11,700 | 44,916 | 30,405 | 11,921 |
| 1950 | 152,271 | 16,410 | 26,721 | 8,542 | 11,680 | 45,672 | 30,849 | 12,397 |
| 1951 | 154,878 | 17,333 | 27,279 | 8,446 | 11,552 | 46,103 | 31,362 | 12,803 |
| 1952 | 157,553 | 17,312 | 28,894 | 8,414 | 11,350 | 46,495 | 31,884 | 13,203 |
| 1953 | 160,184 | 17,638 | 30,227 | 8,460 | 11,062 | 46,786 | 32,394 | 13,617 |
| 1954 | 163,026 | 18,057 | 31,480 | 8,637 | 10,832 | 47,001 | 32,942 | 14,076 |
| 1955 | 165,931 | 18,566 | 32,682 | 8,744 | 10,714 | 47,194 | 33,506 | 14,525 |
| 1956 | 168,903 | 19,003 | 33,994 | 8,916 | 10,616 | 47,379 | 34,057 | 14,938 |
| 1957 | 171,984 | 19,494 | 35,272 | 9,195 | 10,603 | 47,440 | 34,591 | 15,388 |
| 1958 | 174,882 | 19,887 | 36,445 | 9,543 | 10,756 | 47,337 | 35,109 | 15,806 |
| 1959 | 177,830 | 20,175 | 37,368 | 10,215 | 10,969 | 47,192 | 35,663 | 16,248 |
| 1960 | 180,684 | 20,364 | 38,504 | 10,698 | 11,116 | 47,134 | 36,208 | 16,659 |
| 1961 | 183,756 | 20,657 | 39,768 | 11,093 | 11,408 | 47,061 | 36,756 | 17,013 |
| 1962 | 186,656 | 20,746 | 41,168 | 11,258 | 11,889 | 46,968 | 37,316 | 17,311 |
| 1963 | 189,417 | 20,750 | 41,620 | 12,061 | 12,620 | 46,932 | 37,869 | 17,565 |
| 1964 | 192,120 | 20,670 | 42,294 | 12,819 | 13,154 | 46,881 | 38,438 | 17,863 |
| 1965 | 194,592 | 20,404 | 42,963 | 13,563 | 13,679 | 46,807 | 39,015 | 18,162 |
| 1966 | 196,920 | 19,811 | 43,822 | 14,304 | 14,063 | 46,855 | 39,601 | 18,464 |
| 1967 | 199,114 | 19,168 | 44,488 | 14,167 | 15,178 | 47,084 | 40,224 | 18,804 |
| 1968 | 201,184 | 18,506 | 44,978 | 14,338 | 15,748 | 47,621 | 40,827 | 19,134 |
| 1969 | 203,216 | 17,960 | 45,260 | 14,655 | 16,484 | 47,994 | 41,393 | 19,470 |
| 1970 [1] | 205,395 | 17,741 | 45,289 | 15,082 | 17,176 | 48,388 | 41,893 | 19,825 |
| **Projections:** [2] | | | | | | | | |
| 1975: Series C | 217,557 | 19,968 | 42,761 | } 16,610 | 19,205 | 53,927 | 43,583 | 21,503 |
| Series D | 215,588 | 18,187 | 42,592 | | | | | |
| 1980: Series C | 232,412 | 23,245 | 42,037 | } 16,892 | 20,911 | 62,302 | 43,533 | 23,492 |
| Series D | 227,510 | 20,305 | 40,074 | | | | | |
| 1985: Series C | 249,248 | 25,791 | 47,301 | } 14,442 | 20,933 | 71,867 | 43,439 | 25,474 |
| Series D | 240,925 | 22,356 | 42,412 | | | | | |

[1] Data for 1970 are based on the 1960 Census. The total tabulation for July 1, 1970 based on the 1970 Census is 204,835,000. Data by age on this basis are not yet available.

[2] Two of four series projected by the cohort method and based on different assumptions with regard to completed fertility, which moves gradually toward a level of 2,775 children per 1,000 women for Series C and 2,450 children per 1,000 women for Series D. For further explanation of method of projection and for additional data, see "Population Estimates and Projections, Current Population Reports, Series P–25, No. 448," August 6, 1970.

Note.—Data for Armed Forces overseas included beginning 1940. Includes Alaska and Hawaii beginning 1950.

economic conditions. If there is much of it, a margin of vacant homes will appear even though no people leave the city. Hence, estimates of this type are necessary to supplement data on population changes.

## Changes in Preferences and Tastes

Consumers of real estate resources and services include the entire population and range from large corporations to single individuals. Within any real estate market, whether it is the market for industrial property in a certain city, the market for shopping center sites or subdivisions, or the market for rental housing, shifts may occur in the preferences and tastes of the customers involved. Such shifts may be very difficult to identify or to evaluate. Consumers of housing may be attracted by design or style changes; consumers of industrial real estate by efficient and convenient layouts of space; and consumers of retailing areas by ease of access and flexibility. At one time, one set of factors may be in favor; at another time, others will predominate.[2]

Many real estate decision makers rely on their own experience and observation of market changes to guide them with respect to changes in tastes and preferences. In some cases, surveys are conducted by means of questionnaires or interviews. Various types of controlled experiments may also be undertaken.

In many cases, however, the supplier of real estate resources and services anticipates trends in an almost intuitive way. Surveys of customers and potential customers may not reveal basic shifts in desires and preferences since people are not able to indicate preferences for things with which they are not yet familiar. Once available, however, customers may flock to buy. Ranch houses, split levels, and town houses have enjoyed popularity at various times but the determination of why or when has been a difficult process.

## Financing Conditions

Next to incomes, the terms and availability of financing are the primary factors in determining the strength or weakness of demand for real estate. When financing is available on liberal terms and at low interest rates, the demand for property is strengthened. Rigorous financing terms tend to limit demand.

Financing conditions may vary between different sectors of the real estate market. Financing may vary between regions and cities. Generally, financing tends to be more readily available in eastern areas than in southern or western regions.

[2] See Anthony Downs, "Current Economic Trends: Impact Upon Appraisal of Real Estate," *The Appraisal Journal* (April 1971).

As we have pointed out, the mortgage market does not operate independently of the other capital markets. Hence, the availability of financing for real estate projects is dependent in part on the alternative uses for funds in other types of projects.

Information in regard to the terms and availability of funds for real estate financing may be secured from such sources as the Federal Reserve *Bulletin, The Federal Home Loan Bank Board Journal,* the publications of the regional Federal Reserve Banks and Federal Home Loan Banks, from financial newspapers and magazines, and from institutions which engage in real estate finance, such as insurance companies, banks, and savings and loan associations.

### Construction Volume and Costs

The rate at which new additions to supply have been made during recent years should be studied by securing figures from city offices on the volume of construction and the number of demolitions. Such data are made available for a number of cities by the Bureau of Labor Statistics and by several commercial services.

Conditions in the building industry should be analyzed carefully. The availability of labor resources and of building materials and their prices require special consideration. The availability of building sites and the prices of available land need to be determined. Also, special attention should be given to changes and potential changes in building technology since this may affect construction costs. The quality and competence of architects often is a factor of importance and should be related to quality and competence of builders and developers.

Data on construction costs can frequently be secured from the city building department. Local real estate boards often assemble data of this type. Several federal agencies publish information on construction costs for a number of cities, and various commercial organizations also supply such data.

Construction costs must be related to selling prices and rents in order to determine future rates of building. When prices and rents are sufficiently above costs to allow a substantial profit margin, building proceeds rapidly. As the spread is narrowed, the rate of building slows down. Less efficient builders are eliminated. When costs exceed sales prices or capitalized rental income, nearly all building ceases.

One of the important elements in building and developing costs is land and the cost of improving it. When the available supply of improved lots has been exhausted, builders may face very large outlays of funds in order to develop new areas. If the market does not exhibit signs of substantial strength, such large-scale projects may be postponed.

**TABLE 9–3.  New Construction Activity, 1929–1971—Value Put in Place, Millions of Dollars—Department of Commerce, Bureau of the Census**

| Year or month | Total new construction | Private construction | | | | | | | Public construction | | |
|---|---|---|---|---|---|---|---|---|---|---|---|
| | | Total | Residential buildings [1] | | Nonresidential buildings and other construction [1] | | | | Total | Federally owned | State and locally owned [5] |
| | | | Total [2] | New housing units | Total | Commercial [3] | Industrial | Other [4] | | | |
| 1929 | 10,793 | 8,307 | 3,625 | 3,040 | 4,682 | 1,135 | 949 | 2,598 | 2,486 | 155 | 2,331 |
| 1930 | 8,741 | 5,883 | 2,075 | 1,570 | 3,808 | 893 | 532 | 2,383 | 2,858 | 209 | 2,649 |
| 1931 | 6,427 | 3,768 | 1,565 | 1,320 | 2,203 | 454 | 221 | 1,528 | 2,659 | 271 | 2,388 |
| 1932 | 3,538 | 1,676 | 630 | 485 | 1,046 | 223 | 74 | 749 | 1,862 | 333 | 1,529 |
| 1933 | 2,879 | 1,231 | 470 | 290 | 761 | 130 | 176 | 455 | 1,648 | 516 | 1,132 |
| 1934 | 3,720 | 1,509 | 625 | 380 | 884 | 173 | 191 | 520 | 2,211 | 626 | 1,585 |
| 1935 | 4,232 | 1,999 | 1,010 | 710 | 989 | 211 | 158 | 620 | 2,233 | 814 | 1,419 |
| 1936 | 6,497 | 2,981 | 1,565 | 1,210 | 1,416 | 290 | 266 | 860 | 3,516 | 797 | 2,719 |
| 1937 | 6,999 | 3,903 | 1,875 | 1,475 | 2,028 | 387 | 492 | 1,149 | 3,096 | 776 | 2,320 |
| 1938 | 6,980 | 3,560 | 1,990 | 1,620 | 1,570 | 285 | 232 | 1,053 | 3,420 | 717 | 2,703 |
| 1939 | 8,198 | 4,389 | 2,680 | 2,270 | 1,709 | 292 | 254 | 1,163 | 3,809 | 759 | 3,050 |
| 1940 | 8,682 | 5,054 | 2,985 | 2,560 | 2,069 | 348 | 442 | 1,279 | 3,628 | 1,182 | 2,446 |
| 1941 | 11,957 | 6,206 | 3,510 | 3,040 | 2,696 | 409 | 801 | 1,486 | 5,751 | 3,751 | 2,000 |
| 1942 | 14,075 | 3,415 | 1,715 | 1,440 | 1,700 | 155 | 346 | 1,199 | 10,660 | 9,313 | 1,347 |
| 1943 | 8,301 | 1,979 | 885 | 710 | 1,094 | 33 | 156 | 905 | 6,322 | 5,609 | 713 |
| 1944 | 5,259 | 2,186 | 815 | 570 | 1,371 | 56 | 208 | 1,107 | 3,073 | 2,505 | 568 |
| 1945 | 5,809 | 3,411 | 1,276 | 720 | 2,135 | 203 | 642 | 1,290 | 2,398 | 1,737 | 661 |
| 1946 | 12,627 | 10,396 | 4,752 | 3,300 | 5,644 | 1,153 | 1,689 | 2,802 | 2,231 | 865 | 1,366 |
| New series | | | | | | | | | | | |
| 1946 | 14,308 | 12,077 | 6,247 | 4,795 | 5,830 | 1,153 | 1,689 | 2,988 | 2,231 | 865 | 1,366 |
| 1947 | 20,041 | 16,722 | 9,850 | 7,765 | 6,872 | 957 | 1,702 | 4,213 | 3,319 | 840 | 2,479 |
| 1948 | 26,078 | 21,374 | 13,128 | 10,506 | 8,246 | 1,397 | 1,397 | 5,452 | 4,704 | 1,177 | 3,527 |
| 1949 | 26,722 | 20,453 | 12,428 | 10,043 | 8,025 | 1,182 | 972 | 5,871 | 6,269 | 1,488 | 4,781 |
| 1950 | 33,575 | 26,709 | 18,126 | 15,551 | 8,583 | 1,415 | 1,062 | 6,106 | 6,866 | 1,624 | 5,242 |
| 1951 | 35,435 | 26,180 | 15,881 | 13,207 | 10,299 | 1,498 | 2,117 | 6,684 | 9,255 | 2,981 | 6,274 |
| 1952 | 36,828 | 26,049 | 15,803 | 12,851 | 10,246 | 1,137 | 2,320 | 6,789 | 10,779 | 4,185 | 6,594 |
| 1953 | 39,136 | 27,894 | 16,594 | 13,411 | 11,300 | 1,791 | 2,229 | 7,280 | 11,242 | 4,139 | 7,103 |
| 1954 | 41,380 | 29,668 | 18,187 | 14,931 | 11,481 | 2,212 | 2,030 | 7,239 | 11,712 | 3,428 | 8,284 |
| 1955 | 46,519 | 34,804 | 21,877 | 18,242 | 12,927 | 3,218 | 2,399 | 7,310 | 11,715 | 2,769 | 8,946 |
| 1956 | 47,601 | 34,869 | 20,178 | 16,143 | 14,691 | 3,631 | 3,084 | 7,976 | 12,732 | 2,726 | 10,006 |
| 1957 | 49,139 | 35,080 | 19,006 | 14,736 | 16,074 | 3,564 | 3,557 | 8,953 | 14,059 | 2,974 | 11,085 |
| 1958 | 50,153 | 34,696 | 19,789 | 15,445 | 14,907 | 3,589 | 2,382 | 8,936 | 15,457 | 3,387 | 12,070 |
| 1959 | 55,305 | 39,235 | 24,251 | 19,233 | 14,984 | 3,930 | 2,106 | 8,948 | 16,070 | 3,724 | 12,346 |
| 1960 | 54,632 | 38,769 | 22,975 | 17,279 | 15,794 | 4,180 | 2,851 | 8,763 | 15,863 | 3,622 | 12,241 |
| 1961 | 56,292 | 39,144 | 23,107 | 17,074 | 16,037 | 4,674 | 2,780 | 8,583 | 17,148 | 3,879 | 13,269 |
| 1962 | 59,965 | 42,096 | 25,150 | 19,443 | 16,946 | 5,144 | 2,842 | 8,960 | 17,869 | 3,913 | 13,956 |
| 1963 | 64,563 | 45,206 | 27,874 | 21,735 | 17,332 | 4,995 | 2,906 | 9,431 | 19,357 | 4,001 | 15,356 |
| 1964 | 67,413 | 47,030 | 28,010 | 21,786 | 19,020 | 5,396 | 3,565 | 10,059 | 20,383 | 3,898 | 16,485 |
| 1965 | 73,412 | 51,350 | 27,934 | 21,712 | 23,416 | | | | 22,062 | 4,014 | 18,048 |
| 1966 | 76,002 | 51,995 | 25,715 | 19,352 | 26,280 | | | | 24,007 | 3,964 | 20,043 |
| 1967 | 77,503 | 51,967 | 25,568 | 18,985 | 26,399 | | | | 25,536 | 3,475 | 22,061 |
| 1968 | 86,626 | 59,021 | 30,565 | 24,030 | 28,456 | 7,761 | 6,021 | 14,674 | 27,605 | 3,367 | 24,238 |
| 1969 | 93,347 | 65,384 | 33,200 | 25,941 | 32,184 | 9,401 | 6,783 | 16,000 | 27,963 | 3,312 | 24,651 |
| 1970 | 94,265 | 66,147 | 31,748 | 24,156 | 34,399 | 9,754 | 6,538 | 18,107 | 28,118 | 3,312 | 24,806 |
| 1971 [6] | 108,440 | 78,620 | 41,970 | 34,090 | 36,650 | 11,590 | 5,430 | 19,630 | 29,820 | 3,990 | 25,830 |

[1] Beginning 1960, farm residential buildings included in residential buildings; prior to 1960, included in nonresidential buildings and other construction.
[2] Total includes additions and alterations and nonhousekeeping units, not shown separately.
[3] Office buildings, warehouses, stores, restaurants, garages, etc.
[4] Religious, educational, hospital and institutional, miscellaneous nonresidential, farm, public utilities, and all other private.
[5] Includes Federal grants-in-aid for State and locally owned projects.
[6] Preliminary estimates by Council of Economic Advisers.

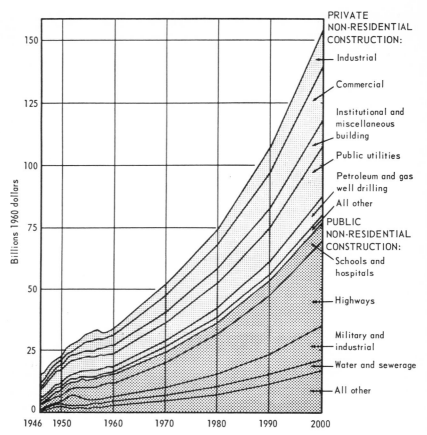

**Fig. 9–1.** Principal categories of nonresidential construction, private and public, medium projections to the year 2000. (Source: *Resources in America's Future,* p. 118.)

## Vacancies

As we indicated above, the vacancy rate is one of the important indicators of real estate market conditions and trends. A surplus of vacant units will tend to retard price or rent increases even when demand is strong. Just what is meant by a surplus or deficit of vacant units cannot be defined exactly. The concept varies from one community to another and from one type of property to another. Normal vacancy for houses is usually considered as something less than 5 per cent, for apartments slightly over 5 per cent, and for business units it may run somewhat higher; but these are only rules of thumb which vary from one place to another.

Whenever the supply of vacant units exceeds a normal percentage, the market tends to be depressed. Competition of owners and sellers seeking tenants and buyers forces prices and rents downward and restrains new construction. A decline in the vacancy ratio, on the other hand, may be reflected in an upward movement of rents and prices.

Information about vacancies in various types of properties is frequently collected by local real estate boards. At times the Post Office Department conducts vacancy surveys in various cities. Often local public utility companies or departments will assemble data concerning vacancies, and the publishers of local directories may gather information of this type at periodic intervals. Conferences with major property managers often provide useful data. It is desirable that vacancy ratios be computed separately for different classes of property, for it frequently happens that one part of a market will have a shortage of space while another has a surplus.

### Price and Rent Trends

Any persistent changes in market prices or rents upward or downward reflect basic market conditions. Sometimes these movements are of short duration, but if they persist for a year or more it may usually be presumed that the trend will continue for a time.

On occasion real estate brokers test the market by advertising a popular type of property at a very reasonable price or rental. They are then able to gauge market conditions by the number of responses received to the advertisement.

Of special importance is the variation between listing and actual selling prices. Similarly the difference between the rental rate asked and finally paid is a reflection of the strength of the market.

The length of time new properties remain on the market before being sold or rented indicates the strength or weakness of demand. When long periods are required to dispose of property, the market is weakening. This assumes, of course, that prices have been set on a reasonably competitive basis.

### Market Activity and Trends

After the factors outlined above have been studied, it should be possible to make reasonably sound estimates of future market trends. This involves determining the present position of the market in relation to past conditions. Variations in market activity are reflected in the number of real estate transfers. Such information may be secured from the volume of deeds recorded in county recorders' offices. The number of mortgages recorded is available from the same sources, as is information about the volume of foreclosures.

Studies of these data covering fairly long periods of time are desirable. Data on deeds, mortgages, and foreclosures may be related to population trends; vacancy ratios; price, rent, and cost indexes; and the volume of construction. Such relationships provide a good indication of the present position of the market with regard to past periods.

### Relative Prices and Relationships

Of major importance in studying market conditions and trends are *relative prices*. For example, construction costs may be rising, but rents and selling prices may be rising even more rapidly. Hence, further construction may be expected to take place despite the advancing costs. Furthermore, an upward or downward trend in prices and rents may cause buyers, investors, and property users to expect still further changes in the same direction and accentuate the trend that has been developing.

A reduction in financing charges may stimulate market activity, even though no other basic change has occurred. Favorable terms of sale, such as smaller down payments and longer periods in which to repay loans, may stimulate the market. Rising incomes may have only a limited effect if real estate rents and sales prices, as well as the prices of other goods and services, are moving up in proportion. In other words *real incomes* rather than monetary incomes deserve primary consideration.

It is well to remember also that real estate resources are in competition with other goods and services for a slice of the consumer's or the businessman's dollar. The real estate market does not operate in a compartment that is separated from other markets. It is an integral part of the entire economic system, and real estate market changes must always be considered in relation to other developments in the local or national economy.

## HOUSING MARKET ANALYSIS

The analysis of a housing market involves application of the pertinent factors outlined above to the residential rather than to other sectors of the real estate market. After careful definition of the specific problem under consideration, the analysis proceeds to a consideration of the major demand, supply, and price factors involved.

## Housing Demand

Expanding economic opportunities will bring people into a city from elsewhere and stimulate the demand for housing. Rising incomes even without expansion of employment may also lead to heavier housing demand. Thus, economic base and similar types of analyses are often helpful in housing market studies.

In relating income levels to housing demand, it is necessary to consider incomes in relation to house prices. As a rule, families cannot afford to pay more than about 2½ times their annual income for a house. Consequently, a good housing market analysis requires that an income distribution of the families in the area be secured. Data of these types are available from census materials by census tracts in metropolitan regions and for cities, towns, and counties. Such census reports also indicate the number of owner-occupied and rental units by price and rent brackets.

Closely related to income, cost, and price factors are financing considerations. If financing is available on easy terms, demand may be maintained even though incomes are not advancing. Conversely, if financing terms are not favorable, housing demand may be reduced rapidly, even though incomes are steady or advancing. Changes in the terms of financing may have an even greater impact on the market than changes in incomes because of the large proportion of borrowed funds that go into most house purchases. For example, extending the term of the mortgage reduces the monthly payments of the home buyer.

## Housing Supply

The supply of new dwelling units can be estimated on the basis of new building permits and the number of water meters or electric meters added. Data of this type can be broken down by districts and can be related to base periods such as those for which census materials are available.

A long period of strong building activity may indicate the possibility of a weakening market, especially if vacancies are rising and new houses are remaining on the market for long periods of time before being sold. Also, construction costs must be studied in relationship to current prices to determine whether it is likely to be profitable for builders to continue high volumes of construction activity.

Efficiency of building and low sales prices will stimulate demand. Larger builders, both those with large-scale on-site operations and prefabricators, have been able to stimulate demand in this way. However, whenever market prices fall below the amount for which the most efficient builders can and will construct houses, few will be added to the supply.

As we have suggested above, changes in design or style may appeal to changing tastes and preferences of house buyers. Changes in technology may make design and style changes possible.

## MARKET ANALYSIS FOR BUSINESS REAL ESTATE

Analysis of markets may be undertaken for a variety of business real estate. Here we will consider briefly shopping centers, individual stores, office space and industrial space. Our discussions will be short and should not be considered as more than suggestive of the types of analyses that may be undertaken.

### Shopping Centers

A market analysis to determine the soundness of a new shopping center requires consideration of special sets of factors in addition to those involved in the analysis of broader divisions of the real estate market. A general outline of a shopping center market analysis is presented below.

1. The size of the trade area is determined by the location of competing centers, by location of mass transportation routes, and by related factors. The time or distance from the center is not the vital factor. Families will drive long distances to reach a large shopping center if there is no similar facility near them. They will not drive even a short distance if they live within walking distance of a major shopping district. Most of the recently developed large regional shopping centers depend upon customers who arrive in automobiles. Families living near subways, elevated stations, or suburban railroad stations often prefer to shop in central shopping districts.

The size of the trade area varies with the type of center. It is broadest for a regional center with a large department store, smaller for a center with a junior department store, still smaller for a center with a variety store as the principal unit, and only neighborhood-wide for a center with a supermarket and drugstore as the chief units. The size of the trade area can best be determined by taking a sample survey of housewives to determine where they shop.

2. After determining the extent of the trade area, the next step is to estimate the number of families in each census tract, community, or district of the trade area. This is accomplished by adding to the number of dwelling units shown by the most recent United States Census the number of new dwelling units added since that time as reflected by building permits, electric meters, or water meters.

3. The average family income in each census tract or community is estimated on the basis of U.S. Census reports. Adjustments for intervening years between the last census and the date of the market analysis can be

made by applying the average increase in per capita income for the state in which the center is located, using the midpoint of the income brackets as the average. Aggregate income of each community is determined by multiplying the number of families by the average income.

4. The next step is to estimate the volume of retail purchases for each type of store planned for the center as of the date of the survey. It is estimated that all families above the lowest income level spend about the same percentage of their incomes for clothing, shoes, furniture, and other fashion goods. The percentage of income which families spend in each metropolitan area in each type of store may be determined by relating total metropolitan area retail sales in each type of store to the total family income of the region or state as indicated by the U.S. Retail Census.

5. On the basis of questionnaires or sample surveys, an estimate may be made of the proportion of their income which families in the area will spend in each type of store planned for the shopping center in its first year of full operation.

6. The total sales of each type of store at the center being studied may be estimated by adding expected purchases from each segment of the trade area, taking into account the competition of other centers.

7. The store area required for the new center is estimated on the basis of expected average sales per square foot for each type of store. Parking area is calculated on a ratio of parking to store area.

8. The cost of constructing the center is estimated on the basis of current square foot cost for the number of square feet of store area required.

9. The rentals are estimated on the basis of percentages customarily paid by each type of store on the volume of sales.

10. The net return is estimated by deducting from the gross rents the annual charges for interest, maintenance of the buildings, real estate taxes, insurance, and allowances for vacancies and management fees.

11. The future sales at the center are based on estimates of the future growth of population and income of the trade area.

### Individual Stores

Surveys may be made for single stores as well as for shopping districts. For example, a survey may be made for the purpose of determining whether a new drugstore or hardware store can thrive in a specific location. In this case, the competition of other stores must be noted, the extent of the trade area from which the local neighborhood draws customers estimated, and the number of families and income of the families in that trade area determined. From these data, the total purchases for the type of store under consideration in the trade area will be estimated. Knowing the experience of their own type or a similar type of store in other neighborhoods with similar populations and incomes, the store company will decide whether sufficient volume of sales could be developed to warrant paying the rents for which stores could be obtained in the given location.

It is always necessary to estimate the potential growth of the trade area. An important factor is the amount of vacant land suitable for new homes in that area. It is desirable to ascertain the future program of builders for new home construction and to consult with telephone company and electric power company engineers as to their predictions for the future growth of the specific neighborhood or trade area.

## Office Space

The potential demand for new office space in a city may be estimated by determining the number of occupied square feet of office space per capita for the metropolitan region. In large commercial and financial cities, 5 to 6 square feet of office space is needed for each person in the metropolitan area. This ratio must be determined for each city, since wide variations prevail. The amount of new office space potentially required may be estimated for each city on the basis of growth prospects and its prospects for development as a regional commercial and financial center.

Such general estimates, of course, should be related to current vacancy ratios, rents, construction costs, and the terms and availabilty of financing. Cycles in office building net income are of longer duration than those of general business. A period of overbuilding may produce a surplus of office space, which depresses rents and net income for a long time thereafter.

It has been estimated that 2 square feet of office space per capita is adequate for most "normal" requirements. Thus, any space above such a figure indicates the extent to which a city is a national or regional office center. For example, San Diego has 2.2 square feet of office space per capita; New York, 16 square feet; and Chicago, 7.5 square feet.

## Industrial Space

In making surveys of available factory space, industrial buildings should be classified into one-story buildings and multi-storied buildings. The buildings should also be classified as to age, condition, and as to whether they have direct switch track connections. There may be a surplus of space in old multi-storied buildings but a scarcity of one-story factory buildings. Rental rates or sale prices of buildings offered for rent or sale should be obtained. Usually surveys of this type are made by the utility companies, such as the Commonwealth Edison Company of Chicago, with a view to attracting new industries to their region.

## MARKET SURVEYS FOR RENEWAL PURPOSES

In planning redevelopment or renewal of residential areas, surveys should be made to determine what types of dwelling units are preferred, how many rooms are desired in typical dwelling units, what proportion should be for sale or rent, and the potential demand in each price range.

### Importance of Interviews

Interviews with a sample number of families in every census tract in a proposed renewal area are often helpful to ascertain how many families desire to move, the relation of the rent paid or the value of their homes to income, what type of dwelling unit is preferred by those who desired to move—row house, apartment, or detached house—whether they preferred to own or rent, and what rent or price they can afford to pay. Such surveys may be used as the basis for deciding what proportion of row houses, detached houses, and apartments should be built in the redeveloped area. Such surveys help to indicate the types of housing units in greatest demand and at what price or rental range. They also enable developers to avoid some of the mistakes that have been made in building large projects without analyzing local housing needs, preferences, and ability to pay.

### Potential Needs and Demands

Careful analysis of the preferences of customers often helps to avoid error in a renewal program or in other types of real estate projects. Such analysis may point toward needs and wants that are not being adequately met by the market (including governmental as well as privately developed programs) and thus form the basis for creative advances over time.

Surveys may also be conducted to determine whether there will be a demand for office buildings, hotels, and stores sufficient to warrant their inclusion in a renewal project. Current trends point to more and more large-scale, multipurpose renewal efforts.

## SUMMARY

This chapter presents general guides to the analysis of various real estate markets. It is essential to know the purpose for which any analysis is undertaken, and purpose indicates whether long-run or short-run considerations will be dominant.

In the analysis of any real estate market, the following factors are usually applicable:

1. General business conditions.
2. Local business conditions.
3. Employment and incomes.
4. General population changes.
5. Special population information.
6. Changes in tastes and preferences.
7. Financing conditions.
8. The volume and costs of construction activity.
9. Prices, rents, vacancy rates, and other indicators of market conditions.

These and related factors help to make estimates of future market changes. Factors related to income are of primary importance in estimating the demand for real estate; of almost equal importance are the terms and availability of financing.

Suggestions related to market analyses for housing, shopping centers, individual stores, office and industrial space, and also for redevelopment and renewal purposes are also presented.

## QUESTIONS FOR STUDY

1. If demand in the real estate market rises, what will happen to prices and rents? Over the longer run what will happen to supply? Explain.
2. Is there usually a relationship between the volume of real estate activity and the level of local business conditions?
3. How do monopoly elements in the real estate market contribute to inner-city housing problems?
4. Describe the processes of expansion in real estate markets; the processes of contraction.
5. Which economic variables might produce a downturn in real estate activity on the national level?
6. What reasons can you give to substantiate the argument that there is a national cycle in real estate market activity. Do you concur in this position? Why or why not?
7. Why does the purpose of a real estate market analysis play such a large role?
8. List and explain the major factors to be considered in making a real estate market analysis.
9. Indicate the types of data in each of the following categories that you could profitably employ in making a market analysis: (a) population, (b) employment, (c) building costs, (d) financing, (e) incomes, and (f) vacancies.
10. What is the relationship of economic base analysis to real estate market analysis?
11. Prepare an outline for estimating population in the current year for the city in which your study property is located.

12. Which special factors would you consider in making a market analysis for a shopping center? For an individual store in a shopping center?
13. How would you go about analyzing the demand for office space in your city? For industrial locations?
14. Why is market analysis important in real estate decision making?

## SUGGESTED READINGS

Lusk, David J., Donald Taylor, and Hugh Wales. *Marketing Research* (3d ed.). Englewood Cliffs, N.J.: Prentice-Hall, Inc., 1969.
Manheim, Uriel. *How To Do Housing Market Research*, Handbook for Local Home Builders Associations. Washington, D.C.: National Association of Home Builders of the United States, 1963.

*Economic Indicators* (published monthly by the Council of Economic Advisers). Washington, D.C.: U.S. Government Printing Office.
*Survey of Buying Power* (published annually in May by *Sales Management*).
*Survey of Current Business* (published monthly by the Department of Commerce). Washington, D.C.: U.S. Government Printing Office.

## STUDY PROJECT 9–1

### The Housing Market of College Town

Frank Olsen, Director of Residences at State College sent the following memorandum to his supervisor, J. A. Jordan, Vice President and Treasurer, State College:

> Students are not renting university housing to the same extent as last year or the year before. Many who would formerly have rented dormitory rooms are renting apartments in town, usually two, three, four or more to an apartment, thus bringing rents into a comparable relationship with dormitory space and giving them whatever benefits they see in off-campus living. Our apartments are renting fairly well; married students find them attractively priced relative to comparable facilities in town. I wonder, however, whether we should proceed with plans to add either to our dormitories or our apartments. I recommend a survey at once so we can make our plans with greater certainty. This survey should cover the apartment house market but should also give us some indication of potential changes in the housing market of College Town in general. If local developers are going to provide adequate facilities, I would recommend that we delay or abandon plans for adding to our housing facilities.

Mr. Jordan replied:

> I agree with your recommendation that a survey of the local housing market in College Town be made. I have called the Bureau of Business and Economic Research and asked if they can do this for us. They can conduct the survey this summer. They will need an indication of the specific types of inforamtion desired. Will you please provide this for Dr. Jack Armstrong, the Director of the Bureau?

A day or so later Mr. Olsen encountered Mr. Jordan at a reception for a visiting lecturer and said, "Jim, about your memo on the housing market. Do you really think the Bureau can handle an assignment like this? I sort of had in mind an outside consulting firm."

"Surveys by outside firms cost a lot of money," Mr. Jordan said. "I think Jack Armstrong runs a good shop. They conducted some student market polls last winter and I had good reports on their work. Seems to me we can give them a summer project and save ourselves some money."

"Well, I don't say they can't do it, but I would feel more comfortable with some real experts surveying our market," Mr. Olsen said.

"The success of the Bureau will depend in part on how well you outline the survey," Mr. Jordan said. "Put together some good instructions and I believe we'll have a good result."

"What kinds of instructions are you thinking about," asked Mr. Olsen.

"Well, you know the things we need. How many apartments are vacant in town? How many are under construction? How many are planned? What about other housing? Are any good houses vacant that married students might rent? What about rents, are they going up or not? How about financing costs? How many students will prefer town housing to college housing. Things like that."

"If we hired an expert consultant, he'd know what to look into," observed Mr. Olsen.

"Probably so," said Mr. Jordan, "but the cost would be high. Let's go ahead with the Bureau, then if we're not satisfied with the result, we can still call in a consulting firm."

"OK—but we may lose five or six months," replied Mr. Olsen.

### Questions

1. Please prepare the memorandum that Mr. Olsen should send to Dr. Armstrong to guide the decisions Mr. Jordan and Mr. Olsen will have to make about their housing programs. Indicate: (a) the general market data needed; (b) the specific formation needed about the college market; and (c) any special types of information that may be helpful. Also indicate possible sources of information of the types needed.
2. Outline a brief housing market analysis for College Town or your home town. What is the outlook for the market in the year ahead?

### STUDY PROJECT 9–2

### Market Survey for Chester Grove Shopping Center

A shopping center has been proposed for the suburban city of Chester. This center is to be called Chester Grove. The developers of the project, Mr. R. A. Maxim and Mr. G. F. Houser, have both been in the real estate business for nine or ten years, but this is their first shopping center project. They have the land under option; the owner wants to participate to the extent of 40 per cent of the selling price of the land. This constitutes eight acres, and he wants $30,000 per acre.

The developers have made estimates of the potential costs and returns for the projected center. They estimate the sales of the center for the first year as in Table 1.

### TABLE 1.    Estimated Sales of Stores at Chester Grove

| Type of Store | Building | Sales | Area in Square Feet | Sales per Square Foot |
|---|---|---|---|---|
| Supermarket | A | $3,000,000 | 18,000 | $167 |
| Furniture | A | 500,000 | 18,000 | 28 |
| Women's lingerie | B | 150,000 | 3,000 | 50 |
| Family shoe store | B | 150,000 | 2,500 | 60 |
| Household appliances, TV | B | 300,000 | 6,500 | 46 |
| Beauty shop | B | 100,000 | 1,500 | 67 |
| Barber shop | B | 60,000 | 860 | 70 |
| Cafeteria | B | 250,000 | 4,040 | 62 |
| Bakery | B | 90,000 | 1,500 | 60 |
| Optician | B | 60,000 | 1,000 | 60 |
| Book store, stationery | B | 100,000 | 1,500 | 67 |
| Drug store | C | 1,000,000 | 15,360 | 65 |
| Cleaning establishment | C | 300,000 | 7,500 | 40 |
| Restaurant | C | 500,000 | 7,860 | 64 |
| Candy | D | 70,000 | 700 | 100 |
| Florist | D | 30,000 | 750 | 40 |
| Greeting cards | D | 40,000 | 550 | 73 |
| Bank | E | – | 1,400 | – |
| Total: all buildings | | $6,700,000 | 92,520 | $ 73.53 |
| Ground area occupied by stores | | | 59,160 | |
| Balance of area for mall and parking or 3.12 times leasable area | | | 289,320 | |
| Total area | | | 348,480 | |

They have also estimated what this might mean in terms of rents as shown in Table 2.

They believe operating expenses will average around 55 cents per square foot of gross leasable area, estimated at 59,160 square feet. This should cover taxes, insurance, exterior maintenance, advertising and management and general administration. This estimate is based on average costs for the area and might vary upward or downward. They believe a vacancy allowance of 10 per cent for local stores would be adequate but that no vacancy allowance would be needed for national chain stores.

**TABLE 2. Estimated Rents of Chester Grove**

| Type of Store | Gross Leasable Area in Square Feet | Minimum Guarantee per Square Foot | Per Cent of Sales | Estimated Sales | Rents Received On Minimum Guarantee 1971 | Rents Received On Percentages 1973 |
|---|---|---|---|---|---|---|
| Building A | | | | | | |
| Supermarket | 18,000 | $2.05 | 1.5 | $3,000,000 | $ 36,500 | $ 45,000 |
| Furniture store | 18,000 | 1.25 | 5 | 500,000 | 22,500 | 25,000 |
| Total Building A | 36,000 | 1.64 | 2 | 3,500,000 | 59,000 | 70,000 |
| Building B | | | | | | |
| Women's lingerie, sportswear | 3,000 | 3.00 | 6 | 150,000 | 9,000 | 9,000 |
| Family shoe store | 2,500 | 2.50 | 5 | 150,000 | 6,250 | 7,500 |
| Household appliances, TV | 6,500 | 1.50 | 5 | 300,000 | 9,750 | 15,000 |
| Beauty shop | 1,500 | 4.00 | 10 | 100,000 | 6,000 | 10,000 |
| Barber shop | 860 | 4.00 | 10 | 60,000 | 3,440 | 6,000 |
| Cafeteria | 4,040 | 2.50 | 6 | 250,000 | 10,100 | 15,000 |
| Bakery | 1,500 | 2.00 | 5 | 90,000 | 3,000 | 4,500 |
| Optician | 1,000 | 3.00 | 10 | 60,000 | 3,000 | 6,000 |
| Book store | 1,500 | 3.00 | 10 | 100,000 | 4,500 | 10,000 |
| Total Building B | 22,400 | 2.46 | 6.6 | 1,260,000 | 55,040 | 83,000 |
| Building C | | | | | | |
| Drug store | 15,360 | 2.20 | 4 | 1,000,000 | 33,790 | 40,000 |
| Cleaners, etc. | 7,500 | 2.00 | 6 | 300,000 | 15,000 | 18,000 |
| Restaurant | 7,860 | 2.00 | 6 | 500,000 | 15,720 | 30,000 |
| Total Building C | 30,720 | 2.10 | 4.9 | 1,800,000 | 64,510 | 88,000 |
| Building D | | | | | | |
| Candy | 700 | 4.00 | 8 | 70,000 | 2,800 | 5,600 |
| Florist | 750 | 2.00 | 8 | 30,000 | 1,500 | 2,400 |
| Greeting cards | 550 | 3.00 | 10 | 40,000 | 1,650 | 4,000 |
| Total Building D | 2,000 | 2.98 | 8.6 | 140,000 | 5,950 | 12,000 |
| Bank | 1,400 | 4.00 | – | – | 5,600 | 5,600 |
| Total All Stores | 92,520 | 2.06 | 3.8 | $6,700,000 | $190,100 | $258,600 |

Construction costs are estimated at $12 per square foot for the 92,520 square feet of buildings; this will provide for paving the parking area, air conditioning, architects fees and interest during construction.

Mr. Maxim and Mr. Houser have not yet arranged a loan. They want some signed leases before approaching a lender. They fear financing costs may be high and are concerned that they may have to give a participation to a lender in order to get a loan.

All of these estimates are overshadowed by their concern about the potential of the area. They have heard that several other shopping centers are under consideration in or near Chester. They fear that even one additional center could be disastrous for their plans if it were built before their center could be put into operation. They are worried about the growth of the Chester area and its competition with the new town of Ardmore that is developing about ten miles away. They can see the potential for one shopping center in the area but no more.

Chester is an area of middle class homes with several new developments in progress. It is estimated that nearly 400 single-family dwellings will be constructed in the area during the year. Several apartment complexes are in the early stages of construction and should add over 1,000 rental units in about 18 months. Good land for development in Chester, however, is in short supply and the land available is going up rapidly in price and in some cases discouraging developers.

The rapid growth of Ardmore is of special concern to Mr. Maxim and Mr. Houser. This new town was started some five years ago approximately ten miles from Chester but in the open countryside where land costs are low and there is plenty of room for development. At first Ardmore grew at a slow and uncertain pace. More recently an electronics industry has located there and growth had advanced sharply. The developers fear that this may mean substantially reduced growth rates for Chester.

### Questions

1. How would you design a market survey for Chester Grove? What types of information are important?
2. How would the growth of Ardmore affect Chester Grove?
3. How much return on investment may be expected in 2 years. Do you feel the estimates presented are reasonably accurate? Why or why not?
4. It is estimated that 300 families can support a shopping center of this size. What does this mean for the future of Chester Grove?

# 10

# Location Analysis:
# Patterns of Land Use

## LOCATION FACTORS IN REAL ESTATE DECISIONS

We have pointed out repeatedly that a real property may be thought of as a fixed but dynamic point on a changeable economic, social and political framework. This framework is made up of the property's immediate environment, its local economy and community, and the broader national and international climate.

In this chapter, we consider location factors related to patterns of land use in the major sectors of cities; in the next chapter, we consider neighborhoods and districts.

### Property Environment

The real estate decision maker has a vital interest in a property's immediate surroundings and in its relationship to other parts of the local area and region. He has an interest in the property's enviroment and in any special physical, economic, governmental or social factors that may improve or impair this environment. We usually refer to these various sets of relationships and particularly to those involving a property's immediate surroundings and its position relative to the local area and region as *location* factors. To a considerable degree, a property's income-producing potential is determined by location factors, conditioned, of course, by market changes and by trends in the local, regional, and national economy.

## Properties as Shares

An urban property may be thought of as a share in the local economy or city and also as a share in a specific area or sector of the city. The economic strength of a city or local economy provides basic support for the values of all of the properties located there. If the local economy expands, however, all properties will not be affected in the same manner or to the same degree; some will benefit greatly, some slightly, and some may be affected adversely.

Similarly, a piece of real estate may be thought of as a share in the immediate neighborhood or district of which it forms a part. A variety of factors are at work constantly to bring about favorable or unfavorable changes in the neighborhoods and districts and in major sectors of urban areas.

## TRENDS AFFECTING STRUCTURE OF LAND USES

Although we have tried to emphasize the importance of location factors in dynamic rather than static terms, it may be helpful to consider briefly some of the forces that are likely to hold particular significance for the real estate decision maker in the years head. As has been said:

Begin with the perspective that the city evolves to expedite the interactions of social and economic activities. The content of these activities is changing, and simultaneously a revolution is taking place in how these activities interact with each other. New organizational factors supplant earlier ones in the evolution of our cities, overcoming inertia and the resistance of entrenched (if vestigial) institutions—sunk capital in the physical plant of the city, legal institutions, behavior patterns. New forces are presenting us with new problems.[1]

### General Trends

We are likely to see gains in per capita incomes and these will hold implications for changes in expenditure patterns and future employment opportunities. Science and technology are bringing major changes in communication patterns. New machines, techniques, and processes are bringing new organizational relationships and hastening the obsolescence of existing plant and equipment which in turn present location decisions. Changes and potential changes in transportation patterns as well as in methods for bearing the costs of transportation are likely to have

[1] Lowdon Wingo, Jr., "Urban Space in a Policy Perspective: An Introduction," in Wingo (ed.) *Cities and Space* (Baltimore: The Johns Hopkins University Press, 1963), p. 11, by permission.

major effects. Less concentration of activity is required due to the nature of the transportation system, the influence of the automobile and improved roads, and related developments. More land can be used efficiently. Problems of air and water pollution will bring efforts toward greater dispersion and distribution of activity.

## Urban Trends

These factors and others related to them, all will have a bearing on the pattern of future land uses. That urban growth will continue is almost beyond question although some slowing down in the rate of expansion seems probable. It is interesting to note that the urban saturation point was almost reached in England in 1890 with 72 per cent of the population living in urban places of 2,000 or more. By 1970 the population in such places had increased only to slightly more than 80 per cent of the total. In the United States 37 per cent lived in urban places of 2,000 or more in 1890, 87 per cent in 1970.[2]

The character of urban growth may change. Present trends suggest further expansion of urban areas with "urban sprawl" continuing as the settled areas spread out. More "interurbias" or "supercities" or new candidates for the designation of "meagalopolis" may emerge as present urban areas grow together. Entirely new cities and towns are emerging such as Reston and Columbia.[3] There may be some tendency to reverse the outward trends as city centers regain some of their earlier appeal as a result of improved transportation and urban renewal programs. Also such tendencies may be reinforced if it becomes possible to spread some of the costs now borne by the central city to suburban areas.

## Competition Between Land Uses

Industrial and commercial locations have tended to spread more widely throughout urban areas in recent years. Residential land uses have become somewhat more fluid; apartment houses are now found mixed up with single-family houses; town houses or row houses are found in a variety of areas. Shopping centers are being scattered throughout urban areas; often a shopping center is a key factor in the success of a new subdivision. Increasingly, industrial developments, many of which are not incompatible with residential uses, are found at scattered locations throughout the urban area. Concepts of "inharmonious" land uses appear to be changing.

---

[2] Homer Hoyt, "The Growth of Cities from 1800 to 1960 and Forecasts to Year 2000," *Land Economics*, XXXIX, No. 2 (May, 1963).

[3] R. Bruce Ricks, "New Town Development and the Theory of Location," *Land Economics* (February 1970).

Downtown business locations compete with locations in outlying areas to an increasing degree.[4] Markets for land generally seem to be broadening as transportation facilities and the increasing use of the car and truck extend the areas over which various land uses can be located to advantage.

The role of the automobile undoubtedly will continue to be a major one in expanding urban land markets. The number of private passenger cars exceeded 89 million by 1970 in comparison to slightly over 20 million in 1933; projections range up to more than 300 million by the end of the century. Of course, a saturation point may be reached before then or new technological advances may shift the demand from automobiles to something else. For example, vehicles that run on "air cushions" may develop. Jet aircraft will play an increasingly dominant role in determining land values of resort areas. Locations that have jet airports and are at the crossroads of international travel routes like Oahu in Hawaii have developed extremely high land values.

The promotional activities of real estate developers and associations of business groups such as the merchants in a shopping center will continue to have a bearing on the competition between land uses. Intercity rivalries also will have an influence.

## Social and Political Competition

Although zoning laws and deed restrictions, as well as other types of regulations, tend to limit competition and channel it into specific directions, there continues to be intense competition between land uses and within classes of land uses. To some degree, zoning laws and related forms of regulation have become another form of competition between land developers, investors, and users. Developers tend to seek those jurisdictions in a metropolitan area that have a minimum of zoning restrictions as to lot size, type of use, utility requirements, and tax levels.

In other words, competition may take social and political forms. Labor and political organizations sometimes provide the basis for competition between land uses and between neighborhoods. Special efforts are being made to disperse rather than to concentrate low income groups.[5] We should note also that all types of business competition cannot be explained by economic considerations alone.

Governmental and political factors will exert growing influences on the future pattern of land uses. Their general character may change;

---

[4] Arthur M. Weimer, "Investors and Downtown Real Estate," Technical Bulletin No. 39 (Washington, D.C.: Urban Land Institute, 1960).

[5] The President's Task Force on Low Income Housing, "Toward Better Housing For Low Income Families" (Washington, D.C.: Government Printing Office, 1970).

for example, there may be a resurgence of interest in local governmental and political activity. Tax sharing between national and local governments may emerge. The effect of a heavier tax burden in one neighborhood than in a competing one will continue to merit the atttention of the real estate decision maker as will such factors as fire and police protection, control of traffic, location of traffic arteries, zoning laws, and the cost of local governmental services relative to their quality.

### Attitudes and Preferences

Cultural factors and attitudes will surely play an important part in determining the future pattern of land uses, as we have already suggested. For example, we have had a strong trend toward home ownership; this may be modified, of course, but we are fairly certain that home ownership will continue to be highly acceptable in most areas and that neighborhoods of home owners may represent relatively stable areas. Efforts are being made to extend opportunities for home ownership to those in very low income groups. Attitudes toward private property, home ownership, appropriate locations for various lands uses, and many others are important in this connection. Prestige factors also change over time and their importance can easily be overlooked.

The tastes and preferences of people relative to real estate may undergo significant changes. The two-house family may become as popular as the two-car family in the not too distant future. Weekend cottages combined with "near-in" apartments appear to be competing effectively with some types of suburban residences. There may be some renewed interest in "near-in" locations in order to reduce commuting time. Many other changes may emerge as well.

Social unrest and pressures are likely to expand. Primarily, these are related to the increased efforts of blacks and other minority groups to gain wider access to housing in many types of neighborhoods. Increased leisure, broader social and cultural interests, longer life for many, and increased interest in political activities, notably on the local level, are likely to have effects on the location of various land uses.

### Physical Factors

Physical factors such as rivers, swamps, land contour, condition of soil and subsoil, and the like will continue to have a bearing on the location of land uses and the shifts that occur. Environmental problems and controls probably will play a role of growing importance. Depreciation resulting from the physical deterioration of structures or from changes in use or fashion will have an influence, in part physical, in part social and economic. The existing transportation system has both physical and economic implications in regard to present and future land uses. Original locations may have been the result of political considerations as well as economic forces. Future changes or extensions will be the product of such factors but will be influenced greatly by the existing transportation system.

## Planning and Renewal

Concepts of urban planning and renewal may undergo some changes. The President's Task Force on Urban Renewal, for example, states:

> The Federal-local government program of land acquisition, replanning, demolition or rehabilitation, and re-sale—defined in law as "Urban Renewal"—is one instrument for meeting urban problems, but it is only one of the instruments. It cannot be expected to cure all the ills of the cities, of which the most serious are poverty and racial discrimination. In fact, unless carefully planned and administered, the urban renewal program inadvertently may aggravate these other problems:
>
> > While Urban Renewal can eliminate slums at a project site, it may, in the absence of other aids, lead to the intensification of slum conditions and housing shortages in other locations.
> > Urban Renewal can provide sites for housing of any price class, but it cannot produce housing for low and moderate income families unless it is combined with programs for aiding low cost housing such as those included in recent housing bills. On the contrary, by wholesale demolition, it has tended to contribute to the shortage of housing, particularly for families of low income.
> > Urban Renewal cannot end racial discrimination, and indeed, the demolition incidental to a change in land use may lead to an intensification of racial concentration and unrest.
> > Urban Renewal may ultimately increase job opportunities, but the demolition entailed in carrying out the plan may, by destroying local sources of employment, temporarily add to the difficulty of relieving poverty.
>
> In addition, Urban Renewal is limited by the resistance of suburbs to the introduction of families of different race and lower income than the norm of the local community. Its effectiveness has also been blunted by vague and conflicting objectives and by complexity in program and administration within the Department of Housing and Urban Development. This problem has been magnified by the confused and complicated relationships among federal agencies concerned with some aspect of urban conditions and between the federal agencies and the state and local governments with which they must deal.
> Nevertheless, if properly administered and supported with related programs for reducing poverty and building low cost housing, Urban Renewal can be a vital tool for alleviating slum conditions and tensions and for stimulating the physical and economic revitalization of the cities, which serve as the hub and crossroads of our metropolitan areas.[6]

[6] The President's Task Force on Urban Renewal, 1970.

The challenging of previously accepted concepts of desirable neighborhood structure and renewal programs by such writers as Jane Jacobs may lead to significant changes. She says, for example, that she has been trying to:

> . . . introduce new principles of city planning and rebuilding, different and even opposite from those now taught in everything from schools of architecture and planning to the Sunday supplements and women's magazines. My attack is not based on quibbles about rebuilding methods or hairsplitting about fashions in design. It is an attack, rather on the principles and aims that have shaped modern, orthodox city planning and rebuilding.[7]

## Anticipating Changes

All this suggests that the future structure and pattern of land uses will be determined by a wide variety of factors, as has been the case in the past. To some extent, past trends will be helpful, but it will be important to anticipate, if possible, the major forces that will affect land uses and interrelationships between them in the future.

## URBAN GROWTH AND CHANGE

Our urban areas are highly complex arrangements of many types of land uses serving a wide variety of people. These urban areas are seldom static; they change constantly. For most American cities change has been stimulated primarily by growth. In a few cases, however, change comes about as a result of decline. In some growing cities there are certain areas and sectors which do not share in the benefits of growth.

Efforts have been made to develop general principles and concepts that will help us to understand the processes of urban change. We will consider some of these efforts and their potential significance for the real estate decision maker.

## Stages of Growth

As cities expand they tend to pass through certain stages of development. For example, a city in the initial stage of development is like a small country town.[8] Here there is little competition among various

---

[7] By permission from *The Death and Life of Great American Cities*, by Jane Jacobs, p. 3. Copyright, 1961, Random House, New York.

[8] Professor N. S. B. Gras has pointed out that the form of the village may either be "nucleated," that is, of a very compact form, which is sometimes called a "heap village," or it may be "nonnucleated," that is, spread out, the houses usually being some distance apart and near the field surrounding the village. One example of this is the so-called "long-street village," which is fairly common in Europe, also in Quebec, Nova Scotia, and Maine. See Gras, *An Introduction to Economic History* (New York: Harper & Row, Publishers, 1922), pp. 53–56.

land uses. In general, the major business center is at the point of origin of the town, which may be a crossroads or a railroad intersection, the point at which a river meets the sea, or some similar focal point which caused original settlement there. A few light industries may grow up; if so, they are usually adjacent to the downtown business center. The homes of the merchants, professional groups, and those receiving higher incomes will be located near the stores and the downtown business area, while the homes of the workingmen will be located near the factories. Hence the town will represent a very simple sort of organization.

However, when expansion continues beyond this stage, possible land uses increase in number and intensity. The area of the city will be expanded as a result of population growth, and the intensity of land use at various points will be increased. Various types of uses to which the land was originally put will give way to "higher" uses, or those which will yield a greater return per dollar of investment. For example, establishments which require relatively large areas in relation to business volume will tend to be crowded out of the central parts of a city because of the competition of other types of enterprises with greater rent-paying ability. Because the more powerful activities are able to force out other land uses, this competition for sites causes a constant movement within the city.

Such competition is most intense when the city is expanding. If a city is declining in economic importance, new demands for space are limited; and it is only the most favored locations which are able to earn substantial incomes. It is during periods of rapid growth that the most noticeable changes occur in the uses to which various parcels of real estate are put.

## Methods of Expansion

A city may expand (1) by growing vertically through the replacement of lower structures with higher ones, (2) by filling in open spaces between settled areas, or (3) by extending the existing settled area.

When the settled area is expanded, growth may take several forms, the most important being (1) *concentric circle* or *ring growth* around the central nucleus; (2) *axial growth,* with prongs or fingerlike extensions moving out along main transportation routes; and (3) *suburban growth,* with the establishment of islands of settlements in advance of the main city area. These types of expansion are characteristic of most larger cities. Baltimore was for a long time a good example of ring growth, while New York, Chicago, and Detroit illustrate axial and suburban development.

When both ring growth and axial expansion occur, a star-shaped city structure results. As Hurd pointed out many years ago:

In their methods of growth cities conform always to biological laws, all growth being either *central* or *axial*. In some cities central growth occurs first and in others axial growth, but all cities illustrate both forms of growth and in all cases central growth includes some axial growth and axial growth some central growth. Central growth consists of the clustering of utilities around any point of attraction and is based on proximity, while axial growth is the result of transportation facilities and is based on accessibility.[9]

## Influence of Topography

A city located in the center of a level plain might be expected to grow outward in rings from the main point of origin. However, most of our cities were located at points where their growth was influenced by hills, rivers, and other topographical features. New York, located first at the southern tip of Manhattan Island, could expand only northward until ferries, bridges, and tunnels made growth in other directions possible. Chicago's growth to the east was stopped by Lake Michigan. In some cases the original topography of a site was changed by grading or filling when it became profitable to undertake such projects. For example, Boston was located on a rather narrow peninsula, but the filling-in of the Back Bay and similar areas provided space for expansion. The lake front in Chicago has been extended nearly a mile eastward from the Loop area. The original area of Miami Beach, Florida, was nearly tripled by pumping sand out of Biscayne Bay. In addition, topographical factors often govern the location of transportation lines, and these in turn influence the direction of city growth by accelerating axial and suburban developments.

## Land Use Patterns

Although we can distinguish central and axial growth in our cities today, a much greater variety and diversity of land uses and changes in land uses have emerged than appeared probable even a few years ago. Few of the earlier theories or explanations of land use patterns are adequate for current and future purposes although they give us some keys to understanding the processes that have gone on. It has been pointed out, for example:

In the era of the Greek cities in the fifth century B.C. a city was considered an artistic creation which should maintain its static form without change. To take care of population growth, the Greeks sent out colonies, like swarms of bees, to found new cities on the ideal model. Plato said that the ideal city should not contain over 5,000 inhabitants, although he, himself was the product of an Athens with 250,000 population. In the Middle Ages most continental

[9] Richard M. Hurd, *Principles of City Land Values* (New York: The Record & Guide, 1924), pp. 58–59.

European cities were surrounded by walls and many, like Milan, Italy, preserved an unaltered form for hundreds of years.[10]

## Concentric Circles

The modern city tended to spread over wider areas as transportation made such dispersion possible. In the 1920's Burgess set forth his concentric circle theory in an effort to explain city form and structure. It is an interesting concept, though not too helpful today.

Burgess said:

The typical process of the expansion of a city can best be illustrated, perhaps, by a series of concentric circles, which may be numbered to designate both the successive zones of urban expansion and the types of areas differentiated in the process of expansion.

He believed that each zone tended to invade the next one by a process called "succession." At the heart of his model was the "loop" with the financial and office district at the center and the central retail district surrounding and penetrating it. Beyond this, as he pointed out:

Encircling the downtown area there is normally an area in transition, which is being invaded by business and light manufacture. A third area is inhabited by workers in industries who have escaped from the area of deterioration but who desire to live within easy access of their work. Beyond this zone is the "residential area" of high-class apartment buildings or of exclusive "restricted" districts of single-family dwellings. Still farther out, beyond the city limits, is the commuter's zone—suburban areas, or satellite cities—within a thirty- to sixty-minute ride of the central business district.[11]

## Wider Dispersion

Burgess' explanation was made obsolete primarily by the automobile; but other factors were at work as well, including rising incomes, advancing technology especially in transportation and communication, the requirements for large amounts of space for single-story factory buildings, tax factors, and others. Noneconomic forces also played a part in this process.

The automobile made possible a wide dispersal of people over a metropolitan area, the wide separation of workers from places of employment, the rise of planned shopping centers with thousands being established, the outward movement of manufacturing, as such land uses

[10] Homer Hoyt, "Recent Distortions of the Classical Models of Urban Structure," *Land Economics* (May, 1964).

[11] Reprinted from *The City* by R. E. Park, E. W. Burgess, and R. D. McKenzie, by permission, University of Chicago Press, pp. 50–53. Copyright, 1925, by the University of Chicago.

became more compatible with residential land uses, improved roads and freeways, and the general broadening of the urban land market.


## SECTOR THEORY—RESIDENTIAL NEIGHBORHOODS

Another general theory of urban structure was developed by Homer Hoyt and set forth in 1939.

If an entire city is thought of as a circle, and if the different residential areas are thought of as wedge-shaped sectors pointing to the center, the high-rent or high-price areas of the city will tend over a period of years to move outward to the periphery in the path described by one or more of the sectors. Similarly, if a certain sector develops originally as a low-rent or low-price area, the balance of that sector is likely to be occupied by low-rent or low-price residences as expansion proceeds outward. The same tendency is typical of intermediate rent or price sectors.[12]

### Bases of Sector Theory

The sector theory is based on the following general tendencies:

1. The various groups in the social order tend to locate in rather definite areas according to their incomes and social positions. While efforts are being made to modify these tendencies, they continue to persist.

2. The highest-income groups live in the houses which command highest prices and rents, while the lower-income groups live in houses which are offered for lower prices and rents. Generally the low-rent areas are located near the business and industrial center of the city and then tend to expand outward on one side or sector of the city, occupying the land which is not preempted by higher-rent residential areas or by business and industrial districts.

3. The principal growth of American cities has taken place by new building at the periphery rather than by the rebuilding of older areas. This means that some of our cities are beginning to resemble a hollow shell, with the major demands for land uses by-passing many of the "near-in" areas. In other cases these "near-in" areas become slums with little possibility of being rehabilitated through ordinary market processes. Heavy subsidies are usually required for renewal to occur.

---

[12] This theory was worked out by Homer Hoyt and first presented in a series of articles in the Federal Housing Administration's *Insured Mortgage Portfolio* (Washington, D.C.: Government Printing Office), Vol. I, Nos. 6–10. See also, his *The Structure and Growth of Residential Neighborhoods in American Cities* (Washington, D.C.: Federal Housing Administration, 1939).

## Factors Influencing Outward Movement

A detailed study of the movements of residential neighborhoods in American cities indicates that the high-grade neighborhoods of a city (measured by price or rent) tend to follow a definite path in one or more sectors of a city. In their expansion, high-grade residential areas tend to move outward along established lines of travel or toward other settled areas. Typically, such growth is toward high ground free from risk of floods. It may spread out into areas distinguished for their natural beauty; for example, along lake, bay, river, or ocean fronts. Growth proceeds toward open country and away from barriers to expansion. Real estate promoters and developers may at times bend the direction of growth. Outlying shopping centers and industrial uses may preempt some land that might otherwise develop into high-grade residences.

Changes will occur with the introduction of new traffic arteries and major road systems. It should be noted that the building of expressways and belt highways around cities has opened up large areas for residential development. In some cases new communities are developed on land areas that are large enough to establish their own character. For example, a high-grade neighborhood may be developed around a golf course. Developments of this type may be found at almost any point as the settled area expands.

## Multiple Nuclei

Changes are always taking place in the growing cities and the student may note the value of new homes built since 1970 and check to see whether the old high-income areas are being extended in the same directions or new high-income areas are being created. With the development of new towns and suburbs, there will undoubtedly be changes in older patterns. There probably is less concentration of high-income families in clusters now than formerly due to the spread of egalitarianism, the avoidance of conspicuous displays of wealth, more widespread crime, and the leveling effect of steeply progressive income taxes.

The multiple nuclei concept was developed by Harris and Ullman as a modification of the sector theory. They stressed the clustering of land uses, especially business uses, and the impact of transportation, topography, and related factors. Family preferences and social customs were considered as major factors in the location of residential land uses.[13]

---

13 Chauncey D. Harris and Edward L. Ullman, "The Nature of Cities," *Annals* of the American Academy of Political and Social Science (November, 1945); Frederick E. Case, *Real Estate* (Boston: Allyn and Bacon, Inc., 1962), pp. 53–54; and Homer Hoyt, "Where the Rich and the Poor People Live" (Washington, D.C.: Urban Land Institute, Technical Bulletin 55, April 1966), maps reprinted in Homer Hoyt, *According to Hoyt* (2nd ed.). (Washington, D.C., 1970), pp. 616–621.

### Individuality of Regions

The great diversity of American cities makes it difficult to set forth general explanations of land use patterns. If the sector theory is viewed as a statement of general tendency rather than applied rigidly, it may be helpful in anticipating land use changes. We should remember that all shifts in the patterns of land uses result from the decisions of people either as individuals or as officials of business firms or governmental or institutional agencies. What motivates them at a given time may be hard to anticipate. They may react in one manner in one region and in another way elsewhere. Hence, the pattern of every urban region tends to have its own unique characteristics and is deserving of special study.

## LAND USE PATTERNS AND BUSINESS DISTRICTS

The central business district of a city can expand in two ways; vertically and laterally. If the expansion is vertical, smaller buildings are replaced by taller ones. Such expansion generally takes place if the central business district remains in one place for a long time and is confined by some barrier and if the city is growing rapidly. The steel-frame skyscraper and the electric elevator have facilitated vertical as against lateral expansion. Indeed the elevator has been called the most efficient form of urban transportation. However, lateral expansion of the central district has been of importance, modified somewhat by the growth of outlying business centers.

### Central District Changes

Major shifts in the location of the central district sometimes occur. In such cases new buildings may be constructed at the edge of the main business district or at other points rather than on the sites of older buildings. In any case the expansion of the central business area forces out less intensive uses.

For example, the large department stores in central cities continued at the same sites such as Macy's in New York, Marshall Field & Company in Chicago, the J. L. Hudson Company in Detroit, and the Dayton Store in Minneapolis. These large stores remained rooted at the same spot for long periods of time because of the convergence of mass transportation routes at their location.

The growth of regional shopping centers has tended to curtail the expansion of existing central business districts. Many of these districts are seeking to hold their customers by building central parking garages, as in the case of the Lazarus store in Columbus, Ohio, and Foley's in Houston. Extensive public parking garages have been built in Chicago,

Baltimore, San Francisco, and other cities for the purpose of aiding central retail districts.

Each type of store has its own trade area and its own optimum size. A central department store with 100,000 square feet or more will have a trade area extending to that of another department store of similar or greater size. For example, the trade area of the Blass department store in Little Rock covers 41 Arkansas counties and is bounded by the trade area of Memphis on the east, Springfield, Missouri, on the north, Fort Smith on the west, and Texarkana on the south. The trade area of the Dayton department store in Minneapolis extends as far as Montana. On the other hand, the trade area of a variety store (such as Woolworth or Kresge) which has 10,000 to 20,000 square feet of floor area and which requires 10,000 to 15,000 families for its support extends only to the boundaries of the trade area of the nearest variety store which may be only two or three miles away.

Clothing stores in the popular-price lines usually tend to concentrate in central business districts or major outlying shopping districts, because women prefer to patronize a center which has a number of stores offering a wide variety of styles so that they can compare apparel as to quality and price. Fashionable women's stores such as Lord and Taylor, on the other hand, sometimes seek solitary locations in the midst of high-income neighborhoods. When several of these higher-price stores locate near one another the sales of all of them tend to increase.

### Potential of Central Districts

Although the central business districts in most cities have now declined in their rate of expansion, they continue to change and to move. The main retail shopping center generally tends to move toward the more fashionable residential areas. For example, the stores in New York City moved up Fifth Avenue. The growth of Chicago, Washington, D.C., and Houston likewise illustrates movements of this type. In a similar manner the development of Miami Beach and the northeast section of Miami has attracted the central business section of the city.

The emergence of "platform cities" has tended to support further growth of the central districts. It has been pointed out, for example, by Perry Prentice:

Making tomorrow's cities twice as big horizontally for tomorrow's twice as big urban population would be impossibly costly in dollars, intolerably costly in wasted land, unbearably costly in added travel time to and from work and to and from outdoor recreation.

Doubling their area by growing up instead of out would cost far less and add only seconds instead of minutes to everybody's travel time.

So whether we like it or not, most urban growth in the next thirty years will have to be up, not out. Otherwise our twice-as-big-cities will strangle in their own sprawl. . . .

. . . horizontal stratification is natural, economical, and desirable between those activities that need and profit by easy access to street and sidewalk vs. those activities of which it can be said that the further above the street the better. This natural stratification makes it easy and logical to use heart-of-the-central-city land over and over again in layers to meet different needs. . . .

Planners are beginning to call cities thus planned in horizontal layers "Sandwich Cities."

Architects, perhaps more artistically minded, are beginning to call them "Platform Cities" to emphasize the great new opportunity offered by the level rooftops above the stores and between the office or apartment towers to bring greenery and outdoor recreation space back to the city. They visualize, for example, space enough for a football field on top of a school, space for tennis courts and swimming pools and children's play between apartment towers, etc.[14]

### Outlying Business and Shopping Centers

Outlying business centers have developed at or near intersections between radial and crosstown transportation lines and the intersections of main automobile highways. Independent shopping centers tend to grow on the periphery of large cities because it is difficult to reach the central downtown shopping area where traffic is congested. The extent to which such centers develop depends on the number of customers in the area and their current or potential purchasing power.

The development of large regional or super regional shopping centers has been a major development in the pattern of urban land uses. The transportation network, the purchasing power represented in the present and potential market area, the location and design of the center, the types of goods and services offered, parking spaces and arrangements, convenience and comfort of customers, attractiveness and general appeal of the center all play a part in determining its success in meeting competition of the central business district and other outlying business centers. The relationship of the shopping center to its general urban environment will play a role in its success. The quality of its management, of course, will be important. Adequate promotion and publicity campaigns often have been of major importance, especially in the early stages of a shopping center's development.

### Types of Shopping Centers

We will consider the various types of shopping centers in greater detail in Chapter 22 but should note here that the major types are the super regional and regional centers; the community centers; and the

---

[14] From a speech to the National Association of Real Estate Boards, by permission.

convenience or neighborhood centers. There are also small clusters of business land uses as well as isolated outlets. For example, supermarkets can be operated successfully in isolated locations with ample parking. Since people buy food more frequently than other things they place a heavy emphasis on convenience in this type of shopping.

## LAND USE PATTERNS AND INDUSTRIAL DISTRICTS

In earlier years heavy manufacturing industries tended to be located in areas near the central retail district. The best transportation facilities were available there. Such locations provided ready access to wharves, docks, or railroad sidings. Central locations also provided broadest access to the labor supply.

Currently the pattern of industrial land uses frequently is quite different from the earlier arrangements. Transportation has improved and made a broader variety of locations available especially with the development of improved roads and the increased use of truck transportation. This has made it possible to bring lower priced land into industrial use. Also it has been possible for industries to seek out locations with favorable tax arrangements relative to the government services provided. Favorable topographical features continue to be important.

Favorable topographical features, transportation facilities, lower-priced land, and favorable tax arrangements now appear to be important along with transportation in determining industrial locations. Transportation facilities have opened up new areas as neighborhoods developed and as truck transportation has grown in importance.

### Bands and Clusters

Heavy industries now tend to follow railroad lines, river valleys, or lake or ocean fronts in long bands of growth rather than to remain near the central business district. Frequently, industrial suburbs develop near the periphery of the city. In some cases a cluster of industries forms a specialized industrial section or industrial park, such as Bush Terminal in Brooklyn, the Clearing District in Chicago, and the Trinity Industrial District of Dallas. Industrial parks have grown rapidly in recent years and have been especially attractive to industries of many types. Some industries now seek locations in the countryside on major highways well away from population centers.

### Influence of Land Values

Industries are usually not able to occupy land which is of extremely high value. Areas which are located in outlying areas represent cheaper land, and the tax burden is usually lower. Hence, it is possible to use more land for storage space. Also, one-story buildings which permit continuity of factory operations can be used. Such structures are more economical than multi-story buildings for many types of manufacturing processes. They permit continuity of manufacturing operations, there is no use of space for elevators or ramps, heavy machinery can be installed in any part of the plant, railroad freight cars and trucks can enter the plant directly, overhead cranes can be installed, and expansion can be arranged more easily.

Industries may locate in suburban and outlying areas because workers' homes are scattered throughout the area and widespread use of the automobile plus improved road networks have tended to eliminate distance as a major factor in attracting an adequate labor supply.

## METHODS OF ANALYZING LAND USE PATTERNS

In order to make estimates regarding future probable changes in the land uses of a city, it is necessary to study past developments with some care. Changes in the internal structure of a city occur slowly. Hence we cannot forecast future probable changes unless we can determine the major trends that have been in operation for a considerable period of time.

### Time Interval Maps

One method for collecting the necessary information is by the use of time interval maps. A photograph or a map of a city at a given moment of time fails to show the dynamic character of the city's growth. Several photographs taken at different time intervals or several maps for different periods reveal the processes of change. Thus, if the location of a certain type of area has changed from one period to another, it is possible to determine the direction and speed with which such movements have occurred by using devices of this kind.

Generally speaking, a period covering at least the time since the end of World War II should be studied. A detailed description should be worked out for a year around two decades ago. Earlier situations should then be compared with current conditions.

If it is possible to undertake careful and intensive research, specific information can be secured from such sources as the Sanborn insurance maps, which show locations of individual structures in many cities for periods as far back as the 1880's. Also, valuable assistance can be secured from the United States quadrangular survey maps, which provide similar information. Older maps of cities can frequently be found that provide valuable data. City histories and old newspaper files often include accounts of the development of particular areas.

It is sometimes possible to compare recent aerial photographs of entire regions with those taken at a former period. Thus in recent surveys of the growth of the Washington metropolitan area, a comparison was made between aerial photographs taken currently with those taken in 1958 and 1937. The marked growth in the urban settled area which had taken place in that period and the direction of growth were clearly indicated.

In the absence of such specific material, or if pressure of time necessitates the use of less refined methods, sufficient information can often be secured by consulting older people who have a reputation for accuracy and good judgment and who are known to be well informed regarding the growth of the city. At least three different persons should be consulted. If there seems to be considerable disagreement among them, additional people should be questioned.

## Land Use Changes

Regardless of the plan of attack adopted, a map (which may be referred to as a time interval map) for each period should be prepared which will indicate the areas occupied by (1) factories and heavy industries, (2) low-rent residential areas, (3) the chief central and outlying shopping or commercial areas, and (4) the more fashionable residential neighborhoods. From these maps a reasonably accurate picture can be secured of the major movements affecting each of these important types of land uses.

Such general maps should then be compared with maps showing the development of the internal transportation system of the city. Maps showing the transportation system at various periods of time can usually be secured from city offices or from the offices of those who are in charge of the transportation system. Similarly, comparisons should be made with existing zoning maps which indicate the restrictions applying to various areas of the city.

When the movements indicated by the maps have been studied and analyzed, the forces of city expansion may be noted and the probable future structure of the city may be estimated. It is generally possible to assume that existing uses will expand outward in the same sector and that the trend of past development will be continued into the future, unless important and powerful forces are in existence or are likely to develop which will tend to cause a change in such trends.

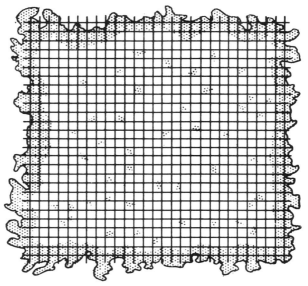

**Fig. 10–1.**   The dispersed sheet. (Source: *Metropolis: Values in Conflict,* p. 98.)

## FUTURE METROPOLITAN PATTERNS

Kevin Lynch has suggested types of patterns for the metropolis of the future. These include the dispersed sheet, the galaxy, the core city, the urban star, and the ring.

### Dispersed Sheet

One of these patterns assumes that there may be a much greater spreading out of urban activities—what Lynch refers to as a "dispersed sheet." He says:

The old center and most subcenters could be dissolved, allowing city-wide activities to disperse throughout the region, with a fine grain. Factories, offices, museums, universities, hospitals would appear everywhere in the suburban landscape. The low density and the dispersion of activities would depend on and allow circulation in individual vehicles, as well as a substantial use of distant symbolic communication such as telephone, television, mail, coded messages.[15]

This is essentially the Los Angeles pattern of the city and was apparently preferred by the late Frank Lloyd Wright. This pattern has high

[15] Kevin Lynch, "The Pattern of the Metropolis," in C. E. Elias, Jr., James Gillies, and Svend Riemer (eds.), *Metropolis: Values in Conflict* (Belmont, Calif.: Wadsworth Publishing Co., Inc., 1964), p. 97.

flexibility, independence, personal comfort, and the like, but its costs would be high and distance would remain a major problem. Also, there would be little local identity and community participation might be limited. (See Fig. 10–1.)

### Galaxy

A second type is outlined by Lynch as a "galaxy of settlements" (Fig. 10–2). Here, growth would not be dispersed evenly over a wide area as in the case of the "dispersed sheet," but would be bunched in relatively small units, each with high density at the center and with low density or no density between the units. It provides for many of the advantages of wider dispersion and solves some of the disadvantages.

### Core City

By contrast the "core city" would pack all urban activity in a small space with high density. Lynch describes it as follows.

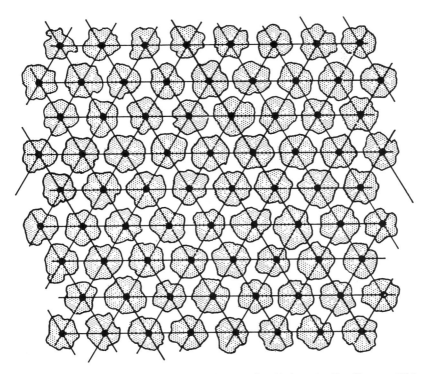

**Fig. 10–2.** The galaxy. (Source: *Metropolis: Values in Conflict,* p. 99.)

Parts of the city might become "solid" with a continuous occupation of space in three dimensions and a cubical grid of transportation lines. (The full application of this plan could cram a metropolis within a surprisingly small compass: twenty million people, with generous spacing, could be accommodated within a cube less than three miles on a side.) Most probably there would be a fine grain of specialized activities, all at high intensity, so that apartments would occur over factories, or there might also be stores on upper levels. The system of flow would necessarily be highly specialized, sorting each kind of traffic into its own channel. Such a city would depend almost entirely on public transport, rather than individual vehicles, or on devices that facilitated pedestrian movement, such as moving sidewalks or flying belts.[16]

The plan would allow for combination with dispersion over the countryside, for example, week-end houses, combining long week ends with work concentrated in the "core" in three or four days per week. This type of arrangement would contrast sharply with the "dispersed sheet" outlined above.

### Urban Star

A fourth arrangement is designated as "The Urban Star" (Fig. 10–3). This would retain the dominant core of the city but would channel growth into axes outward from the center with open spaces between such settled areas. The radii might extend to other metropolitan centers;

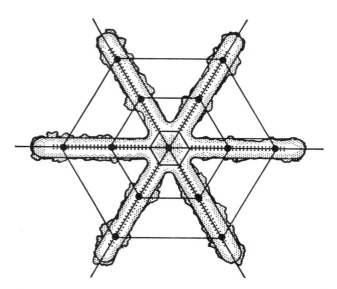

**Fig. 10–3.** The star. (Source: *Metropolis: Values in Conflict,* p. 103.)

[16] *Ibid.,* p. 103 (by permission).

the dominant core would remain with secondary centers. Copenhagen follows this type of growth; it is the type that was emerging before the automobile upset older patterns of growth and it fits the patterns outlined earlier by Hurd and referred to above.

## Ring

Combinations of the above may be made as well. One interesting arrangement is "The Ring," which would have a "doughnut" type of arrangement with low density in the center to make for easy access to the various parts of the ring or rings which would have high densities. This pattern could be combined with week-end houses and similar arrangements in the surrounding countryside (Fig. 10–4).

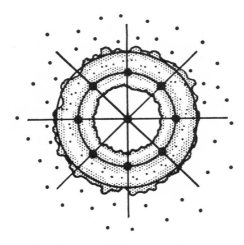

**Fig. 10–4.**   The ring. (Source: *Metropolis: Values in Conflict,* p. 105.

## Diversity of Future Patterns

It is interesting to consider these types of arrangements as models. Some types of cities will fit one model and some others. Various combinations also exist. In the early editions of this book we presented our concept of the "City of the Future" and we reproduce it here again because it combines some of the arrangements outlined above. (See Fig. 10–5).

General explanations of the pattern of urban land uses, however, do not appear to be as helpful to the real estate decision maker as was once the case. Diversity in urban life and in the patterns of land use seems to be increasing. Each situation requires careful analysis by the real

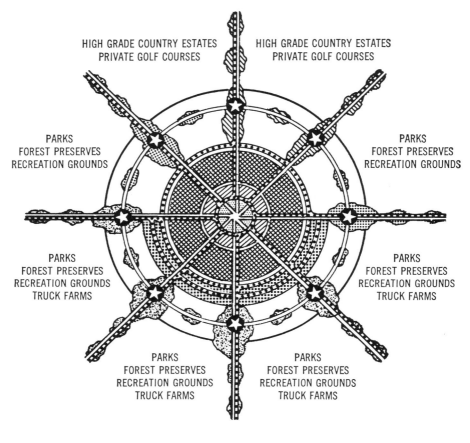

HIGH GRADE COUNTRY ESTATES
PRIVATE GOLF COURSES

HIGH GRADE COUNTRY ESTATES
PRIVATE GOLF COURSES

PARKS
FOREST PRESERVES
RECREATION GROUNDS

PARKS
FOREST PRESERVES
RECREATION GROUNDS

PARKS
FOREST PRESERVES
RECREATION GROUNDS
TRUCK FARMS

PARKS
FOREST PRESERVES
RECREATION GROUNDS
TRUCK FARMS

PARKS
FOREST PRESERVES
RECREATION GROUNDS
TRUCK FARMS

PARKS
FOREST PRESERVES
RECREATION GROUNDS
TRUCK FARMS

CENTRAL BUSINESS AREA
HOTEL AND MULTIPLE APARTMENT AREA
FORMER SLUM AREA
(now converted into parks, parking
lots and automobile highways)
INDUSTRIAL BELT
HIGH RENT AREAS
INTERMEDIATE RENT AREAS
LOW RENT AREAS
OUTLYING BUSINESS CENTERS
AUTOMOBILE HIGHWAYS
RAIL AND STREET TRANSPORTATION

**Fig. 10–5.** A city of the future. (Source: Weimer and Hoyt, 2nd ed., p. 117.)

estate decision maker. He may be aided, however, by general concepts and models of the type outlined above.

### Toward Ecumenopolis?

Are we headed toward a single world city? This suggestion was put forth by Toynbee. He said, for example:

> The megalopolises on all the continents are merging to form Ecumenopolis, a new type of city that can be represented by only one specimen, since Ecumenopolis is going, as its name proclaims, to encompass the land-surface of the globe with a single conurbation.

He goes on to suggest:

> Human affairs are already being swept toward Ecumenopolis by two currents, both of which are strong and which are both flowing in the same direction. Between them, they make the coming World-City a certainty. One of these two currents is the present rapid growth of the world's population, especially among the economically backward and therefore indigent majority. The second current that is making the Ecumenopolis is the simultaneous migration from the countryside into the cities which is taking place in the "developing" and "developed" countries alike.[17]

These concepts certainly are stimulating. They may indicate the direction of future developments. On the other hand new forces, not yet in evidence, may emerge which will modify the trends which Toynbee identifies.

### SUMMARY

Location factors play an important part in real estate decisions; of these, the patterns of land use have special significance. A real property may be thought of as a share in the local economy and also as a share in a particular area or sector of the local community. When a city expands, all properties do not participate in the same degree; the reverse is also true. Factors likely to influence these interrelationships in future years include the anticipated rise in per capita incomes and resulting changes in expenditure patterns; the impact of science and technology on transportation, communication, the environment and the obsolescence of plant and equipment; governmental changes, notably in allocation of costs and benefits; further expansion of the urban area; changing competitive patterns between land uses; social unrest and pressures; and the tastes and preferences of people.

---

[17] Arnold Toynbee, *Cities on the Move* (New York and London: Oxford University Press, 1970), pp. 95–96.

Cities may expand by growing vertically, by filling in open spaces between settled areas, or by extending the settled area. Such expansion may take ring, axial, or suburban forms; and a variety of explanations has developed, including the concentric circle concept, the sector theory, and others.

Land use patterns may be analyzed by comparing changes over a period of years. Special maps may be prepared for this purpose.

Future metropolitan patterns may include the dispersed sheet, galaxy of settlements, core city, urban star, ring, or others. Diversity of urban life and land uses appears to be increasing and this makes it difficult to generalize. Toynbee suggests that the world may be in the process of becoming one city.

## QUESTIONS FOR STUDY

1. Why is location such an important factor in real estate decisions? In the determination of property income?
2. Explain this statement: "An urban property may be thought of as a share in the local economy or city and also as a share in a specific area or sector of the city."
3. List the urban trends that seem most likely to affect the future structure of land uses. Which of these now has a major influence in your city?
4. Explain the changing character of the competition between land uses in recent years.
5. Which social and cultural trends may be expected to affect the pattern of land uses in the future? Which government and political factors? Which of these do you consider most important and why?
6. Why is it important to anticipate future changes in factors influencing land use patterns?
7. What are the methods of urban expansion? How can we expect each of these to affect land use patterns and incomes from real property?
8. Explain the concentric circle theory of city structure set forth by Burgess.
9. Explain Hoyt's Sector Theory. How may it help to anticipate changes in land uses?
10. Compare the growth pattern of New York with that of Los Angeles. How do you account for the difference?
11. Explain the application of the sector theory of city growth to the development of the residential neighborhood in which you live.
12. What are the principal developments affecting land use patterns in business districts?
13. How have industrial districts changed? What have been the major forces causing such changes?
14. How do you account for the great diversity of land use patterns between cities?
15. What are time interval maps? Explain their use.

16. Outline the concept of a "dispersed sheet" as a pattern for the metropolis of the future; the "galaxy of settlements" concept; the "core city"; the "urban star"; the "ring" concept. Which of these do you believe will be the most likely to emerge? Explain.

17. Do you agree with Toynbee's suggestion that we may be moving toward Ecumenopolis? Why or why not?

## SUGGESTED READINGS

HARVEY, ROBERT O., and W. A. V. CLARK. "The Nature and Economics of Urban Sprawl," *Land Economics* (February, 1965).

HOYT, HOMER. *According to Hoyt* (2nd ed.). Washington, D.C.: Hoyt, 1970. Sec. IX.

————. "The Growth of Cities from 1800 to 1960 and Forecasts to Year 2000," *Land Economics*, XXXIX, No. 2 (May, 1963).

————. "Recent Distortions of the Classical Models of Urban Structure," *Land Economics* (May, 1964).

ISARD, WALTER. *Methods of Regional Analysis: An Introduction to Regional Science.* Cambridge: The Massachusetts Institute of Technology Press, 1960. Chap. ix.

LYNCH, KEVIN. "The Pattern of the Metropolis," in C. E. Elias, Jr., James Gillies, and Svend Riemer (eds.), *Metropolis: Values in Conflict.* Belmont, Calif.: Wadsworth Publishing Co., Inc., 1964.

## STUDY PROJECT 10–1

### New Shopping Centers for a Growing Population *

The period from 1948 to 1970 witnessed a fantastic growth in a new type of shopping center—a group of stores set back from the highway with a strip of automobile parking spaces in front or a mall center surrounded by a belt of parking. These planned centers with provision for parking were almost non-existent at the end of World War II. Today there are over 13,000 centers of all sizes in practically all the urban areas of the United States and Canada.

Has the saturation point been reached? Do we have enough shopping centers already built to take care of population growth for the next 30 years?

If the population of the United States increases from 204 million in 1970 to 300 million by the year 2000, as is presently anticipated, approximately 50 million new dwelling units of all types, including low income housing, will be needed to house the added population and to provide for a continued downward trend in number of persons per household. At least 14 million new units will be required to replace obsolete structures and to house families moving from demolished structures, from blighted central ghettos or from small towns or rural areas. Most of the 64 million new dwelling units will be in the suburbs in a continuation of urban sprawl or in new satellite towns around metropolitan urban masses, far from central shopping centers and even from presently planned shopping centers.

* By Homer Hoyt; reproduced by permission of Mortgage Guaranty Insurance Corporation, from *MGIC Newsletter*.

An estimated 12 million of the new units will be mobile homes, all in out-lying areas. As a result of the high cost of building, high land values and high interest rates, at least half or 26 million of the conventional dwelling units will consist of apartments, located mostly in suburban areas, and half will consist of townhouses and detached singly family houses, also mostly in suburban areas.

Concentrations of apartment units and townhouses and detached houses located near radial and belt highways leading to central city areas will create a demand for two major types of shopping centers, regional and neighborhood.

**Regional Centers.** The new regional center will follow the latest model now being built—a shopping center of one million or more square feet of stores, with three or more of the leading department stores and 40 or 50 specialty stores, in an air-conditioned mall surrounded by a belt of parking, on 100 or more acres of land. Apartments and office buildings will be erected on adjacent sites. Such a center will require a sales volume of $70 to $100 million, of which $50 million would be in fashion goods such as women's and men's clothing and shoes. To support such a new center (with families spending 10 per cent of their income in department, apparel and furniture stores) a trade area with aggregate personal income of $1 billion is needed. On the basis of average household incomes of $10,000 in 1970 dollars this would mean 100,000 households or 250,000 persons for each new regional center.

An increase of approximately 100 million in the national population in the next 30 years would require 400 new regional centers. In the period of the 1970's with a population growth of 26 million, there would be a total demand for 104 new regional shopping centers.

**Neighborhood Centers.** Families will travel to regional centers to purchase clothing at the department and apparel stores, which offer the greatest selection in sizes, styles, quality, and price range. But they will tend to go to the nearest large supermarket to buy refrigerated foods, meats, vegetables and also to get drug store items and to patronize the cleaners or the beauty and barber shops. These neighborhood centers, with a 20-30-thousand square foot supermarket, a 10,000 square foot drug store and other local convenience stores, and possibly also a restaurant, a drive-in hamburger or fried chicken carryout, a branch bank and post office, require less than 100,000 square feet of store area on no more than five or 10 acres of land. Such centers, with an annual sales volume of $5 to $10 million, can be supported by as few as 3,000 families with an average income of $10,000, or an aggregate income of $30 million.

Thus an increase of approximately 100 million in the population from 1970 to 2000 could give rise to a demand for well over 10,000 new neighborhood centers. In the period 1970–1980 alone, with the population increasing from 204 million to 230 million, there could be a demand for as many as 3,000 new neighborhood centers.

The demand for new shopping centers does not arise from population growth alone, but from a redistribution of retail sales, particularly in fashion goods. From 1950–1970, when the population of the United States increased by 50 million, or 33 per cent, over 13,000 planned shopping centers were built, of which over 400 were regional centers. In 1950 the sales of department stores outside the central business district were less than $1 billion; in 1970 they probably exceed $30 billion. General merchandise sales in the CBD increased only 3.4 per cent from 1954 to 1958 and declined 3.5 per cent from 1958 to 1963, while the increase outside the CBD was respectively 54 per cent from 1954 to 1958 and 89 per cent from 1958 to 1963.

In addition to the planned shopping centers, there will be a rebuilding of some central retail areas where large office and apartment buildings are planned, as in Bunker Hill and Century City in Los Angeles, Church Street in New Haven, and Market Street in Philadelphia. Central retail areas also will be affected by the construction of new buildings that have stores, offices, garages and apartments in the same structure, such as the John Hancock Building and Marina City in Chicago. There also will be hundreds of isolated stores in the suburbs, particularly supermarkets and discount stores.

Two new types of shopping centers have arisen recently, one is the discount store such as K-Mart, Woolco, Korvette, Zayre and others, which in 100,000 square feet of store area offer a complete line of merchandise, have a supermarket and cater to lower middle-income families. Sales of discount houses increased from $300 million to $3.6 billion, an increase of over ten-fold, in the ten years from 1956 to 1966. The second type is the high fashion center—with stores such as Saks Fifth Avenue, Lord & Taylor, Bonwit Teller, Neiman Marcus that seek to locate apart from regional centers. Lord & Taylor and Saks Fifth Avenue have located stores in the center of the highest income areas of Washington, D.C., and Atlanta.

**Local Differences.** Up to this point I have considered the estimated increase in population and the demand for new shopping centers in the next 30 years for the entire United States. There is however, a vast difference in the anticipated rate of population and household growth between different metropolitan regions. In two books, I estimated the growth of population and the urban land use requirements of leading metropolitan areas in the United States from 1960 to 2000.[1] In some metropolitan areas the anticipated rate of population growth is expected to be exceptionally high, such as Los Angeles, Atlanta, Washington, San Francisco-Oakland, Houston, Dallas, Miami-Fort Lauderdale, New Orleans, Tampa-St. Petersburg, Denver and Phoenix, all of which indicate an increase of 70 to over 100 per cent in the next thirty years. In other metropolitan areas present trends indicate a slower rate of growth owing to a slackening in the basic economic forces which support them. In the Boston, Pittsburgh and Buffalo metropolitan areas, the thirty year growth is estimated at less than 30 per cent. Other metropolitan areas such as New York, Chicago, Philadelphia and St. Louis, while expecting a smaller rate of

[1] Homer Hoyt, *Urban Land Use Requirements 1968–2000*. Homer Hoyt Institute, Research Monograph No. 1, Table 13. Homer Hoyt, *People, Profits, Places,* National Retail Merchants Association, 1969, Table 24. Copies may be purchased from Homer Hoyt, Washington, D.C.

growth will have a large growth in absolute numbers. A growth of population of six million in New York-N.E. New Jersey, four million for Chicago, 900,000 for Baltimore and one million for St. Louis will furnish demand for many more shopping centers. (Any of these forecasted rates of growth may be reversed with declines in basic employment.)

It is not enough to forecast population growth for entire metropolitan areas. Most metropolitan areas are divided into segments, some of which are growing much faster in population and income than other areas. High income growth often moves predominantly in one direction, as north in Chicago, Dallas or Miami Beach, south in Kansas City, west in Philadelphia.

In examining the need for new regional centers there is no rigid formula determining need, such as by taking the average of 2 square feet per capita of the metropolitan area population. Some metropolitan areas such as Dallas and Columbus, Ohio, draw customers to their department stores from counties far beyond the limits of the metropolitan area and have regional centers with 5.4 square feet per capita. Other metropolitan areas, with mass transit facilities such as subways which make it easy to come to central stores, have lower than average space in regional centers. These include New York-N.E. New Jersey with only 0.73 square feet per capita, Chicago-Northwestern Indiana 1.53, and Boston 1.46.[2] In other metropolitan areas with low average per capita regional center footage, new regional centers were planned but not yet opened in September 1968, the date of my survey.

**Construction Costs, Rentals, Profits.** The first planned shopping centers of all types were built when land costs were as low as $2,000 an acre, building costs were less than $10 a square foot for neighborhood centers and $12–$15 a square foot for regional centers. Stores were leased on a basis of $1.00 to a top of $3.00 a square foot minimum against a percentage of sales varying from 1 per cent for supermarkets; 2½ per cent for department stores; 4, 5, and 6 per cent for specialty apparel stores, drug stores and other stores. In early 1970 raw land for a regional center may be priced at $40,000 to $60,000 an acre, building costs for regional centers may range from $20 to $30 a square foot of gross leasable area, and interest rates are 9 to 9½ per cent, with the mortgage lender also demanding a share in the equity. Operating expenses, including real estate taxes, are also rising. The shopping center owner must now receive $5.00, $6.00, or $7.00 a square foot for minimum guarantee in order to break even.

The operator has an opportunity to profit from leases that in addition to a guaranteed minimum also stipulate a percentage of sales. Such terms usually produce an average rent above the guaranteed minimum. The dollar value of retail sales will increase sharply if the inflationary trend continues even at a modest pace. The national personal family income of $770 billion in January 1970 has almost doubled since 1960, when it was slightly over $400 billion. If it doubles every 10 years, it will be $1.6 trillion in 1980, $3.2 trillion in 1990 and $6.4 trillion in the year 2000. Retail sales would increase from $350 billion in 1970 to $700 billion in 1980, to $1.4 trillion in 1990 and to $2.8

[2] *People, Profits, Places,* Table 16, pp. 52–53.

## COMMENTARY

### by Edward E. Edwards *

Homer Hoyt is an outstanding authority on shopping centers and their location, design and financing. He has developed an uncanny ability to estimate sales volume for a complex mix of stores that exist only in a developer's imagination. But that is not too surprising in view of his lifelong interest in population growth and movement and consumer incomes and spending habits.

Dr. Hoyt projects with great confidence a continued growth in number of shopping centers and he may be right. But I cannot help but wonder whether some brand new merchandising idea, one just as revolutionary as the planned shopping center, may not be forthcoming between now and the year 2000, possibly even in the decade of the seventies.

Shopping centers are heavily dependent on the automobile. Their rapid growth paralleled the great increase in number of cars, the construction of our interstate highway system, and the general breakdown of public transportation on which central business districts were so dependent. Discouraging as the outlook is for improved public transportation, a breakthrough could come. If it does, central business districts might revive, but other possibilities must not be overlooked. For example, those regional shopping centers served by the new transportation systems might expand vertically, or into present parking areas, looking chiefly to non-automobile traffic for increased business.

Shopping habits could easily change in thirty years. For example, more selection could be done by television or picture telephone rather than by shopping in stores. Less emphasis may be placed on variety and style, more on quality and price, in which case shopping might be less necessary. Further development toward a service rather than a goods economy could change commodity distribution, although in what direction and to what extent would be difficult to predict.

Until changing trends do develop—and probably for quite some time thereafter—Dr. Hoyt's forecasts likely will be a dependable basis for planners, developers, builders and mortgage lenders.

Financing for the new shopping centers presents fewer problems than have to be faced in the housing field. Mortgage lenders can take an equity position, in a variety of ways, and have some protection from purchasing poor risk. Because of this, mortgagors can bargain for appropriate trade-offs that lessen the burden of the debt and more closely relate loan payments to actual cash flows. One result of this kind of financing should be an improved competitive position for lenders in terms of raising funds. Another result should be better leasing arrangements, with rentals matching tenant's cash flows. Higher land and construction costs plus higher interest rates may make required rentals seem high, but if new centers are well planned and based on accurate analysis of the market, high rents merely demonstrate that land is being put to its highest and best use. About the worst thing that can be said about a shopping center is that its rentals are low.

* As consulting editor in the MGIC Newsletter.

trillion in the year 2000. Department store sales of $40 billion in 1970 will, if this inflationary trend continues, zoom to $80 billion in 1980, to $160 billion in 1990 and to $320 billion in the year 2000. The physical quantity of goods sold will increase less rapidly, but nevertheless faster than the estimated 50 per cent growth in population from 1970 to 2000 because of the greater affluence of the population.

### Questions

1. Do you agree with Dr. Hoyt's conclusions in regard to the potential growth of shopping centers between now and the year 2000? Why or why not?
2. Is it probable, as Professor Edwards suggests in his comments, that some revolutionary new merchandising idea may come along and make present day shopping centers obsolete? What kind of idea might this be?
3. What kinds of developments would again improve the competitive position of the Central Business District relative to shopping centers?
4. Why does financing for shopping centers present fewer problems than financing for housing?

### STUDY PROJECT 10–2

### Urban Planners Play a Game Called City 1 *

Practitioners of the subjective art of city planning have a problem. Their laboratory tools are few. Untested ideas must often be tried out on cities that are real. When errors are made, the effects also are real.

Now urban planners—along with architects, government officials, and educators—are playing a game that shows promise of helping to resolve this difficulty. It is called City 1, and its object is to improve on a hypothetical city. The action is taking place in the basement of a Washington, D.C., building.

At the heart of City 1 is an IBM 1130 computer, which stores the hundreds of bits of information that can affect the make-believe city's growth. The game, defined as an "urban simulation system," was completed in August for more than $100,000, about 70% of it from the U.S. Office of Education. Its developer is the nonprofit Washington Center for Metropolitan Studies, which is heavily backed by the Ford Foundation.

**Assessment.** City 1 is the latest in an evolving family of games, each more elaborate than its predecessor. It has been played by hundreds of people and has been demonstrated in several cities.

Its creators see it as a teaching tool and planning aid for ensuring that urban development is orderly and coordinated. Says Peter House, 31-year-old director of urban simulation systems at Washington Center and developer of the game: "After all, it's cheaper than renting a city."

Participants agree that the game is meaningful and that they have benefited from playing it. Most say they have gained increased awareness of the need to discipline their thinking to prevent uncoordinated planning.

* By permission, *Business Week*, Nov. 16, 1968, McGraw-Hill, Inc.

**The Rules.**    City 1 is played as a series of 90-minute rounds, each equivalent to a year of a city's life. As many as 36 players are divided into nine teams; seven of the teams simulate city departments, two represent citizens' groups and the mass media. The teams must work together; if they don't, chaos results, just as in a real city. "People quickly see the value of cooperating with their opposite numbers in other departments," says William W. Chase, a U.S. Office of Education official.

The teams elect members to the city council, and the players as a group elect a mayor. The teams make their plans for the round, then fill out planning forms that have been distributed by the game's operator, a representative from Washington Center.

The plans are used as a basis for the bureaucracy's estimate of what public action must be taken in the round—what must be done, for instance, about a Highway Dept. request for funds. The council must vote at a specific time on such actions. Those approved must be completed during the round.

**Basis for Decision.**    After plans are made, the Finance Dept. produces a budget, based on its interpretation of departmental requests and expected revenues. The mayor reviews and modifies the budget and submits it to the council for approval. When approval comes, funds are allocated to the departments and the teams carry out their plans.

Built into the game is an arbitrary factor which simulates human differences in a real world.

The game pulls together hundreds of factors, including the human. Players are forced to think through all decisions. A housing development, for example, must have a sewer system. A new plant must have a labor supply. And workers must have places to live and transportation to and from the job.

Also recognized is the fact that most cities are governed by a power structure that usually is aligned with the wealthier elements of the community.

**On the Spot.**    The success of each team's performance—weighed with the opinions of the citizens' and mass media groups—determines its chances of holding political office in the succeeding round.

Action is displayed on a six-foot-square Plexiglas board, which dominates the front of the sloping room. The board is divided into 625 squares, each representing a square mile of land. Models are placed on the board to represent ownership and improvements to land sections, so that players can see how their city would look at game's end.

Both good and bad results are put on the board, and Washington Center officials think the effect may be a bit too realistic if applied to an actual city. House says that city officials usually want their planners to predict a rosy future, and would probably fire one who did otherwise.

**Predecessors.**    The game concept for urban studies did not originate at Washington Center. For example, Allan Feldt's Cornell Land Use Game (CLUG) and Metropolis, developed by Richard Duke of Michigan State University, are well-known in planning circles.

Neither of these, however, is as comprehensive as the center's urban simulation system. Indeed, CLUG is limited to competition between real estate developers, whose motivation is primarily economic gain—and was expanded and adapted to municipal government by the center. Metropolis, on the other hand, is closer to the center's concept, but is a simulation of an actual city, East Lansing, Mich.

## Questions

1. Do you think a simulation exercise such as "City I" can be helpful in connection with city planning? Why or why not?
2. Is an exercise such as "City I" likely to be more effective as a teaching tool than as an aid to long-range planning? Explain.
3. Can a city planner in practice predict other than a rosy future for his city? Why or why not?

# 11

# Location Analysis:
## Neighborhoods and
## Districts

### NEIGHBORHOOD AND DISTRICT FACTORS
### IN REAL ESTATE DECISIONS

As we have pointed out every parcel of real property is a share in its surroundings, in the residential neighborhood or business district of which it forms a part. It is also a share in a sector of the metropolitan area and in the local economy.

It is often said that the three main considerations in real estate decisions are (1) location, (2) location, and (3) location. We have considered some of the broader location factors in our preceding discussions. We turn now to a consideration of the immediate areas surrounding a property, its immediate neighborhood or district. We will indicate some of the types of neighborhood and district analyses that may be helpful to real estate decision makers.

### Purpose and Extent of Analysis

As is true of most types of real estate analysis, studies of neighborhoods and districts are governed to a considerable extent by the purpose to be served. A business executive may have one purpose to be served, a government official another, an individual home buyer still another.

Each will have an interest to be served. An analysis of a neighborhood may be undertaken in connection with a property appraisal. A businessman may be considering a location for a new branch office; a local official may be considering recommendations for changes in the zoning law; a newcomer to the city may be considering the purchase of a house that is for sale.

In some cases a quick inspection may be adequate. In others, detailed and extensive analyses may be required. A prospective home buyer might be interested in a relatively limited area, a mortgage lender might want to cover an extensive area. Purpose and type of interest, thus, will govern the analysis of a neighborhood or district.

### Neighborhoods, Districts, and People

When we refer to neighborhoods and districts, we are likely to think in terms of land area, structures, and other physical factors. Although this is appropriate in a sense, we should remember that these physical factors have significance only as they serve the needs of people. When we refer to neighborhoods and districts, we mean primarily the people who live or work in such places. The people may be influenced by their physical surroundings, but in a final analysis the people control the types of buildings and other improvements that are found in neighborhoods and districts. Thus, we are concerned with the factors that influence the decisions of people, either from a personal or a business standpoint, relative to real estate resources.

There is a tendency for us to think of impersonal forces as determining the future of specific localities. We refer to location factors, to market forces, poltical influences, and the like, often forgetting that when we do this we are really referring to the attitudes, points of view, interests, and objectives of specific persons. In combination, the opinions of large numbers of persons may appear to constitute an impersonal sort of force. Fundamentally, however, we are likely to reach false conclusions if we forget that real properties, neighborhoods, districts, the structure of cities or metropolitan areas all mean little or nothing unless we think in terms of the peope who give importance to them. And it is the reactions, value judgments, hopes, and fears of people that finally result in the assignment of values to real properties, and that give one neighborhood a better reputation than another or give one business district an advantage over others.

In the discussions that follow we often refer to the physical characteristics of neighborhoods and districts. This should not obscure the fact that we are considering factors which are likely to influence the judgments and decisions of people in respect to real estate resources.

## FORCES CAUSING NEIGHBORHOOD CHANGE

The forces which cause people to reach decisions that bring about changes in neighborhoods are of three main types: (1) physical and functional depreciation, (2) the development of more intensive land uses, and (3) changes of residence. Physical wear and tear and the introduction of new materials, designs, and equipment tend constantly to make older structures less desirable places in which to live. As new houses are built, the older ones lose out in competition with them.

Business uses sometimes invade residential areas. The relocation of an industrial district may affect a number of neighborhoods. There is some tendency for families to move as income increases. As people move into a neighborhood, they may be absorbed without any significant change. On the other hand, the movement of new people into an area may replace others already living there.

As a result of the operation of these forces, people are drawn to newer or more desirable areas (as measured by their standards). A number of population movements are taking place more or less constantly in our towns and cities. Some families move into other apartments in the same building, others go next door, across the street, or around the corner. Still other families move long distances within the city or move to other parts of the country, while new individuals and families move into the city. It is estimated that each year about one family in five moves.

### Neighborhood Life Cycle

Those interested in real estate value changes sometimes observe that houses do not wear out but neighborhoods do. Residential neighborhoods tend to pass through periods of early growth, maturity, and decline. A new neighborhood may be entirely built up by a developer, with all facilities complete and no intervening vacant lots. Where the area is subdivided and lots are sold to individual home builders, houses may be built on scattered lots. A development may be arrested with builders going to new areas where entire sections of new houses can be built. Sometimes the advantages of utilities and pavements in the older areas cause new houses to be built in the vacant lots at a later period.

There is no uniform rate of maturity or decline in neighborhoods. The Battery in Charleston, South Carolina, has mainained an attractive residential character for over 200 years. Suburbs often remain attractive for very long periods of time. Examples include various of the North Chicago suburbs, the Westchester County area near New York and the Maryland and Virginia suburbs near Washington, D.C.

Neighborhoods may decline for many reasons; the buildings may become obsolete as to structure, achitectural style, or lot area; new groups of people may enter the area; or certain commercial or industrial establishments may expand and make the area less desirable for residential purposes. Changes in the character of schools often lend to neighborhood decline.

The aging of the population may be a factor. As children grow up to marriageable age, they may find it difficult to buy homes in the old neighborhood or they may prefer to move to newer neighborhoods where their friends are living. As the old residents die, a different social or income group may take their places.

In some cases families move from a central apartment to a suburban apartment, and then into a single-family home. When children reach school age, families tend to move from apartments to single-family homes.

It cannot be assumed, however, that old residential neighborhoods have steadily declined in value after reaching maturity. Houses in old neighborhoods sometimes sell for higher prices than at the time they were built. But the general tendency is to lose out in competition with newer areas.

Some residential neighborhoods are absorbed in new commercial developments. This is rather infrequent, as most central business districts have ceased to expand laterally. The requirement for parking areas near existing shopping districts, however, is creating a demand for old houses near established commercial areas at prices high enough to absorb the cost of the structures.

Thus there is no uniform rule as to the rate of decline in a neighborhood, and each neighborhood should be considered in relation to the general pattern of residential land uses.

## Types of Residential Neighborhoods

The largest proportion of the utilized land in our cities is devoted to residential purposes. However, these residential areas contain many different types of people, properties, and neighborhoods. Although the dividing lines between neighborhoods usually are not sharp, there are great differences between the deluxe residential suburbs at the one extreme and slums at the other.

Neighborhoods might be classified by the types of people who live in them; by type, location, age, and condition of structures; or in other ways. Nearly all of these factors are reflected, however, in the level of rents or prices typical of the various neighborhoods of a city. Hence, the following classification is based on three general levels of rents or prices: high, intermediate, and low; in addition, types of structures and locations are reflected in the subclassifications. This is not a hard-and-fast classification, but will suggest the types of neighborhoods most generally found in our cities.

I. HIGH-RENT OR -PRICE AREAS
    A. Apartment house or town house neighborhoods, located at desirable points
        1. On main mass transportation lines
        2. Near ocean, lake, or river fronts
        3. Near expressways
    B. Single-family neighborhoods
        1. Axial developments
            a. Located along best transportation lines
            b. Located along desirable water fronts
        2. Self-contained areas
        3. Suburban towns
        4. Country estates

II. INTERMEDIATE-RENT OR -PRICE AREAS
    A. Apartment house neighborhoods
        1. Garden types
        2. Walk-ups
        3. Elevator types
    B. Row-house or town house areas
    C. Neighborhoods of two-family structures and small apartment houses
    D. Neighborhoods of single-family homes
        1. Suburban or peripheral developments
        2. "Near-in" areas

III. LOW-RENT OR -PRICE AREAS
    A. Multi-family dwelling areas
    B. Row-house or town house areas
    C. Two-family structures and small apartment houses
    D. Single-family home neighborhoods
        1. Centrally located and near-in locations
        2. Peripheral and suburban locations
        3. Declining country towns

## Density of Population

Ordinarily we think of overcrowded conditions as being undesirable for a neighborhood either from a social or an economic standpoint. In planning for the redevelopment of some of the slum areas of our cities, special efforts are often made to decrease population density. With careful planning, however, high densities can be accommodated as in the case of "platform cities."

The density of population in cities depends on (1) the size of the total population, (2) the speed of the city's internal transportation system, (3) types of structures, and (4) land coverage.

In ancient Rome, for example, a population of 1,000,000 was crowded into an area of five square miles. Most of the residential buildings were 5 or 6 stories high, and the streets were only 8 to 10 feet wide. While the population density in the central portion of our larger cities is still high, improved transportation and more careful land planning have helped to reduce densities.

**Relative Density**

Some indication of the population densities likely to be found in residential neighborhoods may be secured from the following relationships. The population density is around 10,000 per gross square mile in neighborhoods of single-family houses where the lots are 50 feet wide and 100 feet deep and when half the land is allocated to streets, recreation areas, schools, shopping centers, and similar land uses. In row-house or town house areas under the same general conditions outlined above, the population density reaches 30,000 per gross square mile. In 3-story walk-up apartments with 4-room units and with 50 per cent of land covered by the apartment buildings, a density of 50,000 per square mile is reached. Population density ranges from 100,000 to 200,000 per square mile in areas of elevator apartments 8 to 22 stories high with 25 per cent of land coverage.

Sometimes theoretical standards of population density are set up which ignore other important considerations. From the standpoint of light and air, conditions are worse in Chicago walk-up apartment areas, with a density of 70,000 persons to the square mile, where 3-story buildings are crowded together on the fronts of lots, than they are in New York developments which have 8- to 13-story apartment buildings on a 25 per cent land coverage with a density of 180,000 persons per square mile. It is not desirable, however, to impose uniform density rules on all locations. Sites near an express subway station are limited in area and tend to be occupied by families who want the maximum convenience in transportation. Hence, high-rise elevator apartments tend to develop in such locations. The ocean-front land at Miami Beach is limited in extent and tall hotels properly spaced are economically desirable there. Lower buildings can occupy less strategic areas.

## MAIN POINTS FOR NEIGHBORHOOD DECISIONS AND ANALYSIS

We consider here the following items which are likely to influence decisions of owners, buyers, sellers, tenants, or investors and which thus are the major points for neighborhood analysis.

1. Location of the neighborhood with respect to other land uses and the main lines of growth.
2. Land use regulations.
3. The age of the neighborhood.
4. The types of people in the area.
5. The types of buildings and other improvements in the area.
6. Transportation.
7. Nearness to schools, churches, shopping centers, amusement places, and places of employment.
8. Tax burdens and special assessments.
9. Utilities, conveniences, and services.
10. Special hazards and nuisances.

### Land Use Structure and Main Lines of Growth

The relation of each neighborhood to the main lines of city growth and to the structure of major land uses can be determined by inspection. In general, property values are likely to be more stable in areas which are in the main direction of city growth. Neighborhoods which are not likely to participate in the economic advance of the city will tend to decline more rapidly than those which are located more favorably in this respect.

### Protections

The future of a neighborhood may depend on the protections which are set up for it. Zoning laws usually regulate the types of uses to which various areas in a city may be put. To be adequate they must not only indicate the permitted uses in a definite manner, but the uses allowed must be such as to contribute to the future of a neighborhood. In addition, attention should be given to the extent to which such regulations are enforced and the manner of their administration in the light of changing conditions. Height and area restrictions are also of importance, since they help to protect a neighborhood against overcrowding and the dangers likely to result from it.

Regulations of these types are sometimes used by self-seeking groups for their own advantage rather than for public purposes. As a result, zoning ordinances and similar regulations may give a false sense of security to home purchasers or investors.

Restrictive covenants, usually referred to as *deed restrictions*, represent another type of protection. These are private covenants in the deed to property rather than public regulations. Hence, deed restrictions typically may be much more detailed and definite than zoning laws and may regulate such things as cost of buildings, types of structures, setback lines, and related matters.

Deed restrictions are usually set up at the time a new development is started. Thus, much depends on the wisdom and foresight of the developer in such cases, as well as in his decisions with respect to lot sizes, land coverage, street locations, dedication of land to park and playground areas, and the like. Much depends also on the effectiveness of the administration of these restrictions.

An area which is entirely or almost entirely built up is less likely to change rapidly than one which is only partially developed, for in the latter case there is always the possibility of utilizing vacant land for purposes which do not harmonize with existing land uses. Hence, relatively undeveloped areas tend to be less stable than those which are more completely built up, unless adequate restrictions and regulations are in existence. The extent to which vacant areas may be a hazard to neighborhood stability varies somewhat from one city to another, depending chiefly on the rapidity with which the city is growing or changing.

Both natural and artificial barriers may help to protect a neighborhood. Public parks, hills, ravines, and similar barriers may be of great importance to the future stability of a neighborhood.

### Neighborhood Age

In the case of both neighborhoods and people, age is a relative matter. Some age rapidly, others grow old gracefully. There are neighborhoods in some of our cities that are well over 100 years old but are still desirable residential areas with stable property values. Other things being equal, newer neighborhoods which have been sufficiently built up to become established are more likely to be sound investment areas than older ones. However, other things seldom are equal in cases of this type. In analyzing neighborhoods, age should be considered only to the extent that it is likely to have a direct bearing on future property values.

Typically, age brings about deterioration of structures and increases the cost and difficulty of maintaining them. In addition, newer neighborhoods may be planned and developed in a more attractive manner than those which are older.

## The Residents of the Area

Since future development of a neighborhood will be determined to a large degree by the decisions of the people who live there, it is necessary to consider the principal characteristics of these people in the process of analyzing a neighborhood.  Such questions as the following should be considered: What are the typical incomes of residents of the area?  Are there wide variations of income?  What percentage of the people own their own homes?  Which occupations are represented?  How frequently do people move into or out of the neighborhood?  Does the general social organization and tone of the neighborhood make it a place where people like to live for long periods of time?

Typically, a high percentage of owner occupancy indicate a favorable future for a neighborhood.  Owners tend to move less frequently than tenants.  Owners usually take great pride in their dwelling and do whatever they can to maintain and preserve the stability and appeal of the neighborhood.

## Buildings and Other Improvements

Neighborhoods of attractive architectural style tend to be areas of relatively stable land values for long periods of time.  This condition is strengthened if lot sizes are well planned and if the buildings are arranged in accordance with an attractive pattern.

Typically, greater stability of values is assured if all of the buildings in a neighborhood are maintained in good condition.  Obviously, houses which are kept in good condition last longer than those which are allowed to deteriorate, and hence there is less chance for depreciation.

Landscaping, gardens, walks, drives, and accessory buildings contribute to neighborhood advance or decline depending on their general character and maintenance.  The nature of the topography, availability of pleasing views, wooded lots, broad vistas and the like all add to the appeal of an area.  Attractive street layout, provision for drainage, and well-planned traffic flows are all factors of importance.

## Transportation

Adequacy of transportation, like so many other factors involved in neighborhood analysis, is a relative matter.  In small towns all neighborhoods may be within easy walking distance of schools, shopping centers, places of employment, and amusement points.  Some new towns are planned in this way.  In such cases transportation is of little significance in determining a neighborhood's future.  However, in most larger cities, transportation has a vital bearing on a neighborhood.  Transportation must be considered in relation to the present and prospective occupants of a neighborhood. If most of the families in a neighborhood have two cars, public transportation may be of relatively little significance. For many of the neighborhoods in our metropolitan areas, however, public transportation plays an important role. The important point to remember in analyzing transportation is the comparison of services and costs between neighborhoods.

### Civic, Social, and Commercial Centers

Neighborhood stability is increased if a neighborhood is served adequately by grade and high schools, shopping centers, churches, parks, playgrounds, hospitals, amusement places, and other civic, social and commercial centers. If a neighborhood is served by schools of good reputation, there is competition among people to locate there, and property values are supported. In some cities the central downtown business district is capable of serving all neighborhoods adequately; but in our larger metropolitan centers, the services of outlying shopping centers are essential for most residential areas. Similarly, the location of other types of community centers should be considered in relation to the requirements of the neighborhood under consideration, especially with respect to the major differences between competing neighborhoods.

Of special importance also is the extent to which civic, social, and commercial centers add to or detract from the general tone of the neighborhood. These intangible factors often have great significance.

### Taxes and Special Assessments

The burdens of taxation often vary from one neighborhood to another in the same city because of the fact that the assessment process frequently results in the valuation of properties at different percentages of "true" value. If the properties in one neighborhood bear a higher proportionate tax load than those in other areas, instability may result. Thus, it is necessary to study assessment methods and to compare tax burdens in different neighborhoods in order to determine the extent to which uniformity or differences exist.

Property taxes constitute such a heavy burden on real estate owners that an unduly heavy tax load may militate strongly against a neighborhood's future. The average tax burden on homes is high. A property owner is likely to pay in taxes over a period of years an amount equal to more than the price of the building.

While it is always desirable that a neighborhood have adequate streets, sewers, sidewalks, and similar conveniences, their costs sometimes are excessive and are paid for over a long period of time. The special assessments levied for such purposes may be so heavy in a neighborhood that its future will be endangered. Hence, it is always necessary to determine the payments which are outstanding and the length of time during which such payments must be made.

### Utilities, Conveniences, and Services

The utilities, conveniences, and services which may be available in a neighborhood include electricity, gas, water supply, garbage disposal, street lighting, sewage disposal, drainage, street improvements, police and fire protection, and mail delivery. The types of services available and their cost to the user in comparison with other areas of the city should be analyzed carefully. In addition, the types of utilities, conveniences and services available should be considered in terms of what is expected by the residents of the area.

As is true of the factors we are considering here, one area may have a competitive advantage over another if there are great differences with respect to the type, quality, and cost of the utilities and services available. As violence has increased in major cities, the availability and quality of police and fire protection have grown in importance.

### Topography, Hazards, and Nuisances

We have already pointed out how topographical factors may form natural barriers against blighting influences. Such matters as streets with steep grades, soil erosion, and hillside locations may be hazardous to persons and property. Low-lying areas may be subject to periodic floods; the condition of the soil may discourage lawns and gardens.

High-speed traffic thoroughfares create hazards for the residents of a neighborhood; high-tension electric lines involve some risks; locations near airports may be hazardous; nearness to industrial areas or railroad lines or yards may subject an area to noise and other nuisances.

The increase in airplane traffic to many airports may have caused some damage to the property values of residences located in close proximity to airports. The noise developed by large modern airplanes and the danger that there may be crashes in the adjacent areas are both factors of considerable importance in this connection. Just how much damage to property values may be caused by these developments is not too certain, but this is undoubtedly one of the factors to be added to the list of hazards and nuisances which affect residential properties.

### Relative Marketability

All of the factors which we have discussed briefly in the preceding sections have a bearing on the marketability of properties in the area. As a summary of these factors, it may be desirable to consider the degree to which typical properties in the neighborhood will be salable over a period of years and whether they will be more or less salable than similar properties in other areas. We should remember that the high-cost neighborhoods are not always the most stable areas.

As we have pointed out in the earlier part of this chapter, a careful analysis of the factors which have been discussed should give us a fairly reliable indication of the future trend of property incomes and values in a neighborhood and should provide a useful guide to real estate decisions. Such an analysis will be more reliable if proper allowances have been made for local applications of the general tendencies which we have outlined.

## TYPES OF COMMERCIAL AND INDUSTRIAL DISTRICTS

Although there are wide varieties of business (commercial and industrial) areas in our cities, they may be classified into five main groups. Commercial districts include: (1) central business districts, (2) outlying business centers, and (3) isolated outlets and clusters. Industrial districts are of two main types: (1) those used chiefly for heavy industrial establishments and (2) those used principally by light industry. Industrial districts may also be classified by location.

Business uses may radiate out from the center of the city along one or more main traffic arteries. Businesses which require larger amounts of horizontal space, special parking facilities, or large quantities of land are found along these streets. New and used automobile and accessory dealers, filling stations, food marts, supermarkets, and larger grocery stores, farmers' markets, tourist hotels and motels, and the like are located on such streets. "Near-in" parts of such streets may be thought of as a part of the central business district; those farther out may be classified with outlying business centers.

### Central Business District

The central business district is the functioning heart of the city. In it are concentrated the major retail, financial, hotel, service, and governmental activities of the city. The specialized land uses in the central business district typically include retail shopping areas, office buildings, hotels, theater and amusement sections, banks and other financial institutions, government buildings, and, on the fringe, the wholesale district and the light manufacturing area. Transportation routes usually lead to this center.

In the central business district the cost of doing business is high, competition is keen, good sites are at a premium, and there are chances for both great successes and great failures. Almost all kinds of business enterprise may be found there except those requiring large amounts of horizontal space or those dealing in commodities which are low in value in relation to bulk. The establishments with the greatest rent-paying ability obtain the choice sites, with the less desirable space going to other businesses. Generally speaking, the best parts of the central business districts are those with access to the greatest potential purchasing power, as measured by the quantity and quality of pedestrian traffic. Customers are drawn from all parts of the city and from its hinterland or market area, which may extend for many miles in all directions.

### "100 Per Cent" Locations

The types of business which can afford to locate in "100 per cent" business locations and pay the highest rents are department stores, women's apparel stores, shoe stores, men's clothing stores, jewelry stores, drugstores, candy stores, and variety stores. These stores can afford to pay 3 to 6 per cent of their sales in rent on sales volumes ranging from $80 to $200 or more per square foot of floor area, which yields returns of from $2.50 to as high as $15 per square foot in rents. Stores which cannot afford to pay the rents for ground floor locations in the heart of the central business districts include furniture stores (those whose sales rarely exceed $40 per square foot), hardware stores, barbershops, and food stores.

With the rapid development of shopping centers, the downtown areas have suffered in varying degrees from this competition. Certain functions, however, appear to be performed best in central business districts. These include the functions of providing the greatest selection of retail merchandise, highly specialized activities, financial institutions, major office headquarters, theaters and other amusement places, and related activities.

### Outlying Business Centers

Outlying business centers include a variety of districts which may be miniatures of the central business district, regional and super regional shopping centers, smaller shopping centers and neighborhood business streets. Typically the outlying centers do not include transportation terminals. Parking space and the presence of good feeder streets are of considerable importance to such a center.

Nearly all types of enterprises may be found in outlying centers. There has been a tremendous growth of shopping centers of many types. The choice sites go to the establishments with greatest rent-paying ability. Pedestrian traffic is much less significant than in the central area. Parking facilities are one of the major attractions.

Small neighborhood centers usually include only such establishments as appeal to the immediate needs of the people in the area, with little specialization of land use.

### Isolated Outlets and Clusters

Isolated business outlets are single establishments doing business principally on a personal basis, as in the case of a delicatessen in the front of a residence or a beauty shop or dentist's office located in a part of a house or apartment. Increasingly, such stores as Sears Roebuck and various supermarkets occupy isolated locations. Isolated filling stations, restaurants, general stores, and repair garages are found on principal highways. Two or more such outlets may form a business cluster of establishments which complement each other, such as a drugstore, supermarket, and shoe repair shop. Typically they develop on small parcels of land which are designated by zoning regulations for commercial uses and are quite limited in extent. However, the small town or village business cluster is more like the central business district in embryonic form. It usually serves the village and the surrounding countryside, but the establishments located there are not highly specialized.

### Industrial Areas

Heavy industrial areas are being located to an increasing extent in peripheral areas and in the open countryside. Light industry may be found at almost any location. Some light industry may even be acceptable in or near residential neighborhoods. Often there is no noise or odor, grounds are attractively landscaped and the number of employees is relatively small due to highly automated processes. Industrial parks have developed extensively in recent years, typically in outlying locations.

## ANALYSIS OF DISTRICTS

The analysis of commercial and industrial districts varies with the purpose being served. Purpose will govern the extent and intensity of the analysis, the factors given priority and the types of data included. Usually analyses of this type are more detailed and specialized than those of residential neighborhoods, although there are wide variations in practice. In our discussions here we will consider the analysis of central business districts, outlying business districts including shopping centers and the analysis of industrial areas. We try to consider fairly standard approaches, recognizing that from time to time special considerations will require attention. For example, franchises have had a recent popularity; equity financing has increased in importance; and industrial parks have assumed a larger role. Additional changes will be coming along as times goes on and the analyst should be alert to their potential importance.

The more important forces to consider in analyzing various business districts include: (1) the economic potential of the region, (2) intensity of competition, (3) changes in the internal structure of the city, (4) physical factors, (5) transportation, and (6) government policies, including taxes, zoning and planning regulations, traffic controls, protections against crime, fire and other hazards and related policies and regulations.

Industrial districts will be affected by the same forces but their impact may vary somewhat.

### Economic Potential and Type of City

The growth of the central business district will depend on the economic development of the area which it serves, including the city and its market region.

The strength of the central business district will depend to some degree on the type of city—whether an international, national, or regional capital is involved or whether the central district must compete rather directly with outlying business centers in the same area. Differences between office building and retail land uses should be noted. If a city is an international center such as New York, offices in the central districts enjoy some special advantages over outlying centers, and to some degree this may be true of retailing.

To an increasing extent, business is being done on a regional and also on a national basis. For example, businessmen in smaller cities now do their banking to an increasing extent in major regional centers. Many financial activities are tending to center in New York on a national basis.

This suggests that major office building developments will occur in a relatively few cities that will emerge as the principal regional economic capitals of the country. Only in them will it be economical to concentrate the highly specialized activities that result from a minute division of labor which is induced by large scale regional and national operations.[1]

### Intensity of Competition

Although financial activities and others that support major office building types of land uses are likely to be concentrated in the centers of

[1] Arthur M. Weimer, *Investors and Downtown Real Estate*, Technical Bulletin No. 39 (Washington, D.C.: Urban Land Institute, 1960).

principal regional cities, retailing has tended to move outward even in the larger regional and national economic capitals. Similarly there is little likelihood of manufacturing activities, except for some light types, seeing much further development in city centers, regardless of the type of city. The growth of the central business district also depends on the intensity of competition from outlying centers. Outlying business centers, however, may not participate in the general economic advance or decline of the city as directly as the central business district.

Some types of business establishments are more successful if located near competing or complementary firms. Continuity of stores and shops contributes to the value of each of the stores because shoppers like to find a complete asortment of merchandise in one location and often want to compare prices. On the other hand, inharmonious activities will endanger the success of some establishments; for example, a retail store catering to a fashionable group will be affected adversely by the development of a low-priced entertainment and amusement center at a nearby location.

### Internal Structure

Changes in the internal structure of a city are likely to affect all business districts within it. Generally the central business district tends to move in the main direction of city growth, although the location of transportation terminals exerts great influence and usually anchors the central district to a fixed location. Parking difficulties have become one of the main disadvantages of central business districts. The growth or movement of outlying centers depends to a large extent on changes in the internal transportation system and on changes in residential areas. The continued decentralization of our cities indicates that many of the outlying business centers will develop markedly in the years ahead and that new ones will be established.

Other factors which have contributed to the growth of outlying business districts include the development of chain, department, drug, and variety stores adapted to such areas, and the opening in the outlying centers of branches of banks, savings and loan associations, and other financial institutions. Office buildings, sometimes of relatively large size, often develop in outlying centers. The growing popularity of franchising has had a bearing especially on outlying centers in recent years.

### Topography

Topography has a bearing on the growth of a business district, since most business establishments prefer locations on level land. Hence, a business district seldom moves uphill or down a steep incline. Topography also is an important determinant of transportation routes. Low-lying areas are often endangered by floods or require special protections which may be costly. The load-bearing qualities of the soil will affect the cost of building. If there are problems of air and water pollution, they will have an important bearing on the future of an area.

### Government Policies

Taxation, zoning laws, transportation regulations, police and fire protection, and other government policies have a major effect on business districts. Obviously, any decisions affecting the transportation system, including changes of main lines, rates, or related policies, will have a bearing on the future of business districts. Those tax policies are most important which result in different tax burdens for different districts. Frequently the central business district is required to bear an extremely high tax burden, and this may force certain business establishments to seek other locations. In some cases one outlying center bears a higher tax burden than others because of faulty assessment practices or because it is in a sewer or sanitary district or other special tax area which imposes high rates.

Land use regulations are not likely to affect central business districts to a marked degree, but are of major importance in determining the growth of outlying centers. Height and bulk regulations are of greater importance to central business districts.

The increase of crime in our cities has had a greater impact on central districts than on outlying centers although all have been affected to some extent. The adequacy of police protection, thus, has become a factor of growing importance. Fire protection has always been important but increased violence has made it even more so. Again, the problems appear to have been somewhat more important in the central districts.

### Pedestrian Traffic Counts

Estimates of the probable amounts of business which may be expected to develop at a downtown retail location are often based on traffic counts. In making traffic counts, sampling techniques are usually employed. A number of stations may be set up within each block on both sides of the street so that checkers can count the number of persons passing each point for five minutes during each business hour. Traffic intersections are not included, attention being centered at points where people are passing in front of stores. High correlations have been found between the number of pedestrians passing a point and the volume of retail sales, rents, and land values. While it is generally assumed that the average purchasing power of persons within the same business district is about equal, there are often marked differences between the crowds on the two sides of the same street. In some cases pedestrian traffic counts must be modified to allow for shopping by telephone and similar practices.

### Impact of Industrial Districts

Like other types of districts, industrial areas will be affected by the economic development of the region as well as general directions of city growth and changes in the city's internal structure. Transportation facilities have always exercised great influence on the development of industrial districts; with the development of truck transportation, some industry has no longer been tied to main transportation lines. There has been a significant development of industrial plants along belt highways; for example, Route 128 in Boston, the Calumet Expressway in Chicago, and the Pennsylvania Turnpike north of Philadelphia. Heavy industries still require adequate rail or water transportation, and their location and development continue to depend to a large extent on the transportation facilities available and their cost. Topography is of importance in this connection because it may control the development of new transportation lines and because industry tends to follow level and relatively low-lying areas rather than high ground.

Industrial districts may be limited in their development by the amount and kind of vacant land available. They may be influenced also by the rate of functional depreciation of industrial buildings, since some structures of this type are superseded by more efficient ones in a relatively short time.

Regulations pertaining to environmental factors are growing in importance. Relative standards and costs of waste disposal, for example, are entering more and more into industrial location decisions.

In most cities definite limits have been placed on the movement of industrial districts by city planning regulations and zoning laws. Usually, such laws and regulations are liberal in the amount of space allocated to present and potential industrial uses, although restrictive tendencies have become more common.

Tax policies are of major importance in determining the future probable locations and developments of industrial districts. Tax burdens are one aspect of the whole problem of competition for sites and the relative costs of land. Usually, commercial establishments can outbid industries in their competition for space. Industrial establishments often require large ground floor areas, and only the light industries can operate economically in the upper stores of buildings. Hence, high land values are a handicap to heavy industrial development.

To escape high land values and high taxes, many industries have moved farther and farther from the centers of our cities. Industries now cover many parts of the countryside much as farms did in an earlier period. Formerly it was necessary to consider nearness to the homes of workers, but improved transportation and especially the increased use of the automobile have largely eliminated this consideration in determining industrial locations.

## SUMMARY

As with any investigation, it is essential to know the purpose for which neighborhood or district analysis is undertaken. Such analysis may be needed for business, personal, institutional, or governmental decisions. Purpose also helps to determine the type and extent of the analysis undertaken.

A number of classifications of neighborhoods may be employed. This chapter has presented a classification based on levels of rents and prices.

Neighborhood change is the result of the interaction of personal, business, and governmental decisions plus various historical or institutional factors. The primary forces behind these decisions are physical and functional depreciation, type and intensity of land use, and changes in residential patterns.

Many factors in the neighborhood environment will have important influences on decisions. They include location with respect to city growth, protections, types of people and buildings in the area, transportation, civic and social facilities, and governmental factors including regulations and police and fire protection, and taxes.

Neighborhoods tend to go through phases of growth, maturity, and decline. However, the time sequence of these phases is not fixed; some neighborhoods decline rapidly whereas other remain attractive for long periods of time.

Commercial and industrial districts are classified in this chapter into five main groups. In analysis of these districts the following factors are of importance: (1) changes in the economic potential and internal structure of the city, (2) transportation, (3) physical factors, (4) intensity of competition and (5) governmental policies.

## QUESTIONS FOR STUDY

1. Describe the principal forces causing changes in residential neighborhoods.
2. Make a list of the principal factors now affecting the neighborhood in which you live.
3. Which forces are likely to have greatest effect on your residential neighborhood in the next few years?
4. What are the main protections for a neighborhood? Which of these exist in the neighborhood in which you live?

5. How do population movements affect the future of a neighborhood? In analyzing a neighborhood, which population factors would you consider most important?

6. What effect does the condition of structures have on the future of a neighborhood? Does the age of structures have the same effect? Explain.

7. How important is the availability of transportation for the future of a neighborhood? A shopping center? An industrial district?

8. As an investor, would you prefer to invest in industrial or commercial property? Explain.

9. Outline an analysis for a shopping center investment. An industrial park.

## SUGGESTED READINGS

AMERICAN INSTITUTE OF REAL ESTATE APPRAISERS. *The Appraisal of Real Estate* (5th ed.). Chicago: The Institute, 1967. Chaps. 6, 10.

HOYT, HOMER. *According to Hoyt* (2nd ed.). Washington, D.C.: Hoyt, 1970. Pp. 269–96.

WEIMER, ARTHUR M. *Investors and Downtown Real Estate,* Technical Bulletin No. 39. Washington, D.C.: Urban Land Institute, 1960.

## CASE 11–1

### A Neighborhood Decision

George Edwards has just moved to your city and has called several real estate brokers to help him find a house. He is in a hurry to make a purchase because he is scheduled for an overseas assignment which will take two or three months and he wants to get his family settled before leaving the country.

One real estate broker calls his attention to a 15-year-old house located in one of the older neighborhoods of the city. It has been on the market for several months. The neighborhood continues to be an attractive area despite its age. The properties are well maintained. Insofar as Mr. Edwards can determine, the people in the area are the kind with whom he and the members of his family would feel comfortable. Schools, churches, and shopping centers are readily accessible. There is a heavy traffic artery two blocks from the house which must be crossed to reach the school and the shopping center.

Taxes have been advanced in recent years and are now considered to be among the highest for any neighborhood in the city. A bus line is available at the high-speed traffic artery and the area is about a twenty-five minute bus ride from downtown. The broker reports that fire and police protection are adequate. The area is zoned R-3 which means that multi-family buildings could be constructed. However, most of the land area is now used by single-family residences with a few doubles and it would be necessary to tear down older houses to make way for apartments.

The second property suggested by another broker, is less than a year old and located in a new neighborhood. It is approximately the same size, but has a three-car garage in contrast to a two-car garage for the older property.

The development in which the newer property is located is fairly new and is only about a third built up at this time. The property has come on the market within the past week because the owner was transferred to another location. Mr. Edwards is assured that deed restrictions will protect the area and that the limited extent to which the area is built up does not constitute a hazard. It is zoned R-1 which means single-family residential use only. The oldest house in the area is now about two years old so it is not possible to determine how stable the area will be. Most of those living there now are newcomers to the city.

A school is located about a mile away. There is no public transportation. Tax rates are relatively low since the area is located outside the city limits. No city police or fire protection are provided. The county sheriff and his staff are believed able to provide whatever protection may be needed. The city fire department will service the area but a special fee is charged. The property is accessible to city water, but not sanitary sewer.

The first property is priced at $37,500 and the broker believes an offer of $35,000 will buy it. The second is priced at $42,500 and there seems little likelihood of an adjustment since it has just come on the market.

## Questions

1. Which property should Mr. Edwards buy? Justify your selection.
2. Which basic factors would you change in order to reach the opposite decision? Explain.

## CASE 11–2

### Lacey's Department Store

Lacey's department store had served the town of Edgewater for 75 years when Mr. Morgan, the company president decided it was time to consider opening a second store in town. Edgewater had grown to a size of 125,000 and suburban shopping areas had begun to develop. Morgan was afraid that competition from these areas would draw business and profits away from downtown. He wanted to protect the profitability of the Lacey Company.

Last month, Morgan was approached by the agent of a real estate developer who was developing a large enclosed mall shopping center on the south side of town. It would be spectacular, he said, containing 40 stores, including Sears Roebuck and several other national tenants. It would be built at the intersection of two major highways, one of which was an interstate. Therefore, it would be of easy access to small towns in the Edgewater retail trading area. The agent said that he wanted Lacey's because it was a good department store and because of its fine local reputation.

Mr. Morgan also knew of an existing smaller shopping center on the north side of town that had expansion room that would be large enough for a department store. It was located well within the city at the intersection of two principal streets. There was also the possibility of locating a free standing store at a number of locations throughout the metropolitan area. One possibility would be on the west side where most of the higher-priced homes were located.

In the course of his investigation, Mr. Morgan accumulated the following information about the location possibilities. He realized that selecting the right location would be crucial to the success of his business.

**South Side.** The south side of town is largely industrial, but some housing has been developed outside the city limits. All the public housing in town is near the mall site. The location at the intersection of the highways is a definite advantage as far as rural shoppers are concerned, but it is not known how many residents from the north side will drive all the way through town to the mall. It is significant that Sears will be in the shopping center. The rent for Lacey's would be $120,000 per year plus 4 per cent of annual gross sales over $3,000,000.

**North Side.** The north side site is located at a major intersection and is convenient to a large number of townspeople. In a smaller shopping center, there will not be competition from as many other stores. Mr. Morgan thinks he can have a building built and rent it from the owner for a flat rate of 4 per cent of gross annual sales.

**West Side.** The site Mr. Morgan has in mind on the west side is also at the intersection of two principal streets. It is closer to the center of town than either of the other sites, but is nowhere near a highway. He figures the rent on a new free standing store there would run about $80,000 per year. One disadvantage is that there would be no other stores in the immediate area to help draw traffic.

### Questions

1. What advantages and disadvantages of each location can be inferred from the information given?
2. At what level of annual gross sales would the rent on the south and west side stores equal 4 per cent of the gross.
3. At which site do you think Lacey's could do the greatest business? Why?
4. If you were in Mr. Morgan's place, what would your decision be?

### STUDY PROJECT 11–1

### The Future of American Cities—and Suburbs *

Flying over an urban area, one is often prompted to ask: why would anyone want to work in that mess in the center when there are so many "nice" places in the outskirts.

---

* By David L. Birch; reproduced by permission of Mortgage Guaranty Insurance Corporation, from the *MGIC Newsletter.*

A closer look uncovers several plausible reasons. The first is simply tradition. The central city is where it all started. Customs develop, meeting places become familiar, and commuting patterns become established.

But tradition cannot explain the growth in employment that is taking place in most central cities today. As he searched for more positive explanations, Raymond Vernon[1] hit upon three factors that seem to explain central city growth: (1) communication, (2) minimizing the cost of uncertainty, and (3) external economics of scale.

By communication, Vernon meant the personal, face-to-face communication that is so essential when the corporate president meets with the lawyer and the banker to hammer out the terms of a loan or arrange a stock offering. The need for this kind of communication between many different kinds of specialists favors concentration, and hence central city locations.

Minimizing the cost of uncertainty is a fancy way of talking about the fellow who produces advertising brochures. He needs access to five or ten different types of printing processes, none of which he can afford to own himself because his need for any one is so small. So he relies on several different printers to do his work for him. Conversely, the printers with specialized presses rely on a large number of customers to keep their equipment operating at an efficient level. Collectively, this group of suppliers and producers forms a community in which the risks to any single member are minimized. There are many such inter-locking communities in most central cities, all located theer for the same basic reason.

The third rationale for choosing a central city location, the external economies of scale, recognizes that the central city can provide subways, airports, shopping facilities, hotels, restaurants, theaters and other community services that most smaller towns cannot offer. Many businesses, particularly the newer and smaller ones, cannot afford to be without such services, nor can they provide the services themselves.

Of course, we would not expect Vernon's three factors to affect all firms in the same way. Talking face-to-face, minimizing risk, and capitalizing on economies of scale are more important to the banker, the corporate financial staff, the wholesaler, and the small manufacturer than they are to the retailer or the large manufacturer.

It is not surprising, therefore, that natural selection takes place over time, with different sectors of the economy growing at different rates in the central city. The result is a substantial change in the mix of employment. The central city tends to become an elite service center, providing jobs for highly-paid white collar service workers. On balance and over time, this growth in service jobs has more than off-set the decline of retailing and large-scale manufacturing.

However, central city employment has been growing only one or two per cent per year, while employment in suburbs has been growing at a rate of 10

[1] Raymond Vernon, *The Changing Economic Function of the Central City* (CED, 1959).

to 20 per cent. This has led to a decline in the central city share of employment.

**Older Cities Different.** The question asked immediately in the face of these trends is: are all cities behaving in the same way? Intuitively, Phoenix and Albany conjure up quite different images, despite the fact that they are roughly the same size. The same is true of Buffalo and Houston or San Diego and Cincinnati. What would be expected is that the smaller and younger the city, the more rapidly it is growing and the more even the mix of employment within the central city boundaries. To an extraordinary degree, this turns out to be the case.

The implications of this life-cycle effect are many. Most obvious is the relative decline of the older, larger cities over the next 10 to 20 years. A second implication is regional. Most of the smaller, younger cities are in the South and the West.

So far we have been talking just about jobs. When people are added to the picture, an immediate chicken-egg problem arises. Do people follow "natural" shifts in the location of jobs, or do they create such shifts to suit their own preferences? The question is yet to be resolved, but one thing is clear: People and jobs are both moving in the same direction, and that's into the suburbs.

**Why People Move.** When we turn to the natural selection process within cities, things become more complex. People move far more often than jobs. They are constantly searching for an improved way of life. It is important to understand the nature as well as the magnitude of this movement in order to project its future course.

Let us start with a single family. Its history of movement might be diagrammed as in Fig. 1.

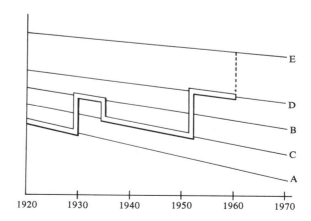

**Fig. 1.  Quality of Neighborhood.**

The lines labeled A, B, C, D, and E represent neighborhoods in the region over time. In 1920, the family moved into neighborhood A from a farm, from abroad, or possibly from another central city, and lived there for 10 years. The neighborhood, already crowded, was running downhill as the housing decayed. Over the ten year period, the family's income went up enough to allow the move to neighborhood B. The gain was only temporary, however, due to the depression, and the family was forced to move to neighborhood C. The war years brought the family head a much better job and, by 1952, he was able to move to neighborhood D. The children were married by this time, however, and they moved to neighborhood E, or beyond. In this process, the family has experienced disjointed and probably very frustrating change, but, in economic and social terms, an upward and not a downward movement is suggested.

When we examine where in the region the family started, and where it ended up, there is a good chance that neighborhood A was in the heart of the central city, while neighborhood D was an inner suburb. The family's movement has been outward as well as upward.

Not every family starts at the same place or moves with the same ease through this system of neighborhoods, of course. A major factor affecting mobility is age. Young families between the ages of 25 and 45 tend to move far more easily and upwardly than do older people. As a consequence, the central cities tend to get left with a more elderly population as out-migration takes place and in-migration slows.

A second factor affecting mobility is wealth. The rich start higher and move more easily, and this has tended to mean out into the suburbs. A close look at the job patterns, though, suggests that this cannot continue forever. As the low skill jobs move out and the high skill service jobs stay and grow in number, and as the ring of decay surrounding the city grows in size and unattractiveness, sooner or later the people who hold the elite jobs in the center will be forced to compare their long, unpleasant commutes with a central city residence. Increasingly they will choose to become central city residents.

There are already signs that this is beginning to take place. Between 1959 and 1967, for example, the percentage of central city families that were "rich" (incomes over $15,000, adjusted for inflation) practically doubled—from 7 per cent to 12 per cent—and the percentage who were "poor" (under $4,000) fell from 22 per cent to 19 per cent.

**What About Race?** A third major factor affecting migration within urban regions is race. Historically, the black migrant from the South was poor, and tended to settle in the central cities where he could find friends and low-cost housing. This trend has led to a substantial build up of black concentrations in our central cities that is approaching 22 per cent to 23 per cent on the average in 1970, with much higher concentrations in some areas.

A careful look at the data, though, suggests that the trend of rising concentrations will not continue forever. In the first place, the absolute flow of blacks into central cities has decreased substantially (from 3.4 per cent per years to 1.8 per cent per year between 1960 and 1968). In the second place, blacks now in urban areas are tending to look more and more like an upwardly mobile group. They are young, their educational attainment is rising rapidly: in the case of the crucial 25–29 year old group, blacks and whites have virtually the same median educational achievement.

Meanwhile, the inner suburbs are decaying. What were once pleasant bedroom communities are now deteriorating, densely packed areas that are virtually indistinguishable from their neighboring central cities. Under these conditions, it would be reasonable to expect blacks to move, first out of ghetto areas into better central city neighborhoods, and eventually, across the central city boundary into the inner suburbs and beyond. With whites waiting in line for luxury apartments, the net result should be a leveling off, and eventually a decline in the black percentages in many central cities.

There are signs that, in fact, all of these things are occurring. The abandonment of the ghettos, particularly in the large northern cities, has become a reality, as can be seen in the following mean growth rate figures for families in central city poverty areas:

|            | 1960–67  | 1967–68  |
|------------|----------|----------|
| White      | −2.90%   | −13.5%   |
| Non-White  | − .01%   | − 8.9%   |

During this same period, the annual growth in the number of blacks in suburban areas jumped from .7 per cent to 8.0 per cent. The result, recently reported by the Census Bureau, has been a 42 per cent increase in the number of suburban blacks between 1960 and 1970 in a sample of 67 metropolitan areas. Most of this growth has taken place since 1966, with cities such as Los Angeles, Washington, New York, Miami, Houston and St. Louis experiencing the greatest black out-migration.

Two key questions remain: (1) is the outward movement of blacks also upward movement—economically and socially—and (2) does it mean integration. These two questions are often treated as one, but they are, in fact, quite separable.

The outward movement definitely seems to have meant upward movement. For the first time in many years, suburban blacks now surpass their central city counterparts in educational achievement and earning power. The domestics and the janitors are being outnumbered by the bankers and the engineers and the professors.

Regarding integration, the picture is much less clear. Beyond tokenism here and there, the general pattern appears to be one of enclaves. It is the same pattern followed by the Jews and the Italians and the Germans who moved into the same suburban neighborhoods one or two generations ago. Eventually there should be integration at the fringes, but it does not yet seem to have taken place to any considerable degree.

## COMMENTARY

### by Edward E. Edwards *

For a decade or more we have been reading, and hearing, that our central cities are doomed, that the processes of urban decay are irreversible without massive inputs of both public and private money, under some well conceived plan of urban renewal. Thus it is encouraging and refreshing to be reminded that cities do have a power of self-renewal, and that our central cities not only can survive but can also become the best of all places in which to live and to work.

If our author is right, most of our older cities must be near the bottom of the long trend toward decay. The movement outward into the suburbs by those who are working their way up the economic ladder is beginning to be matched by the return of people much nearer the top of the ladder. As these trends continue, the level of incomes, the quality of housing, and the ability of the central city to provide necessary public services will increase rapidly.

American cities in their earlier history served as a "melting pot" for immigrants from abroad. Today they are called upon to perform a similar function for the disadvantaged of our own land. That job is a more difficult one, but it can be done, and apparently is being done, according to Professor Birch.

Let's assume for the moment our author is right and that the life cycle in our older central cities is beginning to turn favorably upward. What are the implications? First of all, and as Professor Birch suggests, our close-in suburbs and our newer central cities will soon be experiencing all the ills of urban decay that the older central cities have suffered in the past decade or so. Or they will unless they do a better job of avoiding or dealing with the problem. One possibility for doing better might be for them to begin earlier than did the central cities to do something constructive and many other local government entities that comprise the whole metropolitan area.

A second implication would seem to be the need for the most careful study and planning of new developments on the periphery of all our cities, new and old. If persons living in the decaying inner-city areas are to move through the suburbs to jobs and homes beyond, factories, stores, houses, and community facilities not only must be provided, but their location and their quality must be of the sort that will develop self-supporting communities, rather than bedrooms for commuters into, or work places for commuters out of, the central city. For example, the movement of corporate home offices to the suburbs—or to newer central cities—may turn out to be ill-timed and unsuccessful.

Finally, Professor Birch's analysis very strongly suggests that the central cities and the federal government re-examine their programs for building and rebuilding housing for low income families. Not that low income families should not be better housed, but rather to make certain that the new housing be built in the right location, which would seem to be in the suburbs and beyond rather than in the central city.

---

* As consulting editor in the MGIC Newsletter.

**Summary.** Pulling all these threads together, we find that the central cities in most of our urban areas are going through economic and emographic life cycles. They start first with a homogeneous mix of people and jobs. They grow through annexation and immigration. Sooner or later, though, as their densities and their problems rise, suburbs no longer wish to be annexed, and migrants no longer prefer to settle in the center. The growth slows down. The center then begins to serve more specialized functions. It houses the poor who are still stuck there, and increasingly it houses the rich who cannot bear the pain of commuting.

Taking this model into the future, we can expect significant changes from past trends. The growth of the great northern cities during the first half of the twentieth century will be replaced by growth in the smaller, younger, largely western and southern cities during the next 50 years. It would come as no surprise if these smaller, younger cities experienced the same difficulties that the northern cities have experienced in recent years, including increased concentrations of dissatisfied minority groups.

The large northern cities should increasingly become elite service centers. Employment growth will take place in the services, which should barely offset declines in manufacturing and retailing.

As the poor follow the manufacturing and trade jobs out, and as the rich find it more convenient to settle in luxury apartments, the northern cities should begin to get back on their feet financially. The tax base should improve, at least relative to that of the suburbs, and the tremendous welfare load of today's central cities should be more evenly distributed.

Absorbing the brunt of all this relocation in the large northern cities over the next 10 or 20 years will be the inner suburbs. They should experience agonizing problems of a sort they never dreamed of as recently as 1950 or 1960.

## Questions

1. Do you agree with the explanations developed by Raymond Vernon in regard to the growth of the central city? Why or why not?
2. How does Professor Birch explain the more frequent movement of people than jobs? Do you agree with his explanation? Why or why not?
3. What are the major differences between the mix of employment in central city boundaries in older and in newer cities?
4. Has the outward movement of blacks also been upward movement? How much integration of neighborhoods has taken place?
5. Where is urban growth most likely to occur in the remaining years of the century? What will happen to the older cities? Do you agree with Professor Birch that the outlook for older central cities appears to be good? Why or why not?
6. How might inner suburbs and newer cities avoid some of the problems that older central cities have encountered?
7. Where should housing for low income groups be located? Explain.

## STUDY PROJECT 11–2

### Pollution: Challenges and Opportunities *

The axiom that "real estate value is location" could be stated as "value depends on environment." Certainly investors in real estate, whether mortgage lenders or equity holders, have a high stake in the environment and in controlling the pollution that threatens it.

Mixed emotions arise from the current concern about pollution. Relief, perhaps even joy, must come from the possibility of accelerated action to deal with conditions we know are unquestionably bad; some get worse, almost as we watch. Yet a responsible person will also worry; exaggeration and impatience, though well intentioned, breed too much nonsense.

Pure hearts will not make pure water. Pocketbooks will feel heavy impacts —tens of billions by even conservative estimates. The benefits to be obtained from each program ought to be worth the cost. Society suffers when "good works" deprive it of still better things. How can we proceed wisely?

One characteristic of "the" pollution problem is that its myriads of parts differ tremendously from one place to another. For this reason, if for no other, the various avenues open for seeking efficient improvement must differ in all conceivable respects. That current fashion, looking to Uncle Sam, can lead us astray. Where conditions differ fundamentally from one community to another, there is a presumption against expecting that the most effective action can usually come from federal initiative.

**Local Initiative and Responsibility.** The localized nature of air and water pollution argues strongly for reliance upon local initiative and responsibility, but this characteristic complicates enormously the achievement of efficient solution. Each community's boundaries and legal jurisdiction are restricted. But air and water move. No major local government is sufficiently extensive in area and authority to take all of the action needed to deal with its problems. Neither the regulations it may impose (on business and individuals), nor its own local government activities, can deal with all the air and water which come through it.

Moreover, some of the benefits of any one government's project will accrue to persons outside the area—downstream and downwind. The people of each particular area, therefore, cannot get all the benefits of projects which involve costs and onerous restrictions. As local groups, voters do not have adequate incentive to do all that may be desirable for the broader area. Here we encounter one of the most complex problems of "externalities," of "third party" and "neighborhood" effects. Both costs and benefits extend beyond traditional areas of local government. This "spilling-over" plagues pollution control as almost no other matter of public concern. New metropolitan area, regional, state wide agencies seem essential. But to say this marks only a first step on a road of vastly difficult terrain.

* By C. Lowell Harriss; excerpts reproduced by permission of Mortgage Guaranty Insurance Corporation, from the *MGIC Newsletter*.

## COMMENTARY

### by Edward E. Edwards *

Just what investors in real estate should do about pollution is far from clear. Landowners typically do not suffer from their own polluting; in fact, in a competitive world they more likely benefit from it. They do suffer from the polluting done by their neighbors, both near and distant, and for that reason they should feel some responsibility for the collective action necessary to preserve and protect the total environment. But what action should be taken, how should it be initiated and who will pay for it?

Business firms who could eliminate their own polluting (or that done by their products, as in the case of automobiles) have had three basic and until now perhaps justifiable reasons for not doing so. First, they have been afraid that their added cost (including higher real estate taxes because of increased investment) would give their competitors an unfair advantage. Second, they have been afraid that cooperative action with their competitors might bring them into difficulty with the anti-trust laws. Third, they have been afraid to advocate and support government enforcement of high standards because this might lead to further government regulation. These deterrents to action are rapidly disappearing in the face of a very genuine threat of political action growing out of the consumer movement.

Cities and towns that could quit polluting our air and water have been unwilling to do so, primarily because they would have to incur the cost but other communities would enjoy the benefits. Closely related, however, has been the inability of tax revenues to finance services of direct benefit to the local community. Our author believes cities must incur these necessary costs, even to the extent of re-ordering some priorities, and he cautions against too much reliance on Uncle Sam for funds.

Of special interest to all real estate investors is the suggestion that doing something about pollution should increase the value of some real estate, and that this increase should be added to the tax base. This idea is quite consistent with Professor Harriss' previously expressed views against taxing improvements to real estate. If the property tax applied only to land values, and the assessment of land values reflected changes in location factors, a better environment would justify a higher tax. But a capital investment by the owner to reduce his polluting would not increase his assessment, although it might properly increase the assessment of adjoining property.

The great increase in public awareness to pollution in all its forms may bring significant and perhaps rapid changes in people's wishes as to where and how they will live. Getting away from it all, by spending long week ends away from the city and living in minimum accommodations near the place of employment for only three nights and four days each week, could bring drastic changes in real estate values. So could the re-emergence of public transportation and the declining use of the automobile.

---

* As consulting editor in the MGIC Newsletter.

Some of the country's worst polluters are cities and towns. To pour inadequately treated sewerage into rivers and lakes has seemed cheaper than to cleanse. Municipal facilities sometimes emit more air pollution than is really justifiable. Local governments themselves must incur new costs if pollution is to be reduced toward more livable levels. Very often, however, budgets strained at every point have no evident money for such projects. But some will need doing, even at the sacrifice of other good things, some private, some public. "Reexamining our priorities" is easy to say but hard to do.

Decisions to act on anti-pollution projects offer an opportunity for follow through based upon recognition of a fundamental point: successful projects will make for a better life. Some benefits will be strikingly clear, evident and open. Other benefits will consist of preventing conditions from getting worse. Most often the good results will be diffused, mixed with others; soon they will be taken for granted and pass unrecognized. Measurement of these widely different benfits presents vast difficulties, but the environment will be better. How can a community draw upon the value of these positive results, especially in helping to bring them about, and others to follow?

**Effects on Property Values.**   Local governments should try to exploit one potentiality. Some effects of anti-pollution projects will consist of higher property values. Many projects will improve neighborhoods. River and other water front lands will become more valuable. Sharp real estate operators will begin to take into account even the prospects of success in raising property values. Will not a lot of money be made (especially downstream and downwind) from reducing water and air pollution? I think so.

Cannot special assessments and comparable devices be used to finance projects for improving the environment? Let us try. An alert community leadership on the lookout ought to find ways to use some of the benefits—notably increments in land values—to defray costs. Special assessments of the familiar type offer one opportunity. "Betterment charge" may be a better term, and new concepts and procedures can undoubtedly be devised.

A policy of more general scope, one justifying sustained efforts, is to assure that changes in value are reflected in property tax assessments. Where property values rise because of projects to reduce pollution, such changes can appropriately be put upon the tax rolls, promptly and fully. Value increases can then be used as a base to help pay for local government.

## Questions

1. Where should the responsibility for halting pollution lie—on which level of government or on which individuals?
2. What business justifications are there for halting pollution?
3. How is real estate affected by pollution?
4. Edwards speaks of pollution leading to a change in life styles that would cause "drastic changes" in real estate values. Specifically, to what types of changes was he referring?

# 12

# Appraising Methods:
# The Income Approach

## APPRAISALS AND REAL ESTATE DECISIONS

In this chapter and the following one we will consider appraising methods. Valuations or appraisals are important aids to real estate decisions. They provide one of the major bases for reaching real estate decisions and for developing programs of action for implementing such decisions. Thus, valuations are not usually ends in themselves. Appraisers do not *make* decisions. They provide information and forecasts which may aid business executives, government officials, or individuals in arriving at better conclusions and decisions than might otherwise be possible. If a mortgage lender asks an appraiser to estimate the value of a property for mortgage lending purposes, it is not the function of the appraiser to decide on the merit of the specific mortgage arrangement that the lender has under consideration. An appraiser may help a seller to decide how much to ask for a piece of property or a buyer to decide how much to offer, but the appraiser does not make the final decisions.

Because of this, it is sometimes argued that the appraiser need not know the objective of the valuation he is asked to make—that is, how it is going to be used by the decision maker. If we could find some uniform basis for all appraisals, this might be the case. In view of the many different interpretations of value, however, it is almost impossible for an appraiser to proceed without such knowledge.

### Defining Valuation Problems

Thus the objective which an appraisal is intended to serve—the purpose for which it is made—is of basic importance, not only in defining value, but also in defining valuation problems. Other conditions that are of importance in defining valuation problems include *time*, the identification of the specific *property rights* and the major physical and economic factors involved.

In general, however, the objective of the appraiser may be thought of as that of estimating the present market value of the income potential of a given property. Specific situations, however, may require that he estimate the price that may be obtained in a quick sale; the price that a prospective buyer should offer for the property or a partial interest in a property; and the value of the property for insurance purposes, for mortgage lending purposes, for damages suffered under condemnation proceedings, or for the solution of many other business or personal problems. Thus, definition of the specific valuation problem to be solved is an essential first step in the process of making an appraisal of the rights to a piece of real property.

## Classes of Transactions

For example, Ratcliff has suggested that real estate transactions may be classified in the following ways and that this classification indicates the nature of the appraisal problem that is involved:

1. Transfer of ownership:
   a. Sale.
   b. Purchase.
   c. Trade.
2. Extension of credit secured by real estate.
3. Compensation for damage or loss:
   a. Through condemnation.
   b. For damage compensable under property insurance contract.
4. Taxation:
   a. Assessment for property tax.
   b. Basis for depreciation allowance.
   c. Basis for inheritance tax.
5. Selection of a program of utilization.[1]

## Specific Property Rights

The definition of the problem includes an identification of the specific property rights involved. As we indicated in Chapter 4, a wide variety of interests may exist in the same piece of real state. Usually the appraiser estimates the value of specified property rights rather than the

[1] Richard U. Ratcliff, "A Restatement of Appraisal Theory," *The Appraisal Journal* (January, 1964). See also his article in the April, 1970 *Appraisal Journal* with Bernard Schwab, "Contemporary Decision Theory and Real Estate Investment."

value of the physical land and buildings. He must, of course, identify the physical property, but he is much more concerned with the "rights" to the use of the physical property. He may be called upon to estimate the reversionary right in a leased fee, the value to a tenant of a lease, the air rights over a piece of land, the value of an easement, and many other types of interests. The American Institute of Real Estate Appraisers points out:

Because the value of real property does not solely reside in the physical land and the improvements, the appraiser cannot define his problem precisely until he knows exactly what property rights are involved.[2]

### Date of Valuation

The date of the valuation is another important element in defining appraisal problems. In some cases the appraisal requires that a value estimate be made as of some specified date in the past, rather than in terms of the current date. Such situations often arise in the case of tax problems or valuation for the purpose of settling estates. It may be necessary to estimate value as of some future date as well.

### Physical Real Estate

Another aspect to consider in defining the problem to be solved is the physical characteristics of the real estate. Chapter 3 was devoted to a discussion of physical elements—land and improvements. It was emphasized in that discussion that the physical elements are merely the "machine" for providing property services such as shelter, privacy, protection and the like. Sometimes there is a tendency to overemphasize the importance of the physical property. It is tangible, as contrasted with the intangible legal and economic characteristics of the property. But it is essential to know and consider in the decision making process the major physical characteristics of the property as outlined in Chapter 3.

### Economic Factors

The major economic characteristics of a property should be identified as one of the preliminary steps in defining an appraisal problem. Such factors as the following are important: relationships of the property to its surroundings; its relative position as a share in its neighborhood, district and local economy; its potential economic life; the character of the income it will produce; the cost of producing this income and related factors.

---

[2] *The Appraisal of Real Estate* (5th ed.; Chicago: American Institute of Real Estate Appraisers, 1967), pp. 51–52.

It may be helpful at this point to review several of the economic concepts which help to explain real estate value in order to relate them to specific valuation problems:

1. Income is the fundamental fact of economic life.
2. Like other areas of business, real estate is concerned with income but more specifically with income produced at a fixed site.
3. Income production potentials can be translated into present values by the discounting process. Thus, the value of a real property may be defined basically as the present worth of the future income it may be expected to produce.
4. Future income may be derived from the direct use of a property or from monetary returns it may produce.
5. Estimates of the income that a property may produce require an analysis of:
   a. Governmental and political trends.
   b. Business conditions.
   c. Regional and local economic trends.
   d. The property's real estate market.
   e. The property's location.
   f. The economic characteristics of the property itself.

We have discussed each of these topics in the preceding chapters in this second part of the book. This chapter and the following one conclude that series of discussions. They draw on the background of the discussions of various types of analyses for real estate decisions. More specifically, these chapters relate such discussions to the processes of appraising specific real properties.

## THE APPRAISAL PROCESS

The orderly procedure developed by professional real estate appraisers to help make reliable valuations is known as the "appraisal process." The American Institute of Real Estate Appraisers has recently outlined what is referred to as the "Expanded Appraisal Process." An outline of this process is presented in Figure 12–1.

According to the Institute the appraisal process includes five major steps, the first being the definition of the problem which we discussed above. The physical characteristics of the land and buildings are identified as well as property rights pertaining to them, the date of the valuation is determined and the major economic or value characteristics are defined.

The second step involves a preliminary survey and development of an appraisal plan.

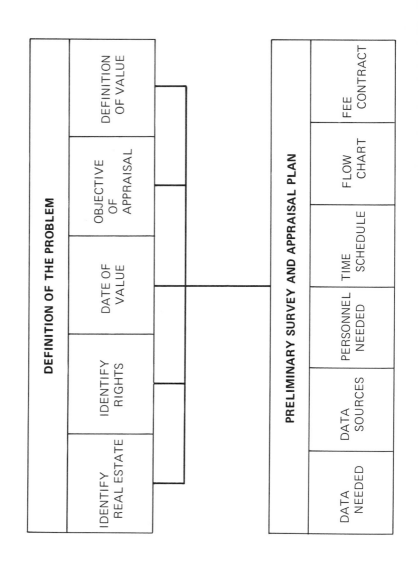

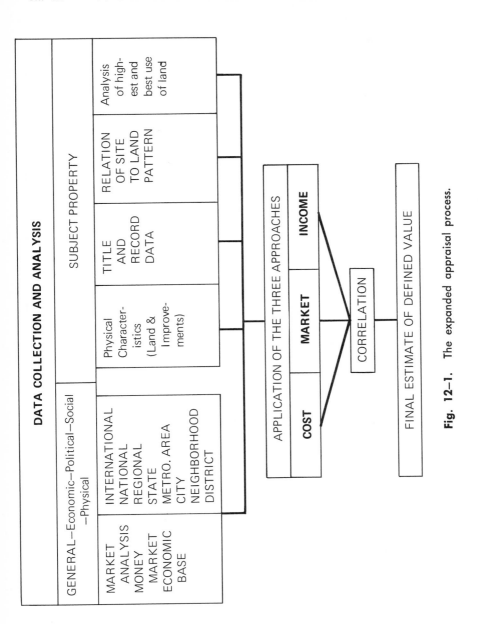

**Fig. 12–1.** The expanded appraisal process.

The third step is the process of data collection and analysis. Information about the real estate is often divided into two main categories: (1) general data which relate to economic, governmental, and market conditions; and (2) data related more specifically to the real estate being appraised.

Having collected and analyzed the available and pertinent data, the cost, market and income approaches are undertaken as the fourth step. The final step in the process involves a survey and correlation of the analyses and a determination of the property's value as defined.

## The Three Approaches

Professional appraisers have developed three principal (or "classic") approaches to valuation problems:

1. Cost approach
2. Market approach
3. Income approach

As we have suggested, the income approach fits best the logic of valuation theory, since all property value is derived from future income, whether such income is in the form of monetary returns or results from the direct use of the property. (The latter are sometimes called *amenity returns* in connection with residential property.) In many cases, however, there are practical difficulties in using the capitalized income method. For example, if you have occupied your own home for a number of years, it may be easier to make an appraisal by the *market approach* than by capitalizing an estimated future income. Again, the appraisal of a public building requires almost inevitably the use of the *cost approach,* since neither income estimates nor comparable sales prices are likely to be available. In most cases (except for single-family owner-occupied homes) all three approaches are used in order that one result may be compared with another.

Regardless of the method used, however, the appraiser must always consider the objective of the appraisal, the property interest represented, the physical real estate and its economic or value characteristics, and the time at which the appraisal is to apply. In almost all cases he will find it essential to think in terms of the income-producing ability of a property even though he is employing the market or cost approaches in his work. Obviously, the costs of developing a site and constructing a building would not ordinarily be undertaken unless anticipated monetary or direct returns were expected to exceed such costs. Similarly, prices, rents, and other pertinent market data reflect more or less accurately the market's estimate of the future income-producing capacity of properties.

### Selection of Method

Three principal factors will guide an appraiser in his selection of the appraising methods to be used for a specific case. Much will depend on (1) the purpose of the valuation, (2) the type of income produced by the property or assumed to be produced under the use program that is projected, and (3) the kinds of data available for use.

In some cases the appraisal problem is stated in terms which specify the method to be followed. For example, an appraiser may be asked to estimate the present value of a lease, which clearly indicates the use of the income method, or he may be asked to report the price which could be obtained for a property in a quick sale, which would require the use of the market method.

As we have already indicated above, the availability of data sometimes dictates the choice of appraisal method. While decisions based on the availability of information may not always be logical, there are times when the appraiser has no alternative. Cases such as a public library, a government building, hospital, a school, a grain elevator, an unused factory building, or a museum are likely to present data problems.

### Method and Income

If the method is not defined, consideration is given to the type of income produced or assumed to be produced by the property. As has been suggested, two principal kinds of returns may be considered: (1) dollars, and (2) direct returns resulting from the use of the property by the owner. Babcock has pointed out how type of income may aid in selection of method. If income is in dollars, it may be derived from several sources, the two main types being commercial rents and business profits.

### Business Profits

If the property earns commercial rents, the income method is indicated. If business profits are involved, they may be due entirely to the real estate or partly to the real estate and partly to the business enterprise. If profits are all due to real estate, the income method is preferred. To the extent that returns to the real estate and the business enterprise can be distinguished, the income method is considered preferable. However, if the returns on real estate cannot be distinguished from other returns, as in the case of a foundry or a railroad terminal, the cost method is generally used.[3]

---

[3] Frederick M. Babcock, *The Valuation of Real Estate* (New York: McGraw Hill Book Co., Inc., 1932), p. 184.

### Direct Use

If returns are in the form of direct use of the property, the income method may be used if such returns can be translated rather accurately into dollars. If, on the other hand, returns from direct use cannot be translated into dollars, the selection of methods hinges on the extent to which market data are available. If there are sufficient market evidences of value, as in the case of comparable properties, the market method would be selected. This is often the case in appraising a single-family owner-occupied residence. However, if there are few or no data available indicating market prices or rents for comparable properties, the cost method is followed of necessity. Typical illustrations of this situation are provided by the problems of appraising a library or a government building.

### Method and Type of Property

As we have pointed out, the appraisal method should be adapted to the type of property. For example, in the case of a large department store on a principal corner of an eastern city, the lot and the building were both owned by the store, thus the property and the business were parts of a total unit. The building was suited for only one purpose, that of a department store. The valuation was derived by capitalizing the percentage of sales the department store could afford to pay as rent. On the other hand, in valuing the property on the opposite corner, an obsolete bank building, the valuation was developed by ascertaining the net rentals that could be obtained from stores on that corner and capitalizing these rentals. That is, an assumed use program was set up. The building in this case was regarded as of no value in appraising the best retail corner in the city, because it had to be wrecked to make way for the new stores from which the highest rent could be obtained. This is an illustration of developing a model of the highest and best use of the site for appraisal purposes.

### Limitations of Appraising Methods

Acceptance of the concept that value is directly related to the present worth of future income does not mean, as some seem to infer, that all appraisals must be made by the income method. Because of specific objectives as defined in the appraisal assignment, the nature of the income, or the absence or inadequacy of data, it may be impossible in many practical situations to use the income method. This does not alter the basic nature of the appraiser's task. Regardless of method used, he is attempting to estimate the value of the earning expectancy. Most real estate decisions will be related to earnings but important modifying factors may be present.

It is often necessary to use sales prices of comparable properties as the basis of valuations and decisions since data may not be available on which estimates of the size or duration of a future income stream can be made. Sales prices of comparable properties, however, indicate what buyers and sellers in the current market believe the present value of that income stream to be.

Construction and development costs are important elements in the valuation of real properties and in decisions regarding them. They enter directly into the valuations of new properties and indirectly into value estimates of older properties. The owner of a vacant urban site can only secure a stream of income from the land, except in the case of parking lots or similar uses, by constructing a building and other improvements on it. If the building is constructed in an area where there is no demand for its services, or the demand is very limited or operating costs are too high for the income produced, then the land may have a zero or even a negative income.

Properties located in declining areas present special problems because of the difficulty of estimating rate of decline, possibility of renewal efforts, and other uncertainties. Market prices of comparable properties often are helpful in the valuations of such properties since they reflect the opinions of buyers and sellers in regard to such uncertainties.

### Investment Preferences, Cash Flow, and Depreciation

A typical appraisal may not in a specific situation reflect the special interests of an investor. For example, an investor may have little interest in the market value of a property but may be especially concerned with the cash flow that it may generate. Or it may be that an investor has a greater concern with the depreciation allowances that a property may generate so that this may be offset against other income than he has with the income producing capability of the property itself. In some cases investors will instruct an appraiser as to their specific interests, in others they will look to cash flow and depreciation types of analyses as by-products of appraisals undertaken for other purposes.

## THE INCOME APPROACH

The capitalization of anticipated net incomes requires that estimates of revenues and expenses be made and that the estimated net income before depreciation be capitalized at an appropriate rate. While the procedures of appraisers vary somewhat, the three main steps usually involved in the process are these:

First, gross income is estimated by computing the total possible income at 100 per cent occupancy of the building and deducting for vacancies and collection losses.

In the second step, expenses are estimated, including allowances for replacement of certain items of equipment and parts of the building which must be replaced because of physical deterioration.

The third step in the use of the income method is capitalizing the net income resulting from the deduction of estimated expenses from gross effective earnings by applying the appropriate capitalization rate or rates. This phase of the process is not simple, even when net income is capitalized in perpetuity. The selection of an appropriate capitalization rate usually means the difference between a sound and an unsound decision. Even more complicated problems arise with the application of one of the residual techniques in which there is the use of one rate for the income attributed to the land and another for the income assigned to the building. A more complete explanation of these techniques follows.

### Application of the Income Approach

The practical difficulties in applying the principle of capitalizing income to actual real estate valuations and related decision problems in the business world are numerous. For example, it has been said by those who are critical of the income approach to valuation problems that the application of the present value concept involves dividing one unknown (the estimated future annual net income) by another unknown (the capitalization rate) to arrive at a third unknown (value).

Thus, if we assume that the annual net income of a particular piece of real property is $1,000 and that the rate necessary to attract investment into properties of this type is 10 per cent, then by dividing, $\frac{\$1,000.00}{.10}$, we find that the estimated value of this property on the basis of capitalizing its anticipated income at a 10 per cent rate is $10,000. (In this case income is capitalized in perpetuity; that is, $10,000 now is equal to $1,000 per year forever in terms of a 10 per cent capitalization rate.)

Although it is true that anticipated future incomes can never be known exactly, buyers, sellers, investors, developers, mortgage lenders, appraisers, and others concerned with valuation problems must make the best estimates possible of the future income that a property can produce. Similarly, while the capitalization rate that will exactly reflect future earnings in present value is unknown, an estimated rate can and must be applied. This process is little different from those which are followed in arriving at many other types of business decisions. For example, a new product is available to a manufacturer. He estimates its income-producing ability, estimates the risks involved, and discounts them to the extent that he believes appropriate. On the basis of these estimates he decides to produce and market the new produce or to pass it by.

## Capital Investment Decisions

Many business decisions involve similar types of postulates and analyses, notably capital investment decisions. As has been pointed out:

> The situation in which a manager is working will tend to indicate the factors to which he gives greatest weight in arriving at capital investment decisions. For example, he may stress the period of pay-back. It may be important to recapture the investment at an early period. Or he may stress returns per dollar of outlay, without respect to the timing of the return. He may emphasize average annual proceeds per dollar of outlay (that is, giving consideration to the number of years and averaging the return per year). The manager may estimate average income on book value of the investment; that is, after depreciation has been charged against the investment. The method considered highly desirable by many managers is the discounted cash flow method; that is, computing the present value of the earnings that will be secured over a period of time.[4]

## Estimating Income

Income estimates are based on the earnings record of the property as well as that of comparable properties, with proper allowances being made for probable future developments. That is, past earnings may be used as an indication of future earnings only if there is reason to believe that the future will be like the past with respect to the subject property. Past income is only a part of the data to be considered by the appraiser. That is why it is important for him to consider general economic trends, governmental and location factors, and local market trends, as well as the specific property being appraised. The difficulties of estimating the future income production of a property are emphasized by a review of urban real estate investment experience. Usually there have been rather wide variations in gross income and even wider variations in net income over a period of years. Estimates of income potential made during periods of prosperity tend to be unduly optimistic. Those made in periods of economic recession tend toward the conservative side.

---

[4] Arthur M. Weimer, *Introduction to Business: A Management Approach* (4th ed.; Homewood, Ill.: Richard D. Irwin, Inc., 1970), p. 419. See also Harold Bierman, Jr., and Seymour Schmidt, *The Capital Budgeting Decision* (New York: The Macmillan Co., 1960), ch. ii; Richard U. Ratcliff, *Modern Real Estate Valuation* (Madison, Wis.: The Democrat Press, 1965), pp. 56–57.

## Need for Careful Estimates

Since the anticipated future income is the most vital element in a valuation, the appraiser should make a careful survey to determine probable future incomes. If an apartment property is being appraised, he should obtain prevailing rents in a number of comparable properties, ascertain the number of vacancies, and study location and market trends for the purpose of determining whether the prevailing rents are likely to continue. The appraiser should determine also what would be a reasonable estimate of vacancy rate and collection loss.

In the appraisal of commercial properties, the appraiser should secure information about rentals on recent leases of comparable properties. Where properties are leased for long terms on net leases to responsible firms, the problems of estimating future income is much less difficult.

The appraiser should be particularly careful in estimating future income after a sustained period of building. Appraisers take into consideration the competitive effect upon the market of new office buildings, new regional shopping centers, new apartment buildings, or new houses. Usually appraisals are made on the basis of price levels as of the time the appraisal report is prepared. In some cases the appraisal problem may require that potential price level changes be reflected.

## Estimating Expenses

In appraising, expenses are defined as all actual cash outlays involved in the ownership and operation of a property during the remaining economic life of the building except those arising from mortgage indebtedness. They do not include vacancy allowances, rent concessions, collection losses, and allowances for depreciation. Professional appraisers use three principal classes of expenses:

1. *Fixed Expenses.* The category of fixed expenses usually includes real estate taxes and property insurance. There may be other types of expenses which are not affected by the operation of the facility. Both taxes and insurance premiums generally are outside the control of even good management, whereas expenditures known as operating expenses may depend heavily on the efficiency of management and the type of tenants. Real estate taxes and other assessments are calculated on the basis of current rates and those which are likely to develop within the next year. Property insurance includes fire and extended coverage, liability, plate glass, elevator, rental loss, and other types which good management would include in the operation of a facility.

2. *Operating Expenses.* Operating expenses include all the cash expenditures in the actual operation of the facility such as utilities (elec-

tricity, gas, water, etc.) repairs and maintenance, supplies, wages and salaries, and a representative management fee for the management of the property. Note that no replacement or capital expenditure is included in this category. Maintenance includes the patching or repair of a roof in order to continue the operation of the facility. Painting and minor repairs are also included in maintenance. Capital expenditures are defined as those which alter the structure, change its use, and increase or decrease its economic life.

3. *Replacements.* Replacements include those expenditures for major parts of the building which wear out or become obsolete and must be replaced in order to maintain the operation of the building. The replacement of a roof is illustrative of this type of expenditure. Inasmuch as these expenditures are not usually annual, it is necessary to amortize or "to spread over a number of years" these particular items. For example, a furnace is considered to have a 20-year life and so the cost to replace a furnace is divided by the number of years of its expected life.

Note that the personal income taxes of the owner are not chargeable to the building and that payments on the mortgage are not operating expenses. If either were included, it is obvious that a comparable property without a mortgage owned by a person in the 20 per cent tax bracket would have a higher value than one with a mortgage owned by a person in the 50 per cent tax bracket, yet both properties might bring the same amount in the open market.

### Accuracy of Records

In estimating operating expenses, the appraiser should be careful to determine the accuracy of the records placed at his disposal. It is usually advisable to compare figures for several similar properties or to consult the officials of real estate management firms who are usually intimately acquainted with operating expenses. In addition care must be taken to include only annual charges; insurance, for example, is often paid for 3-year periods and a division is necessary to reflect annual expenses. Such charges as special assessments may have only a definite number of years to run, and this must be reflected in future expense estimates.

As is the case with income records, the past experiences reported by records of operating expenses are supporting data only. They help to make possible estimates of future expenses, but past experience can be projected only when it appears that the future will resemble the past sufficiently to justify such a procedure. In estimating future operating expenses, allowances must be made for increased wages of building maintenance workers, higher real estate taxes, higher insurance costs, and higher material costs for repairs whenever such increases appear probable. Conversely, probable declines in such items may also be reflected in the estimates. Also, the condition of the structure should be considered since this may affect operating costs.

### Net Income

The ultimate objective of gross income and expense estimates is to produce a representative annual net income figure. Net income for appraising purposes may be quite different from that used by accountants, the Internal Revenue Service, or by investors.

## CAPITALIZATION

As we have pointed out, the value of a property may be considered as equivalent to the present worth of anticipated future incomes. We have considered briefly some of the items which have a bearing on the income-producing capacity of real properties and on the expenses of producing such income.

In order to capitalize income it is necessary to establish a rate which will reflect the risk involved in the particular investment being considered. This rate should reflect the market for all types of investment. An analysis of the investment market should make possible the development of an appropriate rate for the property being appraised.

### The Capitalization Rate

The "cap" rate is that rate used to convert a net income figure into a capital value figure. The accompanying illustration of the capitalization process is a very basic and simple one. Usually it is necessary to employ a more detailed technique than that of "capitalization in perpetuity."

Land earns returns in perpetuity; buildings and other improvements wear out sooner or later, and therefore, like any investment which has a finite life, the investor wants a *return on* his investment as well as the *recapture of* his original capital over the period of the economic life of the depreciable asset. Thus, the capitalization rate for a building is composed of two components: the risk rate (representing the *return on* the investment) plus the recapture rate (representing the amortization each year of the original capital invested).

The amortization of the investment in the building may be compared to an oil well or a gravel pit, which will be used up over a period of time. This is known as depletion. In real estate, we use the term "depreciation" since the asset can to some degree be renewed. In both cases the investor recognizes that he is investing in assets that are being used up at varying rates.

**Capitalization Illustration**

Assume that an investor owns vacant land which he leases at $12,000 per year net for 99 years. Such an investment may be relatively low in risk and the investor may be satisfied with a 6 per cent return. The conversion of $12,000 in perpetuity at 6 per cent produces a value figure of $200,000 ($12,000 ÷ .06 = $200,000). Since land is not a depreciating asset there is no need for the investor to protect himself by "loading" the "cap" rate with a percentage for recapture.

Now let us consider the value of an investment from the standpoint of the entrepreneur who leased the land described above in order to construct a building on it. His primary investment is in the building since he does not own the land. Assume that the annual net income produced by the building after paying all expenses (including the lease on the ground) is $60,000. If an 8 per cent rate will be required to attract him into this type of investment and if the building will wear out (economically or physically or both) in 25 years, the investment in the building will have to be recaptured in that time, hence a 4 per cent rate per year will be used for this purpose (100% ÷ 25 yr. = 4%). (See for example the effect of The Discounting Process in Fig. 12–2.)

The appropriate capitalization rate for this building then is:

| Risk rate | 8% |
|---|---|
| Recapture rate | 4 |
| Capitalization rate | 12% |

The capitalization process then is to divide $60,000 by 12 per cent ($60,000 ÷ .12 = $500,000) indicating a value of $500,000.

**Selection of Rate**

The rate of interest is not the capitalization rate. Theoretically, the term *interest* is used to designate a *return on* capital, and may be composed of two parts: a riskless rate and the rate for risks assumed. Pure interest is riskless interest. The return on government bonds is the closest approximation to riskless interest which can be cited. Such rates vary from time to time. To this basic interest rate we must add an allowance for various risks in arriving at a total risk rate. Such additional risks will vary from property to property.

Incomes from properties with prospects for stable, continued returns merit low rates; those with great risks, higher rates. Such factors as marketability of the property, changes in business conditions, interest rate risk, purchasing power risk, investment preferences, and the like are important risk elements. Also, in some cases allowances are made in the development of the rate for the management of the investment.

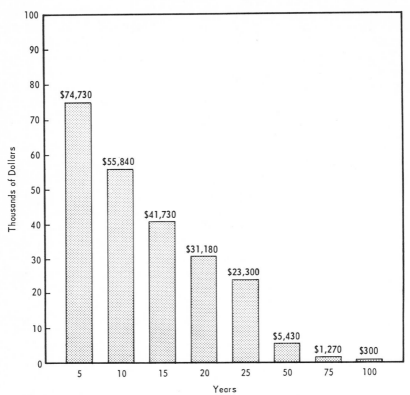

**Fig. 12–2.** Present value of $100,000 at 6 per cent at the end of various numbers of years.

It is obvious that a difference of 1 per cent in the capitalization rate will have a major effect on the value estimate. For example, if an investment is expected to earn a net return of $5,000 per year and is capitalized in perpetuity at 10 per cent, the resulting value estimate is $50,000. However, if it is capitalized at 9 per cent, the result leads to the higher estimate of $55,555. At 15 per cent the value estimate declines to $33,333.

### Investor Opinions

How is an appraiser to know which capitalization rate to select? In most cases he selects a rate which will reflect the opinions of investors at the time. This rate should indicate how much investors expect to receive as a return if capital is advanced on one or another type of property or how much more or less they expect if capital is invested in real estate as against alternative types of investment. In a sense the selection of a capitalization rate is based on an estimate of the opinions of real estate investors. Financial institutions as well as investors themselves provide data of this type which the appraiser may find useful. The final selection of a rate will be an estimate, of course. However, it should be an estimate based on the most reliable information available to the appraiser.

## Summation Method

Sometimes appraisers use a summation method in developing risk rates. For example, they may begin with as near a riskless rate as possible, such as the return on government bonds. To this may be added an allowance for risk, an allowance for lack of liquidity of real estate investments, and an allowance for the difficulty of managing the investment. Thus, to a return of 4½ per cent on government bonds might be added 2 per cent for risk, 1½ per cent for nonliquidity, and 1 per cent for management—or a total rate of 9 per cent.

## Band of Investment Method

If comparable investments in real estate could be financed with a $40,000 first mortgage of 50 per cent of value at 8 per cent, a $20,000 second mortgage of 25 per cent of value at 10 per cent and if equity investors of the balance of 25 per cent would want 12 per cent, these may be related as follows:

|  | Interest Rate | Amount | Per Cent of Total | Weighted Average |
|---|---|---|---|---|
| First Mortgage | 8% | $40,000 | 50% | 4% |
| Second Mortgage | 10 | 20,000 | 25 | 2½ |
| Equity | 12 | 20,000 | 25 | 3 |
| Totals |  | $80,000 | 100% | 9½% |

The weighted average is calculated by multiplying, for the first mortgage, the 8 per cent interest times 50 per cent, the percentage of the first mortgage to the total financing. This is repeated for the second mortgage and the equity, producing a risk rate for this type of property of 9½ per cent.

## Quality Rating Method

Most appraisers attempt to base the risk rate on market experience, as suggested above. In some cases they work out quality ratings and use various grid rating systems to aid them in the selection of a rate. Ultimately, the risk rate selected is a matter of judgment. It reflects the appraiser's estimate of the degree of risk involved, the problems of managing the investment, and general market and investor attitudes.

## Residual Techniques

More difficult problems are encountered in appraising investments composed of a combination of land and buildings and perhaps other improvements. A property is a single income-producing unit, of course, but it is possible to make estimates of the proportion of the income which may be allocated to land on the one hand and to buildings on the other.

For example, suppose that a small apartment house on a 100-foot lot earns a net return of $5,000 per year. If land in this area has been selling for $100 per front foot, one may estimate (by the market method) that the lot has a value of around $10,000 (100 ft. × $100). If investors are expecting a return of 5 per cent on improved land ($10,000 × .05 = $500), then $500 of the earnings may be attributed to the land and the remainder to the building. The remaining $4,500 may be capitalized at a rate which will reflect recapture of the investment over the remaining economic life of the building plus the investors' expectations of earnings from such properties.

## Building Residual

In the building residual approach the residual return is assigned to the building, to use appraisal terminology. The investors demand the same return on the building as on the land (5 per cent is the indicated risk). In addition the investor expects to recapture his investment over a 25-year period, the economic life of the building. The 25-year period calls for 4 per cent per year recapture rate. The capitalization rate is then developed by adding the 5 per cent risk rate to the 4 per cent recapture rate, producing a 9 per cent capitalization rate. The net income to the building of $4,500 then is capitalized at 9 per cent ($4,500 ÷ .09 = $50,000), producing an indicated value of the building of $50,000. The value of the property then is:

| | |
|---|---|
| Land | $10,000 |
| Building | 50,000 |
| Property | $60,000 |

## Land Residual

The example above applies more definitely to properties in mid-life or late life than to properties improved with new buildings. When the net income from a property has the characteristics of an annuity, then the income must be processed in a different way. For example, an investor builds a commercial facility for a "Triple A" credit rating tenant who leases it on a 20-year term for $60,000 per year. Obviously, this is a comparatively low risk venture and the net income will be in equal annual installments over a 20-year period. The building is new and is the highest and best use of the land. The cost to construct the improvements was $500,000, a figure which has been substantiated as a fair and representative cost. The land, however, is an unusual piece of property with no sales of comparable sites available. In this situation it is reasonable to believe that "cost is value"—that the $500,000 cost figure is equivalent to value. In order to establish an estimate of the value for the land, the "land residual" technique and the "present value of level annuities" table may be used. A risk rate [5] of 9 per cent may be estimated for this investment.

Net income of $5,224, to land capitalized in perpetuity at 9 per cent, produces a capital value of $58,044. The value of the building, $500,000, plus the value of the land, rounded to $58,000, totals a value for the entire property of $558,000. If a lower rate on the land should be acceptable, say 8 per cent, then the land value would be increased to $65,300.

**Mathematical Models**

Another problem involves the selection of a capitalization rate which will reflect the trend of income. Several mathematical models or assumptions may be set up, such as level annual returns to the end of the building's life or declining returns at different rates. Babcock, for example, has established four income premises and has set forth tables reflecting the different types of return under appropriate capitalization rates. Various other tables have been prepared, based on different mathematical models or assumptions, including the Hoskold sinking fund and the Inwood tables.

---

[5] Note that when the annuity tables are used that only the risk (return on) rate is used; the use of a term of years (20 years in this example) incorporates the recapture (return of) provision.

| | | |
|---|---|---|
| Net income to the property | | $60,000 |
| Building cost (value) | $500,000 | |
| 9% for 20 years (Table II) produces a factor of 9.128 | | |
| Share required each year from net income to produce 9% return on investment of $500,000 and recapture that amount in 20 years ($500,000 ÷ 9.128 = $54,776) | | |
| Income attributed to building | | 54,776 |
| Net residual to land | | $ 5,224 |

Almost any type may be used, if the appraiser understands the assumptions back of the tables and their meaning in the capitalization process.

In the Inwood method the principal is reduced each year by an amount equal to the periodic payment less the interest on the prior unpaid balance. The Hoskold method assumes that the portion of the investment returned each year is reinvested in a sinking fund at a lower rate of return; hence, the outstanding investment is not reduced.[6]

## Ellwood Method

Drawing on his experience as a mortgage loan officer, L. W. Ellwood developed a concept of valuation known as "mortgage equity."[7] This concept, popularly called the Ellwood Method, considers certain factors which may not be specifically recognized in other capitalization methods. Its primary contribution is the explicit recognition that most property is financed by a mortgage. The mortgage is usually repaid with level, periodic payments which include both a reduction of the mortgage principal and a payment of the interest on the remaining principal balance. As time goes by, the level payment includes a proportionately greater reduction of the principal because the unpaid balance, and consequently the interest payment thereon, is lower. Therefore the value of the equity in the property, which is the difference between the value of the property and the unpaid mortgage balance, increases at an increasing rate over time.

The Ellwood Method recognizes the mortgage factor by taking both the amount of the mortgage as a percent of the value of the property and the various terms of the mortgage into consideration. For example, if the loan is for a large proportion of the appraised value of the property and the amortization period is relatively long, then the Method reflects a higher value. In addition the Ellwood Method allows for the inclusion of an estimate of the change—either an appreciation or a depreciation—in the property's value over time. A projected decrease would, for example, result in a higher "cap" rate and thus a smaller present value estimate. Finally, the Ellwood Capitalization Tables include sections applicable to purchase-leaseback problems and to income tax shelters. In general, the mortgage equity concept incorporates in a more specific manner many elements which investors consider in making investment decisions.

---

[6] Frederick M. Babcock, op. cit., pp. 534 and 561.

[7] L. W. Ellwood, Ellwood Tables for Real Estate Appraising and Financing (2nd ed.; Chicago: American Institute of Real Estate Appraisers, 1967), Chapter 1.

## SUMMARY

Appraisals or valuations are important guides to real estate decisions. Careful definitions of specific valuation problems are important and should include identification of the specific property rights, the date of valuation, the physical property and the related economic factors.

The appraisal process includes three principal methods—the income, market and cost approaches. The selection of method often depends on the type of income, but it may be determined by type of property or simply by the availability of data.

The income approach most nearly fits the theoretical basis of real estate valuation. Its use, however, may be limited by lack of data or the difficulty of translating returns from direct use into monetary returns.

In applying this approach gross income is estimated, an estimate is made of expenses, net income is established and this is capitalized into value. The selection of the capitalization rate often presents difficult problems for an appraiser. Various methods may be used for estimating the capitalization rate, including summation, band of investment and direct market methods.

## QUESTIONS FOR STUDY

1. Why is it important to know the purpose of a real estate transaction before making an appraisal? Outline the principal classes of transactions.
2. Define the Appraisal Process.
3. How might an appraisal made to estimate an asking price for a quick sale of a property differ from one made to aid in settling an estate? Explain.
4. Assume that your home is assessed for tax purposes at $8,500 and that you have been offered $25,000 for the property. You also know that the local savings and loan association will lend $17,500 on it. Which of these amounts indicates the property's value? Explain.
5. Which appraisal method would you use in appraising your study property? Justify your selection.
6. Why is the capitalization of future income the approach most consistent with valuation theory? Why are other methods used?
7. How may type of income influence the selection of appraisal method?
8. What difference would it make in selecting a method if the return on the property were in the form of dollar payments or direct use?
9. If returns to a property are in the form of business profits, how may this affect selection of method? Illustrate.
10. List the steps typically followed in the income approach. Discuss the principal difficulties in each step. Illustrate.

11. Outline the principal methods used to determine capitalization rates. Which one seems best from your standpoint? Why?

12. If gross income from a small apartment house is estimated at $30,000, expenses at $18,000 and if investors are expecting 12 per cent return for investments of this type, what would be a value estimate for this property? Explain.

13. Suppose you knew that you could purchase the apartment house in Problem 12 with a 75% mortgage at 8% interest. You also expect the value of the apartment house to decrease by 20% over the next 10 years. Would it be best to estimate the present value of this property using the Ellwood method? Why or why not?

## SUGGESTED READINGS

AMERICAN INSTITUTE OF REAL ESTATE APPRAISERS. *The Appraisal of Real Estate* (5th ed.). Chicago: The Institute, 1967. Chaps. 2, 4, 15–19.

BABCOCK, FREDERICK M. *The Valuation of Real Estate.* New York: McGraw-Hill Book Co., Inc., 1932. Chaps. xv–xviii.

ELWOOD, L. W. *Elwood Tables for Real Estate Appraising and Financing* (3rd ed.). Ridgewood, N.J.: Published by the author, 1970.

KINNARD, WILLIAM N., JR. *Industrial Real Estate.* Washington, D.C.: Society of Industrial Realtors, 1967. Chap. 12.

———. *Income Property Valuation.* Lexington, Mass.: Heath Publishing Co., 1971.

RATCLIFF, RICHARD U. *Modern Real Estate Valuation.* Madison, Wis.: The Democrat Press, 1965.

WENDT, PAUL F., and ALAN R. CERF. *Real Estate Investment, Analysis and Taxation.* New York: McGraw-Hill Book Co., Inc., 1969. Chaps. 1, 2, 10.

## CASE 12–1

### Samuel Jones' Appraisal and Investment Decision

Samuel Jones would like to buy an income property in his home town of Centerville, Massachusetts. The two most likely possibilities are apartment projects.

One, the Cambridge Arms, was built in 1928. Its 100 units are large and rent for $230 per month. When new, they were almost the only apartments of their type in town and were considered luxury apartments. Maintenance expenses and taxes amount to $100,000 per year, bringing net cash flow to about $176,000.

The other possibility, the Park Chateau Apartment Complex was built in 1965. Geared toward young marrieds, these apartments are not nearly as large and ornate as those in Cambridge Arms. The 120 units rent for an average of $150 per month. Maintenance and taxes run about $80,000 per year.

Mr. Jones must decide which project offers a better investment opportunity. Park Chateau is very popular with the younger set and even has a waiting list so he feels it has a minimum of risk. Because mortgage rates on apartments are running around 7½ per cent, he feels a capitalization rate of 10 per cent would be appropriate.

The Cambridge Arms represents a completely different situation. It is filled now, but that may be because there is a shortage of apartments in town. When newer ones are built, he feels that tenants will be drawn from the oldest eixsting units first. He is also wary of maintenance expenses on such an old building. Therefore he has settled on a capitalization rate for the Cambridge Arms of 15 per cent.

## Questions

1. Using Mr. Jones' figures, what are the values of the two projects?
2. Do you agree with Jones' capitalization rates? How would you change them?
3. Mr. Jones says his decision is made more difficult by the fact that the full-occupancy cash flow for the Cambridge Arms is so much higher than that of Park Chateau. He computes it this way:

|  | Cash Flow | Value |
|---|---|---|
| Cambridge Arms | $176,000 | $1,166,600 |
| Park Chateau | 155,000 | 1,560,000 |

Do you agree with these estimates? If he came to you for advice, what would you tell him?

## STUDY PROJECT 12–1

### Recent Trends in Real Estate Investment Valuation *

Decisions to purchase or develop real estate are capital budgeting decisions of some complexity, due to the relatively slow payback of total capital employed and the vulnerability of the capital asset to obsolescence because the real estate attributes of immobility, durability, and relative inflexibility of use. Nevertheless, investment decisions have generally been made under the influence of oversimplified appraisal approaches to present value theory rather than the rapidly developing techniques of capital budgeting and financial management. It is useful to trace the evolution of real estate theory and the recent infusion of modern capital budgeting techniques into urban land economics. Appraisal technique continues to center its theories for valuing discounted income streams on the truism that the stabilized income stream divided by an overall discount rate equals present value of the investment ($I/OAR = V$). Stabilized income is a very theoretical measure of economic productivity, as it requires determination of economic rent for a given property rather than its actual cash pattern, and deduction of expenses which include both actual cash outlays and accrual reserves for items which have a shorter useful life than the structure as a whole. Net income productivity is therefore an economic concept of net surplus in a base year and this surplus is presumed to be level or declining in a continuous function implicit in the

* James A. Graaskamp, Associate Professor, University of Wisconsin.

selection of the capitalization rate computation. The big debate in the selection of a rate for appraisal is the need to allocate this surplus of productivity between an interest return on capital employed and recapture of the capital outlay. Straight-line capitalization would allocate a flat amount each year to capital recapture as in straight-line amortization of a bond premium charged against coupon income. Income is presumed to fall, to reflect declining interest required on unrecovered balance of the capital. No credit is given for reinvestment potentials of recaptured capital. Hoskold and Inwood capitalization systems recognize reinvestment of recovered capital by accumulating the initial capital outlay in a kind of mathematical sinking fund, reducing the required diversion of net income from profits to recapture, and thereby producing higher values for, the properties. Net income surplus is always considered before payment of interest and principal on loans outstanding and before payment of the federal income tax and is extrapolated for the full useful life of the property—perhaps as much as 50 years. With time the allocation of net income productivity to recapture original investment has been modified by the introduction of residual techniques which recognized some recovery of capital from sale of the land or structural salvage at the end of its useful life. In addition, the reinvestment opportunity value of capital recapture was recognized by the reinvestment assumptions inherent in Hoskold and Inwood techniques.[1] Nevertheless, the essential fallacy remains of leveling economic income while recapitalizing to recognize present value of cash.

A major shift in appraisal valuation techniques occurred with the introduction of the Ellwood capitalization procedures.[2] Proponents of the Ellwood technique point out that the investment projection period should reflect the relatively short span of 5–10 or 15 years which characterizes a single ownership or a single phase in structure utility before major remodeling investment necessitates full revaluation. A relatively short forecast period logically must lead to the assumption that most of the original investment would be recaptured from resale. Income productivity need only be allocated to capital recapture to the degree resale value was less than purchase price; and indeed, the formulation could value the possibility of capital appreciation. The proponents of the Ellwood technique further argue that credit terms have a major influence on market price because real estate equity investment depends so heavily on leverage. The Ellwood technique regards the credit obligation as a further claim on productivity and is therefore concerned with annual cash dividends or cash throwoff (net income less debt service) to the equity investor plus equity proceeds after debt retirement upon resale. All of this is accomplished as in Chart 1 in the method of computing the overall capitalization rate. Net income is modified to an average annual cash concept by the reduction of accrual reserves as expenses to only those items which will be

[1] For a thorough and fair treatment see: *Income Property Appraisal*, William Kinnard, published by Heath Publishing Co., Lexington, Mass., 1971.

[2] *Ellwood Tables I & II*, 3rd ed., L. W. Ellwood; American Institute of Real Estate Appraisers, Chicago, Ill., 1970.

**CHART 1. Comparison of Accounting Definitions of Real Estate Income from Rental Property for Three Present Value Valuation System**

PART I. ANNUAL RETURNS TO INVESTOR

A. Estimate Potential Gross Cash Income: Cash Income from Space Sales

B. Deductions from Potential Gross
1. Normal vacancy
2. Seasonal income loss
3. Collection losses

Traditional appraisal approach

4. Franchise fees, deposits returned, etc.

C. Add "Other" Income from Service Sales

D. Derive Effective Gross Income

E. Deduct Operating Expenses (on Expected Cash Outlay without Accrual Reserves Except for Traditional Appraisal)
1. Fixed expenses
2. Variable expenses
3. Repairs and maintenance
4. Replacements

F. Derive Net Operating Income

Ellwood mortgage equity approach

G. Deduct Annual Debt Service
1. Contract interest
2. Supplementary variable interest
3. Principal amortization

H. Derive Cash Throw-off

I. Add Back Principal Payments and Replacements

Spendable cash budget investment value approach

J. Deduct Tax Depreciation Allowance

K. Derive Taxable Income

L. Determine Income Tax on Real Estate Income

M. Deduct Income Tax from Cash-Throw Off (H)

N. Derive After-Tax Cash Flow

O. Add Tax Savings on Other Income (if K is Negative)

P. Add Surplus from Refinancing

Q. Derive Spendable After-Tax Cash

PART II. RETURNS TO INVESTOR ON RESALE

A. Estimated Resale Price*

B. Deduct Broker's Commission and Other Transaction Costs

Ellwood mortgage equity approach

C. Derive Effective Gross Proceeds from Sale

D. Deduct All Credit Claims Outstanding
1. Short and long term note balances due
2. Prepayment penalties
3. Deduct equity shares to non-owner interest

E. Derive Pre-Tax Reversion to Equity

F. Deduct Tax Claims on Ownership Interest

Spendable cash investment approach

1. Deduct capital gains tax
2. Deduct income tax on disallowed accelerated depreciation
3. Deduct surtax on taxable preferential income

G. Derive After Tax Resale Proceeds to Investor

*Traditional approach would define resale value as salvage value of unencumbered land, thus omitting B–G.

**CHART 2. Comparison of Critical Real Estate Investment Valuation Assumptions for Discounting Real Estate Productivity Returns***

| Traditional Appraisal | | |
|---|---|---|
| 1. Instant investment | 1. Instant investment and disinvestment | 1. Discontinuous series of outlays |
| 2. Continuous income function | 2. Continuous income function | 2. Discontinuous series of receipts |
| 3. Productivity limited to annual economic net income from parcel before debt and income tax | 3. Productivity limited to average annual cash after debt service but before income tax | 3. Productivity is periodic net change in spendable cash from all sources after debt and income tax |
| 4. Simple discounting at arbitrary rate | 4. Weighted average discounting of arbitrary equity rate | 4. Modified internal rate of return |
| 5. Recapture of capital from income except for land value | 5. Recapture of capital from income & resale | 5. Payback of equity from spendable after tax cash and debt from net revenue |
| 6. Projected for full useful life of improvements | 6. Projected for normal operating period 5–10–15 years for typical investor | 6. Projected for elapsed time of outlays and receipts for specific total holding period of investor |

*Small variations on theme are oversimplified for purposes of tabular comparison replaced within the projected period of ownership. While the Ellwood approach moves closer to a cash concept of productivity, it still depends upon instant investment, instant resale proceeds, and income projections as continuous mathematical functions. Chart 2 provides a summary comparison with traditional appraisal methods.

It should be understood that the Ellwood technique is not only intended to improve the relevance of appraisal valuation theory but also is intended to be a system for practical application in the field with the aid of precomputed tables by a number of professional appraisers whose mathematical ability and accounting abilities are no better than any cross section of small businessmen. Real estate decisions have been typically infrequent events related to small enterprises where there is little managerial specialization, and therefore operational techniques need to be easily understood and applied by those making the investment decisions. This constraint of interfacing theory and practice may account for the lag between field methods of valuation and modern capital budgeting theory developed by the upper echelons of banking and corporate staff analysts.

In recent years the scale of real estate enterprise has grown from isolated development of individual sites to the creation of total urban systems more commonly called new towns, shopping centers, planned unit development or industrial–commercial parks. The development process involves increasing capital outlays over development lead time ranging from 3 years for a shopping center up to 15 years for a new town. Both equity and debt capital required limit activity to only the largest corporation with sophisticated accounting and financial specialists. Their multiple profit centers and income tax considerations produce erratic discontinuous streams of receipts. The hidden assumptions of traditional or Ellwood appraisal techniques of instant investment, of continuous income functions, or of productivity limited to that inherent to real estate before the income tax, appear as distortions no longer justified in large part by the need for simplicity. Large sophisticated capital investors are therefore significantly altering current concepts of real estate productivity and valuation.

The fundamental departure of modern capital budgeting from appraisal is related to its emphasis on cash revenue forecasting by periods rather than by projection of a continuous function. Moreover, the traditional real estate assumption of a conventional investment of a single outlay followed by a series of one or more receipts is only a special case of the more general pattern of real estate investment which is a series of outlays followed by or interspersed with a series of receipts. The real estate appraiser is solving his formula by assuming a discount factor for which he has some market evidence to determine the justified outlay which he calls market value or investment value. The capital budget maker attempts to define outlays and receipts in order to solve for the rate of return that would be realized if the schedule were to be accomplished. Typically this rate is the internal rate of return (ROI) modified for cost of capital, which is defined by the capital budgeting people as that rate of interest that will make the future value of the cash proceeds expected from an investment equal to the present value of the cash outlays required by that investment.[3]   Cash outlays are discounted to the beginning of the forecast period at a rate equal to the cost of capital or reinvestment opportunity rate.   Cash proceeds are compounded forward to the end of the forecast period at the cost of capital or reinvestment rate.   Then it is possible to solve for the internal rate of return which will make the future value of cash proceeds equal to the present value of cash outlays.   This technique avoids the problem of solving for the internal rate of a non-conventional investment, that is, one with outlays interspersed with receipts.   More significant than the technical problem of computation is the fact that investors typically experience higher returns to equity in real estate than any other investment alternative, so that the reinvestment assumptions of the internal rate of return do not distort the results when outlays and proceeds are modified.

To determine after-tax spendable cash, it is necessary to provide detail on the calendar of financial events, the sources of proceeds and their income tax classification, operating expenses, financial plans for interest and principal advances and payments, and the possible variance in critical assumptions.   Determination of outlays and receipts for each period involves extensive computation best performed by computer.   As a result, accounting firms, engineering firms, and time-sharing services, as well as institutional investors, have developed a large number of cash flow simulation programs serving various types of real estate investment.   The computer terminal, in particular, should solve interfacing problems of theory and practice which delayed widespread adaptation of the Ellwood approach among appraisers.[4]

While capital provided by mortgage loans secures its recapture from net income and resale proceeds, the equity cash required looks to its payback from all sources of spendable cash attributable to participation in the real estate enterprise.   Productivity can thus be expanded in concept to include a variety of profit centers inherent in the construction process or operating management of the real estate, as well as the deferral of income taxes or the abatement of operating costs of the owner.   Relocation of a manufacturing firm may not only provide economies in occupancy costs for a new building, but may also produce lower marketing, raw material, transportation, and labor-cost savings per unit of production, while increasing income tax deductions and reducing capital investment due to community subsidies to attract new employers.   An increase in net spendable cash and a decline in net invested capital thereby produces a higher return on investment capital.   The developer may find cash profits from land sales, construction contracts, creation of business opportunities within the development such as retailing sites, and captive markets for his insurance agency and mortgage banking house, not to mention the profiable sale of tax losses and investment management.   Such an expanding concept of productivity is looking at a real estate commitment as entree to a consumption

---

[3] The professional appraisal societies have organized a joint educational program as a separate foundation to accelerate introduction of computer terminals in appraisal offices.   More information can be had by writing EDUCARE, School of Business, University of Wisconsin, Madison, Wisconsin 53706.

[4] "How to Assess Investment Proposals," *Harvard Business Review*, Robert H. Baldwin, May–June 1959.

system generating a variety of potential cash flows for the supplier of urban space systems. Each investor may choose to recognize different profit potentials, but the result is that the independent appraiser who does not have access to internal data of the investor cannot predict with accuracy the value of a specific parcel to that investor.

Just as the income stream is undergoing redefinition, so is the assumption of instant reinvestment. Unlike the purchase of a bond, which may involve a cash transfer to the broker within a day or two of the investment commitment, real estate investment involves a series of outlays in the form of earnest money, down payment, construction draws, special improvements for new tenants, and occasional remodeling and deferred maintenance. The actual timing of outlays can be manipulated by the terms of purchase contracts, forms of business organizations such as joint ventures and syndicates, and by terms of real estate credit alternatives. Thus the network of financial events called outlays may be proceeding in part independently of the schedule of anticipated net receipts, although financial solvency obviously requires some correlation between scheduled receipts and scheduled outlays.

Once the valuation system becomes concerned with cash accounting for outlays and receipts, many of the old assumptions for accrual reserves, or average returns on capital, or allocations of streams of revenue between profit and capital recapture, drop out of explicit consideration. Of course, the alternative makes it necessary to detail a whole calendar of specific cash transaction events, to make explicit assumptions as to rates of construction, occupancy, sale, repair and all the other changes which occur in the condition or state of a real estate enterprise system.[5] Immediately, the investor is confronted with the reality that he is making decisions under conditions of uncertainty, uncertainty which cannot be softened by the appraisal assumption of average revenue, implicit sinking funds, and non-existent non-cash reserves. As long ago as 1932, Frederick M. Babcock stated in his classic book *The Valuation of Real Estate*:

> If anticipated income is the basis of valuation, then the valuation process will necessarily include the making of forecasts and predictions. The fact that predictions are difficult to make with accuracy in no way modifies the necessity for making them, and the process of deriving an estimate of present value from a forecast of future income is in no sense to be considered as one of the several alternative methods of valuation.[6]

In short, Babcock advocated the discounting of net return as the only legitimate method of valuation. Several methods have developed among sophisticated investors for dealing with the uncertainty of capital budget projections and assumptions.

Risk in real estate is the variance between expectations and realizations. Such a definition implies that the analyst has a plan which defines his expectation and provides a means of measuring the adequacy of his realization, namely

---

[5] *Management Dynamics—The New Synthesis*, John A. Beckett, McGraw-Hill, 1971.
[6] *Valuation of Real Estate*, Frederick H. Babcock, McGraw-Hill, 1932.

a budget, a monitoring system with feedback, and specific criteria as to what is included in "net profit." Without that premise, the investor may have much anxiety and doubt but has no means of discussing risk. There is no relationship between rate of return, which is a quantitative computation involving fixed variables, and risk, which is concerned with consequences of variance in those quantities. Instead, risk is a manageable factor which can be controlled through planning and monitoring, shifted by contract, reduced through scale of operations, or avoided through a variety of legal escape routes. A real estate project must be analyzed for its potential variance between realization and expectation by evaluating the degree to which its revenues are assured, its costs have been stabilized by contract and technique, and unforeseen future contingencies can be cushioned with conservative financial planning. Long-term upset may be buffered by early recovery of equity capital, coupled with a limit on investor liability, or prearranged formulas for liquidation. Having determined the variance which could be eliminated by contract and by management, it is then necessary to analyze the significance of possible variance in the variables which remain. To some degree, management control of when the money is spent permits an increase in snow removal cost to be offset by a deferred expenditure for maintenance or improvement so that net flows do not gyrate with every variable in the budget.

After the allowance for co-variance within aggregates of revenue, expenses, and capital costs, there still remains some potential for a positive or negative difference between net cash flow expectations and realizations. One method of measuring the significance of these residual variances is facilitated by computer simulation cash flow models. Several sets of optimistic and pessimistic assumptions are run through the model to establish the range of typical outcomes and yields. The possible outcome of the investment is thus bracketed, and if realization seems reasonable by subjective probability standards the investor will proceed. A number of sophisticated investors have created probability or stochastic cash flow simulation models in which variables are described as a single number with a standard deviation or as a range with a median point. These dimension statements on the range and shape of frequency distribution of key variables can take the form of either normal distributions or Baysian curves skewed to the high or the low side. For example, total construction cost might be described as within $400,000 and $500,000 with the median at $420,000, suggesting the overruns may be more costly than unanticipated savings. The computer constructs an array of 100 or more pro forma cash flow statements by choosing on a random basis the necessary variables from the curves of each frequency distribution suggested by the inputs. The computer then calculates the frequency distribution of the 100 fictional financial statements on matters of net income or rate of return in order to provide a probability statement relative to achievement of certain dollar or ratio decision criteria.

Among the variables which affect yield, the most sensitive factors are total capital cost and its derivative, equity cash required "up front" at the start of the investment. Since that is the case, it can be said that the investor predetermines his rate of return by how well he negotiates the price and terms of his purchase. For many years to come there will be a great discrepancy among buyers and sellers (or their agents) in their ability to correctly value the present worth of any given property. A significant portion of profits to be made will therefore go to those who understand the requirements of capital investment valuation and the components of risk necessary to apply the present value of money concept to maximum advantage.

### Questions

1. Explain the formula $I/OAR = V$.
2. Why is "capital recapture" provided for in real estate investment analysis but not for most other types of investments?
3. Are there basic differences between the Ellwood capitalization procedure and the mortgage equity approach?
4. Comment on the statement: "A real estate project must be analyzed for its potential variance between realization and expectation by evaluating the degree to which its revenues are assured, costs have been stabilized by contract and technique, and unforeseen future contingencies can be cushioned with conservative financial planning."

### STUDY PROJECT 12–2

### Computers Can't Do My Appraisal, But . . .*

Computers cannot appraise.

A computer is a precise assemblange of electrical and mechanical hardware and surrounding peripheral equipment. It cannot measure a room; it cannot determine the quality of construction; it cannot evaluate a subdivision; it cannot think. So what is all this about computers and appraisers?

The appraisal field is growing. The information and staff requirements of the appraiser are increasing rapidly; but unfortunately, fees are static. There is a need to get more done and to do it more efficiently and more accurately. There is an urgent need to increase productivity and the quality of appraisals. Most important, appraisers need to get away from the clerical work and get back to appraising. The computer could have something if it could help meet these goals. It can. It does.

**About the Machine.** But before discussing computers and appraising, let's put to rest some of the mysticism that surrounds computers. A computer is not a thinking machine or an electronic monster; it's an elaborate electronic calculator that can perform according to a specific set of instructions. The calculators are extremely fast. This speed and the ability to store and retrieve vast amounts of data make the computer a powerful and sophisticated tool. The computer is a complex machine and nothing more. It cannot think, use judgment, or perform in place of an appraiser.

---

* Dan L. Swango and Gary Williamson. "Computers Can't Do My Appraisal, But . . .", *The Real Estate Appraiser* (Chicago: Society of Real Estate Appraisers, May–June, 1971).

An incorrect attribute that is often associated with computers is that they make mistakes. This belief is analogous to the idea of blaming a typewriter for spelling errors. Neither a typewriter nor a computer makes mistakes. As machines, they are only as accurate and useful as the person using them. A computer is checked and serviced regularly. Parts and electrical components that might fail under extreme conditions are immediately replaced. Furthermore, a computer cannot be subtle. If a power shortage or some remote occurrence affects the computer, the problem should be immediately apparent.

A typewriter receives a continuous series of changing instructions. Computer instructions, unlike typewriter instructions, may be constantly refined until they are absolutely perfect. This set of instructions may then be used when a particular need arises. This set of instructions is called a computer program. The program is often complex and may require many trials before it is perfect. Once the desired program is set up, it can be guaranteed. As an appraiser, it is not your job to do this work; that's up to the programmer, computer expert or systems analyst. The computer company that tries to blame bad results on a computer error is neglecting its responsibility and trying to hide incompetence. You don't have to use these people any more than you have to use a poor typist.

**Computer Systems Are for People.** Another belief is that the user must conform to the computer and follow a specific set of requirements that are generated in some mysterious way. Appraisers should not have to change their operation to meet the demands of the computer system. Machines should follow the dictates of man and not the converse.

There are different models and sizes of computers, and different ways to use computers. Further, the programs that tell the computer what to do may be extremely varied and customized for particular types of users and assignments. Like any type of machine, some computers and programs will not fit your needs as an individual appraiser. What is generally good in some other part of the country, or for some other type appraisal work, may not be acceptable to you in your location, with your type of appraisal assignments. As an appraiser, you may specify the type of programs that you want. It is true, that once established, certain criteria must be followed, but an individual appraiser may specify the criteria according to his needs and desires. This is one test for good, flexible, adaptable computer programs.

The basic idea of the programs is to help the appraiser, or appraisal effort, to achieve greater speed, accuracy and consistency in the application of conventional approaches to value. The computer can do much of the routine, leaving more time for the appraiser to think, to reason, and to analyze. As an advertisement for I.B.M. said, "Machines should work; people should think."

**Applying Computers to Appraising.** The computer programs that are of assistance to appraisers may be divided into three categories.

First, there are programs that store and manipulate large amounts of data. These are the programs that store data and sort it by alphabet or by price (or other criteria) and produce corresponding lists of sales. These programs are characterized by the fact that they process large quantities of data but do not generally change the information provided.

Second, there are specific applications of the computer to appraising and the approaches to value.

There are the applications which are somewhat routine for a given type of property, that is, where there is a logical flow to the processing of data and repetitive work. Where there is logic and consistency in the appraisal of property (or should be!), the computer can be of tremendous assistance. The computer can follow logic in applying adjustments in Market Comparison, in applying cost factors in the Cost Approach, and in calculating formulas used in the Income Approach. These programs act upon the information provided. They do extensive calculations and produce additional information resulting in an estimate of value.

There are areas in the application of any of the approaches to value which are highly dependent upon the judgment and talent of the individual appraiser. Good computer programs of the Type Two category must consider and respect the importance of judgment.

Third, there are auxiliary programs which round out a complete service to the appraiser. In addition to the two categories above, the programs in this category process and display information so that a comprehensive understanding of the data may be obtained. These programs can search for specific data such as comparable sales, and may be used to determine statistical information about the market. For example, the average cost of homes, the range of prices, and the number of homes sold are all easily obtainable. These programs also plot the data so that it may be displayed in graphic form. More advanced analysis such as Multiple Linear Regression may be included.

With these three general categories of programs, let's explore what a customized set of computer programs can do for an individual appraiser. It will be shown how an appraiser can make effective use of the computer. To do so, we are going to discuss a set of appraiser oriented computer programs which were implemented in Tucson, Arizona. These programs will be referred to as illustrative examples only.

The programs take into consideration the logical processing of data as well as the need for individual judgment of the appraiser and the need to consider the uniqueness of each property. These example programs are modular and flexible so they are adaptable to various types of appraisal application in almost any location.

**Type 1 Programs: Stored Information.** Two files of data were established within the computer: (1) *The Single Family Residential Data File* contains a description of financial and physical characteristics of individual single family residential market data; including homes, homes with guest houses, townhouses, and condominium units. (2) *The Land Market Data Bank* contains a number of land sales, giving physical and financial characteristics for each of the sales, covering a great deal of essential and helpful information.

These two files provide for the storage and processing of comments and miscellaneous information. This is particularly important because it gives the users the opportunity to explain features which do not readily lend themselves to rigid numeric coding.

All of the information entering the data files is automatically checked for accuracy and consistency. Individual records may be modified or deleted as desired. For example, if no bedrooms are given for a home, an error is printed for that home. If the size and price do not seem to match, a warning may be given. In the Tucson, Arizona programs now in use, for example, there are 40 checks made on each home before it enters one of the information files.

**Programs that List.** Both the single family residential and the land data are listed on a periodic basis or upon request of a user, to provide current sales information to users. This data may be classified and rated by location, subdivision, zoning or any of various other characteristics. These lists are produced by programs of the first classification.

Thus, the computer is used to provide a comparable sales list, a print-out of properties which have sold, grouped by various cross-indexing methods. Such a system is now in use in the Tucson area and provides information on property sales, and gives a wide variety of physical and financial characteristics. The list is automatically updated, adding new sales and dropping the sales over a certain specified age.

The data collection and list program may be modified for particular communities. In the residential file, for exmaple, in Tucson basements are not an important consideration; however, in the midwest or other parts of the country, they would have to be included.

The comparable sales data file and list is of primary importance. Fresh, complete, and accurate comparable sales data is essential. It means a better appraisal, and an appraisal completed more efficiently.

**Selective Data Retrieval.** Selective data retrieval is an important part of the computer-assisted appraisal concept. The appraiser's foremost problem and most costly and time-consuming effort is in searching for market data. Selective data retrieval is of even greater importance than the sales list of comparable properties described above. Appraisers need to have a central data bank, and be able to request information by convenient remote terminal. This should cover sales of any properties which meet specific requirements, with data retrieved after specification of any combination of financial, physical or locational characteristics.

The appraiser may receive the desired information by visual display (a TV screen), or teletypewriter or computer print-out list. This greatly facilitates appraisal work and saves appraisers time and money. Since a great deal of an appraiser's time and effort is spent in searching out market data and trying to find properties which have certain characteristics similar to his subject property, the selective data retrieval program is appreciated by both independent appraisers and institutional appraisers.

The program used in Tucson is not limited to selections by date, price or bedroom in the single family home category or limited to land of only a certain size or zoning description. It has the capability of select records by any variable or by any combination of characteristics that are given in the source information.

For example, it is possible, for any given location, to find all the sales of three bedroom-two bath homes, between 1500 and 1800 square feet, from $25,000 to $35,000, which are currently offered for sale or which have sold during the last six months. The characteristics and the categories are flexible. The properties so found may then be used for (1) comparable sales by the appraiser, (2) automatically applying cost and conventional market data approaches to value, and (3) further statistical processing (to be discussed next).

In other words, it is possible to request comparable sales from the data bank for any property type and use the comparable property for manual or computer-assisted application of the Cost Approach and Market Data Comparison Approach or for statistical analysis.

**Type 2 Programs.**   The following three programs, which aid in estimating value, are all programs of the second classification.

**Conventional Cost Approach by Computer.**   The Cost Approach program used in the Tucson program is flexible and the cost factors in the program are changed to meet the changing costs of the various building components. For application of the Cost Approach to a particular property, a rating sheet is simply filled out which describes the subject property including judgment factors as to quality of components, condition of components, effective age, remaining economic life, and such. The computer does the rest: applying the cost factors, summing, depreciating, and adding land value according to instructions.

The Cost Approach, using a computer, is particularly good for (1) insuring consistency and (2) handling mass appraising with speed and accuracy while still leaving room for all important judgments by the appraiser.

**Conventional Market Data Comparison Approach by Computer.**   In the conventional Market Data Comparison Approach used in our program, a rating sheet is filled out which describes the subject property including judgment factors as to location, quality, and condition. The computer then applies plus and minus adjustments as necessary (in dollars or percentage adjustments) for the particular property type, and may compare the subject to possibly dozens of similar sales. The adjustments are flexible, meet each property type specifically, and insure consistency in logical comparisons of comparable data. The adjustments in the Market Data Approach are programmed for particular locality and are completely flexible to meet the reality of the market situation. They may cover different adjustments for different property types in different price strata. This approach, too, is excellent for insuring consistency in handling mass appraising and increasing both speed and accuracy. Again, in all programs and systems, there is ample room for the appraiser's judgment, since appraising is still something of an art; perhaps even more than a science.

**The Income Approach.**   In the Income Approach the value of the property is estimated by capitalization of the net income expected from the property, considering expenses, taxes, yield on investment, etc. The Income Approach by computer makes use of present value and future worth tables, as well as capitalization formulas which have been programmed by appraisal and computer firms. There are many such programs which are widely available to appraisers at the present time.

**Type 3 Programs: Statistical Inference.** Statistical information and displays of market data are possible, using the programs we employ. The display and statistical programs present the data in a coherent and concise form. For example, in a given set of data the programs can be used to determine the relationships between square footage and price, between types of construction and price, between bedrooms and bathrooms or between any requested variables. These may be shown on a chart, or graph, or they may be analyzed by various types of statistical analysis. The relative importance of the various factors is thus shown. The common items of mean, median, modes and standard deviation may be easily obtained.

**Multiple Regression Analysis.** Currently, appraisals of property are usually made by using one or more of the three approaches to value, each of which is used to simulate the thinking of buyers and sellers in the marketplace.

A new and promising approach, which is not currently in wide field use, is multiple regression analysis in which the unknown, value, is "forecast," based on the relationship and interaction of the various known characteristics, or independent variables, of the subject property. Hundreds of sales may be analyzed to find a relationship between the various independent variables (or influencing factors such as size, number of bedrooms, construction, etc., or in the case of land, front footage, square footage, zoning, location, etc.) and the sales price—the dependent variable.

The relationships thus found may then be applied to the independent variables (characteristics) of the subject property in order to predict sales price or estimate market value for the subject. This may be done for improved property or for vacant land. In this way hundreds of comparable sales are analyzed in arriving at an estimate of value instead of only a handful. In addition, accuracy and confidence interval may be statistically known.

Multiple regression analysis will provide a pure market basis upon which to make an estimate of value rather than having the estimate influenced by cost information, as is presently the case. We believe the market application of multiple regression analysis is promising in the field of real estate appraising both for single and multi-family income property, as well as land and some commercial properties.

A logical outgrowth of this system is that the input of information about the subject property, including judgment factors, would be fed by push-button telephone or terminal directly into the computer facility, which would return, almost instantaneously or with a short turnaround period, the multiple regression analysis considering hundreds of comparable sales applied to the subject property. This information could be returned by TV screen to teletypewriter.

**Capabilities.** The programs described herein are all related and serve one another. The output from one program may become the input to another program. For example, the selective data recall program may be the input to one of the list programs, or cost, or market approaches, or to a statistical program.

The program may be modified, added to, or deleted, whenever necessary. This is important to any good appraisal computer program. It must meet the needs of the appraiser in his locality for his type of work. A good system may be refined and customized to best serve the needs of a particular locality or user.

**Other Possibilities.**    The appraisal profession in most locations could use maps showing values and locations presented by grid or topographic lines, and statistical information on sales and listing activity by properties and location. This could easily be derived from the sales data banks and listing banks mentioned above.

The computer does not produce an appraisal. It can utilize and manipulate data and information given it so that the information and results of information processing are readily available to the appraiser. The appraiser can use more data in his analysis. He can spend more time thinking and less time in clerical detail covering routine work needing little analysis. With current and accurate data and information he can have more confidence in his decisions, more substantiation for his value estimates, and produce his "product" more efficiently. The computer does not replace the appraiser in any way; it simply does the "idiot" work and allows him time to think, to analyze, and to do a much better job for his client.

## Questions

1. Why can't computers appraise? Explain.
2. What can computers do to assist the appraiser in reaching his decision?
3. Do you feel that it is necessary for the appraiser to check his calculations by the use of multiple regression analysis?
4. What appears to be the likely future use of computers in appraising? In investment decisions?

# 13

# Appraising Methods: Market and Cost Approaches

## THE MARKET APPROACH

In the preceding chapter we paid special attention to the income approach to valuation problems. We will turn our attention now to the other two major approaches—the market and cost approaches.

The process of estimating value by the use of the market approach includes four principal steps: (1) analysis of the property under consideration; (2) selection of comparable properties; (3) analysis of comparable properties; and (4) comparison of the subject property and those selected for comparative purposes.

### Analysis of Subject Property

The property under consideration is analyzed in terms of its use and potential uses, characteristics of the land, characteristics of the structure or potential new structures, location factors, market trends, regulations and restrictions affecting the property and related factors. The detail with which this analysis is carried out will vary with the type of property and purpose of the appraisal. In many cases, established forms are used; for example, savings and loan associations, insurance companies, banks, and other mortgage lenders often indicate rather specifically the factors to be included in a property analysis.

In making comparisons most appraisers are careful to consider the time of the sale, the conditions of the sale, the characteristics of the property, its location and selected market and governmental factors. Sometimes appraisers use a grid system to help make comparisons.

### Selection of Comparable Properties

Other properties having the same or nearly the same characteristics are selected. The appraiser has available or secures information about these properties to use for comparison with the subject property. Generally properties are selected for comparative purposes which have been bought in the open market (without such compulsion as forced sales) and for which price information can be obtained. Other information which is used in the absence of price data includes listings or offers to sell, offers to purchase, and rentals. Only "arms length" transactions should be used. Recent sales data are much more reliable than those going back a year or more.

### Analysis of Comparable Properties

The information about the comparable properties is analyzed carefully. For example, sales data are considered with respect to the number of sales involved, the period of time covered, the terms of the sales (including down payments, financing arrangements, and the like), the motivating forces back of the sales, if discoverable, and the degree of market activity, including the rate of turnover of properties.

### Comparison of Subject and Selected Properties

Comparisons between the subject property and comparable properties are made, either on an over-all ("chunk") basis or by the use of cubic- or square-foot units or other units of comparison, such as number of apartments or seats in a theatre.

Appraisers follow various techniques in carrying out the process of making comparisons between properties. In some cases, detailed rating forms are used to assist in the process. Typically, comparisons are made at least with respect to physical factors, location, market and related economic factors, and governmental and regulatory influences.

Physical factors include: (1) site and accessibility; (2) size and shape of the lot; (3) size, style, and functional plan of the building; (4) condition of the building; (5) materials of construction; (6) number of apartments, rooms, offices, or other space units; (7) equipment in the building and its condition; and (8) life expectancy of the building and other improvements.

## PROFESSIONAL RESIDENTIAL APPRAISAL

| | |
|---|---|
| Ins. Value, 100% $.......... | Loan Number.................. |
| Ins. Value "As Dep." $.......... | Loan Reported.................. |
| No. of dwelling units .......... | $.................. |
| Masonry.... or Frame.......... | Final Estimate of Market Value |

STAPLE PICTURE HERE

PURPOSE: Mortgage_____ Insurance_____ Collection_____

Request by: Mr(s)_____
builder—seller—attorney—buyer—broker

Phone_____ Date _____

To inspect   Mr(s)_____
Contact   Phone/Key at_____

Owner's Value: $_____ Name _____

For general use:

ADDRESS:_____
CITY/COUNTY: _____ BLK_____ LOT_____
SUBDIVISION: _____

INDICATE NORTH

SQ. FT. AREAS
HSE: _____

SKETCH EXTERIOR PLAN—SHOW DIMENSIONS

## N E I G H B O R H O O D   D A T A

PROXIMITY OF PROPERTY TO:

| | Less ¼ mi. | ¼ to 1 mi. | 1 mi. + | Trans. to | | TRENDS: | INC. DEC. STAB. | GENERAL ECONOMICS: | | | | |
|---|---|---|---|---|---|---|---|---|---|---|---|---|
| Downtown Area | | | | | | Income Level | | TYPICAL RESIDENT'S GROSS INC. | | | | $/yr. |
| Local Shopping | | | | | | Population | | TYPICAL OCCUPATION | | | | |
| Grammar School | | | | | | Housing Units | | TYPICAL PROPERTY VALUES: | LOW | HIGH | MODE | % DEVEL. |
| High School | | | | | | Density Pop./Unit | | Single Family Residences | | | | |
| Expressway Access | | | | | | Ave. Prop. Values | | 2-12 Family & Condominium | | | | |
| Other: | | | | | | Ethnic Compos. | changing | Condominium & Multi-Family | | | | |
| | | | | | | Remaining Economic Life | yrs. | Non-Residential Uses | | | | |

TYPE OF DEVELOPMENT: One____Few____Many____ Builders. UNITS PER YR.    TYPICAL FINANCING: CONV._____INS._____Ln./Val._____%

## S I T E   D A T A

| LOT SIZE | x | | x | | x | | x | | Corner | | Inside | |
|---|---|---|---|---|---|---|---|---|---|---|---|---|
| ZONING | | | HIGHEST AND BEST USE OF SITE: Present | | | | or | | | | | |
| IMPROVMTS. | Asphalt St. | | Conc. St. | | Curbs | | Sidewalks | | Alley | | Driveway | |
| UTILITIES | Gas | | Elect. | | Water | | San. Sewer | | Storm Sewer | | Well | Septic |
| EASEMENTS (DETRIMENTAL TO VALUE): | | | | Party Wall | | Driveway | | Sidewalk | | Other | | |

Describe Easements:

## B U I L D I N G   D A T A   TYPE   AGE   ACT. EFF.

| E X T E R I O R | | | | Good Avg. Poor | I N T E R I O R | | | | | Good Avg. Poor |
|---|---|---|---|---|---|---|---|---|---|---|
| FOUNDATION | Conc. | Block | Brick | | WALLS & CEIL. | Drywall | Plaster | Wood | | |
| | Bsmt. | Crawl | Slab | | FLOOR | Conc. | Tile | Wood | Carpet | |
| WALL CONST. | Frame | Veneer | Block | | CENT. HTG. | Air | Water | Steam | SPACE | |
| WINDOWS | Metal | Wood | Type | S & S | FUEL | Gas | Oil | Elect. | Coal | |
| ROOFING | Asphalt | Blt. Up | Wood | | FUR./BOIL. | Age | HWH | Gals. | A/C | |
| SIDING | Wood | Alum. | Stucco | | ELECT. | Amps | Fuse | Cir. Br. | O/S | |
| GAR.-CAR PT. | Frame | Veneer | Block | | BATH(s) # | Age | FLR/Walls | Ceramic | Other | |
| # Cars | Det'd. | Att'd. | Blt.-in | O'H Door | BATH FIX(s). | Lavs. | W.C.s | Tub(s) | Shwr(s). | |
| OTHER | Gutters | Porch | Patio | | KITCHEN | Age | Cb. & St. | Adq. | Inadq. | |
| REMARKS: | | | | | | O/R | Dishw. | Disp. | Ex. Fan | |
| | | | | | OTHER | Firepl. | | | Flr. Plan ▷ | |

| FLOOR | ROOMS | LIVING | DINING | KITCHEN | #BEDRM | CLOSETS | BATHS #FIX. | | #APTS. | DEPRECIATION | IF NOT TYPICAL, DESCRIBE |
|---|---|---|---|---|---|---|---|---|---|---|---|
| BASEMENT | | | | | | | | | | PHYSICAL DETERIORATION | |
| 1st FLOOR | | | | | | | | | | | |
| 2nd FLOOR | | | | | | | | | | FUNCTIONAL OBSOLESCENCE | |
| 3rd FLOOR | | | | | | | | | | | |
| ATTIC | | | | | | | | | | ECONOMIC OBSOLESCENCE | |
| TOTAL | | | | | | | No. Units | | | | |

**Fig. 13–1.** Professional residential appraisal.

**DEFINITION OF MARKET VALUE:*** "Market value contemplates the consummation of a sale and the passing of full title from seller to buyer by deed, under conditions whereby:
1. buyer and seller are free of undue stimulus and are motivated by no more than the reactions of typical owners;
2. both parties are well-informed or well-advised and act prudently, each for what he considers his own best interest;
3. a reasonable time is allowed to test the market; and
4. payment is made in cash or in accordance with financing terms available in the community for the property type in its locale."
°Society of Real Estate Appraisers

## COST APPROACH TO VALUE:

LAND VALUATION—(ZONED:_____): _____  F.F. or S.F. × $/F.F. or $/S.F. = $_____

+ SITE IMPROVEMENTS: "AS IS" driveway, landscaping, etc. .......................... +_____

other:_____                                            TOTAL ........ $_____

BUILDING VALUATION—REPLACEMENT COST

| BLDG. | AREA | UNIT COST | COST NEW | AGE ACT. | AGE EFF. | PHY. | DEPRECIATION FUNC. | ECON. | TOTAL | DEP. VALUE |
|-------|------|-----------|----------|----------|----------|------|--------------------|-------|-------|------------|
| MAIN  |      |           |          |          |          |      |                    |       |       |            |
|       |      |           |          |          |          |      |                    |       |       |            |
|       |      |           |          |          |          |      |                    |       |       |            |
|       |      |           |          |          |          |      |                    |       |       | +_____  |

**INDICATED VALUE from COST APPROACH** ▷ $_____

## MARKET DATA APPROACH TO VALUE:

| ADDRESS OF COMPARABLE SALES | A | | B | | C | |
|-----------------------------|---|---|---|---|---|---|
| SALE PRICE OF COMPARABLE | | $ | | $ | | $ |
| ADJUSTMENT FOR DATE OF SALE | $ (−) | (+) | $ (−) | (+) | $ (−) | (+) |
| AGE & OVERALL CONDITION | | | | | | |
| SIZE & UTILITY | | | | | | |
| MODERN KITCHEN, BATH, HEATING | | | | | | |
| GARAGE & PORCHES | | | | | | |
| SITE & LOCATION | | | | | | |
| OTHER | | | | | | |
| SUB-TOTALS | $ (−) | $ (+) | $ (−) | $ (+) | $ (−) | $ (+) |
| TOTALS | | $ | | $ | | $ |

**INDICATED VALUE from MARKET APPROACH** ▷ $_____

## INCOME APPROACH TO VALUE: (if applicable)

ESTIMATED MONTHLY RENTAL: $_____ × GROSS MONTHLY MULTIPLIER (_____) =

**INDICATED VALUE from INCOME APPROACH** ▷ $_____

MARKETABILITY "AS IS": Good_____ Average_____ Fair_____ Poor_____ _____

REMARKS:

**CORRELATED FINAL ESTIMATE OF MARKET VALUE,**   AS OF_____, 19____  $_____

I (We) certify that to the best of my (our) knowledge and belief the facts and data used herein are true and correct, and that I (we) personally inspected the property from the inside and the outside, and that I (we) have no undisclosed interest, present or prospective therein.

_____  _____
field appraiser                    reviewing appraiser

MARKETABILITY "AS REPAIRED": Good_____ Average_____ Fair_____ Poor_____ _____

| NEEDED REPAIRS: | CURABLE ITEMS | EST. COST |
|-----------------|---------------|-----------|
|                 |               |           |
|                 |               |           |
|                 |               |           |

COR. ESTIMATE OF MARKET VALUE $_____
EST. CONTRIBUTION TO MARKET VALUE FROM REPAIRS ... +_____

## CORRELATED ESTIMATE OF MARKET VALUE, AS REPAIRED:   $_____

17-PRA   PROFESSIONAL RESIDENTIAL APPRAISAL   ACCOUNTING DIVISION, 111 E. WACKER DRIVE   CHICAGO, ILLINOIS 60601

Location factors include: (1) the general reputation of the neighborhood or district in which the property is located; (2) the desirability of the area as a place to live or do business; (3) the presence or absence of adverse conditions; and (4) the economic future of the city or area (see Chapters 8, 9, 10 and 11).

Market factors include present and anticipated sales prices, rentals, ease or difficulty of financing, volume of transfers, preferences for various types of properties, construction costs, and anticipated changes in market trends (see Chapter 9). Degree of marketability, currently and in the future, is one of the major considerations in determining comparability of properties for appraisal purposes. Related economic factors include: (1) earnings, (2) operating expenses, (3) competitive position of the property, and (4) special features.

Governmental and regulatory factors include: (1) tax rates and assessments, (2) zoning and building regulations, (3) deed restrictions, (4) traffic regulations, (5) police and fire protection, and (6) public improvements, such as streets, utilities, schools, and related facilities.

### Gross Income Multipliers

In some cases, appraisers develop value estimates by comparing gross incomes of the property being appraised with like properties. This involves the use of a multiplier based on experience and rules of thumb. One such rule of thumb is that value will be equal to 100 times gross monthly rent in the case of residential rental property. Such rules of thumb, of course, may be dangerous and misleading. The proper application of the gross income multiplier requires the development of an appropriate multiplier for the property being appraised. The reliability of the multiplier depends directly upon the quality of the data available. A large number of comparable sales should form the basis for a multiplier. Following is an example of the development of a multiplier:

| Comparable Properties | Sales Price | Gross Income | Indicated Gross Income Multiplier |
|---|---|---|---|
| A | $100,000 | $10,000 | 10.00 |
| B | 109,000 | 9,900 | 11.01 |
| C | 92,000 | 10,100 | 9.11 |

An indicated multiplier from these three examples would be in the range of 10. To complete the illustration, assume that the gross income of the property being appraised is $11,200, then 10 times this figure produces an indicated market value of $112,000. More sales would be desirable, of course, to develop a more reliable conclusion. The gross income figures used in this example are on an annual basis. For certain types of properties which are rented on a monthly basis, such as apartments, it is common practice to develop multipliers using gross monthly incomes.

Investors often base their decisions on some multiple of gross income, both in the real estate field and in other fields. In some cases appraisers use current gross incomes in this process and in others a stabilized or adjusted annual income is established. The multiplier used varies with the type of property, economic life of the property, current investment preferences, and other factors.

### Problems of Applying Multipliers

The principal problem involved in the use of gross income multipliers arises from the fact that for many types of properties expenses do not change in the same proportion as gross incomes. That is, if gross rents advance, net incomes are likely to advance even more rapidly if many expense items, such as taxes and insurance, do not move up in the same degree or at the same rate as gross rents. The opposite is also true: When gross rents decline, net incomes may decline even more rapidly.

There is some justification for the use of gross incomes in the case of single-family residences, because expense ratios do not appear to vary in the same degree as in the case of larger residential or commercial properties.

When a value is estimated by using a rent multiplier, the selection of this multiplier must be made with care. Rent multipliers will vary between rental ranges; they will differ for properties in the same rental or value range, depending on the appeal and competitive position of such properties; and there will be variations depending on the remaining economic life of the property.

This process of valuation by the use of gross income multipliers may be considered a variation of the capitalized income method but more frequently is used in connection with the market method, since the multipliers employed may be developed by using data on the market prices of comparable properties and the relation of such prices to gross incomes.

### Sources of Market Information

Standard sources of information are insurance atlases, showing the dimensions of the land and buildings; the assessor's record cards, which usually show dimensions of the land and buildings, the assessed valuation, and data on sales; city zoning maps; real estate atlases, showing the occupancy of each store in the principal shopping districts; airplane maps of cities; the county recorder's records of leases and deeds; published accounts of transactions in newspapers and real estate magazines; files of real estate brokers and financial institutions; records of title companies; and interviews with brokers and clients.

Most appraisers follow the practice of building voluminous files of information. These are sometimes referred to as an appraiser's "data plant." The computer makes possible the storage and retrieval of a large volume of data. It may play a big role in future appraisal data plants.

## THE COST APPROACH

The cost or "cost to produce" method is used widely by appraisers. Many terms are used with reference to costs, including actual cost, historical cost, original cost, reproduction cost, cost to produce, and replacement cost, to mention but a few.

### Actual Cost

This term usually refers to the amount actually expended in the development or acquisition of a property. Hence, the same property might have different actual costs under different conditions; it may have cost $4,000 to acquire a lot and $20,000 to build a house, an actual cost of $24,000; however, the property may have been sold for $27,500 and this amount would then represent actual cost to the new owner.

### Original Cost

This term often is intended to refer to the cost of construction rather than to subsequent sale price. Here again, however, problems arise. What is to be included in cost of construction? Will contractors' profits be included? Financing costs? Other charges? Also, there is the problem of accounting practice, which tends to identify original cost with the acquisition cost to the present owner.

### Historical Cost

The concept of historical cost has also been used to designate original construction costs, but almost any cost which has been previously incurred is a matter of history and might properly be included in this term.

### Cost Concept in Appraisals

Because of the many terms and meanings in common use, we need to define what we mean by cost in real estate appraisal practice. A number of terms have been used such as "estimated cost of replacement of building" and "required investment exclusive of land," the former referring to the costs involved in replacing a similar structure itself, whereas the latter includes all costs incurred in improving a site. In the latter group are included (1) building costs, (2) carrying charges, (3) financial costs and interest, and (4) equipment and fixtures. Typically appraisers use current costs less depreciation.

Difficult problems are involved also in deciding what to include in replacement or reproduction costs when buildings are in mid-life or late life. Most appraisers tend to use the terms *cost of replacement* and *cost of reproduction* synonymously, taking both terms to mean the *present cost of a property of equivalent utility.* The investor is concerned with an acceptable substitute. He is not interested in a replica. For learning purposes we will emphasize the "cost to produce" concept and thereby avoid becoming involved in the conflicts described above.

### Bases of the Cost Approach

A "cost to construct new" estimate with land value added is usually considered as establishing the upper limit of the value of a property. The *principle of substitution* serves as the basis for this position. There is an inherent danger, however, in accepting this conclusion without careful review.

When a new building is constructed, the owner would not ordinarily undertake the project unless he believed that the return which the new property is expected to earn would more than justify the costs incurred. Hence, it is quite appropriate in the case of a new structure (assuming highest and best use of the site) to compute a return on the investment required to improve the land and to impute the remainder of the anticipated income to the land, as we explained above in our discussion of the income method.

The appraisal of an older building raises the depreciation problem. *Current cost to produce less depreciation* is the principle applied to such properties in valuation by the cost approach. While investors are concerned with estimates of this type, there are many problems involved in the use of the cost approach in the case of older buildings. Market prices of comparable properties often provide more reliable guides in such cases.

When valuations are based on costs less depreciation, current construction costs should be used. As a general rule, when there are available sales data on a number of buildings of the same type as an older building being appraised, the market approach is preferable. It reflects obsolescence but does not exaggerate physical depreciation.

Despite these difficulties, there are cases in which the appraiser has no alternative but to use the cost method in the case of older properties. The purpose of the appraisal may necessitate the use of this method, or it may be found impracticable to proceed in any other manner because of the lack of pertinent data. If proper considerations are given to the problems and difficulties involved, reasonable value estimates may be made. This is likely to be true if it is possible to relate such data to market prices or to the income production of comparable buildings. Often, an older structure would not be replaced. In some cases, it might even have a negative value.

### Backward vs. Forward View

The fundamental difficulty with the cost method, except in the case of new structures, is that the appraiser's view must of necessity be directed backward rather than forward. The income method stresses future probable returns; the cost method may emphasize past experience of the property rather than its future. The original decision to construct a building may have been made at a time when it was justified by expectations; however, subsequent events may justify the original expectations or prove them to be in error. The key to the solution of the problem is the treatment of depreciation in terms of the ability of the property to perform its functions in the future rather than only in terms of past events.

### Steps in the Cost Approach

The steps in the cost approach are:

|   |   |   |   |
|---|---|---|---|
| 1. Market value of the land | | | \$ x x x |
| 2. Cost to produce new the buildings | \$ x x x | | |
| 3. Less accrued depreciation | x x x | | |
| 4. Indicated value of the building "as is" | | | x x x |
| 5. Indicated market value of the property | | | \$ x x x |

In the appraisal of new properties, cost estimates may be based on a quantity survey of the actual expenditures involved, or unit cost methods may be used. Special factors may arise in specific cases which cause costs to be well above or below the average for properties of the type under consideration. Unit costs are based on averages which are reduced to square feet, cubic feet, or some similar unit.

In some cases blueprints are used as the basis for making cost estimates for buildings that are to be constructed. Appraisers usually do this by the application of a unit cost factor, with allowances for extras or deficiencies.

Building costs include all of the expenditures required to construct a building—costs of materials, wages, contractors' fees or profits, architects' and engineers' fees, and allowances for extras and contingencies. Sidewalks, driveways, landscaping, and the like are also included, as well as costs of accessory buildings. To these are added carrying charges, financial costs, and equipment costs.

Carrying charges include costs incurred during the period of construction and the time that elapses before the building is put into operation, such as taxes and insurance during construction, costs of working capital, and expenses involved in rental campaigns. Financing costs include interest on invested capital or borrowed funds during the construction period, as well as discounts, commissions, consulting fees, related legal expenses, and the like. Costs of such equipment which becomes a part of the real estate are included, although furniture and removable equipment may or may not be included, depending on the valuation problem involved.

Market value of the land is usually estimated by the comparative method, although the actual amount paid for the land may be a guide if it is comparable to current prices of similar sites.

As we have pointed out above, cost of construction new does not provide a usable result for the valuation of older structures unless allowances are made for depreciation, earlier defined as "loss in value from all causes."

### Depreciation and Obsolescence

Buildings and the equipment in them wear out over time. This usually takes place gradually. This process is referred to as *depreciation* as we have seen and may be contrasted with *depletion* or the using up of a natural asset, commonly used in the case of oil wells.

Loss of value not only results from wear and tear but from the development of more and better buildings and equipment and from general economic changes. We typically use the term *obsolescence* to describe this process. Obsolescence, as we have seen, may be functional or economic, the former relating to conditions within a property, the latter to external changes. Physically a building may be in excellent condition but will lose value if another building (usually a newer one, but the time difference may not be great) performs the same function more efficiently or more attractively.

In recent years as rates of change have accelerated, value losses from obsolescence have grown increasingly important. Higher discount rates are required in connection with many real estate decisions in order to reflect higher risks of obsolescence.

### Methods of Estimating Depreciation

There are a number of methods in use for estimating depreciation, such as the straight line, weighted rate, reducing balances, and sinking funds; however, their application without modification is likely to result in wide margins of error because of the differences in the definition of depreciation and the variations in the care and maintenance of different properties.

The care and maintenance given to different properties are not reflected in many of the depreciation tables which are used. Two methods are often adopted to deal with this problem: (1) the quantity survey of observable depreciation with allowances for curable and noncurable defects, and (2) the effective age device.

## Quantity Survey

In the quantity survey method, a survey is made of the building and points of depreciation are divided into curable and noncurable classes; the cost of making the repairs and alterations necessary to remedy the curable defects is then computed and added to the estimated loss in value due to noncurable defects. Physical deterioration, functional and economic obsolescence, and other causes of loss in value may be treated in this manner.

## Effective Age

The effective age of a property may or may not coincide with the actual age—the numbers of years since construction. A building may be 25 years old and the average life for structures of the type under consideration may be 50 years, but the estimated remaining economic life of the building may be 40 years. Hence it is more like a 10-year-old building than a 25-year-old building. An appropriate depreciation percentage may then be applied on the 10-year basis to provide an estimate of value loss. This method has the advantage of forcing the appraiser to consider the future economic life of the building rather than to deal only with past events.

## Depreciation Tables

The application of depreciation tables often exaggerates the loss of value of well-maintained properties. There are examples of residential structures 50 years old that sell in the market for half of their present cost to build new, and yet, on the basis of the types of depreciation tables often used, would be almost valueless. Tests of all depreciation tables should be made by comparing market prices of old buildings with valuations based on current costs less depreciation. Rapidly rising construction costs, of course, offset many depreciation allowances, and structures over 20 years old have frequently sold for more than their original cost. When used, depreciation and obsolescence allowances should be deducted from the most recently available cost of construction estimates.

### Depreciation Techniques

Three techniques are used rather widely to reflect depreciation for various types of properties. The straight line technique provides for equal yearly charges. It is figured by subtracting salvage value, if any, from original cost (or cost to replace new today) and dividing the difference by the useful life of the building.

The declining balance technique accelerates depreciation charges in the early life of the property. For example, the investor may charge twice the straight line rate on the undepreciated balance. Thus, a building with a 40-year life would be depreciated at a rate of 2½ per cent per year using straight line. With the declining balance technique, the rate can be doubled to 5 per cent. On a $100,000 property, the first year's depreciation would be $5,000. The second year, it would be 5 per cent of $95,000, or $4,750, and so on.

The sum-of-the-years'-digits technique is the other accelerated depreciation technique. It provides that a changing fraction be applied to the depreciable base, which remains constant. The numerator is the number of years of useful life left and the denominator is the sum of the years' digits. Thus, for a building with a cost less salvage value of $15,000 and a useful life of 5 years, the denominator would be $1 + 2 + 3 + 4 + 5 = 15$. The depreciation schedule is as follows:

| Year | Calculation | Depreciation |
|---|---|---|
| 1 | 5/15 × $15,000 | $ 5,000 |
| 2 | 4/15 × 15,000 | 4,000 |
| 3 | 3/15 × 15,000 | 3,000 |
| 4 | 2/15 × 15,000 | 2,000 |
| 5 | 1/15 × 15,000 | 1,000 |
| Total | | $15,000 |

For properties with long useful lives, the following formula provides a technique of determining the denominator:

$$D = N \frac{N + 1}{2}$$

where:

$D$ = Sum-of-the-years'-digits denominator
$N$ = Estimated useful life

In the example of the $15,000 property with a useful life of 5 years, $N = 5$ years, and the denominator is 5, then $D$ equals $5(5 + 1)/2 = 15$.

## Land Value

The market value of the land is developed from actual sales, offers, listings or leases of vacant land considered comparable to the land being appraised. The only source of land value is from the market inasmuch as land cannot be "produced" or "built" like buildings. Sales or other market information about similar sites provides a basis for estimating the market value of land for use both in the cost approach and the capitalized income as well as the market approach.

Another method of determining land value is to set up a model of a hypothetical building that represents the best use of the site. The rents for this building are estimated on the basis of comparable rents in the vicinity, or sometimes by actual offers of responsible prospective tenants. Operating costs are estimated on the basis of comparable buildings. The land residual technique outlined in Chapter 12 in the discussion of the income method is then followed.

A number of tables, such as *depth tables* and *corner influence tables,* have been prepared for use by appraisers. Depth tables are based on the theory that added depth will increase the value of a standard lot, but at a diminishing rate. Although this idea may have validity for some types of lots, particularly those used for commercial purposes in older parts of cities, its application to residential lots is questionable since some variations in depth have little effect on the value of homesites. These concepts have little applicability in shopping centers or in industrial areas.

Corner influence tables are of great value as an aid to the valuation of sites for downtown office buildings and for smaller retail stores located on corners with frontage on two important streets. Such tables have practically no utility in the valuation of regional shopping centers, industrial properties, and most types of residential properties.

## Plottage Value

If a city zoning ordinance requires that detached homes have a minimum frontage of 60 feet, a single 30-foot lot would have little or no value, but if two 30-foot lots were joined together they would have a greater value than the sum of the two lots as separate units. This increase of value obtained by combining lots into a larger tract is known as plottage value. Value increases in such cases until the assembled tract is large enough for the maximum utilization of the site.

Recent changes in land uses have increased the size of plots necessary for the highest and best use of land. Now it is considered desirable to acquire a number of blocks for one downtown project so that streets can be closed, and the buildings placed on the basis of 25 per cent land coverage, oriented so that they will have the best view, and provided with the maximum light and air.

Department stores have found that plottage value can be obtained by acquiring an entire block so that the values of the main street are carried over to the side street. Rockefeller Center in New York City obtained a plottage value by erecting a series of buildings on a tract of several blocks, which permitted open plazas and yielded higher rents for the office space than buildings with 100 per cent land coverage.

Factories gain plottage value from combining several properties, which permits more efficient layout of the plant and which avoids congestion of city traffic and policing of factory buildings on every side. Retail stores achieve plottage value by combining several tracts of land, which permits automobile parking near the store. The planning of complete communities of many acres and even many square miles suggests the growing importance of the plottage concept.

The power of condemnation is often necessary in order to assemble a large number of parcels at reasonable cost, because the owners of the last remaining parcels will usually demand a price so high as to defeat the entire project. Sometimes private firms assembling a tract will pay a nuisance value for one single parcel if it is in the middle of the proposed development, but if it is on the edge, development can often proceed without it.

**Valuation for Tax Assessment Purposes**

The cost method is used widely in appraising real estate for tax assessment purposes. A land value map usually is prepared by estimating current front foot values for every block in a city, with square foot values being prepared for industrial properties and acreage values for certain vacant land. These values do not necessarily represent full market price, but they should reflect the relative desirability of the different residential neighborhoods in the city and the relative value of business and industrial properties. Usually the assessor consults with local real estate brokers to secure a proper relativity of land values.

The building values generally are estimated on a reproduction cost basis. All the buildings in the community are classified according to types, which are determined by materials of construction, quality, height, area, plumbing facilities, and related items. Then square foot or cubic foot costs are established for each type. This cost may be a percentage of the current cost, which is to be preferred, since that is the cost which may be most easily ascertained, or it may be the costs in what is considered a normal year.

After all the buildings in the city are classified by types, field staffs visit every property, classify it as to type, take its external measurements, note the material of construction, type and quality of equipment, and related items. The age of the building is determined for depreciation purposes, either from building permit records or from the architectural type and appearance of the building.

Assessments derived by the method of construction costs for buildings should be checked against recent sales. Properties that sell for less than their reproduction cost less depreciation plus land value are probably suffering from obsolescence for which allowances should be made.

The foregoing methods are generally used in wholesale assessments for taxation purposes. It is not possible to secure sufficient current sales data for all types of properties, particularly factories, office buildings, and large stores, to base assessments upon sales. In the case of commercial properties, rentals paid on current leases should be analyzed in making assessments. Valuations based largely on cost less depreciation can be related to values based on income by adjusting land values or the amounts allowed for obsolescence.


## CORRELATION

The final step in the appraisal process is correlation and conclusion. The appraiser reviews his efforts and makes an estimate of value. The appraiser in his summary statement selects those factors which have the greatest influence on the value of the property.

### Factors Influencing the Judgment of Appraisers

Although the making of value estimates should be an objective process, there is little doubt that appraisers frequently are influenced by the state of the real estate market at the time an appraisal is made and by popular opinions. During periods of prosperity, when the real estate market is very active and the income from real estate is high, appraisers may tend to project this favorable income situation far into the future. On the other hand, during periods of extreme depression, when the volume of sales is limited and the return on real estate is low, appraisers may forecast a continuation of this low-income condition for a long period of time.

Similarly, prevailing opinions regarding the character of certain neighborhoods or sections of the city or the popularity of one or another type of property may influence the judgment of appraisers. For example, appraisers may continue to predict an optimistic future for fashionable residential neighborhoods for some time after such areas have started to decline. Similarly, certain types of commercial property (for example, some downtown stores) which have had a long record of past success often are expected to continue to maintain such a record even though forces are in operation which will tend to limit their future earning power.

Competent appraisers try to avoid pitfalls of this type. They try to study objectively all of the factors which will affect the future income-producing power of the properties which they appraise. Other appraisers, however, do little more than rationalize the popular beliefs prevailing in the real estate market.

## The Use of Data

The best protection for an appraiser against current market psychology is the use of factual information. As we have indicated above, many appraisers follow the practice of collecting voluminous files of data for use as an appraisal tool. However, appraisals are not the product of such data; they are the result of the appraiser's judgment. The data available to him are of importance because they help him to formulate sound judgments. They supplement rather than supplant the judgment of the appraiser.

In order to use data, an appraiser or other analyst must understand the basic processes of collecting, classifying, and analyzing them. A considerable portion of appraisal data is statistical in nature, and its use is governed by sound statistical practice.

## General Rules for Using Data

Such general rules as the following apply to the use of data:

1. *Isolated facts* are relatively useless. The facts used should have a direct bearing on the appraisal.
2. Observations must be sufficiently *numerous* to be representative.
3. The items of information collected must conform to *accuracy standards;* for example, *errors* should tend to cancel out rather than to be cumulative.
4. The sample collected must be *characteristic* of the area or problem or of the "universe," to use statistical terminology.
5. The data must be *classified* or *arranged* systematically, the basis of the classification varying with the purpose involved.
6. Analysis is carried on for the purpose of determining points of *similarity and difference* between items and classes or groups.

Too frequently, appraisers overemphasize one item of information and fail to put it into a proper relationship with other data. In many cases too few data are collected; conclusions may then be based on information which is not typical. During a boom period nearly all information may be weighted in the same direction and reflect the immediate market situation and immediate future expectations only, rather than long-range trends.

Basically, the use of data means borrowing from the experience of others. The complexities of real estate value problems are so great that few people can carry enough information around in their heads to solve them. Programs of data collection, assembly, and analysis are growing in importance in the field of real estate valuation, aided by the expanding use of the computer.

Although theoretical concepts have not changed a great deal, except for some refinements, more elaborate sets of relationships can now be developed in a practical manner through the use of the computer. It should be recognized also that major changes have occurred that complicate the application of various value theories and principles. For example, the old depth and corner influence concepts have little or no applicabiilty for the modern regional shopping center. Recognition must be given to the increasing importance of governmental influences, ranging all the way from farm price supports, transportation developments, and zoning laws to general federal programs for the maintenance of long-term prosperity.

## The Appraisal Report

Appraisal reports may be relatively simple statements or involved and detailed reports, depending on the purpose of the appraisal and the complexity of the problem. Many firms use standard forms for appraisal reports. In such cases the appraiser has a definite guide as to the requirements of his client. In some cases a brief statement in the form of a letter or memorandum serves as an appraisal report.

With the growing importance of appraisals and with the development of standards of practice by such groups as the American Institute of Real Estate Appraisers and the Society of Real Estate Appraisers, appraisal reports have tended to become more standardized than was formerly the case. A suggested recommended format of a formal appraisal report is shown in Figure 13–2.

## Main Parts of Appraisal Report

Usually a formal report contains three main parts: (1) an introduction, (2) the analysis and conclusions, and (3) the supplementary data in the form of appendixes or annexes. The introduction may include a brief description of the type of property being appraised; a photograph or photographs of the property; and in addition (if the report is of some length) a table of contents and title page as well as a statement of the appraiser's qualifications.

FORMAT FOR THE APPRAISAL REPORT

Letter of Transmittal—

  "As requested . . . . . . . . . ."
  Identify property appraised
  Any other special comments needed

Part I—Introduction

    a. Title page
    b. Picture(s)
    c. Table of contents

Part II—Description, Analysis and Conclusions

    d. Brief identification of property, legal description, and rights being appraised
    e. Definition of defined value
    f. Date as of which the defined value estimate applies
    g. National (International) Market and Business Conditions Analysis—specifically as these factors affect the subject property
    h. Economic Base Analysis (City, Region, Area, and/or State)
    i. Analysis and application of real estate market conditions and trends—specifically as they apply to the subject property
    j. Neighborhood (District) Analysis—location factors, including zoning, utilities, trends, etc.
    k. Site description, analysis of functional utility, and statement of highest and best use (including zoning, utilities, taxes)
    l. Indicated defined value of the land
    m. Building description and analysis
    n. The cost approach—indication of defined value from this approach
    o. The market approach (comparison)—indication of defined value from this approach
    p. The capitalized income approach—indication of defined value from this approach
    q. Correlation and final estimate of defined value
    r. Certification of value
    s. Limitations and qualifying statements, contingent and limiting conditions
    t. Qualifications of Appraiser

Part III—Addenda

    u. Maps, plats, pictures
    v. Detailed statistical data
    w. Other detailed reports too long or complex to include in the body of the report
    x. Any other supporting data

**Fig. 13-2.**   The appraisal report.

The second part, which is really the body of the report, usually includes the following: (1) purpose or objective of appraisal, (2) legal description of the property, (3) property data (building and site), (4) location data, (5) market information, (6) a detailed outline of the value estimate, including reasons for selection of the method used and the main steps required in its application to the problem, (7) interpretation of the estimate, and (8) certification of the estimate.

The third part of the report includes maps, supplementary photographs, blueprints, floor plans, and other information. Materials of this type are ready for use if necessary but are supplementary to the first two parts of the report.

Current practices vary in the use of the letter of transmittal. In Figure 13–2 the letter is used only to "convey" the report to the reader. Many appraisers, however, use the letter of transmittal to summarize the report, pointing out major conclusions and matters of great import in the appraiser's development of his conclusion.

The appraisal report, regardless of the type or format used, is the appraiser's sole vehicle to convince the reader of his logical procedure in reaching a defensible conclusion. It must be clear, concise, and convincing.

## SUMMARY

The market approach to valuation problems enjoys widespread use. It is especially helpful when markets are active and information about sales is readily available. Careful comparisons are made between the subject property and similar properties for which market information may be available. Physical, location, market and governmental factors are included in such comparisons.

In some cases gross income multipliers are used in connection with the market approach. Such multipliers are sometimes used also with the income approach. Appraisers often enounter special problems in the application of gross income multipliers.

Market data are of great assistance to appraisers. Often they build "data plants" to assist them in their work.

The cost approach includes an estimate of land value usually by the market method, an estimate of the cost to produce the building or buildings and other improvements new, and if the building or other improvements are not new, this estimate is adjusted to reflect accrued depreciation. Various methods may be employed to make required adjustments for depreciation and obsolescence.

The cost approach has widespread use in valuations for tax assessment purposes. The cost approach often is used when lack of data prevents the application of another approach.

The results of a valuation are carefully correlated and presented in the appraisal report. Appraisers are required to exercise careful judgment and to maintain an objective point of view. They try to follow established standards of practice in the analysis of data and in the correlation of results.

The appraisal report may be presented in greater or lesser detail, depending on the requirements of the appraisal. Typically such reports include an introduction, analysis and conclusions, plus supplementary data.

## QUESTIONS FOR STUDY

1. Which appraisal method would you use in the valuation of the house in which you live? Why is this method better than others?
2. If capitalization of future income is the appraisal method most consistent with the theory of value, why are other methods also used? For what purposes are these other methods applied?
3. Outline the principal steps in the market approach. Illustrate each.
4. What are the principal problems likely to be encountered in using the market approach?
5. What does the gross income multiplier method have in common with the capitalized income method? How is it related to the market method?
6. Which of the three valuation methods would you recommend for use in the valuation of: (a) the administration building of your college or university? (b) your own home? (c) a newly constructed home that you might be interested in buying? (d) your local post office building? (e) your city's newest shopping center?
7. How may the age of a building influence the choice of valuation method?
8. Outline the main steps in using the cost approach. Illustrate.
9. Why is the cost method easier to apply to new than to older structures? Discuss some of the difficulties involved in using this method for old structures.
10. Which methods do appraisers use in making estimates of depreciation? Which one is best? Explain. Define straight line, declining balance, and sum-of-the-years'-digit techniques to reflect depreciation.
11. Why is the cost approach in valuations used for tax assessment purposes?
12. Explain how "the use of data means borrowing from the experience of others."
13. Outline the principal risks in using data. Illustrate each.
14. What is usually included in an appraisal report?

## SUGGESTED READINGS

AMERICAN INSTITUTE OF REAL ESTATE APPRAISERS. *The Appraisal of Real Estate* (5th ed.). Chicago: The Institute, 1967. Chaps. 12–15, 21, 23, 24.

BROWN, ROBERT KEVIN. *Essentials of Real Estate*. Englewood Cliffs, N.J.: Prentice-Hall, Inc., 1970. Chap. 8.

DAVID, PHILIP. *Urban Land Development*. Homewood, Ill.: Richard D. Irwin, Inc., 1970. Pp. 87–111.

HOAGLAND, HENRY E., and LEO D. STONE. *Real Estate Finance* (4th ed.). Homewood, Ill.: Richard D. Irwin, Inc., 1969. Chap. 8.

KAHN, SANDERS A., FREDERICK E. CASE, and ALFRED SCHIMMEL. *Real Estate Appraisal and Investment*. New York: The Ronald Press Co., 1963. Chaps. 8, 13, 14.

KINNARD, WILLIAM N., JR. *Income Property Valuation*. Lexington, Mass.: Heath Publishing Co., 1971.

## CASE 13–1

### Appraisal of Westside Shopping Center

Mr. John Smith
1627 Lincoln Street
Metropolis, Indiana

Re: Westside Shopping Center
1350 West 15th Street
Metropolis, Michigan

Dear Sir:

At your request, I have examined the subject property for the purpose of estimating the market value as of March 30, 197—, for fee simple title free of encumbrance to the real estate which is more particularly described as Lots #25, 26, 33 and 34 of the West Manor Subdivision of a part of the northeast quarter of the northwest quarter of Section 17, Township 6 North, Range 3 West, in the City of Metropolis, Livingston County, Michigan, the plat of which is recorded in the Office of the Recorder of Livingston County.

I have inspected the subject property and the surrounding neighborhood and considered the factors affecting its market value. Based upon my knowledge of real estate values and my experience in this field and particularly upon the facts which relate to the subject property, the more pertinent of which are included in the attached appraisal report, it is my opinion that the market value of the subject property, as above described, is $275,000.

Respectfully submitted,
Richard I. Brown, CPM, MAI

**Identification of Property.** Legal Description: The subject property is legally described as:

Lots #25, 26, 33 and 34 of the West Manor Subdivision of a part of the northeast quarter of the northwest quarter of Section 17, Range 6 North, Township 3 West in the City of Metropolis, Livingston County, Michigan, a copy of which is recorded in the Office of the Recorder of Livingston County, Michigan.

*Summary of Salient Facts and Conclusions*

| | |
|---|---|
| Land Area | 37,125+— square feet; 225 front feet |
| Building Area | 14,097+ square feet |
| Ratio of improved land to parking area | 1 to 2.4 |
| Market Value indication by replacement cost, less depreciation, plus land value approach | $272,000 |
| Market Value indication by income capitalization approach | $277,000 |
| Market Value indication by market approach | $274,000 |
| Conclusion of Market Value | $275,000 |
| Economic rent | Approximately $2.00 per sq. ft. |
| Estimated local taxes | $5,234 |
| Estimated net operating income | $28,000+ |

Street Address: The subject property is known by the street address of:

1350 West 15th Street, Metropolis, Michigan.

**Property Rights Appraised.** The property rights appraised are those of fee simple title free of encumbrance. Liens, mortgages and other encumbrances, if any such exist, have not been considered as factors affecting value.

**City Data.** Metropolis, Michigan, is the county seat of Livingston County, Michigan. It is situated on State Roads #57, 66 and 83, U. S. Highways #40, 41 and 231 and Interstate 65. It is 50 miles northeast of Flint, Michigan.

The 1970 population, according to the U. S. Census, was 31,357, an increase of 11.3% over the 1960 figure. The population of Livingston County was 59,225 in 1970; 50,800 in 1960; and 36,534 in 1950.

Metropolis has several large factories of major corporations. These include General Motors, General Electric, RCA, and Bristol-Meyers. Total employment in industry is approximately 8,500 persons. Metropolis also has considerable employment in agriculture, meat packing, and mining. The Peabody and Ayrshire Coal Companies employ a total of approximately 900 persons.

Shopping areas in Metropolis are concentrated principally in three areas: Downtown, Eastgate Shopping Center on the east side at the intersection of U. S. 40 and Interstate 65, and Westside Shopping Center at 1350 West 15th Street. The pattern of shopping seems to be that major purchases are made downtown and that the outlying centers serve more for daily needs and convenience purchases.

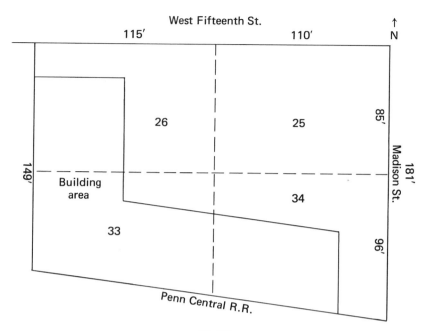

PLAT
Part of West Major Subdivision
City of Metropolis, Livingtson County, Indiana

**Exhibit A**

**Neighborhood Data.** The subject property is bounded on the north by 15th Street, on the east by Union Street, on the south by apartments and on the west by a service station. The area is characterized by high-density housing and numerous commercial establishments such as service stations, fast food franchises and an automobile dealership.

**Site Data.** A plat of the site (Exhibit A) shows the property to be a trapezoid, having a frontage of 225 feet on the south side of West 15th Street, a west line running north and south 149 feet, a south line running diagonally northwest and southeast along the railroad right-of-way, and an east line measuring 181 feet. The total land area is computed to contain 37,125 square feet. The topography is level and at street grade. There are no descernible soil or subsoil conditions which would affect the highest and best use of the land or its marketability. City sewer, both storm and sanitary, city water, gas, electricity and telephone are available at the site. Fifteenth Street has a platted width of 40 feet, is paved with concrete and has curbs, gutters and sidewalks on either side, as does Madison Street.

**Zoning.** The subject property is zoned B-3 which is a classification for "General Business Use."

**Assessment and Taxes.** Records in the Office of the Township Assessor indicate that the land is assessed at a total of $20,870, the improvements total $48,730, and the total assessment is $69,600 for the year 197_, payable in 197_. Taxes for this township are currently assessed at the rate of $7.52 for each $100 of assessed valuation. It is computed that the taxes for the year 197_, payable in 197_ for the subject property will amount to $5,233.92.

**Description of Improvements.** The improvements on the subject property consist of a one-story masonry structure with a flat roof and no basement, built along the south and west sides of the property. All of the walls except the south and west walls are faced with brick and those two walls are concrete block. The roof structure is designed so that there is a six-foot overhang projecting over the sidewalk, which runs in front of and on the ends of the building. All foundations are poured concrete slabs, and roofs are covered with tar and gravel, and the downspouts are aluminum. Part of the windows are double-hung and part are plate glass store windows all set in aluminum sash. The subject property is divided into thirteen storerooms.

**Replacement Cost, less Depreciation, plus Land Value Approach.** The nature of the subject property made it extremely difficult to find sales of comparable parcels of land in Metropolis. It was finally concluded that two transactions, adjusted, provide the best indication of the land value and they are described as follows:

#1. The Wamper Lot. This lot is designated as Lot No. 10 in West Manor Subdivision and has a frontage of 68 feet on the north side of Fifteenth Street, directly across from the subject property, and has a depth of 261.38 feet. It contains a total of 17,774 square feet and was recently purchased at a price of $57,500. The agreement with the former owner of the property is that he will remove the existing improvements at no expense to the purchaser.

$57,500/17,774 sq. ft. = $3.24 per square foot

At the date of purchase of this property, it was not zoned for commercial use and it is estimated that an adjustment of 110% in the sale price is appropriate to reflect this lack of zoning. The difference between the frontage and size of the Wampler Lot and the frontage and size of the subject property indicates that this lot lacks a certain plottage value which is possessed by the subject property and it is estimated that an adjustment of 115% is appropriate to reflect this difference. Total adjustment 126.5% × $3.24/ sq. ft. = $4.10/ sq. ft., the indicated value of the subject property.

#2. Property situated between 6th and 7th Streets and between Adams and Jefferson Streets, containing a total of 78,870 square feet (which does not include all of the property in the block) was recently purchased as a site for a motel at a cost of $280,000.

$280,000/78,870 sq. ft. = $3.55 per square foot

At the date of purchase this property was not zoned for business use and it is estimated that an adjustment of 110% is appropriate to reflect this difference between this transaction and the subject property; $3.55/ sq. ft. × 110% = $3.90/ sq. ft., the indicated value of the subject property by comparison with this transaction. Analyzing these two sales which appear to be the most nearly comparable of recent date, leads to the conclusion that the present market value of the subject property is $4.00/ sq. ft.

   37,125 sq. ft. @ $4.00/ sq. ft. = $148,500

**Site Improvements.**    The subject property contains a total of 39,080 sq. ft. of which 14,097 is improved with the building. This leaves a total of 23,028 sq. ft. of land area which is paved. It is estimated that the cost of this paving is 30¢ per square foot.

   23,028 @ 30¢ = $6,908.40.

Improvements: By reference to Boeckh's Manual of Appraisals (6th ed.) page 331, it is found that the base cost of the building is $134,955.

|  |  |
|---|---|
| Site Improvements | $   6,908.40 |
| Building | 134,955.00 |
| Total Replacement Cost New | $141,863.40 |

Say—$142,000

**Depreciation.**    It is estimated that the total physical deterioration, both curable and incurable, amounts to approximately 10% of the replacement cost new or $13,499.

In analyzing the rent schedule, the tenancies and the operation of the subject property, it was concluded that the total functional obsolescence, both curable and incurable, amounts to $13,499.

Since the highest and best use of the land has been found to. be in its present use as a shopping center and in view of the present and anticipated future population density in the immediate surrounding area, it is difficult to imagine a location which would be better for this type of an improvement and therefore it is concluded that the subject property does not suffer from economic obsolescence.

| | | |
|---|---|---|
| Physical Deterioration—10% | | $14,200 |
| Functional Obsolescence—10% | | 14,200 |
| Economic Obsolescence | | –0– |
| Total Depreciation | | $28,400 |
| Summary: | | |
| Land Value | | $148,500 |
| Replacement cost of improvements | $142,000 | |
| Less depreciation | 28,400 | |
| Depreciated Replacement Cost | | 113,600 |
| Indicated Market Value | | $262,100 |
| Rounded to | | $262,000 |

**Market Data Approach.** A careful analysis of the City of Metropolis failed to reveal any recent property sale reasonably comparable to the subject property in physical terms. One transaction was found on the south side of Third Street between Maple and Oak Streets. It is an automobile dealership. The actual selling price was $253,000, a figure which is in marked contrast with an offer of $278,000 which the seller refused to accept in January of 197_. It seems well established that this was a case of a distressed seller and that the transaction would be aptly described as a good buy. After careful consideration, it is estimated that this property could have been sold, granted a reasonable time, at a price of $280,000.

The gross monthly rental being developed by this property at the date of sale was $3,460. Dividing the adjusted sale price by the gross monthly rent gives a monthly gross rent multiplier of 81.

The actual monthly gross rents received from the subject property during the fiscal year ending 197_ amounted to $3,384.05. Multiplying this figure by the gross rent multiplier of 81 gives an indicated value of the subject property of $274,108.05.

Rounded to     $274,000

**Income Capitalization Approach**
*Annual Rent Schedule:*

| Room Number | Annual Rent |
|---|---|
| 1 | $6,500 |
| 2 | 1,800 |
| 3 & 5 | 4,020 |
| 4 | 4,200 |
| 6 | 1,920 |
| 7 | 1,400 |
| 8 | 1,836 |
| 9 | 2,564 |
| 10 | 1,800 |
| 11 | 2,100 |
| 12 | 2,700 |
| 13 | 9,800 |

*Estimated Stabilized Operating Statement:*

| | | |
|---|---|---|
| Income: | | |
| Stabilized Rent (Adjusted from Annual Rent) | | $40,608.66 |
| Vacancy and Collection Loss (3%) | | 1,218.26 |
| Effective Gross Rent | | $39,390.40 |
| Operating Expenses: | | |
| Heat | $ 330.00 | |
| Electricity | 285.00 | |
| Maintenance: | | |
| Building exterior | 800.00 | |
| Building interior | 650.00 | |
| Building lot | 460.00 | |
| Management | 1,579.00 | |

Taxes:

| | |
|---|---:|
| Gross Income | 474.00 |
| Real Estate | 5,234.00 |
| Insurance | 930.00 |
| Miscellaneous | 631.00 |
| | 11,373.00 |
| Operating Income | $28,017.40 |

An investigation indicates that mortgage money is generally available in Metropolis for an investment of this type at from 8 to 8¼ per cent. An adjustment for risk factors of the property being appraised raises this rate to 8½ per cent as an acceptable rate of return.

| | |
|---|---:|
| Operating Income | $28,017.40 |
| Land Requirements ($148,500 @ 8½%) | 12,622.50 |
| Income Attributable to Improvements | $15,394.90 |
| $15,394 capitalized at 12% (8½% + 3½% recapture) | $128,284.00 |
| Plus land value | 148,500.00 |
| Total | $276,784.00 |
| Rounded to | $277,000 |

**Correlation and Conclusion.** Each of the approaches to value contains certain inherent advantages and certain dangers. In the replacement cost, less depreciation, plus land value approach, the advantage is that it is particularly applicable to a property which reflects the highest and best use of the land and which is of relatively new construction. The danger in this approach lies in the difficulty in estimating accurately the degree of depreciation which a property has suffered and the greater the degree of depreciation suffered the less the reliability which can normally be placed upon this approach. The advantage of the market data approach is that this is the one commonly employed by buyers and sellers in the market place. The disadvantage is the difficulty of accurately comparing the known sales with the subject property and particularly in understanding the motivations of the buyers and sellers. The income capitalization approach is of particular value in analyzing properties of the type which are normally owned for the income stream which they produce. The disadvantage of this approach is the difficulty of estimating accurately the income and expense and supporting an opinion as to the proper rate of interest, since the operation of the capitalization process multiplies a small error in any of these items into an error of great magnitude in the final result.

The range of the three approaches is from $272,000 to $277,000 which is a variation of approximately 2% and both the high and low figures appear to have about the same degree of support. It is therefore concluded that the market value of the subject property, as of the appraisal date, March 30, 1972, is $275,000.

CERTIFICATE OF APPRAISAL

The undersigned certifies that:

1. He has personally inspected the subject property and considered the factors affecting its value.
2. He has no present or contemplated future interest in the property.
3. Neither his employment nor his compensation is contingent upon the values estimated herein.
4. This report has been made in conformity with the standards and rules of professional ethics of the American Institute of Real Estate Boards of which he is a member.
5. In his opinion, the market value of fee simple title free of encumbrance to the land, land improvements and buildings constituting the subject property as of March 30, 197_, is $275,000.

Richard I. Brown, C.P.M., M.A.I.

Date: April 20, 197_

## Questions

1. What could be done to improve the quality of this appraisal?
2. How would the results of the income approach be changed if the net operating income were $35,000? If the capitalization rate were 7 per cent plus 2 per cent recapture rate?
3. What are the weaknesses of the market comparison approach in this case? What would be the result if the gross rent multiplier had been 94 and the monthly gross rent from the subject property $2,900?
4. What would be your conclusion in the replacement cost approach if the Wampler Lot had sold for $72,000 and the motel site for $310,000?
5. How does an appraiser arrive at a depreciation figure? Outline the advantages of each of the three methods that are in widespread use for estimating depreciation.
6. What is the present value of Westside Shopping Center's operating income over the next 30 years? (Assume it will remain constant.) Which capitalization rate should be used to determine this? (If the rate you choose is not in the table, round off to the next higher rate in the table.
7. How does the present value arrived at in question 6 compare to the appraised value in the income approach?

# III

# REAL ESTATE
# DECISION AREAS

Part III considers various decisions in the production, marketing and financing of real estate resources and services.

The first two chapters cover production and include the subjects of subdividing, land development and building. Study projects for Chapter 14 call attention to various problems related to land planning and development. In addition there is a case study of Sans Souci Estates for analysis and discussion. Chapter 15, covering the general subject of building, includes a case study on the projected expansion of a housing corporation as well as a study project taken from the well-known Kaiser Report, *A Decent Home,* and provides an overview of the housing industry. There is also a project which outlines various types of high-density housing.

The following two chapters deal with real estate marketing including discussions of brokerage and promotion and property management. Chapter 16 dealing with brokerage includes a case study of the A & A Realty Company, reprinted from Professor Fred E. Case's book, *Real Estate Brokerage.* There is also a case on the Timberlake property and a study project "The Six Great Motivators" by William B. O'Connell. Chapter 17 on Property Management provides a study project on the rental of single family units as well as one entitled "Renters Turn Militant" which outlines some developments in the area of tenant discontent, reprinted from the *U. S. Savings and Loan News.*

The final three chapters deal with the general subject of financing. Chapter 18 considers major methods and instruments of finance. It provides a study project discussion on improvements that could be made in the home mortgage by Professor Edwards. Financial institutions and agencies are reviewed in Chapter 19. A study project by Professor R. J. Saulnier, "Maintaining an Adequate Flow of Funds into Home Mortgage Markets," reviews some of the potential developments in this area. The final chapter, dealing with mortgage lending, includes a case study of a specific mortgage loan application, as well as a comparison of some British and American practices in this area through an interview of Sir Hubert Newton by Professor Edwards.

# 14

# Production: Subdividing and Land Development

## DEVELOPMENT DECISIONS

The production of real estate resources is usually thought of in terms of the physical processes of land development, improvement, and building. These physical processes, while often intricate, have significance primarily because they provide people as individuals and as members of economic, governmental or social groups with real estate resources and services. Thus, the developer of a large project is in effect the developer of a community. The developer of a small subdivision creates at least a part of a neighborhood. A few have developed entirely new towns.

The manner in which land is developed, the size of the lots, the types of streets installed, the services and utilities provided, the quality and price level of the houses built, the business and community facilities provided, and related factors—all have a bearing on the kind of community or neighborhood that ultimately will result. Thus, early decisions have long-range effects. They may have a major role in determining the general quality of life in the area.

### Short-Range and Long-Range Interests

Typically, those who develop and sell land are interested primarily in providing properties that will be immediately attractive to potential buyers and hence readily salable. The concern of the real estate broker is similar to that of the original subdivider since his primary interest is in immediate sales. In both cases, however, the long-term success of these firms depends on the effectiveness with which the properties serve the needs of the buyers.

The interests of financial institutions and other investors are almost always of a longer-term nature. This is because the funds which are advanced are typically repaid over a great many years. Similarly, the interests of property managers tend to be of a long-term nature.

Long-term investors and mortagage lenders are concerned that the properties developed and the communities and neighborhoods of which they are a part will continue to be desirable places in which to live and work over a number of years. Properties that remain desirable over long periods of time represent less financial risk than those involved in financing other properties.

### Production Alternatives

If you were going to buy an automobile, you would probably visit one or more dealers, select the type and model you wanted, pay in cash or arrange the necessary financing, and drive the car away. You would hardly think of manufacturing it yourself or having it built entirely to your order.

If you wanted a house, however, you might consider these alternatives: you could go to a builder or a real estate broker and buy a house, either a used one or a new one, in somewhat the same way you would buy a car. Or you might buy a lot, install a water and sewage-disposal system, build a road, buy the necessary materials, and construct a house, either by your own efforts or by engaging a contractor to do the work for you. You might arrange for a prefabricated house dealer to put it up for you. You might buy a lot in a subdivision that had been carefully planned and in which all of the various utilities and streets had been installed. The developer of the subdivision might also be a builder and he might agree to build a house for you, either one planned by your own architect or one constructed from plans the builder had available.

Much the same type of situation would face a business firm wishing to develop its own place of business. A piece of land might be bought and a contractor engaged to erect the desired type of structure. Or a developed lot in an industrial park or district or a shopping center might be leased or bought and arrangements made for constructing a building.

### Production Processes

In the real estate business the production of real estate resources is usually thought of as including only the processes of land development and building. Of course, in an economic sense the production of real estate resources or services includes all of the processes of developing the site and constructing the improvements, as well as financing, marketing, and property management. It involves the creation of facilities for the production of income at fixed locations, whether these incomes are in the form of direct use of the property, as in the case of an owner-occupied home, or a place of business that is owned by the firm, or in the form of monetary returns to an investor.

## Management of Building and Development Firms

A wide variety of business firms are engaged in subdividing and land development activities. Frequently, such activities are combined with building operations. In some cases, an individual buys land and holds it for future development, sometimes subdividing it himself and installing the necessary facilities, sometimes selling it to others who do this. In some cases, several persons form a syndicate to engage in land development. Sometimes a real estate brokerage firm undertakes to develop land and sell the lots, or contracts with a builder to provide completed properties for sale.

Land development and building enterprises may be individual proprietorships, partnerships, or corporations. They may be operated as syndicates or trusts or in other ways. Some of the largest of our corporations have gone into land development and building operations from time to time.

Regardless of how they are set up, every firm engaging in subdividing or land development activities must perform the basic management functions of determining objectives, planning to achieve them, organizing resources, and controlling operations. Leadership is necessary to direct, activate and set the process into motion.

Each firm must utilize the resources available to it, that is, the abilities of people, capital goods, land, or other resources, in the process of producing and marketing the goods and services it provides. It must do this at prices in excess of costs if it is to remain in business very long.

We are concerned chiefly with subdividing and land development in this chapter and with building processes and problems in the next. In recent years, large-scale developers have tended to combine subdivision, land development, and building operations. In some cases complete communities, even entirely new towns, have been developed, including commercial and industrial structures as well as housing and community facilities. Major corporations often are involved including ITT, U. S. Steel, Chrysler, Gulf Oil and others along with National Homes, Redman, Guerdon, Weyerhaeuser and others with more traditional relationships to this field.

## Types of Products

We should be careful to note, however, that whether a real estate firm is engaged in land development, building, brokerage, property management, or financing activities, it must perform production and marketing as well as financing activities. Although we refer to land development and building firms as being engaged in production activities, we use this term to refer to what they do for the community as a whole. Similarly, we refer to brokerage firms and property management firms as marketing enterprises because they perform marketing functions for the public. They must both produce and market their services, however, as well as arrange to finance their own programs.

## Decision Factors

Of special importance in decisions related to land development are careful market analyses and the predictions of probable market changes based on them. Analyses of general and local business conditions often play an important part in such decisions. In addition, consideration is given to construction costs and trends, availability and cost of financing, price trends, and government policies especially as related to taxes, public improvements, and zoning and similar regulations. All of these factors will affect cost-return-risk relationships which are basic to decisions regarding land development.

Various types of costs are of importance in land development. These may be grouped as (1) economic, (2) social, (3) time, and (4) supersession costs. Economic costs include the costs of the labor and capital resources required to make land ready for use. Social costs include the disruptions and inconveniences that may be involved. Time costs largely relate to the waiting period required for land to "ripen" to productive uses. Supersession costs are incurred in scrapping existing improvements to make possible new land uses.

Strategic factors such as the timing of the development relative to competitive operations, the size of the effort, pricing policies, and the like will usually affect the decisions that are made. Attempts will be made to anticipate the decisions of competitors insofar as possible.

Decisions will finally be based on such matters as (1) the objectives to be accomplished by means of the project, (2) potential cost and return relationships, modified as necessary by tax considerations, (3) risk factors, (4) relationship of the project under consideration to others, and (5) the timing of the effort and the time required for it to pay out.

## STAGES IN THE DEVELOPMENT PROCESS

The main activities essential to a new development include the following:

1. Analyzing market conditions (determining the need for and the proper time for the proposed development).
2. Selecting an appropriate location.
3. Analyzing the principal features of the selected tract and developing preliminary plans and design.
4. Purchasing the location and establishing a method of financing. In the case of a shopping center, a leasing campaign will be carried on before financing is arranged.
5. Designing the layout of the area, locating the principal facilities, and determining relationship between public and private land uses; dividing the remaining portions of the land into parcels of such sizes and shapes as appear to be best adapted to the anticipated uses.
6. Securing approval of government authorities as required.
7. Arranging protections against risks by means of insurance and bonds.
8. Installing utilities, streets, and the various conveniences necessary for the development.
9. Establishing restrictions and methods for regulating land use.
10. Selling parcels or proceeding with construction.

### Market Analysis

Prior to undertaking a new land development project, it is essential that the general conditions of the market be understood. In addition, the subdivider or developer needs information about the potential market for the specific types of products which he intends to sell. If he plans to sell lots, he needs to know something of the demand for lots of the type and price range he is considering. If he intends to subdivide and completely develop a tract of land, constructing houses, apartments, a shopping center, or other buildings on the lots, he will need information about their salability or rentability. Hence, the real estate developer will begin by considering the need for additional real estate resources. He will consider the available supply and current price and rent ranges in the light of potential demand. Land development calls for one of the specific applications of the market analysis procedures outlined in Chapter 11.

Generally, land development activity is greatest during periods of prosperity and high incomes. In periods of recession relatively little activity is undertaken. History indicates that all too frequently land is developed during boom periods more rapidly than it can be absorbed by the market. For example, at the end of the boom of the 1920's, Chicago and its suburbs had enough lots to house over a million additional persons living in detached houses. Thus, the *timing* of a new subdivision or development is of basic importance to its success.

A heavy volume of land development does not mean that all old subdivisions will be used. Many never will be because of poor locations, financial involvements, and other reasons. Premature subdivisions have created numerous problems, not only for the subdivider himself but for the community at large. Careful market analyses should help to prevent such occurrences.

These analyses should include a consideration of the principal demand, supply, and price factors having a bearing on the specific project under consideration. The principal demand factors are the trends of employment and incomes of the potential customer group and the terms and availability of financing. From the standpoint of supply, the availability of competing facilities and the potential development of competing projects are of prime importance. Relative prices and rents for old and new accommodations of a similar size and type need careful consideration. Costs of development require careful study.

One should always remember in making analyses of this type that relatively long-range predictions are required. Only in exceptional cases is a subdivision completely developed and sold in the space of one or two years. In most cases the process goes on over a longer period of time. Often it is advisable to develop a tract in sections to be sure that the market will absorb the new properties.

### Location of New Housing

Just as poor timing may result in unsuccessful developments, improper locations lead almost inevitably to developments which fail to become desirable additions to our real estate resources. The proper location of new real estate developments leads to orderly expansion. The successful development of a new area requires a careful study of the past trends of city growth and structure and the location of competing or complementary areas. The discussions in Chapters 10 and 11 are applicable to problems of this type.

Location factors of special importance in decisions relating to a new housing development typically include the following:

1. The site should be favorably located with respect to the needs of the population for the type and class of development planned.
2. The site should not require undue development costs and be free from natural hazards.

3. Protections should be available in the form of natural barriers, zoning, or deed restrictions; if not available, they should be set up.
4. The site should be reasonably accessible in terms of time and cost of travel.
5. The planned development should put the properties in a favorable competitive situation relative to competing developments in terms of general attractiveness, lot sizes, parking areas, utilities and conveniences, roads and streets, and parks, schools, shopping centers and other public and community facilities.

## Location of Commercial and Industrial Developments

The factors which are of major importance in the location of commercial and industrial real estate developments are: (1) available transportation facilities, (2) topography and the nature of the soil and subsoil, (3) the relationship of the area to other parts of the region, and (4) the location and character of competing sites.

In most cities the location of commercial and industrial developments is limited by zoning laws as we have seen. Recently, however, the location of such developments at points far removed from the center of cities has often placed them beyond the control of zoning regulations. While this gives the developer greater flexibility of operations, he will usually consider the relationship of a new commercial or industrial subdivision to the probable future pattern of growth and to the way in which the transportation network is likely to develop.

## Analyzing the Selected Tract

Experienced developers make careful analyses and surveys of tracts prior to reaching decisions to purchase them. It is necessary to determine the usability and marketability of *all parts* of the area. Substantial losses can be avoided if advance consideration is given to the less desirable portions of a tract. A competent engineer or land planner should study the area and prepare layouts of the tract.

One student of the subject said:

Marketing subdivisions may be compared to marketing beef. The butcher pays so much a hundred for the carcass, and the subdivider pays so much an acre for his land. When the butcher retails, he charges according to the choiceness of the cut. He must charge enough for the porterhouse and tenderloin to take care of the waste and the cheap cuts.[1]

It should be noted also that the first properties marketed may have to be priced somewhat lower than those sold after the area has been

---

[1] Statement by the late Stewart Mott.

partially developed. The earlier purchasers frequently require a price inducement for bearing a portion of the risk of a new project.

Cost of development must be studied with great care. Such costs vary widely. Flat land, of course, requires less preparation than rough terrain. An area which is to be densely settled requires heavy streets and sidewalks and large water mains and sewers. Less densely settled areas require streets, and sidewalks may not be needed. Utility lines, however, will need to be longer in proportion to the number of people in the area.

Improvement costs should be related to traffic load, number of families per acre, and the character of the layout of lots and services. The buying power of the residents must be considered with care.

The largest elements in the improvement bill are the costs of streets and walks. Costs of sanitary sewers (and, except in areas of very low density, storm sewers) and water mains are added, as are costs of grading, draining, and landscaping, as well as the cost of engineering service. The cost of gas and electric service requires advance payments, but usually is reimbursed as the service is put into use.

Factors of importance in studying both costs of development and marketability include (1) topography; (2) limitations established by zoning ordinances and other regulations; (3) accessibility to places of employment, to schools, and to shopping, amusement, and civic centers; (4) location with respect to other neighborhoods and special attractions such as golf courses; (5) taxes; (6) potential special assessments; and (7) future probable management, financing, and maintenance costs.

### Purchasing and Financing

The purchase of land for a new development is similar to the buying of other real estate. Options may be acquired; in some cases land may be purchased on contract; or it may be bought outright. Often the developer arranges to "take down" portions of an area paying over a period of time. This arrangement may be helpful both to buyer and seller—in the former case to avoid tying up large blocks of funds and in the latter because of tax considerations. The usual complex legal formalities are involved as in all real estate transactions. Of course, it is especially important to the land developer that title matters be definitely settled and that as much red tape as possible be eliminated if parts of the development are to be sold.

Brokers are often commissioned by developers to find suitable tracts or to assemble land where diversity of ownership is involved. The difficulty of assembling tracts of sufficient size for economical development has been one of the main factors preventing the redevelopment of "near-in" areas and has accelerated the trend toward city decentralization.

Increasingly real estate developments are being financed by equities with lending institutions taking "a piece of the action." Provision has been made by several states whereby large institutional lenders may develop and own real estate projects. Many operators rely on borrowed funds to a large degree. Construction financing usually is provided on a short-term basis but may be tied in with mortgage arrangements. Mortgages may be insured by the Federal Housing Administration or guaranteed by the Veterans Administration or insured or guaranteed by private mortgage insurance companies.

## Designing the Layout

The decisions reached in regard to the number of lots to be laid out, the areas to be used for business purposes, land dedicated to public use, the utilities and conveniences to be installed, and the restrictions to be established all involve detailed study of numerous factors. For example, the type and extent of street improvements are limited on the one hand by minimum essentials for decent living and on the other by the amount which prospective buyers or tenants can pay over and above such minimum requirements.

Local customs, climate, and soil conditions play a large part in determining the types of roads and streets constructed. The general plan for developing the tract will determine the road and street pattern. Courts or cul-de-sacs with proper turning space help to reduce traffic hazards; adapting the road system to the topography of the area not only adds to the attractiveness of many lots but also helps reduce costs.

The size and shape of the lots will be dependent on the anticipated land uses, on topographical features, on local planning regulations, on the income levels of prospective purchasers, and on the proposed price or rent scale. In earlier years many developers attempted to subdivide an area in such a way that the greatest possible number of lots would be obtained. Present-day practice dictates the division of an area into the greatest number of *readily salable lots*. Land planners and engineers have made substantial progress in solving problems of this type. (See, for example, Fig. 14–1.)

The inclusion of park and playground areas in the plan of a subdivision adds greatly to the attractiveness and salability of many lots. The extent to which land in a tract will be dedicated to parks and playgrounds will be influenced, of course, by the nearness of the development to established facilities of this type. Also, provision should be made for shopping center sites, schools, churches, and related facilities. In some

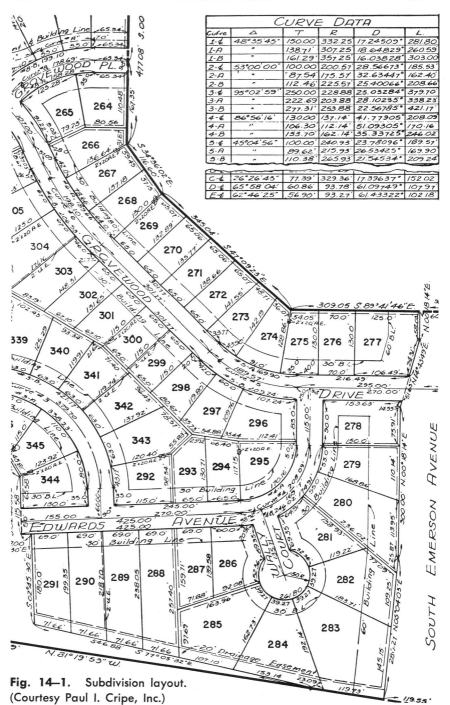

**Fig. 14-1.** Subdivision layout.
(Courtesy Paul I. Cripe, Inc.)

cases special features such as lakes, golf courses, community centers or others are built into a development.

### Guidelines for Neighborhood Planning

The following suggestions serve as guidelines for neighborhood planning:

1. Heavy through traffic should be discouraged.
2. Extension of major streets should be planned in advance.
3. Traffic should flow toward thoroughfares.
4. Minor streets should enter major streets at right angles.
5. Dead-end streets should be avoided. (Courts with cul-de-sacs which provide adequate turning space, however, are often desirable.)
6. Streets should fit contours of irregular land.
7. Short blocks are not economical.
8. Plan commercial sites where needed.
9. Provide school and church sites.
10. Parks are a definite community asset.
11. Preserve natural features of site for improved appearance.
12. Deep lots are wasteful.
13. Plan lots of adequate width.
14. Avoid sharp-angled lots.
15. Plan wider corner lots.
16. Make lot lines perpendicular to street.
17. Plan lots to face desirable views.
18. Protect lots against adjacent nonconforming uses.
19. Protect residential lots against major street traffic.
20. Provide for adequate parking.
21. Develop special features to improve marketability.
22. Protect the environment.

### Securing Government Approvals

With few exceptions, it is necessary to secure the approval of various government agencies before land development programs may be carried out. State and local planning regulations typically require that plans for each new subdivision be approved. Detailed plats and working drawings for a proposed tract or subdivision showing the lots; position of streets; type and quality of streets, curbs, and sidewalks; land dedicated to public use; and related matters are presented to the proper authorities for approval. In some cases modifications are required. Sometimes approval is denied. Tax matters must be cleared in some cases.

State governments typically require the submission of plans for provision of water and for sewage disposal in order to safeguard public health. Approval must be secured to gain access to state roads. Some states require the submission of evidence of ability to deliver title to lots and in other ways undertake to protect the public against fraud and misrepresentation.

Federal regulations usually to do not apply to subdivision development unless federal highways, taxes, or similar matters are involved or unless FHA or VA financing is desired. Approval must be secured for the proposed development from appropriate FHA and VA offices if such financial plans are to be used. Federal regulations may be involved if a subdivider needs to gain access to federal roads or if there are liens against the projerty resulting from a failure to pay federal taxes, or if the project involves use of the federal urban renewal program.

## Protections Against Risks

Before any work is undertaken in the development of the physical subdivision, various protections usually are arranged against such risks as injuries to persons or property. Usually this is done through insurance coverage under a "manufacturer's and contractor's liability" policy. Also it is customary to arrange for performance bonds if contracts are let for such work as grading, utility installation, and the like. Such bonds provide a guarantee through an insurance company that work will be completed according to the contract that has been arranged.

Long and Gregg make this statement:

While the provisions of contract bonds vary somewhat with different owners, they follow similar lines. First, when an owner advertises a project for bidding, he normally requires all bidders to accompany their proposals with a guarantee, usually in the form of a Bid Bond or certified check. The bid bond generally guarantees that, if awarded the contract, the principal will (1) enter into the contract and furnish the required performance and payment bonds or (2) pay the owner (up to the limit of the bid bond penalty) the difference between the principal's price and the cost of awarding the contract to the next higher bidder.

The Performance Bond guarantees to the owner that the contractor will complete the project within the scheduled time, for the agreed upon price, and in strict accordance with the plans, specifications, and contract. If the contractor fails to perform, the surety on the performance bond may undertake to finish the work or pay the owner the excess cost (up to the bond penalty) of having the work completed by another contractor.

Ordinarily, a separate Payment Bond is also given to guarantee that the contractor will discharge his bills—and often those of his subcontractors—for labor and material used in the project, although this obligation is sometimes included in the performance bond.

Construction contracts occasionally require the builder to guarantee the project, or certain portions thereof, against defective workmanship and materials for stated periods of time. Although this protection is normally afforded under the performance bond, some owners ask for a separate Maintenance Bond for the purpose. The underwriting of construction contract bonds will be discussed later.[2]

## Utilities and Conveniences

The problems involved in the provision of utilities and conveniences vary so widely from one development to another that it is difficult to make general statements about them.

In the long run, the use of sanitary sewers is more desirable than the use of septic tanks. Problems of pollution are multiplying in many areas with inadequate sewage disposal systems. City water is to be preferred over individual wells. In some cases there is no way to avoid such alternative arrangements, however. Sometimes community water or sewerage systems may be established and operated by the property owners in the area.

Telephone and power companies usually extend their services to a new development without cost to the developer. Other utility companies usually make an installation charge with provision for refund if a sufficient number of users move into the area. Installation of underground utility mains and laterals prior to street surfacing helps to reduce costs. However, installation far in advance of needs should be discouraged.

Walks are usually required when there is a density of five houses or more per acre. Finished grading, lawns, and suitable planting help to enhance the appeal of a new development. If there are railroads, heavy traffic arteries, or other features likely to be objectionable to residents of the new area, screen planting or the construction of solid fencing or walls may be desirable. The developer should give consideration to provisions for street lighting, fire protection, and electrical, telephone, and gas services. Underground wiring adds greatly to the attractiveness and long-term appeal of an area.

Usually contracts are let for the various types of work that are necessary. Generally this will be done by entering into one contract for grading, another for road or street installation, another for sewer installation, and the like. Sometimes a general contract is let and the general contractor may sublet parts of the work.

## Public and Private Regulations

The establishment of restrictive covenants and plans for regulating a new development should be considered as an essential part of the developer's functions.

[2] Reprinted with permission from Burgoon, J., "Surety Bonds and Underwriting," in John D. Long and Davis W. Gregg, *Property and Liability Insurance Handbook* (Homewood, Ill.: Richard D. Irwin, Inc., 1965), pp. 829–30.

The types of restrictions established will depend on the extent to which zoning laws and land planning provisions regulate land uses, as well as on the character of the new development. In some places new developments are regulated by master plans established by local planning authorities. Standards for new subdivisions and developments may be established by such authorities. Zoning laws are usually the most important method for carrying into effect the master plan of a local authority. In some cases, however, this method is inadequate. The protection afforded by suitable covenants is of primary importance in the areas which lack the benefit of adequate and effective zoning. Protective covenants are an important supplementary aid in maintaining neighborhood character and values. The extent of zoning protection is limited to governmental exercise of the police powers of maintaining and promoting public health, safety, and welfare. Protective covenants, being agreements between private parties, can go much further than public regulations in meeting the needs of a particular development and in providing maximum possible protection.

Usually the developer needs to establish more specific and detailed regulations than are set up by public bodies if he is to assure the orderly and stable development of the new area. Deed restrictions are the most effective means for accomplishing this purpose. They may control land uses, lot sizes, design and size of structures, position of structures on lots, nuisances, price ranges, land coverage, architectural factors, utility easements, and related matters. Deed restrictions should provide suitable enforcement provisions, be recorded in the public land records, and be superior to the lien of any mortgage that may be on record prior to recording the protective covenants. In some cases a "homes association" or "property owners' maintenance association" is organized to administer such regulations.

Protective covenants may also contain various special conditions such as regulations governing individual water supply and sewage-disposal systems, for example, requiring conformance to stated standards; protection of sites for community facilities such as parks, schools, and shopping centers; and related matters. Occupancy restrictions, of course, may not be enforced by the courts.

The FHA provides this advice:

Protective covenants should provide suitable enforcement provisions, be recorded in the public land records and be superior to the lien of any mortgage that may be on record prior to the recording of the protective covenants. The proper form of protective covenants varies in the different states. A generally acceptable and enforceable form is a written declaration by the owner of the entire tract which is recorded in land office records. Sometimes in small developments, the covenants and conditions are stated on the recorded plat.

When a separate declaration is made, it is good practice to record it simultaneously with the recordation of the subdivision map.[3]

### Marketing a New Development

The process of marketing a new development depends on the types of properties established and the objectives of the developer. If the subdivider wants to sell lots directly to users, quite a different marketing program will be set up than for a large-scale housing development or other type of project.

In the case of a subdivision it is considered good practice to develop and market one part of the area at a time. Relatively few subdividers today follow the practice which was common a generation ago of simply dividing raw land and selling unimproved lots on an indiscriminate basis. Orderly development almost never resulted from such practices. Today the subdivider typically installs streets and roads and makes provision for essential utilities as a minimum. He may also build houses or other structures on the lots, either for sale or for rent.

When houses are built for sale, good practice dictates that houses be grouped rather than scattered. "Model houses" and "open houses" are often employed as selling devices. Auctions of lots were typical of practices a generation ago, but in relatively few cases are they used as a marketing method today.

Resort communities often market lots with a great deal of fanfare. They may advertise widely, make offers to transport prospects for long distances to see the development, conduct competitions, offer prizes and do many other things to promote sales.

In case a subdivision is only partly developed and the developer finds it difficult to complete his project, he may improve his chances for success if he places new restrictions on the land through the cooperation of the property owners, resubdivides into lots of proper size to fit the current market, vacates unnecessary roads, and eliminates insofar as possible objectionable features.

If a rental housing project is developed, the marketing process is quite different, since house services rather than the houses themselves are being sold. Marketing operations are discussed in greater detail in Chapters 16 and 17.

### RECENT TRENDS IN LAND DEVELOPMENT

Most of the new single-family homes built in the United States since the end of World War II have been constructed in new subdivisions on the periphery of existing cities or in vacant interstices between the older

[3] FHA *Underwriting Manual.*

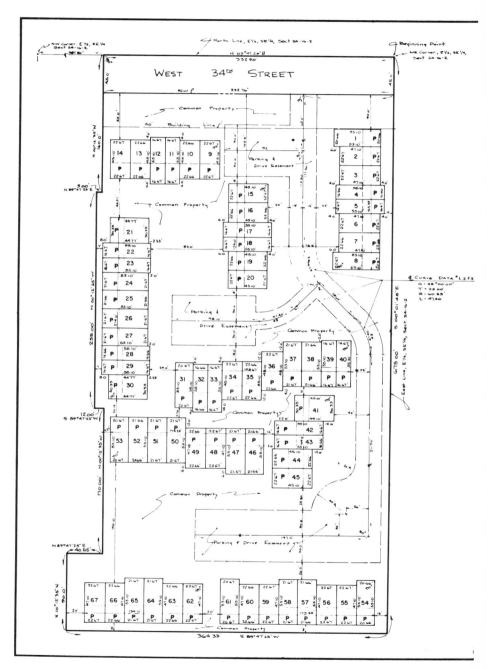

**Fig. 14–2.** Tara Town House on the Green addition—section 1.

I hereby certify that the within plat is true and correct and represents a survey of a part of the East Half of the Southeast Quarter of Section 24, Township 16 North, of Range 2 East in Marion County, Indiana, being more particularly described as follows:

Beginning at the Northeast corner of said Half Quarter Section, running thence South 00 degrees 01 minutes 48 seconds East upon and along the East line of said Half Quarter Section a distance of 675.00 feet to a point; running thence South 89 degrees 47 minutes 25 seconds West and parallel with the North line of said Half Quarter Section a distance of 364.33 feet to a point; running thence North 00 degrees 12 minutes 35 seconds West a distance of 90.00 feet to a point; running thence North 89 degrees 47 minutes 25 seconds East a distance of 40.55 feet to a point; running thence North 00 degrees 12 minutes 35 seconds West a distance of 170.00 feet to a point; running thence South 89 degrees 47 minutes 25 seconds West a distance of 12.0 feet to a point; running thence North 00 degrees 12 minutes 35 seconds West a distance of 255.0 feet to a point; running thence North 89 degrees 47 minutes 25 seconds East a distance of 5.00 feet to a point; running thence North 00 degrees 12 minutes 35 seconds West a distance of 160.00 feet to a point on the North line of said Half Quarter Section a distance of 991.81 feet North 89 degrees 47 minutes 25 seconds East of the Northwest corner of said Half Quarter Section; running thence North 89 degrees 47 minutes 25 seconds East upon and along said North line a distance of 332.90 feet to the place of beginning, containing 5.214 acres, more or less.

The area designated as "Common Property" contains 3.244 acres +.

This subdivision contains 67 lots, numbered 1 thru 67 inclusive and "Common Property" as indicated. The size of lots and widths of streets are shown on this plat in figures denoting feet and decimal parts thereof.

This survey was made by me during the month of May, 19--.

Witness my signature this      day of              , 19--.

James E. Dankert
Registered Land Surveyor #4028

NOTE:   All Lot Lines are parallel
        or perpendicular to the
        North ½, ¼ Section Line
P = INDIVIDUAL   PATIO
    ON EACH LOT

# TARA  TOWN  HOUSE
# ON  THE  GREEN  ADDITION
# SECTION  ONE

residential communities. Developers have had the opportunity to lay out a new design of streets and a different lot size from the old pattern. Winding streets and cul-de-sacs often replaced the old rigid design of streets and lots. Planning the new subdivisions created an extensive field of activity for land planners.

Vacant land on the edge of cities becomes ripe for house building when sewer and water mains are extended from the central city or its principal built-up suburbs. Most of our new housing developments have been constructed in areas closely adjacent to the older settled areas and have been a mass extension of urban growth from the main urban body.

Houses in high-priced residential developments have been constructed on larger lots of one or more acres, in areas separated from the concentrated urban mass by green belts. Some entire communities have been built, as in Pittsburgh, which are in open areas, and which have their own sewage-disposal system and water system. Other communities have relied on individual septic tanks, which have sometimes, under certain soil conditions, become objectionable and polluted the area. Many cities, villages, and counties in the United States have sought to regulate density of residential development by requiring minimum lot sizes.

### Land Scarcity

As a result of heavy suburban building activities, there is a growing scarcity of vacant sites for new single-family homes that are close to sewer and water lines in some of the larger metropolitan areas. The travel time between home and work has gradually been lengthening as the distance to new suburban developments increases and as automobile traffic congestion continues to rise. This has been responsible in part for the increased demand for apartments which are located near places of employment. Apartments have also become a part of various outlying suburban developments.

### Planned Unit Developments

Because of the scarcity of improved land and rapidly rising land costs, efforts have been made to use land with greater intensity in residential developments but still to provide for adequate open areas and privacy. This has led to what we often refer to as "planned unit developments." In these, townhouses and apartments are used rather than single-family detached houses but provision is made for laws, gardens and play areas that are carefully related to the dwellings.

### Large-Scale Developments

Large-scale, carefully planned developments are being undertaken to an increasing degree. Often 600 to 1,200 or more acres are involved. Such developments may include single-family units, garden and high-rise apartments, and town houses. Provision is made for recreation areas, shopping centers, schools, and related facilities. In some cases entire cities or "new towns" are being planned from the beginning. Columbia will have 150,000 residents when development is complete. This development owns a 14,500 acre tract of land between Baltimore and Washington, D.C. Developments in the Washington-Baltimore area include King's Park West, 500 acres; Colton, 1,600 acres; and Reston, another "new town," 7,000 acres.

## PROBLEMS OF LAND DEVELOPMENT AND URBAN GROWTH

Subdividers and land developers have sometimes been criticized for lack of foresight in arranging for the orderly expansion of urban areas, for premature subdivisions, for the poor planning of new areas, for attempts to make excessive profits, for unsound financing plans, and for failure to establish adequate regulations and controls.

Although land developers have contributed their share to present-day problems of land utilization, governments have been relatively inactive until recently in establishing the regulations necessary for orderly developments and in setting up a realistic framework within which competitive forces could operate.

### Long-Term Growth

Some progress has been made in recent years. Planning has been extended to cover metropolitan areas in some cases. Carefully developed plans for long-term growth have been worked out for a number of localities including both urban and rural areas. In some cases zoning may prescribe minimum lot sizes of from one to four acres, and this is permissible if for health or safety purposes; however, if large areas are set up as a requirement in order to limit growth, such regulations may be unconstitutional. Despite the progress that has been made, much remains to be done in this field.

### Rising Standards

Higher standards are being followed in many subdivision developments. These include larger lots, wider streets, better curbs and gutters, and improved storm and sanitary sewers and water mains. Increasing restrictions are being placed on private wells and sewage-disposal systems. The importance of larger-scale developments to reduce costs is being stressed, as well as reduction in the scattering of developments, and the need for expansion of community facilities to keep up with land needs. Regional planning and the coordination of public facilities on a metropolitan basis are being accorded increased attention.

## Public and Private Division of Labor

The improvement of land development in the future will require the very best efforts of both public and private business administration. Recognition must be given to the development of a sound division of labor between government and private enterprises. Possibly new governmental devices will have to be developed in order to provide a sound framework within which the private developer can operate.

On the other hand, private practices must improve. We can hardly expect this to happen unless the necessary inducements are present. Private business practices respond more definitely to promises of profits and sound investments than to preachments by public-spirited citizens. Realistic recognition of this should help city planning commissions and other public bodies in their work. Advancement in the field of land development will result chiefly from a many-sided attack on current problems by private enterprises and public agencies.

## Consumer Demands

The demands of the consumers as a result of higher housing and business standards will exert continuous, even though often indefinite, pressure toward better land development.

The importance of the consumer as a force toward improved standards is emphasized in this statement:

And there's still another direct influence to better land planning, design and the expanded use of newer and better materials, an influence that is already pushing the trend toward better quality construction. The influence: Today's buyer isn't being *forced* to buy a home. The shelter shortage is a thing of the past. Today's buyer demands higher quality and better design. If he doesn't find it one place, he'll look somewhere else. Tomorrow's home buyer will be no different. He'll also demand a bigger and better property for his dollar.[4]

---

[4] Statement by John Schmidt and Arthur Goldman.

## SUMMARY

The terms *subdividing* and *land development* describe the activities of those firms and individuals engaged in the production of real estate resources. Decisions at this stage have long-range importance, since the manner in which these functions are performed has considerable impact on the eventual character of the property and of the community or neighborhood of which it forms a part. Developers and builders usually are interested in immediate or early sale of the properties involved, and their outlook is esentially short run. Users, investors, and property managers, however, typically take a longer-range view, since their interests are tied in with the development of the community and the future income-producing potential of the properties.

Although subdividers and developers are engaged in the production of real estate resources, each firm must arrange the financing of its own operations and the marketing of its own products. These products may be raw land, partially or completely developed lots, and perhaps buildings and other improvements. The timing of development and subdividing is of extreme importance in determining a project's success, and therefore should be based on careful market analysis. Planned Unit Developments are growing in importance.

Location, timing, and costs all are important factors in the production of real estate resources. Financial institutions and other investors exercise much influence on decisions to produce real estate resources. Governmental approvals also are important, particularly with respect to building permits, zoning laws, and insuring or guaranteeing of mortgages through FHA or VA if such arrangements are desired. Approvals also are required to insure conformity with local use and occupancy regulations and with public health requirements. The influence of the consumer of housing is highly important in developing improved standards.

## QUESTIONS FOR STUDY

1. Suppose that you are planning the introduction of a proposed "Woodland Acres" subdivision. What market factors would you consider in determining whether or not this new subdivision might be successful?
2. What factors would be most important in determining the location of this subdivision?
3. Should you include commercial, residential, and recreational sites in the plan for the "Woodland Acres" subdivision? Explain.
4. Would you plan to include land for apartment houses as well as for single-family homes? Explain your position.
5. In your planning for the subdivision, what allowances should you make for

traffic patterns? If the land is irregular in contour, how should the streets be laid out?

6. Outline the principal regulations that would help to assure the orderly development of a subdivision.

7. Why is timing so important in new land developments?

8. Make a list of the important costs involved in developing land, and describe them.

9. Are greater public controls needed over private subdivision developments? Give reasons for your position on this question.

10. Are the interests of a land developer typically of a long-term or short-term nature with respect to a specific project? Explain.

11. What factors determine the way in which a tract of land should be subdivided into lots?

12. What are the most important items that should be included in protective covenants?

13. What is meant by a "planned unit development"?

14. Are large-scale developments likely to increase in importance?

## SUGGESTED READINGS

AMERICAN INSTITUTE OF REAL ESTATE APPRAISERS. *The Appraisal of Real Estate* (5th ed.). Chicago, The Institute, 1967. Chaps. 6, 7.

LONG, JOHN D., and DAVIS W. GREGG. *Property and Liability Insurance Handbook.* Homewood, Ill.: Richard D. Irwin, Inc., 1965. Chaps. 53, 55, 57.

NATIONAL ASSOCIATION OF HOME BUILDERS. *Land Development Manual.* Washington, D.C.: The Association, 1969.

SELDIN, MAURY, and RICHARD H. SWESNIK. *Real Estate Investment Strategy.* New York: John Wiley & Sons, Inc., 1970. Chap. 4.

U. S. SAVINGS AND LOAN LEAGUE. *Construction Lending Guide.* Chicago: The League, 1964.

## CASE 14–1

### Sans Souci Estates

The purpose of this case study is to illustrate the nature of land development decisions.

The Flamingo Development Company, subdividers and builders since 1953 purchased 40 acres in the Eastwood section of a West Coast metropolitan area. The Eastwood section had its greatest development in the post-World War II years when land formerly used for growing citrus fruits was developed with low- to medium-priced homes financed by VA-guaranteed and FHA-insured mortgages. Though the heyday of Eastwood has passed, the Flamingo Development Company believes that there is a strong market in Eastwood for medium-priced conventionally financed homes.

The Flamingo Development Company decided to call the 40-acre development Sans Souci Estates. The land to the north, south, and east is almost fully developed. The houses built in the immediate post-World War II period are in a general price range of $16,000 to $18,000. The homes most recently built are larger and sell in the general price range of $24,000 to $26,000. San Souci Estates is about three miles from Eastwood Shopping Center, a major regional center.

The Flamingo Development Company considered three alternative land patterns:

1. A gridiron pattern with lot sizes ranging from 50 x 110 feet, to 55 x 125 feet. This plan would provide for 160 lots. Total costs as follows:

| | | |
|---|---|---|
| (a) | Surveying | $  8,100 |
| (b) | Grading | 12,000 |
| (c) | Sewers | 25,000 |
| (d) | Roads and curbs | 45,000 |
| (e) | Water mains | 14,800 |
| (f) | Street lights and corner signs | 3,100 |
| | Total Cost | $108,000 |

2. A gridiron pattern with lot sizes ranging from 70 x 110 feet to 75 x 125 feet. This plan would provide for 120 lots with costs as follows:

| | | |
|---|---|---|
| (a) | Surveying | $ 7,600 |
| (b) | Grading | 12,000 |
| (c) | Sewers | 22,000 |
| (d) | Roads and curbs | 41,400 |
| (e) | Water mains | 13,000 |
| (f) | Fire hydrants | 3,000 |
| | Total Cost | $99,000 |

3. A curvilinear street pattern with cul-de-sac. Lot sizes would range from 70 x 110 feet to 75 x 125 feet except some irregularly shaped lots of at least 7,500 square feet. This plan would provide for 120 lots.

| | | |
|---|---|---|
| (a) | Surveying | $ 7,800 |
| (b) | Grading | 12,000 |
| (c) | Sewers | 23,000 |
| (d) | Roads and curbs | 43,000 |
| (e) | Water mains | 13,200 |
| (f) | Fire hydrants | 3,000 |
| | Total Cost | $102,000 |

Eastwood has a comprehensive zoning plan. The restrictions applicable to the Sans Souci Estates and the neighboring area provide, among other things, that:

1. No buildings or land shall be used except for the following purposes:
   a. Single-family dwellings
   b. Parks and playgrounds owned and operated by a governmental agency
2. No buildings shall be erected having a height in excess of two and one-half stories or 35 feet.
3. No main building shall be erected unless the following yards and lot area are maitained:

    a. A front yard of not less than 20 feet or 20 per cent of the depth of the lot, whichever is the lesser of the two

    b. Side yards of not less than 5 feet or 10 per cent of the width of the lot, whichever is the lesser of the two

    c. Rear yard of not less than 25 feet or 25 per cent of the depth of the lot, whichever is the lesser of the two

    d. A lot area of not less than 5,000 square feet, and the lot frontage shall not be less than 50 feet in width

The Flamingo Development Company plans to provide the following restrictive covenants:

1. All the lots herein described are declared to be residential in character, and no dwelling or structure, except a private dwelling house, designed to accommodate one family only, and garage and outbuildings appurtenant thereto, shall at any time be erected or maintained on any building lot.

2. No building or fence of any character shall be constructed upon any lot in this tract without the approval as to location, height, and design first having been obtained from Grantors or their nominee. No dwelling or structure erected on the property shall be erected closer to the front boundary line of the property than the setback shown upon the map of the tract on file and accepted by the city of Eastwood.

3. No person shall reside in any dwelling or structure until and unless the construction has been completed.

4. No boundary or fence exceeding 7 feet in height above the ground shall be constructed upon said property.

5. No store, shop, or factory shall be erected or placed on any lot, nor any business or trade conducted or maintained thereon.

6. No fowl or animals other than reasonable and usual number of household pets, such as domesticated dogs, birds, and felines, shall be permitted.

7. No lot shall be subdivided or portion thereof sold, transferred, or conveyed, excepted that a portion thereof may be transferred or conveyed for the purpose of forming a part of an adjoining lot, but no lot shall be left with a principal frontage of less than 50 feet or an area less than 5,000 feet square.

8. No noxious or offensive activity shall be allowed in the tract, nor shall anything be done which may be or become an annoyance or nuisance to the neighborhood.

9. All covenants and restrictions are to run with the land and shall be binding on all parties and all persons claiming thereunder until July 1, 1978, at which time said covenants and restrictions shall automatically extend for successive periods of ten years, unless by a vote of the majority of the then owners of the lots it is agreed to change said covenants and restrictions in whole or in part.

10. If the parties hereto or any of them or their heirs or assigns shall violate or attempt to violate any of the covenants or restrictions herein, it shall be lawful for any person or persons owning any other lots in the development or subdivision to prosecute any proceeding at law or in equity against the person or persons violating or attempting to violate any such covenant or restriction, and either to prevent him from so doing or to recover damages or other dues for such violations.

The Flamingo Development Company purchased the property with a down payment of $40,000, and executed a purchase-money blanket mortgage for the balance of $160,000. The mortgage calls for payment of $40,000 or more annually plus 8 per cent interest. There is no prepayment penalty. The mortgage has a release clause providing that 10 acres will be released for each $40,000 payment on the mortgage. There is no subordination clause. The Flamingo Development Company is considering the alternative of developing the land in 4 units of 10 acres each, 2 units of 20 acres each, or 1 of 40 acres.

The Flamingo Development Company has, in addition to their capital equipment and the $40,000 equity in the land, the sum of $100,000 in cash available for the development of Sans Souci Estates. Flamingo Development Company also has contact with a number of investors who would be willing to participate in the development on a joint-venture basis. The investors would be willing to furnish the capital and participate in 50 per cent of the profit.

### Questions

1. On what basis did you think the officials of the Flamingo Development Company decided that this land was ripe for development?
2. Which of the three alternative land patterns would you choose? Explain your choice. Can you think of any more desirable ways of developing the property than those enumerated?
3. Would your choice of land patterns be any different if you were going to build instead of just subdivide? Explain.
4. How much would each lot cost under each of the three alternative arrangements?
5. How many acres would you develop at one time: 10 acres, 20 acres, or all 40 acres? How would you decide?
6. Would you add to or eliminate from the deed restrictions? Why?

### STUDY PROJECT 14–1

### Attractiveness of Low-Rise Suburban Apartment Developments

John L. Schmidt, the U. S. Savings and Loan League's director of architectural and construction research raises the following questions as to the attractiveness of low-rise suburban apartment developments.

Are the buildings attractive when viewed at a distance? Are the spaces between them in scale?

Does the project's overall design seem to take advantage of natural land features? Has the developer taken care to retain trees and other natural growth?

Are the buildings fitted into the topography, or has the topography been flattened to make way for the buildings?

Do the project's outside areas show evidence of good maintenance and housekeeping?

Is the landscaping attractive and tasteful? Or is it inadequate and poorly maintained, perhaps with bare spots that would be ugly in dry weather and muddy when it rains?

Is the space between the buildings pleasant to look at?

Are there play areas especially designed for children? Are they located where the sounds of children playing will not annoy tenants?

Are the buildings attractive when viewed close-up? Do the exterior fixtures appear of good quality?

Does the general parking plan seem practical and convenient?

Are parking facilities located relatively close to the building entrances, and is the path from the car to the building pleasant?

Is access to the units convenient, or are some tenants forced to do excessive walking and stair-climbing?

Do the building entrances provide protected stair enclosures? Especially, do stairs to upper units provide protection from rain, snow and ice?

Are views from inside the units attractive? And do lower-level units have good ventilation and natural light?

Are so-called "private" balconies really private? Especially, are they reasonably isolated from noisy play areas?

Do all special facilities, including swimming pools and clubhouses, also show good maintenance and housekeeping?

### Questions

1. Which of the factors mentioned do you consider most important?
2. Do you think of additional factors that might be considered in determining the attractiveness of a low-rise suburban apartment development?

### STUDY PROJECT 14–2

### Street Patterns and Land Planning *

In a typical residential development the street pattern is not an important sales feature. Usually a curvilinear plan, it is like that of competitive subdivisions. Because it is not distinctive, it attracts little attention from the sales department or the buyers. Because the street plan is seldom talked about, most developers do not think of it as a merchandising feature.

The very fact that most street plans look alike gives a great advantage to the developer who does something better than average. An imaginative plan becomes a talking point, a sales attraction and a major factor in creating a good neighborhood. A good street pattern helps create a good environment.

* Urban Land Institute Technical Bulletin #57, *Open Space Communities in the Market Place* (Washington, D.C.: Urban Land Institute, 1966), pp. 28–32.

A carefully-planned street pattern is the very heart of a land-use plan. It makes the best use of changes in elevation and of natural features. It saves beauty spots and provides visual pleasures. It lets pedestrians, bicycle riders, and motorists get easily and conveniently from one place to another. It helps keep the automobile in its place and makes life safer and more bearable for walkers and cyclists. A good plan creates numerous small neighborhoods and gives them individuality. Once people understand these features, they want them because they all add up to better living.

This study reveals that people are quick to see and appreciate ideas like cul-de-sacs and clusters. In the communities described below, the better street patterns have been important sales features.

**Communities Where Street Patterns Are Popular Features.** *Parkwood,* near Durham, North Carolina, has an outstanding street plan. People living there are well aware of how the streets are laid out and what benefits this carries. In describing what they like about the community, they list the street layout second only to the greenbelts. Most families there live on a cul-de-sac, or a short loop street, a semi-circular "eyebrow," or a secondary street with little traffic.

"The street layout is what attracted most people and it gives them a feeling of being off the main street," said one home owner. Another said, "Circular streets are much safer for small children." Another said, "The dead-end streets have extra recreation areas." Another said, "The street layouts here are more interesting than in other places and are more attractive." Because it is better for family living, the unusual street pattern here was an important asset in helping to get Parkwood started when it was considered far out of town.

At *Village Green,* New Jersey, all but six of the 72 houses are on one of the three short loop streets. People like the street pattern because it makes each neighborhood quieter and safer. There is no through traffic and even the milkman, mailman, and garbage truck make only one pass around the loop, rather than going down and back as in a cul-de-sac. The three loop streets form three private neighborhoods, with which each group identifies itself.

At *Crofton,* the principal feature of Mott & Hayden's land plan is a loop street encircling the property. This wide, boulevard street carries all the main traffic and lets both home owners and visitors get quickly from one place to another. Fully as important are the series of short streets that lead from the collector street to numerous quiet neighborhoods. The street plan, in combination with a beautifully landscaped golf course, form small neighborhood clusters that are quiet and individual. The developer asked the planners for as many cul-de-sacs as possible and there are about 26. These and the fairway lots sell first and at premium prices. Almost all intersections are T's or 3-way, and not the more dangerous 4-way crossings. The street plan shows clearly on a three-dimensional model of the entire community and is used by salesmen as a major sales feature. (*See plan.*)

*See Pines Plantation* is another example of how a carefully thought out street plan can increase lot values. Land planner Hideo Sasaki of Harvard wanted to provide as many waterfront and water-view lots as possible. Instead of run-

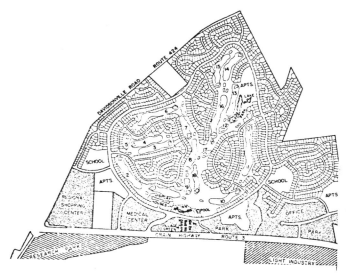

Crofton's excellent plan has been highly marketable. The 210-acre golf course creates many small neighborhoods and several hundred premium golf-course lots. Open space, many cul-de-sacs, and variety of housing types help create nteresting, attractive environment. Total area: 1,300 acres.

ning his main road one lot back from the water, as is commonly done, he put it from five to seven lots back. From this main road a series of cluster roads project towards the water. What makes the plan work is a walking path on a wide right-of-way which all families may use to get to the water. Because everyone can walk to the beach, no one feels like a second-class citizen. As a result, houses back from the water sell well. Instead of one row of high-value lots, developer Charles Fraser has up to seven in some areas. Fraser believes such a cluster plan works best when each house in a cluster harmonizes with the others both in design and in color.

*The Bluffs:* nearly one-third of the land on this 300-acre parcel in the Irvine Ranch in California's Newport Beach has been devoted to parks, green areas, and recreation. The garden homes, townhouses, commercial, school, and church areas are all served by two major curving thoroughfares which are inter-connected at two points. Trailing off from the two major looping thoroughfares are a series of smaller loops which furnish back door and garage access. There are five separate groups or subcommunities. The entire area is criss-crossed with greenbelts which afford further separation of the five main residential clusters and also separate residential areas from commercial, educational, recreational and the club complex. It is significant that in California, where it is sometimes said that no one walks unless he is in the mountains or on a golf course, the plan of The Bluffs has encouraged walking. Some 42 per

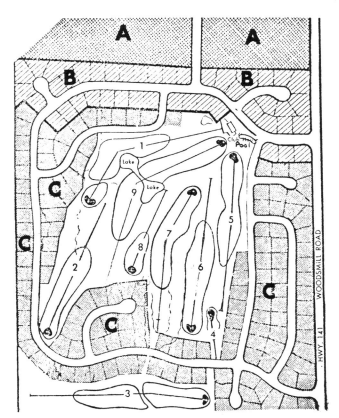

*Four Seasons* in St. Louis uses 47 acres for a highly successful golf course, which has club house and pool (upper right). The course is par 35, 2,900 yards in length. The total project has 138 acres, 130 homes, and 298 apartments.

cent of people there said they walked more, and 63 per cent said it was safer. Walking was a sales attraction for 31 per cent. Most parents are aware that children may walk more safely to school. The streets and the green areas form a separation between people and cars, and show that this is a community designed for people, not automobiles.

**Street Plans in Small Developments.**   A good street plan for a ten or twenty-house neighborhood has as much potential value as in larger developments—perhaps more, because the value of each lot represents a larger proportion of the developer's income. A good street plan can easily add $1,000 to each lot value.

The most common mistake in many small developments is to put a perimeter street on the outside of the property and to face houses on what may be heavy-traffic streets. An interior loop or several cul-de-sacs would provide just as many lots, perhaps even more, and give home buyers more privacy, individuality and safety.

At *New Mark Common*, in Rickville, Maryland, Edmund Bennett uses such a plan. His site is 96 acres but the principles will work on smaller parcels. A major feature is that all single-family houses face on short, private streets—none on a through street. All houses face inward, rather than outward toward busy streets and older houses or apartments. The cul-de-sac streets create small, attractive neighborhoods that give salesmen something to talk about. Almost every lot thus becomes a valuable lot. A main collector street brings people easily and quickly through an attractive entrance and to their homes or townhouses, or to the neighborhood center. Close attention was paid to making it easy for children to get from their homes to the central swimming pool and community building.

Bennett's plan (drawn by his architects Keyes, Lethbridge, and Condon, with suggestions from Sasaki, Dawson, DeMay Associates) which was supervised by Robert Ledermann, also shows how to combine townhouses and single-family houses. Townhouses are clustered around a small artificial lake, the village green, and community center. A valuable by-product of this fine plan was the speed with which it was approved by the town planning board. The first houses are now under construction.

**Walking and Bicycle Paths.**  Special paths take space, cost money, and involve maintenance. How successful are they?

A quick answer is that they are used if the planner has been correct in anticipating where people want to go, especially children. This is not easy. Paths which lead nowhere are a waste of space.

Children will use paths that are short cuts from their homes to a nearby school, swimming pool, or favorite store. Such paths are safer than sidewalks along busy streets that have intersections, and many times safer than if children walk or ride bicycles in a street. Paths leading to a nearby elementary school which are safe for small children to use are a great benefit.

Townhouses or garden apartments lend themselves especially well to paths which lead to community features such as a pool or play areas. At Reston, there are numerous black-topped paths from townhouses to the lake, community center, shops, pool, and other features. These paths are much used and people talk about them.

**Plan Street Patterns for Expansion.**  Some street patterns do not work well because they were planned for an area that was later expanded. In one otherwise excellent community the developer now realizes that his main entrance road, which is also the collector street, does only one-third of the job it should because it ends too soon. Since it was planned he had added additional community features such as a marina, a community center, and scattered model houses. The main road does not serve them, nor some of his newest neighborhoods. Consequently in later sections there is too much auto traffic on narrow streets and his salesmen waste much time showing prospects around.

At another large subdivision the planner had no understanding of how to handle Sunday crowds, including how they would drive from the entrance to the principal features and model houses. As a result, visitors drive from place to place in a roundabout route, are often lost and probably many give up and go home. The street pattern was not designed for visitors.

### Do's and Don'ts on Street Layout

• Do plan your entrance street after visualizing what people will see as they drive in your entrance and at successive stages along your principal street. Give them some visual interests and surprises. Remember that the entrance road is the first sample of your environment.

• Do use as many cul-de-sacs as you can.

• Do plan short, private streets with clustered houses.

• Do remember that guests' cars will be parked at the end of cul-de-sac streets and provide room for them.

• Do think about how the school bus will get around, about delivery trucks, children walking, children on bicycles and make it easy for all of them to get from one place to another.

• Do tie your principal features together with one collector street if possible: entrance, pool, shops, club house, model houses, or whatever features you want visitors to see on a Sunday tour.

• Do remember that a good street plan will give you far better and more interesting townhouses or apartments.

• Do think ahead and avoid dangerous intersections and traffic bottlenecks that could occur when your community is finished and most families have three or even four cars.

---

• Don't run a straight street if you can curve it.

• Don't face houses on a heavy traffic street if you can face them on quiet, interior streets.

• Don't use a small turn-around at the end of a cul-de-sac.

• Don't use dangerous 4-way street intersections when 3-way T's are 14 times safer.

• Don't be satisfied with the first or second street plan suggested. Early plans can always be refined and improved.

• Don't start by letting your engineers freeze the street patterns. Begin with land planners who are concerned with creating a good environment and fine sites for your buildings. Then see the engineers.

• Don't forget that many families will have three or four cars and will need places to park them—but not on the streets.

• Don't permit a through street that will draw outside traffic from other subdivisions which could jam your residential streets and attract fast drivers.

• Don't forget that a good street pattern which creates individuality and privacy and safety can give your sales force something special to talk about.

• Don't overlook the fact that, if you are building townhouses or garden apartments, you should locate your streets to create as many down-hill lots as possible, and fewer up-hill lots. Down-hill lots permit you to have a three-story rear elevation with a recreation room and a walk-out door to a patio. When buyers have a choice, such units are most popular.

## Questions

1. Compare planned unit developments with the traditional method of developing residential neighborhoods. Which do you prefer? Compare the relative advantages of each method.
2. What problems may be encountered in getting approval of a PUD from the proper governmental agencies?
3. Which risks are involved in developing an unconventional subdivision such as those described?
4. Which of the "Do's and Don'ts on Street Layout" do you agree with? Which would you eliminate? Are there any additions you could make to the list?

# 15

# Production: Building

## RELATION OF BUILDING TO LAND DEVELOPMENT

In the preceding chapter we considered the functions and some of the problems of the land developer and subdivider. We pointed out that in many cases building and land development were integrated operations, while in others they were carried on separately. Obviously, the completed product is composed of land and buildings, hence the best results are often achieved when the processes of land development and building are integrated and there is close coordination between them.

New real estate resources are the result of at least six processes: (1) *initiating*, (2) *planning*, (3) *land development*, (4) *building*, (5) *financing*, and (6) *marketing*. As we pointed out in the preceding chapter, all of these processes except building are involved in land development if a project is undertaken solely for the purpose of marketing lots. When we include construction, however, many of these activities become more complicated.

### Building Processes

The building process itself requires the performance of these principal functions: (1) *initiating*; (2) *planning*, including the design and engineering of the building (this is chiefly the responsibility of the architect in order to meet the program requirements of the developer); (3) *financing*, including construction loans and financing the sale of the final product; and (4) *construction*, including purchase of the materials and equipment, employment of labor, and assembling and installing the materials and equipment. This is largely the work of the contractor and subcontractors and may be appropriately thought of as a fabricating or manufacturing process.

431

## Construction Enterprises

The business firms engaged in construction range all the way from very small organizations to large companies operating on a regional, national, and in a few cases an international basis. In some cases major corporations are involved in construction projects. General contractors and subcontractors are included. Lumber and building supply dealers form a part of this industry. Prefabricated house manufacturers and the manufacturers of building materials and equipment play a major role in the construction field. The firms in this industry, as in others, may be individual proprietorships, partnerships, or corporations. Syndicates may be set up for large projects.

Each of these business firms must establish its own objectives and manage its resources as effectively as possible in trying to attain its objectives. Its owners and managers must establish plans to achieve objectives, organize resources, and control operations. Leadership plays a big part in the success of enterprises in this field. Even in small construction enterprises, large amounts of money are involved. Hence, owners and managers must be able and willing to undertake big risks. This often requires courage of a high order plus good judgment and organizing ability as well as a sense of timing.

## Construction Decisions

As we suggested in the preceding chapter, a number of complicated factors are involved in decisions to undertake new land development programs. Such programs frequently include building as well as land development. Primary decisions are made by the owners of the land. They may sell off the land in stages thus helping to finance the project. Such arrangements may help them with their tax problems. Those who lend money to developers almost always play a major role in such decisions. Construction loans usually are for short periods. In some cases they are tied in with mortgage financing.

Since long-term commitments usually are necessary in the field of investors, it becomes extremely difficult to estimate potential costs, returns, and risks with any degree of accuracy. Sometimes developments contemplate relatively quick sale and recapture of investment as in the case of a small subdivision and building operations with all properties designed for sale. In other cases, long-term investments are involved as in the case of an apartment house, shopping center, or office building.

Typically, the firms engaged in building activities have only a short-run interest in these projects. Such firms may have a general or a special contract for a construction project. But even in short-run periods many uncertainties exist. Costs may vary widely in the space of a few months. There may be sudden changes in weather conditions. Labor problems may cause expensive work stoppages. It may be impossible to get delivery of key materials. These are all parts of the risk undertaken by the building contractor when he assumes responsibility for a project.

In some cases, a builder will take a part of his compensation in stock of the new development. He then has both a long- and a short-term interest in it, the length of the term depending on the type of development. The interests of brokerage firms and bonding companies, however, are almost always short-term in character.

## INITIATING AND PLANNING

The preliminary stages of a building operation include initiating and planning. Each of these stages will depend on the type of initiator, the size of the operation and the care with which planning is carried out.

### Types of Initiators

A real estate development may be initiated by an individual for the sole purpose of providing himself with a place to live. He will probably buy a lot, consult an architect, arrange financing, and make arragaments with a contractor, who will secure the necessary materials, equipment, and labor.

The initiator may be a builder who is undertaking a new development for the purpose of building and selling houses or building and renting houses or apartments. An industrial firm may initiate a project such as an addition to existing plant facilities or the erection of new plants. A merchant may want to build a store. A private investor may develop a shopping center or an apartment house. A carpenter may decide to build a few homes for sales. Almost anyone with savings or credit may initiate a building project.

### Size of Operations

The size of the operation may range from a single house or the conversion of an old dwelling into several efficiency apartments to the development of a community or a new town. The resources available, condition of the market, risks-cost-return relationships, and objectives of the developer—all will affect the scope of the project. The Levitt organization (now a division of I.T.T.), for example, has developed entire communities in Long Island, eastern Pennsylvania, and New Jersey. An entire town has been developed as a retirement community at Sun City, Arizona, by

Del Webb. The developers of the Irvine Ranch in California created a major city. "New towns" such as Reston and Columbia represent an important new trend in the building industry.

During recent years, industrialized home manufacturers have become an important part of the building industry. They have been of major importance in the housing field but have also engaged in shopping centers and related developments. Mobile home manufacturers have occupied a prominent place in the residential field. Building materials and equipment manufacturers have influenced the methods of both large- and small-scale on-site builders. Through research programs they have made improvements in the use of materials and in the efficiency of building processes.

Regardless of who initiates a building project, plans must be made, financing arranged, and construction carried out. In some instances the initiator may perform all of these functions himself. In projects of any size, however, specialists usually perform various parts of the process.

**Planning Construction**

Planning is usually the work of the owner or developer and the architect designer or engineer. The developer determines the type, price range, and quality of structure. On the basis of this information, the architect plans the building. This includes the following activities: (1) schematic design including preliminary sketches and estimates of probable construction costs and time; (2) design development which comprises preliminary design drawings, outlining specifications, and probable cost estimates; (3) preparation of construction documents—working drawings, specifications, and all documents necessary for bidding and construction; (4) construction with the architect providing general supervision and project inspection.

The preliminary sketches which an architect prepares are diagrams of the building which give a clear picture of the proposed arrangement, showing the location and size of the rooms, the general appearance of the structure, the equipment to be included, and the position of the structure on the lot. Preliminary cost estimates are often made on the basis of these sketches.

After definite agreement has been reached on all points between the developer and the architect, working drawings are prepared which show the exact size and location of all walls, partitions, and rooms, the material to be used at various points, and all details of construction. Specifications are then written which supplement the drawings, establishing the quality of materials and workmanship, and indicating how the work is to be executed.

## FINANCING

Ordinarily the contractor does not finance construction. Usually he provides only the working capital for current operations either from his own funds or from bank or individual loans. In some cases a pool is made up by the builder and other private investors, with profits being divided and the arrangement dissolved at the completion of a project. In most other manufacturing processes, of course, the producer finances the operation. In the case of construction, however, the owner or developer and the ultimate consumer may both become involved in the financing of production.

### Advances

A fairly typical arrangement is that of the construction loan under which a financing institution agrees to advance funds at various stages of the building process. Upon completion of building, the construction loan is typically supplanted by a mortgage. In other cases the permanent mortgage is recorded and payments are disbursed at various stages of construction. In some cases a commitment is given with provision for merging of short-term construction loans and long-term financing.

### Conditional Commitments

In the case of residential building, the builder usually arranges for individual mortgages for his houses and assigns the mortgage to the purchaser. Many lending institutions engage in construction financing in the hope of securing mortgages. The use of FHA "conditional commitments" to insure loans usually provides the owner or developer with sufficient credit to enable him to finance all or substantial portions of construction. Commitments from the Veterans' Administration for loan guarantees are often used in a similar manner. In some cases lenders may take "a piece of the action" and become part owners.

### Business Properties

Industrial plants are usually financed by the firms which own or intend to use them. Commercial properties may be financed by private investors or by owning or using enterprises. Insurance companies are important in this field. Again, there is often a fusion of construction and long-term financing. Sale and lease-back arrangements have been used widely as a method of financing commercial properties.

## Equities

Some larger financial institutions now develop properties and rent them. In such cases they finance the entire operation from start to finish. In other cases they take "a piece of the action" on a variety of bases.

## Cumbersome Processes

Except for the latter type of arrangement, most of the financing of construction is cumbersome. This is due chiefly to the fact that the property rather than the credit of the developer or contractor is the principal security. Laborers and subcontractors are protected by mechanics' liens, an arrangement which also reflects this situation. Thus, financial institutions can exert great influence on construction operations because of their dominant position in providing the necessary credit advances.

## BUILDING OPERATIONS

Generally speaking, building operations fall into two categories: (1) those accomplished by a builder-developer-contractor employing an architect or a designer either on a fee basis or as a member of his staff; and (2) those accomplished by an individual who lets the work to a contractor but employs an architect to administer the contract for the owner, as in the case of a custom-built house project.

## Bids

Bids are usually invited from several general contractors, although contracts may be let without competitive bidding. If bids are invited, the contract is normally awarded to the lowest bidder, unless his figure is so low that there is doubt about his ability to do a satisfactory job. Bids may be taken on the following bases:

1. A fixed price for the entire project.
2. Cost plus a percentage for profit (usually 10 per cent).
3. Cost plus a profit percentage, say 10 per cent, but with a maximum limit established.
4. Cost plus a percentage with a maximum upper limit, with provision for dividing any savings between contractor and developer.
5. Cost plus a fixed fee.

Other methods may be used as well, but the above arrangements are typical. The fixed price method is used very widely. Contracts for mechanical work may be let separately with a general contract covering the rest of the project.

A single contract may be awarded to a general contractor, or various contracts may be let for specific parts of the project. If the former plan is followed, the general contractor typically parcels out certain phases of the work among subcontractors. In the case of some large projects, all of the work may be sublet. In either event, the construction process is seldom carried out by a single organization.

### Division of Work

The general contractor usually reserves for himself such work as he is equipped to handle. This may be excavating, putting in foundations, masonry, carpentry, or other work. Figure 15–1 illustrates some of the interrelationships in building operations.

The types of work for which subcontractors may be used include roofing, plumbing, lathing, painting, tiling, heating, electricity, and structural iron work. A subcontractor may be a building supply jobber or dealer, but more frequently such suppliers sell materials to the general contractor or to one or more subcontractors. Many materials are originally processed by building supply manufacturers, who sell them directly to contractors or through supply dealers. Restrictive practices sometimes surround these operations, as we shall see in a later section.

### Work Force

After all contractual agreements have been arranged and provision has been made for the required materials, the necessary labor force is hired and the actual work of construction is carried out. Many different types of labor are required even in the construction of a single-family dwelling. From twenty-five to forty-five crafts may be involved in relatively simple house-building operations. As many as eighty occupational groups may be engaged in a large-scale building project. Because of the complexity of the building process many organizations are using programmed evaluation and review techniques, usually referred to as PERT. This is a process for using the computer to plan and control the building operation in a way which enables the most advantageous route or "critical path" to be followed in completing the process. Through these methods the various efforts involved can be coordinated in the most effective way.

Because of the high degree of organization typical of building labor, the contractor and subcontractors frequently arrange for the necessary labor through a union official. Since the degree of labor organization varies from city to city, workers are sometimes hired directly. Contractors seldom maintain anything resembling a permanent work force, although a skeleton organization may move from job to job. Usually other laborers are recruited as needed for each job.

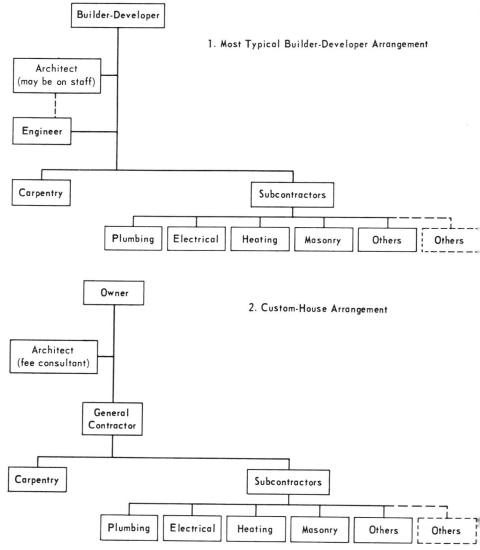

**Fig. 15–1.**   Organization of building operations.

It has been estimated that skilled labor accounts for more than 70 per cent of all building labor. This is due in part to the fact that many workers are classified as "skilled" even though they may not perform skilled operations.

## Completion

The building process is completed when the owner or developer accepts the structure as finished and final payments have been made. The period between the letting of contracts and the completion of construction may be as short as several weeks in the case of prefrabricated operations. It may cover several months or even a year or two or longer for large projects.

## BUILDING COSTS

Except for such prefabrication of structural parts or equipment as takes place, the "manufacturing" of a building occurs at the site. Hence, costs vary with local situations.

### Architects' Fees

Architects' fees usually are 6 to 8 per cent of the cost of a structure, except on very small projects where the percentage is higher. Fees vary with services performed. When an architect performs "full services" and handles the job for a client, a fee of 8 to 10 per cent may be quite reasonable. In some cases an architect may be engaged on the basis of a one-time development cost plus royalties if the designs are to be repeated. A 1 to 1½ percentage of cost may be a reasonable fee in such cases.

### Local Variations

Building costs vary widely between localities because of differences in the local availability of materials and resulting transportation costs. Furthermore, building costs vary greatly due to differences in climate. Not only do insulating and heating costs vary greatly from one part of the country to another, but so do the requirements for foundations, glazing, roofing, and many other items.

### Materials Distribution

The contractor may buy his materials and supplies in several ways. Usually the channels for distributing building materials are similar to those of many other products: from manufacturer to wholesaler or jobber to retailer and then to the consumer, who in this instance, however, is represented by the contractor.

In some cases manufacturers maintain control of the distribution process down through the retailing level; in others they sell to wholesalers who distribute through their subsidiaries or sell to independent dealers. The typical lumber dealer generally handles a wide variety of materials, though usually there are separate dealers in hardware, paint, wallpaper, and similar items. Plumbing materials, linoleum, tile, heating equipment, and electric wiring often are installed by local dealers. Larger builders, however, may absorb these functions.

Although the dealer serves the contractor in numerous ways, such as maintaining his inventory for him and frequently promoting business and helping to arrange financing, there are numerous instances of special arrangements which favor the more substantial builders or which limit in various ways the introduction of certain new products into a local market.

### Labor Costs and Efficiency

All types of labor in the building trades usually receive high wages on an hourly or daily basis. Approximately half of the cost of most structures is required to pay the labor bill. Because the degree of labor organization varies widely from locality to locality, there are wide differences in labor costs.

The actual cost of materials in place depends upon the efficiency of labor. When building is at low ebb, bricklayers tend to lay more brick than when jobs are plentiful. Some contractors, subcontract all or nearly all work, putting it on a price basis; and the resulting in-place costs are often low even though the weekly wages of workers on such projects are among the highest in the building trades.

### Other Costs

Other expenditures typically incurred in the usual construction project include costs of construction loans; building permits; workmen's compensation; liability, unemployment, and other types of insurance; social security taxes; sales taxes; contractors' overhead; and the maintenance of equipment. In some instances the payment of "side money" and bonuses represents substantial amounts.

## LARGE-SCALE PRODUCTION OPERATIONS

Significant advances have been made in the application of standardization and large-scale production methods to the building industry. There are three principal types of developments which are tending toward the industrialization of building. They are (1) simplification and standardization of parts by manufacturers; (2) adaptation of factory methods to production at the site by large-scale contractors and builders; and (3) prefabrication of virtually complete structures for assembly at the site. Two main types may be identified: panelized structures and modular structures.

A number of preparatory operations are now carried on away from the site with manufacturers preparing precut lumber, roof framing, stairs, pre-hung doors and windows, cabinets, and similar items. In addition, much equipment assembly is completed prior to delivery to the site.

## Simplification and Standardization

Standardization of house plans and designs has been progressing for some time and has brought economies through reduction in costs of design and increased efficiency of labor. The standardization of plans,

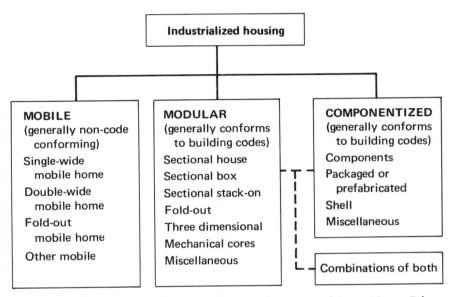

**Fig. 15–2.** Industrial housing. (Source: *Savings and Loan News*, February, 1971.)

designs, and materials, as well as more manufacturing of parts away from the site, has brought economies to nearly all types of builders. In addition, large-scale builders have adapted factory methods to production at the site. Industrialized housing firms manufacture virtually complete units for assembly.

## On-Site Factory Methods

Large-scale builders now arrange for workers to move from one operation to another, organizing the work with a relatively high degree of efficiency as in a factory operation. In part, this has been made possible by the introduction of a number of laborsaving devices including power excavating, grading, and hoisting machinery; electric saws and drills; concrete, mortar, and plaster mixes; spray guns for paint; and power sanders. The introduction of some of these laborsaving devices, however, has been resisted by the unions, as has the use of precut and prefabricated materials which are delivered to the site for assembly.

### Prefabrication

Prefabrication has made significant progress in the recent years. Economies of substantial proportions have been achieved both in production and distribution processes. Great progress has also been made in purchasing materials and equipment on a large scale for assembly in factories and delivery as a more or less complete package. Prefabrication has probably led to greater mechanization of traditional building processes as well, not only for houses but also for large-scale projects such as office buildings. It has also helped to stimulate the use of "modular" methods of production.

With the solution of various manufacturing problems, greater emphasis is being given to the marketing and financing of prefabricated houses. Prefabrication has gained wide acceptance. Prefabricated houses including mobile homes now dominate the small-house field. Many local building codes do not now exclude prefabricated houses. They create numerous problems, however, for mobile home developments. Sometimes union rules tend to cancel the economies resulting from improved production methods.

### Marketing Practices of Prefabricators

Local dealer representatives are one method of marketing prefabricated homes. Similar arrangements are typical of the mobile home field. This permits local acquisition of land and the utilization of and adaptation to local labor and supply conditions. It also aids in the developing of local sources of financing. Future developments in the production process and in distribution will depend to a large extent on whether financing arrangements will meet the requirements of this industry.

Specific arrangements for local dealerships vary widely. Some manufacturers control them very closely, and others have rather informal working relationships with their dealers. Integrating of manufacturer and local dealer activities is especially important in connection with advertising and sales promotional campaigns. Another arrangement is the company owned dealership. The parent company in such cases controls the entire process from factory through financing and sale to the ultimate buyer. This arrangement has some advantages but may or may not have local connections as in the case of an independent builder-dealer.

One of the major problems of local dealers or company owned dealerships in the housing industry arises from the fact that land cannot be prefabricated. As we saw in the preceding chapter, the costs of acquiring and developing land are often very great. Sometimes the financial requirements for land development are beyond the resources of local dealers and beyond their ability to command the necessary credit through traditional channels. Hence, some house manufacturers have established special financial programs to assist local dealers in their programs of acquiring and developing land.

### Mobile Homes

Some builders and developers have made use of mobile homes in recent years. Many types are 14 feet wide and have a length of 60 feet or more. Limitations are imposed by highway regulations for moving mobile units. These vary widely. In some cases two units are combined on a "double wide" basis. Some combined units contain as many as two baths and four bedrooms.

Specialized manufacturers have developed in this field including Skyline, Fleetwood, National and others. Large scale plants provide efficient production methods. Assembly usually includes major appliances and furniture. Thus, when delivered a unit is ready for almost immediate occupancy.

There are usually local retail outlets selling directly to the public. Mobile home park developers provide parking spaces usually on a monthly rental basis. Frequently these developers are local people; in some cases building organizations go into this field and operate on a wide basis. In some cases mobile home parks are very attractive and carefully planned and developed; in others the parks leave much to be desired.

Mobile homes have been popular in part because they are classified as personal property and carry personal rather than real property taxes. Financing usually can be arranged without difficulty even in tight money periods although the rates are usually high.

## BUILDING INDUSTRY TRENDS

Despite its problems the building industry has made progress in a number of directions in recent years. Of special importance are advances in (1) technology, (2) engineering and architecture, and (3) management. Problems persist, however, in a number of areas including labor, materials distribution, and government-business relationships.

## Technology

Technological advances include the development of new products, improved uses of old products, and more efficient production methods resulting from new machinery, prefabrication, and modular construction. Product changes range all the way from better heating and lighting equipment, air conditioning, and cooking and other kitchen equipment to improved uses of glass, better insulation, and the use of aluminum covering for exteriors. Technology may soon give us even better basic systems of construction, improved finishes for both interior and exterior application and such mechanical devices as automatic cleaning equipment, luminous walls, and "instant cooking." Even the sewerless toilet may not be too many years away.

## Engineering and Architecture

Engineering and architectural advances include improved space planning, more efficient layout of buildings, better combination of building materials, and many related developments. Even houses in the lower price ranges have been given the benefit of good architectural design and planning.

## Management

Management has improved the processes of planning, organizing, and controlling operations. Longer-range planning has characterized the activities of subdividers and builders. Seasonal fluctuations have been reduced by careful scheduling of work so as to allow for colder weather operations. The increased diversity of materials and products used in construction has necessitated better managerial planning and scheduling. Many builders have been able to improve their organizational arrangements through better division of work and more effective supervision. The use of PERT and related "critical path" methods has been widespread. Controls have improved in part because of rising costs and in part because of tax considerations. Inventory controls have been improved in the construction industry but also there have been advances in inspections, in cost accounting, and in budgeting.

## Restrictions

As competition has grown more intense, greater emphasis has been placed on improved products and methods and on cost cutting. The industry continues to suffer from restrictive building codes, restrictive labor practices, and from its dependence on the development of regional supporting facilities by government to allow for new land development. Many builders, of course, continue to follow outmoded practices. Informal agreements sometimes result in price fixing and the reduction of competition.

Because of restrictive practices, the introduction of new products and methods often is retarded. There has been some tendency to revise building codes in order to introduce greater flexibility, but many localities follow requirements that are unduly restrictive. Building operations have been limited by the slow pace of many local governments and other agencies.

Although problems persist, the building industry can take credit for significant advances in recent years. It holds numerous opportunities for young people who have energy, imagination, and a willingness to pioneer. Government has made special efforts through such programs as "Operation Breakthrough" of the Department of Housing and Urban Development. Government financing programs have improved and expanded. Special attention has been devoted to the problem of low income housing.

## Labor Organizations

Building labor is highly organized in most cities. Many organizations continue to follow craft rather than industrial lines. Jurisdictional disputes are among the more difficult problems of the building industry and at least some of these would be eliminated if labor were organized on a different basis.

The attitudes of labor unions in the building trades have tended to retard the introduction of laborsaving machinery and devices. There has also been insistence that production be limited to prescribed speeds. Featherbedding rules are common. While one can hardly blame the individual worker for resisting the introduction of laborsaving machinery and for not wanting to work himself out of a job, union leaders have often been slow to recognize that these policies are shortsighted and not in the ultimate interests of the workers. In the long run, the earnings of workers are limited by their productivity. Laborsaving devices aid in the process of increasing output per worker. If this were not the case, China and India would have the highest wage levels in the world, since they have few laborsaving devices in use and the proportion of labor to capital employed in production is high.

The building trades have succeeded in establishing high hourly or daily wage scales. In part this is an attempt to compensate for seasonal and cyclical variations in construction activity, and in part it is the result of a high degree of labor organization and the strategic position of building labor which enables it to enforce its demands.

Limitations on the number of apprentices who are trained, the relatively disorganized condition of some employers, the small scale of a number of building operations, and the policies of trade-unions in resisting the introduction of laborsaving devices all help to explain the success of labor organizations. Not only are wage scales high, they are relatively inflexible downward. Even during recession periods, wage rates tend to be maintained at high levels. Productivity of workers, however, tends to increase in such periods.

It is probable that considerable benefit would result from a more flexible wage scale, both for labor and for the builder and consumer. It may be that some form of annual wage arrangement is the answer to these problems. The nature of employment in the building trades, however, with laborers moving from one job to another as projects are finished, is a real obstacle to the establishment of an annual wage.

Improved labor relations would be highly beneficial to the construction industry. Ordinarily the number of wage disputes is higher in this field than in most others, and the elimination of some of the lost time and the added risks which result would benefit worker and employer alike.

## Materials Distribution Problems

The materials distribution system now results in highly competitive pricing. The emergence of "cash and carry" lumberyards and builder-dealer merchandising connections contribute to the intensity of competition. Because of his dominant position in many local communities, the materials dealer must be reckoned with by manufacturers and builders alike. In some cases dealers organize and establish more or less fixed prices and working agreements, thus reducing competition. The combination of the functions of dealer and builder in the prefabricated house industry has broadened competition.

Construction materials dealers serve building contractors in a number of ways. They may help with inventory problems, in promoting business and sometimes with short term financing.

## Government and Building

As we have suggested, the building codes of a number of cities make excessive requirements and hinder the introduction of new structural materials. In addition there are fire-prevention, elevator, and related codes, as well as occupancy regulations. Codes are seldom changed as often as necessary to keep abreast of industrial developments. Also, the administration of building codes frequently leaves something to be desired. Progress toward performance codes is being made, however, and significant improvement may be expected in the years ahead.

Licensing laws for architects, contractors, engineers, and even work-men in certain building trades are in force in a number of states. While their objectives are desirable, they often lead to restraints and virtually monopolistic practices. The property standards and minimum construc-tion requirements set up by the FHA have had desirable effects, but have also added to the regulatory problems faced by the building industry. The Federal government has influenced building through improvement of fi-nancing practices as a result of the work of the Federal Home Loan Bank System, and the Federal Home Loan Mortgage Corporation (Freddy Mac), the Federal Housing Administration, the Veterans' Administration, the Government National Mortgage Association, and the Federal National Mortgage Association. The Bureau of Standards has helped to develop and improve materials as well as to establish better criteria for judging the performance of materials. The Department of Commerce (especially the Bureau of the Census) and the Federal Home Loan Bank System have prepared much information about housing markets. The Department of Housing and Urban Development through its "Operation Breakthrough" program has attempted to stimulate innovation.

Limited progress has been made in eliminating restrictive and monop-olistic practices in the building industry. Local zoning laws and city plan-ning regulations affect building activities, and local tax burdens must be reckoned with constantly. The laws governing the sale, transfer and mar-keting of new real estate developments often are not adapted to present-day requirements.

## Place of the Building Industry in the National Economy

The building industry is one of our largest, and is mainly responsible for the quantity and quality of our real estate resources. A number of other industries are dependent wholly or partially on building, such as lumber, cement, steel, brick, building stone, glass, hardware, and others. The solution of many of our housing problems must await improvements in the building industry. Building activity is one of the main determinants of prosperity and is an important index of general business conditions. Because of the importance of the industry in our economy, great advan-tages would result from improvement in the efficiency of its operations and from a lessening of the cyclical and seasonal fluctuations to which it has been subject in past years.

A statement prepared by John L. Schmidt and Arthur S. Goldman summarizes some of the major changes that are going on in the build-ing industry, particularly as it relates to housing. Among other state-ments, the following is especially significant.

American home building has progressed more in the last decade than it did during the first 50 years of the 20th Century. But even though we today enjoy

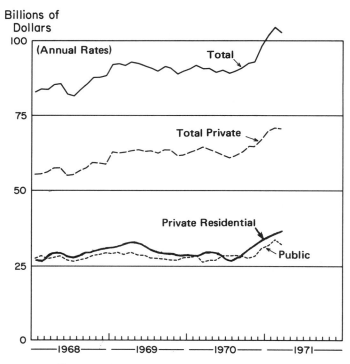

**Fig. 15–3.** New construction expenditures.

the highest standard of housing in the world, we still stand at the threshold of a whole new era of better housing. We stand at this threshold today, but we have not crossed it because technology is far, far ahead of practice.

Admittedly, successful home builders are introducing new materials and new building methods. But still, home building remains the most fragmented industry in the country, one that is hamstrung by zoning ordinances, building codes, labor difficulties and the inertia of habit. The result—a gap between what architects and engineers know *how* to do and what builders are *permitted* to do.

The gap between knowledge and practice also is widened by the paradox of poor public acceptance. Here we find a typical house buyer who "demands" newer, better and more economical methods and materials, yet one who tends to label new and better materials or methods as "cheap or flimsy substitutes." But one thing is encouraging—the search for cost savings. The search for cost savings is probably home building's greatest motivation to change; we can be thankful that this is a never-ending search.

The attack on costs during the next 10 years will focus on the untapped potential efficiencies of conventional construction and on development of other systems of building.

How and in what ways will this attack on building costs take place? We can expect significant changes on three fronts: The ways we use land; the methods used in construction; and the quality and character of design.[1]

## The Building Industry's Industrial Revolution

The large amount of experimentation going on in the building industry may be comparable to the experiences of other industries during the earlier phases of their industrial revolutions. As a result of this experimentation, the building industry has already taken on quite a different appearance in the past decade or so. This is probably the most important reason for optimism in regard to the potentialities of this field.

As Lyle C. Bryant has pointed out,

Industrial revolutions are never accomplished overnight. As we look back over industrial history, however, the striking fact is that almost every industry has had its "revolution," each heralded by a period of seething unrest and experimentation much like what we see in the building industry today.[2]

### SUMMARY

The building process consists of the planning, financing, and construction of buildings upon improved land. Land development and building operations often are combined. Construction firms range in size from very small to very large builders. Construction is a risky business, involving substantial sums of money.

Almost anyone with savings or credit may initiate a building project, whether he is an individual desiring a residence or a large operative builder. Whether the project is a single residence or an entire community, it must be planned, financed, and constructed. Various specialized parties such as architects, contractors, and subcontractors are involved in the physical operation, while financing usually is arranged through one or another type of financial institution. Decisions about construction are made primarily by property owners and developers, subject to the veto of lenders and the influence of various specialists, notably architects and engineers.

In recent years, the building industry has realized advances in technology, engineering and architecture, and management. Of particular importance have been the development of simplification and standardization, the use of factory methods of production at the building site, and prefabrication of materials for assembly at the site. Materials distribution,

---

[1] John L. Schmidt and Arthur S. Goldman, "Design and Construction Advances Need Lender Support," *Savings and Loan News* (September, 1963), p. 67. Revised, 1971.

[2] Lyle C. Bryant, unpublished manuscript.

governmental factors, and labor relations remain as critical problem areas. In labor, extensive organization of the building trades into many different craft unions, and the instability of employer-employee relationships have tended to result in jurisdictional disputes, featherbedding, and resistance to technological advance. Significant changes may be anticipated in methods of using land and carrying out construction as well as in quality and character of design.

## QUESTIONS FOR STUDY

1. What are the main processes involved in the development of new real estate resources?
2. Describe the principal steps in planning for the construction of a single-family residence. Would the planning be any different in the case of an apartment building?
3. What are the two principal types of building operations in terms of the role of the architect?
4. Can you suggest ways in which the financing of building construction might be improved?
5. What is the relationship of the subcontractor to the contractor? Why does the contractor sublet parts of his contract?
6. Why do building costs vary between regions of the country?
7. Explain the important advantages of prefabrication and modular construction; the main advantages of large-scale on-site construction.
8. Indicate ways in which the marketing practices of prefabricated housing manufacturers differ from those of other builders.
9. If you bought a mobile home, you would be getting a considerably different product than if you bought a house. Describe the differences in both the product and the transactions involved.
10. How might labor practices in the building industry be improved?
11. Would you favor the establishment of an annual wage in the building industry? Why or why not?
12. What are the principal advantages of building codes? In what ways may building codes hinder construction activities?
13. Outline the principal current trends in the building industry. What are the principal changes that appear to lie ahead?

## SUGGESTED READINGS

KRATOVIL, ROBERT. *Real Estate Law* (5th ed.). Englewood Cliffs, N.J.: Prentice-Hall, Inc., 1969. Chap. xxii.

NATIONAL COMMISSION ON URBAN PROBLEMS. *Building the American City* (The Douglas Report.) Washington, D.C.: U. S. Government Printing Office, 1968. Part V, Chaps. 1, 2.

THE PRESIDENT'S COMMITTEE ON URBAN HOUSING. *A Decent Home* (The Kaiser Report). Washington, D.C.: U. S. Government Printing Office, 1968. Pp. 113–22.

NEWCOMBE, ROBINSON. *Mobile Home Parks,* Technical Bulletin 66. Washington, D.C.: Urban Land Institute, 1971.
U. S. SAVINGS AND LOAN LEAGUE. *Construction Lending Guide.* Chicago: The League, 1964.

## CASE 15–1

### Housing Corporation Considers Expansion

Housing Corporation has 20 years experience in the home building industry. The company's principal operation is the manufacturing of house components which are then sold to franchised builders. This activity had been the basis for the company's growth. In addition, Housing Corporation also has a large mortgage banking capability and a division experienced in the on-site construction of both single family and multi-family homes. In 1967, Housing Corporation sales were just over $50,000,000 and after-tax earnings were just under $500,000.

In 1968, Housing Corporation had completed its fourth consecutive quarter in which the earnings for that quarter exceeded the earnings for the prior corresponding quarter. Management was convinced that this strong earnings trend was likely to continue for a number of years into the future. Principally as a result of its earnings performance, the price of the company's stock advanced considerably with respect to most other issues in its industry. The price earnings ratio was well above 30 times earnings.

With this in mind, the company undertook a modest acquisition program with some general criteria.

1. Any acquisition must be profitable and have been profitable.
2. All acquisitions should either expand the company's current activities or enter new areas within the shelter industry.
3. The management of the acquired company must be willing to stay after the acquisitions and must be capable of continuing the prior rate of growth.
4. The acquisition must be done for stock and preferably as a pooling of interest.
5. No major capital investment should be required beyond the ability of the acquired company to finance itself.
6. The acquired company must be of significant size relative to Housing Corporation.

By the summer of 1968, Housing Corporation had made one major acquisition—a mobile home company with four plants. In the fall of 1968, another acquisition opportunity was presented to Housing Corporation. This was Riverview Estates.

Riverview Estates began in 1958. The company's only business activity was to develop a substantial resort retirement community on a large lake about 30 miles from a medium sized city in a southern state. The climate in this area was substantially superior to the north but still had four seasons, including a brief and generally mild winter season.

Riverview was the successor to a group originally formed to develop this parcel of ground with a view toward one acre tracts with relatively expensive homes to be occupied primarily for retirement or second home use. Initial sales in the 1961–1965 period were largely for cash with 1-acre tracts selling for $1,000 to $2,000; 107 lots were sold during this period. Many of the better view lots were sold and a number of very fine residences built. The original developer promised the lot purchasers that water would be available and that he would grade and pave the roads.

However, the original developer became over-extended and when his sales program did not meet expectations, he was unable to continue the project.

Riverview acquired the land in 1965 and commenced an aggressive program bringing customers from cities within a 200-mile radius to the development and selling the lots to these purchasers with low down payments (generally 10 per cent or less) with the balance financed over a 10 to 15-year period. The lots were sold on contract so that if a customer failed to keep monthly payments current the lot could be repossessed rather than foreclosed. The legal maximum interest rate for land contract sales was charged. In addition, Riverview agreed to provide the developments promised by the original developer and in addition to establish a community center, camping facilities, golf course, etc.

Because Riverview was undercapitalized, its management made arrangement with Land Investment Co. to assist in financing. Land Investment advanced Riverview 50 per cent of the unpaid balance of any contract provided it approved the credit worthiness of the purchaser. Land Investment charged Riverview the same interest on its advances that it received from the contract purchaser. Thus, Riverview had no cash outflow for interest. Lot prices were increased to a range of $1,500 to $3,000. The proceeds received from Land Investment were used to provide the marketing services, sales commissions and with a balance available for improvements, land mortgage payments and general overhead.

There was an increase in the sale activity but not enough acceptable sales were made to insure Riverview of the ability to meet its land mortgage payments.

Accordingly Riverview entered into an agreement with Nationwide Salesmen, Inc., to provide for a better marketing organization. Nationwide Salesmen, which was a new organization, formed by two experienced land marketing men, agreed to provide a sales organization, advertising and sales promotion efforts, as well as advance a modest sum to initiate promised physical improvements. For their services, Nationwide Salesmen were to receive 45 per cent of the selling price. Because of their previous successful record, Nationwide Salesmen convinced Riverview that if Riverview would maintain a continuous development program, they could increase the selling price of lots from $3,000 to the $6,000 range. Nationwide Salesmen performed very well. Sales increased significantly.

However, Riverview did not fare too well. It received approximately 60 per cent of the selling price and immediately had to pay 45 per cent of the selling price, or 75 per cent of total receipts, to Nationwide Salesmen, which made it difficult for Riverview to meet costs for land mortgage payments, improvements, and overhead. Because of their forceful personalities and their success in holding up their end of the bargain, Nationwide Salesmen, continually pressed Riverview to step up the development program beyond the financial capability of Riverview. Riverview was profitable but its cash flow was not adequate to sustain the business. If the development work could have been postponed until Land Investment had been repaid, then Riverview would have had more than ample funds to meet the promises to the lot purchasers. The situation became untenable for the principal of Riverview and because of its cash position, it elected to sell out.

The projects record at this time was as follows. From 1965–1967, sales averaged about 125 lots each year. Through July of 1968, 260 lots had been sold. This left a potential of about 1,550 lots to be sold during the duration of the project.

In mid-1968, the project included an entrance way, a pool, and 81-slip marina and restaurant, some paved roads in fair condition, a water system, and a campaign area. A golf course had been designed for the area but had not yet been built. Some 40 houses had been constructed.

In addition to its selling capacity in the project with Riverview, Nationwide Salesmen also owned a sizeable development in a northern state. This property included 412 acres with a substantial amount of frontage on a large lake. Roads had already been constructed. There was an estimated 750 lots in the area, of which approximately 75 had been sold. This property also had a boat house, a swimming pool, club house, and several small cottages and other buildings. Nationwide Salesmen also owned 1,500 acres of undeveloped land in a western state.

Financial statements for Housing Corporation, Riverview Estates, and Nationwide Salesmen, Inc., are attached (see following pages).

## Questions

1. Should Housing Corporation acquire Riverview community?
2. Should Housing Corporation acquire Nationwide Salesmen, Inc.?
3. What price should be paid for any acquisition that is recommended?

## STATEMENT OF FINANCIAL POSITION—June 30, 197_

(Amounts in thousands)

| | Housing Corporation | | Riverview Estates | | Nationwide Salesmen, Inc. | |
|---|---|---|---|---|---|---|
| | 1968 | 1967 | 1968 | 1967 | 1968 | 1967 |
| **ASSETS** | | | | | | |
| Current Assets: | | | | | | |
| Cash | $ 2,793 | $ 1,936 | $ 20 | $ 15 | $ 36 | $ — |
| Receivables | 15,984 | 14,670 | 130 | 55 | 397 | — |
| Inventories | 16,570 | 10,958 | 170 | 99 | 334 | — |
| Prepaid expenses | 484 | 604 | — | — | — | — |
| | 35,831 | 28,168 | 320 | 169 | 767 | — |
| Investments and Other Assets: | | | | | | |
| Subsidiaries not consolidated—at equity in underlying net assets | 8,245 | 7,838 | — | — | — | — |
| Land held and notes receivable on land sales | 12,189 | 12,198 | 570 | 150 | 54 | — |
| Other | 2,369 | 2,515 | 35 | 30 | 4 | — |
| | 22,803 | 22,551 | 605 | 180 | 58 | — |
| Property, Plant and Equipment: | | | | | | |
| Net of depreciation | 7,547 | 8,052 | 170 | 126 | 356 | — |
| | $66,181 | $58,771 | $ 1,095 | $ 475 | $ 1,181 | $ — |

## LIABILITIES AND SHAREHOLDERS' INVESTMENT

| | | | | | | |
|---|---:|---:|---:|---:|---:|---:|
| Current Liabilities: | | | | | | |
| Payables and accrued expenses | $ 7,138 | $ 3,154 | $ 445 | $ 92 | $ 289 | $ — |
| Current installments on long-term debt | 923 | 786 | 254 | 130 | 95 | — |
| | 8,061 | 3,940 | 699 | 222 | 384 | — |
| Long-Term Debt: | | | | | | |
| 5¾% Subordinated convertible debentures | 14,554 | 15,000 | — | — | — | — |
| 6% Notes payable | 3,358 | 3,637 | — | — | — | — |
| Other | 2,019 | 1,088 | 444 | 460 | 714 | — |
| | 19,931 | 19,725 | 444 | 460 | 714 | — |
| Shareholders' Investment: | | | | | | |
| Capital stock | 2,417 | 2,362 | 150 | 150 | — | — |
| Capital surplus | 11,125 | 10,416 | 33 | 33 | — | — |
| Retained earnings | 24,829 | 22,478 | ( 231) | ( 390) | 83 | — |
| | 38,371 | 35,256 | ( 48) | ( 207) | 83 | — |
| Less: Treasury stock | 182 | 150 | — | — | — | — |
| | 38,189 | 35,106 | ( 48) | ( 207) | 83 | — |
| | $66,181 | $58,771 | $ 1,095 | $ 475 | $ 1,181 | $ — |

## STATEMENT OF EARNINGS—For Six Months Ended June 30, 197_

(Amounts in thousands)

| | Housing Corporation | | Riverview Estates | | Nationwide Salesmen, Inc. | |
|---|---|---|---|---|---|---|
| | 1968 | 1967 | 1968 | 1967 | 1968 | 1967 |
| Revenue | $30,266 | $22,535 | $ 1,173 | $ 203 | $ 537 | $ — |
| Cost of sales | 24,849 | 18,422 | 168 | 62 | — | — |
| Operating expenses | 3,442 | 3,933 | 729 | 158 | 404 | — |
| | 28,291 | 22,355 | 897 | 220 | 404 | — |
| Operating profit | 1,975 | 180 | 276 | ( 17) | 133 | — |
| Financing subsidiaries earnings | 678 | 553 | — | — | — | — |
| Earnings before federal income tax | 2,653 | 733 | 276 | ( 17) | 133 | — |
| Provision for federal income tax | 1,326 | 389 | 141 | ( 9) | 69 | — |
| Earnings for the period | 1,327 | 344 | 135 | ( 8) | 64 | — |
| Retained earnings of prior periods | 23,502 | 22,134 | ( 366) | ( 382) | 19 | — |
| Retained earnings at end of period | $24,829 | $22,478 | $( 231) | $( 390) | $ 83 | $ — |

## CASH FLOW STATEMENT—For Six Months Ended June 30, 197_

### (Amounts in thousands)

| | Housing Corporation | | Riverview Estates | | Nationwide Salesmen, Inc. | |
|---|---|---|---|---|---|---|
| | 1968 | 1967 | 1968 | 1967 | 1968 | 1967 |
| Cash generated from operations: | | | | | | |
| Net income | $ 1,327 | $ 344 | $ 135 | $( 8) | $ 64 | $ — |
| Depreciation | 731 | 738 | 12 | 9 | 17 | — |
| | 2,058 | 1,082 | 147 | 1 | 81 | — |
| Other source and application of cash: | | | | | | |
| Trade payable and expense accruals | 1,493 | ( 688) | 309 | 94 | 244 | — |
| Long term debt | 1,122 | 234 | 28 | 20 | 5 | — |
| Receivables | (1,029) | ( 129) | 32 | — | ( 300) | — |
| Lot sales contracts | — | — | ( 433) | ( 60) | — | — |
| Plant and equipment | ( 429) | ( 537) | ( 38) | ( 40) | ( 10) | — |
| Land acquired and development costs | (2,620) | ( 405) | ( 191) | ( 72) | — | — |
| Land used or sold | 927 | 344 | 168 | 62 | 16 | — |
| Inventories | (3,084) | ( 289) | — | — | — | — |
| Financing subsidiaries | ( 325) | ( 265) | — | — | — | — |
| Other assets | 551 | ( 252) | ( 2) | — | ( 6) | — |
| Other cash received (used) | (3,394) | (1,987) | ( 127) | 4 | ( 51) | — |
| Net cash (used) generated from operations | $(1,336) | $( 905) | $ 20 | 5 | $ 30 | $ — |

## STUDY PROJECT 15-1

### An Overview of the Housing Industry *

Is it possible for American housing producers to build and rehabilitate a total of 2.6 million housing units a year? Does the economy have the resources —business skills, trained manpower, capital, land, technical ability—for such a large expansion of housing production?

Can American housing be produced more efficiently? Are there new ways to build houses more quickly and more cheaply?

A summary of the answers to these questions about American housing production is assayed in a brief overview.

**The Distinct Features of the Housing Industry.** The "housing industry"— defined here to include all firms which share in the receipts of expenditures for housing—is one of the most complex in the American economy. The firms which perform the critical function of putting together the finished housing unit make up the heart of the industry. These home assemblers include home-builders, contractors, home manufacturers (and their dealers) and mobile home producers. These firms procure their materials from an extraordinary range of building products manufacturers, from tiny millwork plants to some of the nation's largest corporations. Distribution of these materials from man-ufacturer to assembler is carried out primarily by specialized wholesalers and retailers—lumberyards and hardware stores, for example. Acquisition and preparation of land for the ultimate construction of housing commonly involves real estate brokers, lawyers, title insurance companies, surveyors, and civil engineers, and possibly land planners and landscape architects. Engineers and architects are sometimes involved in design. Much on-site construction work is characteristically performed by specialty subcontractors; painting, plumbing, and electrical work, for example. Financing, needed both by the builders to complete construction and development and by buyers to finance purchase of completed units, is available through a battery of lending institutions. Opera-tion of apartments may involve superintendents or management firms. Main-tenance of housing adds to the cast of characters—for example, repairmen, janitors, remodeling firms, and domestic workers.

Thus, the housing industry is made up of literally millions of business en-terprises. Most are small and specialized, and competition throughout the industry is characteristically fierce. It is incorrect to speak of the need to in-volve private enterprise in housing production; the housing industry is already one of the most important parts of the private enterprise system.

The housing industry has extremely ill-defined boundaries. Many building and contracting firms are involved not only in housing but in other kinds of light construction. Lenders and real estate brokers who service this industry do much of their business in other areas. Producers and distributors of mate-

---

* An excerpt from The Kaiser Report, of the President's Committee on Urban Housing, *A Decent Home* (Washington, D.C.: U.S. Government Printing Office, 1968), pp. 113–17.

rials tend to serve the entire construction market, rather than to specialize in residential construction. Craftsmen and laborers may be building houses one week, but working on missile silos the next. Significantly, the Bureau of the Census does not consider home building to be an industry at all. For example, the Census counts contractors as part of the construction industry, and merchant homebuilders as part of the real estate industry.

The housing process can be divided into several phases:

First, the preparation phase: potentially developable land is identified and plans are developed.

Second, the production phase: the site is prepared, financing is arranged, and the housing unit is constructed.

Third, the distribution phase: the house or apartment is marketed. This recurs throughout the useful lifetime of the structure.

Fourth, the servicing phase: the housing unit is repaired and maintained. This continues until the end of its economic or physical life.

The participants and the process and the external influences which affect them are graphically illustrated in Fig. 1.

**Housing is the Most Important Consumer Good in the Economy.** Housing, broadly defined, is the premier U.S. consumer good. Americans spend over $100 billion annually to buy, rent, operate and maintain their places of residence. About half goes for direct housing expenditures (such as rents or mortgage payments) and the remaining half for utilities, furniture, domestic help, and other household items. In addition, residential structures and their sites constitute almost one-third of the national wealth: more than one-quarter of new capital investment each year goes into housing.

Most money spent on housing goes to pay for use of existing housing. But new housing is a major expenditure, too. Roughly 10 per cent of the Gross National Product each year is devoted to construction of all kinds; residential buildings are the object of roughly one-third of this amount. Recently the cost of private residential construction has averaged approximately $25 billion per year. About $5 billion of this is spent for additions to and alterations and repairs of existing housing.

The importance of housing in the economy underscores the need for efficient operation. If the cost of building new housing can be cut by 5 per cent (with no corresponding drop in value), this will result in an annual savings in the American economy of $1 billion. Similarly, American consumers would save $1 billion for every 1 per cent reduction in the total cost of owning, renting, and operating their residences.

**A House is an Unusual Product.** Housing's distinctive characteristics require a production and merchandising system unlike those typical in manufacturing.

*Housing is Tied to Land.* The fact that housing developments are inevitably associated with land operations has numerous consequences. Land development has historically been regulated primarily by local governments who typically impose a battery of building and mechanical codes, zoning ordinances, and subdivision regulations on potential builders. The tradition of local regulation of building contributes to the localization of markets. Builders, lend-

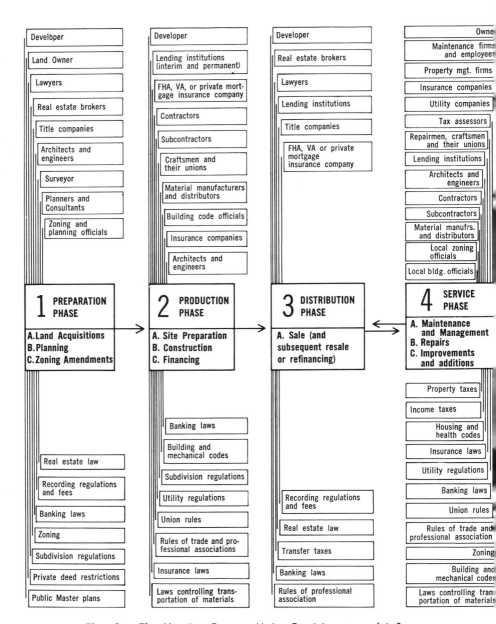

**Fig. 1.** The Housing Process Major Participants and Influences.

ers, and real estate brokers often must learn a new set of rules each time they venture from their home territory. The fact that housing units are immobile also means that their value is heavily influenced by the neighborhood in which they are situated. Builders must be concerned not only with whether the structure itself will appeal to the market, but also with whether there will be any demand for that structure on the sites where it can be built. Its ties to the land leads to housing's transferability being governed by cumbersome and often archaic procedures of real property law.

*Housing is Durable.* A house or apartment building, if structurally sound when built, may last for generations. Repair and replacements can remedy whatever deterioration in materials may occur, and may even forestall market obsolescence. The dominance of the existing stock in the market means that housing production can be deferred for long periods (during wars or depressions, for example). The annual rate of production of new housing can—and does—vary widely. In addition, the durability of housing leads to a level of expenditures for repair and maintenance that is usually high in comparison to most other goods.

*Housing is Bulky.* The sheer size of housing units and their components places strong pressure on the industry to minimize storage costs and handling expenses and to avoid the transportation of major elements where possible. The shipment of three-dimensional prefabricated houses is costly compared to shipment of the unassembled materials. Manufacturers of sectionalized houses, or mobile homes, who assemble materials at a convenient place and then ship the finished product to final site, have been successful primarily where they have not had to compete with modern line-assembly operations on the sites themselves. Many large homebuilders who have studied the problem believe that, if good production management is used, it is usually more efficient to assemble the structures on their sites. On-site assembly requires a complex system of supply of both materials and labor to diverse and shifting locations. The constant shifting of job sites has brought into being rather unique institutions in the construction labor market. The fact that much of the work is done in the open also means that it is vulnerable to daily weather conditions.

*Housing is a Large Expenditure Item.* Housing represents the largest single fraction of most family budgets. As a consequence, both homebuyers and owners of rental units usually make their purchases on credit, characteristically through a loan secured by a mortgage on the property. Housing therefore is tied to the money market and interest rates to a degree far beyond that of any other consumer purchase.

*Housing Comes in Many Varieties.* A housing decision involves numerous smaller decisions. The consumer can choose a single-family unit, as almost 75 per cent of all American households do. If he does, it may be detached, connected to another as a duplex, or connected to many others as a rowhouse. If multi-family housing is preferred, the choice includes, among others, small walk-up apartments, garden apartments, and high-rise elevator buildings. Form of tenure represents another major choice. The housing consumer may choose to own his dwelling (as a solid majority of American family households do), join a cooperative, enjoy ownership in a condominium, or rent his unit over the long term, or on a shorter basis in a hotel or motel. The consumer must also consider space requirements in relation to his prospective residence. A shopper may have strong feelings about style and design. The consumer must also decide what features he wants in his residence—air conditioning, storage space, appliances. Those who design housing units are forced to make decisions on quality at every step in their work. They must choose grades of lumber for shingles, the thickness of gypsum board, the quality of thermal and sound insulation, even the luxuriousness of water faucets and touch plates behind electrical switches.

The consumer's choice of residence might still be rather simple if the only issues were style, size, quality, and form of tenure. Such choices must be made in many other purchases. What makes the housing decision truly complex is that the choice of a unit necessarily involves choice of location. (This is usually true even for mobile homes.) Thus, the consumer is likely to be keenly aware of the quality of neighborhood facilities—schools, shops, parks— and of the transportation problem he will face if he lives in that location. Every location is unique. Buildings which are structurally identical but on different sites may vary widely in their appeal to consumers. The housing producer must not only be concerned that he build an appealing structure, but also that the structure be located in a neighborhood where people will want to live.

The highly individual character of housing demand has forced the housing industry to offer an exceptionally wide range of units. Mass-produced standardized units are often difficult to market because of the variations in consumer demands. In fact, in recent years, over one-third of all new single-family homes have been custom-tailored to the desires of their first occupants. Individuation in the market is increasing. In the early 1950's, large tract builders were able to build and sell thousands of identical units on contiguous parcels. Today, housing consumers are much more discriminating; tract builders now find it necessary to offer a range of models.

**The Housing Industry Is Unique and Complex.** The methods of producing housing have evolved in response to these characteristics of its product. Laymen are inclined to wonder why houses are not produced like automobiles through a highly capitalized, factory assembly-line production process. There are several reasons; one is that factory assembly has often proved to be more expensive than on-site assembly, because of high overhead and transportation costs. Much can be done to improve the efficiency of housing production, but even a high-technology housing industry might have little in common with assembly-line manufacturing industries.

With the major exception of the mobile home industry (and to a lesser extent the home manufacturing industry) the present characteristics of the housing industry are these:

*Localization.* The fact that housing is tied to land and locally regulated has meant that most builders, real estate brokers, and mortgage lenders (at least savings and loan associations) restrict their activities to rather small geographical areas. Only a handful of homebuilders look for nationwide market possibilities.

*Fragmentation.* The variety of the housing product has led to fragmentation of the industry into an elaborate complex of interlocking producing units. Different structures require different combinations of skills. Thus, the industry tends to work through *ad hoc* arrangements for each specific job. The practice of subcontracting, which is prevalent in the industry, is not necessarily irrational, and in fact, is often an efficient response to the need to meet many specialized demands. It is not clear whether greater vertical integration in the industry—that is, permanent alignment of a broader range of skills under the umbrella of a larger organization—would greatly increase efficiency in production. One clearly adverse result of fragmentation, however, has been an inadequate amount of research and development.

Trade associations have evolved to diminish the effect of this fragmentation. For example, in addition to providing technical services to its members, the National Association of Homebuilders has been effectively involved in the councils of government on housing policy, economic issues and other questions affecting the housing industry.

*Lack of Size.* With the major exception of some building materials manufacturers and a few distributors and lending institutions, most firms involved in the production and distribution of housing are relatively small. Smallness is characteristic not only of most builders, contractors, and subcontractors, but also of architectural and engineering firms, real estate brokers, and real estate management and maintenance firms. The smallness of these firms results primarily from the industry's localized and fragmented nature. There are, however, additional reasons for the smallness and light capitalization of construction firms. The rate of housing production is rather erratic, both on a national basis, and especially in each local market. The main causes of this instability are seasonal fluctuations in production (which now seem to be based mainly on tradition in as much as winter protection has been demonstrated to be completely feasible), the sensitivity of the industry to the supply of credit, and the dominance of the existing stock in the market. The erratic rate of output forces construction firms to try to keep their continuing overhead to a minimum, thus discouraging capital investment and assembly of large central staffs.

*Dependence on Outsiders.* The firms which make up the heart of the industry—primarily homebuilders and contractors—are dependent on larger enterprises not primarily engaged in housing. They are usually too small to bargain on an equal basis with the larger firms on the periphery of the industry. Thus financial institutions probably constitute the single most important locus of power in the industry. Builders and contractors have little influence over the rate of technological development in the industry: most innovations are introduced by building materials manufacturers.

### Questions

1. Indicate the types of firms that are classified here as "home assemblers."
2. What percentage of the gross national product on the average goes into construction of all kinds annually? What part of this goes to housing?

3. What are the four "phases" outlined as descriptive of the housing industry's major types of activities?
4. Why are most firms involved in the production and distribution of housing relatively small?
5. On the basis of this discussion where do you see the greatest opportunities for improving the housing industry?

### STUDY PROJECT 15–2

### Types of High-Density Housing *

**The Townhouse.** Suburban "townhouse" designs today are a marked reformation of the old monotonous city row house pattern. Variety and selectivity are keys to creation of a pleasant, new atmosphere. Careful introduction of open yards, strategically placed in a comprehensive land plan of interior walkways, playgrounds, private patios, and parking areas, accomplish this.

Several types of plans falling into the townhouse category include:

*1. The Terrace or Patio Unit.* Essentially a conventional detached house with the front and rear yards walled for privacy. Portions of the yard walls or the dwelling walls may be shared by adjoining units. (See Fig. 1.)

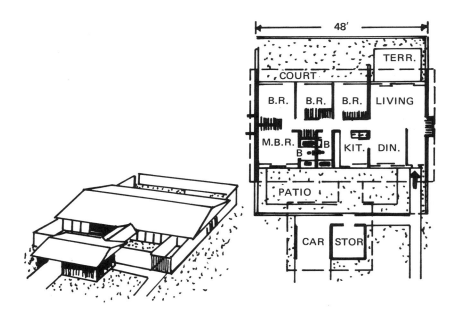

**Fig. 1.** Levitt's Eastwood Model.

* Reprinted by permission from the National Association of Home Builders *Land Development Manual* (Washington, D.C.: The Association, 1969), pp. 164–67.

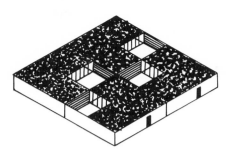

**Fig. 2.**   The Court or Atrium House.

**Fig. 3.**   The Row House.

**Fig. 4.**   Maisonette and alternate maisonette showing a corridor extending through the center of the townhouse group separating two units on the grade level while providing access to the third unit above.

2. *The Court or Atrium House.* Usually a single-story unit with the enclosed rooms wrapped around a private open yard. (See Fig. 2.)

3. *The Row House.* A narrow dwelling usually two or three stories high. (See Fig. 3.) There are also the stacked or "maisonette" row units, more commonly found in Canada and Europe, and back-to-back row units with two or three units sharing parallel party walls. (See Fig. 4.)

**Garden Apartments.** The garden apartment building has come to mean a low two- or three-story walk-up structure of units planned at densities which allow substantial green spaces. Among variations of the usual garden apartment plan idea is one very similar to the back-to-back townhouse sometimes referred to as the "piggy-back" plan. By placing back-to-back units above the "through" apartments a circulation corridor is eliminated in favor of more frequent stairways. A more completely zoned plan in terms of noise is the combination of two-level units one above the other.

Other plans achieve grade level patios at each dwelling unit of the apartment structure by terracing the earth, truly creating a garden for every unit of the development.

Finally, there is a trend in new design for higher density housing with a sloped cross section which creates outside terraces from a portion of the roofs of the dwelling units. Numerous examples of this technique have been built in Europe on steeply sloped land. Substantially larger and more exposed outdoor space is immediately accessible from the indoor living space than is possible with balconies. (See Fig. 5.)

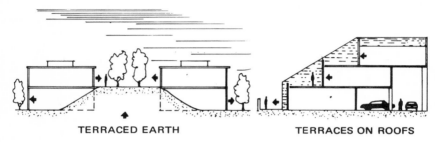

TERRACED EARTH                    TERRACES ON ROOFS

**Fig. 5.**

**Medium and High-Rise Residential Structures.**    The medium-rise (from four to six stories) and high-rise categories (over six stories) have certain economic disadvantages of construction because of fire and building code regulations, addition of elevators and more complex equipment, and interior parking requirements.    Common shapes of structures are the block (which becomes a "tower") and the slab with numerous variations and combinations such as the "T" block, double rectangle, curved slabs, and hollow squares.

### Density of Development

A fundamental problem which plagues builders, developers, and planners, and undoubtedly the least understood, is establishing the proper residential densities in zoning ordinances and planning documents. Thus far, no generally recognized standards have been established which may be applied to setting a density regulation with full understanding of its environmental effects. Such densities still are set by crude "rules of thumb" and by "planners' bias."

People and places are the parts of the problem.    Communities identify the need to regulate density with the adequacy of existing public facilities such as streets, schools, and sewer and water utilities.    In this case, the communities primarily are concerned with controlling population density.    Another part of the problem is *building* density, or more properly, "intensity."    This relates to the question of building height and bulk versus the amount of land left for recreation, parking, and nuisance insulation purposes.    There are, in fact, so many different identifications of density in use in different ordinances and planning publications that the actual *objectives* of many regulations are left in confusion. References to persons per acre must be translated into dwelling units by ratios of the average number of persons in a household. This varies according to the size of dwelling units and the location of the area compared to surrounding areas of a city. Some regulations specify density according to the number of habitable rooms and even bedrooms per acre. Density is usually computed in terms of "net acres" of land but references to "gross density" are sometimes found.

Net density represents the number of dwelling units per acre devoted to residential buildings and accessory uses within the site but excluding land for public streets, parking, parks and playgrounds, and other nonresidential uses. Gross density is computed on the basis of gross land area including area devoted to streets and other nonresidential uses, plus one-half of bounding streets and one-quarter of bounding street intersections. Neighborhood density is another term commonly used when "gross density" is not intended to include major commercial, industrial, or institutional land uses such as schools and churches.

Related to control of population density is control of building intensity. The objective is to assure adequate open space at ground level to accommodate circulation, service, possibly recreational needs, and also to assure privacy and adequate sunlight. Standards adopted usually regulate the amount of building coverage on the property, distance between buildings on the same lot, and the height of construction. When standards for height and coverage are combined, the result is an "index" of building bulk known as the floor area ratio (FAR). (See Fig. 6.)

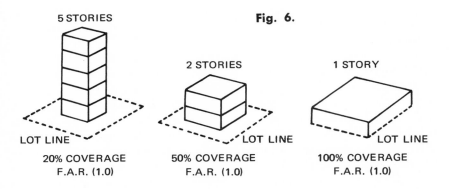

Fig. 6.

5 STORIES · LOT LINE · 20% COVERAGE · F.A.R. (1.0)

2 STORIES · LOT LINE · 50% COVERAGE · F.A.R. (1.0)

1 STORY · LOT LINE · 100% COVERAGE · F.A.R. (1.0)

### Questions

1. Of the units described, which would you prefer to live in? What are the advantages that make it preferable to you?
2. For what reason was the floor area ratio index developed?
3. What are the components used to determine net density? gross density?

# 16

# Marketing: Brokerage and Promotion

## DECISIONS IN REAL ESTATE MARKETING

The basic decisions in regard to the marketing of real estate are made by present and prospective property owners who must decide whether to buy or sell, at which prices, on what terms, and at what time. Sellers or buyers may be individuals, business firms, or governmental or institutional agencies. The motives behind decisions to buy or not to buy, or to buy more or less, or to sell or not to sell, or to sell more or less may arise from a variety of sources.

Of major importance are objectives, which in turn may vary widely. For example, the owners and managers of a business firm may decide to buy land to allow for future expansion, an individual investor may be concerned with increasing the return on his capital or with improving his tax position, or the head of a family with providing a better home for his wife and children. The same objectives may motivate both purchases and sales, as for example a business firm may sell to another in order to move to a new location, but at the same time both may thus assure space for future growth. Of course, opposing objectives may also lead to purchases and sales.

### Factors Influencing Decisions

Factors that influence decisions of this type may include: (1) Anticipated changes in the trend of general and local business conditions are important; for example, differences of opinion may exist about trends of expansion or contraction or the rates at which they occur. (2) Anticipated changes in real estate markets or in specific sectors of such markets may lead to decisions as to property purchase or sale. (3) Prospective changes in money market conditions may have a strong impact on such decisions. (4) Probabilities of change in location influences may be important—for example, belief in the rapid expansion of a new subdivision or in the future of a new shopping center may lead to decisions to buy; belief in no expansion or slow expansion may lead to decisions to sell. (5) Finally, there is always the matter of the alternatives open. A property owner may be forced to liquidate his holdings quickly in order to meet pressing personal or business problems. A business firm may be forced to buy a particular property because it is the only one which will allow it to expand at its location. Pollution problems may dictate sales.

Other factors may play a part as well, including probable changes in government or political conditions, anticipated changes in technology, possible population movements, international uncertainties, and the like. Those we have outlined give some indication of the factors that are likely to play a major part in decisions to buy or sell real property.

### Role of Brokers and Sales People

Because the processes of buying and selling real estate are complex and the market is not well organized, the decisions of prospective buyers and sellers often are facilitated, influenced, and translated into action by brokers and sales personnel. We pay special attention to their work in this chapter. Our attention will center on such topics as the major characteristics of real estate marketing, real estate brokerage and sales organizations, listing procedures and arrangements, relationships between owners and brokers, processes and methods involved in the selling of real estate, promotion programs including advertising and public relations, sales contracts, financial factors in sales, title transfers, and various possibilities for improving the marketing of real estate.

### Characteristics of Real Estate Marketing

The marketing of real estate involves all of the processes of bringing together buyers, sellers, and users of real properties or property services. It frequently includes assistance in making financial arrangements to carry out sales or leases. Often provisions for the management of properties are involved as well. Buyers and sellers, lessors and lessees, of course, can negotiate directly and often do. Brokers, however, play a major role in many real estate transactions—serving, essentially, as negotiators and counselors. They play a more important part in the marketing of real estate than do brokers and middlemen in many other fields.

Because of the nature of the real estate market there is wide room for bargaining, since prices are not set with the same precision as in many other types of markets. The original asking price of a seller of property may be much higher than any bids that can be secured. Gradually the broker works out adjustments. He tries to find the potential user or investor who can secure maximum advantage from the property. He informs the seller of sales prices or rents for comparable space. In some cases he may be careful to keep the potential buyer and the seller apart until the final closing. In other cases he will bring them together and skillfully guide the interview.

Since it is often difficult for sellers and buyers alike to secure adequate information about property values, current prices and rents, financing arrangements, and the like, the broker performs the function of supplying such information. In addition, the broker helps to avoid errors in the complicated process of selling real property. As has aptly been pointed out:

It is sometimes thought that all a real estate broker needs to start him in the business is a fairly presentable automobile and a decent suit of clothes. It is true that many enter the business with little more than this. Their exit is likely to be as easy as their entrance. The successful broker knows the city in which he operates and particularly the neighborhood in which he hopes to make sales. It is axiomatic that he cannot know too much about the property he has for sale or rent. On occasion he may say too much, but he can never know too much. He must have the capacity for winning the confidence of those with whom he deals. Few buyers or sellers of property know its value or can acquire the facility of learning it. They must lean heavily upon the representations of the broker. They will not do this unless they trust him.[1]

## Types of Customers

Many large corporations include real estate departments in their organizations for the purpose of arranging for the use and management of the properties that are needed for their operations. Such departments often work with local real estate brokers in making arrangements for the sale, purchase, leasing or financing of real properties. The bulk of the work of brokers, however, is carried out for individuals, families, small businessmen, and small investors. Because of their knowledge of the local market, familiarity with properties, and skill in negotiating, brokers are usually able to market properties to greater advantage than those who own them. The work of brokers may range from simple transactions such as the sale of a single-family home to complicated arrangements involving the sale, financing, and leasing of large blocks of properties.

---

[1] By permission from *Real Estate Principles,* 3d ed., by Henry E. Hoagland, p. 286. Copyright, 1955, McGraw-Hill Book Co., Inc., New York.

### Selling Organizations

The organizations engaged in real estate brokerage include many types, ranging from one-man offices to brokerage departments of large real estate firms. A large real estate firm will usually have brokerage, management, leasing, insurance, mortgage, and appraising departments. Some of the more aggressive ones even have their own construction crews. In addition there may be separate departments for advertising, collections, accounting, and legal work. (See Fig. 16–1.) Both the brokerage department of a larger organization and the one-man office perform the functions of securing listings, advertising, selling properties, arranging for the closing of deals, and related activities. In the smaller organization the broker, often with the aid of a secretary or assistant, will perform all of these functions himself. In larger organizations the broker will have a number of salesmen in addition to office personnel; and he may have specialists in charge of legal, advertising, and appraising work. The salesmen may work under the direction of the broker or a sales manager, and they may specialize in residential, business, or industrial properties.

Usually we refer to the owner of a real estate agency as a *broker,* and to those who assist him in the marketing of properties as salesmen. A Realtor is a member of a local real estate board which is affiliated with the National Association of Real Estate Boards (NAREB). The term *Realtor* is copyrighted by this organization and may be used only by authorized persons.

## BROKER–OWNER RELATIONSHIPS

Whenever an owner of real estate employs the services of another to assist him in the sale of a property, he enters into an agency or brokerage agreement in which he lists the property for sale. The legal rules governing the relationship between an owner and a broker are a special branch of the law of agency—every broker being an agent, although not every agent is a broker.

The relationship between the owner and broker is established by an agreement between the parties. Such agreements may be oral or they may be written contracts. (See Fig. 16–2.) In a majority of states, agreements between principal and broker need not be in writing, although written agreements are preferable and some states have set up definite statutes requiring that such agreements must be in writing.

The authority given to a broker by the owner may be of a general or a special nature; for example, if the broker is to manage an apartment or office building for the owner, the agency will be general, but if the owner lists a piece of property with the broker for sale, the agency is usually spe-

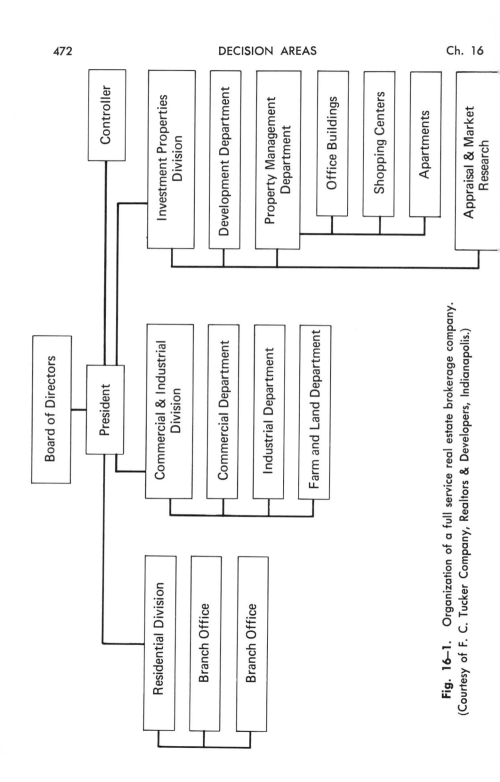

**Fig. 16–1.** Organization of a full service real estate brokerage company. (Courtesy of F. C. Tucker Company, Realtors & Developers, Indianapolis.)

**APPROVED STANDARD FORM**

Adopted by the Indiana Real Estate Association, Inc.
And for Use of Members only

## LISTING CONTRACT

................*August 5*.........................., 19.......

To *Neighborhood Realty Co.*................................................

In consideration of your listing for sale and undertaking to find a purchaser for the real estate described on the reverse side of this contract, I or we hereby grant and give you the exclusive right and authority to sell or exchange the same for a period from *August 5*..................., 19......., to *November 5*..............., 19......., and represent that no other exclusive agreement is now in force with any other Realtor or broker.

In the event you find a purchaser ready, willing and able to buy said real estate, or should said real estate be sold by or through you, ourselves or otherwise, during said time for the price and upon the terms named on the reverse side of this contract, or for any other price or terms, or consideration acceptable to me or us. I or we hereby agree to pay you as commission a sum equal to _6_ per cent of the sum for which said property is sold or exchanged; but not less than $100.00, and you are hereby authorized to accept an earnest money deposit with any offer to purchase said real estate. Said deposit may be retained by you until settlement is made. Should purchaser fail to complete said purchase said earnest money deposit shall be applied first to your advertising and other expense and the balance shall be divided equally between us. I or we also agree to do and to perform all that may be necessary to enforce the contract made with the purchaser for the property described herein and collection of any money due.

It is agreed that you, or your representatives and all prospective purchasers shall at all reasonable times have access to said premises and appurtenances located thereon for the purpose of inspecting the same.

I or we agree the price stated herein includes all mortgages, unpaid special assessments and any balances due for furnaces, or miscellaneous equipment now on or attached to the premises.

If said real estate is sold or exchanged within six months after the expiration of the term of this agreement to any person, firm or corporation with whom during the exclusive period of this listing you, your representatives or myself or ourselves had negotiations relative to the purchase of said property for said price stated herein or for a price and upon terms acceptable to me or us, I or we agree to pay you a commission equal to _6_ per cent of the gross sale or exchange price thereof, provided, however, that this extension clause shall not be applicable and binding during the term said real estate is relisted with some other licensed Realtor under an exclusive listing contract upon or after the term of this listing agreement.

This contract is enforceable without relief from valuation and appraisement laws and with attorneys fees.

I or we also agree to furnish a complete abstract of title showing a good and merchantable title to said real estate, or a Title Insurance Policy for the sale price of said real estate. I or we also agree to execute and deliver a good and sufficient warranty deed or land contract for the same to whom you direct. To induce you to enter into and accept this contract I or we hereby warrant that the undersigned is or are the sole and only owner or owners of the property above described and that the within mentioned encumbrances are the only and all encumbrances against said above described property. I or we further represent that the statements on the back hereof are made by me or us and that the same are true and are a part of this agreement. I or we have read the foregoing contract and thoroughly understand the contents thereof, and have received a duplicate thereof, and agree to give possession on or before......*30*......days after final closing of transaction. You are hereby authorized to put a "FOR SALE" sign on said real estate.

This contract is binding also upon my or our heirs, administrators, executors or assigns. 
Owner *Joe Doakes    3420 N. Delaware    876-5432*
                        Address                              Telephone

Owner *Mary Doakes*.................................................................

The undersigned accepts this authority to sell and agrees to the terms of said contract

this....*5th*....day of.*August*................., 19.......

*Neighborhood Realty Co.*............ Realtor

**Fig. 16—2a.**   Indiana standard listing contract—front.

Approved Form—Adopted by the Indiana Real Estate Association, Inc.
And for Use of Members only

## IMPROVED PROPERTY

Street No. 3420 North Delaware City Indianapolis
Legal Description Lot #58 in John Platts Addition to the
City of Indianapolis, Marion County, Indiana.

Size of Lot 100 X 200     Kind of Roof asph. shingle Foundation cement block
Which Side of Street West     Front Porch yes   Rear Porch yes
Type of Home 1-story bungalow    Bath, Kind 1 full
Built of frame - wood siding    Heated by oil   Cost
When Built 1925   Garage rear    City Water yes Gas yes Electric yes
Kind of Floors hardwood    Septic Tank no   Sewer city
Kind of Trim yellow pine with fir doors    Screens yes Storm Windows yes
Schools { Grade #56    Front Drive conc. Walks, Kind conc.
      { High Shortridge    Insulation ceiling Water Heater 30 gal.
      { Parochial St. Mark's    Street Paved yes Water Softener no
Fireplace in living room    Assessed Value $6,750.00
Plaster or yes   Dry Wall    Taxes per Annum $386.40
Open Stairway to basement    Mortgage of $7,650.00 Int. 5½ %
Rooms, 1st Floor 5   Bed Rms. 2    Monthly Mtg. Paym't's $85.00
Rooms, 2nd Floor none Bed Rms. none   Mortgagee Indiana National Bank
Closets, 1st Fl. 4   2nd Fl. none    Bal. Due on Land Contract $ none
Venetian Blinds yes    Principal none Interest none
Decoration painted    Paym't's on Land Contract none
Attic none   Basement full    Holder of Land Contract none
Barrett Assessment none    Fire Insurance $15,000 Exp. Jan. 18
Will Exchange for no exchange    Price $18,000.00
Terms of Possession 30 days    Terms cash or cash and
Owners Telephone Number 876-5432    assumption of mortgage
REMARKS:

Listing Agent Bill Darr

**Fig. 16—2b.** Indiana standard listing contract—reverse.

cial. Ordinarily, the duty of a broker is merely to find a purchaser who is ready, willing, and able to purchase in accordance with the terms laid down by the owner.

Other authority may be given, such as the right to show the property, to put up signs, to advertise, or even to sign the contract of sale. If the agent departs from his authority, the owner may be liable; nevertheless, if the principal or the agent has acted in such a manner that his action would be reasonably believed to have been authorized, as interpreted by persons in the community where the agent acted, or even though the agent has exceeded his authority and there has been no reliance, the principal is responsible if he ratifies the agent's act. If the owner does not ratify, the broker may be responsible to the third party.

The broker is expected to act in good faith always and to exercise reasonable care and diligence. If higher prices are offered than are asked, the agent is obliged to indicate this fact to the owner and not to use such knowledge to his own profit. A universally accepted rule of agency is that an agent cannot serve two principals. This rule applies to brokers. Thus, a broker cannot represent both the buyer and the seller unless both know of the arrangement and consent to it. Then the broker must act with absolute impartiality.

### Types of Listing Agreements

The agreements which are drawn up between an owner and a broker may be of various types, the most important being (1) open listing, (2) exclusive agency, and (3) exclusive right to sell contracts. In addition, an arrangement called "multiple listing" exists in some cities.

Such agreements, when entered into, will usually include, in addition to the parties to the contract: a sufficiently accurate description of the property to make it possible to prepare a sales agreement, and the terms of the sale, including the broker's commission, the length of time for which the property is listed, and any special conditions to be fulfilled.

In an open listing contract the owner may employ as many brokers as he chooses. A time limit may or may not be set. The broker making the sale collects the commission; but the owner may sell the property himself, in which case no commission is paid. If a contract is drawn up in which the designated broker is the only agent of the owner, an exclusive agency agreement exists. In such cases the broker receives a commission if sale takes place as a result of the efforts of anyone but the owner. A third type of agreement is provided in the exclusive-right-to-sell contract. Under such an agreement the broker is the only person who may sell the property (except for the owner) during the period of the agreement, and he is entitled to a commission even if sale results from the efforts of the owner himself.

# EXCLUSIVE AUTHORIZATION AND RIGHT TO SELL

## CALIFORNIA REAL ESTATE ASSOCIATION STANDARD FORM

1. **Right to Sell.** I hereby employ and grant_____, hereinafter called "Agent", the exclusive and irrevocable right to sell or exchange the real property situated in

_____, County of _____, California described as follows:

_____

2. **Term.** Agent's right to sell shall commence on_____, 19_____ and expire at midnight on

_____, 19_____.

3. **Terms of Sale.**

(a) The price for the property shall be the sum of $_____, to be paid as follows:

_____

(b) The following items of personal property are to be included in the above-stated price:

_____

(c) Agent is hereby authorized to accept on my behalf a deposit upon the purchase price in an amount to be not less than $_____.

(d) Evidence of title to the property shall be in the form of a California Land Title Association Standard Coverage Policy of Title Insurance in the amount of the selling price to be paid for by _____

(e) I warrant that I am the owner of the property or have the authority to execute this agreement. I hereby agree to permit a FOR SALE sign to be placed on my property by Agent named herein.

4. **Compensation to Agent.** I hereby agree to compensate Agent as follows:

(a) _____ % of the selling price if the property is sold during the term hereof, or any extension thereof, by Agent, on the terms herein set forth or any other price and terms I may accept, or through any other person, or by me, or _____ % of the price shown in 3.-(a), if said property is withdrawn from sale, transferred, conveyed, leased without the consent of Agent, or made unmarketable by my voluntary act during the term hereof or any extension thereof.

(b) the compensation provided for in subparagraph (a) above if property is sold, conveyed or otherwise transferred within 180 days after the termination of this authority or any extension thereof to anyone with whom Agent has had negotiations prior to final termination, provided I have received notice in writing, including the names of the prospective purchasers, before or upon termination of this agreement or any extension thereof. I further agree to register these names and exclude them from any exclusive agency and/or exclusive right to sell listing I may grant to any licensed real estate broker within 180 days of the termination of this authorization or any extension thereof.

5. If action be instituted on this agreement to collect compensation or commissions, I agree to pay such sum as the Court may fix as reasonable attorney's fees.

6. I authorize the Agent named herein to cooperate with sub-agents selected by him.

7. This property is offered without respect to race, creed, color, or national origin.

8. In the event of an exchange, permission is hereby given Agent to represent all parties and collect compensation or commissions from them, provided there is full disclosure to all principals of such agency. Agent is authorized to divide with other agents such compensation or commissions in any manner acceptable to them.

9. I agree to hold Agent harmless from any liability or damages arising from any incorrect information supplied by me or any information I fail to supply.

10. Other provisions:

_____

11. I acknowledge that I have read and understand this Agreement, and that I have received a copy hereof.

Dated _____, 19_____.    _____, California

| | |
|---|---|
| Owner | Owner |
| Address | City - State - Phone |

12. In consideration of the execution of the foregoing, the undersigned Agent agrees to be diligent in endeavoring to obtain a purchaser.

_____
Agent                                    Address - City

By _____

Phone                                    Date

FORM A-11-Rev.

REVISED    CPS

**Fig. 16–3.** California standard listing contract.

| ML # 2120 | MUNICIPALITY | ADDRESS | SECTION |
|---|---|---|---|
| | Rumson, N.J. | 20 Ross Place | |

| NAME | PHONE | B.R. & B. | PRICE |
|---|---|---|---|
| Harrison Rhodes & Helen D. | 842-2222 | 5    3½ | $60,000 |

| CONST. Brick & Frame | STYLE Colonial | AGE 6 years |
|---|---|---|
| L. B.   Listing Broker's Name | LOT FR. 200   SIDE 200   REAR 200 | AC Approx. 1 |

| ROOMS | LOWER LEVEL | 1ST FLOOR | 2ND FLOOR | 3RD FLOOR | | |
|---|---|---|---|---|---|---|
| | | | | | GAR. Attached CAR. 2 | |
| | | | | | HEAT Hot Water Baseb'd FUEL Oil COST $400 | |
| HALLS | | 8x26 | | | F. P. In Living Room & Den | |
| L. R. | | 15x26 | | | LAUNDRY  Off Kitchen | |
| D. R. | | 15x15 | | | SCR. Combin. Aluminum S. S. | |
| KIT. | | 14x18 | | | APPLIANCES Electric Range, Wall Oven, Dishw'r | |
| DEN | | 15x18 | | | PERS. PROP. Carpeting in L. Rm. | |
| GAME RM. | 15x22 | | | | TAXES $1,265        YR.   19 | |
| SUN RM. | | | | | MTGEE Local Bank      BAL. $30,000 | |
| M.B.R. | | | 15x22 | | RATE                VA - FHA - CONV. | |
| 2nd B. R. | | | 12x16 | | PAYT $214.94 (pr.&int.)REM. YRS.   20 | |
| 3rd B. R. | | | 12x14 | | WHY SELLING  Relocating | |
| 4th B. R. | | | 10x12 | | POSSESSION  60 Days | |
| ADD B. R. | Maid's | | | | OPEN HOUSE  10/5/ | |
| BATHS | | 1½ | 2 Tile | | APPRAISERS (Note: Usually 3 brokers chosen) | |
| PORCH | | 14x20 | | | CONDITION  Excellent | |
| PATIO | | 12x20 | | | KEY AT Lock box (Call first)  EXP. DATE 1/4/ | |

BASEMENT Full and Dry

Owner's Address If different from above:

REMARKS: Master bdrm. has dress. rm., 2 closets; game rm. is panelled; patio
is flagstone & has new awning. House is fully air-conditioned. Kitchen has
breakfast area. Grounds are beautifully shrubbed; many tall trees.

| LOT 4   BLOCK 20   MAP  Borough of Rumson | ASSESSED LAND $9,000   IMPROV. $36,000 |
|---|---|

IN CONSIDERATION of the services to be performed by the undersigned REALTOR, herein called Broker, a participant
in the RED BANK AREA MULTIPLE LISTING SERVICE, and/or by other participants in the said Service, the undersigned owner, herein called owner, does hereby authorize and give to Broker the exclusive and irrevocable right to sell the above
described property at a price of $ 60,000       and further agrees to pay the member selling said property a commission of
six per cent of this or any other price accepted by the undersigned.  In the event said property is sold, traded or exchanged
through any source during the term of this agreement, the undersigned agrees to pay the aforesaid commission to the member
listing said property or his nominee.  The authority to sell shall automatically terminate six months from the date hereof. Commission will be due and payable at title closing.  Above member reserves the right to cancel this contract if the listed price is
15% or more above the evaluation made by said members.

The undersigned hereby acknowledges receipt of this agreement and receipt of the New Jersey Attorney General's interpretation
of the Fair Housing Act.

DATE: June 1        19

George Bassett
(Witness)

Harrison Rhodes                L.S.
(Owner)

Accepted by: Frances Doakes
(Listing Broker)

Helen D. Rhodes   L.S.
(Owner)

It is mutually agreed that no FOR SALE signs shall be displayed during the term of this agreement.

**Fig. 16-4.** Multiple listing form. (Courtesy Red Bank Area Multiple Listing Service, Red Bank, New Jersey.)

## Multiple Listing

While most owners prefer to dispose of their properties as quickly as
possible, they often find it difficult to decide between an open listing,
which engages the interest of a large number of brokers, and an exclusive-
right-to-sell agreement, which places responsibility on a specific broker
and assures him a reward for his efforts. In order to secure the major

advantages of both methods, some real estate boards have set up "multiple listing" systems. Where such arrangements exist, the broker with whom a property is listed also lists it with other members of the organization. If he sells the property himself, he receives the full commission; if another sells it, the commission is split on a predetermined basis between the selling broker and the one with whom the property was listed. In some cities, multiple listing systems are compulsory for registered brokers or those who are members of a local association or board—that is, every member of the board is required to list all properties with the organization. More generally, however, an optional system exists. The use of the multiple listing system preserves many of the advantages of the exclusive-right-to-sell contract, and at the same time extends the scope of the market by including as many brokers as possible.

Experience has indicated the basic ingredients for a successful multiple listing system. Note, for example, this statement:

> One of the oldest and most successful multiple-listing agencies is the Southwest Branch of the Los Angeles Realty Board established in 1921 and in continuous operation since that time. In any particular year, depending upon market conditions, this board may have anywhere from 3,000 to more than 15,000 listings from which its members can make sales. The volume of business transacted through this board runs into millions monthly since the board estimates their average listing value at $100,000. The Board bases its success on the following principles: (1) a listing must be submitted in writing within thirty-six hours after it is signed, (2) no listing may be reported sold and removed from the active sales list until both the buyer and seller have signed, (3) listing terms cannot be changed if they increase the difficulty of selling, (4) no listings can be canceled in less than forty days unless the owner pays the full commission rate, (5) the board cannot interfere in the operations of any member's operations, and (6) all brokers must deal directly with the owner and not through the multiple board.[2]

## Broker's Authority

Except where a broker's employment is definitely indicated as exclusive, it is assumed that a nonexclusive agreement exists. In such cases as many listings may be made with as many brokers as the owner wishes, all being terminated in various ways, such as the destruction of the property, bankruptcy, insanity, or death of either party, and by mutual consent or by revocation. Thus, in most situations, the owner may revoke the broker's authority without incurring any liability, unless he does so in order to avoid paying a commission after the broker has introduced him to a prospect.

[2] Frederick E. Case, *Real Estate* (revision of *Modern Real Estate Practice*) (Boston, Allyn and Bacon, Inc., 1962), p. 376.

In cases where there is doubt of the broker's right to a commission, it is necessary for him to show that he was actually employed; that he was the "procuring cause" of the sale, that he exercised good faith; that he produced the customer on the seller's terms; that the customer was ready, able, and willing to buy; that the contract was consummated within the time limits, if any were set, and that a completed transaction was brought about if the contract required it.

## Securing Listings

A real estate broker must have listings before he can sell any property. The listings may be thought of as his merchandise, as the stock of goods on the shelves of his store. In ordinary periods, relatively little difficulty may be encountered by a broker in securing listings. His business acquaintances, the owners of property with whom he has dealt, and former customers may provide him with an adequate stock of merchandise. There are times, however, when brokers must make special efforts to secure listings, especially when the market is active.

Brokers may advertise, indicating their desire for listings; they may call on or write letters to property owners who may be willing to dispose of their properties; they may canvass management firms to determine whether rental properties are for sale; they may canvass financial institutions who hold foreclosed properties or who have clients with properties for sale; and they may engage in numerous other related activities. In some cases, brokers have carried on house-to-house canvasses inquiring whether home owners are interested in selling their properties. There has been much argument among brokers as to the effectiveness of this doorbell ringing technique.

All the above suggests that a broker's acquaintances in the business community, his reputation for efficient service, and the quality of his advertising are of major importance in securing listings. These same factors are also of basic importance in the selling of properties once they are listed with him.

Some real estate firms combine brokerage with property management. In such a combination the property management activities of the firm may yield a number of listings for the brokerage department. Since the firm is serving the owners through the management of properties, the owners are very likely to ask the same firm to sell such properties as are to be placed on the market.

## Terms of Listing Agreement

It is not only important for the broker to secure listings; he must also obtain them under favorable conditions. If an owner lists a property at a price which is far above the market, there is relatively little chance for the broker to market it, regardless of how much effort and money he spends. Real estate brokers often say, "A property well listed is half sold." By this they mean that the property is listed at a price and on terms which are reasonable in relation to current market conditions. Sometimes also they mean that the period of the listing is long enough to allow the broker to carry out a careful sales campaign.

### Listing Policies

Brokers prefer that properties be listed under exclusive-right-to-sell agreements for periods of at least ninety days. In the case of special-purpose property a longer period may be desirable. Typically the broker's commission is 5–7 per cent of the sales price, although a lower percentage is sometimes paid in the case of more expensive properties.

In some cases, brokers accept listing on terms that are not realistic. As a result, the properties cannot be sold; later, negotiations have to be carried on with owners and prices and terms adjusted to levels that should have been worked out originally. Some brokerage offices refuse to accept listings unless prices and terms are realistic. This saves the time of salesmen, eliminates renegotiations, and speeds up the turnover of property listings. Other offices will accept listings on almost any terms in order to prevent competitiors from getting them, then renegotiate if possible before the end of the time involved in the original listing agreement. The first type of policy is probably to be preferred. The latter works reasonably well in a period when markets are expanding rapidly but in other periods properties listed on nonrealistic bases can waste sales effort and advertising expense, and result in painful renegotiations and general frustration.

The obtaining of listings under favorable conditions is often the primary factor in the success of a real estate brokerage organization. In some cases, a broker may ask several of his salesmen to give an independent estimate of the price that can be secured for a property before it is listed for sale. The salesman who calls on the owner to arrange the listing is armed with this information. Records of sales in the area in which a property is located and information about sales prices for comparable properties are usually considered before a listing is arranged. The public records may be checked to determine if possible the amount that the owner paid for the property. In these ways brokers are often able to avoid delays in the sale of property because the original asking price is too high.

Brokers sometimes arrange for an independent appraisal in order to establish a reasonable asking price. Some real estate boards set up committees for this purpose in order to facilitate the work of brokers.

## THE SELLING OF REAL ESTATE

In boom periods the selling of real property may amount to little more than taking orders. When demands are high and brokerage offices have long lists of live prospects who are anxious to secure desirable space, relatively few sales problems are encountered. Such periods are relatively rare, however, and even in boom periods there may be many people who would like to buy but who are unable to meet the prices demanded by owners.

Usually, therefore, every brokerage office will maintain a list of prospects. These are secured from answers to advertisements, from acquaintances of the broker or his salesmen, from tenants in buildings managed by the firm or others, from financial institutions, and from other business firms. Prospect files are kept alive by frequent analysis in order that dead cards may be eliminated and live ones substituted.

### Matching Properties and Customers

The primary job of the real estate broker or his salesmen is to match properties and customers. Only in the case of new construction can the property be tailor made to fit the customers' needs, whether a residence, a store, or a factory building is involved. Matching properties and customers requires a detailed knowledge of the property on the one hand and the needs of the customer on the other. It is important to recognize that *exchange must be a mutually beneficial proposition if an enterprise system is to function.* Too often people think that in a business transaction one of the parties must gain an advantage. Or salesmanship is thought of as a series of hocus-pokus procedures and mumbo-jumbo phrases whereby the customer is forced to act contrary to his wishes or best interests. Both of these ideas are fallacious.

Exchange must be mutually beneficial; both the seller and the buyer must gain or expect to gain otherwise no exchange will take place. The buyer must want the property more than the money and the seller must want the money more than the property. The broker's job is to arrange a meeting of minds between buyer and seller, and basically that means finding a property suitable to the buyer's needs at a price that is mutually agreeable to both parties.

In some cases other factors also are involved. For example, the broker may find it necessary to help the buyer arrange for financing; legal difficulties may require solution; tax problems may complicate the seller's or the buyer's situation; it may be necessary to arrange for extensive alterations or repairs; or special arrangements may be necessary for closing the deal, such as escrow agreements and the like. In some cases, because of emergencies, it may be necessary to buy or sell quickly.

### Qualifications of Brokers

This brief summary of the processes involved in selling real estate suggests that a broker and the salesmen who work for him need a broad knowledge of a number of subjects and a detailed knowledge of real estate and the factors which have a bearing on real estate values. A broker should be able to analyze properties in terms of their adequacy for the uses which a prospective customer may wish to make of them. Similarly, he should be able to analyze the customer's needs and match these with appropriate properties. He needs a detailed knowledge of real estate financing, subdividing and land development, building activities, the local real estate market, and general and local economic trends which bear on real estate values. He should know enough real estate law to recognize those situations which require competent legal advice. In addition, he needs a knowledge of office organization and procedure, commercial correspondence and business communications, advertising media and methods, and related information.

Much has been said about the importance of a pleasant personality for a real estate broker. While tact, good humor, and the ability to persuade are important, there are many successful brokers who have less than the average share of these qualities. Tact and good humor cannot take the place of knowledge, judgment, imagination, organizing ability, and hard work. Even so we should recognize that those who know how to "win friends and influence people" are more likely to succeed than those who do not have such abilities.

### Selling Methods and Strategies

The right kind of salesmanship has a very important place in the equipment of the broker and in the whole process of marketing real estate. By the "right" kind of salesmanship we mean the correct analysis of properties and customers' needs, the presentation of *facts* rather than opinions about properties, and the exercise of imagination to help the customer see the possibilities of the properties under consideration.

As has been indicated, selling starts with listing. Realistic pricing and related sales terms are a primary factor in real estate sales. Following listing, a selling strategy needs to be worked out. The broker or a member of his staff needs to think in terms of potential buyers, people who may lead to potential buyers, competitive properties, alternative plans for developing sales, the selection of the alternative offering most promise, and then action in terms of advertising, sales promotion activities, brochures, sales kits, and the like.

Basically, the selling of real properties involves exactly the same processes used in selling other types of goods and services. Specific methods vary widely, depending on the type of property being marketed, the personality of the salesman, and the kind of customer. To a large extent selling is a psychological process about which it is difficult to generalize. Methods that are successful if employed by one salesman will fail if used by another. Every successful salesman must study himself as well as the property and the customer. He must determine in advance how he can best bring about a meeting of minds.

Methods which will help to bring about the sale of one type of property may be ineffective if used in connection with another. Also, the types of selling methods which will produce desired effects in the case of one group of customers often fail if used in dealing with another group. Probably the only statement with general validity is that adequate information, carefully and honestly presented, is the most useful selling device available.

### Adequacy of Information

For the real estate salesman, adequate information about the subject property includes a knowledge of the exact location, size, and shape of the lot and detailed data about the building or buildings involved, especially with respect to such items as age, type of construction, number of stories, floor area, and potential monetary or direct returns. He should know the type of depreciation schedules that may be set up. He should be acquainted with the district in which the property is located and understand the relationship of the district to the growth and structure of the city. In addition he should be familiar with sales which have recently been made of similar types of property, the values of competing properties in the area, and the trends of prices and rents for properties of the type under consideration. All of this information has little value, however, unless the salesman applies it to specific sales problems. Basically, this means property analysis with a view to matching the customer's requirements.

### Steps in the Sale

The steps in a sale are sometimes listed as (1) attention, (2) interest, (3) belief, (4) conviction, and (5) action. In some cases a sixth, satisfaction, is added. Sometimes these steps are reduced to (1) attention, (2) interest, (3) desire, and (4) action.

Regardless of how divided, the sales process is not really a series of separate steps. It is a continuous process in which the customer's mind may have passed through the earlier steps listed above before he sees the salesman. The good salesman directs the interview with the customer, but only in rare cases will he undertake to dominate it. He will try to lead the customer to a final decision by suggestion, by providing additional information, and by answering objections.

He may lose his leadership in a sales interview if he fails to keep up with the customer, turns the interview into an argument, or lets it become a visit. Analysis of the customer will help to avoid such mistakes. Another cause of failure in selling is losing the confidence of the customer. Misrepresentation of facts, attempts to conceal undesirable features rather than admitting them frankly, and exaggeration, all lead to loss of confidence. Such simple things as failure to keep appointments may undermine confidence. Loss of confidence also results if the salesman is unable to provide adequate information.

Ordinary courtesy and good manners are essential to the successful salesman. Lack of consideration, overbearing attitudes, and the like may be very costly.

Every salesman should use nontechnical language. Even businessmen are not familiar with all of the technical language used in real estate transactions. The house buyer may be puzzled by such terms as *equity, elevation, cubic content, masonry construction, amortization,* and many other terms which are used commonly by those associated with real estate. The avoidance of technical language prevents confusion in the mind of the customer and facilitates the selling process.

## PROMOTION

We use the term "promotion" to include all types of activities and programs intended to aid the sales process. In the real estate field this will encompass advertising, open houses, displays and related efforts, and public relations programs. We emphasize particularly the areas of advertising and public relations in these discussions.

Advertising and public relations serve the dual purposes of securing listings of properties to sell or rent on the one hand and of facilitating the selling or renting processes on the other. In most types of enterprises advertising and public relations activities are used primarily as an aid in selling. In the real estate business such efforts also help to secure the merchandise for the broker to market. Similarly, a real estate financing institution by its promotion efforts will appeal to both savers and borrowers.

Effective public relations programs require two-way communications between a firm and its public. It is important for the firm to know what the public thinks of it and its programs. Then proper steps can be taken to correct undesirable impressions or to add to points of strength. In all types of promotion programs it is well to remember that ideas have wide appeal and that originality is often the key to success.[3]

Evaluation of public relations programs is extremely difficult. If coupons are used in advertising, it is possible to estimate the impact of the advertisements involved. In most cases, however, it is not possible to measure very closely. In a final analysis, success depends on the total volume of business generated over a period of time.

### Promotion Strategy

To be effective, promotion programs should be planned with a view to furthering the objectives of the organization. Formulation of effective programs requires careful analysis of the firm's business and its market. It is necessary also to budget carefully the resources that will be allocated to the various phases of the programs that are evolved. In short, a careful *promotion strategy* is needed. This will cover such factors as the type of programs to be undertaken, the size of the effort, relationships between programs, and relations to the competitive situation. For example, if it is anticipated that a competitor will expand his promotion efforts, it may be desirable to expand even more and to start sooner. Or expansion of a competitor's advertising program, for example, may be countered by a reduction in advertising effort but by expansion of direct sales programs. As is true in other fields, promotion strategy depends to a considerable extent on anticipated changes in market conditions, public attitudes, governmental influences, and programs of competitors.

The fundamental questions of *what* is to be sold, *where*, and *to whom* require analyses of the properties that are for sale or rent, the services that may be provided by the firm, and the markets in which the firm will compete. Careful market analysis, as outlined in Chapter 9, often is helpful in planning promotion programs. Different types of programs may be indicated depending on whether the market is expected to advance, decline, or continue at the same level.

### Economic Soundness of Promotion and Advertising

The economic soundness of promotion programs and especially of advertising has been debated for some time. Some economists have taken a highly critical position relative to advertising and to many other forms of promotion. False and misleading advertising, of course, is harmful. All

---

[3] See Albert W. Frey and Jean C. Halterman, *Advertising* (4th ed.; New York: The Ronald Press Co., 1970), pp. 226–29.

types of promotion, however, should not be condemned on this account. New products could hardly be introduced and brought to a wide market without promotional efforts. The function of informing customers and potential customers about a product is important. In some cases people appear to prefer the glamor and reassurance of advertising programs to cheaper prices.

### Types of Real Estate Advertising

Real estate advertising may be classified according to purpose, media used, and the form in which it is presented. In terms of purpose, three main types may be distinguished: primary institutional, name, and specific.

*Primary institutional advertising* pertains to real estate in general and has for its chief purpose the creation of favorable public attitudes toward real estate, investments in real estate, or the people engaged in the real estate business. From a competitive standpoint every type of commodity is in competition with every other type for a slice of the consumer's dollar. Institutional advertising is designed to aid real estate in this competition. Such organizations as the National Association of Real Estate Boards, local real estate boards, the American Bankers Association, the U.S. Savings and Loan League, the Mortgage Bankers Association, and various associations of builders carry on advertising of this type.

*Name advertising* has for its main purpose the popularizing of the name, activities, and reputation of a specific real estate firm. Name advertising is designed to appeal to the owner who may wish to list his property for sale or rent, to the saver and borrower, to the contractor and property buyer or user. Such advertising may include spot announcements on radio programs, business cards in the classified advertising columns of newspapers, or the sponsoring of special publicity programs.

For example, a firm may distribute quarterly or monthly "Letters" containing comment on economic and business conditions. Such letters may form the basis for news releases as well.

*Specific advertising* pertains to individual properties and property services. Its purpose is to aid in the selling or renting of a specific property. The most widely used type is classified newspaper advertising, which usually combines name and specific appeals.

Some advertising which appears to be specific may in fact pertain to several properties. It has been said, for example:

What appears to be a presentation of facts about some specific property may be only a blind advertisement, the contents of which could apply to any one of several parcels listed with the broker. In answer to inquiries which may be generated by the advertisement, a quick-thinking broker may decide which of several properties he wishes to show the prospect.[4]

## Major Advertising Media

The major advertising media for most Realtors are newspapers, magazines, radio and television. In addition, signs, posters, direct mail, streetcar or bus cards, office displays, and a miscellany of items such as blotters, matchbooks, calendars, letterheads, and others are often used.

Since the market for many types of real estate is local in nature, the newspaper fits such advertising requirements rather specifically. Newspapers reach a heterogeneous group of readers. The reading life of a newspaper is very short; usually it is read as soon as received and then discarded. The average time spent in reading it is about twenty minutes.

There are various advantages and disadvantages to advertising in morning or afternoon papers or in daily or Sunday editions. Much real estate advertising is concentrated in the classified sections of Sunday editions, since greater circulation may be provided, readers have more leisure time, and in the case of residential properties much of the "shopping" is done on weekends. The Sunday editions combine many of the advantages of the newspaper and magazine media for the real estate advertiser.

Magazines have a longer reading life than newspapers and are often read more carefully. However, few magazines are directed toward a specific local market, and hence products which are sold in national or regional markets are more likely to be advertised in this medium.

Thus, industrial properties are likely to be advertised in magazines that reach various industry groups, farm properties in farm journals, and resort and recreation properties in magazines stressing outdoor activities, sports, and recreation. Advertisements relating to properties that may appeal to retired people are found in a number of magazines.

Display and classified advertising are the two main kinds which appear in newspapers and magazines. Real estate firms use classified advertising to a predominant extent, although in special cases display advertisements are used. Preferred space in a newspaper is usually considered to be the right-hand column on the right-hand page, the front or back page of a section, and the positions next to reading matter. Such spaces often command extra rates.

## Other Forms of Advertising

As we have suggested Realtors often make use of direct mail advertising, signs and posters, displays, novelties and other types of advertising.

---

[4] Hoagland, *op. cit.*, p. 324.

Direct mail advertising includes letters, folders, booklets, cards, leaflets, and the like. It is the most selective of all types of advertising. However, it is relatively costly in terms of cost per reader, but selectivity may make such costs relatively low. Effectiveness of direct mail advertising depends on the copy used and especially on the mailing list which is prepared. In some cases direct mail is sent to persons of influence such as financial executives and others who are in a position to refer customers.

Mailing lists may be based on prospect files, names of people visiting open houses, respondents to advertisements, city directories, members of civic clubs, and the like. In some cases mailing lists for specific purposes may be purchased.

Radio and television are among the major media, with the latter currently achieving phenomenal results for many advertisers; but both are less selective than newspapers. [5] Television affords the additional power of demonstration. Short announcements or spots on local stations are preferable for most real estate purposes. Programs, especially on television, quickly reach prohibitive costs. Use of either or both of these media should be carefully coordinated with other advertisements for maximum effectiveness.

"For Sale" or "For Rent" signs on properties are among the oldest forms of real estate advertising. They have been generally successful. Usually they carry the broker's name, office location, and telephone number. "Sold" signs are sometimes used to attract future listings. A suburban operator north of Chicago found signs pointing to, and briefly describing, his subdivision were his most effective media.

Posters are used in connection with the sale of new developments or the renting of space in larger buildings. Car or bus cards are often used to advertise a real estate firm rather than specific properties.

Displays are not used widely in the real estate field. Some brokers display in their offices photographs of properties which they are marketing. A few use window displays. Often displays at home shows or other occasions are utilized. These types of advertising may be effective, but they reach limited audiences and hence may be relatively costly.

Many real estate firms use calendars as a form of name advertising. Some make use of novelties, blotters, and similar devices.

## Motivation Research

In recent years, advertising specialists have given considerable attention to motivation research as a means of finding out why some adver-

---

[5] A. W. Frey and J. C. Halterman, *op. cit.*, chap. 14.

tising messages are more effective than others. Through motivation research, attempts are made to determine why prospective buyers react as they do to products or services or to the advertisements used in attempting to sell them. For example, are people more interested when considering the purchase of a home in shelter, comfort, conveniences, or in the prestige of home ownership? Why have colonial style houses had such a strong appeal over many years? Is this because many people think of a little white house in an attractive location, perhaps with a white fence around it, when they think of a home? Through motivation research, attempts are made to answer questions like this about consumer preferences.

Motivation research has revealed that the home owners of today differ in some respects from those of yesterday. Home ownership is currently viewed as an investment rather than in terms of a permanent, deep-rooted family association. Although the home has kept the traditional values of thirty years ago such as security, shelter, privacy, independence, pride of ownership, and the like, the owner tends to view his home today more as an investment, a form of saving, and a means of building an equity.

Motivational research techniques are used to uncover ways to understand the ultimate consumer of real estate better and to gain a better perspective on his feelings toward the purchase of a home and the assumption of a mortgage, as well as his attitudes toward lending institutions.

### Public Relations and Publicity

The term "public relations" may be used in such a broad sense as to include almost every type of activity that a firm or the members of its staff may undertake. Many public relations programs try to develop a broad understanding between the business firm and the public it serves or the public at large.

Such understanding requires that two-way communication be established and maintained between the firm and its public and the public and the firm. As a result of such a program, those who operate a real estate firm should be able to determine what the public thinks of it, where its points of strength and weakness may lie, and the types of programs that will add to its strength and shore up its weaknesses.

The primary purpose of most public relations programs is that of winning the approval of the community and the public. This may be done in a variety of ways. In the real estate field, special attention is often given to community activities, especially those that are likely to lead to community betterment such as work on the solution of tax or other government problems, assistance in land planning or zoning programs, or help in the improvement of schools, parks, and other community facilities. Those in the real estate business usually have information and experience of a type that enables them to make real contributions to the solution of such community problems. Such efforts may bring favorable public reaction to the firm, develop close association with community leaders, and generally assist other aspects of the firm's promotion programs.

**Publicity Programs**

A real estate firm may be able to publicize many of its activities or those associated with it through the news columns of newspapers or radio or television news broadcasts or in related ways. A regular program of providing news releases may be very productive if carried out with imagination and efficiency. The following events may have news value if stories are prepared properly for release:

1. The sale or lease of an unusual property.
2. Announcement of a new building program.
3. Special or unusual arrangements for financing sales.
4. Office expansion or announcement of a new location for an office.
5. Promotion of personnel.
6. Firm activities designed to recognize unusual services of its personnel.
7. Volume of sales or rentals for a quarter or a year.
8. Personal activities of staff members, especially of a professional type, such as attending conventions, study groups, special courses, institutes, and real estate board or other trade association activities.
9. Community service of officers or staff members.
10. Sponsorship of home shows.
11. Modernization and repair programs.
12. Any activities relating to the improvement of housing or living conditions.

Best results are secured if the job of preparing and releasing publicity is assigned to one member of the staff or if the broker makes it a special part of his own activities. Whoever handles publicity must become acquainted with the editors, financial editors, or real estate editors of local papers and those who prepare and present the news programs of local radio and television stations. Sometimes local and national trade association publications provide outlets for publicity releases as well.

## CLOSING THE SALE

When a buyer and seller are brought together, the broker's function may be completed. However, he may be authorized to act for either party in drawing up a contract of sale, or he may give advice during this stage of the transaction. Once such a contract has been drawn up, the broker may collect his commission even though the transaction is not completed.

After the broker has brought seller and buyer together, a purchase-and-sale agreement is usually drawn up. Of course, a sale of real estate may be made without a preliminary contract, the seller executing and delivering a deed and the buyer paying the purchase price; but in practice such transactions are rare. In some cases the agreement is a land contract or a contract for deed, which may be a method of selling real estate on the installment plan. Sometimes the buyer secures an option to purchase, which is an agreement to buy a stipulated property at a certain price within a designated period. For this option the buyer pays a certain sum, which is usually applied on the purchase price if the transaction is completed. In some cases exchange agreements are drawn up in which properties are traded, rather than sold for money. Exchange agreements differ little from ordinary contracts of sale; but they are double in form, and the price is paid in whole or part by property.

Buyers and sellers may also be brought together by auction sales, which may be voluntary or involuntary. In voluntary auction sales, the terms of sale are written in advance. After the property is sold to the highest bidder, the transaction becomes a private matter between him and the owner. Involuntary auction sales usually result from the desire to satisfy a lien. Such sales must be public, adequate notice must be given, and various legal formalities must be satisfied.

The drawing up of a sales agreement is an important step in the selling process, since it is the first evidence of a meeting of minds between the buyer and seller. Contracts should be carefully drawn. It is always wise to arrange a written statement which contains all of the items about which the parties have agreed. (See Fig. 16–5.) Such an agreement is preliminary to a sale; if consideration is given, an option contract is formed which may bind the parties for a period of time during which various matters may be investigated. In some cases an escrow agreement is made.

### Main Items in Contract for Sale

A contract for sale should cover at least the following items: (1) the parties, (2) legal description of the property, (3) the price and financial

**APPROVED STANDARD FORM**
**INDIANA REAL ESTATE ASSOCIATION, INC.**
Marott Hotel Arcade—2625 North Meridian Street—Indianapolis, Indiana
**OFFER TO PURCHASE REAL ESTATE**

To_____Neighborhood Realty Co._____, Realtor

_____Indianapolis_____, Indiana

September 3_____, 19__

The undersigned, hereinafter called purchaser, hereby agrees to purchase from the owner, hereinafter called the seller, through you as broker, the real estate known as No.___3420 North Delaware_____St., in the City (or town)

of_____Indianapolis_____, County of_____Marion_____, State of Indiana, the legal description of which is:

Lot Numbered Fifty-eight (58) in John Platt's Addition to the City of Indianapolis, as

per plat thereof in Plat Book 29, Page 112, in the Office of the Recorder of Marion County,

Indiana,

and to pay as the purchase price therefor the sum of

Seventeen Thousand and 00/100 - - - - - - - - - - - - - - - - - - -DOLLARS ($_17,000.00__)

payable as follows:

One Thousand and 00/100 - - - - - - - - - - - - - - - - - - - -DOLLARS ($_1,000.00__)

as earnest money deposited with the broker herewith, which shall be applied on the purchase price at the closing of this transaction, and the balance of the purchase price shall be payable in accordance with Paragraph___2___as hereinafter set forth:

**PARAGRAPH 1 (SALE BY DEED)** The balance of the purchase price shall be paid in cash upon delivery of warranty deed.

**PARAGRAPH 2 (SALE BY DEED ASSUMPTION OF MORTGAGE)** A down payment of

Nine Thousand Three Hundred Fifty and 00/100 - - - - - - - - - - - -DOLLARS ($_9,350.00__),

of which the earnest money is a part, subject to a mortgage now of record in unpaid amount as of___June 30,__19__of

Seven Thousand Six Hundred Fifty and 00/100 - - - - - - - - - -DOLLARS ($_7,650.00__),

interest at_____%, monthly payments of $__85.00_____, including principal and interest_____

which the grantees agree to assume and pay at date of closing.

**PARAGRAPH 3 (SALE BY CONTRACT)** The balance of the purchase price shall be paid as follows:

A down payment of_____DOLLARS ($_____)

of which the earnest money deposit shall be a part, and the balance of

_____DOLLARS ($_____)

shall be paid under the terms of the approved Indiana Real Estate Association, Inc., form of LAND CONTRACT to be executed

by the parties at the closing of the transaction, the interest rate therein to be_____%. Monthly payments of $_____

**PARAGRAPH 4 (SALE ON OTHER BASIS)** If neither Paragraphs 1, 2, or 3 is applicable, then upon the following terms:

_____

_____

_____

Purchaser shall have complete possession on__or before 30 days after delivery of a General Warranty Deed. Failure by seller to surrender possession on date of delivery of deed or land contract shall not make the seller a tenant of purchaser, but in such event seller shall be obligated to pay purchaser $__10.00_____ per day as liquidated damages for each day seller holds over, and this provision shall not deprive purchaser of any other legal or equitable remedy available under the law.

Rents, if any, and interest on mortgage indebtedness, if any, shall be prorated as of date of closing.

Insurance shall be (prorated) (cancelled) as of date of closing.

Taxes shall be prorated as of the date of closing, that is to say, seller shall be charged with and pay taxes on said real estate payable in the current year and for that portion of taxes payable the following year calculated as of the date of closing, and purchaser shall pay all taxes subsequent thereto. Seller shall be charged with and pay all delinquent payments on assessments for public improvements, if any, and all payments on such assessments currently due. Purchaser shall pay all assessments for public improvements becoming payable and becoming a lien after date of closing.

Purchaser shall be furnished, at seller's expense, a complete and merchantable abstract of title continued to date as quickly as the same can be prepared, said abstract to show a merchantable or insurable title to said real estate in the name of the grantors who will execute and deliver a general warranty deed (or contract of sale if so specified herein) conveying said real estate (or in the case of a contract of sale, agreeing to convey) in the same condition as it now is, ordinary wear and tear excepted, free and clear of all liens and encumbrances except as stated herein and subject to easements or restrictions of record, if any. However, if sellers have Owners Title Insurance, in that event purchasers shall be furnished, at sellers' expense, an Owners policy of Title Insurance in the amount of $_17,000.00_____. Should additional time be required for making or continuing such abstract, or for correcting defects of title, reasonable extension of time shall be given.

This transaction is to be closed within___10___days after said abstract showing merchantable title or binder for title insurance is delivered.

This offer is void if not accepted in writing on or before 12:00 o'clock noon of__13th__day of__September__, 19__.

This purchase includes such lighting fixtures, window shades, venetian blinds, curtain rods, linoleum cemented to floors, storm sash, screens, awnings, fences, clothes poles, laundry tubs, shrubbery, traverse rods, drapery cranes, water heater, gas burner, oil burner, stoker, heat regulator, water pump, sump pump, pressure tank, water softener, towel racks and bars, door bells or chimes, lattices, television tower, antenna and rotor now installed or in use on the premises. Seller guarantees that all of the above accessories or appliances are fully paid for or will be fully paid for, at the final closing of this transaction, unless otherwise herein stated.

The risk of loss or damage to improvements on said real estate or a substantial portion thereof by fire or otherwise, until delivery of deed or contract, is assumed by seller, and if all or a substantial portion of said buildings are so destroyed or damaged prior to execution of said deed or contract of sale, this agreement at the election of the purchaser shall not be binding upon the purchaser, and in such event any earnest money deposited shall be returned to the purchaser.

The said earnest money deposit above mentioned shall be returned in full to purchaser promptly in event this proposition is not accepted. In the event this proposition is accepted, and purchaser shall, without legal cause, fail or refuse to complete the purchase of said real estate in accordance with the terms and conditions hereof, said earnest money deposit shall be retained by the broker under his listing contract with said seller and shall be applicable to the broker's and the seller's damages, but seller may also sue for specific performance or pursue any other legal remedy available to seller under the law.

**Fig. 16–5.** Offer to purchase real estate.

arrangements, (4) title, (5) time and place of closing, and (6) various special items. As in all other contracts, the parties must be legally competent and capable of entering into contracts. For example, the capacity of married women is usually defined by statute. Similarly, the ability of a corporation to contract is indicated by its charter. In real estate contracts it is always wise to require signatures by both husband and wife in order to remove any doubts about dower rights. Also, if purchasers are to take title as *joint tenants* or *tenants in common,* it is necessary to indicate this fact. Good practice dictates that both parties to a contract should sign it in duplicate, each retaining a signed copy.

## Property Description

While a property is usually designated by street and number during the early stages of a transaction, it is usually necessary to describe it more exactly in the sale contract. The description need not be as detailed as it is in the deed, but it must be accurate. Property may be located by metes and bounds, that is, with reference to certain landmarks, roads, rivers, streets, corners, or other designated points, and then described by a certain number of feet in various directions from a starting point. In most cities property may be located by a plat or subdivision map which is filed in the land records office. Lots and blocks are numbered on such a plat and descriptions can easily be made. Property may also be designated with reference to government land surveys; that is, with respect to north and south lines or *principal meridians,* east and west lines or *base lines,* townships, and sections, as outlined in Chapter 4.

## Price and Financial Arrangements

The financial arrangements between the buyer and seller must be set forth exactly in the contract of sale. Of greatest importance are the following: (1) price, (2) the deposit on contract, (3) the amount of cash to be paid on closing, (4) existing mortgages and purchase money mortgages, and (5) miscellaneous items.

The price of the property that is agreed to by buyer and seller is of basic importance. It is usually the primary ingredient in the transaction. Usually the purchaser is required to make a deposit at the time the contract is drawn up. This deposit is called earnest money and is used to bind the transaction. Typically, it represents at least 10 per cent of the purchase price, the amount varying according to the agreement between the parties. In case the buyer fails to perform the terms of the contract, this amount may be forfeited to the seller, who may then use it to pay any commission which he owes a broker.

The amount of money to be paid to the seller at the time the deal is closed should also be designated in the contract. Sometimes the exact form of payment is indicated. For example, a certified check may be required. It is necessary to indicate specifically the amount to be paid at the time closing takes place in order to make certain that there has been a complete understanding between the buyer and seller.

Since most real estate is mortgaged, it is necessary to make some arrangement regarding the mortgages, if any, which are in force. A recorded mortgage is an encumbrance on the property, and the purchaser takes the property subject to it. The mortgagee may proceed against the land after sale to a third person. The third person, however, does not subject his personal assets to the payment of the mortgage unless he assumes it. If he does, it is important that the contract of sale indicate in detailed form the terms of existing mortgages.

In some cases real estate is sold subject to a *purchase money mortgage* —that is, the seller agrees to take back a mortgage for a certain part of the price. In such a mortgage the general rules governing all mortgage transactions regulate the relationship between the parties. Ordinarily such mortgages are subordinate to any existing mortgages in force.

Various miscellaneous items governing the financial arrangements between the buyer and the seller should also be indicated. For example, taxes may be delinquent or payable at some future time, and there should be a definite agreement regarding the amounts which each party shall pay. Also, arrangements must be made regarding special assessments, rents, insurance, water charges, and other similar matters.

In order to guard against uncertainty, it is desirable that a complete statement be drawn up indicating the purchase price, the amount to be paid on deposit, the amount to be paid at the time the transaction is closed, the presence of existing mortgages and the method of their disposal, agreements regarding purchase money mortgages, and an itemized statement of any other financial arrangements which are involved.

### Title Problems

Before a piece of real estate can be transferred, it is necessary to determine the condition of the title. Because of the many uncertainties surrounding the title to a piece of property, careful investigations must be conducted before a transaction can be completed. A contract of sale usually provides that the seller shall furnish a good, merchantable title.

It may also require the furnishing of a complete abstract or summary history of the *chain of title*, which includes all deeds and other instruments of record since the original grant of land by the government. The buyer may require some form of title insurance or a certificate of title. Typically, all of these matters are indicated in the contract, together with certain defects or encumbrances which the buyer is willing to waive.

Also, the contract usually specifies the form of deed which the seller will deliver, indicating whether a warranty, quit-claim, bargain-and-sale, or other type of deed is to be given. In ordinary transactions the buyer demands a full covenant warranty deed in which the seller takes all responsibility for the validity of the title. In some cases a bargain-and-sale or special warranty deed is all that can be demanded; for example, this would be the case in purchasing from a trustee or the executor of an estate. Such a deed limits the personal liability of the seller. It is seldom used in a free conveyance, for most purchasers are unwilling to buy a title that may be valueless. Usually the party who is to draw the deed and pay the expenses is indicated in the contract; otherwise the seller cares for these matters.

While it is not necessary to indicate the time and place of closing, it is desirable to include such provisions in the contract. In addition, contracts often include clauses in regard to the payment of broker's commissions, loss or damage by fire, limitation of seller's liability in case of defective title, provisions allowing the purchaser to assign the contract, as well as provisions regarding fixtures and personal property, making time the essence of the contract, leases, and various other subjects.

### Compliance

After the contract of sale has been signed, each party must comply with its conditions. If the property does not comply with its description or the title is not as the vendor agreed, he must see that the conditions of the contract are met. A check of the property description may indicate that it does not coincide with the tract which the buyer specified. Similarly, encroachments may be discovered; that is, a building on the land may be partially located on adjoining land, or a building on adjoining land may encroach on the seller's property. Any substantial difficulty of this type may render the property unmarketable. On the other hand, slight encroachments may be of little consequence. Where one property is separated by a party wall, that this actually bounds the property must be determined.

Of greater difficulty, however, is the problem of determining the status of title. The buyer usually requires a title search to be made as soon as a contract of sale has been entered into so that he may know the status of the title. The seller may be required to furnish an abstract of title, a guarantee policy, or a certificate of title. An abstract will present a complete history of the property, and an attorney's opinion is made on this to the buyer. However, a title company may make a search and, upon the payment of a certain amount, issue a title insurance policy. The value of certification or guarantee depends on the character of the assuring agency. Title insurance usually provides that the insuring company will indemnify the assured according to various agreements; for example, (1) the insuring company may guarantee that the *record of title* is good except for certain noted defects or (2) it may insure against unknown defects. In some states a system of title registration simplifies the process of examination of title.

When the buyer's attorney receives an abstract, he checks it and advises the buyer as to the status of the title. If defects are discovered which the seller cannot or will not correct, or if no title insurance or other guarantee against loss is provided, the buyer may refuse to complete the transaction. Usually the seller is expected to provide a good, merchantable title.

### Closing Processes

After all problems of the type outlined above are settled, the parties to the transaction and their lawyers meet at the time and place appointed for closing. The deed must be checked regarding description, parties, signatures, acknowledgments, and other items. Also, other instruments such as mortgages are examined. At the closing, adjustments are determined, insurance policies transferred, other details settled, and the deed is delivered to the buyer, who then pays the purchase price. The buyer is entitled to immediate possession unless otherwise specified. As soon as the transfer is completed, the buyer or his attorney records the deed and other necessary instruments.

At the time of closing a closing statement is prepared in which real estate taxes, insurance, and rents are prorated. (See Fig. 16–6.) The seller normally pays taxes and insurance up to the time of closing and receives credit for taxes or insurance paid in advance. Similarly the seller receives rents up to the time of closing and gives credit to the buyer for rents paid to the seller but accruing after the date of closing. It also shows how the commission is to be distributed. This closing statement is the final accounting of the transaction and is an important record.

### Escrow

Sometimes an obstacle arises so that closing cannot be completed. In such cases, if the parties do not desire to arrange another meeting, the transaction may be completed in *escrow;* that is, the purchaser may have the papers delivered to a third person who holds them until all matters are cleared up and then delivers them to the proper parties.

Martin makes the following summary statement in regard to escrow arrangements:

To transfer interests in realty a large number of documents have to be drawn and a great many things have to be checked. The buyer usually has

**APPROVED STANDARD FORM**
**INDIANA REAL ESTATE ASSOCIATION, INC.**
2625 N. Meridian St.          Indianapolis 7, Ind.

## CLOSING STATEMENT

October 10          , 19

**Seller(s)** Joe Doakes and Mary Doakes    **Buyer(s)** Jack Byers and Betty Byers
**Address** 3420 N. Delaware St. **Phone** ME 1-1451 **Address** 1846 Lark Avenue    **Phone** ME 1-1775

### FINAL CLOSING STATEMENT

ADDRESS OF PROPERTY 3420 N. Delaware St. **Lot No.** 58 **Addition** John Platt's **City** Indianapolis

• • • • •

|  | Buyer | Seller |
|---|---|---|
| Purchase Price |  | $ 17,000.00 |
| Unearned Insurance Premium____yrs.____mos.____days |  | 41.50 |
| Escrow deposits, Taxes, Insurance, |  |  |
| Earnest money deposit_____ September 3 _____, 19____ | $ 1,000.00 |  |
| Additional down payment, if any, _____, 19____ |  |  |
| Balance 1st mortgage held by___The Indiana National Bank | 7,310.00 |  |
| Interest 1st mortgage from___July 1, 19___to October 10, 19 | 115.63 |  |
| Balance _____, 19____ |  |  |
| Interest from_____to |  |  |
| Real Estate Taxes—Spring_____Fall____19 | 193.20 |  |
| Prorated Rent, from___January 1, 19___to October 10, 19 | 298.64 |  |
| (Note: In this example purchaser is given credit for the pro-rated taxes. In other sample closing statement taxes are treated as an expense.) |  |  |
| Balance due sellers | 8,124.03 |  |
|  | $ 17,041.50 | $ 17,041.50 |

### SELLERS EXPENSE

| Cash received by ___Neighborhood Realty Co._____**Realtor** |  | $ 1,000.00 |
|---|---|---|
| Continuation of abstract by___Brown Abstract Co.____**Co.** $ | 52.50 |  |
| Documentary Stamps_____ |  |  |
| Funds, if any, advanced to Seller(s)_____ |  |  |
| Brokerage Commission ___Neighborhood Realty Co.___**Realtor** | 850.00 |  |
| Balance due ___Sellers_____ | 97.50 |  |
|  | $ 1,000.00 | $ 1,000.00 |

**Conditions:**
Possession to be given buyers on or before_____ November 9, _____, 19____
Abstract of Title delivered to_____ Buyers
_____keys for premises delivered to Buyers.
_____copies of survey given to Buyers.
Assignments of Insurance sent to_____ Sam Actuary _____19_____**Agent**
$15,000.00 Insurance, Term 3-year Expires July 20, / Premium $160.57 Co. American Mutual Insurance Co.
Assignment of Escrow Deposits sent to_____, 19____
Next payment on Mortgage due by Buyers_____ November _____, 19____, Amount $_____
Next payment of Real Estate taxes due from Buyers _____, 19____
Notice to tenant, if any_____, 19____ Rent due_____, 19____ Amt. $_____

Accepted by                          Accepted by

_Jack Byers_
Jack Byers          **Buyer**          _Joe Doakes_
_Betty Byers_                          Joe Doakes          **Seller**
Betty Byers          **Buyer**          _Mary Doakes_
Neighborhood Realty Co.___**Realtor**   Mary Doakes          **Seller**
                          By ___Bill Farr_____
                                        **Salesman**

**Fig. 16–6.** Closing statement.

to have time to get his money together to pay some of the expenses and to assemble the down payment. Financing usually changes in some way in the sale of the property. In some parts of the country a specialized company, called an "escrow company," has arisen to do these jobs. The escrow holder, as these companies are called at law, cannot take a position adverse to either the buyer or the seller. It is a neutral holder. Escrows are frequently done in the offices of financial institutions such as commercial banks.[6]

### Enforcing the Contract

If either party to a contract fails to perform the agreement, various remedies are available to the other party. Such a failure to carry out the contract does not affect the broker's right to a commission, but it may interfere with the completion of the transaction.

If a seller changes his mind, the buyer may follow several courses of action: (1) He may sue the seller for *specific performance*. It should be noted in this connection that most real estate contracts may be specifically enforced; that is, the court, may force either party to carry out his agreement exactly, but this is discreptionary with the court. (2) The contract may be rescinded, and the buyer can ask for his purchase money back, together with any costs which have resulted from the contract. (3) The buyer may sue the seller for breach of contract and damages.

On the other hand, if the purchaser refuses to carry out his part of the agreement, the seller may similarly sue for specific performance, or declare the contract void and the earnest money forfeited, or sue for damages.

### Trade-in Problems

One of the problems of real estate marketing which requires solution is that of trading in one property for another. The problem is particularly acute in the case of single-family homes. For example, if the buyer of a new house could trade in his old house in much the same manner that he trades in his old car on a new one, many transactions would be facilitated. In some cases builders and brokers have worked out their own arrangements to provide for trade-ins. Much remains to be done, however, in this field.

A closely related problem arises from the increasing number of people who are required to move from one city to another because of changes in their work assignments. Some companies guarantee certain managerial employees against loss if they are required to move to conform to company programs. Usually an independent appraisal is made and if the

<hr>

[6] Preston Martin, *Real Estate Principles and Practices* (New York: The Macmillan Co., 1959), p. 161. By permission of The Macmillan Co.

owner of the house who is forced to move finds it necessary to sell for less than the appraised value, the company makes up the difference. If a national network could be developed in some manner which would permit the turning in of a property in one city to a broker for sale and the purchase of a house in another city from another but perhaps affiliated broker with appropriate arrangements to tie both transactions together, the transfer of people between locations would be facilitated.

## SUMMARY

Basic decisions in real estate marketing are made by present and prospective property owners who are motivated by a variety of factors. Brokerage and promotion play a large part in real estate marketing due to the difficulties of bringing buyers and sellers together. Selling organizations vary in size and degree of specialization. Listing of properties for sale often is the key to successful sales; listing agreements of various types may be arranged. Multiple listing systems are expanding in popularity. Processes of selling real estate resemble those in other fields but knowledge of real estate resources is essential.

Promotion includes all types of activities and programs that help and support the sales effort. Advertising, displays, open houses, public relations programs, and related activities are all parts of promotion. Publicity programs often are used to good advantage by brokerage firms.

Upon completion of a sale, a purchase-and-sale agreement usually is drawn up pending final arrangements. Financing often is worked out by the broker. Title problems sometimes create difficulties. When all matters are worked out, a final closing statement is set up. In some cases escrow agreements are used. Contracts finally arranged may be enforced specifically or alternative arrangements may be worked out.

## QUESTIONS FOR STUDY

1. Why do brokers play such an important role in the marketing of real properties?
2. What is meant by "listing"? How does a broker obtain listings?
3. How do you interpret the statement "a property well listed is half sold"?
4. Differentiate among the various types of listing contracts employed by brokers. If you were a broker, which would you prefer? If you were a small manufacturer desiring to sell your property, which type of listing contract would you prefer? Why?
5. The ABC Corporation is transferring its local plant manager, Mr. Carson, to the home office in another state. He has to dispose of his home within 30 days, and asks you to sell it for him. Mr. Carson wants $27,500 for the property. After inspecting the property, you decide that it will not bring

more than $25,000 in the current market and may have to be sold for even less in order to complete a sale within 30 days. What action would you take under these circumstances?

6. "Exchange must always be a mutually beneficial proposition." Why? Is this statement consistent with the attempt of a firm to maximize its profits? Explain.

7. Indicate ways in which the selling of real estate differs from the selling of other commodities.

8. Define "promotion" as it pertains to real estate sales. What is meant by a "promotion strategy"?

9. Prepare illustrations of the principal types of real estate advertising. Which types of advertising would be most effective for residences, investment property, industrial property?

10. Distinguish between public relations and publicity.

11. If the seller of a certain real property changes his mind after signing a sales contract, what remedies are available to the buyer?

12. What essential items need to be covered by a contract for the sale of real estate?

## SUGGESTED READINGS

BROWN, ROBERT KEVIN. *Essentials of Real Estate*. Englewood Cliffs, N.J.: Prentice-Hall, Inc., 1970. Chaps. 4, 12.

CASE, FREDERICK E. *Real Estate Brokerage*. Englewood Cliffs, N.J.: Prentice-Hall, Inc., 1965. Chaps. 6, 7, 9.

FREY, ALBERT, and JEAN C. HALTERMAN. *Advertising* (4th ed.). New York: The Ronald Press Co., 1970. Chaps. 2, 3, 15.

LUSK, HAROLD F., CHARLES M. HEWITT, JOHN D. DONNELL, and JAMES A. BARNES. *Business Law: Principles and Cases* (Second Uniform Commercial Code Edition). Homewood, Ill.: Richard D. Irwin, Inc., 1970. Chaps. 5, 18, 30.

OTTESON, SCHUYLER F., WILLIAM G. PANSCHAR, and JAMES M. PATTERSON. *Marketing: The Firm's Viewpoint*. New York: The Macmillan Co., 1964. Pp. 539–42, 556–62.

## CASE 16-1

## A & A Realty Company

The A & A Realty Company is a partnership consisting of two partners and two salesmen. They operate in a community of about 40,000 adjacent to a major metropolitan area and specialize in the sale of properties in the $12,000 to $22,000 class. They have been in operation since 1928 and have a membership in the local real estate board. They believe that the success of their firm is built on their selling program, the chief characteristics of which are:

1. SELECT A LOCATION. Each of the men in the firm is assigned to a particular section of the town, and it is his responsibility to know about all properties which are being offered for sale in this area and to know about all persons who might wish to purchase property in this area. Each man is expected to spend a good portion of his time going from

door to door in his area asking about properties which might be for sale or seeking persons who might wish to purchase properties. Their slogan is: "Ring doorbells, ring doorbells, ring doorbells," and they believe that this is the cornerstone for any brokerage operation.

*a. Do you believe that the emphasis on a policy of this kind will be successful in a majority of real estate sales?*

*b. How would you supplement such a program in order to develop sales projects?*

*c. What kind of training would you give the men who are going to do the doorbell ringing?*

2. GET TO KNOW THE NEIGHBORS. The firm urges each salesman to get acquainted with the people in the neighborhood in which he operates. They believe that this is important, not only because a friendly neighbor will encourage sales, but because it will also make it easier to find prospective clients. Neighbors often know friends or relatives who would be interested in moving next door.

3. HAVING SOMETHING TO OFFER. Each salesman is encouraged to return to the persons in his area who have had business with the firm and to offer the services of the firm to them. This includes such things as helping them to find contractors when they want to repair their houses, keeping them informed as to new city activities which might affect their neighborhood, and similar services. They believe that if the former clients come to rely on the salesman both as a friend and as a source of valuable information, they will be willing to keep him informed about possible future business.

*d. What other services do you believe this firm could render? How would you make such services "services" and not "nuisances"?*

4. GET LISTING IN WRITING. This firm believes that all the listings which they obtain should be exclusive listings, and the reasons why they believe this are:

4.1 While listing is given to a number of agents, no one works on it.

4.2 An exclusive listing means that one office is concentrating its interest and talents on the property.

4.3 One person will be responsible for obtaining the best offer and there will be only one offer and, therefore, no confusion.

The listing contract which they use in the one advocated by their real estate board and it provides for exclusive listing.

*e. Do you believe it is necessary to get listings in writing?*

*f. Do you think this firm is correct in insisting on an exclusive listing?*

*g. What other device can be used with exclusive listings to disseminate information about the property?*

*h. Do you think that the information listed on the listing contract is sufficient, or would you want additional information about the property?*

5. USE A CHECK SHEET IN SELLING PROPERTY. When a listing has been obtained through the firm, this listing is then assigned to one of the salesmen. The information is furnished the salesman on a sheet of paper which fits into a small notebook, and he is expected to follow up

on the listing until he has obtained a client.   On the reverse side of the notebook sheet are listed the steps which the salesman is expected to follow in selling the property.   These steps include:

5.1   Calling on any prospects which the salesman has developed through his own contacts.

5.2   Talking with the persons who are currently occupying the property which is to be sold.

5.3   Calling on the neighbors in person, notifying them that the property is to be offered for sale and asking them if they have anyone who they would like to have move in.   The call is then followed up with a letter within the next few days.

5.4   Salesman should arrange to place a sign on the property announcing that it is for sale.

5.5   Classified advertising is prepared and an insertion schedule is arranged.   This firm specializes in the use of the morning paper.

5.6   Property listings with the local Realtors' group.

5.7   Letter is sent to other agents telling them about the property, particularly when the property has unusual characteristics which might meet someone's particular needs.

5.8   Letters are sent to the various personnel men throughout the city, particularly those with big companies, informing them that the property will be available in the near future.

5.9   The salesman is required to determine how much of a mortgage can be obtained on that property and to be fully informed about any financial plans in connection with the property.

5.10   Salesman handling the property is expected to call the owner at least once every two weeks and to tell him what has been done and what is being done in order to sell the property.

5.11   After the property has been sold, a card is sent to the neighbors introducing them to the new owner of the property.

6.   SHOW PROPERTY TO PROSPECTIVE CLIENTS.   Before a prospective client is taken to a home, the salesman should inform the people occupying the property and arrange for an appointment.   As the prospects are being taken to the property, the route should be arranged so that they will be shown the most favorable parts of the neighborhood in which they will be living.   When they arrive at the house, the salesman should first talk about the outside of the house, pointing out both the strength and the weakness of the house.   This firm has found it successful to point out the defects and let the prospects sell the salesman on how easy it would be to remedy them.   This firm emphasizes that women buy houses, and that the sales talk should be built so as to appeal to the women.   They also believe that emotions sell houses and that the sales program should be designed to emphasize those factors which would appeal to the emotions, such as beautiful fireplace, unusual views, and unusual architectural treatments inside and outside the house.

When the firm has arranged for an appointment to show a house, they send the people occupying the house a small pamphlet (Exhibit C) which shows how the people living in the house can help the sale; however, this will be successful only when the people occupying the house are selling the house.   Many times, the persons in the house will be renting it and will not be anxious to have it sold. In this case, the salesman must plan his program so as to have minimum interference with the occupants of the house.

*i. Evaluate the strength and weakness of this program, and indicate how you would improve it.*

*j. What steps would you take to show a house which is occupied by persons who do not want the property to be sold?*

*k. Do you think a sales training program of any kind is necessary for a salesman in this program? If so, what would you include in such a program?*

7. CLOSE THE SALE. After the prospect has indicated that he will be interested in buying the property, the salesman is encouraged to put the prospect's offer in writing and to urge the giving of earnest money. They believe that the earnest money should be an amount equal to the commission that the firm will receive for the sale of the property. Once the offer has been written out, the firm presents the offer to the owner and lets the offer speak for itself. They urge the seller to review the offer and to try to decide whether he would be willing to sell the property under the terms and conditions as outlined in the offer. Once the seller has agreed to sell, the firm calls in their attorneys and, with the attorneys, completes the papers necessary to close the transaction.

*l. What items do you think should be included in the written offer? How would you convince a prospect that he should be willing to put his offer in writing? to give earnest money?*

8. SUPPLY A SALESMAN'S HANDBOOK. The firm believes that each salesman should be encouraged to keep with him a handbook in which he has the following information:

8.1 Prospects
8.2 Listings
8.3 Payment books from savings and loan associations
8.4 Tax rates

*m. Can you think of any other items which should be included in the salesman's handbook? How would you expect the salesman to use this handbook?*

## CASE 16–2

### The Timberlake Property

On May 25th of this year Steven L. Timberlake and his wife, Marcia M. Timberlake, of 2426 Southwinds Drive, called the office of Leader Realty. They stated that they are moving to another city and would like to have Leader Realty sell their home. On May 26, Arthur Hall, a salesman for Leader Realty called on the Timberlakes at their home, a limestone ranch house on the east side of Southwinds Drive. They asked him to list their property for sale and gave him the following information.

1. They want the listing period to be 90 days, effective June 2.
2. They will give possession on or before 20 days after closing.

3. The legal description is lot #4, Willinston's Addition to the City of Melbourne, Green County, Indiana.
4. The lot is 80 feet wide and 100 feet deep.
5. The Timberlakes do not wish to exchange their property for another.
6. The assessed value of the property for tax purposes is $5,600—$1,000 of which is land, and $4,600 of which is improvements.
7. The annual tax rates are: last year payable this year—$8.40 per $100; this year payable next year—$8.70 per $100.
8. The First National Bank of Melbourne holds an FHA mortgage on Timberlake's property. Mortgage payments, including principal, interest, property taxes and insurance are $135 per month. The mortgage balance, after the May 1 payment, was $11,002. Payments are due the first of each month. Annual rate of interest is 5½ per cent plus ½ per cent mortgage insurance.
9. Fire insurance of $14,500 is carried on the property. The present policy expires at midnight, September 4.
10. Listing price: $15,500.
11. The Timberlakes will accept cash or cash and assumption of mortgage.

On June 12, Hall showed the property to Mr. Henry R. Wurthman and his wife, Elaine C. Wurthman. They express interest in purchasing the property. On June 14, the Wurthman's asked him to complete an offer to purchase form, including the following terms.

1. Purchase price: $14,500.
2. Assume outstanding mortgage and cash for balance.
3. Earnest money deposit of $2,000.
4. Liquidated damages for late vacancy at $17.00 per day.
5. Closing to be within 12 days after showing merchantable title.
6. The offer shall expire in 8 days.
7. Purchasers will have possession on or before 17 days after closing.

On June 18, the Timberlakes accept the Wurthman's offer. Closing is to be July 6.

### Questions

1. Why is there a need for both husband and wife to sign?
2. What type of listing agreement is this?
3. Which steps does the salesman take, once the property is listed, to find buyers?
4. What happens after the offer to purchase is accepted?

### STUDY PROJECT 16–1

#### Six Great Motivators *

Competition for savings is by far the greatest now that it has been since World War II. Our public relations effort must be intensified, expanded and made even more effective if we are to keep our place in the sun and if we are

* An article by William B. O'Connell in *Saving and Loan News*, as reprinted in *Director's Digest* (March, 1959), pp. 21–24, and revised by the author, 1971.

to continue approximately the same rate of growth that we have enjoyed recently.

To a very great degree, the success of these efforts will depend upon the measure of understanding we have of the basic emotions and impulses—motivational forces—that govern people. I think it can be argued that this understanding of people is the paramount consideration involved in developing our various public relations and promotional programs.

Some years ago, the advertising people gave the fancy-sounding title of "motivation research" to the job of understanding people. It is this understanding of people and why they act as they do that might be called the golden key to public relations success.

The first important motivational force that has direct influence on public relations activities is that people like to feel that they are needed. This basic desire to be needed suggests a variety of approaches as far as public relations programs are concerned.

One such approach is that people's savings are needed to build a safe future for the family. Another is that their savings are needed now so that the saver can enjoy new and wonderful products of the future. Still another approach is that savings are needed to provide the fuel of capital for the expansion and growth of our economy. And a fourth approach is that savings are needed for patriotic reasons—currently this patriotic reason is the fighting of inflation.

The second great basic motivational force which can influence our public relations programs is that people like to be successful. An obvious major public relations approach here is that people who save are successful people because they have mastered the problem of putting away part of what they earn. Similarly, people like to feel that they are part of a successful, progressive enterprise, which accounts, incidentally, for the sense of proprietorship that many families display in the growth of the savings association in their community.

The third great force that should affect public relations planning is that people like a sense of physical well-being.

There are at least three considerations here that apply to public relations programs—office quarters, personnel and the dress of personnel. With respect to office quarters, the building of new buildings, the remodeling or modernization of old quarters has played a vital part in developing new business. With respect to personnel, people like warm, friendly employees to handle their affairs. As to the dress of personnel, studies have shown that people are greatly impressed by the appearance of other people; this suggests that employees be suitably and conservatively attired.

The fourth great moving force affecting public relations programs of associations is that people like to feel secure.

The search for security has brought remarkable changes in American life. It has developed a tremendous life insurance industry; it has inspired passage of unemployment compensation and social security laws; it brought the Blue Cross and Blue Shield health insurance into being; it caused the establishment of literally thousands of private retirement and pension plans.

.   .   .   .   .   .   .   .   .   .   .   .   .   .   .   .   .   .

There is still another element involved in the search for security, and that is the seeking of assurance that savings placed with a savings association are safe. In the past 10 years I have given a great deal of thought and study to this matter and long ago reached the conclusion that public confidence in the safety of our institutions is more vital to our prestige than anything else.

This suggests immediately the necessity of placing repeated emphasis on such factors of safety as sound and careful management, including auditing, the federal-agency insurance of savings accounts and the assistance available through the Federal Home Loan Bank System.

The fifth great motivational "mover" is that people like to be appreciated. Look for opportunities to say "thank you" in many different ways, not only to persons when they open new accounts but on the anniversary dates of the day on which the accounts were opened. You can say "thank you," too, to persons who have shown consistency and regularity in adding to their accounts.

The sixth great mover is that people like to be informed.

This is more true today than it ever was. Our educational levels have advanced generation by generation, and today a higher percentage of youngsters go through college than went through high school 50 years ago. As a result, the hunger for knowledge and information is more active than ever before.

### Questions

1. How might the "six great motivators" be applied to the public relations program of a real estate brokerage firm?
2. Compare the discussion of motivation research in this study project with that presented in Chapter 16.

# 17

# Marketing: Property Management

## CHARACTERISTICS OF PROPERTY MANAGEMENT

In this chapter we consider the marketing of property services rather than the properties themselves. This general field, usually referred to as property management, has developed rapidly in recent years.

Our attention will center at the outset on several basic definitions of management and property management, the reasons for the development of this field, the requirements of property managers, the major types of managements and the professional management organization.

### Basic Definitions

Because terms often have special meanings in different fields, we will define the ways in which the terms management, administration, and property management are used here.

The terms *management* and *administration* are used in relation to all types of organized activities. As we suggested in our discussions in the introductory chapters, we use these terms interchangeably in most situations to identify the processes of using resources effectively in the attainment of desired objectives. In this broad sense, the term *management* may be applied to all types of business and to all aspects of the real estate business.

The term *property management,* however, has come to have certain special connotations in the real estate business. Although the owner of a property might manage it himself, the term *property management* usually is applied to situations in which someone other than the owner performs the management function. Because of this type of usage that has grown up in the real estate field, we tend to use the term *administration* in relation to broader managerial processes and the term *management* in the specialized sense of property management as indicated above. Although we use the term *property management* in the customary narrow sense, it will be understood that when an individual owner or a business firm manages a property, the principles and methods of the property manager may be applied.

### Reasons for Property Management

The increasing complexities of many problems associated with the managing of real properties, together with the fact that some owners know relatively little about real estate principles and practices, accounts in large part for the development of this specialized branch of the real estate business. Absentee ownership, use of trustee arrangements, tax factors, technological developments, and growth of the corporate ownership of real property have contributed to the development of property management. In addition, it is often difficult for some owners to maintain favorable income-expense relationships for their properties.

### Inflexible Resources

Certain conditions create special types of problems for the manager of real property. The durability of real estate necessitates managerial planning over longer periods of time than is necessary for many other types of business. Furthermore, real properties are economically inflexible—that is, once they are improved their uses are relatively fixed for long periods. Hence, to a large extent the manager is called upon to operate properties so as to get as large a return as possible from relatively fixed resources.

Current expenses are only slightly more flexible than the basic investment. Many important operating expenses, such as taxes, insurance, and interest charges, are usually beyond the control of the property manager. Hence, a slight decline in gross income usually means a considerably larger decline in net returns.

As we have said before, the fact that real properties are fixed in location means that the manager cannot move a property to those who desire its services; rather, they must be induced to come to it. For the same reason, the property cannot escape adverse developments affecting a city or a neighborhood or district.

## Requirements of Property Managers

While property management is a specialized branch of the real estate business, a knowledge of the basic principles which explain the utilization of real estate is helpful in developing a successful operation. Thus, good management requires adequate information about the economic base and future prospects of the city in which a property is located. Knowledge of the structure of the city and its characteristics of growth and development are extremely helpful in the planning of long-range management programs. The manager should understand the forces affecting the specific districts or neighborhoods in which properties under his management are located. In addition, he should be familiar with the forces affecting the market for the types of real estate he is managing. Market information is needed almost constantly and should be kept up to date and analyzed currently. With such knowledge, the property manager can adjust rental schedules and certain types of expenditures in accordance with changes in the market.

Apartment houses, office buildings, loft buildings, stores, and dwellings are the types of property most frequently operated under the direction of specialized property managers. Farm management has grown in importance in recent years. Some shopping centers and industrial districts are operated by management organizations. Each type of property involves special problems of management, but the general principles of management are the same for all.

## Relation of Management to Ownership

The relationship between managers and owners has been well summarized as follows:

The real estate manager is the agent of the owner. His legal position is similar to that of the manager of a branch office or branch store. He is a general agent—that is, an agent vested with general power involving the exercise of judgment and discretion. He is usually empowered to transact all business connected with the property entrusted to him. The property manager is generally authorized to negotiate leases, collect rents, make ordinary repairs, keep the premises in a rentable condition, pay taxes, and perform many other additional services. He is a fiduciary and must use his best efforts to further the legitimate interests of his principal. The principal is liable for the acts of his manager, done within the scope of his authority.

The manager may be authorized to keep the property insured, take care of tax matters, such as attending hearings on tax assessments. However, in all his activities, he must comply with the instructions of the owner. The manager cannot lawfully substitute his judgment for the judgment of the principal (owner).

The manager owes a duty to keep accurate accounts and to make an accounting to the owner at such periods as have been agreed upon, and also at any time the principal requests one. The manager owes a duty not to commingle the money of the owner with his own money. He should keep a separate account for money handled for each owner. If he does not keep separate accounts, he makes himself personally liable to the owner for all money of the owner coming into his hands.[1]

## Management Contracts

Frequently, the property manager's relationship with the owner is defined by a specific contract. When such a contract is drawn up, it includes a description of the property to be managed, the length of time for which the agreement is to run, removal and cancellation provisions, the amount of compensation to be paid the manager, and the duties and powers given to him. As in all other contracts, the parties must be legally competent; and all terms of the agreement must be stated definitely and exactly. Since the manager is the owner's agent, the general law of agency governs such relationships, but the use of a specific contract eliminates many special problems.

Typically, such contracts are drawn up for specific periods with provisions for renewal, the owner often reserving the right to cancel the agreement by giving the manager adequate notice of such intention. Management contracts should present a complete list of the functions to be performed by the manager and should provide for complete centralization of authority in the manager with respect to all work undertaken in connection with the property. Sometimes management contracts are set up with a trial period of three or six months.

Compensation is usually computed on the basis of a percentage of gross collections, 5 to 8 per cent being a "normal" management fee, although other arrangements are not uncommon. The amount of compensation and the manner of computing and paying it should be specified in the manager's contract.

## Types of Managements

The management functions may be performed by individual agents of the owner or by a management company which operates a number of properties for many different owners. Frequently a real estate office conducting a general brokerage business will include a property management department in its organization. Some economies are effected by this arrangement, and the selling process is often facilitated if a buyer

[1] Harold F. Lusk, *Law of the Real Estate Business* (rev. ed.; Homewood, Ill.: Richard D. Irwin, Inc., 1965), p. 34. See also Robert Kratovil, *Real Estate Law* (5th ed.; Englewood Cliffs, N.J.: Prentice-Hall, Inc., 1969), chap. x.

knows that the firm making the sale is willing to manage the property. While the average property management department seldom produces large revenues, it is a source of steady income, a factor of considerable importance to real estate firms during periods of limited market activity.

### The Professional Management Organization

In order to perform the manifold functions required of management, various employees must be hired; where the scope of operations is broad, a complete organization must be set up. (See Fig. 17–1.) If a number of buildings are involved, superintendents may be hired for each one of sufficient size to require a full-time person. Of course, janitors must be hired and supervised, as well as other laborers, including repair and maintenance men and others. In larger management organizations, special functions, such as collecting rents and hearing complaints, may be delegated to specific people. Similarly, advertising may be handled by one department, tenant selection by another, and legal matters by a third department. Accounts always require special attention, and accounting departments are normally provided in all offices of any size.

The management of a property often involves certain responsibilities which cannot be departmentalized and which are on the borderline between the functions of the manager and the owners. In some cases, these are handled in part by attorneys.

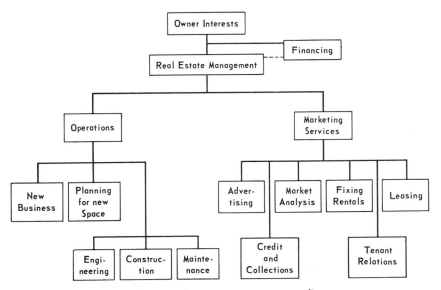

**Fig. 17–1.** Real estate management diagram.

## PROPERTY MANAGEMENT FUNCTIONS

The functions performed by property managers include the general management processes of establishing objectives, planning to achieve them, organizing resources, and controlling operations. The property manager also performs the functions of (1) planning space, (2) marketing property services, (3) conserving the property and its surroundings, and (4) supervising the operation of the property, which will include among other things the maintenance of accurate records and accounts. The manager is expected to keep the owner informed regarding the property and its operation and to consider with him any significant changes in policy.

In the performance of his functions the property manager must consider the interests of three parties: the owner, the tenants, and "the party of the third part," the members of the community in which the property is located. The owner is concerned with potential changes in the value of the property and is interested especially in securing a reasonable return on his investment. Tenants are interested in the space and equipment provided, their condition and maintenance, their cost to them, and the special services and conveniences which may be provided. The community has a continuing interest in property management policies, since they will have a direct bearing on the advance or decline of the property involved and its environment.

### Planning Space

If a manager has adequate information about the local market, his advice to the owner, architect, and builder will be of great value in planning a new building or in modernization and repair programs. A competent manager is able to advise concerning the type of building accommodations most readily marketable, the competitive position of various types of properties in the market, and the many special requirements of prospective tenants. Also, he usually knows something of the most economical methods for arranging rooms, halls, and storage space.

In the case of older buildings, managers must accept the space available and utilize it as efficiently as possible. Sometimes it is possible to alter the arrangement of an older building, but whether or not this should be done depends on the possibilities of securing adequate return on the additional investment required.[2]

---

[2] James C. Downs, Jr., *Principles of Real Estate Management* (9th ed.; Chicago: Institute of Real Estate Management, 1967), chap. v.

### Establishing Rental Schedules

Once a building, regardless of type, is constructed, the manager must fix a rental schedule and enter the market. Fixing a rental schedule calls for an accurate knowledge of such matters as the character of competing space, rents currently charged, the nature of the potential demand, the special requirements of prospective tenants, and the various advantages and disadvantages of the location. A general level of rents is determined first, from which the manager is able to develop a rental schedule for the individual quarters. Specific rates, however, are determined on the basis of market conditions. If net income is to be maximized, rents must be adjusted carefully. For example, if rents are too low, all of the space will be rented; but the total return will be less than what might be realized under a higher rental schedule. On the other hand, if rents are too high, the increase in the number of vacancies will reduce income. The determination of a rental schedule for a building is one of the basic functions of a manager, and to a large extent his success or failure depends on the care with which this work is done.[3] Also, the process of adjusting rental schedules is never complete—rents must follow the market, rising when the demand for space is strong and diminishing when demand falls off. Constant analysis of all factors affecting the market is essential in the performance of this function.

### Attracting Tenants

With the establishment of a rental schedule, it becomes necessary for the manager to secure tenants. Promotion programs as outlined in the preceding chapter may be helpful. If the building is new, it may be necessary to advertise and solicit for tenants. A new building opens with a competitive advantage, for it usually makes available all of the newest facilities. The opening of a new building is always detrimental to existing buildings, even if it is only a small structure. When a large new office or apartment building is opened, the existing structures must face stiff competition. Tenants of existing buildings are made conscious of the advantages of the new building through advertising and systematic solicitation. If special concessions are offered by the new building or if rental schedules compare favorably with those of existing structures, there will be a tendency for tenants to move from their old quarters to the new building.

The process of advertising space requires great care, for it is easy to waste funds on improperly directed advertising. If the management or-

[3] The Sheridan-Karkow formula is often used to determine the rental value of office space.

ganization is sufficiently large, this function may be performed by a special person or department. If not, it is often wise for the manager to employ outside assistance in this work.

In established management organizations, the number of prospective tenants who will call at the office in search of accommodations is frequently large. This is especially true in the case of people seeking residential space, particularly if the management office has developed a reputation for fair dealing and courteous treatment of tenants over a period of time.

In the process of attracting tenants, the wise manager is careful to consider both short- and long-range factors. To a large extent, the condition of the market will govern the specific procedure followed—a buyer's market calls for a different program from that suitable in a seller's market. The original rental campaign continues until complete or nearly complete occupancy is achieved. Thereafter, the problem of management is to hold tenants and to meet the competition of other buildings, both old and new.

The successful manager is familiar with current vacancy rates in various types of properties in the city. There is probably no such thing as a normal vacancy, although a vacancy ratio of around 5 to 8 per cent for office buildings and 5 to 10 per cent for apartment houses is generally considered normal. A manager's own vacancy situation is always significant, since it helps to determine policy changes.

### Selecting Residential Tenants

It is very important that the character of tenants be investigated carefully at the time a building is being opened for occupancy, especially in the case of large apartment houses, since tenants give a building the reputation of being either desirable or undesirable. If a manager can secure a highly desirable group of tenants in the first instance, many of his renting problems will be solved for some time in the future. Downs lists the following factors as being of major importance in selecting residential tenants: stability, housekeeping ability, child care, living habits, tenant compatibility, and social responsibility. The housing of more than a dozen families under one roof requires exceptionally careful selection of tenants. Hence the apartment house manager often requires a signed application for a lease, accompanied by a deposit, in order to allow time for investigation. Then the actual lease is signed later.

### Selecting Tenants for Office Buildings

The manager of an office building faces a number of special problems in selecting his tenants. He must always be on the alert against certain types of tenants, especially those whose businesses are likely to involve unethical practices. He must decide whether he desires a few large tenants or a number of small ones, a specialized tenancy or a general one. Usually, property managers prefer to have enough leading firms operating in a certain line of business to create a "center," but not so many that the exodus of such a group will result in the loss of a large percentage of the tenants. In connection with the selection of commercial tenants, attention should be given to such factors as the ability, aggressiveness, and progressiveness of the firms under consideration as well as tenant reputation, service requirements, and expansion requirements.

Medical buildings, because of their particular physical requirements, are an exception. In larger cities, physicians tend to congregate in certain buildings and expect the property manager to enforce high standards in the selection of tenants.

With the expansion of its activities, the federal government has become an important customer in the market for office space. Its leasing requirements and policies differ somewhat from those of the average tenant. For example, annual rent may not exceed a fixed percentage of the fair market value of space leased, and the cost of repairs and alterations may not exceed a stated percentage of the first year's rental. Leases are made on a government form. Sometimes a 30-day cancellation clause is required in order to permit a move to governmentally owned space if it becomes available, and the time of the lease seldom runs longer than the end of the fiscal year (June 30).

### Other Functions

In addition to planning space, establishing rental schedules and attracting and selecting tenants, the property manager performs the functions of leasing space, conserving property and supervising building operations. We will discuss each of these topics in the following sections.

### LEASING PRACTICES

Property managers ordinarily arrange all leases for the space they operate. However, leases are not used for all types of property, and the extent of their use varies from one part of the country to another, depending on the statutes of various states. About 50 per cent of the management offices which operate residential buildings require tenants to sign leases for at least one year. In some states leases for one year or longer must be in writing to be valid; in others, oral leases are valid for as long as three years. In many cases residential space is rented on a month-to-month basis, and the tenants are free to move or the owner or manager can request tenants to move if either party gives appropriate notice.[4]

### Security Required

It is not customary to require the tenant to post any security when leases for residential property are signed. A lease ordinarily binds the owner and manager very effectively because the property serves as security and guarantees performance of the terms of the contract. But unless the tenant is financially responsible and has assets which can be attached if the lease is broken, it is difficult to enforce a lease of this type.

When leases run for periods of longer than a year, which is common practice in the renting of stores, loft building space, or offices, definite lease agreements are usually drawn up, with liquidated damage provisions for failure to perform the contracts. Since business firms usually possess more financial responsibility than individuals, property owners and managers have greater protection in such cases. When leases run for long periods of time, they are usually considered to involve many special problems not normally a part of the functions of property management.

### Legal Relationships Established

From a legal standpoint, a lease is a transfer of possession and the right to use property to the tenant for a stipulated period, during which the tenant pays rent to the owner. At the end of the period the right of possession reverts to the owner of the fee. It is a contract containing various terms and conditions, the most important being the agreement to pay rent. To be valid, such a contract must be entered into by parties who are legally competent; and it must describe the property, the term or period of the lease, the rent, and special covenants of the contracting parties completely and exactly.

Special problems which may be anticipated in the lease include such items as the exact dates on which the lease begins and ends, arrangements governing the agreement in case of damage to the space, such as may result from fire, and termination of the lease in case of complete destruction of the building or the relationship which shall exist between tenant and owner in case a new building is constructed.

Other points which are often included in the lease are these: (1) reservation by the manager of the right to enter upon the premises for inspection, (2) specific uses to which the property may be put, (3) restriction or regulation of subleases, (4) control of the placement of signs and other things which may affect the appearance of the building,

---

[4] Subject to rent control regulations, if in force.

X 48—Form of Apartment Lease Approved by the Committee on Real Property of The Association of the Bar of the City of New York.

JULIUS BLUMBERG, INC., LAW BLANK PUBLISHERS
80 EXCHANGE PLACE AT BROADWAY. NEW YORK

**Lease,** made the 12th day of December 19 , between
John Land 400 West 66th Street, Manhattan,
New York
hereinafter called the Landlord, and
Robert Money 5000 Riverside Drive, Manhattan,
New York
hereinafter called the Tenant.

WITNESSETH: The Landlord hereby leases to the Tenant, Apartment 5B on the Fifth floor,
in premises, 400 West 66th Street Borough of Manhattan , City of New York,
hereinafter called the building, to be used as a private dwelling apartment, and not otherwise, for a term to commence
January 1st 19 and to end December 31st 19 unless sooner terminated as hereinafter
provided, at the annual rent of $ 1800.00 payable in equal monthly installments of $ 150.00 each in advance on the first day of each calendar month during the term, the first of said installments to be paid on the signing of this lease.

The parties hereto further agree as follows:

1st. The Tenant will pay the rent as herein provided.

2nd. The Tenant will take good care of the leased premises, fixtures and appurtenances, and suffer no waste or injury; make all repairs to the leased premises, fixtures and appurtenances necessitated by the fault of the Tenant, his family, guests, servants, assignees or under-tenant; conform to all laws, orders and regulations of the Federal, State or Municipal governments, or of any of their departments, and regulations of the New York Board of Fire Underwriters, applicable to the leased premises, but shall not be required to make any expenditure to comply therewith unless necessitated by his fault; and save harmless the Landlord from any liability arising from injury to person or property caused by any act or omission of the Tenant, his family, guests, servants, assignees or under-tenants; repair at or before the end of the term, all injury done by the installation or removal of furniture and other property; and at the end or other expiration of the term, surrender the leased premises in as good condition as they were at the beginning of the term, reasonable wear and damage by fire or other casualty excepted.

3rd. The Tenant will not, without the Landlord's written consent, make any alteration in the leased premises and will not deface or permit the defacing of any part of the leased premises which will increase the rate of fire insurance on the building; will not use any shades, awnings, window air-conditioning units or window guards, except such as shall be approved by the Landlord; will not keep or harbor any animal in the leased premises without first obtaining the written consent of the Landlord; will not permit the accumulation of waste or refuse matter; and will not assign this lease or underlet the leased premises or any part thereof without the Landlord's written consent, which consent the Landlord agrees not to withhold unreasonably.

4th. The Tenant will observe and comply with such reasonable rules as the Landlord may prescribe on written notice to the Tenant for the safety, care and cleanliness of the building, and the comfort, quiet and convenience of other occupants of the building.

5th. The Landlord shall furnish, insofar as the present facilities of Landlord provide, the following services: (a) Elevator service; (b) Hot and cold water in reasonable quantities; (c) Heat at reasonable hours during the cold seasons of the year; (d) Air-conditioning during the warm seasons of the year.

6th. The Landlord shall have the privilege of furnishing the electric current consumed at the leased premises, and current so furnished shall be paid for by the Tenant at the rates charged for similar consumption by the local public utility company. If the Landlord furnishes the Tenant with telephone service, the Tenant shall pay for each call at the rate established by the Landlord, but the Tenant shall not be precluded from obtaining telephone service direct from the telephone company. Charges for electric current and telephone service shall be deemed additional rent, and for non-payment of same the Landlord shall have the same remedies as for non-payment of the fixed rent.

7th. In case of damage by fire to the building, without the fault of the Tenant, if the damage is so extensive as to amount practically to the total destruction of the leased premises or of the building, or if the Landlord shall within a reasonable time decide to rebuild, this lease shall cease and come to an end, and the rent shall be apportioned to the time of the damage. In all other cases where the leased premises are damaged by fire without the fault of the Tenant, the Landlord shall repair the damage with reasonable dispatch, and if the damage has rendered the premises untenantable, in whole or in part, there shall be an apportionment of the rent until the damage has been repaired. In determining what constitutes reasonable dispatch consideration shall be given to delays caused by strikes, adjustment of insurance and other causes beyond the Landlord's control.

8th. If the leased premises, or any part thereof, are taken by virtue of eminent domain, this lease shall expire on the date when the same shall be so taken, and the rent shall be apportioned as of said date. No part of any award for the leased premises, however, shall belong to the Tenant.

9th. If the Tenant defaults in the performance of any of the covenants or conditions herein contained, other than the covenants to pay rent, or if any conduct of the Tenant or occupants of the

leased premises shall be objectionable, the Landlord may give to the Tenant ten days' written notice thereof, and if such default has not been cured or the objectionable conduct stopped within said ten day period, then at the expiration of said ten days the Landlord may give the Tenant five days' notice of the termination of this lease, and at the expiration of said five days' notice the term of this lease shall expire, and the Tenant shall then surrender the leased premises to the Landlord, but the Tenant shall remain liable as hereinafter provided. In case of default by the Tenant in the payment of rent, or if the ten day notice above provided for shall have been given and the ten day period shall have elapsed without curing such default or stopping the objectionable conduct, and the five day notice above provided for shall have been given and the five day period shall have elapsed, or if the leased premises become vacant or deserted, the Landlord may at any time thereafter resume possession thereof by any lawful means, and remove the Tenant or other occupants and their effects, by dispossess proceedings, or otherwise, without being liable to prosecution or damages therefor, and hold the premises as if this lease had not been made. In any such case, the Landlord may at the Landlord's option relet the premises or any part thereof as agent of the Tenant or otherwise, and receive the rent therefor, applying the same first to the payment of such expenses as the Landlord may have incurred in connection with such resumption of possession and reletting, including brokerage, cleaning, repairs, and decorations, and then to the payment of rent and performance of the other covenants of the Tenant as herein provided; and the Tenant agrees, whether or not the Landlord has relet, to pay to the Landlord the rent and other sums herein agreed to be paid by the Tenant, less the proceeds of the reletting, if any, as ascertained from time to time, and the same shall be payable by the Tenant on the several rent days above specified. The Tenant hereby waives all right of redemption to which the Tenant or any person claiming under the Tenant might be entitled by any law now or hereafter in force.

10th. The failure of either party to insist in any instance on strict performance of any covenant hereof, or to exercise any option herein contained, shall not be construed as a waiver of such covenant or option in any other instance. No modification of any provision hereof and no cancellation or surrender hereof shall be valid unless in writing, and signed by the parties.

11th. If this lease is assigned by the Tenant, or the leased premises are underlet or occupied by anybody other than the Tenant, the Landlord may collect rent from the assignee, under-tenant or occupant, and apply the net amount collected to the rent herein reserved, and no such collection shall be deemed a waiver of the covenant herein against assignment and underletting, or the acceptance of such assignee, under-tenant or occupant as Tenant, or a release of the Tenant from further performance of the covenants herein contained.

12th. This lease shall be subject and subordinate at all times to the lien of existing mortgages and of mortgages which hereafter may be made a lien on the premises. Although no instrument or act on the part of the Tenant shall be necessary to effectuate such subordination, the Tenant will, nevertheless, execute and deliver such further instruments subordinating this lease to the lien of any such mortgages as may be desired by the mortgagee. The Tenant hereby appoints the Landlord his attorney in fact, irrevocably, to execute and deliver any such instrument for the Tenant. If any underlying lease to which this lease may be subject shall terminate, the Tenant shall attorn to the owner of the reversion.

13th. All improvements made by the Tenant to the leased premises which are so attached to the freehold that they cannot be removed without material injury to the premises, shall become the property of the Landlord.

14th. Any notice by either party to the other shall be in writing and shall be deemed to be duly given only if delivered personally or mailed by registered or certified mail in a postpaid envelope addressed (a) if to the Tenant, at the building in which the leased premises are located, and (b) if to the Landlord, at the address, if any, noted on the lease, or, if none, then to the building, provided, however, that if either party admit, either in writing or under oath, the receipt of notice, evidence of service in accordance herewith shall not be necessary.

15th. The Landlord shall not be liable for damage or injury to person or property occurring within the leased premises, unless caused by or resulting from the negligence of the Landlord or any of the Landlord's agents, servants or employees, in the operation or maintenance of the leased premises or the building.

**Fig. 17—2a.** Lease form. (Prepared by The Association of the Bar of the City of New York. Published by Julius Blumberg, Inc., New York.)

16th. If the making of repairs or improvements to the building or its appliances, or to the leased premises, other than those made at the Tenant's request or caused by the Tenant's negligence, shall render the leased premises untenantable in whole or in part, there shall be a proportionate abatement of the rent during the period of such untenantability.

17th. Interruption or curtailment of any service maintained in the building if caused by strikes, mechanical difficulties, or any other cause beyond the Landlord's control, whether similar or dissimilar to those enumerated, shall not entitle the Tenant to any claim against the Landlord or to any reduction in rent, nor shall the same constitute constructive or partial eviction, unless the Landlord shall fail to take such measures as may be reasonable in the circumstances to restore the service without undue delay.

18th. During the four months prior to the expiration of the term, applicants shall be admitted at all reasonable hours of the day to view the premises until rented; and the Landlord and the Landlord's agents shall be permitted at any time during the term to examine the leased premises at any reasonable hour; and workmen may enter at any time when authorized by the Landlord to facilitate repairs in any part of the building; and if the Tenant shall not be personally present to permit any such permissible entry into the premises, the Landlord may enter same by a master key, or forcibly, without being liable in damages therefor and without affecting the obligations of the Tenant hereunder.

19th. Neither party has made any representation or promises, except as contained herein, or in some further writing signed by the party making such representation or promise.

20th. The Landlord covenants that the Tenant, on paying the rent and performing the covenants hereof, shall and may peaceably and quietly have, hold and enjoy the leased premises for the term herein mentioned.

21st. The provisions of this lease shall bind and enure to the benefit of the Landlord and the Tenant, and their respective successors, legal representatives and assigns. The Landlord shall be released from, and the Landlord's grantee shall be liable for, all liability of Landlord hereunder accruing from and after each grant of the reversion.

22nd. The Landlord acknowledges receipt from the Tenant of $ 150.00 as security for the performance of the Tenant's obligations under this lease. To the extent that said sum shall remain unapplied to such performance after the date fixed as the end of the term or after the earlier expiration of the term pursuant to paragraphs 7th or 8th hereof, said sum shall be returned by the Landlord to the Tenant if the Tenant shall have surrendered possession of the leased premises to the Landlord as herein provided.

IN WITNESS WHEREOF, the parties hereto have signed this instrument, the day and year above written.

In the presence of:

*John Land*
Landlord

*Robert Money*
Tenant

**Fig. 17–2b.** Lease form—reverse.

and (5) definition of the rights of the tenant in case of condemnation proceedings.

## Rents and Concessions

The rents fixed in a lease may be of several types: (1) a flat rate for the period covered; (2) a graded or step-up rental; (3) a percentage rental varying with the amount of tenant's gross or net income; or (4) a rental which is adjusted by reappraisal of the property at certain times.[5] Also, various combinations of these types of leases may be worked out. For example, a lease on a business property might be drawn up which provides for a minimum flat rent, plus a percentage of the tenant's gross business receipts if they exceed a certain stipulated amount. In the case of long-term leases, such an arrangement is often desirable to guard against important changes in the value of money.

---

[5] Reappraisal leases have seldom worked out advantageously, since it is difficult to secure an adjusted appraisal which will be acceptable to both landlord and tenant.

# LEASE
### (NON-RESIDENTIAL - SHORT FORM)
#### CALIFORNIA REAL ESTATE ASSOCIATION STANDARD FORM
##### THIS IS INTENDED TO BE A LEGALLY BINDING AGREEMENT—READ IT CAREFULLY

_____, California

_____ 19____

_____Lessor, and

_____Lessee,

agree as follows:

1. Lessor leases to Lessee and Lessee hires from Lessor those premises described as:_____

_____

_____

together with the following furniture and fixtures:_____

_____

(Insert "as shown on Exhibit A attached hereto" and attach the exhibit if the list is extensive.)

2. The term of this lease shall be_____
      (years/months)

commencing _____, 19____ and terminating _____

_____, 19_____. Any holding over by Lessee with Lessor's consent beyond the term of this lease shall be a month to month tenancy at the rental and upon the applicable terms of this lease except as specified here:_____

_____

3. Lessee is to pay rent as follows: $_____

_____

_____

The rent shall be paid at _____
or at any address designated by the Lessor in writing.

4. Lessee also agrees to pay upon execution of this lease, in addition to rent, a security deposit of $_____. Said deposit will be returned to Lessee by Lessor or his successors upon full performance of the terms of this lease.

5. Lessee agrees to pay for all utilities except_____

_____

which shall be paid for by Lessor.

6. Lessee has examined the premises and all furniture and fixtures contained therein, and accepts the same as being clean and in good order, condition and repair, with the following exceptions:_____

_____

7. The premises are rented for use only as_____

_____

8. Lessee shall not disturb, annoy, endanger or inconvenience other tenants of the building or neighbors, nor use the premises for any immoral or unlawful purposes, nor violate any law or ordinance, nor commit waste or nuisance upon or about the premises.

9. Lessee shall keep the premises rented for his exclusive use in good order and condition and pay for any repairs caused by his negligence or misuse or that of his invitees. Lessor shall maintain any other parts of the property and pay for repairs not caused by Lessee's negligence or misuse or that of his invitees.

10. Lessee shall not paint nor make alterations of the premises without Lessor's prior written consent.

11. This lease will terminate if the premises become uninhabitable because of dilapidation, condemnation, fire or other casualty for more than 30 days. Rent will be reduced proportionately if the premises are uninhabitable for any shorter period.

12. With Lessee's permission, which shall not unreasonably be withheld, Lessor or his agent shall be permitted to enter to inspect, to make repairs, and to show the premises to prospective tenants or purchasers. In an emergency, Landlord or his agent may enter the premises without securing prior permission from Tenant, but shall give Tenant notice of such entry immediately thereafter.

13. Lessee shall not let or sublet all or any part of the premises nor assign this lease or any interest in it without the prior written consent of Lessor. Lessor's consent thereto shall not unreasonably be withheld.

14. If Lessee abandons or vacates the premises, Lessor may at his option terminate this lease, re-enter the the premises and remove all property.

15. The prevailing party may recover from the other party his costs and attorney fees of any action brought by either party to enforce any terms of this lease or recover possession of the premises.

16. Either party may terminate this lease in the event of a violation of any provision of this lease by the other party.

17. Time is of the essence. The waiver by Lessor of any breach shall not be construed to be a continuing waiver of any subsequent breach.

Lessor: _____          Lessee: _____

Lessor: _____          Lessee: _____

For these forms, address California Real Estate Association, 520 So. Grand Ave., Los Angeles 90017. All rights reserved. Copyright, May 1970, by California Real Estate Association.

FORM LSF-14

CITIZEN PRINT SHOP—20M

**Fig. 17–3.** California standard lease form.

Concessions or special services provided by the owner may be such as to create a wide gap between the real and the nominal money rent. Thus, a rental may be set at $125 per month for an apartment, with a concession of one month's rent, which means in fact that the real charge is $114.58 per month. Managers often make such arrangements instead of cutting rents, because they believe that it will be easier, when the market warrants a return to the old level, to raise rents by eliminating concessions than by reinstating a schedule previously abandoned. The provision of special equipment, or, in some cases, the payment of moving expenses in order to get the tenant in are other examples of concessions.

### Duration of Leases

Different provisions are to be found respecting the duration of the lease:

1. Tenancies for a fixed or definite term.
2. Tenancies for a periodic term, subject to termination upon notice (tenancy "from month to month" or "from year to year").
3. Tenancies for an indefinite period, subject to termination with notice (tenancy at will).

Sometimes leases hold over—that is, the tenant stays after the expiration of the lease. If this happens, as a general rule the owner has the option of either taking proceedings to dispossess the tenant or of assuming that the lease has been renewed for another term.

Once a lease has been drawn up and signed, it may be terminated by expiration of the agreement, by eviction of the tenant by the owner, forfeiture of the lease by the tenant, or voluntary surrender and acceptance. Each of these methods of terminating the lease, except the first, is governed by detailed legal regulations.

### Express and Implied Covenants

As in the case of most real estate contracts, leases contain certain express and implied covenants, the landlord or lessor guaranteeing possession and quiet enjoyment and promising that the property will be suitable for use. The lessee guarantees to pay rent, to use the property in a stipulated fashion, and to care for the premises. In accordance with the latter agreement, the lessee is usually required to carry certain insurance for the protection of the property, although this varies with the type of property involved. In the case of business property the lessee is often required to assist in the payment of taxes if they reach a certain point. Such an agreement in a lease is called a *tax participation clause.*

## CONSERVATION OF PROPERTY

The property manager is responsible for the maintenance of the property so that its economic life may be as long as possible. This means that he must follow a regular program for making repairs and replacements.

### Modernization

At times modernization will be undertaken. For example, older office buildings have frequently been able to compete effectively with new buildings because their managers have devised modernization programs giving them many of the desirable features provided by newly produced structures. The complete interior modernization of an older building represents a huge outlay, but it may be carried out on a piecemeal basis over a period of time. Thus, special attention may at one time be given to a particular floor that seems to have "gone dead," at another time to the space which is being rented to new tenants, and at still another time to that occupied by important tenants whose leases are up for renewal. When such a program is carried out over a ten- or twelve-year period, no great outlay is necessary at any one time; and the program can often be financed out of increased earnings resulting from the changes themselves. The operation of office buildings has been virtually revolutionized by automatic elevators, air conditioning, increased use of electrical equipment, and improved office layout and design.

### Repairs

The careful planning of repair programs over a period of time, and the proper allowance for such work in the budgetary setup of the organization, are important functions of good property management. In apartment house management it is usually safe to allocate one month's rent per year to normal repairs and decorations. Another 5 per cent of the income is usually set aside for painting, roofing, renovation of heating equipment, and other types of repairs which do not arise every year but must be paid for over varying periods of time.

### People Factors

Successful conservation of a property requires that attention be given not only to the physical condition of the structure, but also to the quality of the tenants and to the properties and people in the surrounding neighborhood. Property managers frequently have real opportunities for the up-grading of an area by the careful and systematic selection of tenants as well as by following adequate maintenance and modernization programs. Neither a property nor its environment can be thought of in connection with management programs without giving careful consideration to the people living or working in the property and in the area.

Thus the property manager is involved with process of *community organization* even though he seldom thinks of himself in such a capacity. Physical facilities take on meaning only in relation to people and the various interrelations between the people who may be involved. The property manager can benefit from the work of the sociologist and social psychologist as well as that of the engineer and architect.

## SUPERVISING BUILDING OPERATIONS

The day-to-day and month-to-month operation of a building involves a multitude of activities. The competent manager constantly checks receipts and outlays in order to maintain a proper relation between different income and expense items, such as upkeep, conservation, and improvement of the property. Such a ratio will vary with conditions in the market, the age of the property, and the special objectives of the management program.

Building operation includes the jobs of collecting rents, caring for insurance and taxes, and purchasing and using supplies, in addition to many related activities. Valuable information on this subject and related management problems will be found in the publications of the Institute of Real Estate Management of the National Association of Real Estate Boards, especially the *Journal of Property Management*.

### Collecting Rents

It is necessary to collect rents in order to obtain income in the case of a leased property. While the large majority of tenants will pay promptly if asked punctually and in a proper manner, at least 10 per cent of the potential collections are likely to cause problems. Many collection systems fail because threats are made and never carried out. The making of threats is a last resort of the manager and is used as a collection device by the careful manager only after all others have failed. Informal reports from property managers indicate that the best collection procedure is simply to demand what is due at the time it is due; follow-up notices after a five-day interval often are helpful and if not heeded another notice requesting a call at the management office may be effective. Managers for the most part appear to believe it is wrong to have the tenant feel that a collector will be sent if payment is not made; rather the tenant should feel that it is his obligation to handle the payment.

It is common knowledge that many tenants of residential properties take offense at being asked to pay their debts, regardless of how adroitly they are handled. Insofar as possible, the wise manager will try to determine whether or not difficulties of this kind of likely to arise before the tenant is accepted. Credit reports and careful analysis of references are useful in this connection, and in some cities real estate boards or property managers' associations maintain files of information covering a large number of tenants. Some delinquency always will develop, since a few people follow the policy of moving every few months, to the chagrin and loss of managers and owners. An average rental loss of 5 per cent is not uncommon. Of course, the management office can create a great deal of good will by granting extensions of time for payment when they are honestly deserved. In order to grant such favors, however, it is necessary to secure a considerable amount of knowledge regarding the tenants involved.

Collections are not such a difficult problem in the case of business properties or office buildings, since the tenants are more likely to pay their obligations in a prompt and businesslike manner. Even here the collection problem sometimes becomes burdensome and must be handled firmly and tactfully, unless it is apparent that the tenant is unable to pay. Then steps are taken to obtain possession of the property without delay.

## Providing Insurance

The property manager may be responsible for placing insurance and paying for it regularly. Normally, fire insurance in an amount equal to approximately 80 per cent of the replacement cost of buildings is carried (80 per cent coinsurance). Sometimes in the case of large buildings this is supplemented by use and occupancy insurance—that is, insurance against the loss of rent resulting from destruction of a building.

Public liability insurance typically is carried for all buildings. Also, boiler and plate glass insurance are necessary in some cases; and if rent collectors are employed, good practice requires that they be bonded. Insurance against theft, tornadoes, and other hazards is also carried by many management organizations. Good management often can effect substantial savings in insurance by eliminating various risks or by the use of coinsurance, thus securing the benefits of reduced insurance premiums.

## Taxes and Fees

The payment of taxes and special assessments, as well as of local license and inspection fees, requires careful and prompt attention by a property manager. In some instances, where the taxes on a building appear to be out of line with those on similar structures, the management can effect savings by calling this fact tọ the attention of the proper tax officials. Errors are sometimes made by tax officials who may estimate the value of a building by its external appearance rather than by its earning power. This is especially true of large office buildings or apartment houses. The preparation and submission of accurate statistical materials to the proper tax officers, presenting data on earning power, is often a helpful method of attacking this problem. Problems of this type often arise in connection with older buildings which have been assessed at high values during years when their earning power was great, but for which tax adjustments were not made as income-producing ability declined.

### Tenant Relations

The basic opportunity available to every property management organization for building good will arises from its numerous relationships with the tenants. Such good will is an important asset—one that can be created only over a period of time. As one management official has said, unlike the broker, the property manager does not sell the prospect once; he must keep him sold. The effectiveness with which this selling process is carried out is a good measure of tenant-landlord relations.

Many managers follow the practice of writing or visiting every new tenant within 30 days after he has moved into a building in order to let the tenant know that his welfare is being considered and to provide him with an opportunity for bringing any complaints to the attention of the manager. This is done in the belief that hunting for trouble will lead to fewer demands on the part of tenants. However, many managers do not share this view. Much depends on the type of tenant involved. Some managers write to desirable tenants who have moved from a building, thanking them for their considerate treatment of the property and for their patronage. Such letters often lead to favorable indirect advertising.

In the management of a large building, it is necessary to follow the principle of seeking the greatest good for the greatest number. Frequently, there will be tenants who will not recognize the rights of other occupants of the building and who will not take proper care of the quarters they are renting. When this happens, it is best to request the removal of such tenants as soon as possible, for they can quickly destroy much of the good will the management has built up.

### Handling Complaints

Complaints and requests from desirable tenants require a sympathetic hearing, even when they are unreasonable, as is often the case. Impatient treatment of minor complaints often results in the loss of a desirable tenant. The policy of establishing general rules to which exceptions cannot be made has provided many managers with a convenient device for refusing impossible or difficult requests. General rules also help to avoid the charge that the management is playing favorites. Especially in office or apartment buildings, any special concessions are soon discovered. Tenants resent any appearance of favoritism on the part of management and are likely to demand similar concessions themselves.

In the management of office buildings special devices for creating good will are frequently employed. Among these are found the provision of safety vaults, parking accommodations, libraries and conference rooms, and even the publication of a house organ. Many such devices are beyond the resources of the average building; but every manager, by the exercise of foresight and imagination, can find many ways of cultivating the good will of tenants.

## Management Records and Accounts

In order to control operations effectively, a manager needs adequate records of all transactions and accurate accounts of all operations. Probably no single aspect of property management requires more attention. Without adequate and accurate accounting methods, it is impossible for the manager to render the proper reports to the owner. Without proper accounting he cannot determine the success of the policies he is following and he will lack precise knowledge of the points at which savings can be effected.

The type of accounting system which a manager will use depends in large part on the magnitude of his operations, the size of the building or buildings under his supervision, and the characteristics of the manager. Bookkeeping machines and the use of addressograph plates for rent bills, employees' names, and Society Security numbers are often justified in larger offices.[6] Possible short cuts, as the elimination of various forms, must always be considered from the standpoint of savings secured and effects on standard accounting procedure.

Some managers follow a policy of requiring the preparation of data periodically on the basis of unit costs—for example, rental rates per square foot or per room, cost of heating per cubic foot, annual expenses per unit, per room, or per square or cubic foot, and similar reductions of various items of income and expense to unit bases. Such records are often useful in determining efficiency of operations, but their value depends in part on the records available and the uses to which they can be put. If sufficiently extensive data are involved and they can be put to a variety of uses, access to a computer may prove to be desirable.

---

[6] John G. Held, "Property Management Through Automatic Bookkeeping," *Journal of Property Management* (Fall, 1963).

Reorganized buildings often have special requirements in their trust indentures calling for the allocation of a certain portion of the net income to specific accounts, such as bond retirement. Certain items such as net income, extraordinary expenses, and others are frequently defined in such indentures in a manner that does not conform to customary management or accounting procedure. This creates special problems. Again, institutional owners, such as insurance companies and banks, often require the use of accounting forms designed for general uses which do not fit the needs of specific buildings.

## PROFESSIONAL MANAGEMENT ORGANIZATION

The chief professional organization in the property management field is the Institute of Real Estate Management. It was established in 1933, first as an organization of management firms but later (1938) as a professional society of qualified individuals. Membership is limited to those who can meet stated experience, educational and ethical standards, and can successfully pass designated examinations. Those selected for membership may make use of the designation CPM (Certified Property Manager).

The Institute has done much to further the development of the property management field. It publishes *The Journal of Property Management* and various other reports and studies. It provides for a ready exchange of experience among members. It stimulates educational programs and encourages the continuing personal and professional development of its members. In addition, it helps to present the entire field in a favorable light with respect to the investing and renting public, thus performing a highly valuable public relations function.

Another nation-wide organization is Building Owners and Managers Association International (BOMAI). Membership in BOMAI is primarily made up of owners and managers of office buildings. This organization provides educational programs and the means for furthering the professional development and ethical standards of its members and publishes various reports and studies, including BOMAI's Office Building Experience Exchange Report dating back to 1920. The official publication of BOMAI is *Skyscraper Management.*

## SUMMARY

Property management refers to the performance of the managerial function with regard to real estate resources by specialized individuals or firms rather than by the owners of properties. It is increasing in scope and importance because of the growing complexity of tax, legal, and managerial factors. Although property management refers to a specialized activity, its principles and methods may be applied successfully by those who manage their own properties.

The property manager, who may be part of a brokerage firm, has the legal status of general agent for principals who are the property owners, and therefore seeks to achieve the objectives of the owners, which usually means obtaining the best possible return from the relatively fixed resources of land and buildings.

The primary functions of property management include planning space, marketing property services, conserving the property and its surroundings, and supervising the operation of the property. These functions include such activities as establishing and adjusting rental schedules; selecting tenants and collecting rents; repair, maintenance, and building operation; arranging for insurance; tenant relations; and the keeping of accounts and records. The property manager should be cognizant of developments within the community or neighborhood which affect the income-producing ability of his principal's property.

## QUESTIONS FOR STUDY

1. How do you explain the growth of property management in recent years?
2. In what ways may the following factors create problems for the property manager? (a) The durability of real property. (b) The economic inflexibility of real properties. (c) Inflexibility of operating expenses. (d) Fixity of location of real property. (e) Uniqueness of each piece of real property.
3. Assume that you are managing the Hilltop Apartments, owned by the widow of the late J. Randolph Hilltop. (a) Make a list of your specific duties as manager of this property. (b) What are your obligations to Mrs. Hilltop, as owner of the property? (c) How would you expect to be compensated? (d) What factors would you consider most important in establishing the rental schedule for the building?
4. Suppose that you take over the management of an office building and find that the rents being charged there are approximately 10 per cent above the rents of comparable properties. Vacancy rates, however, have been about the same. Would you conclude that this rental schedule was too high? Why or why not?
5. Give reasons why you believe that it is or is not desirable to establish general rules for all the tenants in a building.
6. What is meant by "hunting for trouble" in connection with tenant relations? Indicate reasons why this is or is no ta sound management practice.
7. Differentiate between flat rate, graded, percentage, and reappraisal leases.
8. The small office building that you are managing has a replacement cost of $400,000. How much insurance should be carried on this building? If more than one type of insurance is necessary, list the different types and reasons why each should be carried.

9. As manager of the property in question 8 you discover that the taxes are apparently higher than taxes on similar properties. What action would you take? Is it your responsibility as property manager to take any action at all?

10. List the factors you would consider in selecting tenants for an apartment building. In what ways can careful selection of tenants help lengthen the economic life of the building?

## SUGGESTED READINGS

Brown, Robert Kevin. *Essentials of Real Estate.* Englewood Cliffs, N.J.: Prentice-Hall, Inc., 1970. Chap. 14.

Downs, James C., Jr. *Principles of Real Estate Management* (9th ed.). Chicago: Institute of Real Estate Management, 1967.

Kratovil, Robert. *Real Estate Law* (5th ed.). Englewood Cliffs, N.J.: Prentice-Hall, Inc., 1969. Chap. xxix.

Lusk, Harold F. *Law of the Real Estate Business* (rev. ed.). Homewood, Ill.: Richard D. Irwin, Inc., 1965. Chap. xviii.

## CASE 17–1

### The Omnibus Realty Company

The Omnibus Realty Company has decided to expand operations to include property management. The various members of the firm have recommended alternative policies and have given a brief statement of the advantages of each of the alternative policies as revealed in the following minutes of a company meeting.

*Mr. Omnibus:* Gentlemen, today we will consider some alternative policies for the property management department which we are planning to add to our operation. First, we will consider the question of flexibility of rents.

*Mr. Maxim:* If we are to maximize the income for our property owners, it will be necessary to adjust rents frequently in accordance with changes in market conditions. Also, this means changing rents for occupied apartments, not just changing rents as space becomes available.

*Mr. Axim:* We should not be so concerned with maximizing scheduled gross income. If we raise rents frequently we may find large vacancy and collection losses and high expenses. That is, we may expect that tenancy turnover will be quite high and maintenance expenses would rise. I, therefore, believe the policy should be only to raise rents when space becomes available or under conditions where our rents fall substantially below the prevailing market rental levels. Not only will this maximize long-run net returns but I think it leads to better tenant relations. I don't anticipate any problems because of rent differentials due to different dates of beginning occupancy.

*Mr. Novis:* Wouldn't the requirements for long term leases solve this problem for us?

*Mr. Omnibus:* Some interesting questions have been raised. We will consider these and come back to them later. Let's now turn to the question of selection of tenants.

*Mr. Maxim:* Since we are trying to maximize income I see no reason to ever let an apartment stay vacant as long as there is someone willing to pay the rent. Therefore, as long as a prospective tenant seems able to pay and is of apparently good character, I think that we owe it to the property owners to immediately rent the space and thereby minimize vacancy losses.

*Mr. Axim:* While it is true that we do not wish to have vacancy losses, I think that if we carefully select our tenants we will have a lower turnover and thus less vacancies. This should also minimize losses since we may then select a good caliber tenant, not to mention the possibilities of minimizing repair expenses and other maintenance charges. I don't think that we need to check back to see if the ancestors of prospective tenants came over on the Mayflower, but I would at least like to see a policy of requiring an application and a deposit giving us sufficient time to check credit references and background.

*Mr. Novis:* Checking out the tenants seems to be a good idea, but I think that most prospective tenants would be offended if we questioned their character. Therefore, why don't we just adopt a policy of accepting tenants if they make a nice appearance?

*Mr. Omnibus:* Well, this brings us to the question as to whether we should require leases which will spell out the terms of our agreement.

*Mr. Maxim:* Since I think we should have flexible rent and therefore short term leases or no leases at all, the question comes down to how we should spell out the terms of the agreement. We may from time to time desire to change the rules by which we operate; therefore, I would rather not commit ourselves as to terms of tenancy. The alternative of setting up general rules posted in the building and in our office letting all tenants know what we expect and what we will do would be sufficient. In this way we have the flexibility of changing our rules and yet the tenants can know what is expected of them by merely looking at our rules from time to time.

*Mr. Axim:* When we lease a space for a period, whether it is short or long, I think the terms of the tenancy should be specifically spelled out and should be held for the period. Therefore, I believe that all the essential elements of the agreement should be contained in a lease and if changes are necessary they would be made at time of renewal. In this way, the tenants having signed the lease will certainly know what is expected of them and what they may expect of us.

*Mr. Novis:* There are certain conditions of the lease which we will want to have written in order to be enforceable. And therefore I think that we ought to adopt a policy of requiring written leases. As for operational rules, we may desire to vary these from property to property so why not just inform the tenant whenever an issue arises? In this way, we can always adjust to the situation.

*Mr. Omnibus:* This brings us to the general area of tenant relations. I would like you gentlemen to render opinions on collection of rents and policies for providing maintenance and repairs.

*Mr. Maxim:* I think the less contact we have with the tenants the less difficulties will arise. Therefore, I would be in favor of a policy of having the tenants mail their checks to the office. With regard to repairs, when the building needs repairs, the tenants will certainly let us know. So I would not be in favor of going out and looking for things to do.

*Mr. Axim:* Good tenant relations in the long run can mean more income for our property owners. I think we should have considerable personal contact with our tenants. Therefore, I recommend that a representative of the office call for the rent on the due date and at that time inquire as to any needs, complaints or recommendations on the part of the tenants. Also, preventive maintenance is important for prolonging the economic life of the property and hence the earnings of the property so I recommend periodic inspection of the property to see that it is being kept up. Deferred maintenance in the long run can be costly. While such a policy may mean a lower net income for some period, in the long run we will benefit the property as well as the tenants.

*Mr. Novis:* In regards to rent, I don't think people like to be reminded, so I would be in favor of having them mail their checks. As for maintenance, if we go ahead with our plans to provide our own maintenance crews we might as well keep them busy by having them going to each of the properties and doing whatever they see necessary rather than waiting for someone to complain.

## Questions

1. Which of the suggested policies would you recommend? Explain your reasons for each of your policy recommendations.
2. Do you agree that all arguments presented for each of the alternative policies were valid? Explain.
3. Have you made any implicit assumptions as to the type of property the property management department would be handling? If so, what are these assumptions?
4. Evaluate for Omnibus the inspection and tenant relations policies described as follows: The firm of Applegate and Smith, Property Managers, follows the practice of making an annual inspection of each property under the firm's management to determine the general conditions of each. The tenants are not interviewed at the time of the inspection, as tenants are prone to ask for a large amount of repair and renovation work. Mr. Smith states: "Given the slightest opportunity, most tenants will ask for almost anything; yet if they have to call at the office or write a letter asking that certain things be done, fewer complaints come in. In fact, many tenants will do minor repair jobs themselves rather than make a complaint."

## STUDY PROJECT 17–1

### A Closer Look at the Rental of Single-Family Units [*]

When we talk with our colleagues in the management profession, invariably the subject of single dwellings management arises. You, as well as I, have had the experience of hearing someone say that the management of single dwellings is a non-profitable nuisance, one which many managers will not touch. Someone will say there are too many problems, and not enough profits. Lets examine single family dwellings critically, and see if the profits really need to be so small, and the problems so large.

How would an alert manager approach the management of single dwellings? Why do owners rent single family dwellings?

1. Absentee owner transferred out of town—for some reason he doesn't want to sell just now. Maybe depressed market—if he sells now—can't get investment back. Maybe he hopes transfer is temporary, and if he comes back, he certainly wants his own home back. Maybe he has no reason—but we know he has sentimental attachment to it. He can't give it up—not yet, anyway.

2. Estates—owner gone, heirs have no need for the house—executor can let the house set vacant during probate, or rent it, and add the income to the estate.

3. Builder of tract homes—sales are slower than anticipated. Inventory of unsold homes—with payments—hurts. So he offers them for rent, to help him make those payments. This trend is growing—in fact it was noticed and commented on in the September *House and Home* magazine. "Hint of New Trend in the Housing Market—One Family Homes for Rent."

The biggest surprise was spotted by real estate analyst Roy Wenzlick of St. Louis: 2.8 per cent of new homes built in 1963 are being rented instead of sold. A year ago the percentage was negligible. Why are builders renting their homes? The trend is so new that answers from owners provide no clear reason. Most of them are renting homes that have remained unsold for a long while simply to keep them from standing idle. A new census look at house building shows merchant builders are taking 6–7 months to sell a home after completion now.

A new NAHB forecast for housing the rest of the decade indicates the trend to one-family homes for rent may continue. Says NAHB, 9.1 million single family homes will be built this decade, including those already built, but only 7.1 million will be sold. The remaining 2 million will be either rented or vacant. NAHB predicts demand for rental and sale quarters will be about equal. And the new sampling of market prospects among renters shows the rental of a house might be an important sales tool. A survey of 19,000 renters in all 50 states by Panelboard Mfg. Company of Newark shows many renters are fearful about taking on the chores of home-ownership and would like trial

[*] Reba E. Claytor, C.P.M., *Journal of Property Management*, XXIX, No. 6 (July–August, 1964), pp. 309–13.

runs as renters. Some want builders to rent homes on trial before buying. Others want builders to take homes back if families decide to move.

From the sound of that article, management of single dwellings is going to boom in the next decade. I know a builder in Castro Valley, with a tract called Sleepy Hollow. He built 400 homes, and upon selling 300, found he was paying out far more of his profit in income tax than he was keeping. He thought about this, and upon the advice of his tax consultant, stopped selling homes. He rented the last 100, and sells a few each year. He has a lifetime retirement, for each year his homes increase in value, and he carries back mortgages or deeds of trust on part of the payment. His homes now, just 4 years after selling the first one, sell for $3000–$4000 more per home than the original sales price.

**A Need and a Challenge.** I have mentioned a few of the reasons why homes come on the rental market, and you can think of many more. The important point is that—if homes are being rented, management is needed. And where there is a need for management there is both a challenge and an opportunity for the CPM.

What problems are there in managing single dwellings? I don't think they are much different from a multiple unit building. The techniques and methods differ. We must always ask what we should charge for rent. What is the fair rental value of this property? As in multiple dwellings, the rental agent must know his market, and set a realistic evaluation. Keep in mind though, that with one single dwelling, you never have a 5 per cent or 10 per cent vacancy factor. It is 0 or 100 per cent. If that house would rent immediately at $150, but might take 3 months to rent at $175, if it would rent at all at that price—the owner who held out for $175 per month would have collected $225 less in the first year than the owner who rented immediately for $150.

It is difficult for owners to realize this concept when we talk of rental value. A friend and fellow manager—dramatizes this well with a $5 bill. He shows the bill to the owner—and asks what the reaction might be if he tore the bill into tiny pieces and threw it away. Most owners respond that they'd think he needed to have his head examined. He turns the tables on them and explains they are doing about the same thing every day their $150 per month house is idle and unrented. Convince the owner that he has only time to sell, and that a day's rent lost due to vacancy is gone—it can't be recovered. Convince him to be realistic about the rental value.

He must not expect to make a profit on renting a single dwelling. In fact, in my area, he's lucky to break even. His motivation for renting single dwellings must be something other than profit. His motivation may be simply to preserve his asset—until he can later decide what to do with it.

. . . . . . . . . . . . . . . .

**Some Specific Problems.** If you properly merchandise your single dwelling, you'll find a tenant, then you will have the problems of management to meet. Some problems exist here that are absent in multiple units. One might be the gardening. With a large apartment building, you hire a gardener. Often an owner has left valuable plants and shrubs that must be maintained. Most tenants will water, some will cut lawns, but few will weed, spray, and fertilize. If the grounds are extensive, and with valuable plants and large lawns, the owner must retain a professional gardener. Rarely can he regain this cost in additional rents.

If the grounds are modest and without extensive plantings, owners expect the tenant to keep and maintain them. Expecting and getting are often far different. We help to boost the tenant's good intentions with a clause in our lease, stating that if he doesn't do the work, we'll hire a gardener to do the work, and add the cost to the rent. This device has worked for us more than once, when a tenant has been derelict in his duty, and we've called to say unless the lawn was shaped up, we'd have a professional gardener start working the first of the month. We have never yet had to hire a gardener, under those circumstances.

In a single dwelling lease, we usually require a substantial security deposit. This should be at least equal to one month's rent, but definitely not applicable as the last month's rent. For this reason, we never make the amount exactly equal to a month's rent, always a little more or less.

I make it clear that this deposit may never be used as the last month's rent. This security deposit is worth nothing if it is gone before the tenant moves out. It is refunded after the tenant has moved, returned the key, and the house checked and found to be in good condition. In the case of a furnished house, the deposit should be higher, particularly if the owner has left his own furnishings which are usually of higher quality than found in normal rental units. Only with an adequate security deposit can one insure the owner against loss.

Once the house has been rented, the management problems become routine. There is little difference in management of homes as compared to managing multiple units. After all, if you have 58 single dwellings, you have the same number of tenants as you'd have in a 58-unit multiple—only a little more spread out. There is, of course, more travel time caring for maintenance, repairs, showing, inspections. For this reason, if you will manage single dwellings you must build a volume. If you have 6 houses in a 6 block area, it takes little more time to inspect 6 than 1.

Accounting is especially important when you manage single dwellings. Certainly it must be simple—streamlined. When you have an account where the income is only slightly greater than the expenses going out, ask the owner to provide you with a "kitty" to handle unexpected expenses such as maintenance and repairs.

Many of you may be thinking—it sounds good—but how can we do all this work for the small fee involved, and still make a profit?" My answer—you can —if you:

1. Establish realistic fees.
2. Build volume.
3. Take full advantage of the by-products of management.

Lets elaborate—

1. Forego the idea of per cent of gross for your fee. Charge a minimum fee that will cover your cost and return a profit, even though it be a nominal profit. The fee must be based particularly on your individual costs of handling.

So, you must make a cost analysis of your management department, so you are sure that every home pays its own way. Our firm includes 6 per cent monthly management fee based on monthly rent, but with minimum fee of $10 per dwelling. Also 10 per cent supervision on all maintenance and repair items. Quick arithmetic shows a $200 per month house yields fees of $24 per month or $288 per year, without any extra fees for supervision or maintenance, and without any other benefits from management.

2. If you build a volume, of say 200 accounts, you can see you will be approaching a gross revenue of about $60,000 per year. This begins to add up to something worthwhile. Also with volume, per unit costs of handling go down, and thus profits go up. The same bookkeeper needed to handle $30,000 per year gross could, with proper accounting procedures, handle the $60,000 gross. One rental agent can show 2 or 3 homes in one area in little more time than it takes to show one house only.

3. Fringe benefits—or side benefits from management. The most obvious is management into sales. Previously the absentee owner was mentioned. He still has sentimental attachment, and elects to rent rather than sell. Time proves that after several years of renting, that sentiment weakens, the roots he had in the neighborhood begin to wither, his hopes for returning home dim, maybe if he still hopes to return, his family size may have changed, making the home no longer fit his needs. One year, when the lease is coming up for renewal, you will receive a letter asking your opinion on selling at this time. This will be a good listing as you will be asked for your opinion of price. Motivation is strong—as expenses go on while income may be nil if he didn't renew a lease. One management firm counts on their management department to yield 12 to 14 good listings per year from absentee owners, and from management of single dwellings.

Another side benefit may be insurance on the property. You will be asked for advice on the amount and kind of coverage desirable. You are in a prime spot—the insurance account can be yours, along with its extra income to you.

Maybe the owner will need to refinance. If so, you can provide this service for him, for a fee.

None of these are necessarily large commissions, but they are bread and butter, and can be regular. Occasionally, you will find that what you thought was bread is really cake. Some years ago, I agreed to manage a house for an absentee owner. It was a nice house, but at $10 per month commission. I managed it for several years, until the owner returned to occupy the home again. He had been pleased with the service, and later, upon coming into an inheritance, he decided to invest in income property, and came to me. Over the years we've helped him to buy and sell over a million dollars worth of property—and we manage his holdings. He presently owns about one-half million in property, which we manage. This came to us because we pleased one owner with our management of his single dwelling.

No one can deny that there are problems in handling another person's single dwelling. But—do not forget—one man's problems become another's opportunities. And where there are opportunities, there are potential profits.

## Questions

1. Explain why owners rent single-family dwellings.
2. How can the property manager best serve the needs of the owners of single-family houses who put them on the rental market?
3. Why is vacancy such an important problem in this field?
4. What are some of the by-products in the management of single-family homes?
5. Why does the author recommend a minimum fee rather than a percentage of gross?
6. What are the principal "fringe benefits" of this type of activity?

## STUDY PROJECT 17–2

### Renters Turn Militant

**"Another Increase?—Like Hell!"**    Pardon his pique, but the apartment dweller has just looked at his new lease. Rent, it says, will go up again. Just sign on the line and mail it in.

No longer content to pay up or move out, more and more renters are staying put and pitting their might against the most basic traditions of property rights.

Their common cause is tenants' rights, a movement now making its force felt in the form of tenant unions, rent strikes and pressures for rent controls in cities across the nation.

From the lowest and, increasingly, on up to the most affluent income ranges, the protesters are fed up with more than what they consider unwarranted rent gouging. They also point to poor building maintenance, inadequate security, unfair leases and lack of control over building management policies.

To their landlords, of course, the protesters spell trouble. Signs in hand, marching and chanting, picketing renters create an unfavorable image and hard-to-fill vacancies at some future time. Mass evict them, if possible at all, and the problems become even worse.

Though a building owner has much to lose in a situation like this, his losses may not be nearly as great as the lender's whose mortgage happens to cover his property.

**One Association's Experience.**    Ask Robert McConkey, vice president of $574 million Perpetual Building Association of Washington, D.C. His association holds the loan, a conventional, on a 214-unit, garden-type apartment development forced into receivership by rent-striking tenants.

Rather than paying their landlord, 40 tenants of the Trenton Terrace Apartments more than two years ago began making their rent payments to a tenants' council escrow account. The end result was a slow loan for Perpetual as funds fell short for mortgage repayments.

The tenants complained that there was no legal obligation to pay their rent so long as housing code violations went uncorrected—a contention backed, in part, by the U. S. Supreme Court in a case involving another group of renters.

Perpetual, obviously, is unhappy with its investment, which currently stands at some $1.2 million, counting property operating expenses. However, the association had reason to expect much different results when its loan was made in 1967.

At the time, McConkey says, the mortgage was made to a "sound owner." What went wrong was when the owner transferred title to an investment syndicate which "lacked the best motivation."

The syndicate, he states, turned to "incompetent management" to take charge of the property. McConkey blames the management firm for "inadequate screening" of tenants who, in some cases, took poor care of their apartments or failed to keep up their rent payments. In other cases, he says, "adequate leases were not signed by all tenants."

What's more, "a proper maintenance program was not established or maintained by the agent and not insisted upon by the owners," McConkey says.

The strike, McConkey says, was precipitated when the property manager attempted to raise rents as maintenance declined. It wasn't long before Perpetual had to step in and name a receiver to salvage the property when mortgage repayments were shut off completely.

The receivership action was taken in lieu of foreclosing the mortgage. Not yet ready to give up on its investment, Perpetual hopes to make substantial property improvements under Federal Housing Administration rehabilitation lending authority.

The ultimate goal is to increase rentals and generate income. The building, in which low-income renters pay $93 monthly for one-bedroom apartments and $105 for two bedrooms, had 90 vacant units in late January, McConkey reports.

**Uniting the "Silent Majority Types."** No isolated instances, the Trenton Terrace tenants' revolt exemplifies a problem familiar not only in Washington, D.C., but in such diverse locations as New York City, Detroit, Chicago, St. Louis and Berkeley, Calif.

Beyond the bounds of their own buildings, renters throughout the country have gone so far as to organize state and local units to press their demands.

One group, the New Jersey Tenants Organization, claims more than 200,000 members, many of them middle-class "silent majority types," according to NJTO President Martin Aranow. The group's actions have included more than 40 rent strikes, mainly in protest against proposed rent increases.

According to Aranow, the strikes resulted in the withholding of rents totaling some $1.8 million. Five strikes forced cancellations of rent increases, 30 succeeded in spreading out rent hikes from one year to five-year terms and eight ended in tenant acceptance of rent increases in return for improved building maintenance and security. Other examples of tenant power:

> In Washington, D.C. middle- and upper-income families have participated in at least seven major rent strikes in recent months. In one case, the Tenants Council of Tiber Island-Carrollsburg Square, a luxury high-rise development, forced the management to cut a proposed rent increase ranging as high as 32 per cent to a maximum of 12 per cent.

In Ann Arbor, Mich., 1,200 college students living off-campus private housing held back $70,000 in monthly rent payments to force a reduction in rentals charged to be "enormous to astronomical." Most of the students came from families of more than modest means.

In St. Louis, a public housing rent strike involving some 1,000 families succeeded in rolling back rents to a limit of one-fourth of family income. Before the nine-month strike began, rentals had taken as much as 42 per cent of income.

In Texas, the Great Houston Apartment Dwellers, Inc., last year began offering to file legal complaints against landlords for a fee. Within six months after its formation, the group had filed more than 1,000 complaints and enlisted 600 members.

**Stimulation from a Nerve Center.**    To further strengthen their hand, at least 250 renter groups have linked forces with the National Tenants Organization, which considers itself the nerve center for the overall tenants' rights movement.

With a shoestring budget and only six staff members, the NTO, founded only two years ago in Washington, D.C., has emerged as a potent force for change in traditional landlord-tenant relationships.

Says its executive director, Anthony Henry, "I see NTO not just as a means of dealing with the housing problem in this nation but as a means of demonstrating that people who appear to be unorganizable can be organized and can wield power in their own behalf and can begin to make changes in their living situation."

Although most of its efforts have been directed toward improving living standards in public housing, NTO estimates that roughly 20 per cent of the approximately 500,000 renters it claims to represent are of the middle class.

By providing a "communications link," the organization believes that all of its members can "learn from each other's strategies and struggles," even though their particular grievances may differ, says one NTO official.

Toward this end, the organization publishes a monthly newsletter, provides other informational services and conducts frequent workshops on tenant organization.

One example of NTO's approach to renter dissension is contained in excerpts from a draft of a "how-to-do-it" handbook. "Before going on a rent strike," it is advised, "tenants must have some kind of a working organization. Ten per cent of housing units or 15 families are enough to start a strike if the tenants are together. If the housing project is very large, then a lesser per cent will do."

The draft handbook urges tenants "to lay the groundwork for the strike by building their case against the landlord. The more you know about the landlord and his building, the less he can trick you by giving you untrue information."

For example, rent strikers are urged to gather information about "the building, to show its bad condition." Next, "expose" the landlord, it is recommended, if he owns other buildings in disrepair or has "unfavorable political, social or business connections."

Still further, in a point most pertinent to lenders, the draft handbook counsels rent strikers to gain information about "the mortgage holder." What type of information the NTO has in mind is not made clear.

**What Stirs Renters the Most.**   As NTO indicates, most rent strikes center on poor building maintenance, a situation recently confirmed by Chicago's Urban Research Corporation.

In a special study of "The Tenants' Rights Movernment," conducted in 1969, Urban Research found that "poor maintenance" grievances headed the list of 89 cases of renter unrest surveyed in cities across the nation.

For lower-income renters, the survey showed, "poor maintenance" usually involved charges of substandard housing, building code violations, and unsafe and unsanitary conditions.

In particular, complaints took note of "rats and roaches, stopped-up plumbing, faulty wiring, crumbling plaster, uncollected garbage and broken windows," according to the study.

For higher-income renters, it added, poor maintenance often meant inadequate housekeeping, including unclean stairs, hallways and lobbies as well as unkept grounds.

Though not directly cited in the Urban Research study, complaints of poor maintenance from the more affluent also have focused on such matters as the lack of storm windows and screens, air conditioners that don't work and janitors who don't, either.

While "poor maintenance" was the primary complaint of all groups combined, middle- and upper-income families were most vociferous in their objections to high rents and unreasonable rent increases, the Urban Research study found.   Counting lower-income occupants of both private and public housing, rent cost complaints were uncovered in 34 per cent of the cases surveyed.

The next most frequent complaint centered on the "lack of tenant control," which generally involved tenant demands for a say-so over the policies of the buildings in which they live.

In the case of public housing, the study learned, demands of this type usually called for tenant representatives on housing authority boards.   For other renters, including privately housed lower-income families, the demands sought "recognition of a tenant organization and creation of a tenant board or landlord-tenant board to hear grievances and determine policies regarding such things as rent increases and lease provisions."

Not far behind "lack of tenant control" were complaints about "inadequate security."   Included in this category were broken locks or buzzer systems, the absence of locks on entry or garage doors, and poor or broken lighting on stairs, hallways or outside grounds.

To express their discontent with existing conditions, 75 per cent of all renters studied by Urban Research moved to organize unions of various types to take collective action.   At the same time, legal action was initiated in 55 per cent of all cases studied.

According to Urban Research, one legal step involved "going to court or to a hearing before some official body, such as a housing authority or code violation board."   In other cases, renters were found to be "actively seeking" legislation in the areas of rent control, rent withholding receivership and non-retaliatory evictions.

Nearly one-fourth of all renters surveyed went even further by withholding rents, the study found, while 20 per cent engaged in protest marches and other types of demonstrations.

Though not without setbacks, the tenants' rights movement has managed to score some significant gains where they count most—in the courts and among lawmakers.

For instance, the U. S. Supreme Court, in a case that could have national implications, has upheld the principle that apartment tenants in Washington, D.C. have the right to withhold their rents if the buildings in which they reside contain housing code violations or are improperly maintained. The ruling backed a lower court finding that "the law must recognize the landlord's obligation to keep his premises in a habitable condition." Landlords, the ruling added, "should be as accountable for the products they provide as are other sellers of goods and services."

Under this decision, a renter could petition the courts for the right to withhold some or all of his rent for application toward the correction of alleged property deficiencies.

Tenants in New Jersey now have the same right under a like decision handed down recently by their state supreme court. The court held that if a landlord fails to keep his property in good repair, he essentially has violated a lease agreement and his tenants may use rent payments to make repairs.

Still other cases have emerged, including two others involving renters in Washington, D.C. In one case, the U. S. Supreme Court upheld a lower court ruling that completely invalidated leases signed at a time when building code violations existed. The other case maintained the principle that a landlord may not evict a tenant who complains to housing authorities about alleged code violations.

**Retaliation Against Retaliatory Evictions.** Described as a "barrier to tenant activism" by Urban Research, "the fear of a retaliatory eviction" for reporting building code violations has been eliminated by lawmakers in states such as Illinois, Michigan and New Jersey.

"It is these laws, coupled with the large amounts of free legal representation now available to the poor through the [Office of Equal Opportunity] Legal Services, that have prompted the rapid rise of rent strikes and other activities of tenants in low-income housing," the research firm states.

It adds that OEO has made at least $42 million available to 265 community legal aid programs "to enable them to increase their services to include more free legal assistance in rapidly changing areas of law, particularly housing law."

Rapidly changing it is. In addition to those laws barring retaliatory evictions, several states have enacted legislation permitting tenants to place their rents in the hands of the courts until their landlords correct housing code violations. Similarly, laws on the books of some other states allow rents to be withheld in substandard buildings and turned over to court-appointed receivers who see that repairs are made.

### "One-Sided" Leases Also Rile Apartment Renters

Along with their other major grievances, renters often point to alleged inequities in what has been called the "one-sided lease."

What disturbs renters the most in such agreements are provisions including:

- Confessions of judgment clauses, which authorize a landlord's attorney to appear in court and plead guilty to an alleged lease violation on behalf of a tenant without prior notice to the tenant.
- Waivers of tort liability, which exempt a landlord from liability for damages or injuries to persons or property, even if damages or injuries result from personal actions of the landlord or his agent.
- Waivers of notice, which allow a landlord to terminate a lease without notice if, in the landlord's opinion, a tenant fails to live up to any lease provision, no matter how minor.
- Re-entry clauses, which give a landlord or his agent the right to enter a tenant's apartment at "all reasonable times."
- Security deposit agreements that fail to spell out how such funds are to be used or when, if at all, they are to be returned.

Concerned with these provisions, a select panel of the American Bar Foundation recently developed a proposed "Model Residential Landlord-Tenant Code" to effect major reforms. The code, for example, would:

- Prohibit confession of judgment clauses in leases. Landlords insisting on the retention of these clauses would be charged with a misdemeanor and made subject to a fine of up to $200.
- Prohibit waiver of liability clauses. Such clauses have been ruled meaningless, anyway, in lease agreements inasmuch as no renter can legally sign away his right to damage awards if he is injured through his landlord's negligence.
- Liberalize waivers of notice in favor of tenants. In cases other than nonpayment of rent, a landlord would have to demonstrate the legitimacy of a lease obligation a tenant has breached.
- Clamp down on re-entry provisions. A landlord would be required to give a tenant at least two days' notice, if possible, of his intention to enter the tenant's apartment. Furthermore, entry would be limited to usual business hours.
- Provide more protection for security deposits. A landlord would be able to keep such advance payments only if a tenant defaulted on his rent or if the funds were needed to pay for tenant-caused damages.

Eventually, its drafters hope the proposed model code will be adopted by state legislatures across the country. As noted in the proposal's introductory remarks, existing law "allows the landlord to discriminate in favor of tenants who give him the least trouble—those who do not organize tenant unions, complain to code enforcement officials nor complain to him about stopped-up toilets. A landlord can effectively stifle legitimate desires and free speech without threatening his own profit."

| | |
|---|---|
| HEIRS, ETC.<br>CONFESSION<br>OF<br>JUDGMENT | 17. TENANT (and if more than one person's name appears as TENANT, each of them jointly and severally) irrevocably authorizes any attorney of any court of record in any State of the United States from time to time to appear for TENANT (and each of them) in such court, to waive process, service and trial by jury, to confess judgment in favor of OWNER, OWNER'S heirs, executors, administrators, successors or assigns and against TENANT (and each of them) for any rent and interest due hereunder from TENANT to OWNER and for OWNER'S costs and reasonable attorney's fees, to waive and release all errors in such proceedings and all right of appeal and to consent to an immediate execution upon the judgment. |

A third type of remedy, the "repair-and-deduct" statute, is now in effect in at least six states. Laws of this nature permit renters to make minor apartment repairs themselves and then deduct the cost of the repairs from their rent.

Still another remedy, rent control, has long been familiar in New York City. It's now either appearing or getting a hearing elsewhere as well. Examples:

- In Rhode Island, legislation enacted last year freezes public housing tenant rent payments for one year after tenant income has increased.
- In Cambridge, Mass., the city council last year passed a rent control ordinance which, in effect, rolled back local rents to the levels of April 1969.
- In Yonkers, N. Y., a recently authorized third-party beneficiary contract agreement provides for rent increase negotiations between city officials and landlords for the benefit of tenants. Similar programs also have been worked out in Mt. Vernon, White Plains and New Rochelle, N. Y.
- And in Washington, D.C., Rep. Frank Annunzio (D, Ill.) introduced legislation in Congress last year to freeze rents at their June 1, 1969, levels within the District. Annunzio and other renters in a luxury highrise earlier had engaged in a rent strike against what the congressman called "profiteering and rent gouging of the worst sort."

**Making Voices Heard.** Although Annunzio's bill failed to make headway, official Washington has not exactly ignored the tenants' rights movement. Witness, for example, a statement of policy issued last year by the Department of Housing and Urban Development.

The statement, though not an order, strongly urged local public housing authorities to appoint tenants to their governing boards. "The rapidly mounting desire by tenants of low-rent public housing to make their voices heard, to share in the decision making process and to achieve a feeling of belonging," said HUD, "argues strongly for local communities' consideration of providing for tenant representation."

What the department wants, explains Norman V. Watson, HUD's acting assistant secretary for renewal and housing management, is for local housing authorities to begin showing "greater sensitivity" to the "seen and expressed" needs of tenants.

Watson believes that "the single most critical critical need in public housing today is to improve communications and relations between management and tenants." What has happened instead, he says, is a tendency to "view the rising chorus of complaints and demands from tenants as a power struggle and a threat to management's authority.

"In my opinion, tenants are the manager's greatest potential resource for achieving good management," Watson adds. "Most tenants are not out after the executive director's job. What they want is a well-managed project and a management staff that is sympathetic and responsive to their needs and inspirations."

Though Watson refers directly to the management of public housing, his remarks may be equally relevant to many owners and managers of private rental housing.

Good communications between landlord and tenant certainly are critical, agrees Joseph Murray, vice president of Shannon and Luchs, a property management firm in Washington, D.C.

For example, Murray recommends close attention to preventive maintenance, prompt and courteous response to renter complaints, and insistence on good management by a professional.

When rents are to be raised, he urges that tenants be told at least 60 days in advance, that financial data be provided to justify the increase and that there be evidence of property upgrading or an improvement in service.

**More Tips for Better Relations.**    Adding to this list, the acting director of the National Apartment Association of Houston calls for "making rent increases reasonable and *explaining* rent increases." Moreover, cautions Ed Coleman, increases must be predicated on "providing the type of housing for which the renter is paying" and doing "everything you can for the money he is paying."

Coleman, whose 23,000 NAA members include apartment owners, investors and managers, acknowledges that "there is some legitimate basis for the tenant movement." He blames a large share of the troubles on the hiring of poorly trained property managers.

Too often, after taking great pains to assure his investment is sound, Coleman says, the owner or developer will "turn the whole thing over to some flaky person who doesn't know a thing about what's going on. This is sort of like A.T. and T.'s board of directors going down to wino's alley and asking somebody to run their corporation."

Coleman adds that "we have a long, long way to go" in the field of property management.

Hoping to get there faster is the Institute of Real Estate Management, an affiliate of the National Association of Real Estate Boards.

To achieve this goal, the IREM has established a Certified Property Managers (CPM) designation, which it awards only to individuals who pass stringent courses and prove their qualifications through "education, high ethical standards and experience," according to James F. Cannon, the trade association's executive vice president.

"Our goal," he says, "is to build respect for the designation to create an image that there are criteria which one can look to for well-trained, experienced managers. We want it known that there is a professional group that can look out not only for the investor's interest but the tenant's interest as well."

Cannon affirms that his organization's 2,700 CPMs and CPM candidates clearly "recognize that tenants have rights," including "a clean place to live, maintenance of property and rentals at a price comparable to what other rental housing commands in a given market."

Qualified property managers, he adds, can be expected to keep close watch over property cash flows, maintenance reserves, building security, rent collections, vacancy factors, tax and utility cost projections, and major appliance inventories.

He states further that the trained property manager can provide valuable assistance in helping determine various maintenance and cash flow cost factors relating to the particular design of an apartment building.

**Look for a Good "Track Record."** These functions, of course, not only benefit the property owner but also provide added protection for the mortgage investor.

One large savings association, $325 million Western Savings of Phoenix, agrees wholeheartedly. First of all, each apartment loan made by the association is looked at from the standpoint of the property's "economic feasibility" —a factor which covers "soundness," projections of operating expenses, overall plan and "whether facilities are adequate," states Executive Vice President Gary Driggs.

However, beyond these standards, the association goes a long step further and stipulates in its mortgages that it has the right to approve a particular property manager or a change in property management.

The idea is simple enough. "Unless we know who the management is going to be," Driggs states, "we don't want to make the loan."

Western Savings' standards call for a property manager to be experienced, have a "track record of good management and be knowledgeable in its field," Driggs says.

With 15 per cent of its $275 million in mortgage investments now in apartments, the association has had no problems arising from tenant unions and rent strikes. Nor does it expect to. "You won't have a rent strike," Driggs declares, "unless you have bad management."

**The Vacancy Factor.** Based on its experience with rent strikers, Washington's Perpetual Building Association can vouch for the importance of good property management. In fact, the association today "would definitely put in an apartment loan commitment that it has the right to approve a management firm or a change in property management," according to Vice President McConkey.

"Our current policy" on apartment lending, he adds, would include "the right of the association to approve a transfer of ownership subject to our loan." What's more, the association would take a "closer look at the cash flow and income and expense statement, including a requirement that at least semi-annually audited income and expense statements be furnished."

While standards like these may help produce sounder loans and happier tenants, he says, a better solution to today's renter unrest lies in the production of more housing.

With available housing generally in short supply, renters often find fewer options to move into new quarters when existing conditions may call for a change of address. Instead, the renters frequently stay put and stir up trouble.

Given the resources, associations stand to play a major role in overcoming today's housing shortages by increasing their investment in apartment construction. Current projections are that apartments will account for well more than 50 per cent of new housing starts in the near future.

Indeed, as President John Naisbitt of Urban Research Corporation has indicated, "By the end of the '70's, in a fundamental shift in American habits and dreams, more people will be living in apartments than in houses. There will never again be a housing boom—only apartment-building booms."

### Questions

1. Do you think tenant union and rent strikes are likely to increase in the future? Why or why not?
2. What types of property management practices would help to reduce frictions between tenants and owners?
3. How important is good property management for solving tenant relations problems?

# 18

# Financing: Methods and Instruments

## CHARACTERISTICS OF REAL ESTATE FINANCE

In this chapter and the two which follow, we consider the subject of real estate finance. This chapter deals with the methods and instruments used in the financing of real estate resources and projects; Chapter 19 with the principal institutions and agencies operating in this field; and Chapter 20 with mortgage lending programs and risks.

As we have pointed out repeatedly, the terms and availability of financing play a major role in decisions affecting the development, marketing, ownership, and use of real estate. For example, most purchasers of real property, whether they are business firms or individuals, must borrow a part or all of the funds needed to pay for the desired property. Similarly, most builders, land developers, and subdividers must borrow a part or all of the funds needed to finance construction and land development.

Like most other commodities that have economic value, real estate resources may be pledged as security for loans. Although the principles of finance involved are similar to those explaining other types of financing decisions and programs, the major characteristics of real properties, particularly their long life, fixed locations, and relatively limited marketability, have brought about the development of numerous special practices and policies.

## Major Characteristics

Of the various characteristics of real estate finance the following are of major importance:

1. The terms and availability of credit in the real estate field depend in part on conditions in the general capital markets. Real estate is in competition with other types of investment opportunities for the funds with which to finance the purchase, development, or use of real estate resources. During tight money periods real estate and especially housing has not been an effective competitor for funds.

2. Although some short-term financing is used, especially in the case of construction projects, most of the financing in the real estate field is long term in character. Real properties and even repairs on real properties last for long periods of time and investments in them are relatively fixed.

3. Loans typically are made against the security of real properties, and mortgages or similar instruments are used to pledge the borrower's interests. The processes required to mortgage real estate are complex and technical. They vary greatly from place to place.

4. Because of the long-term nature of real estate financing, special risks are involved. These arise from changes and anticipated changes in business conditions, government programs, inflationary or deflationary forces, local economic conditions, location factors, the property itself, consumer preferences, market changes including interest rates and property values, legal factors, and administrative arrangements.

5. Real estate resources and projects may be financed by means of equity (owner's) or borrowed funds. Or leases may provide for the use of property without the necessity of financing ownership.

## Equity Funds

Whenever fee ownership is to be acquired, the prospective buyer faces several alternatives. If he can pay the entire purchase price out of savings or other funds, no financing problem is involved. Conversely, when the seller is willing to sell "on contract" without down payment, no equity funds need be raised. In most cases the buyer will have available some portion of the purchase price and will borrow funds for the remainder. Sometimes he is unable to provide the necessary down payment from his own resources and is faced with the problem of assembling sufficient equity funds.

Thus the buyer of a house may borrow against his life insurance or his automobile, or use personal credit to raise funds from relatives or other sources to assemble the necessary equity funds. A business firm may borrow by pledging other real properties or other assets. It may issue securities to raise funds for this purchase and for other purposes. Or other available funds may be used.

The equity for real estate developments such as apartment houses, office buildings, and shopping centers is often secured by organizing a corporation and selling stock. In some cases, the services of architects, engineers, and builders are paid for in whole or in part by means of stock. Sometimes the owner of the land will take all or part of his payment in the form of stock. Although the developer's equity position is diluted by the stock payments to others, less cash has to be raised when stock payments are used.

Partnerships, syndicates, and trusts may also be formed to provide for the assembly of equity funds for real estate developments. Estates, foundations, unions, and limited dividend corporations have also engaged in the equity financing of a number of housing projects, many of which have had a long record of success.

In more recent years various financial institutions were given authority to make equity investments in residential income-producing housing. Such investments may represent a "piece of the action" or be owned outright, with or without mortgage financing. In addition, life insurance companies are authorized in all but a few states to make equity investments in nonresidential income properties. Such investments have expanded rapidly in recent years. Under certain conditions various savings and loan association and mutual savings banks may acquire land for development.

### Investment Decisions

The factors which play a major role in investment decisions will vary depending on whether equity or debt investments or combinations of them are under consideration. There will be differences also between individual and institutional investors. Decision factors of these types are considered at greater length in Chapter 20.

### Borrowed Funds

The borrowing of funds for the purpose of financing fee ownership of real estate is accomplished largely by the use of the mortgage, the trust deed in the nature of a mortgage, bonds, and land contracts. Other arrangements are also possible but are of less importance. Construction financing may be accomplished by a short-term loan or under various types of mortgage arrangements. Property improvements may be financed by the use of open-end mortgages or by the use of personal credit. The purchase of equipment is sometimes financed by means of a "package mortgage," as well as by the use of personal loans or installment credits. Of major importance, however, is the mortgage, and we shall give special attention to the processes of mortgage financing.

## The Mortgage [1]

A mortgage creates the existence of a debt and requires a pledge of property to secure it. Technically the mortgage note admits the debt and contains an agreement to repay it in accordance with specified conditions. The mortgage pledges the property as security for the obligation. The note makes the borrower personally liable for the obligation, and he cannot simply abandon the property to avoid payment of the debt. It is possible, however, to create a mortgage without the mortgage note; and in that case the borrower has no personal liability.

## Definition of a Mortgage

At common law a mortgage amounted to a conveyance of an estate to the mortgagee, which conveyance became void upon the performance of the terms of the mortgage. Today it is considered more in the nature of a lien upon the estate to secure the performance, normally a money payment, specified in the instrument. The term *mortgage* is commonly used to denote the instrument by which such interest in property is transferred. Any instrument or legal form which conveys an interest in property for the purpose of giving security is in effect a mortgage, regardless of its form.

Several of the terms used in the above definition require further clarification. We have already pointed out that a *deed* is an instrument that conveys title to real property. A *conveyance* is a transfer of the interest in property from one person to another. In mortgage transactions the debtor or borrower is called the *mortgagor*. The creditor or lender is called the *mortgagee*. The period for which the mortgage is made is called the *term*.

In order that a conveyance of the type required in a mortgage transaction be valid, it must be in writing, must be executed by the mortgagor with all the formality prescribed by the statutes of the particular state in which the property lies, and must be delivered to the mortgagee. The laws of the state in which the property is located govern the mortgage transaction.

---

[1] For a more complete discussion, see Harold F. Lusk, *Law of the Real Estate Business* (rev. ed.; Homewood, Ill.: Richard D. Irwin, Inc., 1965), chap. xv. See also Robert Kratovil, *Real Estate Law* (5th ed.); Englewood Cliffs, N.J.: Prentice-Hall, Inc., 1969), chap. 20.

**THIS MORTGAGE,** made the 1st  day of    May      , nineteen hundred and

**BETWEEN**    JOHNATHAN. WHITE, residing at 711 Front Street,
in the City, County, and State of New York

, the mortgagor,

**and**       WILLIAM W. JONES, residing at 115 Lenox Hill Avenue,
in the City, County, and State of New York

, the mortgagee,

**WITNESSETH,** that to secure the payment of an indebtedness in the sum of ********************
TEN THOUSAND ($10,000)*****************************************dollars,

lawful money of the United States, to be paid on or before the 1st day of May, 19  ,

with interest thereon to be computed from the date hereof, at the rate of         6      per centum
per annum, and to be paid on the   1st  day of   May      19   , next ensuing and semi-
annually  thereafter,

according to a certain bond,
note or obligation bearing even date herewith, the mortgagor hereby mortgages to the mortgagee

**ALL** that certain plot, piece or parcel of land, with the buildings and improvements thereon erected, situate,
lying and being in the Village of Lyons, in the County of Wayne, State of
New York, and bounded and described as follows:

BEGINNING at a point on the southerly side of One hundred and
seventh Avenue (Wayne Avenue) distant forty feet westerly from
the corner formed by the intersection of said southerly side of
One hundred and seventh Avenue with the westerly side of One
hundred and thirty-fifth Street (Clinton Avenue) running thence
southerly parallel with One hundred and thirty-fifth Street one
hundred feet; thence westerly parallel with One hundred and
seventh Avenue forty feet; thence northerly parallel with One
hundred and thirty-fifth Street one hundred feet to said southerly
side of One hundred and seventh Avenue and thence easterly along
said southerly side of One hundred and seventh Avenue, forty feet
to the point or place of beginning.

SUBJECT to covenants, restrictions and reservations contained in
former instruments of record and to encumbrances of record.

**TOGETHER** with all right, title and interest of the mortgagor in and to the land lying in the streets and
roads in front of and adjoining said premises;

**TOGETHER** with all fixtures, chattels and articles of personal property now or hereafter attached to or used
in connection with said premises, including but not limited to furnaces, boilers, oil burners, radiators and
piping, coal stokers, plumbing and bathroom fixtures, refrigeration, air conditioning and sprinkler systems,
wash-tubs, sinks, gas and electric fixtures, stoves, ranges, awnings, screens, window shades, elevators, motors,
dynamos, refrigerators, kitchen cabinets, incinerators, plants and shrubbery and all other equipment and
machinery, appliances, fittings, and fixtures of every kind in or used in the operation of the buildings standing
on said premises, together with any and all replacements thereof and additions thereto;

**TOGETHER** with all awards heretofore and hereafter made to the mortgagor for taking by eminent domain
the whole or any part of said premises or any easement therein, including any awards for changes of grade of
streets, which said awards are hereby assigned to the mortgagee, who is hereby authorized to collect and receive the proceeds of such awards and to give proper receipts and acquittances therefor, and to apply the
same toward the payment of the mortgage debt, notwithstanding the fact that the amount owing thereon may
not then be due and payable; and the said mortgagor hereby agrees, upon request, to make, execute and
deliver any and all assignments and other instruments sufficient for the purpose of assigning said awards to
the mortgagee, free, clear and discharged of any encumbrances of any kind or nature whatsoever.

**Fig. 18–1a.** Mortgage form—sheet 1. (Courtesy The Title Guarantee
Company, New York.)

**AND** the mortgagor covenants with the mortgagee as follows:

1. That the mortgagor will pay the indebtedness as hereinbefore provided.

2. That the mortgagor will keep the buildings on the premises insured against loss by fire for the benefit of the mortgagee; that he will assign and deliver the policies to the mortgagee; and that he will reimburse the mortgagee for any premiums paid for insurance made by the mortgagee on the mortgagor's default in so insuring the buildings or in so assigning and delivering the policies.

3. That no building on the premises shall be altered, removed or demolished without the consent of the mortgagee.

4. That the whole of said principal sum and interest shall become due at the option of the mortgagee: after default in the payment of any instalment of principal or of interest for fifteen days; or after default in the payment of any tax, water rate, sewer rent or assessment for thirty days after notice and demand; or after default after notice and demand either in assigning and delivering the policies insuring the buildings against loss by fire or in reimbursing the mortgagee for premiums paid on such insurance, as hereinbefore provided; or after default upon request in furnishing a statement of the amount due on the mortgage and whether any offsets or defenses exist against the mortgage debt, as hereinafter provided. An assessment which has been made payable in instalments at the application of the mortgagor or lessee of the premises shall nevertheless, for the purpose of this paragraph, be deemed due and payable in its entirety on the day the first instalment becomes due or payable or a lien.

5. That the holder of this mortgage, in any action to foreclose it, shall be entitled to the appointment of a receiver.

6. That the mortgagor will pay all taxes, assessments, sewer rents or water rates, and in default thereof, the mortgagee may pay the same.

7. That the mortgagor within five days upon request in person or within ten days upon request by mail will furnish a written statement duly acknowledged of the amount due on this mortgage and whether any offsets or defenses exist against the mortgage debt.

8. That notice and demand or request may be in writing and may be served in person or by mail.

9. That the mortgagor warrants the title to the premises.

10. That the fire insurance policies required by paragraph No. 2 above shall contain the usual extended coverage endorsement; that in addition thereto the mortgagor, within thirty days after notice and demand, will keep the premises insured against war risk and any other hazard that may reasonably be required by the mortgagee. All of the provisions of paragraphs No. 2 and No. 4 above relating to fire insurance and the provisions of Section 254 of the Real Property Law construing the same shall apply to the additional insurance required by this paragraph.

11. That in case of a foreclosure sale, said premises, or so much thereof as may be affected by this mortgage, may be sold in one parcel.

12. That if any action or proceeding be commenced (except an action to foreclose this mortgage or to collect the debt secured thereby), to which action or proceeding the mortgagee is made a party, or in which it becomes necessary to defend or uphold the lien of this mortgage, all sums paid by the mortgagee for the expense of any litigation to prosecute or defend the rights and lien created by this mortgage (including reasonable counsel fees), shall be paid by the mortgagor, together with interest thereon at the rate of six per cent. per annum, and any such sum and the interest thereon shall be a lien on said premises, prior to any right, or title to, interest in or claim upon said premises attaching or accruing subsequent to the lien of this mortgage, and shall be deemed to be secured by this mortgage. In any action or proceeding to foreclose this mortgage, or to recover or collect the debt secured thereby, the provisions of law respecting the recovering of costs, disbursements and allowances shall prevail unaffected by this covenant.

13. That the mortgagor hereby assigns to the mortgagee the rents, issues and profits of the premises as further security for the payment of said indebtedness, and the mortgagor grants to the mortgagee the right to enter upon and to take possession of the premises for the purpose of collecting the same and to let the premises or any part thereof, and to apply the rents, issues and profits, after payment of all necessary charges and expenses, on account of said indebtedness. This assignment and grant shall continue in effect until this mortgage is paid. The mortgagee hereby waives the right to enter upon and to take possession of said premises for the purpose of collecting said rents, issues and profits, and the mortgagor shall be entitled to collect and receive said rents, issues and profits until default under any of the covenants, conditions or agreements contained in this mortgage, and agrees to use such rents, issues and profits in payment of principal and interest becoming due on this mortgage and in payment of taxes, assessments, sewer rents, water rates and carrying charges becoming due against said premises, but such right of the mortgagor may be revoked by the mortgagee upon any default, on five days' written notice. The mortgagor will not, without the written consent of the mortgagee, receive or collect rent from any tenant of said premises or any part thereof for a period of more than one month in advance, and in the event of any default under this mortgage will pay monthly in advance to the mortgagee, or to any receiver appointed to collect said rents, issues and profits, the fair and reasonable rental value for the use and occupation of said premises or of such part thereof as may be in the possession of the mortgagor, and upon default in any such payment will vacate and surrender the possession of said premises to the mortgagee or to such receiver, and in default thereof may be evicted by summary proceedings.

14. That the whole of said principal sum and the interest shall become due at the option of the mortgagee: (a) after failure to exhibit to the mortgagee, within ten days after demand, receipts showing payment of all taxes, water rates, sewer rents and assessments; or (b) after the actual or threatened alteration, demolition or removal of any building on the premises without the written consent of the mortgagee; or (c) after the assignment of the rents of the premises or any part thereof without the written consent of the mortgagee; or (d) if the buildings on said premises are not maintained in reasonably good repair; or (e) after failure to comply with any requirement or order or notice of violation of law or ordinance issued by any governmental department claiming jurisdiction over the premises within three months from the issuance thereof; or (f) if on

**Fig. 18—1b.** Mortgage form—sheet 1, reverse.

application of the mortgagee two or more fire insurance companies lawfully doing business in the State of New York refuse to issue policies insuring the buildings on the premises; or (g) in the event of the removal, demolition or destruction in whole or in part of any of the fixtures, chattels or articles of personal property covered hereby, unless the same are promptly replaced by similar fixtures, chattels and articles of personal property at least equal in quality and condition to those replaced, free from chattel mortgages or other encumbrances thereon and free from any reservation of title thereto; or (h) after thirty days' notice to the mortgagor, in the event of the passage of any law deducting from the value of land for the purposes of taxation any lien thereon, or changing in any way the taxation of mortgages or debts secured thereby for state or local purposes; or (i) if the mortgagor fails to keep, observe and perform any of the other covenants, conditions or agreements contained in this mortgage.

15.　That the mortgagor will, in compliance with Section 13 of the Lien Law, receive the advances secured hereby and will hold the right to receive such advances as a trust fund to be applied first for the purpose of paying the cost of the improvement and will apply the same first to the payment of the cost of the improvement before using any part of the total of the same for any other purpose.

16.　That the execution of this mortgage has been duly authorized by the board of directors of the mortgagor.

*Strike out this clause 16 if inapplicable.*

This mortgage may not be changed or terminated orally. The covenants contained in this mortgage shall run with the land and bind the mortgagor, the heirs, personal representatives, successors and assigns of the mortgagor and all subsequent owners, encumbrancers, tenants and subtenants of the premises, and shall enure to the benefit of the mortgagee, the personal representatives, successors and assigns of the mortgagee and all subsequent holders of this mortgage. The word "mortgagor" shall be construed as if it read "mortgagors" and the word "mortgagee" shall be construed as if it read "mortgagees" whenever the sense of this mortgage so requires.

**IN WITNESS WHEREOF,** this mortgage has been duly executed by the mortgagor.

IN PRESENCE OF:

*Deborah Behrmann*　　　　　*Johnathan White* (Seal)

| STATE OF NEW YORK, COUNTY OF New York　ss: | STATE OF NEW YORK, COUNTY OF New York　ss: |
|---|---|
| On the 1st day of May 19 before me personally came Johnathan White | On the 1st day of May 19 , before me personally came Deborah Behrmann the subscribing witness to the foregoing instrument, with whom I am personally acquainted, who, being by me duly sworn, did depose and say that he resides at No. 12 Mockingbird Lane, New York, New York; that she knows Johnathan White |
| to me known to be the individual described in and who executed the foregoing instrument, and acknowledged that executed the same. | |
| | to be the individual described in and who executed the foregoing instrument; that he, said subscribing witness, was present and saw him execute the same; and that he, said witness, at the same time subscribed her name as witness thereto. |
| (Seal) *Christopher Robin* Christopher Robin Notary Public, State of New York No. 00-0000000 Qualified in New York County Commission Expires March 30, 19 | (Seal) *Christopher Robin* Christopher Robin Notary Public, State of New York No. 00-0000000 Qualified in New York County Commission Expires March 30, 19 |

**Fig. 18–1c.**　Mortgage form—sheet 2.

## Lien vs. Title Theory

In the earlier stages of the development of the law of mortgages, the actual possession of property, as well as the title to it, passed to the mortgagee or lender during the period of the loan. If the debt was not paid in full and in accordance with all of the requirements on the day it became due, all of the rights of the mortgagor or borrower were forfeited. As mortgage transactions developed, experience indicated that the possession of the property was not necessary in order to secure the lender against loss. Consequently, the law was changed to permit the mortgagor to retain possession as long as the mortgage was not in default.

At the present time some states provide that the title, as well as the possession of the property, is kept by the mortgagor, the mortgage being regarded merely as a lien and not as an actual conveyance of title. These are called lien theory states, as contrasted with title theory states, in which the law more nearly resembles the earlier concept.

The arbitrary forfeiting of all rights in the property by the borrower in case he defaulted on the debt worked considerable hardship on the mortgagor, particularly in those cases where the value of the property was considerably greater than the debt. This aspect of the earlier law of mortgages was also changed. At the present time, all states require that some legal steps be taken by the mortgagee after default of the debt before the property can be proceeded against for debt payment. Such legal steps are called *foreclosure*, and this may take a number of forms. There are still wide variations between the states. Usually this process provides for the public sale of the property under the foreclosure laws, with the mortgagee securing repayment from the proceeds of the sale and the mortgagor being allowed to keep any surplus which remains. If a sufficient amount is not realized, the lender may secure a deficiency judgment against the borrower. (This is not the case in all states, however.)

## TYPES OF MORTGAGES

Mortgages may be classified by degree of priority, by method of repayment, financing requirements and whether insured or not. There are also blanket, package and open end mortgages as well as purchase money mortgages.

### Degree of Priority

Any mortgage which is subordinate to a mortgage or mortgages on the same property is a junior mortgage. The degree of priority is usually indicated by referring to the instrument as a first, second, third, and in some cases fourth mortgage; but the public records must always be consulted to determine which claims against the property have precedence. Also, a junior mortgage may become a senior lien if prior claims are paid. Obviously, junior mortgages typically contain more risk than senior mortgages, and consequently they usually yield a higher rate of return and are not written for long periods.

There are cases where a deed in the form of an absolute conveyance is used to transfer the title to the property. It may contain no reference to any debt or condition, indicating that it is really given as security for a debt. Such a legal instrument may be a mortgage in legal effect if it is actually given for the purpose of securing a debt and if this fact can be proved in the courts.

## Method of Repayment

Various methods of repayment may be provided in a mortgage agreement. If no payments on the principal are made during the term of the mortgage, it is called a *straight term* mortgage. If repayment is made in accordance with a definite plan which requires the repayment of certain amounts at definite times so that all of the debt is retired by the end of the term, the mortgage is *amortized*. If parts of the debt are repaid during the term of the mortgage and part remains to be paid when the debt falls due, it is called a *partially amortized* mortgage. Various combinations of straight term and amortized mortgages may be used; for example, a straight term mortgage may allow amortization in part or in entirety according to the terms of the instrument; or an amortized mortgage may be converted into a straight term agreement under certain conditions. In some cases mortgages "balloon out" with a big final payment at the end of the term. Frequently the balloon mortgages are used with renewal options that provide refinancing of the final payment with conventional mortgages at current rates of interest. This arrangement helps the lender to adjust to interest rate risk.

## Insured, Guaranteed, and Conventional Mortgages

Mortgages that are insured by the Federal Housing Administration or guaranteed by the Veterans' Administration are usually referred to as insured or guaranteed in contrast to others which are referred to as conventional mortgages. Private systems of mortgage insurance and guaranty have grown in importance. In the past decade, the Mortgage Guaranty Insurance Corporation (MGIC) is a case in point. FHA, VA and private mortgage insurance plans will be discussed in greater detail in the next chapter.

Mortgage insurance and guarantees have stimulated the use of high loan to value ratio and long term mortgages and this has broadened the housing market. Both down payments and monthly payments are reduced through such arrangements. Apartment house financing has also been aided by mortgage insurance. Cooperative and condominium ownerships along with subsidized rent and interest plans have also been important factors in stimulating the apartment house market.

## Variable and Fixed Interest Rate Mortgages

Inflationary tendencies have created special types of risks for mortgage lenders. One method of adjusting to such risks is the use of variable rate mortgages; arrangements are made for the mortgage interest rate to advance or decline with some index of changes in the cost of money such as the prime rate. Adjustments usually are made at stated intervals. Similar problems have stimulated the increased use of prepayment penalties when mortgages carry fixed interest rates. Also, shorter maturities have been introduced by some lenders who use fixed rates to allow for frequent readjustments of such rates.

## Special Financing Requirements

Special types of mortgages have developed in response to particular types of financing requirements. For example, the blanket mortgage assists in the financing of new developments, the package mortgage allows for the financing of equipment and fixtures under the mortgage and the open-end mortgage provides for future advances to the borrower using the same instrument. Purchase money mortgages are often used in financing a new project. Each of these will be discussed briefly here.

## Blanket Mortgage

This type of mortgage "blankets" several or a number of pieces of property. It is often used in the financing of new developments. As sales are made, releases are granted to remove the properties that are sold from the blanket mortgage. For example, an individual buyer of a lot in a new subdivision development typically will make a large enough down payment to provide for the release of his lot from the blanket mortgage. In many cases the seller of the land may take back a purchase money mortgage and arrange for releases under it. Corporate mortgages may make use of blanket arrangements and arrangements which include "after-acquired" property clauses may be thought of as in effect blanket mortgages.[2]

## The Package Mortgage

Because of the increasing amount of equipment used in homes and the special problems arising from financing the purchase of such equipment,

---

[2] Henry E. Hoagland, and Leo D. Stone, *Real Estate Finance* (4th ed.; Homewood, Ill., Richard D. Irwin, Inc., 1969), p. 57.

a number of financial institutions make use of the so-called package mortgage. Practices vary between states, but usually provision is made for financing the equipment under the mortgage which is set up to finance home purchase. The various items of equipment included must be designated exactly and made a part of the mortgage agreement. Usually, only equipment which has a relatively long, useful life is included in such arrangement. The Federal Housing Administration insures mortgages of this type and has developed an extensive list of equipment which is considered to be eligible for inclusion in mortgage agreements. Such items of equipment as the following are included: plumbing accessories, air-conditioning systems, awnings, blinds, cabinets and bookcases (not built in), dishwashers, fireplace accessories, floor coverings, garbage disposal units, laundering equipment, radiator covers, ranges, refrigerators, screens, storm doors, and the like.

The package mortgage, by financing equipment, makes homes easier to sell and the homeowner has one monthly payment to cover the house and the appliances. Usually, also, the package mortgage reduces costs to the homeowner.

## The Open-End Mortgage

If an ordinary mortgage is set up with provisions for securing future advances to the borrower, an open-end mortgage is created. In recent years such arrangements have been made by various mortgage lenders in order to allow the borrower to secure funds for the maintenance and improvement of the mortgaged property. Some legal difficulties may arise in case other liens or judgments are placed against the property before additional funds are requested under the open-end provision. However, many mortgage lenders have adopted this type of mortgage in order to discourage the borrower from using short-term loans to finance necessary improvements to the property. Such loans may impair his ability to carry his regular mortgage obligations. At the same time the improvements may be desirable to maintain the property in good condition. The use of the open-end mortgage appears to be gaining in popularity, since the borrower can obtain financing for improvements on the basis of the terms and interest rates set up in the original mortgage.

## Purchase Money Mortgage

This type is used when an owner of property sells to a buyer. It is a conventional mortgage in which the owner becomes the mortgagee rather than a financial institution or some other source of funds. The purchase money mortgage is given to the seller of a property as part payment of the purchase price and is used to consummate the sale when other arrangements can't be made.

## THE PROCESS OF FINANCING REAL PROPERTY

There are many different ways in which buyers and users of real estate may finance their transactions. Most common is the use of the mortgage and trust deed. Other devices include the land contract and lease with option to purchase. The first to be discussed is the mortgage.

### Mortgage Elements

Two basic elements must be present in order for a mortgage to exist: a *debt* and a *pledge of property to secure the debt.* If either of these elements is lacking, no mortgage agreement exists. The debt may have been incurred prior to making the agreement or simultaneously with it, or it may come into existence after the date of the agreement. A mortgage which is given to secure a debt already in existence is subject to prior mortgages and liens, even though these are not recorded. This is due to the fact that the lender did not rely upon mortgage security at the time the loan was made. Hence, the law holds that he has not been injured by any failure to record such prior claims and will not protect him against them.

If a mortgage is given to secure advances to be made in the future, the amount of such loans need not be stated in the mortgage and may be at the option of the mortgagee. However, it is customary to fix a maximum amount in such an agreement. There is no question regarding the validity of such mortgages, but the rights of subsequent mortgagees and others who secure claims against the property differ widely from one state to another.[3]

### Ownership Interest

In order for anyone to mortgage a piece of property, he must actually possess a stated interest in the property he is offering as security. In general, any interest in real property which can be sold or assigned can be mortgaged. But, as we have already pointed out, the interests that one may own in real property are many and varied. Thus, the mortgagee must always be certain that the mortgagor actually possesses the title to the

[3] In general, the law states that the making of such advances is optional with the mortgagee, and if those who hold junior liens against the collateral notify the mortgagee of their claims and direct him not to make further advances, then such advances will be inferior to the junior claims.

property which he claims to have.[4] His title may be clouded and he himself may not be aware of it. Taxes, special assessments, prior mortgages, mechanics' liens, attachments, judgments, or court orders may leave little actual ownership for the borrower to mortgage. Similarly, private or public restrictions may so limit the use of a property that it is incapable of earning the type of return which is expected of it. Rights of dower and curtesy, easements, reservations, encroachments, prior liens, and rights of tenants are all possible claims that may interfere with the setting up of a satisfactory mortgage agreement. Such matters must always be determined by a competent lawyer or title company.

## Property Description

A careful and accurate description of the property is of major importance, since this eliminates uncertainties regarding the location or extent of the property which is mortgaged. Usually it is sufficient to describe the property by referring to it in the same way that it is described in the deed or as the number of a lot shown on a recorded map, but personal investigation and inspection help to avoid mistakes and misunderstanding. Surveys by competent engineers should be made whenever questions arise which are likely to create future problems.

In general, the property should be designated with accuracy, the amount of the debt indicated, the terms of repayment, the exact conditions under which the conveyance is made, and any special promises or agreements that are a part of the contract.

## Strict Foreclosure

The legal steps that must be taken by the mortgagee or lender for the purpose of having the property applied to the payment of a defaulted debt are called *foreclosure*. Legally there is a distinction between *strict foreclosure* and *foreclosure by sale*, although the latter method has come to be used so generally that most people have this in mind when they speak of the process of foreclosure.

One of the early developments of the law of mortgages relieved the borrower from forfeiting his property through failure to pay within the time set, provided he paid within a reasonable time thereafter. The time

---

[4] Under certain circumstances a mortgage will be held to convey an interest which the mortgagor or borrower did not own at the time the agreement was made. For example, the mortgage might contain a provision by which the mortgagor stated and guaranteed that he had good title to the property. If he did not have such title and later acquired it, the law will hold that such title actually passed to the mortgagee or lender at the time the agreement was made. This is permitted because it would be unjust to allow the borrower to benefit by his own wrong.

was determined by a court of equity. This process made it necessary for the mortgagee to institute a court action in order to determine that a reasonable time had elapsed. In case sufficient time has been allowed, he was able to secure a decree foreclosing or terminating all rights and interests of the mortgagor in the property. Such an action by a court constitutes strict foreclosure. The decree given by the court under strict foreclosure proceedings does not order a sale of the property but confirms the absolute title to it in the mortgagee or lender.

Strict foreclosure is still used in many states, but is permitted only under special circumstances. For example, this method may be proper in cases where the value of the property does not exceed the debt and the mortgagor does not contest the action. It is also proper in cases where the mortgage is in the form of an absolute deed without any written condition or agreement to reconvey. As we have indicated, however, the method most generally used in this country to collect a defaulted mortgage debt is foreclosure by sale. There is considerable variation from state to state in regard to the methods and practices followed.

In most states the mortgagee has several remedies from which he may choose the one best suited to his purpose. Where there is no prohibition by statute, he may pursue all of his remedies, concurrently or successively. He may sue for judgment on the note, which can be collected out of other property owned by the debtor, and at the same time start foreclosure proceedings. In some states a judgment for the debt may be taken in the foreclosure action and will stand against the debtor to the extent that it exceeds the amount realized from the foreclosure sale. In other states separate court action must be brought to make up any deficiency.

### Foreclosure by Sale

The two methods of foreclosure by sale most commonly used are (1) foreclosure under power of sale contained in a mortgage or deed of trust, and (2) foreclosure by court action resulting in a decree of sale.

If the mortgage instrument expressly authorizes the mortgagee or trustee to sell the property in the event of default, the laws of many states permit him to do this so long as he follows the procedure prescribed by statute. Whether or not the mortgagor has the right to redeem the property within a certain period after sale depends entirely upon the laws of the state in which the property is located. Some states allow no redemption after a sale of this type. Others provide that the mortgagor may redeem the property within a certain period after sale if he pays the costs of the sale and the full amount of the debt.

Many states require that all foreclosure sales must result from court action even though mortgages and deeds of trust contain powers of sale.

Under this arrangement a suit is brought by the mortgagee against the mortgagor and all parties who have acquired an interest in the property subsequent to the mortgage.

The law provides that the rights of no person shall be affected by a decree unless he is before the court. Because of this regulation, it is important for the mortgagee to search the record carefully in order that all persons who have acquired rights in the property may be made parties to the proceedings and properly served with summonses or otherwise brought before the court.

Usually the decree directs the sheriff to sell the property to the highest bidder after public notices of the time and place of sale as prescribed by statute. The purchaser at the sale may receive a deed from the sheriff conveying an absolute title, or he may receive merely a sheriff's certificate which will become a conveyance of the title within a specified period if the property is not redeemed within that time.

## Redemption

The interest of the mortgagor in the property prior to foreclosure is frequently called the *equity of redemption*. This should not be confused with the *statutory right of redemption*, which is a legal privilege recognized in certain states. In some states the mortgagor, and frequently junior lien holders as well, are given the right to redeem the title upon payment of the redemption price within a certain time after the foreclosure sale. This redemption period ranges from six months in some states to two years in others. Some states allow the mortgagor to retain possession of the property during the redemption period, while others give possession to the purchaser and allow him to retain it unless the property is actually redeemed within the time allowed.

In some cases a mortgagor is unable to pay his debt but is willing to convey the property to the mortgagee in order to satisfy the claim. By doing this he is relieved (if the mortgagee agrees) of personal liability, the danger of future deficiency judgments, and the unpleasant publicity frequently associated with foreclosure proceedings. Such a proposal is often agreeable to the mortgagee, for it relieves him of the expenses and delays connected with foreclosure proceedings. Under some conditions, the lender may even pay the borrower a sum of money for title to the property. However, a deed of this type must be considered carefully by the mortgagee before he accepts it because of the fact that its validity depends upon the intention of the parties involved and on other special circumstances.

## Trust Deed

The trust deed in the nature of a mortgage [5] is an instrument which provides for the conveyance of title to a third party who holds it *in trust* as security for the payment of an obligation by a borrower. The creditor is called the *beneficiary,* the *legal holder* or the *mortgagee.* The party holding the title for the period of the loan is called the *trustee.* The trustee, then, is holding the stakes, with instructions to reconvey title to the debtor when the debt is repaid or to sell the property in event of default. Sales proceeds are applied to the payment of the debt, with any surplus remaining payable to the borrower. In a few states, this instrument has virtually supplanted the mortgage, and it is commonly used the country over in transactions involving substantial amounts of funds. In a number of states, the trust deed can be foreclosed by trustee's sale without any court proceedings. However, in most states, the trust deed is virtually identical to the mortgage and is legally considered as such.

## Mortgage Bonds

When several persons or a group of persons lend money on the security of a property, mortgage bonds may be issued. A customary procedure is to give a mortgage or a trust deed to a trustee, who holds it for the benefit of the bondholders. In such cases, the mortgage is accompanied by a trust agreement, which sets forth in detail the rights of the bondholders in the security and the duties of the trustee. For example, a corporation may wish to borrow an amount which is greater than any one person wishes to lend. In such a case the corporation may convey its property to a trustee and provide for the issuance of bonds against it. Such bonds can then be sold to the public generally and the debt distributed among a great many persons. In cases of this type, the trustee acts on behalf of all of the bondholders. If foreclosure and sale become necessary, the trustee pays over to each bondholder his share of the proceeds.

## Land Contract

The land contract, or contract for a deed, is a written agreement by which a property is sold to a buyer who agrees to pay in installments the established price with interest over a specified period of years. Generally a down payment is required, although the amount is usually nominal, 10

---

[5] The trust created for holding a trust deed in the nature of a mortgage should not be confused with the "naked" or "dry" trust. The latter is created solely to hold title to property and is not associated with any debt. In fact, it performs no functions other than to hold title for the convenience of the transferor. The "naked" trust is common in Illinois and a few other states.

per cent or less of the purchase price being common. Under the land contract, the seller retains title until the agreed payments have been made by the purchaser. Frequently, however, the agreement provides that when the installment payments have reached a specified percentage of the purchase price (for example, one half), the seller will give a deed or transfer title under a regular mortgage as security for the remaining payments. The most appealing factor to the purchaser is probably the generally low down payment required. Buyers can sometimes secure property under land contract where the down payment necessary under a conventional mortgage would obviate the transaction. Retention of title makes it relatively easy for the seller in most states to avoid the cumbersomeness of conventional mortgage procedure in enforcing the terms of the contract. The land contract, however, poses certain dangers for the unwary purchaser. Generally the contract is not recorded; hence the purchaser may lose this protection. He may lose his equitable interest, as well as use and occupancy upon default. It is also possible that the seller may lose, through foreclosures of prior liens, the right to convey title before the purchaser is in a position to demand it.

A variety of state laws apply to land contracts. In some states the seller is considered to be the owner until complete payment is made much like installment sales contracts. Other states consider the land contract to be much like a mortgage.

### Lease with Option to Purchase

This arrangement may be thought of as a type of land contract. The prospective buyers can get use of the property and protect occupancy in case he decides to buy. Usually the lease payments become the down payment and the arrangement can become a more typical land contract.

### Uniform Mortgage Laws

Efforts are being made to develop uniform mortgage laws in the various states. If this could be accomplished it would facilitate the development of regional and national markets in conventional mortgages. Competition of federally and privately insured and guaranteed mortgages has stimulated efforts in this direction.

## CONSTRUCTION FINANCING

Individuals and firms engaging in the development of real estate, whether the task be road building or house building, rarely have sufficient funds to carry a job to completion without some form of financing. Personal or company capital is supplemented with loans, advances from purchasers, and credit from material suppliers and subcontractors. The various sources of financing can be combined in many ways, and, of course, not all of them are used in every building venture.

Construction financing varies according to the requirements and charistics of the participants in a particular building project. In the same construction job, the originator or sponsor and subcontractors may require financing for themselves, but may also provide financing for others. For example, an individual or firm for whom a structure is being built might obtain a loan to finance the project and also make personal advances to the builder, who in turn, operates between advances on a commercial line of credit and credit from subcontractors and material suppliers.

### Interim and Long-Term Financing

The most common type of construction financing is the construction loan granted to the originator or sponsor of the building project in which the proceeds of the loan are disbursed as construction progresses. A construction loan may be either one or a series of short-term notes which are drawn at intervals during the construction and refinanced when the project is completed, or a single long-term loan in which the principal is advanced in installments. Thus, construction financing may be either interim financing or an integral part of long-term financing.

A short-term construction loan is not necessarily a mortgage loan, although the long-term loans are nearly always secured by a mortgage on the real estate being improved. Established building firms frequently obtain construction financing through an unsecured line of credit, just as other types of firms borrow on their general credit. Individuals or companies having special structures custom-built for them, such as residences or stores or factory buildings, typically have to pledge the property being developed in order to obtain construction funds.

### Disbursement Schedules

Many different construction-loan disbursement schedules are in use. They are not influenced by whether the loan is long or short term. Some systems permit payouts as certain phases of the project are completed; for example, 25 per cent of the loan is paid out when the foundation is completed, 25 per cent when the structure is under roof and rough plumbing and wiring are installed, 35 per cent when the structure is completed and ready for occupancy, and 15 per cent after the period for filing mechanics' liens has elapsed. Other payout systems permit the borrower to draw loan funds in amounts equal to a certain percentage of the cost of the work completed for which payment has not already been made. The final balance of the loan is disbursed upon completion. Some systems simply require the builder to submit all bills to the lender, who in turn pays them and gives the builder the balance of the loan account upon completion. The Federal Housing Administration and the Veterans' Administration require three inspections during construction on residential units which are to be eligible for insurance or guaranties, so the payouts on FHA and VA projects are usually related to the required inspections.

### Regulations and Policies of Lenders

Whether construction financing is interim financing or a part of a long-term loan depends on regulations and on the policies of the lender granting the loan. The financial and operating characteristics of the borrower, of course, will be a factor of importance. National banks are permitted to grant loans for construction purposes without regard to mortgage security.

Federally chartered savings and loan associations, by contrast, are permitted to grant loans on the security of real estate which is to be improved with the proceeds of the loan. Therefore, a federally chartered savings and loan association can finance construction with ordinary mortgage loans in which the principal is advanced during construction. Efforts are being made to allow these institutions to engage in construction financing in much the same manner as a bank.

Some lenders and some borrowers are not interested in long-term mortgage financing. Commercial banks are often willing to finance building operations as a commercial venture but do not care to invest in long-term mortgage loans. Other lenders may be willing to finance construction on a short-term basis so that they can temporarily avoid committing funds on a long-term basis. Building firms engaging in custom construction are often not concerned with long-term financing but only with financing the project during the construction period.

### Suppliers and Subcontractors

Material suppliers and subcontractors participate in construction financing by granting credit to builders and owners while a project is being brought to completion. Credit from suppliers and subcontractors can be used either to supplement or to replace construction loans.

### Standby Arrangements

Various types of standby arrangements may be used in connection with construction loans. For example, a standby commitment for permanent financing may be necessary to facilitate construction financing. If money markets ease the developer may let the standby commitment expire and secure financing from other sources.

## USE OF LEASES IN LIEU OF FINANCING

As we indicated previously, property users in some instances employ leases to avoid the financing problems arising from fee ownership. In some cases the line of demarcation between certain forms of leasing agreements and various mortgage agreements is barely discernible, although from a strictly legal standpoint distinctions do exist. Many business firms have made use of leases in acquiring the use of various types of properties in recent years. Leasing has been used to an increasing extent by chain store organizations. Industrial and public utility firms have also made use of such arrangements. Probably the most important reason for this development has been the need of business firms while they are expanding to conserve capital for current uses rather than to commit it to long-term fixed uses. Rising prices and high income taxes may also contribute to the need for current capital. Under leasing arrangements no fixed debts are created and no debt is reflected upon the financial statements of a firm. Thus it may sometimes be referred to as "off balance sheet" financing. There are some income tax advantages in the leasing arrangement, since rent is considered a business expense while repayment of the principal of a mortgage is not. Interest on a mortgage, however, is considered a business expense.

### Types of Leases

A number of types of leases are in use, ranging from the ordinary short-term lease, in which a business firm or individual rents an existing property and pays periodic rentals for the duration of the lease, to long-term amortized leases. Under long-term amortized leases, a business firm may arrange to have a site purchased and improvements constructed for it by an individual or a company for lease back to the firm. Under this type of arrangement, the rentals will often completely amortize the investment and also provide a return to the lessor. At the end of such a period, title to the property vests in the lessee. In this instance the lease is almost identical, from an economic standpoint, with the purchase of a property with a 100 per cent loan amortized in a given period. In legal terms, of course, this is not the case.

Different types of business organizations follow various arrangements in regard to leases. For example, a grocery chain organization ordinarily will not lease an outlet in an outlying shopping center for more than five or ten years. However, arrangements are usually made for renewal at the option of the chain store organization. Some department and variety stores have leased outlets in so-called "100 per cent" retail locations for 30 years or longer; but even in such locations, shorter terms are used with increasing frequency. Leases for long terms often include provisions for payments based upon a percentage of the dollar volume of business. This arrangement is commonly called a *percentage lease.* Sometimes there are *graded* or *step-up leases,* with the rental moving from one level to another in accordance with the specific agreements that have been made. When the lessor has the responsibility for taxes, insurance, and property maintenance, the arrangement is called a *gross lease,* in contrast to a *net lease,* in which the lessee assumes that responsibility.

## The Buy-Build-Sell Lease

Sometimes a property which is needed by a business organization is not available at the time and in the location desired. In such instances business firms may buy land in the desired location, build the type of structure and other improvements that are needed, and then sell the property to individual or institutional investors, arranging to lease it back after the sale. This is known as a *buy-build-sell lease.* Such plans provide properties of exactly the type desired, and only temporary financing needs to be obtained by the business organization wishing to use the property. Safeway Stores pioneered this type of arrangement.

In some cases arrangements are made whereby the property may be repurchased by prearrangement. Usually this arrangement is called a *rejectable offer.* The lessee states that the lease is to be cancelled and offers to repurchase on the basis of the original arrangement. If the offer to repurchase is not accepted by the lessor, the lease is cancelled.

## The Sale-Leaseback Arrangement

The buy-build-sell lease outlined above is a specialized type of the sale-leaseback arrangement, which is more commonly associated with the sale of existing properties with arrangements for leasing them back. Such arrangements enable a business firm to raise funds for working capital purposes without surrendering the use of the property which has been owned up to that point. Many of the early sale-leaseback arrangements were made with educational institutions, foundations, and charitable organizations, which enjoyed tax exemptions. However, changes in the revenue laws provided for the taxation of such organizations at full corporate rates on rentals received from properties that were leased to the extent that borrowed funds were used.

Life insurance companies have acquired the right to invest in income properties, and they have been one of the more important sources of funds for arrangements of this type. More recently, pension funds have played an important role in this field. Many of the earlier sale-leaseback arrangements contained options to repurchase; but because questions were raised regarding the tax status of such arrangements, repurchase agreements are not currently being used to any great extent. Renewal provisions, however, are almost always used.

### The Long-Term Ground Lease

The ground lease system dates back to English and colonial procedures. Ground leases once played an important part in the development of business properties, and are still employed in a few localities, particularly in Pennsylvania, Hawaii, and Maryland, as a means for real estate financing. The long-term ground lease usually runs for 99 years and may be renewable forever. It applies only to the land, and arrangements are usually required for improving the land within a specified period of time. Such improvements then serve as security for the lease and insure continued occupancy by the tenant. These leases are almost always "net" in form. Because of difficulties that arose with arrangements of this type during the depression years, most business firms have tended to prefer package deals that secure both land and building under a single long-term lease.

## DEBT-EQUITY COMBINATIONS

Inflationary tendencies with their high interest rates have brought increased use of a variety of debt-equity combinations in real estate finance. These "piece of the action" types of plans include percentages of gross or net income, joint ventures and other types of arrangements. It is quite often referred to as "participation" by the lender.

### Percentage of Gross Income

Under this plan the lender gets an added return over and above the interest on the mortgage on the basis of a percentage—usually two to four percent—of the gross income. Closely related is an arrangement which provides for a percentage of the gross income after a specified dollar volume is reached. No added "kicker" is available to the lender until the property achieves a degree of success. Typically the participation is on the basis of 20 to 30 per cent of the gross above the target volume.

### Percentage of Net Income

Although a variety of arrangements are possible a typical one is a purchase-leaseback of the underlying land with a percentage of net income tied into the ground lease along with a lease-hold mortgage on the improvements. Often there are arrangements which allow no prepayment for a period—usually 10 to 12 years or provide for a substantial prepayment penalty. Arrangements of this type often allow the lender to participate to the extent of 25 to 50 per cent of the net income after debt service.

### Joint Ventures

Many different types of joint ventures have been worked out. Typically the developer has no money in the venture; he provides for the management, construction, marketing and promotion. The lender provides all of the money required. The developer and the lender then may share on a predetermined basis—usually 50 per cent—in the net proceeds after debt service.[6]

### Other Arrangements

Many types of plans have been developed and are in the process of development to provide new combinations of debt and equity financing. For example, efforts are being made to develop a plan whereby the lender on a single family home will participate in the gains which may result if the property is sold. If the owner sells his house and realizes a $1,000 gain, the lender would get some participation, this amount based on a predetermined percentage.

### SUMMARY

Because of the high unit value of real properties, most parties in the real estate field rely heavily on borrowed funds to accomplish the development, construction, or purchase of real estate. Thus, the terms and availability of financing are important factors in real estate decisions.

Like many other economic goods, real estate may be pledged as security for borrowed funds. Because of fixity of location, long life, and limited marketability of real estate, special practices and instruments have been developed for use in the financing of real properties.

[6] For a more detailed discussion, see R. A. Stuart Miller and James C. Kafes, "Mortgage Participation: Effect on Real Estate Investments," *The Appraisal Journal* (April, 1971).

This chapter emphasizes the method of financing through use of mortgages and related instruments like trust deeds in the nature of a mortgage, bonds, and land contracts. Mortgages, which are evidences of debt and pledges of property as security, are classified by degree of priority, method of repayment, insured, guaranteed and conventional types, variable and fixed interest rates, and special financing requirements including blanket, package, open end and purchase money mortgages.

The most common course of action in the event of default on a mortgage is foreclosure by sale. Most states make allowance for the interest of the mortgagor by establishing redemption provisions.

Various types of leases may be employed by users of real estate resources who do not care to undertake the financial responsibility of ownership.

Debt-equity combinations are gaining in popularity. Of special importance are percentage of income arrangements and joint ventures.

## QUESTIONS FOR STUDY

1. How are the terms and availability of real estate credit related to conditions in the general capital markets?
2. Over the past year assume that conditions in the mortgage markets, particularly for single-family homes, have been highly competitive. Business expansion is increasing the demand for funds for plant and equipment expenditures. What effect do you believe this is likely to have on the home mortgage market? Explain your position.
3. List the chief sources of equity funds for investment in real estate.
4. Differentiate between each of the following pairs: (a) A first mortgage and a second mortgage. (b) A senior mortgage and a junior mortgage. (c) A conventional mortgage and an insured or guaranteed mortgage. (d) An amortized mortgage and a straight term mortgage. (e) An open-end mortgage and a package mortgage. (f) A fixed and variable interest rate.
5. Indicate the various types of action available to mortgagees in the event of default on a mortgage
6. Describe the process of financing a construction project.
7. Explain the difference between the buy-build-sell lease and the sale-leaseback arrangement.
8. Why do some firms prefer leasing arrangements to the alternative of financing ownership of the real estate resources they employ?
9. Which of the various types of lease arrangements would you prefer, and in each case give reasons to explain your preference, if you were in business as: (a) A real estate manager for a chain of grocery stores? (b) A property manager for a shopping center? (c) A physician leasing office space? (d) A general manager of a small, single-plant manufacturing firm?

10. In purchasing a new home for your family residence, would you prefer to assume a "conventional" mortgage or an "insured" mortgage? Why? Explain the relative advantages and disadvantages of each.

11. Why are debt-equity combinations growing in importance?

## SUGGESTED READINGS

HOAGLAND, HENRY E., and LEO D. STONE. *Real Estate Finance* (4th ed.). Homewood, Ill.: Richard D. Irwin, Inc., 1969. Chaps. 1–10.

MARTIN, PRESTON. *Real Estate Principles and Practices.* New York: The Macmillan Co., 1959. Chap. ix.

U. S. SAVINGS AND LOAN LEAGUE. *Construction Lending Guide.* Chicago: The League, 1964.

## CASE 18–1

### Flynn *et al. v.* Kenrick *et al.* *
### 285 Mass. 446, 189 N.E. 207 (1934)

This was an action by Nellie T. Flynn and others (plaintiffs) against William A. Kenrick and others (defendants). Judgment for plaintiffs and defendants appealed. Judgment affirmed.

Property was sold under an agreement of purchase and sale, containing the following recital: "Said premises are to be conveyed on or before September 1, 1930, by good and sufficient warranty deed of the party of the first part, conveying a good and clear title to the same, free from all incumbrances except a first mortgage of $5,000 . . . and for such deed and conveyance the party of the second part is to pay the sum of $6,500 of which $100 has been paid this day, balance above mortgage, are to be paid in cash upon delivery of said deed." According to the contract the property was deeded to the purchasers. The mortgage debt was not paid, and on foreclosure the property was sold for $4,500 and a deficiency decree was entered against the mortgagor, which he has paid. Suit is brought against the purchaser by the mortgagor to recover the amount paid on the ground that the purchaser agreed to pay the mortgage debt. The deed was drawn subject to the mortgage.

CROSBY, J.—It has long been held in this commonwealth that where land is conveyed subject to a mortgage the grantee does not become bound by mere acceptance of a deed to pay the mortgage debt. In the absence of other evidence, the deed shows that the grantee merely purchased the equity of redemption. If a deed contains a stipulation that the land is subject to a mortgage which the grantee assumes or agrees to pay, by his acceptance of the deed the law implies a promise to perform his promise. The contention of the defendants that they purchased merely the plaintiff's equity of redemption and did not assume and agree to pay the mortgage cannot be sustained in view of the agreement, the deed, and the agreed facts. The agreement recites that the

* Harold F. Lusk, *Business Law: Principles and Cases* (4th ed.; Homewood, Ill.: Richard D. Irwin, Inc., 1946), p. 306.

defendants for such conveyance are to pay "the sum of Sixty-five hundred dollars of which One Hundred dollars have been paid this day, balance above mortgage, are to be paid in cash upon delivery of said deed." It thus appears that for the deed and conveyance the defendants agreed to pay the sum of $6,500; that $100 was paid on the date of the agreement, and on delivery of the deed $1,400 was to be paid. The words "balance above mortgage" properly construed mean that the defendants having paid $100 obligated themselves to assume and pay the mortgage, and that the balance above the mortgage of $1,400 is to be paid upon the delivery of the deed.

The words of the deed "for consideration paid" interpreted in the light of the agreement mean that the defendants under the terms of the agreement are to pay $6,500 as the entire consideration. This seems to have been the construction put upon the agreement and the deed by the parties, as it is agreed that after the defendants entered into possession of the property they paid the interest installments on the mortgage until July 7, 1932. The agreement of the defendants to pay $6,500 for the property is equivalent to a stipulation that they assumed or agreed to pay the mortgage.

### Questions

1. Why is the mortgagor suing the purchaser?
2. What facts most influenced the decision of the judge in this case?
3. What is meant by purchasing a property "subject to a mortgage?"
4. Do you see any hazards in purchasing a property subject to a mortgage? Explain.

## CASE 18–2

### Boysun v. Boysun *
### 140 Mont. 85, 368 P.2d 439 (1962)

This was an action by Mike E. Boysun (plaintiff) against John C. Boysun and Tillie Boysun, his wife (defendants), to quiet title to certain land. Judgment for Mike E. Boysun, and John C. and Tillie Boysun appealed. Judgment affirmed.

John C. and Tillie Boysun owned a farm which was mortgaged for $4,400. They were in default on their payments and delinquent in the payment of their taxes, and the mortgage was threatening to foreclose.

John was unable to borrow money to pay the mortgage. Mike offered to purchase the land subject to the encumbrances. He stated at the time that it was worth no more than the encumbrances. John and Tillie executed a quitclaim deed conveying the farm to Mike. Mike orally agreed to reconvey the farm to John or to convey it to a purchaser if John found one. Thereafter John and his family moved to another state. Mike worked the farm in 1953 and 1954 and paid the taxes from 1951 through 1958.

* Harold F. Lusk, *Business Law: Principles and Cases* (Uniform Commercial Code Edition; Homewood, Ill.: Richard D. Irwin, Inc., 1966), pp. 781–83.

In the early part of 1954 John told Mike that he had a purchaser who would pay $11,000 for the farm but Mike wished to keep the farm. Thereafter, Mike sent money to John, and the amount sent plus the amount Mike paid to discharge the encumbrances on the farm amounted to $11,000. John and Tillie claim that the quitclaim deed was to secure a loan and asked the court to hold it to be a mortgage. John claimed that the money Mike sent him was a loan.

JAMES T. HARRISON, CHIEF JUSTICE. The ultimate question of whether a transaction was intended by the parties to be a mortgage or a sale rests on the intention of the parties at the time of the execution of the instrument, and to establish this intention the courts will examine the surrounding circumstances.

It has been repeatedly held that the evidence to prove that a deed, absolute on its face, was intended to be a mortgage must be clear and convincing. However, this rule is subject to some modification in situations where there is an option to repurchase or a conditional sale. The general rule is that if there is doubt whether a sale or a mortgage was intended, the court will be inclined to resolve the doubt in favor of the mortgage.

John and Tillie in this action rely heavily on the Murray case. In that case this court listed a number of facts and circumstances which, if present, tend to confirm the view that the transaction was a mortgage and not a sale. These factors are as follows:

(a) The transaction in its inception had for its purpose a loan, not a sale.

(b) The grantor was in financial distress at the time of the transaction.

(c) The price which the grantee claims he paid for the property appears to have been grossly inadequate.

(d) According to grantee's own theory, the transaction did not amount to an absolute sale, but to a conditional sale; that is, a sale with an option to grantor to repurchase.

John and Tillie list the four factors and allege that they are all present in the instant case. We have some difficulty with this assertion. The third principle relied on in the Murray case is based on the inadequacy of the price the vendor received for his property. The adequacy of consideration must be tested by conditions existing at the time of the transaction.

In *Titus* v. *Wallick*, the court held that in order for evidence of a disparity between the consideration for a deed and the value of the land to be of weight, it is essential that there be a satisfactory showing of such disparity.

There is no evidence in the record to support John and Tillie's allegation of a disparity between the purchase price and the value of the land at the time of sale. The only statement as to the value of the land at the time the deed was executed was the testimony of Mike Boysun. He stated the reason he would not loan money against the property was because it was not worth any more than what was against it.

In addition to the above-stated facts there are two elements present in the instant case which were not present in the Murray case. A deed, though absolute on its face, will be construed as a mortgage whenever it is shown that the instrument was intended to secure a debt. However, a debt must be shown to exist between the parties, as a mortgage is a mere incident of the debt.

In the Murray case there was testimony in the record that the parties intended the money paid to be a loan and that a debt was created between the parties. In the instant case, Mike Boysun testified that the agreement between the parties was that any time John paid the money spent by Mike on the property he was to get the property back. John's testimony supports this theory that he received an option to repurchase. His testimony indicates that he felt no obligation to pay any money back to Mike, but rather he had an option to do so if desired.

John and Tillie place considerable emphasis on the fact that Mike Boysun while testifying stated that John had a year or two to redeem the property. They cite this to show that a mortgage was intended. We feel little weight should be given to such statements made by a layman, especially in a situation such as the present wherein it is evident from the legal tangle of the parties that they knew little, if anything, about the law.

The second factor which is present in the instant case, which is absent from the Murray case, is the preponderant and inescapable fact that the option to repurchase was exercised. The testimony of two disinterested witnesses established the fact that in the Spring of 1954, John Boysun exercised his option to repurchase. In addition to exercising his option the testimony in the record establishes that he received his option price.

### Questions

1. What is the nature of a mortgage under common law? In a title theory state? In a lien theory state? Which type state do you believe Montana is?
2. What are the four factors which, under Montana law determine that a transaction is a mortgage and not a sale? Which ones are met in this case? Which are not met?
3. Does Mike's payment of $11,000 abrogate John's right to repurchase? Why or why not?

### STUDY PROJECT 18-1

### The Home Mortgage: A Prime Case for Product Improvement

At the present time, a home mortgage no longer offers much attraction to any investor. It cannot compete effectively with other instruments in the money and capital markets. Whether this unhappy condition is a permanent one may be debatable, but even if only temporary, it likely will be recurring. Thus the possibilities for product improvement need to be examined, especially in view of the great need for an expanding flow of funds into house-building during the decade of the seventies.

Research and experimentation actually are long overdue. The inability of either the conventional or the government insured or guaranteed mortgage to attract adequate funds has been apparent for some time. Progress in the

* By Edward E. Edwards; reproduced by permission of Mortgage Guaranty Insurance Corporation, from the *MGIC Newsletter*.

private sector has been discouraged by laws and regulations that effectively prohibit innovation or the adoption of new ideas that might have come out of research. Meanwhile, laws and regulations, both state and federal, continue to prescribe what may well be obsolete methods of financing home ownership.

The most obvious defect in the home mortgage from the investor's point of view is its lack of protection from purchasing power risk and from interest rate risk. While conventional (but not FHA and VA) lenders have always had the right to put in an escalator clause to protect them from rising interest rates, they have not been encouraged to do so by their regulatory authorities and have in fact been discouraged from doing so by the fixed rates available on government insured and guaranteed loans. A more direct way of protecting against interest rate risk, namely, underwriting mortgages with short maturities and only partial amortization, has been largely prohibited.

**The Direct Reduction Loan.** Here we begin to see the dangers in enforcing regulations that have been drafted on the basis of past experience rather than future needs. The short-maturity, partial or non-amortized loan that was typical of much of the home financing a generation or so ago caused all kinds of difficulty during the great depression, when borrowers could not pay and lenders could not or would not renew. To protect both the borrower and the lender, the fully amortized, equal monthly payment, long-term, direct reduction mortgage became virtually a requirement for institutional lenders. While the direct reduction loan might have served its purpose if we had had another major depression, we have apparently learned how to avoid that catastrophe and the result is that lenders now have their portfolios filled with mortgages yielding rates appropriate to a decade or more ago, but far under today's market.

This illustration is not meant to be an argument for a return to short-term lending, but rather a bit of evidence that rigidly enforced uniformity does not always provide the right answer. Unless lenders—and borrowers—have freedom to explore and innovate, constructive changes in home financing practices are not likely to occur.

But let's return to the direct reduction, fully amortized loan and look at some of its other features. When this type of financing was imposed, one of the arguments for it was that it would require the borrower to begin immediately to reduce his debt. And this was true a generation ago, when interest rates were low and typical maturities were 12 or 15 years. For example, a borrower under a 5 per cent, 15 year mortgage would, under the terms specified, reduce his indebtedness by 25 per cent during the first 5 years, and by 58 per cent during the first 10 years. But today, with terms such as 8 per cent and 30 years, even if there are no points involved, the required reduction in principal during the first 5 years is only 5 per cent, and only 12 per cent during the first 10 years. (If underwritten with three points, the balance does not even drop to the amount actually borrowed until after 38 months.)

When the above arithmetic is combined with today's higher loan-to-value ratios, it should be rather obvious that the direct reduction loan no longer gives the lender or investor the protection from financial risk that it was assumed to do. Even the basic assumption, however, may not have been valid, since the equal monthly payment actually bore little relationship to the borrower's ability to pay, except perhaps, during the early months of his home ownership. If borrowers are unable to pay, lenders have the right, but are not required, to adjust terms to changed conditions; but if borrowers, as a result of rising means, are able to pay more, lenders cannot require them to do so.

Little wonder that the turn-over of mortgage portfolios has slowed down. Borrowers are not required to increase their principal payments in line with their increased ability to pay. Nor are they encouraged to reduce their debt by advances in the rate of interest on their mortgage as rates advance in money and capital markets. (Here we might well reflect on still another element that discourages early repayment. Home owners are permitted to deduct their mortgage interest from their taxable income, even though they do not include in their taxable income any imputed rent for the home they occupy rent free.)

**Purchasing Power Risk.**    Even if lenders could get their principal back sooner and could increase interest rates with market changes, the home mortgage would still be an undesirable investment in an inflationary economy. Under the mortgage terms, one hundred percent of any appreciation in the value of the home goes to the home owner, even though the home was purchased largely or entirely with the lender's money. All that the lender gets back for reinvestment are depreciated dollars. That prospect just isn't very attractive to investors anticipating—or fearing—more inflation.

Mortgage lenders have been, and have been permitted to be, innovative in protecting themselves from purchasing power risk in the financing of income properties. Equity "kickers" are now common features as are also provisions for interest rate adjustments and for relating principal payments to the borrower's ability to pay. If home mortgages are to compete effectively for funds, something similar must be developed for them. This would seem to be much more likely to occur if lenders had freedom to innovate rather than having to wait for bureaucratic changes in regulations.

Not all of the difficulty centers in Washington, however. State usury laws seriously interfere in the competitive market for funds. Foreclosure laws in many states add unnecessarily to the risks and uncertainties of mortgage lending. Of greater importance for future changes, the legal rights of both the occupants and those who put up the money are the result primarily of state legislation. If wholly new methods of financing home occupancy are to emerge, these must be reflected in and made possible by state legislation.

For single-family homes, legal ownership financed by a mortgage is about the only way a family can obtain possession and have reasonable assurance of continued occupancy. For families strongly motivated toward eventual debt free ownership, this legal arrangement and the direct reduction mortgage undoubtedly work quite well, or would if mortgage funds were readily available at reasonable cost. Modern families, however, have many other aspirations than a debt free home, and many other possibilities for the investment of their savings than paying off a mortgage. If their major interest in a home is assured occupancy, they should and probably would be willing to trade off a part of their prospects for capital gains for advantages such as smaller down payment or smaller or more flexible monthly payments.

**New Financing Arrangements.**  A logical financing arrangement would seem to be one that would assure the occupant of continued tenure, that would permit him at his option to become the owner, but until he chose to exercise his option would not require him to invest very much in the house. (This sounds like a long-term lease with option to purchase, and that may be the answer, but a wholly new legal arrangement may be needed.)  Such an arrangement might be an effective one for attracting investment funds into single family homes, since it could permit the investor (who under present law probably would have to become the legal owner) to share in any appreciation resulting from inflation.

This kind of financing would require either that present mortgage lenders be able to take an equity position in what we probably would still call owner-occupied homes, or that a third party enter into the home financing plan.  The third party might well be a brand new type of home-finance corporation, building or buying homes for occupancy by families willing to pay current housing costs and to assume some of the risks of home ownership, but also wanting some protection from inflation.  Such a corporation, unlike prseent home financing institutions, would have full access to the money and capital markets, being free to issue both debt and equity paper of whatever terms investors would buy.  Also, it would—or should—be able to mortgage individual homes, under terms that would give the mortgage lending institution some protection from both interest rate and purchasing power risk.

The major argument against this sort of innovation probably would be that families would much prefer the present arrangement of legal ownership with a mortgage.  This argument has little merit unless mortgage funds are readily available.  Even if families have access to traditional mortgage financing, the rate of interest may well be so high that they would prefer something different.  Home financing institutions should have freedom to offer them a choice.

## Questions

1. What is a direct reduction loan?  What are Edwards' objections to it?  Do you agree or disagree with them?
2. Who has purchasing power risk under the present mortgage setup?  What is the nature of that risk?
3. What new financing arrangements does the author recommend?  Do you agree with his recommendations?

# 19

# Financing: Institutions and Agencies

## TYPES OF INSTITUTIONS

In the preceding chapter we considered some of the more widely used methods and instruments of real estate finance. We turn now to a review of the principal institutions and agencies operating in this field: commercial and mutual savings banks, savings and loan associations, and life insurance companies. We consider briefly individual lenders, mortgage brokers and companies, pension funds, real estate investment trusts, and other sources of funds for real estate projects and programs.

### Stock or Mutual Institutions

The principal institutions engaged in real estate finance are organized either on a stock or on a mutual basis. Thus there are stock and mutual life insurance companies, mutual and stock savings and loan associations, and mutual savings banks; commercial banks typically are organized as stock companies. Virtually all of the institutions in this field are organized as corporations, but in the case of mutuals ownership rests with members—that is, policyholders in the case of mutual life insurance companies, savers in the case of mutual savings and loan associations and mutual savings banks.

### Federal or State Charter

Regardless of how organized, most financial institutions must secure special federal or state charters in order to do business. Thus, they are granted at least a limited monopoly position. This is not true, of course, of individual investors and certain mortgage and investment companies that are also real estate lenders.

## Public and Quasi-Public Agencies

Financial institutions are influenced in their decisions and programs by public and quasi-public agencies and policies to a greater extent than most other business organizations. Thus financial institutions in the real estate field are influenced by Federal Reserve and Treasury policies just as are all financial institutions. In addition, there are a number of agencies that affect real estate financing programs rather directly, particularly in the housing field. These include the Federal Home Loan Bank System and its subsidiary The Federal Home Loan Mortgage Corporation; the Veterans' Administration; and the Department of Housing and Urban Development, which includes the Federal Housing Administration, Community Development Programs, Urban Renewal Programs, the Government National Mortgage Association and others. The Federal National Mortgage Association operates on a quasi-private basis. Also, the Federal Land Banks, the Farm Home Administration, and several other agencies are important in the financing of farms and rural housing.

## Savings and Loan Associations

Savings and loan associations, referred to in various parts of the country as homestead associations, building and loan associations, savings associations, and cooperative banks, are one of the most important sources of funds for real estate financing, especially in the field of housing and home ownership. These institutions typically make over half of the nonfarm home mortgages and hold about the same proportion of the total mortgage debt on one- to four-family nonfarm homes.

These institutions specialize in residential mortgage financing. Many of their loans are made on the security of single-family houses, although they also finance multi-unit residential structures both for rental and ownership under condominium arrangements, and, to a more limited extent, smaller commercial, industrial, and institutional properties. They have authority to invest to a certain extent in the obligations of municipalities and to make loans to finance college education. Besides mortgages, their investments typically are limited to United States government bonds and home improvement loans. In some cases they may own and develop subdivisions. They may also finance mobile homes and vacation homes as well as certain types of home equipment.

### Savings and Loan Development

Originally patterned somewhat after the building societies of England, the early organizations of this type started as small mutual benefit societies, typically being dissolved whenever all members had acquired homes. This terminating arrangement was supplemented gradually by other plans, until today there is no necessary relationship between the members of the associations who save and those who borrow. In terms of actual operating procedures, however, savings and loan associations now more nearly resemble mutual savings banks than the old mutual benefit societies from which they developed. Some states provide for stock or guaranteed stock types of organization, as well as mutuals.

The growth of savings and loan associations was encouraged considerably by the establishment of the Federal Home Loan Bank System in 1932 and the system of federally chartered institutions in the following year. In addition, the establishment of the Federal Savings and Loan Insurance Corporation, with the insurance of savings accounts was of major importance to the growth of these associations. Their growth in the 1950's and 1960's was rapid, total assets rising from $8.7 billion in 1945 to over $200 billion in 1971.[1] There are around 5,700 savings and loan associations in operation. Of these, over a third have federal charters; the remainder have state charters. However, the state-chartered institutions hold less than half of total assets. Most savings and loan associations qualify for insurance of savers' accounts through the facilities of the Federal Savings and Loan Insurance Corporation.

Partly as a result of their growth and pressure from competitive institutions, and partly because of the heavy governmental demands for funds, savings and loan associations were subjected to corporate income taxes in 1951. Prior to that time they had qualified for tax preference as cooperative societies.

Savings and loan associations generally emphasize local areas in their lending operations. They were early pioneers in the development of the amortized mortgage. They may buy mortgages originated in other areas or sell local mortgages to lenders elsewhere. These associations, however, pride themselves on being local thrift and home-financing institutions. Many of them have attained large size, with a number in the billion dollar and over category. The general trend is toward a smaller number of associations of larger than current average size.

In some states branch operations are authorized. Generally these are states in which banks also have authority to establish branches. A few associations operate over entire regions, such as Farm and Home Savings

---

[1] For detailed information, see *Savings and Loan Fact Book* (annual) (Chicago: U. S. Savings and Loan League).

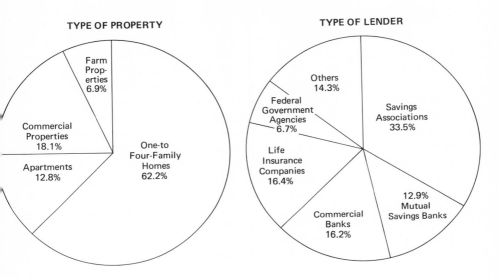

**Fig. 19–1.** Percentage distribution of mortgage loans outstanding, year-end 1970. (Source: Federal Reserve Board.)

and Loan Association of Nevada, Missouri, with branches in Texas and the Pacific First Federal of Tacoma, Washington, with branches throughout Washington and Oregon.

### Mutual Savings Banks

Although savings and loan associations have developed throughout the country, mutual savings banks have been concentrated largely in the New England and Middle Atlantic states. These banks are especially important in Massachusetts, New York and Connecticut, with more than one-third of all mutual savings banks in the country being in Massachusetts. They are also important in a few widely scattered cities such as Philadelphia, Minneapolis, and Seattle. Most of these banks are old and firmly established institutions with a long record of experience in real estate investments covering, in some cases, more than a century. Real estate investments ordinarily represent a considerable proportion of their total assets. Mutual savings banks, with their emphasis on thrift, have been well adapted to the requirements of real estate financing, since time deposits represent a large proportion of their total disposits. These institutions hold about 13 per cent of the total mortgage debt on one-to four-family nonfarm homes.

## Commercial Banks

Commercial banks have always been an important source of funds for real estate financing, and they have extended their activities in recent years. Banks have always been regulated rather closely in regard to mortgage lending, the principal limitations being on the ratio of the loan to the appraised value of the property and/or the term of the loan.

National banks may lend on housing on fairly liberal terms. However, if the mortgages are guaranteed by the Veterans' Administration or insured by the FHA, other restrictions do not apply.

State banks are also regulated with respect to their mortgage practices. As a practical matter, state laws do not vary so widely with respects to mortgage practices as was once the case. The activities of the federal government have tended to iron out many variations. In addition, banks have become more interested in real estate mortgages.

Mortgage lending, however, is relatively less important for commercial banks than for some of the other types of lending institutions. Typically, the mortgage lending activities of a bank are carried on by its mortgage loan department. The size and complexity of such a department varies with the volume of business.

The importance of commercial banks in real estate financing is greater than would be indicated by their direct mortgage investments. They play a significant role in the short-term financing of building operations, where frequently permanent financing is often assumed by some other type of lending institution upon completion of construction. Commercial banks also extend credit to other financial institutions, which then supply long-term real estate credit. Thus, commercial banks in such instances finance the mortgage inventories of other institutions. In some cases they engage in "warehousing" operations, holding mortgages for short terms under agreements with other lenders to repurchase them. Also, many banks acquire mortgages on real estate security in the exercise of trust functions; these loans do not appear on the banks' records of assets. Trust funds are sometimes invested in junior mortgages. In terms of direct investments, the real estate mortgage portfolios of commercial banks have tended to increase.

## Life Insurance Companies

Life insurance companies are one of the important sources of real estate mortgage credit. While some life insurance companies prefer to finance larger projects, the operations of many of them have been extended into the field of small-property financing as well.[2]

In general, insurance companies have been attracted to larger real estate projects, in some cases taking "a piece of the action," in others limiting their financing to mortgages. Often their loans are made through local mortgage brokers or correspondents who act as their representatives. In some cases the insurance companies make loans through their own representatives who are direct employees of the companies which they represent. Many insurance companies buy mortgages, leaving the servicing to be done by local brokers or originators of mortgages who receive a commission for this work.

### Mortgage Banking

Mortgage brokers and mortgage companies perform mortgage banking functions, financing a variety of activities. Typically they channel funds from large institutional investors to owners and users of properties. As has been pointed out:

> The modern mortgage company is typically a closely held, private corporation whose principal activity is originating and servicing residential mortgage loans for institutional investors. It is subject to a minimal degree of federal or state supervision, but has a comparatively small capital investment relative to its volume of business, and relies largely on commercial bank credit to finance its operations and mortgage inventory. Such inventory is usually held only for a short interim between closing mortgage loans and their delivery to ultimate investors.[3]

Mortgage brokers usually represent an insurance company or other financial institution. Mortgage companies may deal with a number of institutions and agencies. Usually these organizations place funds of lenders or originate mortgages and sell them, retaining a servicing fee. Servicing includes collecting interest and principal payments and often the disbursement of funds for taxes and insurance on the mortgaged properties.

In some cases, mortgage companies deal heavily in second mortgages and other junior liens, often originating such loans and selling them to private investors.

Mortgage companies have helped to channel funds between short- and long-term capital markets and have facilitated the movement of funds between primary and secondary mortgage markets. In some ways their operations resemble those of bond dealers.

[2] For detailed information about the lending activities of life insurance companies, see *Life Insurance Fact Book* (annual) (New York: Institute of Life Insurance).

[3] Saul B. Klaman, "The Postwar Rise of Mortgage Companies," *Occasional Paper 60* (New York: National Bureau of Economic Research, Inc., 1959), p. 1.

## SPECIAL SOURCES OF FUNDS

Among the various sources of funds for real estate financing are pension funds, real estate investment corporations, syndicates, real estate investment trusts, individuals and others. We will consider each of these briefly.

### Pension Funds

In recent years various pension funds have become a source of support for the financing of real estate projects. Usually such funds are administered under a trust arrangement. Their principal purpose is to finance retirement programs for participants. Such trusts may be administered by an official of the company or union under which the program is operated. In some cases, funds of this type are administered by insurance companies under appropriate annuity contracts. In such cases, of course, the funds are invested by the insurance companies. Often commercial banks administer pension funds for the companies involved.

While the bulk of the investments of pension funds has tended to center in government and corporate bonds, mortgage investments have been growing in importance and probably will continue to do so. Usually mortgages are purchased that have been originated by banks, mortgage companies, and other lenders. Mortgage investments of pension funds have tended to be concentrated in FHA-insured and VA-guaranteed loans.

### Real Estate Investment Corporations

Real estate investment corporations are well known among the intermediaries that have developed to allow investors to channel funds into the real estate market. The real estate investment corporation and the syndicate are fairly widely used. The real estate investment corporation may be a builder and developer or may be a corporation that has a special interest in the real estate field and offers its securities to the public for purchase.

### Syndicates

Syndicates are limited partnerships in which the principal participants are usually the general partners and have unlimited liability, but provision is made for limited partners who may receive and share proportionately in profits but have no voice in day-to-day operations. Their liability is limited to their investment.

## Real Estate Investment Trusts

Real estate investment trusts have a long history, being started more than 100 years ago in Massachusetts. The development occurred because Massachusetts law did not allow corporations to hold real estate for investment purposes, but trusts were permitted to make such investments. The early trusts were closely held but subsequently offered shares of beneficial interest to the public. They expanded beyond the New England area and prospered until a Supreme Court decision in 1935 determined that they should be taxed as regular corporations thus removing an earlier tax advantage. Federal regulations subsequently gave real estate investment trusts an advantage equal to that of the regular investment company or mutual fund. The development of rules and regulations provided that the trusts should comply with detailed regulation by the Treasury Department and they became in essence closed-end investment trusts with major investments in real estate and mortgages. As has been pointed out,

To qualify for preferred tax treatment, the trusts must: (1) pay out 90 per cent of their net income to shareholders; (2) have at least 100 shareholders; (3) permit no more than 50 per cent (in value) of their outstanding stock to be owned by or for five or less individuals; (4) be investors and not merchants of real estate; (5) derive 90 per cent of their gross income from rent on real property, interest, and gain on the sale of securities and real estate; and (6) derive 75 per cent of their gross income from real property interest, gain on the sale of real property, and shares of other trusts and "other" real estate sources. The last clause allows 15 per cent of gross income to come from dividends and the sale of other securities, and 10 per cent to be derived from any source permitted by the other requirements.[4]

## Individuals

The lending practices of private individuals vary so widely that only the most general statements can be made about them. Often private individuals take greater risks than could be accepted by lending institutions. Sometimes noneconomic considerations govern the actions of private individuals, as in the case of a father who sells his son a house and takes back a mortgage on generous terms. Regardless of their methods, or the motives behind their actions, private individuals are an important source of funds for real estate financing. This is especially true of junior financing arrangements, particularly in the residential field.

4 Glen E. Taylor, and E. Norman Bailey, "Real Estate Investment Trusts," *Business Horizons*, VI, No. 2 (Summer, 1963), p. 74.

### Non-Financial Institutions

Foundations, colleges, universities, and other non-financial institutions often invest in real estate mortgages. Some institutions of this type have invested large amounts of money in this manner. In addition, cooperative societies and cooperative credit unions have some importance in this field.

### State and Local Governments

State and local governments have not occupied a place of major importance in the provision of funds for real estate financing in this country. However, several states have made special provisions for home loans for veterans. Provision has been made for local public housing authorities, redevelopment activities, and similar arrangements by state and local governments. Loans and subsidies of various types are made to local authorities by the Public Housing Administration for various purposes such as redevelopment, slum clearance, and public housing programs.

## THE FEDERAL GOVERNMENT AND REAL ESTATE FINANCE

In some degree, the federal government has had an interest in real estate finance from the time of its establishment. Early programs for the disposition of the public domain included many financing problems. The Homestead Act included financial features. Other programs might be cited as well.

The enactment of the Federal Farm Loan Act in 1916 marked the beginning of the government's present activities in the financing of farms. Although the United States Housing Corporation operated during World War I, it was subsequently liquidated; and present federal programs in the housing field date largely from the early 1930's. World War II, the Korean War, the war in Indo China, and extensive defense programs have all influenced federal programs in the housing field.

It is not our intention to review all of the federal activities in housing and related areas, but rather to concentrate on those that have a primary bearing on real estate finance.[5]

[5] We do not cover, for example, the activities of the PWA Housing Division, the Resettlement Administration, various activities of the WPA, TVA, and the U.S. Housing Authority. Also, we do not include discussions of war housing programs or those of the National Housing Agency, the RFC, or the RFC Mortgage Company. And although the history of the HOLC (Home Owners' Loan Corporation) is highly interesting and was a most successful operation of the Federal Home Loan Bank Board, it is more of historical than current interest and will not be included here.

For a review of federal housing programs, see *A Decent Home*, Report of the President's Committee on Urban Housing (Washington, D.C.: U. S. Government Printing Office, 1969), pp. 51–73. See also Study Project 6–1.

### General Monetary and Credit Policies

Financial and other lenders in the real estate field are influenced greatly by general money market conditions and by Federal Reserve policies. The Federal Reserve may influence the availability of funds by pursuing policies designed to produce varying degrees of easy or tight money market conditions. The impact of such policies often is uneven as between different money markets and financial institutions.[6] Mortgage interest rates typically respond rather slowly to general money market changes. Insured and guaranteed loans have carried fixed interest rates, thus necessitating the use of discounts or premiums to adjust to market changes. Usury laws present special problems in many states. Therefore, when yields on government and corporate bonds rise, there is a tendency for funds to move out of the mortgage market into such investments; when bond yields decline, funds tend to move back into the mortgage market. The mortgage market is not a good competitor for funds when interest rates are high.

Because the Treasury Department is such a large user of funds, the policies followed in borrowing either for new purposes or to refinance older bond issues, including interest rates offered, maturities of bonds, and the like, are bound to affect money markets generally and the mortgage market as well. Thus, those who lend funds to finance real estate projects attempt to anticipate changes in money markets and in Federal Reserve and related monetary policies. The impact of such changes is felt rather directly by financial institutions and through them by borrowers.

### Federal Agencies

The various federal programs are coordinated by a number of agencies. We will review some of them here including the Federal Home Loan Bank System, the Veterans' Administration as it pertains to VA loans, the Department of Housing and Urban Development, including the Federal Housing Administration, the Government National Mortgage Association and other agencies. We will consider the Federal National Mortgage Association here.

### Federal Home Loan Bank System

The Federal Home Loan Bank Act was passed in 1932 and has had important consequences for urban real estate finance. This Act set up a

---

[6] See Edward E. Edwards and Arthur M. Weimer, *Cyclical Fluctuations in Residential Construction* (Bloomington, Ind.: Business and Real Estate Trends, Inc., 1967).

system of twelve regional banks (later changed to eleven, then back to twelve) administered under a board of directors and allowed membership to all state and federally chartered financial institutions, other than commercial banks, which engaged in long-term home financing and conformed to certain requirements. The large majority of the membership in the ensuing years was comprised of savings and loan associations. The various Federal Home Loan Banks, which in a sense serve as reserve banks in their regions for their members, may make loans directly to their member institutions but not directly to private investors. While the government subscribed to a substantial block of the stock of these banks originally, provisions were set up for the retirement of these subscriptions over a period of years through the purchase of stock by member institutions. Since 1951, the capital stock of the Federal Home Loan Banks has been owned entirely by their member institutions.

Dot indicates location of each regional Bank.
Puerto Rico and the Virgin Islands are in District 2.
Alaska, Hawaii and Guam are in District 12.

Source: Federal Home Loan Bank Board.

**Fig. 19–2.** Federal home loan bank districts. (Courtesy of U. S. Savings and Loan League.)

Membership in the Federal Home Loan Bank System consists primarily of savings and loan associations plus a few savings banks and a handful of insurance companies. Of the savings and loan association members there is an almost equal division between federally chartered and state chartered institutions.

The main idea back of the establishment of the Federal Home Loan Bank system was the forming of a central pool of funds which might be used for mortgage purposes and which would tend toward the development of a national mortgage market. It was patterned somewhat after the central mortgage financing institutions of Europe, such as the Swedish Town Mortgage System. The stated objectives of the system were to relieve financial strains on home owners and financial institutions during the depression emergency, to assist in the revival of home construction, and to strengthen the institutions specializing in the financing of home ownership.

### Federal Savings and Loan Associations

As a part of the Home Owner's Loan Act of 1933, provision was made for a system of Federal Savings and Loan Associations. Such associations are incorporated under federal law, being chartered by the Federal Home Loan Bank Board either as new associations or as converted state-chartered institutions. They are required to become members of the Federal Home Loan Bank System. The basic purpose of this legislation was to meet a need in many communities for more adequate home financing facilities by providing for local institutions throughout the country which would operate under a uniform plan incorporating the best operating principles and practices of savings institutions specializing in home financing. These "federalized" institutions have access to funds, in addition to those provided by their own members, by borrowing from the Federal Home Loan Bank of their region either on their own unsecured notes or on the security of mortgages or from other sources.

### Federal Savings and Loan Insurance Corporation

Provision was made in 1934 for the insurance of the savings and investment accounts in saving and loan associations by Title IV of the National Housing Act. Under this legislation, savers' and investors' accounts were insured at first up to $5,000 and later up to $20,000. Membership in the Federal Savings and Loan Insurance Corporation is compulsory for federally chartered institutions and is optional for state chartered institutions.

### Veterans' Administration Loans

Under the Servicemen's Readjustment Act of 1944, the Veterans' Administration was authorized to guarantee veterans' loans secured by real property. Subsequent amendments included various other veterans. Varying arrangements were made from time to time as to amounts and terms of the loan guarantees. A financial institution may be guaranteed against loss on loans to honorably discharged veterans up to a stated percentage of a property's value but not beyond stated amounts and terms.

Mortgage loans of this type are made by all types of financial institutions as well as by private lenders. Interest rates have been fixed at various levels.

Mortgage lenders often prefer loans guaranteed by the Veterans' Administration to those insured by the FHA because in case of default, and after all reasonable efforts to make adjustments have been exhausted, the lender may file a claim for the full amount of the guaranty to be paid in cash by the Veterans' Administration.

Experience with VA loans has been highly favorable. Sometimes interest rates are set at levels below those dictated in the competitive market and this has resulted in substantial discounts. The Government National Mortgage Association and the FNMA may help to provide a market at such times.

### Department of Housing and Urban Development

In 1965 Congress authorized the establishment of the Department of Housing and Urban Development (HUD).[7] It includes the Federal Housing Administration, The Government National Mortgage Association, and various public housing and urban renewal programs

The Housing and Home Finance Agency was established in 1947 for the purpose of coordinating various federal activities in the housing field. The Federal Home Loan Bank System, which was a part of this agency originally, was subsequently restored to its position as an independent agency. The HHFA and its constituent agencies became the basic elements in the Department of Housing and Urban Development.

### The Federal Housing Administration

The Federal Housing Administration was set up by authority of the National Housing Act of 1934. While the original provisions of this Act have been modified by subsequent legislation, the main functions of this agency have followed a rather uniform pattern. Basically, FHA is an insurance agency of the government, insuring lending institutions against loss in the financing of mortgages and loans made in accordance with the requirements of law and the administrative regulations of the FHA. While the FHA program has been altered from time to time to meet changing conditions, insurance of mortgages as provided in the original Act is generally continued. The continuing activities of the FHA include property-improvement loan insurance or Title I loans, home mortgage insurance on

---

[7] Public Law 89–174, 89th Congress, September 9, 1965 (79 Stat. 667).

one- to four-family dwellings or Title II loans, the insurance of mortgages on rental housing projects, and related programs. Special arrangements have been made to facilitate the construction of housing in problem areas. Provisions have also been made for the insurance of mortgages on cooperative housing, mortgages on publicly owned housing, farm housing, and for the insurance of loans for other purposes.

The mortgage insurance system established by the FHA enabled commercial banks to engage more heavily in real estate financing than had been possible prior to the provision of such insurance. In addition, the mortgage lending activities of many other types of financial institutions were facilitated. All lending institutions that wished to participate in the FHA program, however, were required to become approved mortgagees and to meet the standards established by the FHA for such approval.

### The Federal National Mortgage Association

In the National Housing Act of 1934 provision was made for the establishment of national mortgage associations to serve as a secondary mortgage market. Further, in 1935, the RFC Mortgage Company was established to provide an agency within the Reconstruction Finance Corporation which could enter directly into the mortgage field by purchasing mortgages on various types of property and by lending directly on mortgage security. Until 1938, no national mortgage associations had been established; hence the Federal National Mortgage Association was set up in that year as a subsidiary of the RFC, with funds provided by the RFC Mortgage Company. The FNMA ("Fanny May") provided a market for insured mortgages and enabled institutions to sell their mortgages, retaining the servicing fee.

With the liquidation of the RFC Mortgage Company under 1947 amendments to the RFC Act, the FNMA became the sole government agency serving as a secondary mortgage market. It was made the sole possible national mortgage association in 1948. The Housing Act of 1948 authorized the FNMA to purchase not only mortgages on one- to four-family houses insured by FHA but also FHA-insured mortgages on rental property and mortgages guaranteed by the Veterans' Administration.

In 1954 the FNMA was rechartered as part of HHFA to help provide a continuing secondary mortgage market. In 1965 it was made a part of the Department of Housing and Urban Development, and subsequently was transferred in 1968 into a private corporation. Since that time the FNMA has been engaged primarily in secondary mortgage market operations. Of special importance have been its weekly auctions. These provide for weekly announcements of commitments available and approved sellers may submit bids, including price and terms. Sellers provide for

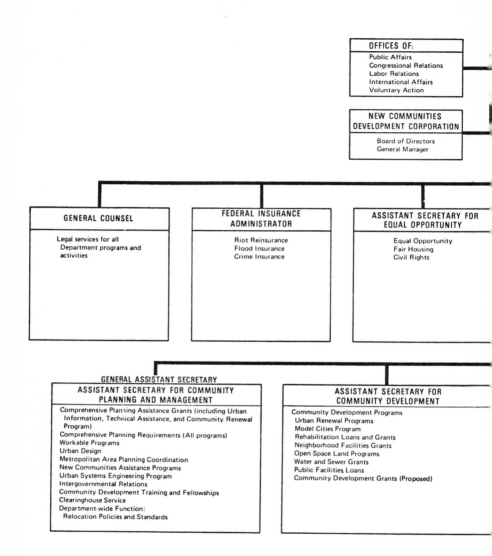

**Fig. 19–3.** Department of housing and urban development.

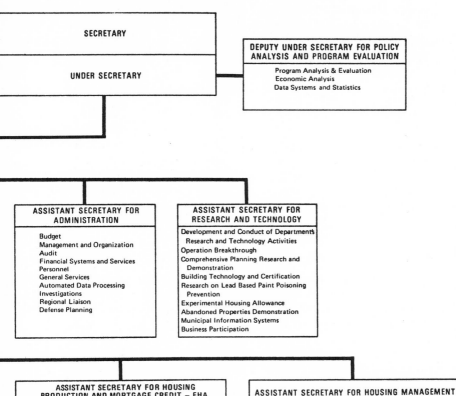

**SECRETARY**

**UNDER SECRETARY**

**DEPUTY UNDER SECRETARY FOR POLICY ANALYSIS AND PROGRAM EVALUATION**

Program Analysis & Evaluation
Economic Analysis
Data Systems and Statistics

**ASSISTANT SECRETARY FOR ADMINISTRATION**

Budget
Management and Organization
Audit
Financial Systems and Services
Personnel
General Services
Automated Data Processing
Investigations
Regional Liaison
Defense Planning

**ASSISTANT SECRETARY FOR RESEARCH AND TECHNOLOGY**

Development and Conduct of Department's
  Research and Technology Activities
Operation Breakthrough
Comprehensive Planning Research and
  Demonstration
Building Technology and Certification
Research on Lead Based Paint Poisoning
  Prevention
Experimental Housing Allowance
Abandoned Properties Demonstration
Municipal Information Systems
Business Participation

**ASSISTANT SECRETARY FOR HOUSING PRODUCTION AND MORTGAGE CREDIT – FHA**

Mortgage Insurance for Housing and Related Facilities (including
  Mortgage Servicing for Single-Family Programs and Premium
  Collection for Multifamily Programs)
Mortgage Insurance, Interest Reduction, and Rent Supplements
  for Low, Moderate, and Middle Income Housing
Production of Low-Rent Public Housing, College Housing, and
  Housing for the Elderly
Financial Assistance for Non-Profit Sponsors
Mortgage Insurance for Rehabilitation
Interstate Land Sales Disclosure
Government National Mortgage Association
Department-wide Functions:
  Market Analysis
  Housing Construction and Design Standards

**ASSISTANT SECRETARY FOR HOUSING MANAGEMENT**

Management of Contracts for Interest Reduction (Sec. 235, 236,
  243), Rent Supplement, College and Elderly Housing
Management and Disposition of Acquired Properties, including
  Government Held or Assigned Properties under Mortgage
  Insurance Programs
Mortgage Servicing for Multifamily Mortgage Insurance Programs
  (excluding Premium Collection)
Management and Modernization of Low-Rent Public Housing,
  including Tenant Services
Revolving Fund for Liquidating Programs (including Advances
  for Public Works Planning, Advance Acquisition of Land, and
  Alaska Housing)
Department-wide Function:
  Counseling Services

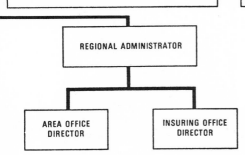

**REGIONAL ADMINISTRATOR**

**AREA OFFICE DIRECTOR**

**INSURING OFFICE DIRECTOR**

servicing. Recently, FNMA has been authorized to deal in conventional as well as government insured and guaranteed mortgages. Lenders selling mortgages to this agency are required to conform to its regulations. From time to time, FNMA may sell mortgages as well as buy them.

### Government National Mortgage Association

The Housing and Urban Development Act of 1968 established the Government National Mortgage Association (usually referred to as "Ginny Mae") as a part of the Department of Housing and Urban Development to administer the various special assistance programs that had formerly been a part of FNMA's operations. Among its more important functions, GNMA issues various guarantees of securities that are backed by mortgage loans. Various management and liquidation functions are performed by GNMA as well.

### Federal Farm Programs

Various federal programs for the provision of assistance in financing farms and farm homes and other buildings have been carried on since the enactment of the Federal Farm Loan Act of 1916. Under this act, the federal land banks were established to provide financial assistance for farmers by means of loans made through national farm loan associations for periods of five to forty years on the basis of first mortgages on farms. The borrower is required to purchase stock in the Land Bank that makes the loan in the amount of 5 per cent of the loan that is arranged.

Joint stock land banks were also set up in 1916 but were discontinued in 1933. At that time, the Federal Farm Mortgage Corporation was established to administer Land Bank Commissioner loans. These were discontinued in 1947. The Farm Security Administration was set up in 1937 and subsequently was replaced by the Farmers Home Administration. Direct loans are provided through this organization to farmers for acquiring ownership and for constructing and repairing farm homes and other farm buildings but only in case financing cannot be arranged through other sources. The Farmers Home Administration also provides for the insurance of certain farm mortgages. Subsequently a program for the financing of low rent housing for domestic workers was added along with provision for financing certain cooperatively used and rented housing as well as for low and moderate income families in smaller cities and towns.

### Other Federal Programs

Federal programs include various arrangements for the financing of public housing and urban renewal projects. In more recent years the latter have been concerned especially with "neighborhood" development programs. Various rent supplement and below market interest rate programs have been introduced. In recent years the so-called Section 236 (rent supplement) and 235 (interest supplement or home ownership) programs have accounted for a significant volume of low and moderate income housing. In the rent supplement programs tenants pay 25 per cent of their incomes toward rent and the remainder is provided as a subsidy. In the interest rate supplement programs the home buyers must put at least 20 per cent of their incomes toward the mortgage. The difference between the 20 and 25 per cent in the homeowner and rental program is accounted for by the homeowner's payment of utility, maintenance and repair charges himself. Programs are administered by the Department of Housing and Urban Development.

The Model Cities Program was established in 1966 and provides for broad scale attacks on various urban and neighborhood problems. The National Housing Partnerships concept was introduced to attract capital from a variety of sources into the housing field. It makes use of the limited partnership arrangement.

In addition a variety of grants are available for demolition projects. Rehabilitation loans and grants are provided under specified conditions. There are also college housing loans and various loans and programs to help provide housing for senior citizens. In addition programs have been introduced to help develop new towns and new planned communities through loans to developers.

Various other agencies such as the Small Business Administration and the Department of Transportation play roles of importance in this field.

## SUMMARY

This chapter describes the nature of the more important institutions and agencies operating in the field of real estate finance. Particular attention was directed to the activities of commercial and mutual savings banks, savings and loan associations, and life insurance companies. Individual lenders, mortgage brokers and companies, real estate investment trusts, and pension funds also may be important suppliers of funds.

Financial institutions are subject to extensive influence and control exercised by governmental agencies. To some extent this results from the partial-monopoly nature of financial institutions which must obtain special permission in order to operate. Much governmental influence is indirect, resulting from the effect of Federal Reserve and Treasury policies on the supply of funds and the level of interest rates.

Government activity in the housing field has led to the establishment of a number of agencies, all of which influence or regulate private real estate decisions to some extent. These agencies include the Federal Home Loan Bank System, the Veterans' Administration, and the Department of Housing and Urban Development, with its component parts.

The programs and policies of private financial institutions and of governmental agencies are important factors in determining decisions in the real estate field. These institutions and agencies influence, among other factors, the availability of real estate credit, the desirability of alternative investments, and the methods by which real estate is financed.

## QUESTIONS FOR STUDY

1. Who are the principal borrowers in the real estate mortgage market? Who are the principal lenders?
2. Describe the functions performed by mortgage brokers in the financing of real estate. How important are these functions?
3. Which financial institutions are most important in real estate finance? What reasons can you give to explain their importance?
4. Describe the purpose and primary operations of the Department of Housing and Urban Development.
5. Explain the roles played by insurance companies, savings and loan associations, mutual savings banks, and commercial banks in the financing of real estate. Do commercial banks have any particular advantages or disadvantages as compared with other institutions engaged in real estate finance? Explain.
6. Which of the financial institutions involved in the real estate field are likely to enjoy most rapid growth in the next decade? Why?
7. Explain the relationship between Federal Reserve policies and the availability of mortgage funds. How is the supply of mortgage credit related to general money market conditions?
8. In what way can the operations of the Treasury Department affect the terms and availability of mortgage funds?
9. Describe the structure and organization of the Federal Home Loan Bank System. How do its activities influence the financing of real estate?
10. Are there any significant differences between FHA-insured mortgages and VA-guaranteed mortgages? If so, explain what these differences are.
11. Do you think the federal government will play a larger or smaller role in the area of real estate finance in the years ahead? Are there likely to be marked differences between urban and rural real estate in this regard?

## SUGGESTED READINGS

AMERICAN SAVINGS AND LOAN INSTITUTE. *Savings and Loan Principles* (rev. ed.). Chicago: The Institute Press, 1961.

COMMISSION ON MONEY AND CREDIT. *Money and Credit.* Englewood Cliffs, N.J.: Prentice-Hall, Inc., 1961. Chaps. i, vi, vii.

COMMISSION ON FINANCIAL STRUCTURE AND REGULATION. *Report.* Washington, D.C.: U. S. Government Printing Office, 1971.

EDWARDS, EDWARD E., and ARTHUR M. WEIMER. *Cyclical Fluctuations in Residential Construction*. Bloomington, Ind.: Business and Real Estate Trends, Inc., 1968.

HOAGLAND, HENRY E., and LEO D. STONE. *Real Estate Finance* (4th ed.). Homewood, Ill.: Richard D. Irwin, Inc., 1969. Chaps. 11–15, 23–29.

KLAMAN, SAUL B. *The Postwar Rise of Mortgage Companies*, Occasional Paper 60. New York: National Bureau of Economic Research, Inc., 1959.

MAISEL, SHERMAN J. *Financing Real Estate: Principles and Practices*. New York: McGraw-Hill Book Co., Inc., 1965. Chaps. i–v.

TAYLOR, GLEN S., and E. NORMAN BAILEY. "Real Estate Investment Trusts," *Business Horizons*, VI, No. 2 (Summer, 1963).

## STUDY PROJECT 19–1

### Maintaining an Adequate Flow of Funds into Home Mortgage Markets

There has been much discussion recently of what might be done to moderate the impact of tight money on the home mortgage market. A more useful approach to housing problems might be to consider what is needed to maintain at all times an adequate flow of funds into home mortgage markets.

The following ten suggestions are offered as an answer to this more basic question.

**1—Overcoming Inflationary Expectations.** The absolutely essential element in any program for assisting the home mortgage market on a constructive and lasting basis must be to overcome inflationary expectations. So long as inflation persists, one can only improvise solutions to a continuing shortage of funds for home financing. There are improvisations that will help, even where inflationary expectations persist, but it has to be a losing battle until the struggle against inflation has been won.

**2—A Federal Budget Surplus.** Next, an anti-inflation policy designed to avoid a harsh impact on the home mortgage market must rely heavily on fiscal restraint. Present policies are having an adverse effect on housing primarily because they rely too much on high interest rates. What is needed is a large budget surplus. Given that, the problem of helping the homebuilding industry would to all intents and purposes be solved.

**3—Incentives To Increase Private Savings.** Just as savings by the federal government through a budget surplus would help the mortgage market, so would an increase in personal savings. And there are things that could be done to accomplish this, beginning with the tax system. One of the anomalies of federal tax arrangements is that they encourage borrowing for home purchases but do nothing to promote the thrift that is essential if credit is to be made available on a noninflationary base. Actually, by tightening the rules on taxation of interest income, practices in recent years have moved in the opposite direction.

° By Raymond J. Saulnier; reproduced by permission of Mortgage Guaranty Insurance Corporation, from the *MGIC Newsletter*.

A powerful stimulus could be given to saving by extending tax exemption to income earned on thrift accounts, subject to a reasonable upper limit. In my judgment there is an urgent need for such a move. Tax deferral would be a lesser but important incentive. Restricted withdrawal savings accounts already enjoy this privilege, but these accounts would almost certainly be more widely used in thrift institutions if the funds could be invested in equities. Although this would draw financing into the homebuilding market only to the extent that the funds were invested in real estate equities, the availability of such a plan at thrift instituticns might also attract savings in conventional form, thus aiding the home mortgage market. In any case, a widening of the tax deferral privilege deserves close study.

**4—Flexibility in Rate of Return on Mortgage Portfolios.** Most problems faced by the home mortgage market would be resolved if earnings on mortgage portfolios could be made sufficiently flexible to keep them broadly in line with alternative investment yields. Basically, the problem is that long maturities and fixed interest rates keep the average yield on mortgage portfolios from rising except slowly as open market yields rise, making it difficult to lift the return paid on savings and thus to hold them against the pull of disintermediation. An obvious way to correct this would be to have a variable division of payments between interest and retirement of principal, with the division perhaps determined automatically in some relation to the cost of savings to the lending institution.

Although it is not clear that a variable yield mortgage would have the same marketability as the fixed-interest, level-payment, long-maturity home mortgage, this possibly should not be dismissed out-of-hand. Obviously, there is work to be done to devise a mortgage instrument that will combine flexibility of return with investment acceptability.

**5—Wider Lending, Investing and Other Service-Rendering Authorities.** Most discussions of the problem of assisting thrift institutions assume they would be better able to compete for savings if they had wider lending, investing and other service-rendering authorities. But it seems reasonable to believe they would earn a competitively adequate rate of return if the yield on a mortgage investment portfolio were adjusted flexibly under a variable-yield mortgage instrument. Conversely, lacking this flexibility, a widening of the lending and investing authorities of thrift institutions would divert funds from the home mortgage market. What this suggests is that the industry should concentrate mainly on making mortgage investment yields more flexible.

It is conceivable, however, that widening the service-rendering authorities of thrift institutions would help them attract and hold savings. Proposals to this end deserve objective examination, though I would expect better results from an extension of the tax deferral privilege, as proposed under point 3.

**6—Flexibility in Rates Payable on Savings.** Next, thrift institutions need greater freedom to fix rates on savings according to their own lights. Like all ceilings, limitations on the amount that can be paid for savings—whether imposed by statute or administrative ruling—do not hold interest rates down until they become unrealistic in relation to the market, at which point they suppress rate increases at the cost of diverting funds from home mortgage investment. At the earliest possible moment, the monetary authorities should begin dismantling all present ceilings; steps to this end should be high on the agenda of the new Commission on the Structure and Regulation of Financial Institutions.

**7—Branches, Mergers, Conversions and Chartering.**   Recent studies show that location is crucial in the ability of a thrift institution to attract new savings accounts and to hold old ones.   There is need, accordingly, to give institutions greater freedom to establish new offices.   Neighborhoods change, new ones are created, and population densities are altered rapidly nowadays, and financial institutions that gather savings in small amounts from large numbers of individual savers need more freedom to adapt themselves to these facts.   Clearly, a fresh look at federal and state regulations regarding the establishment of branches is needed.

At the same time, there is need to reexamine law and administrative practice regarding mergers, conversions and the chartering of financial institutions. These, too, are matters that should be high on the agenda of the new Commission on the Structure and Regulation of Financial Institutions.

**8—Removing Obstacles to Flow of Funds into Mortgage Investment.**   The next requirement for helping the home mortgage market is to remove obstacles to the flow of funds into mortgage investment.   State usury statutes that set maximum interest rates below the rate of return available on alternative investments are a case in point.   A number of these have been adjusted upward recently, but others remain.   In addition, interest rate ceilings imposed on federally-insured, guaranteed mortgages either by statute or administrative edict need to be eliminated.   Time after time, a failure to adjust these ceilings to increases in open market yields has starved the home mortgage market of funds.   And because this always occurs when credit is most urgently needed, the result cannot help but be awkward.   The obvious conclusion is that ceilings should be eliminated.   If some type of monitoring is thought necessary to determine whether rates charged are higher than competitive markets require, surely there is enough ingenuity in the world to devise a system that would be effective without relying on fixed ceilings.

**9—Increasing Flow of Savings into Mortgage Investment.**   The economy's institutional structure has changed sufficiently in the past few decades to suggest the need for innovations to help channel funds into the home mortgage market.   Specifically, it would be constructive to find ways to attract a larger portion of funds gathered on a contractual basis in pension funds and similar pools of capital.   The new mortgage-backed, federally-guaranteed security issued under the Government National Mortgage Association is a promising step in this direction.   But not so the proposals that would require financial institutions to invest some stated percentage of their resources in home mortgages. This dirigist approach collides head-on with the philosophy of competition and I would not want to see it gain any support whatever.

**10—Direct Federal Support of the Home Mortgage Market.**   Under this heading, let me first register complete dissent from suggestions that the Federal Reserve System make direct purchases of home mortgages.   Similarly, I dissent from proposals for supplemental cash reserves—presumably applicable only to commercial banks—that would vary by type of loan according to norms set by Federal Reserve authorities. Whatever may be the implications of such a proposal for control over the money supply, it would assign to the Federal Reserve responsibilities for national planning and resource allocation so extensive as obviously to require basic reconsideration of the system's political accountability.

Actually, there are many ways for the federal government to supply funds to the homebuilding industry without involving a potentially inflationary creation of bank reserves or without catapulting us into a hastily contrived system of bureaucratically-determined resource allocation. Credit can be extended directly or indirectly to home financing institutions, to builders or to homeowners by government in any one of a variety of ways. Funds can be made available on a subsidy or nonsubsidy basis, and availability can be selective in any manner desired. The crucial question is not how to do it—which is simple enough —but how much aid should be given and how much can be funded, considering other budget priorities.

However, two suggestions for changes in present arrangements under which the federal government makes credit available to the home mortgage market are pertinent. First, the informal arrangements under which the Federal Reserve system can provide liquidity to mutual savings banks should be made formal and explicit. Second, steps should be taken to minimize competition for funds between home financing institutions and federal agencies that sell their securities in open markets. Ironically, this competition oftentimes draws funds out of home financing institutions to make them available, circuitously, to the home mortgage market. Proposals have been made on numerous occasions to end this pointless competition by better coordination of the investment banking operations of federal agencies with the overall needs of the capital markets. All that remains is actually to initiate the need arrangements, presumably under the aegis of the Treasury.

### Questions

1. Which suggestions potentially offer the greatest boost in the amount of home mortgage funds? What problems might be encountered in putting these into practice?
2. Even if considerable additional money is injected into the home mortgage market, would that have a beneficial effect on housing starts? Explain.

# 20

# Financing: Mortgage Lending

## IMPORTANT OF MORTGAGE CREDIT

Although we may ordinarily think of finance as a matter of borrowing and lending, it is important to recognize that nearly all types of decisions in the real estate field now have important financial aspects. Decisions to buy, build, lease, sell, improve, and use real estate all involve financial considerations. Thus, the administration of real estate finance is almost as broad a field as real estate administration in general.

### Financing Property Use

One way to narrow the concept of real estate finance is to center attention primarily on two ways of viewing the subject: (1) how to finance the use of real property, and (2) how to invest in real estate without responsibility for the use of it.[1] In connection with the first point, the arrangements that are made may range from complete equity ownership on the one hand to leasing arrangements on the other. Some type of mortgage arrangement, however, is the most widely used method of financing the use of real estate.

[1] Suggested by Edward E. Edwards, Fred T. Greene Professor of Finance, Indiana University. Professor Edwards points out that nonfarm mortgage debt rose from $30 billion in 1945 to $260 billion in 1963 to $418 billion in 1970. In 1945 the mortgage debt was 12 per cent of the publicly held federal debt; in 1963 it exceeded the federal debt; in 1970 it also exceeded it. See his article "Changing Character of Real Estate Mortgage Markets," *Journal of Finance*, XIX, No. 2, Pt. I (May, 1964).

### Investment Without Responsibility for Use

In connection with the second point made above, a wide variety of methods of investing in real estate may be employed without being responsible for its use, including complete equity ownership of leased property, various equity and debt combinations of leased property, savings and loan accounts, Federal Home Loan Bank obligations, and others. Again, however, various types of mortgages represent the most widely used methods of investing in real estate without incurring responsibility for the use of the real estate.

### Equity Investments

As we have suggested, real estate investments may range from equities to mortgages; a variety of combinations of equity and debt interests may be arranged. As we pointed out in Chapter 18, many kinds of methods and instruments are available to facilitate real estate investments including leases which may be used as a means of financing the use of property.

Equities may range from 100 per cent of the investment in a piece of real estate to a thin one or two per cent. Equities may be combined with debt financing in many ways. Debt investors may take a "piece of the action." General and limited partnerships may be set up; these in turn may be combined with various forms of debt investments. For example, percentage leases may be used under various arrangements. Many other types of combinations may be worked out as well. The popularity of different arrangements will vary with money market conditions, investor preferences, general economic trends, and other things.

### Investment Decisions

Although both equity and debt investors will be concerned with estimating risks and returns there will be significant differences in the priorities and emphasis which will be given to these and related decision factors. For example, equity investors may consider both financial and nonfinancial risks and rewards. Home owners may be especially concerned with the nonfinancial aspects of their investment decisions, for example. Individual investors may place a high priority on cash flow. In judging investment opportunities, they may select from a variety of alternatives using the "indifference value" of cash flows, total returns, degrees of risk and related factors as guides.

Both debt and equity investors, of course, will give careful consideration to the present value of the future returns and benefits that may be anticipated from an investment. The discount rate will play a major role in such decisions.

In estimating the degree of certainty and uncertainty which will be faced, investors may use a variety of ways of undertaking to assess the future. They may think in terms of probabilities. They may assume various attitudes toward risk and make estimates as to the extent to which various types of risks may be acceptable. The decisions of investors in such cases may be analyzed in terms of utility curves. Investment decision models may be developed. Illustrations of these types of decision factors are presented in Study Project 20–2, "Contemporary Decision Theory and Real Estate Investment" at the end of this Chapter.

### Mortgages

Since we cannot cover the entire range of methods of financing the use of real estate or investing in it, we will center our attention in this discussion on mortgage credit and the administration of mortgage risk. In mortgage transactions, we always have a borrower and a lender. Their decisions will be influenced by the objectives they hope to achieve, anticipated relationships between costs and returns, degree of risk involved, and the alternative arrangements that may be available.

### Risks and Returns

The mortgage lender is concerned with the soundness of the projects he finances and the conditions under which he may carry the risks involved. The lender's decision to advance funds will be affected by his estimate of the income prospects of the borrower, the market trends likely to affect the property, and the return on the investment relative to the risk involved, probable yield on other investments, interest rate risk and purchasing power risk. When general and local prospects appear to be favorable, the lender will tend to be more liberal in his financing than when the outlook is more uncertain. At times virtually no credit may be available for mortgage financing because lenders are much more interested in liquidity than in yield.

The borrower's decision to use mortgage credit will turn primarily on his estimate of the return he can earn on the borrowed funds relative to their cost and the risks involved. In some cases, of course, he must borrow to protect an earlier position he has taken.

### Public Interest

Problems of mortgage financing are important to the public as well as to borrowers and lenders. The public at large is interested in the proportion of savings going into real estate projects and in the efficiency with which such savings are used. Mortgage lending plays a major role in channeling savings into real estate projects.

## MORTGAGE LENDING POLICIES AND PRACTICES

The lender is primarily concerned with the repayment of his loan with interest over a number of years. While liberal financing terms facilitate the programs of the developer, broker, owner, or user of property, conservative financing terms may prevent them from undertaking unsound ventures. In many respects the lender with his long-range point of view thus serves as a stabilizing force in the real estate market.

### Lender Conflicts

The lender, however, faces numerous conflicts in his own policies. Ultraconservative practices usually limit his earnings. Liberal financing may lead to numerous foreclosure problems. The overoptimism of a boom period may lead him to extend credit on terms that are too liberal for the life of the mortgages which he makes. Such overoptimism, moreover, may cause booms to run greater extremes than would otherwise be the case. By contrast, highly conservative practices in boom periods may limit developments which are needed for the orderly progress of his community. Also, ultraconservative practices during the depths of a recession may prolong the agony of such a period.

### New Financing vs. Old

The mortgage lender who is financing new real estate projects is helping to create competition for properties which stand as security for mortgages that he has already made. If a new type of construction is being featured by a builder, the mortgage lender who finances him may find that such properties are not marketable if foreclosure becomes necessary. Or, if successful, such a project may produce properties that cause rapid obsolescence of properties that the lender is already looking to as security for mortgages. On the other hand, if the mortgage lender fails to finance a progressive builder, he may cut himself off from a good market for his investment funds.

The mortgage lender tends to object to government regulation during prosperous times; yet he cannot object too strongly because he may find it necessary to rely on the support of the government when the cold wind of a recession paralyzes his operations. Government policies are the primary factors in the creation of inflationary or deflationary tendencies in the economy.

### Key Role of Mortgage Lender

The mortgage lender, whether he is a banker, a savings and loan association official, a representative of an insurance company, or a private investor, thus provides an interesting study of contrasts and conflicts. His policies often contrast sharply with those of others in the real estate field. His own objectives and policies are often in serious conflict with one another. Yet he is one of the key figures in the real estate business. His decisions have important long- and short-range effects, both on real estate in general and on the success or failure of specific projects for the development, marketing, ownership, and use of real properties.

## Management Problems of Lenders

Like other business firms, the owners and managers of the institutions engaged in real estate finance must determine objectives, develop plans to achieve such objectives, organize resources effectively, and control operations to assure conformity with plans. Of special importance in the successful management of such institutions is the care with which the risks involved in mortgage financing are estimated and the effectiveness of the programs develop to carry these risks.

The various institutions engaged in mortgage finance have essentially the same management problems. (See Fig. 20–1.) It is necessary to attract savings, and at costs that permit successful lending operations. The required personnel must be selected, hired, trained, and organized into an effective work team. Proper locations must be selected and developed for the place or places of business. It is necessary to generate the required loan volume, and more specifically to select the risks to be underwritten. After loans have been made, they must be serviced, and all mortgage loans as a group, or the *portfolio,* must be administered in a manner that makes the total loan program successful. The decisions and programs undertaken in order to accomplish these things will be influenced by anticipated changes in business conditions, in money markets, in real estate activity, and in government policies. Of special importance are anticipated changes in interest rates and the price level.

Like the managers of other types of business activities, the managers of mortgage lending institutions have the general problem of securing the required resources on sufficiently favorable terms to carry on the programs believed to be essential in achieving selected objectives. In our discussions here, will not undertake a review of all of these topics. Our attention will center primarily in the management of the risks that are involved in mortgage financing.

## RISKS IN LENDING

The individuals and institutions engaged in lending funds on the basis of real estate mortgages assume various types of risks. The successful administration of these risks is a complicated process. Although

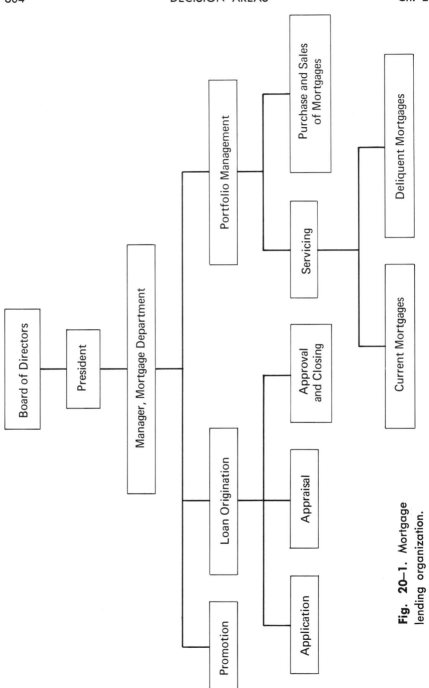

**Fig. 20–1.** Mortgage lending organization.

individual investors who finance real estate projects may make their decisions in regard to the risks they assume on informal bases, institutional lenders have developed rather definite procedures for arriving at decisions and for carrying them out.

The following steps typically are involved. After an application for a mortgage loan is made, a preliminary analysis is undertaken. If the results are favorable, the property to be pledged as security for the loan is appraised. The credit status of the borrower is determined. Final decisions are then reached, often being made by a loan committee. Once the loan becomes a part of the portfolio of the institution, it must be serviced throughout the period of its life. That is, interest and amortization payments are collected, and taxes and insurance payments are arranged.

Sometimes the loans are refinanced, and this may be a source of risk. If refinancing occurs early in the life of the loan, the costs of servicing the mortgage may exceed returns. Hence, some mortgage loans contain prepayment penalties. Refinancing usually results if competitive conditions change. Thus, it is desirable that loans be well adapted to the needs of the borrower and to his financial ability on rates and terms that are likely to be competitive at least for a reasonable period of time. For example, some mortgages provide for variable interest rates. In some cases equity interests are combined with mortgage lending.

### Sources of Risks

The risks involved in mortgage financing vary widely from one project to another, but they tend to arise from essentially the same sources. These sources affect both the borrower and the lender. Both must assume various risks. The borrower may lose his property and the income it may bring, plus (in some cases) other resources as well. The lender may lose yield on the funds advanced and may even lose all or part of the principal amount. The borrower has to decide how much he can afford to pay for borrowed funds in relation to the return he expects to receive from using them, recognizing the risks that are assumed in pledging his property. The lender has the problem of adjusting risks to the cost of funds and the return secured as a result of lending them. Although we pay special attention to the risks of the lender in this discussion, it is important to note that the risks of both the borrower and the lender arise from the same general sources.

### Interest Rate and Purchasing Power Risk

Both the borrower and lender face the uncertainties of interest rate risk. Arrangements may be made for shifting this risk to borrower or lender or for sharing or pooling or insuring it. Similarly, both face risks of changes in the purchasing power of the dollar. Inflation favors the borrower, deflation the lender.

### Borrower and Property Risks

The borrower may be unable to meet his obligation under the mortgage loan. This will bring him losses, of course, and may also bring losses to the lender. The yield on the investment may be impaired. The property pledged as security for the loan may decline in value, and as a result the amount realized from its sale may not be adequate to cover the unpaid balance of the loan plus foreclosure and related costs. Finally, the lender runs the risk that the other assets of the borrower may not be adequate to make up the difference.

### Estimating Risks and Returns

The lender thus has the problem of estimating the risk involved in a mortgage loan in relation to the return that may be realized. If risks are considered to be high, it may be possible to make adjustments by charging higher interest rates, arranging for variable interest rates, taking "a piece of the action," that is, participation in ownership in some way, lending for a short period of time (although in some cases this may increase rather than reduce the risk), or lending a relatively small amount in relation to the value of the property. In some cases, of course, the risks may be considered too great to make adjustments to them. Also, some lenders have fairly standardized lending plans and will only select those loans that fit these plans, rejecting others which might be acceptable under proper conditions by other lenders.

In order to estimate the borrower and property risks involved, most lenders analyze (1) the borrower, (2) the property, (3) the market, (4) legal rules and regulations, and (5) problems of administering the loan.

### Insurance of Risks

Some risks can be insured. For example, the hazards of fire, windstorm, public liability, and similar uncertainties can be transferred to a major extent to appropriate insurance companies. Certain hazards in defects to title to property may be shifted to a title insurance company. Credit life insurance may be used to help meet the risk of the borrower's death or disability. Even interest rate risk might be insured if the necessary plans were available. Almost all other types of risks, however, must be assumed by the lender in advancing funds on the basis of real estate security unless mortgage insurance or guarantees (public or private) are used. Thus, the risks of the lender on real estate security, are numerous and complex.

## LINES OF DEFENSE

Against these various types of risk there are several lines of defense. The first of these is the borrower's income-producing ability. If this is sufficient, the pledge of property need not be used. If not, or if the original borrower sells his property to a less desirable credit risk, the property becomes the second line of defense. In some cases a foreclosure of the property does not recompense the lender for the entire amount of his advance. Such conditions frequently arise where property is foreclosed during periods of depression. The mortgagee may then sue the borrower and receive a deficiency judgment, the value of which depends on the borrower's assets. (Its value varies also from state to state.)

The deficiency judgment forms the third line of defense. In cases where the borrower's assets are sufficient, such deficiency judgment is valuable security, since it cannot be evaded except by bankruptcy. Of course, if a deed is given in lieu of foreclosure, the third line of defense is not available to the lender. We should remember, also, that forced sales usually occur during depression periods when deficiency judgments are most likely to be valueless.

High levels of economic activity both nationally and locally often help in carrying mortgage risks. Recognition must be given, however, to the effect of inflation or deflation on long-term mortgage loans. In most of the fifties and sixties, inflation proved to be the major problem. The seventies are in the process of writing their history and mortgage lenders, borrowers, governmental agencies and the public at large will find it necessary to adjust to the effects of changes in interest rates and the value of the dollar. Lines of defense against these risks are in the process of being developed.

### Borrower Risks

All lenders of money are vitally interested in the individuals or companies that obligate themselves to repay a loan, even though a property is offered as security. Although individuals and companies may borrow for various purposes, two main groups may be designated: (1) individuals wishing to finance the ownership of homes, and (2) individuals and companies financing real estate projects for business and income-producing purposes.

Analysis of risks arising in connection with the first group of borrowers requires that attention be given to the following: (1) the borrower's personal fortune, (2) income, (3) the type of work in which he is engaged, (4) future prospects for economic advance or decline, (5) health, (6) age, (7) the number of people dependent upon him, and (8) the extent of his various obligations or potential obligations of a personal and business nature. Certain personal characteristics require consideration, including his reputation for fair dealing and prompt payment of obligations and his ability to manage his personal affairs.

Analysis of risks arising in connection with the second group of borrowers designated above necessitates a consideration of (1) the financial status of the person or company involved, and (2) the income-producing ability of the project which is to be financed. If the borrower is a corporation, the lender has no recourse to the incomes or assets of individuals, and hence attention must be directed to the condition and earning capacity of the company and the economic soundness of the project involved.

### Property Risks

Analysis of the uncertainties arising in connection with the pledge of a specific parcel of real estate as security for a mortgage requires a consideration of all the factors likely to affect its value during the period of the loan. In addition, it is necessary for the mortgagee to consider such questions as: (1) the value of the property in relation to the amount of the loan requested; (2) the property's economic life, structural soundness, and durability in relation to the term of the loan; (3) its inherent income-producing ability in relation to the amount of the loan, plus interest and servicing charges; and (4) its present and prospective competitive position in the market. Basically, the lender tries to make certain that the market value of the property will exceed the unpaid balance of the loan throughout the life of the mortgage.

The economic life of a property is a function of its location, design, structural soundness, and marketabiilty. Analysis of the income-producing ability of a property requires a consideration of its adaptability to the uses to which it is put and the potential demand for the type of services it is yielding in relation to the probable future supply likely to become available. An estimate of potential income-producing ability, however, is of little value unless considered in connection with the amount of the loan plus interest and servicing charges during the period of the financing contract. Like so many other problems of this type, it is difficult to consider a single factor except in relationship to others. For example, property changes will affect the borrower. A sudden decline in a property's value may cause the borrower to sell or to abandon his interest in it.

## Market Risks

Since investments in real estate typically are not liquid, the degree of marketability is an important risk element. For example, special purpose buildings are generally not so easy to market as other types, and hence involve a greater amount of uncertainty. Similarly, expensive residences are often hard to sell for amounts that even approximate the original investments in them. Also, their degree of marketability is usually limited in small cities. The competitive position of the property in the market at the time and under probable future market conditions is of primary importance in the analysis of mortgage risk.

Sudden declines in markets have a profound effect on mortgages made just prior to such changes. Such mortgages have not been *seasoned*—that is, reduced in value by amortization payments. When a borrower has reduced the principal on a high loan-value loan only slightly, he may be inclined to abandon the property if the amount still due on the mortgage is greater than the current market price of the property. Thus, greater risks of loss appear to be concentrated in the early years of the life of a mortgage. We should note, however, that a period of inflation could help the borrower to achieve a strong position if he had not paid down the loan at all. Also, the type of property may have a great deal of bearing on risk. For example, a 30 per cent loan on a vacant lot might go into default while an 80 or 90 per cent loan on a well-built and properly located house that the borrower wanted to keep as his home might prove to be highly successful.

## Legal Risks

We have pointed out that the laws regulating real estate finance are much more complex and involved than those regulating many other types of transactions. For example, the lender must determine whether the borrower is capable of mortgaging the property, whether he actually owns it or such interest in it as he claims to possess, and the extent of all preceding claims outstanding against it. In some cases zoning laws or deed restrictions may limit the uses to which a property may be put and seriously impair its earning power. In some parts of the country foreclosure laws are very favorable to the borrower and foreclosure costs are high. In others, such laws favor the lender.

## Administrative Risks

In drawing up a loan agreement, the lender assumes various risks of an administrative nature. Allowances for such risks can be made in numerous ways, no one of which is completely separated from the other. The ratio of loan to value, the interest rate, the term of the loan, the method of repayment, and the amount of initial or continuing servicing charges must be adjusted to each other in specific situations if allowances for administrative risks are to be made.

Traditionally, a low loan-value ratio was believed to be sufficient protection against most risks. However, difficulties often arise because values are frequently overestimated. For example, a loan-value ratio of 60 per cent might afford little protection to a lender if the transaction were entered into during a boom period when the value of the property was estimated at a high figure. Shrinkage of value might soon result in a loan-value ratio of 100 or even 110 per cent or more.

Again, a low loan-value ratio might bring about a situation in which the borrower was forced to resort to second- or third-mortgage financing, the costs of which might be high enough to impair his ability to meet the obligations of all the mortgages; or the borrower might refinance his mortgage at an early date, with the result that the mortgage would not have earned enough to pay the cost of putting it on the books. Similarly, a low loan-value ratio might afford slight protection against various uncertainties if the loan had an extremely long term, during which no repayments of principal were made, but during which the property depreciated rapidly. By contrast inflation might move up a property's value.

The interest rate must also be considered in relation to other factors and with respect to the possibilities of price level changes during the term of the loan. For example, provisions which allow the interest rate to fluctuate with general price level changes reduce such risks. Variable interest rates are used by a growing number of mortgage lenders.

The term of the loan represents similar problems. Unless the term is considered in relation to the method of repayment, it has little significance. Risks may be guarded against to some extent by the plan of repayment. Thus a 20-year loan on an amortized basis may contain less risk than a 10-year straight term loan, depending on the rate of amortization. It should be noted in this connection that an amortization plan which provides for large payments during the earlier years of a loan usually contains less risk than one providing for a uniform rate of repayment or one requiring larger payments during the later years of the term, or a so-called "balloon" payment at the end. Also, a lender may think that liberal loans are justified during boom periods if they are amortized. Hence he may increase his risks simply because he thinks he has a device for meeting them.

Again, conservative appraisals, in the minds of some lenders, may be balanced by liberal loans, or high interest rates by longer-term loans. Thus every device for reducing risk may become a risk element itself if the administration of a mortgage lending program is weak.

Amortized mortgages are not sound risks simply because they are amortized. Like other risk elements, amortization must be adjusted to all of the factors bearing on the probable success of the mortgage arrangement. Further, it is always necessary to bear in mind that real estate credit is of a long-term character, and therefore a financing transaction may fail because the loan agreement was not adjusted to the longer-range risk factors in a specific situation, such as purchasing power risk.

### Portfolio Management

Obviously the risks assumed in one mortgage loan may offset in part the risks assumed in another. There is thus somewhat less total risk in an entire loan portfolio than in all of the loans individually. Typically, all of the loans made will not go into default at one time. Loans made at an earlier period that have been partially amortized may help to carry the risks of recently made loans. Variable interest rate mortgages may be balanced against fixed rate loans. Insured and guaranteed mortgages may be balanced against those that are not insured or guaranteed.

Nevertheless, the management of the mortgage loan portfolio requires contant attention. In some cases it may be desirable to sell loans in order to meet current demands or to improve yield on the entire portfolio. Or in other cases buying loans may be indicated. These processes have been facilitated by the use of FNMA and by GNMA-mortgage backed securities. Sometimes geographic spreading of risks may dictate the sale or purchase of loans, especially if the institution may only originate loans in a given area.

In some cases it may be advisable to undertake the financing of new developments by providing construction loans in the interest of securing from such activities a volume of mortgage loans that may remain in the portfolio for a long time.

A mortgage loan portfolio cannot be managed without regard to the over-all programs of the institution. For example, provision of adequate liquidity may at times necessitate the sacrifice of yield by shifting funds from mortgages to government bonds or other securities that have the desired liquidity. In some cases considerations of this type may dictate the distribution of loans between conventional, insured, and guaranteed mortgages.

Anticipated changes in money market conditions, in real estate activity, or in government policies or programs may also influence the decisions taken in the management of a mortgage loan portfolio. For example, if money markets are expected to become tight with rising interest rates, lending volume may be restricted in the hope of securing higher yields later.

## Defense Against Interest Rate
## and Purchasing Power Risk

As has been suggested above, variable interest rates may be set up to shift the risk of interest rate advances to the borrower. Such practices seem likely to increase in the years ahead. They may be coupled with prepayment penalties attached to fixed interest rate mortgages in order to shift a major share of the risk of declining interest rates to borrowers.

It may be that new devices may be developed for handling interest rate risk. For example, since neither the borrower nor the lender have much if any control over conditions, it may be desirable to establish a program for insuring interest rate risk, at least on home mortgages. Whether such a program could be developed successfully remains to be seen. Professor Edward E. Edwards has recommended that such an effort be undertaken.[2]

Defenses against purchasing power risk to date are largely of the type that relate the value of the principal of a mortgage to price level changes. Thus, if the amount due on a mortgage varied with changes in the consumer price index, for example, or some other price index, the lender would be able to shift purchasing power risk to the borrower in the event of inflation, but would be assuming greater risk in the event of deflation. It is sometimes argued that the lender gains from inflation as well as deflation uunder present mortgage arrangements which typically do not make provision for price level changes. Thus, it is contended that if prices rise the value of the property which stands as security rises and hence reduces the risk that the loan will not be repaid. Even if the dollars repaid are worth less, the risks have been reduced. On the other hand if price levels decline the lender is repaid in dollars of higher value, hence stands to gain as well. It is doubtful, however, that the reduction in risk in case of price level advances compensates for the loss of purchasing power in the dollars used to repay the loan.

If inflation persists and becomes a growing problem we are likely to see increased efforts to adjust to risks of price level advances. Some efforts along these lines have been made in various South American countries and in Israel.[3] Various countries have experimented with bonds that change in value with price level changes.

---

[2] Privately circulated memoranda, 1970–71.

[3] Harold Robinson, "Readjustable Mortgages in an Inflationary Economy—A Study of the Israeli Experience," *The Journal of International Law and Economics,* January, 1971.

## SUMMARY

Primary decisions in real estate finance are made by borrowers and lenders. Although their objectives differ, both borrowers and lenders assume risks, and need to administer their financial programs so as to carry such risks.

The borrower runs the risk of losing his property and the income it produces, and perhaps other losses as well. His decision concerns the estimate of the return he can earn on borrowed funds and whether this exceeds the costs, with appropriate allowance for risks.

Lenders must assume several noninsurable risks. The lender may lose all or part of the principal sum, as well as the interest income. There is the danger that the borrower will not be able to meet the obligation, that the mortgaged property may decline in value and not be adequate to cover the unjaid balance, and that the borrower may not have sufficient assets to make up the deficiency. The lender is concerned with the return on his investment relative to the risk involved and the returns on alternative investments. Once the loan is made, his primary interest is in the repayment of the principal amount, with interest, within the specified time.

The risks assumed by both borrowers and lenders arise from the same general sources. These sources are the income-producing ability or other resources of the borrower, the value and income-producing ability of the property, and the uncertainties of market conditions. Legal and administrative risks are important. Inflation and deflation will have major effects on borrowers and lenders with interest rate and purchasing power risks of prime concern.

Financial institutions engaging in real estate finance have the problem of attracting the savings of individuals and business firms on terms that will permit profitable lending. They also have the problems of managing mortgage portfolios as well as the usual types of management problems common to most business enterprises.

## QUESTIONS FOR STUDY

1. List the principal sources of risk to lenders in the financing of real estate. Can these risks be avoided? Explain.
2. List the factors you would consider in evaluating an individual borrower. Which factors would you consider most important?
3. Would the same factors be important in analyzing a commercial borrower? Explain any additional factors that should be considered in the case of the commercial borrower.

4. Which government economic stabilization policies are of major importance to a mortgage lender? Why?

5. Which type of risk is represented by each of the following, and how does it apply? (a) loan-to-value ratio, (b) term of the loan in relation to the life of the property, (c) the interest rate, (d) the rate of amortization, and (e) the borrower.

6. If real estate values decline sharply, can any adjustments be made to prevent a mortgage from going into foreclosure? Please comment.

7. Give reasons why most real estate transactions involve small equity and heavy reliance on borrowed funds. Is this a desirable state of affairs? Explain.

8. What is meant by a "seasoned mortgage"? Explain any differences in risk between seasoned and unseasoned mortgages.

9. Outline the possible conflicts of interest involved in the lending policies of financial institutions in the real estate field. How may these conflicts be resolved?

10. What are the principal ways in which lenders can adjust to differences in risk as between alternative lending opportunities?

11. Suggest some of the different forms that legal risks may take.

12. If a financial institution pursues a policy of conservative lending but makes liberal appraisals, would you consider this an inconsistent policy? Why or why not? What reasons could you advance in defense of such a policy?

13. What is the reasoning behind use of the loan-value ratio as a protection against risk?

## SUGGESTED READINGS

EDWARDS, EDWARD E., and ARTHUR M. WEIMER. *Cyclical Fluctuations in Residential Construction.* Bloomington, Ind.: Business and Real Estate Trends, Inc. 1968.

FEDERAL HOUSING ADMINISTRATION. *Underwriting Handbook* (rev. ed.). Washington, D.C.: U.S. Government Printing Office.

HOAGLAND, HENRY E., and LEO D. STONE. *Real Estate Finance* (4th ed.). Homewood, Ill.: Richard D. Irwin, Inc., 1969. Chaps. 18–20.

MAISEL, SHERMAN J. *Financing Real Estate: Principles and Practices.* New York: McGraw-Hill Book Co., Inc., 1965. Chaps. vi–xi.

WENDT, PAUL F., and ALAN R. CERF. *Real Estate Investment, Analysis and Taxation.* New York: McGraw-Hill Book Co., Inc., 1969. Chap. 10.

## CASE 20–1

### Mortgage Loan Application, Railroadmen's Federal

John and Mary Doe are building a house in suburban Indianapolis, just outside Noblesville, Indiana, and would like to mortgage it with the Railroadmen's Federal Savings and Loan Association. As a member of Railroadmen's Federal loan committee, you must evaluate the mortgage loan application (see Fig. 1). The following questions, among others, must be answered.

# RAILROADMEN'S FEDERAL SAVINGS AND LOAN ASSOCIATION OF INDIANAPOLIS
## MORTGAGE LOAN APPLICATION
### (Please Print)

DATE............................................................ NO.............................................

PROPERTY ADDRESS.................................................. OCCUPANT..............................

NAME (Husband) .................................................. BUSINESS PHONE.......................

NAME (Wife) .......................................JOINT TITLE...... HOME PHONE.........................

MAILING ADDRESS.................................................. ZIP CODE...............................

To Railroadmen's Federal Savings and Loan Association:

I/we hereby apply for membership in Railroadmen's Federal Savings and Loan Association and desire to borrow from said Association **the sum of** $............................for the purpose of securing said credit and in order to assist the Association in acting upon my/our request for such credit, I/we furnish the following as a true and correct statement, with reservations, of my/our financial condition.

AMOUNT OF LOAN DESIRED..............................INT. RATE..........%. TO EXTEND...........YRS. STANDARD ☐ REG. ☐

PURPOSE OF LOAN................................................................................................

..........................................................................................................................

DATE OF PURCHASE......................PRICE PAID $....................DOWN PAYMENT $.................. Home ☐   Investment ☐

### EXISTING INDEBTEDNESS

Present Holder......................................................Loan No.................Date of Loan................

Original Amount $........................Balance as of..................$..................Ahead $................

Delinquent $...................Original Appraisal $......................Date................

### PERSONAL

Husband's Age..................No. of Dependent Children..............Ages..............

Employed by................................................Length of Service..............

Address................................................Position..............

Previous Employer................................................Length of Service..............

Wife's Age..................Employed by................................

FINANCIAL DATA / INCOME:

| FINANCIAL DATA | | INCOME | |
|---|---|---|---|
| Bank Account . . . . . | $.................... | Base Pay . . $.................... | |
| Savings Accounts . . . . | $.................... | Ave. Overtime . $.................... | |
| Savings Accounts . . . . | $.................... | Net after Deductions . . . | $.................... |
| Other Assets . . . . . | $.................... | Net income from business or profit . | $.................... |
| Net Worth in Mortgagor's Business . | $.................... | Dividends . . . . . . | $.................... |
| Other Real Estate Owned: | | Net Rents . . . . . | $.................... |
| Location ..................... | | Pensions (Type....................) | $.................... |
| Mortgage $..........@..........mo. Eq. | $.................... | Income from other sources: | |
| Location ..................... | | ..................... | $.................... |
| Mortgage $..........@..........mo. Eq. | $.................... | ..................... | $.................... |
| Total Value of All Property . | $.................... | Total Net Income . . . | $.................... |

### CREDIT DATA

Present or Previous Obligations:

1. To:......................................................Address.....................................................

   For:..................Opened..................Balance $..................@ $..................Per..................

2. To:......................................................Address.....................................................

   For:..................Opened..................Balance $..................@ $..................Per..................

3. To:......................................................Address.....................................................

   For:..................Opened..................Balance $..................@ $..................Per..................

### For Office Use Only

APPRAISAL

Lot Size...................x...................

Land Value $...........................

Improvements $...........................

Out Buildings $...........................

Total Value $...........................

Date...........................

### LOAN COMMITTEE ACTION

We have examined this application and recommend, subject to final approval of the Board of Directors, the granting of a loan to applicant as follows:

Amount $......................at the rate of............% for..............years.

The loan to be a standard or................loan under the regulations and by-laws of this Association, for the purpose set forth in the applications and no other purpose. Subject to the following conditions:

A ☐   B ☐   C ☐   D ☐   E ☐          Date.....................................
                                              Chairman

## Fig. 1a.   Mortgage loan application

Remarks

..........................................................................................................................

| ESTIMATED MONTHLY PAYMENTS | | ESTIMATED FUNDS REQUIRED | |
|---|---|---|---|
| Principal and Interest . . . . | $.......................... | Purchase Price . | $.......................... |
| Insurance . . . . . . . | $.......................... | Processing Costs | .......................... |
| Taxes . . . . . . . | .......................... | Loan Costs . | .......................... |
| Other . . . . . . . | .......................... | Other . . | .......................... |
| Total . . . . . . . | $.......................... | Total . . | $.......................... |
| Broker | | Less: | |
| Builder | | Earnest Money | $.......................... |
| Other.......................................... | | This Mortgage | .......................... |
| Address.......................................... | | | |
| Telephone.......................................... | | Total Estimated Funds Required . . | $.......................... |

Net Amount of Life Insurance $.........................Beneficiary...............................................................

Inspection Time.........................................................................Key.....................................................................

The undersigned agrees to reimburse the Association for all expenses incurred, including appraisals, title reports, credit reports and cost of collection, in the event that the loan is rejected by the Association because of condition of title unsatisfactory to the Association or because of falsity or omission in any statement contained in this application. The undersigned further agrees to reimburse the Association for all expenses incurred by it in the event that the undersigned refuses to accept the loan requested herein or refuses to execute such documents as are necessary to perfect the Association's lien on the above-described property.

What Legal Action Have You Ever Had Taken Against You?...............................................................................

..........................................................................................................................

THE UNDERSIGNED AGREES THAT THIS LOAN MAY BE CANCELED BY THE ASSOCIATION IF DISBURSEMENT IS NOT MADE WITHIN 90 DAYS FROM THE DATE OF THE APPLICATION.

SIGNATURE.............................................................SIGNATURE...................................................

Application prepared by...........................................

Credit Report Approved.........................................................By........................................................

IS SUBJECT PROPERTY
SOLD ON CONTRACT?

For Office Use Only
**NORTH**

**Fig. 1b.** Mortgage loan application—reverse.

## Questions

1. Describe the nature and extent of the interest rate and purchasing power risks to Railroadmen's Federal.
2. How would you evaluate borrower risk in this case?
3. The surrounding houses range in value from $10,000 to $15,000. Does this represent property risk?
4. Would you make this loan without insurance or guarantee? Would you make it at all?

## STUDY PROJECT 20–1

### Can We Learn From the British?

*Prof. Edwards:* Sir Hubert, your mortgage markets appear to be less affected than ours by tight money. For example, the British building societies continued their rapid growth during periods when our thrift institutions were experiencing great difficulty holding their savings. How do you account for this?

*Sir Hubert:* I think that undoubtedly one of the reasons for the continued rapid growth of building societies in Britain is the fact that as money market yields alter, we can adjust our rates of interest on existing mortgages. This enables us, when necessary, to increase the rate of interest which we pay to our savers and so remain competitive with the general level of interest rates. The power is a power to vary up or down, but when money markets are tight, it is our ability to increase portfolio yields that keeps us competitive. That is why we can offer our savers a before tax equivalent rate of over eight percent.

Apart from being able to vary interest rates, building societies enjoy a very great measure of public confidence in their stability as a result of legislation laying down minimum requirements for liquidity and reserves and as a result of the work of the Building Societies Association. They also are so widely spread that it is safe to say that there are building society offices in every town in Britain able to give the necessary service to the public. We have been in the business for over one hundred years, and as you know, societies are permitted to establish branches nation-wide.

*Prof. Edwards:* Would you recommend a variable rate mortgage, one with an escalator clause, as a standard practice in our country?

*Sir Hubert:* Yes, but I don't know whether now would be the right time to start. If lenders had had the right to raise the rate of interest, they would have benefited greatly in recent years. But the most appropriate time to begin the variable rate mortgage would be when interest rates are low.

*Prof. Edwards:* Is the way savings accounts are taxed in your country a significant factor in maintaining a flow of funds into the building societies?

*Sir Hubert:* Yes, I certainly believe so. As you know, the societies pay income tax at a special composite rate on the interest we pay to our savers. This makes the interest actually received by the saver tax exempt income.

The composite rate is the average rate payable by all personnel buildings society investors—those liable for income tax at the standard rate and those not liable to pay income tax at all. This saves the Inland Revenue a lot of work as they do not have to assess separately the interest received by each individual saver.

The composite rate currently is 32.25 per cent, as compared with the standard rate of income tax in Britain of *41.25 per cent.* This means that the equivalent before tax return on an investment rate of 5 per cent to a person

---

* An interview with Sir Hubert Newton, conducted by Professor Edward E. Edwards; reproduced by permission of Mortgage Guaranty Insurance Corporation, from the *MGIC Newsletter.*

paying tax at the standard rate is just over 8½ per cent. But the cost of the building society of a 5 per cent investment rate is only about 7¾ per cent. The gross return to the saver who is not liable for income tax remains at 5 per cent.

The tax paid feature—plus ready withdrawal and the convenience of the services—all measure up to a worthwhile investment. It is my considered opinion that much of the success of the building society savings account is due to the fact that people do not have to bother with income tax or the interest earned other than to show it on the return as a nontaxed item.

Some years ago when the late Sir Stafford Cripps was Chancellor of the Exchequer, there was a move by the government to abolish the composite rate. We did make a stand against the abolition and were successful.

The general view of my colleagues here in Great Britain is that so long as the composite rate falls below the standard rate, it is sound policy to continue the arrangement.

*Prof. Edwards:* Your new Prime Minister seems to believe that Britain's economic problems—inflation, housing, balance of payments—are aggravated by the low level of saving. As you know, many of us in the United States think the same way about our situation. You may or may not agree, and in either case I would like your comment, but I am especially interested in any thoughts you may have as to how a nation can increase its rate of saving. Can thrift be taught? What can thrift institutions do to increase the total volume of saving rather than just try to increase their share?

*Sir Hubert:* I agree that many of Britain's economic problems are aggravated by the low level of saving. You know that our rate of saving and investment as a proportion of gross national product is one of the lowest in the industrialized world and that a great deal of new investment is being raised out of taxes. A higher level of saving would, in my opinion, enable taxation to be reduced and would increase the incentive to work harder and earn more. I think it is possible to increase the total volume of savings but the lead must come from the government. They must create the right economic climate.

Certainly steps must be taken to curb inflation and to make saving worthwhile. These could include tax concessions on regular savings and education that the equity cult is not really the answer to cope with inflation. The recent substantial fall in equities has educated a good many.

To my mind the whole question turns on the actual purchasing power of the current unit and people these days are much more alive and alert to what happened in Germany a generation ago and what has happened and continues to happen in France and in the Latin American countries.

The stability of currency, therefore, is the real problem which faces the government if it is to attract savings in any shape or form.

*Prof. Edwards:* You have been instrumental in trying to build a National Register of Home Builders, and to assure home buyers that the home they buy from a registered builder will be free from defect. How does this work? Who actually insures or guarantees the home buyer? Do mortgage lenders require this insurance or guarantee?

*Sir Hubert:* The National House Builders Registration Council is working very well. Almost all building societies now require a new home to be either covered by NHBRC certificate or built under the direct supervision of a qualified architect or surveyor.

For some three or four decades now the "jerrybuilder"—as he is known in this country—has "got away with it" and purchasers have been very dissatisfied. The government recognizes that good building is essential; that people should not be faced with substantial repair bills—and indeed bills for reconstruction in some cases—and that every house newly-built should carry a guarantee against defects.

The registration program, however, is a voluntary one, but the government-of-the-day left the builders in no doubt that if they did not register voluntarily, then the program would be made compulsory.

*Prof. Edwards:* Briefly, just how does the registration plan work?

*Sir Hubert:* A registered builder agrees to make good any structural defect. Failure to do so results in his being dropped from the register. In addition he pays a fee of £8.80 (approximately $22) per house to the Council which provides for a guarantee through a leading insurance company in the event of a builder's failure to correct any structural defect. Inspectors from NHBRC also visit the houses at intervals during construction.

*Prof. Edwards:* Thank you, Sir Hubert. I know that our readers, many of whom you know personally, will enjoy your comments on what's happening in the housing and home finance fields in Britain.

### Questions

1. Does the British experience with variable rate mortgages suggest that this method be used more widely in the U. S.? Why or why not?
2. Should the U. S. develop tax arrangements for saving accounts that are similar to those of the British Building Societies? Explain.
3. Is the U. S. beginning to face problems like those of Britain that arise from savings levels that are too low?
4. Should special savings incentives be developed for the U. S.? If so, what types do you think would be most effective? If not, do you believe long term savings flows will be adequate to meet the housing and other capital needs of the U. S.?
5. Should the U. S. try something like the National Home Builders' Recognition Council in Britain? Why or why not?

### STUDY PROJECT 20-2

### Contemporary Decision Theory and Real Estate Investment [*]

Decision theory is a familiar term in the progressive business world; its application in investment decision making is commonplace—except in the area of real estate investment.[1]

[*] By Richard U. Ratcliff and Bernhard Schwab. By permission, from *The Appraisal Journal*, April, 1970.

[1] See Hertz, D. B., *Risk Analysis in Capital Investment*, Harvard Business Review, January–February, 1964; Grayson C. Jackson, *Decisions Under Uncertainty: Drilling Decisions by Gas and Oil Operators*, Boston: Harvard University—Division of Research, 1960; Smith Barney & Co., "*Investment Decision Making: New Perspectives and Methods*," 1968.

This paper will not explain why real estate appraisal and investment literature is almost void of such esoteric terms as: time value of money; probabilities; or utility functions;—all of which are used extensively in modern investment decision theory. Rather, this paper will attempt to bring real estate investment decision making up to date; it will focus on the relevance and usefulness of modern business decision theory and the concepts on which it is built in relation to this process.

A model will be used to illustrate exactly how investment decision making can be applied to a specific real estate investment decision. A conscious and orderly application of rational decision making can replace—and improve upon —the typical process which involves the largely subconscious and intuitive employment of much the same components.

**Financial Rewards.** Modern decision theory recognizes that investment decisions in real life are made on the basis of considerations which often go beyond or may be inconsistent with, the maximizing of financial rewards. Real estate investments illustrate this to the extent to which they reflect goals of prestige, personal pride, or the satisfaction of land ownership. For example, how does one express the various degrees of pride in real estate ownership, a pride reflecting an attitude which enters into the decisions of many individual investors? How does one reflect the unreasoned biases such as preferences for certain forms of architecture and distates for other?

In addition, there are other types of considerations which are subject to quantification but are so complex that few investors make the attempt. Investment decisions are thus, not the simple maximizing decisions of classical economics; they involve many incommensurables as well as many subjective elements. Each investor, whether a person or a corporation, reflects in his investment decision a very complex mixture of: goals, values systems, biases, degrees of analytical ability, stocks of applicable knowledge, and financial situations, etc. A clear picture of the financial implications of an investment decision enables one to assess the amount of money required to satisfy such non-monetary desires as pride of ownership and prestige, thereby clarifying the investor's thinking regarding a particular property.

There are innumerable measures of financial performance such as the accountant's net income, taxable income or yield on investment. However, *cash flow*, i.e., the dollars remaining in the hands of the investor after he has met all prior claims of: operating expenses, financial obligations—usually lease and mortgage payments in the case of real estate—and income taxes will serve as the most practical basis for investment in our model for real estate investment decision making. Spendable cash on hand is an understandable concept and plays a major and often exclusive role in investment decision making.

**Judging Investment Opportunities.** Before an investment decision can be made, the investor must determine—for each alternative investment opportunity —the capital amount which he would equate with its prospective financial rewards (cash flow), i.e., he must determine the capital *"indifference value"* of the prospective financial rewards. The investor must select, from alternative investment opportunities, that choice for which the cost of acquisition bears the most favorable relationship to its indifference value. For example, if the investor determines that the capital sum indifference values of three alternative investments are $10,000, $50,000, and $100,000, he may: (1) disregard the first because the seller of the first property is asking $25,000; and (2) not consider the last option if he has only $50,000 capital available. However, if the owner of the $100,000 property is willing to sell for $50,000, the investor could acquire the property at one-half its worth to him.

*Present Value of Future Returns.* All benefits from a prospective real estate investment are generally viewed as future benefits. Trained appraisers and financial analysts know the theory and practice of expressing these future benefits in terms of the present value, i.e., value at the time of the investment decision. A $1,000 sum in hand today is worth more to its possessor than a perfectly reliable promise of $1,000 five years from today. At 6% interest compounded annually, the $1,000 held today would grow substantially in 5 years to a total of $1,338. From another viewpoint, $747 in hand today could grow—through investment at 6% and the operation of compound interest—to $1,000 in five years. It is thus a matter of financial indifference whether I have $747 in hand or a reliable promise to pay $1,000 in 5 years—assuming the workings of compound interest at 6%. In any form of investment decision, the time-value of money should be considered; equal weight should not be accorded to a dollar expected to be received a year from now and to a dollar which will not be available for five years.

*Discount Rate.* In analyzing an investment in terms of the cash flow which it generates, the cash flow is determined by: (1) the periodic cash flows over the terms of ownership; and (2) the net proceeds from the liquidation of the investment at the end of the holding period. The indifference value of these future rewards—expressed as the total capital presently in hand—is then determined. This requires the utilization of a conversion ratio, i.e., a discount rate which mathematically equates the expected future returns and the present indifference value. In an intuitive and subjective investment decision, the investor would move directly from the rewards to the capital amount without using arithmetic. However, our objective approach to investment decisions involves a series of steps employing quantitative judgments.

The discount rate is an essential link between future benefits and present or investment value; and must be determined before the investor can proceed with the actual analysis. This is a subjective decision which does not entail considerations of risk and uncertainty. These considerations are taken into account at another point in the decision making calculations. The discount rate should reflect the investor's personal time preference for money. Utilizing the "alternative opportunity rate," i.e., the average annual rate of profit per dollar invested expected from alternative investment opportunities, is a simple but insufficient substitute.

For example, consider a man of 65 on the verge of retirement who is contemplating the purchase of a small apartment structure as an investment. He expects to hold it for about 10 years and then sell it before his death. He has made forecasts of the property's cash productivity over the next 10 years and an estimate of its liquidation value at the end of this period. He intends to live off the income for a time and then liquidate the investment to simplify estate problems at the time of his death. One can see the complexities of selecting a discount rate which will convert these forecasts into a capital sum which he will accept as a fair exchange for the prospective rewards from the investment. It should be noted that alternate investment opportunities taken alone are not the sole or final determinants of the discount rate.

*Non-Monetary Considerations.* In actual situations, non-monetary considerations enter into the time value of money. Not all the benefits of ownership can be measured in dollar returns; some investors find satisfaction from the prestige of property ownership or a traditional sense of security just in owning real estate. This type of psychic income enters into the time value of money; and, when dollar returns are supplemented by intangible rewards, the discount rate applied to the dollar income will tend to be lower. Another factor is the relationship between (1) the time pattern of the cash flow and (2) the financial needs and investment objectives of the investor. For example, a doctor with substantial income will attach a lower time value to the cash flow during the years in which his professional income continues, and a high value to the returns after his retirement.

Where intangibles are not involved, the return on an alternative riskless investment is probably the best basis for establishing the time value of money or discount rate. The investor can decide the capital amount which he would equate with a guaranteed annuity of $10,000 per year for 10 years (or some other amount in the general range of the annual cash flow expected from the property and for the expected period of holding). Table 1 sets forth the discount rates which equate annuities of $1 per year and the indifference values as present lump sums. Thus, an indifference value of $56,500 related to an annuity of $10,000 for 10 years indicates a discount rate of about 12%.

### TABLE 1.  Indifference Values for Annuities of $1 per Year at Various Discount Rates

| Annuity in years | Discount Rate as a Percent | | | | | | |
|---|---|---|---|---|---|---|---|
| | 6 | 7 | 8 | 9 | 10 | 11 | 12 |
| 1 | 0.94 | 0.93 | 0.93 | 0.92 | 0.91 | 0.90 | 0.89 |
| 2 | 1.83 | 1.81 | 1.78 | 1.76 | 1.74 | 1.71 | 1.69 |
| 3 | 2.67 | 2.62 | 2.58 | 2.53 | 2.49 | 2.44 | 2.40 |
| 4 | 3.46 | 3.39 | 3.31 | 3.24 | 3.17 | 3.10 | 3.04 |
| 5 | 4.21 | 4.10 | 3.99 | 3.89 | 3.79 | 3.69 | 3.60 |
| 6 | 4.92 | 4.76 | 4.62 | 4.49 | 4.35 | 4.23 | 4.11 |
| 7 | 5.58 | 5.39 | 5.21 | 5.03 | 4.87 | 4.71 | 4.56 |
| 8 | 6.21 | 5.97 | 5.75 | 5.53 | 5.33 | 5.15 | 4.97 |
| 9 | 6.80 | 6.51 | 6.25 | 5.99 | 5.76 | 5.54 | 5.33 |
| 10 | 7.36 | 7.02 | 6.71 | 6.42 | 6.14 | 5.89 | 5.65 |

1. Present Value of $1 per annum. Values for other terms and discount rates can be secured by reference to any standard set of compound interest tables.

*Certainty and Uncertainty.* Investment decisions are never based on *any* certainty, e.g., on guaranteed financial rewards. All business decisions require forecasts or predictions of outcomes which are necessarily based on inadequate information and unpredictable circumstances. The degrees of uncertainty range from almost reliable predictions (such as the return on government bonds) to highly speculative outcomes which are often characteristic of mining stock.

In real estate investment, the future financial rewards which require prediction are: (1) the periodic cash flow over the term of ownership, and (2) the net proceeds from the liquidation of the investment at the end of the holding period. The investor—with limited information and often limited understanding—makes his own best possible predictions. He will have some judgment, explicit or intuitive, on the odds (or chances) that the actuality will be higher than his prediction, or that it will be lower; and his feeling regarding the degree of uncertainty with respect to his prediction will influence his investment decision. Statisticians have technical and more precise concepts for expressing these common-sense and universally used judgments to describe the possible variability of a prediction. These must be explained because our investment decision model will require that the investor convert his judgments on uncertainty into quantitative terms.

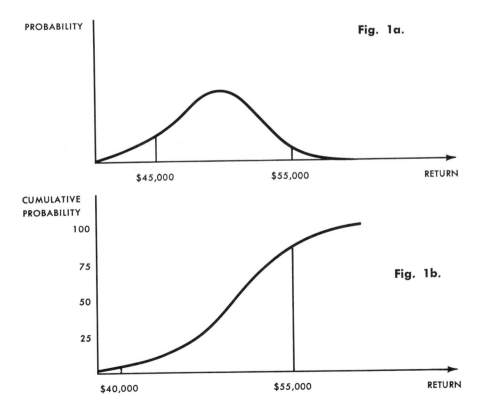

Statisticians often express probabilities of some event occurring in terms of the number of chances out of 100, or some variation of this expression. For example, in predicting the future selling price of property, one might say that there is a 10 out of 100 chance that it will sell for more than $55,000 and a 20 out of 100 chance that it might bring less than $45,000. If there is some basis for judging the odds all up and down the line of possible selling prices, we could derive a curve like Figure 1a where the vertical scale is the odds expressed in terms of the number of chances out of 100 and the horizontal scale is the range of possible selling prices. For certain kinds of properties like a fairly new tract house or standard design where there is ample market information and plenty of recent "comparables," the predicted range of possible selling prices will be narrow and the curve will look like Curve A in Figure 2,

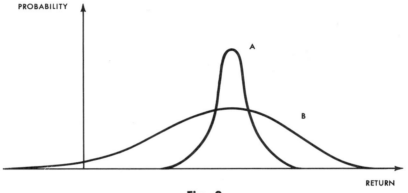

**Fig. 2.**

which reflects the fact that the forecast can come very close to what the property will actually bring because the person making the forecast is well-informed and skilled in analyzing the real estate market. But for other kinds of property such as an expensive luxury home with few comparables and a style of architecture which will not appeal to many buyers but which might appeal greatly to a few, Curve B in Figure 2 will reflect the fact that the forecaster cannot be very certain of his prediction and that the actual selling price might fall anywhere within a rather wide range of values. In both Curves A and B, the vertical height of the curve at various points along the value scale indicates the forecaster's best judgment of the odds that the actual selling price will fall upon that value. More precisely, such curves give the probability of the selling price falling within a certain range, this probability simply being proportional to the area under the curve within that range.

It is often convenient to use another form of expression for the same predictions which are the basis for Curves A and B in Figure 2. Figure 1b uses the same basic predictions and the same scales of odds and dollars, but shows the odds in cumulative form, i.e., at each point along the selling price scale, the height of the curve is the sum of the odds or chances at all lower prices up to that point. Thus at $40,000, this sum can be read on the odds scale at 10, which means that there are 10 chances out of 100 that the property will sell for $40,000 or less. The curve also tells us that there are 90 chances out of 100 that it will sell for $55,000 or less which means that there is a 10 out of 100 chance that it will bring more than $55,000. It is a commonplace that actual investors think in these terms of the chances that a property will bring more or less than a certain price, but it is also true that they rarely express these expectations in just this form. To do so infers a degree of precision of prediction which most practical men would say is impossible and unrealistic. On the other hand, it seems clear than an educated guess will generally be better than no explicit judgment at all. Certainly one of the reasons why investors do not attempt to express the expected odds in actual numbers, is that they would not know how to incorporate this judgment in their investment calculation. Our model will offer this opportunity.

**Attitude Toward Risk.**    In the evaluation of investments whose returns are subject to uncertainty, the investor's attitude toward risk plays an important role; this attitude is clarified through quantitative expression. Investors are conditioned by the risk characteristics of the benefits expected to flow from the investment. Some investors place a high value on certainty; others will accept various degrees of uncertainty or risk of loss, depending on the offsetting possibilities of large gains.

Consider two investment propositions, A and B, which are described by the probability curves shown in Figure 2. Both propositions may yield the same average return; however, proposition B involves considerably more uncertainty than proposition A—it represents a greater gamble, with a possible potential for large gains but also for large losses. Thus, while the most probable expected returns may be equal for both propositions, the investor may prefer one proposition over the other. A conservative investor, being averse to risk, may reject proposition B and accept proposition A—even if proposition B should yield a somewhat higher expected return than proposition A. The ranking of investment alternatives will generally be significantly influenced by the investor's attitude toward risk; i.e., by the relative values which he places on positive cash flow and on losses.

The investor's attitude towards positive cash flow or losses can be represented graphically by deriving a "utility curve" as shown in Figure 3. In this graph, the vertical distance between the curve and the horizontal line is a measure of the value placed on a given investment outcome (gain to the right or loss to the left). It follows from Figure 3 that the positive value placed on the gain of the first $20,000 is greater than the value placed on the gain of an additional $20,000. In other words, the value placed on a gain of $40,000 is less than twice the value on a gain of $20,000. Furthermore, the negative value or disutility placed on a loss of $20,000 is as large as the positive value placed on a gain of $35,000—i.e., a 50% chance of making a profit of $35,000 would be offset by a 50% chance of losing $20,000. Similarly, a 50% chance of making a profit of $100,000 would be offset by a 50% chance of losing $24,000.

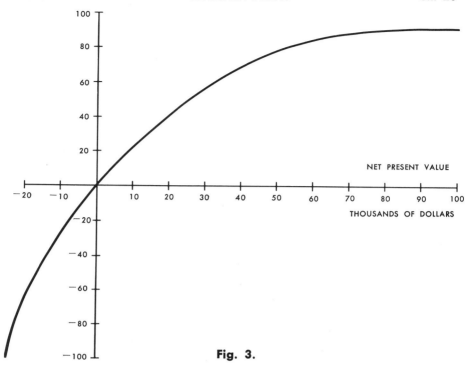

**Fig. 3.**

## Derived Utility Table (from Figure 3)

| Net Present Value (Thousands of Dollars) | −25 | −20 | −15 | −10 | 5 | 15 | 25 | 40 | 60 | 80 | 100 |
|---|---|---|---|---|---|---|---|---|---|---|---|
| Investor's Utility | −100 | −65 | −45 | −25 | 12 | 32 | 50 | 70 | 85 | 90 | 92 |

The Figure 4 curves illustrate various possible utility functions. Figure 4a represents the most liberal position where almost equal values are assigned to gains and losses. Figure 4c represents the most conservative position—the highest degree of risk aversion (the negative value on the loss of a given amount far exceeds the positive value placed on a gain of the same amount).

Thus, before being able to make intelligent and consistent investment decisions, the investor has to ask himself consciously the values which he places on possible gains and losses. The majority of real estate investors will: (1) most likely have a utility curve somewhat averse to risk (following the general curvature as shown in Figures 4b and 4c); and (2) place higher negative values on losses than positive values on commensurate gains. Few investors would undertake an investment with a 50% chance of a loss of $100,000, even if there is a 50% probability of making a profit of $10,000. Most investors

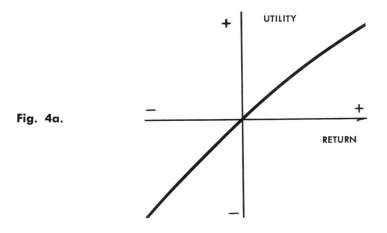

Fig. 4a.

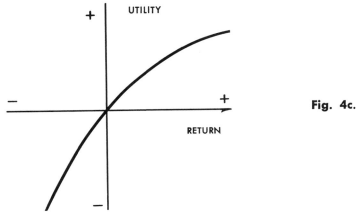

Fig. 4c.

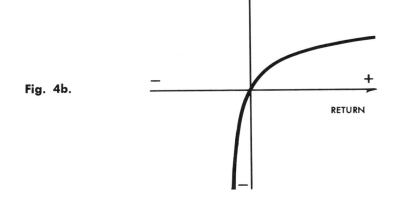

Fig. 4b.

will prefer investment proposition A over proposition B in Figure 2. Again, the investor's particular utility curve may vary over time—e.g., the negative value placed on losses is likely to depend on his general financial position and prospects—and, hence, will be revised periodically.[2]

**Real Estate Investment Decision Model.** All considerations which enter into investment decisions can not be translated in quantitative terms; however, those elements which can be identified have been identified. A model combining these selected quantities into a final investment decision has been developed; the investor must supply the following inputs:

1. A forecast of the most probable periodic returns as cash flows from the property and a forecast of the net cash proceeds from liquidation at the end of a period of ownership.
2. A qualification of this forecast in terms of a probability distribution. Three forecasts of cash flow and liquidation proceeds, each at a different level of probability, must be made.
3. The selection of a discount rate representing the investor's time preference of money.
4. An expression of the investor's personal utility curve.

A standardized format has been developed which could be used by any investor when evaluating property investments. This format is presented in connection with the investment analysis example which follows; the entries and calculations for a hypothetical investment analysis are presented. While the general concepts are applicable to a variety of investment situations, this format was designed for investment decisions related to income-producing real property.

*Overall Structure.* Considering the uncertain nature of investment, three probability levels have been selected for evaluation. Each level is in the form of an after-tax discounted cash flow forecast and reflects a different chance of realization. Rather than utilizing a continuous probability distribution, these discrete points were evaluated in correspondence to three probability levels. The three points evaluated are: (1) "Low" (L); (2) "Most Probable" (MP); and (3) "High" (H).[3] These probability points were arbitrarily chosen so that the estimated probability of doing either worse than the pessimistic point (L) or better than the optimistic point (H) is 10%, as shown in Figure 5. At the mid-point the probability is 80% or the most probable (MP) outcome.

The three probability points provide a basis for establishing an expected utility for each probability level. The total expected utility to the investor for

---

[2] For a detailed description on how an investor may derive his utility function, see the excellent article by R. O. Swalm, *Utility Theory—Insights into Risk Taking,* Harvard Business Review, November–December, 1966. Some standard text-books on modern decision theory which may be useful in this context are Hadley, G., *Introduction to Probability and Statistical Decision Making: New Perspectives and Methods,* San Francisco: Holden Day, 1967; and Horowitz, I., *An Introduction to Quantitative Business Analysis,* New York: McGraw-Hill, 1965.

[3] The number of points to be evaluated can be increased if additional accuracy is desired; thus, for particularly risky propositions with wide fluctuations of possible returns, one may decide to use five rather than three probability levels.

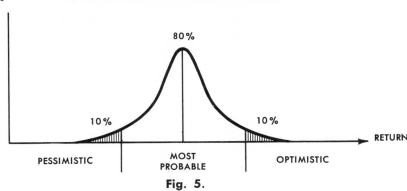

**Fig. 5.**

the property under evaluation is then the sum of the expected utilities for each of the three probability levels. From the expected utilities at the three levels, the final step is to derive the "cash indifference acquisition price," which is the maximum amount which the investor would be willing to bid for the property under the estimates and assumptions made.

**A Standardized Investment Analysis Format.** The proposed standardized investment analysis format can be applied to any income property. The example income property is a three story, frame apartment building in the final stages of construction. The apartment contains nine studio and fifteen single-bedroom suites and is similar in construction, style and attributes to other apartments located in the same general area. The area is in transition; old single-family residences are rapidly being replaced by low-rise apartment blocks (a process which has gained momentum during the past five years). Although favorably located with respect to the central business district, shopping facilities, transportation arteries, and a popular recreation area, the apartment building will be subject to increasing competition both from within the area and from rapidly growing competitive areas.

**Case Study and Format Description.** Each of the in-put estimates and calculations require a detailed explanation.

*Section A—Basic Parameters*

Item (a). Property identification—Schwabcliff Gardens
Item (b). Probability levels
        (1) High (H) = 10 out of 100 (.10)
        (2) Most Probable (MP) = 80 out of 100 (.80)
        (3) Low (L) = 10 out of 100 (.10)
Item (c). Depreciation method. The double declining balance method based on a 5% straight line rate was selected from among the methods permitted for income tax calculation.
Item (d). Marginal tax rate—50%. This is the marginal tax rate of the investor on total income from all sources used to measure benefit from tax loss, if any, on the income property investment. It is assumed that the investor is incorporated and has a large source of other income not related to the investment under analysis. Therefore,

**TABLE 2. Probability Level—Low**

| Year | 1 | 2 | 3 | 4 | 5 | 6 | 7 | 8 | 9 | 10 |
|---|---|---|---|---|---|---|---|---|---|---|
| Discount factors at 6.0% | .943 | .890 | .840 | .792 | .747 | .705 | .665 | .627 | .592 | .558 |
| (6) Gross income (full occupancy) | 38,880 | 38,880 | 38,400 | 37,600 | 37,200 | 36,600 | 35,800 | 35,000 | 34,200 | 33,400 |
| (7) Occupancy rate | .70 | .90 | .94 | .94 | .94 | .92 | .92 | .90 | .90 | .90 |
| (8) Effective gross income | 27,220 | 34,990 | 36,100 | 35,340 | 34,970 | 33,670 | 32,940 | 31,500 | 30,780 | 30,060 |
| (9) Operating expenses | 14,750 | 15,500 | 16,000 | 16,200 | 16,400 | 16,600 | 16,800 | 17,000 | 17,250 | 17,500 |
| (10) Interest on mortgage | 17,480 | 17,160 | 16,800 | 16,400 | 15,990 | 15,530 | 15,020 | 14,460 | 13,850 | 13,180 |
| (11) Book value of building | 205,000 | 184,500 | 166,050 | 149,450 | 134,500 | 121,050 | 108,950 | 98,050 | 88,250 | 79,420 |
| (12) Depreciation allowance | 20,500 | 18,450 | 16,610 | 13,450 | 14,950 | 12,110 | 10,890 | 9,810 | 8,820 | 7,940 |
| (13) Taxable income | −25,510 | −16,120 | −13,310 | −12,210 | −10,870 | −10,570 | −9,770 | −9,770 | −9,140 | −8,560 |
| (14) Taxes | — | — | — | — | — | — | — | — | — | — |
| (15) Benefit of tax shield | 12,750 | 8,060 | 6,650 | 6,100 | 5,430 | 5,280 | 4,880 | 4,880 | 4,570 | 4,280 |
| (16) Annual mortgage principal | 3,400 | 3,720 | 4,080 | 4,480 | 4,890 | 5,360 | 5,860 | 6,420 | 7,030 | 7,700 |
| (17) Mortgage principal payments (cumulative) | 3,400 | 7,120 | 11,200 | 15,680 | 20,570 | 25,930 | 31,790 | 38,210 | 45,240 | 52,940 |
| (18) Unpaid mortgage principal | 180,600 | 176,880 | 172,800 | 168,320 | 163,430 | 158,080 | 152,210 | 145,790 | 138,760 | 131,060 |
| (19) Cash flow after taxes | 4,350 | 6,670 | 5,880 | 4,370 | 3,130 | 1,470 | 150 | −1,490 | −2,780 | −4,040 |
| (20) Discounted cash flow after taxes | 4,100 | 5,940 | 4,940 | 3,460 | 2,340 | 1,040 | 90 | −930 | −1,650 | −2,250 |
| (21) Discounted cash flow after taxes (cumulative) | 4,100 | 10,040 | 14,980 | 18,440 | 20,780 | 21,820 | 21,910 | 20,980 | 19,330 | 17,080 |

the investor's marginal tax rate is 50% on all of the property income (other than capital gains which are taxed at the maximum rate of 25%). Similarly, losses on the property provide tax benefits which are offset at the marginal tax rate against other income in the same year in which the loss occurs.

Item (e). Discount rate—6%. This rate reflects the time value of money to the investor. This discount rate reflects a safe rate of return which can be obtained by this investor in riskless investments such as government securities.

Section B—Initial Acquisition of Property. The following entries can be established prior to acquisition of the property and are thus subject to little uncertainty.

| | | |
|---|---|---:|
| Line 1. | Estimated acquisition price | $275,000 |
| Line 2. | Initial mortgage debt | $184,000 |
| | Interest rate—9½% | |
| | Term—20 years | |
| | Amortization—constant annual payments on interest and principal | |
| Line 3. | Initial equity | $ 91,000 |
| Line 4. | Depreciation base (estimated value of building) | $205,000 |
| Line 5. | Estimated land value | 70,000 |

Line 1: Estimated acquisition price. The investor must make an initial assumption as to the most probable acquisition price of the property; it is required: (1) as a basis for a derived assumption on mortgage financing; and (2) on the initial depreciation base for the analysis which follows. In the case of an existing property this price will be based on the asking price; it will reflect the investor's estimate of how this price may be modified in the bargaining process. For a proposed project not yet in existence, the price of acquisition would be the sum of the acquisition price of the land plus estimated costs of the improvements. The results of this analysis will be a value which will show through comparison whether the initial estimate of the cost of acquisition represents a favorable overall investment opportunity.

Line 2: Initial mortgage debt. This input is the total amount of mortgage debt which can be raised for this property, given the above estimated acquisition price.

Line 3: Initial equity. The difference between lines 1 and 2.

Line 4: Depreciation base. Estimated value for building.

Line 5: Estimated value for land. The difference between line 1 (estimated acquisition price) and line 4 (estimated value of building).

Section C—Operating Costs and Revenues (see Tables 2, 3 and 4). At this point the analyst must estimate the number of years which the investor expects to retain property ownership before sale and liquidation of his investment. A ten-year period has been used in the case example.

One set of forecasts and calculations is required for each of the three selected probability levels. The projections for the Low (L) level represent estimates of productivity factors with only a 10 out of 100 probability of a lower actuality; at the other end of the scale, the High (H) projections are

**TABLE 3. Probability Level—Most Probable**

| Year | 1 | 2 | 3 | 4 | 5 | 6 | 7 | 8 | 9 | 10 |
|---|---|---|---|---|---|---|---|---|---|---|
| Discount factors at 6.0% | .943 | .890 | .840 | .792 | .747 | .705 | .665 | .627 | .592 | .558 |
| (6) Gross income (full occupancy) | 38,880 | 39,600 | 40,800 | 42,000 | 43,200 | 43,800 | 43,800 | 44,400 | 44,400 | 45,000 |
| (7) Occupancy rate | .75 | .90 | .98 | .98 | .98 | .97 | .96 | .95 | .95 | .95 |
| (8) Effective gross income | 29,160 | 35,640 | 39,980 | 41,160 | 42,340 | 42,490 | 42,050 | 42,180 | 42,180 | 42,750 |
| (9) Operating expenses | 14,000 | 14,750 | 15,000 | 15,000 | 15,000 | 15,500 | 15,500 | 15,500 | 16,000 | 16,000 |
| (10) Interest on mortgage | 17,480 | 17,160 | 16,800 | 16,400 | 15,990 | 15,530 | 15,020 | 14,460 | 13,850 | 13,180 |
| (11) Book value of building | 205,000 | 184,500 | 166,050 | 149,450 | 134,500 | 121,050 | 108,950 | 98,050 | 88,250 | 79,420 |
| (12) Depreciation allowance | 20,500 | 18,450 | 16,610 | 14,950 | 13,450 | 12,110 | 10,890 | 9,810 | 8,820 | 7,940 |
| (13) Taxable income | −22,820 | −14,720 | −8,430 | −5,190 | −2,100 | −650 | 640 | 2,410 | 3,510 | 7,880 |
| (14) Taxes | — | — | — | — | — | — | 320 | 1,200 | 1,750 | 3,940 |
| (15) Benefit of tax shield | 11,410 | 7,360 | 4,210 | 2,590 | 1,050 | 320 | — | — | — | — |
| (16) Annual mortgage principal | 3,400 | 3,720 | 4,080 | 4,480 | 4,890 | 5,360 | 5,860 | 6,420 | 7,030 | 7,700 |
| (17) Mortgage principal payments (cumulative) | 3,400 | 7,120 | 11,200 | 15,680 | 20,570 | 25,930 | 31,790 | 38,210 | 45,240 | 52,940 |
| (18) Unpaid mortgage principal | 180,600 | 176,880 | 172,800 | 168,320 | 163,430 | 158,080 | 152,210 | 145,790 | 138,760 | 131,060 |
| (19) Cash flow after taxes | 5,690 | 7,370 | 8,320 | 7,880 | 7,510 | 6,430 | 5,350 | 4,590 | 3,540 | 4,180 |
| (20) Discounted cash flow after taxes | 5,370 | 6,560 | 6,990 | 6,240 | 5,610 | 4,530 | 3,560 | 2,880 | 2,090 | 2,330 |
| (21) Discounted cash flow after taxes (cumulative) | 5,370 | 11,930 | 18,920 | 25,160 | 30,770 | 35,300 | 38,860 | 41,740 | 43,830 | 46,160 |

| Year | 1 | 2 | 3 | 4 | 5 | 6 | 7 | 8 | 9 | 10 |
|---|---|---|---|---|---|---|---|---|---|---|
| Discount factors at 6.0% | .943 | .890 | .840 | .792 | .747 | .705 | .665 | .627 | .592 | .558 |
| (6) Gross income (full occupancy) | 38,880 | 40,200 | 42,000 | 43,200 | 45,000 | 45,600 | 46,200 | 46,800 | 47,400 | 48,000 |
| (7) Occupancy rate | .90 | .98 | .99 | .99 | .99 | .99 | .98 | .98 | .98 | .97 |
| (8) Effective gross income | 34,990 | 39,400 | 41,580 | 42,770 | 44,550 | 45,040 | 45,280 | 45,860 | 46,450 | 46,560 |
| (9) Operating expenses | 12,500 | 12,800 | 13,000 | 13,000 | 13,000 | 13,150 | 13,500 | 13,500 | 14,000 | 14,000 |
| (10) Interest on mortgage | 17,480 | 17,160 | 16,800 | 16,400 | 15,990 | 15,530 | 15,020 | 14,460 | 13,850 | 13,180 |
| (11) Book value of building | 205,000 | 184,500 | 166,050 | 149,450 | 134,500 | 121,050 | 108,950 | 98,050 | 88,250 | 79,420 |
| (12) Depreciation allowance | 20,500 | 18,450 | 16,610 | 14,950 | 13,450 | 12,110 | 10,890 | 9,810 | 8,820 | 7,940 |
| (13) Taxable income | −15,490 | −9,010 | −4,830 | −1,580 | 2,110 | 4,250 | 5,870 | 8,090 | 9,780 | 11,440 |
| (14) Taxes | — | — | — | — | 1,050 | 2,120 | 2,930 | 4,040 | 4,890 | 5,720 |
| (15) Benefit of tax shield | 7,740 | 4,500 | 2,410 | 790 | — | — | — | — | — | — |
| (16) Annual mortgage principal | 3,400 | 3,720 | 4,080 | 4,480 | 4,890 | 5,360 | 5,860 | 6,420 | 7,030 | 7,700 |
| (17) Mortgage principal payments (cumulative) | 3,400 | 7,120 | 11,200 | 15,680 | 20,570 | 25,930 | 31,790 | 38,210 | 45,240 | 52,940 |
| (18) Unpaid mortgage principal | 180,600 | 176,880 | 172,800 | 168,320 | 163,430 | 158,080 | 152,210 | 145,790 | 138,760 | 131,060 |
| (19) Cash flow after taxes | 9,360 | 10,230 | 10,120 | 9,680 | 9,610 | 8,870 | 7,960 | 7,430 | 6,680 | 5,960 |
| (20) Discounted cash flow after taxes | 8,830 | 9,100 | 8,500 | 7,670 | 7,180 | 6,250 | 5,290 | 4,660 | 3,950 | 3,320 |
| (21) Discounted cash flow after taxes (cumulative) | 8,830 | 17,930 | 26,430 | 34,100 | 41,280 | 47,530 | 52,820 | 57,480 | 61,430 | 64,750 |

estimated to have only 10 out of 100 chances of being exceeded. The Most Probable (MP) projections are estimated to have an 80 out of 100 chance of being realized. In the case at hand, for example, the low projections of gross income reflect the possibility of a decline in income due to increasing competition which may depress rental rates. The rent-up period may be extended and the ultimate level of occupancy could continue at an unfavorable ratio. Operating expenses are projected to start at a high point and to increase substantially during the ten-year period. Note that the mortgage interest, the principal repayments and the allowances for depreciation are the same for each probability level. In this example, the projections of gross income, occupancy rates and operating expenses thus determine the differences in after-tax cash flows obtained at the three levels of probability.

The total accumulated discounted after-tax cash flow from operations appears on line 21 in year 10. This figure is carried forward to Section E of the analysis and added to the discounted cash flow from the sale of the property in order to obtain the total discounted return from the investment.

*Line 6: Gross income with full occupancy.* Assume 100% occupancy and derive the gross income for each year of the assumed holding period.

*Line 7: Occupancy rate.* Estimate the actual occupancy rate for each year (in per cent).

*Line 8: Effective gross income.* Line 6 multiplied by line 7.

*Line 9: Operating expenses.* Estimate of total annual expenses incurred in operating the property.

*Line 10: Interest on mortgage for each year.*

*Line 11: Book value of building at beginning of each year.* Initial building value less accumulated depreciation allowances.

*Line 12: Depreciation allowance.* This is based on the book value derived from line 11 and the depreciation method as specified in Section A.

*Line 13: Taxable income.* Line 8 (effective gross income) minus line 9 (operating expenses), line 10 (interest on mortgage), and line 12 (depreciation allowance).

*Line 14: Taxes.* Based on line 13 and the investor's marginal income tax rate as specified in Section A, if the taxable income is positive.

*Line 15: Benefit of tax shield if taxable income is negative.* A negative value in line 13 can benefit the investor—it enables him to offset such negative income against taxable income from other sources. Enter the savings in tax derived from reductions of other taxable income using the marginal tax rate from Section A.

*Line 16: Annual principal payments on mortgage.*

*Line 17: Principal payments on mortgage* (cumulative). For each year, the sum of all previous annual entries from line 16 (example: entry for year 3 equals sum of entries for years 1, 2, and 3 from line 16). This gives the total amount of mortgage principal repaid up to the current year.

*Line 18: Remaining principal on mortgage.* Line 2 (initial mortgage debt) minus line 17 (total amount of mortgage principal repaid up to that year).

*Line 19: Annual cash flow after taxes.* Sum of line 13 (taxable income), line 15 (benefit of tax shield if taxable income is negative), plus line 12 (depreciation allowance) minus line 16 (principal payments on mortgage), and minus line 14 (taxes).

*Line 20: Annual discounted cash flow after taxes.* Yearly entries on line 19 are multiplied by the discount factors, i.e., the present values of $1 at the selection discount rate which are to be entered for each year.

*Line 21: Discounted cash flow after taxes* (cumulative). For each year, the sum of all previous annual entries from line 20—this gives the total discounted cash flow accumulated at the end of that year.

*Section D—Investment Liquidation.* The selling price of the property at the end of the assumed holding period is estimated for each of the three probability levels. (See Table 5) Capital gains—as defined under U.S. tax law—are determined and the maximum tax rate of 25% is applied; the capital gains tax is then deducted from the selling price. Finally, the principal outstanding on the mortgage is deducted to determine the net cash flow to the investor on the sale of the property. The resulting cash flow is then discounted to present value figures. Under Canadian tax laws, the excess depreciation or capital cost allowance must be recaptured at the investor's marginal tax rate and the capital gains (excess of selling price over initial purchase price) are non-taxable. In order to use this analysis in Canada, some minor changes in format are thus required in this section of the analysis.

## TABLE 5

|  | L | MP | H |
|---|---|---|---|
| Line 22: Estimated selling price | 245,000 | 295,000 | 325,000 |
| Line 23: Book value of property | 149,420 | 149,420 | 149,420 |
| Line 24: Capital gains | 95,580 | 145,580 | 175,580 |
| Line 25: Taxes on capital gains | 23,890 | 36,390 | 43,890 |
| Line 26: Net to seller | 90,050 | 127,550 | 150,050 |
| Line 27: Discounted net to seller | 50,250 | 71,170 | 83,730 |
| (Discount factor = .558. .the present value of $1 in 10 years at 6%) | | | |

*Line 22: The estimated selling price of the property.* Expected market value at the end of the assumed holding period.

*Line 23: Book value of the property.* At the end of the assumed holding period —line 5 (initial value of land) plus line 11 (depreciated book value of building).

*Line 24: Capital gains.* Line 22 (estimated selling price of property) minus line 23 (terminal book value of property).

*Line 25: Taxes on capital gains.* Case example assumes U.S. tax laws.

*Line 26: Net proceeds to seller.* Line 22 (estimated selling price of property) minus line 25 (taxes on capital gains) and line 18 (remaining principal on mortgage).

*Line 27: Discounted net to seller.* The entry on line 26 is multiplied by the discount factor.

*Section E—Utility Calculation* (see table 6). Each investor has a unique utility function which reflects his attitude toward risk. The first step in this section is thus to quantify this individual utility function in the form presented in Figure 3 (including its derived table). The investor's attitude is expressed as a series of points which represent the relative utilities of dollar gains and losses. These points are plotted according to: (1) a horizontal dollar scale of gains and losses, and (2) a vertical scale of relative utilities and disutilities— as in Figure 3. They are then connected to form a curve from which a utility table can be derived from readings along the curve. This curve and table are essential before the utility calculation step can be completed. The curve and table in Figure 3 represent the utility function of our hypothetical investor.

## TABLE 6

|  | L | MP | H |
|---|---|---|---|
| Line 28: Total discounted return (21+27) | 67,330 | 117,330 | 148,480 |
| Line 29: Initial equity (from line 3) | 91,000 | 91,000 | 91,000 |
| Line 30: Total return to initial equity (28÷29) | .74 | 1.29 | 1.63 |
| Line 31: Difference: total return—initial equity (28−29) | −23,670 | 26,330 | 57,480 |
| Line 32: Utility factor (from utility table) | −90 | 52 | 83 |
| Line 33: Percent probability | .10 | .80 | .10 |
| Line 34: Expected utility (32×33) | −9.0 | 41.6 | 8.3 |
| Line 35: Total expected utility for this property (L 34 + MP 34 + H 34) |  |  | 40.9 |

Entered on line 28, is: (1) the total discounted return for each of the three probability levels which represents the total appropriate cumulative discounted cash flow from operations (Section C, Line 21) and (2) the discounted net to seller at liquidation (Section D, Line 27). These returns are related to the initial equity as (1) a ratio in Line 30, and (2) a dollar difference in Line 31—for each probability level. By referring to the utility table in Figure 3, these dollar differences are converted to utility factors (Line 32). Each utility factor must be weighted (Line 33) according to the chances of achieving each level in order to derive the expected utility for each of the three levels (Line 34). The sum of the three weighted utilities (40.9 in this example), represents the total expected utility for this property according to: (1) the productivity predictions at the three levels of probability and (2) the utility function defined by the investor.

*Line 28: Total discounted return from investment.* This gives the cumulative total net return, appropriately discounted, derived as the sum of line 21 (discounted cash flow after taxes, cumulative), and line 27 (discounted net to seller from investment liquidation).

*Line 29: Initial equity.* Same entry as in line 3.

*Line 30: Ratio of total return to initial equity.* The present value of the cumulative net return as a percentage of initial equity (line 28 divided by line 29).

*Line 31: Difference—Total return less initial equity.* The amount by which the total cumulative discounted return to equity differs from the initial equity. (Line 28 minus line 29).

*Line 32: Utility factor.* Derived by reading from the table, based on Figure 3, the utility value corresponding to the dollar difference derived in line 21 (excess or deficit on recapture of initial equity).

*Line 33: Percent probability for this probability level.* 10% for L (Low) and H (High), 80% for MP (Most Probable) probability levels, as established in Section A.

*Line 34: Expected utility at each probability level.* Line 33 (percent probability) times line 32 (utility factor).

*Line 35: Total expected utility for this property.* Sum of expected utilities for each probability level (L, MP, H) from line 34.

*Section F—Summary Evaluation*

*Line 36: Total adjusted difference*—$19,000; dollar equivalent of line 35, from Figure 7.

*Line 37: Cash indifference value*—$294,900; line 1 plus line 35.

The final step is to convert the total expected utility for the property to a dollar figure by referring to the derived utility curve. The utility measure of 40.9 from Line 35 can be converted to about $19,000; this amount represents the excess in discounted return to the investor over the initial equity under the assumptions of productivity, probability and utility.

The cash indifference value (line 37) is the initially assumed acquisition price of the property plus the $19,000 premium which the investor would be justified in paying under the assumptions. Had the total expected utility for the property been a negative figure, the investor's cash indifference value would have been less than the initial acquisition price; the investment thus would probably not be made at or above the acquisition price. In any case, the cash indifference value provides the investor with a point of reference which reflects his own estimates and notions of productivity, risk and utility; it is a "value to the investor" against which (1) he may judge the seller's asking price and (2) which will guide him in his negotiations.

The result of this investment analysis is, in part, a function of initial estimates of: (1) the acquisition price, (2) financing pattern, and (3) depreciation base. If the Cash Indifference Value is substantially different from the assumed Acquisition Price, the analyst may re-work the analysis utilizing new assumptions on financing and the depreciation base which conform more closely to the calculated Cash Indifference Value. Mortgage lenders and tax authorities often base their value decisions closer to the calculated Cash Indifference Value than to the originally assumed Acquisition Price.

**Conclusions.** In every field of human decision making technological progress has been largely a matter of reducing uncertainty; certainty can rarely be assured. The X-ray plate and the electro-cardiogram require the skilled interpretation of the physician and are not positive indicators which eliminate uncertainty. The analytical model presented here is no more than a small step toward reducing uncertainty in judgments on real estate investments. It requires explicit consideration of components in the decision making process which are treated intuitively and often sub-consciously by the analyst. Though the variables are not capable of exact measurement, if recognized and thoughtfully considered, they may be given relative numerical expression. The final decision benefits by this kind of narrowing of uncertainty, though much uncertainty remains.

*Application.* A similar formal investment evaluation scheme was recently introduced in a manufacturing enterprise by one of the authors. Within three two-hour training sessions, a reasonable operating knowledge of the procedures —including the underlying business theories of discounted cash flow, probability, and utility—was conveyed to the decision makers. Once the method was instituted, the necessity for thinking propositions through in all their ramifications and consequences, and the availability of quantitative results, served to stimulate and guide the investors' resourcefulness in the search for better alternatives; it generated consideration of alternative financing arrangements, alternative locations, and other alternative solutions.

This investment evaluation procedure was first introduced in 1967 in a company with only $1 million sales per year. Since that time, it has been successfully adopted by the parent company, a diversified medium-sized enterprise, for corporate evaluation of divisional projects. There is no reason why these concepts and procedures which have proven themselves in investment evaluation in a manufacturing context should not prove equally beneficial to investors in the real estate sector by providing a systematic framework to guide experience and judgment in an increasingly complex and competitive decision making environment.

### Questions

1. What are the principal factors which investors typically consider in making judgments regarding real estate investment opportunities?
2. How can non-monetary factors be given consideration in real estate investment decisions?
3. How can the probability of events occurring in the future be expressed in a way which will aid investment decisions?
4. What is meant by cumulative probability?
5. How may attitudes toward risk affect investment decisions?
6. What is meant by a "utility curve"?
7. Do you believe the analysis followed in the case study reflects useful approaches to real estate investment decisions?

# IV

# SPECIAL PROPERTIES
# AND PROBLEMS

The final section of the book discusses various special properties and problems. Chapter 21 concentrates on housing trends and problems. There are two study projects, one by Philip M. Klutznick on "Housing Myths and Realities" and another by Miles L. Colean on "Operation Breakthrough."

Chapter 22 considers various types of business real estate. Two case studies are presented, one of the Western Savings and Loan Association of Denver and the other of the A B Chemical Company.

Farms and other Rural Real Estate are considered in Chapter 23 which includes a brief study project on farm management.

This is followed by a discussion of international real estate trends, with a study project which compares urban problems from an international standpoint.

The final chapter, entitled Toward Improved Real Estate Administration, is itself a type of study project since it raises various questions and possibilities regarding real estate administration in the years ahead.

# 21

# Housing Trends and Problems

## HOUSING NEEDS AND WANTS

The housing problems of the 1970's will reflect the needs and wants of the people for housing relative to its availability. Needs will result from population growth as well as from changes in the age distribution of our people. Needs will arise also from the movement of people from place to place. Although population is always a basic factor in housing needs and wants, incomes are essential to translate needs and wants into effective demands. Thus, people will get the housing they are willing to pay for either directly or through subsidies or other arrangements. Effective demands will reflect the percentage of income which people are willing to spend for housing relative to other things. Many things will affect decisions on housing expenditures including the priorities which people assign to various needs, availability of funds and their cost, the technology available for use by the housing industry, the effectiveness with which housing can be marketed and managed and others.

Various estimates of housing needs have been made. Perhaps the most widely known is the estimate made by General Electric's Center for Advanced Studies called TEMPO, for the President's Committee on Urban Housing or Kaiser Committee. This estimate indicated a need for 26 million new or rehabilitated housing units for the period 1968 to 1978.[1] Various other estimates have been made as well. We will not

[1] See the report of the President's Committee on Urban Housing, *A Decent Home* (Washington, D.C.: U.S. Government Printing Office, 1968), p. 39.

undertake to make such estimates here, but rather to indicate the factors that will have a bearing on future housing needs, wants, demands and supplies.

## Population Growth

Population estimates vary considerably. It now seems likely that the total population will increase from 204 million in 1970 to around 300 million by the year 2000 but current trends suggest that totals may fall short of this estimate rather than exceed it. For example, the Commission on Population Growth and the American Future outlines a number of possible changes in rates of population growth.[2] The estimates for intermediate periods indicate that population will approach 230 million by 1980 and 240 million by 1985.

If the population grows to 300 million, however, some 50 million new dwelling units of all types—single-family, multi-family, high-, moderate-, and low-income housing—may be needed by the end of the century to provide for the added population and to improve housing quality at the rate of advance of recent years. It has been estimated that some 14 million dwelling units will be needed to replace obsolete structures and to house families moving from structures that will be demolished or moving from slum or declining areas.

## Age Distribution

Not only will the total population increase but there will be significant changes in its age distribution as well. For example, there will be some growth but of modest proportions in the under-5 age group in the 1970's. The age group from 5–13 will decline in numbers; the 14–17 group will hold steady; there will be some gain in the 18–24 year age group. Of special significance, however, will be the very substantial increase in the 25–34 age group. As many as 12 million may be added in this bracket. This is the age when many families are formed, thus rapid growth in this age bracket will have special significance for housing. The 35–44 age group will increase slightly and the 45–54 group will decline slightly. The age bracket over 54 will register significant gains. Growth in the older age groups suggests the prospective need for more retirement homes and it may spell some expansion in the second house market.

## Population Movements

The American people have always been a mobile people and they continue to follow this pattern. We have pointed out that on the average

---

[2] An Interim Report of the Commission on Population Growth and the American Future (Washington, D.C.: U. S. Government Printing Office, 1971).

approximately one out of five families moves each year and of the group moving, it has been estimated that one out of five moves from one area or region to another.

In recent years the principal population movements have been from farms and rural areas to cities and from the central parts of the cities to suburban and outlying areas. There have also been movements to the South and West.

The movement from the farms and rural areas has slowed down substantially and may affect housing requirements only slightly in the years ahead. The outward movement from the center of cities not only to the suburbs but into the surrounding countryside seems likely to continue. Even though efforts have been made to induce people to move back to the central city, it seems probable that the major movements will continue to be outward. Some moves back to the central city have occurred and more may take place particularly if the so-called "platform city" develops to a greater extent. The outward movement of people from central cities, however, seems likely to carry beyond the suburbs into the countryside. Also, more new towns probably will be developed. All of these population changes and shifts will spell additional needs for housing in new locations.

## Living Standards

Past trends suggest that people will not only need more housing in the future but that they will want housing of higher quality. This may take no more and possibly a smaller percentage of income than at present. There is a tendency for people to spend smaller percentages of income for housing as their incomes rise; also production efficiencies will help. A half century ago about a fifth of a consumer's dollar went for housing, now it is around an eighth and it may go lower.

At the same time quality of housing may improve; for example, more than two-thirds of new housing is built with more than one bath; almost all new dwelling units have air conditioning; and better designs and quality of materials are generally in evidence.

It is possible, of course, that past trends will not prevail. People may deliberately reduce their standards of living, perhaps hoping that this will help to solve some of our social and environmental problems. It is doubtful that the number who may do this will be sufficiently large to affect long term trends, but the possibility should be recognized.

Another possibility is that people will prefer to spend more of their incomes on other things and less on housing than in the past. For example, production efficiencies and cost reductions in other areas might have such a result; or people may change their value scales in ways that favor other things relative to housing.

From a public policy standpoint people may determine that no one should have a lower housing standard than a predefined level. To a degree housing codes do this now; but many are not enforced. In the future standards for minimal housing may be raised and enforcement may become more rigorous. People may also wish to have a large portion of their tax dollars allocated to provide better housing for those in lower income groups; as a result those in higher income brackets may have relatively less to spend for housing.

It is not possible to estimate very exactly the trend of developments in housing; some possibilities are suggested by the above discussion but we should recognize that events may unfold in entirely different ways.

### Future Consumer Wants

What kinds of housing will consumers want in the future? How will such wants be determined?

Consumer opinion surveys and similar types of investigations can determine with reasonable accuracy which types of properties and property services appear to be most popular currently and in the near future. Greatest contributions to improving products, however, have usually been made by those who are able to anticipate the wants of the people, often before they themselves were aware of them. People did not know whether they wanted color television before it was made available; when it became available, it was difficult to determine how much people would be willing to pay for it.

Much the same thing is true of housing. If the original pioneers in the prefabricated housing industry, for example, had asked people if they wanted such a product, in all probability few prefabricated houses would have been produced. Such pioneers in new building methods, designs and marketing practices, however, have found a widespread acceptance of their products once they were made available at attractive prices.

An interesting analogy may be drawn from the automobile field. Market studies often brought striking similarity of styles and types. As a result, however, foreign cars began to find a market here and they in turn have influenced domestic styles and types.

## FACTORS IN POTENTIAL HOUSING DEMAND

Housing demand is primarily a reflection of (1) incomes and income prospects, (2) terms and availability of financing plus anticipated changes in financial terms, (3) preferences of consumers for housing or for other goods and services or for savings and (4) cost and price factors, including materials, labor, land, financing, and others. Also population forces play a role in establishing overall housing needs as we suggested above.

The demand for housing involves more than the desire and willingness to pay for shelter, comfort, and privacy. It includes prestige and status factors, particularly in the case of home ownership. Prestige factors, however, may also be of importance in regard to rental housing, especially in the higher rental ranges.

It is important to recognize the interrelationships between housing demand factors. For example, incomes and income prospects may be indicative of a strong demand for housing but may be offset by unfavorable financing terms or by high costs and prices. Similarly, recent and projected population growth suggests that housing needs will be high in the 1970's. If incomes do not expand, however, or if financing is not available on favorable terms, there may be little expansion in housing demand despite the pressures of population. Or again, people may prefer to spend more or less on travel, automobiles, amusements, education, or other things than on housing.

## Impact of Incomes on Demand

Of major importance to an understanding of changes in the demand for housing is the trend of personal incomes, both in monetary and in real terms. In 1929, for example, income per capita after taxes, measured in terms of 1964 dollars, was $1,273. By 1933, it declined to $938 (again in terms of 1964 dollars), or a drop of 26 per cent. In 1970, per capita disposable (after tax) income was $3,003 in current dollars or $2,402 in 1964 dollars. Rising incomes have tended to emphasize qualitative factors in housing demands.

As income levels move upward, the luxury and qualitative aspects of housing tend to increase in importance. Conversely, as incomes decline, the utilitarian aspects of housing demand tend to increase in relative importance.

When real incomes are high and tending to go higher, the demand for all types of residential real estate, with the possible exception of that renting at very low levels, must be considered in terms of its luxury aspects. In a sense, of course, nearly all housing as we know it today is a luxury. All of the people in the country could be provided with shelter in barracks for a small fraction of the investment that is represented by our current housing supply and for a small fraction of the annual costs of the housing services that we enjoy. When incomes are high, however, people are not satisfied with modest housing accommodations. Quality factors gain in importance.

## Competition Between New and Old Housing

During periods when demand is unusually strong and before building programs can add appreciably to the available supply, the prices of older houses and the rents for older apartments move up along with the prices and rents for newer accommodations. As the number of dwelling units increases, however, older houses begin to lose out in competition with newer, more modern structures. Hence the prices and rents of older properties level out and begin to move downward before newer properties are affected.

Eventually, if there are great additions to supply or if incomes begin to move downward, some of the older properties may be able to compete more effectively as consumers try to reduce their living expenses. Often older properties are not encumbered with heavy carrying chargs and gain in relative competitive position. As newer properties are refinanced or other adjustments are made to cyclical changes, they will move into a more favorable competitive position relative to older structures.

When incomes are high and consumers stress the qualitative and luxury aspects of housing, the rate at which dwelling units grow obsolete increases. Hence there is a tendency for older houses to lose out in their competition with newer accommodations. Considerable emphasis at such times is placed on modernization and repair programs for older properties.

## Filtering

Most of us occupy housing that someone has used before; some of this housing is owned, some rented. The term "filtering" or "filtering down" has been applied to the process of moving dwelling units from higher to lower income users, much as automobiles filter or move from those who own them as new cars and those who own them later on.

The filtering process has not worked as well in housing as in the automobile market, in part because surplus supplies are needed for the process to work and in part because the housing market has a number of barriers to open competition that interfere with the easy movement of dwelling units from one user to another. Of major importance among such barriers is fixity of location, of course; in addition, zoning and deed restrictions play a part as do various types of discrimination as to race, color and creed.

Filtering works better in some parts of the housing market than in others. It works best in the middle price and rent ranges, fairly well in the higher ranges. It works only to a limited extent in the lower price and rent ranges.

As Perry Prentice has pointed out:

Trade-up (another name for filtering) . . . works best but not well in the middle brackets, where Bill Levitt once traced as many as nine trade-up moves made possible by one new home he had sold, and no doubt there were still more beyond where he stopped tracing. It works best but only feebly in the higher priced field. It doesn't work at all below the poverty line.

He goes on to say,

If we could meet the housing needs of the poor with good used homes as the flood of good used cars meets their auto needs, then we could upgrade our housing expenditures and concentrate on building the kind of homes that will be needed to satisfy the rising expectations of tomorrow's much more affluent market.[3]

## Doubling-Up

The sharing of dwellings by families, or doubling up, often is widespread during periods of housing shortages or in recessions. It is a commonplace practice among many in lower income groups. Even in prosperous periods and in cases where there is no economic necessity, some families double up for a variety of reasons. A young married couple may live with in-laws until an apartment or house is located. Three or four single persons may share an apartment. An elderly couple may live with a son or daughter in order to help look after children so both of the young people may work. Or there may be doubling up in order to look after those who are ill or incapacitated. For the most part, however, economic reasons are primarily responsible for doubling up.

## Income Subsidies

Housing demand results not only from what people spend for housing out of their own incomes but also from what government does with tax dollars. The tax dollars may have both a direct impact as in the case of direct subsidies or an indirect one as in the case of tax exemptions. For example, funds expended for public housing add to housing demands, for practical purposes almost as directly as funds expended by private citizens from their after-tax incomes. Similarly, rent supplement programs such as the Section 236 programs, add to housing demand; in much the same way the interest supplement programs under Section 235 do also.

On the other hand there are some indirect subsidies that also tend to stimulate housing demand. For example, a home owner pays no

---

[3] Perry I. Prentice, "Trade-up and Trade-in—Important Forces for Housing Policy Confidential Paper for CED, April, 1971. Reproduced by Permission.

income tax on the indirect income, that is, the value of the house services he derives from occupying the house. If he has a mortgage on the house he can deduct interest charges and depreciation when computing his federal income tax. By contrast a tenant cannot deduct his rental payments or any part of them.

Thus, when we try to estimate the impact of income on housing demand we need not only to consider direct incomes but the impact of subsidies and related adjustments as well.

### Impact of Economic Policies

Government policies have a considerable influence on how incomes are spent in general but especially in the housing field. The impact of economic stabilization efforts through the medium of monetary and credit policies has been unusually heavy in the housing field. Tight money policies leading to higher interest rates soon price most home mortgages out of the market. Home financing institutions like savings and loan associations with a large inventory of lower interest rate mortgages cannot compete for funds because they cannot pay the higher rates that the market sets under such conditions. As a result housing carries an unusually heavy burden in such stabilization periods. If policies of this type are continued, they will have an unfavorable effect on demand for as well as the production of housing in the future.

Economic policies which lead to inflationary tendencies increase desires for home ownership relative to renting. The opposite tends to be true under deflationary conditions. We should note also that inflationary expectations usually lead to high interest rates and these tend to have a depressing effect on housing markets even though interest in ownership may be high.

Prospective home owners prefer to enter the market when interest rates are favorable in the hope that they will be protected against future price and interest rate advances. Variable interest rates, however, may become more common and make it difficult to work out such arrangements.

Policies which attempt to hold down costs favor housing relative to other goods and services because of the relatively high levels of costs of land and buildings. On the other hand policies that may tend to undermine ownership such as rent controls tend to be unfavorable for the housing field.

Policies that favor housing such as special financing arrangements of the FHA or VA type or the Section 235 or 236 types or those of the Federal Home Loan Bank Board or GNMA tend to stimulate housing demand in comparison to the demand for other things. Elimination of such restrictions as usury laws would have a favorable effect as would greater flexibility in building codes.

Other policy areas might be discussed as well; for example, the entire field of property taxation relative to the taxation of other things is important. Our discussion, however, is intended to suggest the types of factors that may affect future housing demand rather than to present an exhaustive discussion of the forces involved.

### Financing

Since few home buyers have the funds to pay for a house when it is bought, financing terms and conditions play an important role, especially in the demand for single-family homes or for apartments under co-operative or condominium arrangements. Thus when down payments are low, terms of mortgages are long, and interest rates and costs are low, a tremendous stimulus is given to the demand for owner-occupied homes. The buyer uses a small amount of his own funds and a major amount of a financial institution's or other lender's funds to make the purchase.

When money markets are tight and funds for home financing are not readily available, the demand for single-family homes declines more or less sharply, even though incomes may continue to be high. At such times the demand for rented living accommodations may increase. Builders may wish to shift to the construction of apartment houses. Financing of residential income properties may lose out to other fields as interest rates rise. Promoters and developers will expand their operations when financing terms are favorable unless they can operate by using equities. Then lenders can demand and get "a piece of the action," that is, an equity participation.

Savings and loan associations play a major role in the home financing market as we have seen. They specialize in this type of business and do not tend to move into and out of the mortgage market as conditions in the other financial markets change. Insurance companies and savings and commercial banks, which enjoy broader investment powers, tend to shift their activities between the various capital markets as yields and investment opportunities change.

There are widespread differences of opinion as to the relative desirability of specialized financial institutions to channel funds into housing investments. Some contend that all financial institutions should have the same broad investment powers, allowing people to compete for the funds they want. Others favor specialized institutions, contending that mortgages seldom have been strong competitors for funds under high interest rate conditions and hence that housing, along with small business and small municipalities soon gets priced out of the market under highly competitive [4] conditions. Some have argued for the earmarking of specific percentages of the assets of specialized institutions for investment in housing; this has been suggested especially for pension funds, which to date have had limited investments in this field.

Also there are a variety of issues in regard to the extent of financial subsidy that should be provided. The rent and interest rate subsidies, for example, such as are provided under Sections 235 and 236, have grown in importance. There are arguments that special incentives toward saving would be a better approach to a subsidy arrangement than direct assistance. Thus, if savings were plentiful, interest rates would be reasonable and housing could compete for funds in the open market.

## FACTORS IN POTENTIAL HOUSING SUPPLY

The supply of housing has been accumulating for many years. It now includes over 68 million dwelling units up from 58.3 million in 1960. A large proportion are single-family homes but there are many doubles, duplexes, small apartment houses, large apartment houses and complexes, town houses, row houses and other types. This supply of dwelling units includes vacation cabins and cottages. It includes slum dwellings and exclusive residences, simple dwellings or deluxe living quarters. The diversity of dwellings as to type, age, condition, location, quality, architectural style, construction materials and other classifications is very great.

This country has been described as a nation in which we agree to disagree. We allow for a wide variety of values, interests, priorities, objectives, life styles, and preferences. There are few areas where this is more in evidence than in housing. Some people spend far beyond their means on housing, preferring to achieve some sort of balance by cutting down in other areas; others spend far less than they could afford on housing, preferring expenditures on automobiles, travel, entertainment or other things. Some get housing for little or nothing as in public housing projects or military personnel or government officials with official residences.

Thus, we make use of our existing housing supply in many ways. In some cases it is used with great intensity as in cases of slum housing where many people occupy small spaces in order to reduce the cost per person or where two or more families "double up" for economic or personal reasons. In other cases dwelling units stand idle for many

---

[4] See Irwin Friend, *Study of the Savings and Loan Industry* (Washington, D.C.: U.S. Government Printing Office, 1970), especially "Summary and Recommendations."

months out of the year because the owner has another home or is on extensive travel or is too ill to occupy the space.

## Repair and Maintenance

All housing deteriorates over time or is damaged by use to a greater or lesser degree. Carefully planned repair and maintenance programs prolong the life of existing properties and add to their utility and attractiveness. We encourage repair and maintenance by special financing arrangements, in some cases making it possible to do this under existing mortgages. Title I programs under the FHA provide for the guarantee of loans made for repair and maintenance purposes. Many savings and loan associations have special financing plans for modernization and repair programs. As our dwelling units have become increasingly mechanized, the costs of maintaining equipment of many types has gone up and its condition is of major importance to the enjoyment of the dwelling unit. Heating and air conditioning units, electrical and gas systems, disposals, dryers and dehumidifiers, vacuum cleaners, refrigerators, radio and TV sets and many other things all call for almost constant repair and attention along with the basic structural parts of the dwelling unit.

## Reductions in Supply

Each year a small percentage of the existing supply of dwelling units is lost through fire, windstorm, earthquake, flood, accident or deliberate demolition. Some residential structures are demolished because they are no longer fit for use, others because they are in the way of a new road or street or renewal project or other improvement. There are many dwellings which undoubtedly should be demolished and would be if an adequate supply of other housing were available. The percentage of demolitions varies from year to year and, of course, varies considerably from place to place, reflecting differences in local conditions. The growing number of abandoned houses, especially in city centers may step up the demolition rate.[5]

Changes are occurring almost continuously in the quality of our housing supply as well as in the quantity of dwelling units. Physical depreciation goes on day by day and year by year. Newer and better housing units bring obsolescence to those in the existing supply. To some extent these tendencies are counteracted by remodeling, repair

[5] See George Sternlieb, "The Abandoned Building as a Clue to the Future of the American City," for the U.S. Senate Subcommittee on Housing and Urban Affairs of the Banking and Currency Committee, 1970.

and modernization programs. Changes are turning some neighborhoods into slums at the same time that renewal and related programs are rescuing others. Thus, despite the apparent permanence of the housing supply, it is undergoing constant change.

### Additions to Housing Supply

Each year we add to our supply of housing. Although some estimates of needs indicate production requirements that would average around 2.6 million new or rehabilitated dwelling units annually, we have only on occasion approached such a volume. In peak years with housing starts nearing the two million level and if mobile homes are added, we have not been greatly below such a target. Even at a 2.5 million level, annual additions to the supply would represent less than four per cent of the total.

Additions to the housing supply annually range from deluxe single-family homes to smaller homes, doubles, duplexes, garden apartments, high rise apartment complexes, vacation homes and others. Mobile homes now are a significant factor in our annual additions to the housing

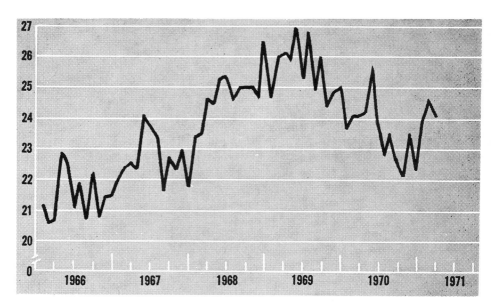

**Fig. 21-1.** Median sales price of new homes sold—in thousands of dollars. (Source: U. S. Department of Commerce, Courtesy of U. S. Savings and Loan League.)

supply.  Public housing developments account for some new units, some new units are subsidized in varying degrees, some are provided on a purely private basis, some are financed by government directly, some through government assistance, others through private financial arrangements.  Some new housing is in the central city, some in suburban and outlying areas, others in the open countryside.  Some new housing is built by conventional methods, some is of manufactured, prefabricated or modular construction, and as we have suggested some is provided as mobile homes.

## Mobile Homes

A very large percentage of the mobile homes are "mobile" only at the time they are delivered to the site.  Few are ever moved.  Many are located in attractive parks, some on golf courses or lakes; some, however, are found in less attractive locations.  We should distinguish between mobile homes of this type and the "travel trailers," which are designed to move readily, being towed by a car or truck.  Mobile home production exceeded the 400,000 unit level in 1969 and was just short of it in 1970.  Travel trailers, though popular, seldom have reached more than 20 per cent of this level.  There are also house cars, land yachts, and self-propelled and largely self-contained vacation homes that go by a variety of names.  These types are gaining in popularity but are as yet a small factor in the overall supply of housing.

## Modular Housing

The term modular housing has been assigned to units that resemble mobile homes but that may be assembled in a variety of ways from "double wide" mobiles to large scale arrangements such as were popularized at Montreal's Expo several years ago.  Many production problems have been encountered but progress has been made in this field.  Industrialized housing firms have given special attention to this area.  It seems likely to be a significant factor in the future housing supply.

## Production Problems

As we have seen in our earlier discussions, the production processes involved in the construction of buildings have improved over time but still have a long way to go if costs are to be brought into line with those in other fields.  HUD's "Operation Breakthrough" has been a recent effort to stimulate innovation in the housing field and especially in the production of new housing.  (See Study Project 21–2 at the end of this chapter.)

We have discussed various production problems in our discussions in Chapters 14 and 15. All we wish to add here is the observation that improved production processes will mean much to our future housing supply. Any improvements that will provide more house for less cost will help housing in its competition for a slice of the consumer's dollar. Such improvements may range from achitectural, engineering and structural to land planning and zoning to finance, marketing and government regulations.

Much has been said about restrictive building codes and much needs to be done in this area. National performance standards would be extremely helpful. But there are restrictions in many other areas including finance, entry into building trades, marketing practices and others.

### Marketing Changes

There is increasing recognition that land development holds the key to most successful house-building operations and to stable future residential neighborhoods. It may be that greater gains in the future will be made in the areas of land development and in marketing than in any other phase of housing.

The combination of land development, building, and marketing has been helpful to both conventional builders and prefabricators. The careful coordination of these activities, plus assistance provided for the local dealer by the manufacturer of prefabricated homes in land assembly and planning, market analysis, scheduling of building programs, and financing, have been of major importance in the success of prefabrication. Company owned prefabricated dealerships and large-scale on-site builders have also provided many of these advantages.

There continues to be great need for the simplification of real estate transfers. This would benefit especially the residential market, with its numerous small transactions and its relatively uninformed buyers and sellers, especially in the owned-home field. With the great progress that has been made in other areas, it is to be hoped that the transfer of title, insurance of title, abstracting, and the many other phases of the process of property transfer may be simplified in future years.

Other marketing developments of importance include the increased role being played by property managers, and the development of programs for trading in houses.

As we indicated above, more and more residential properties are being managed by professional property managers. The success of the property manager in increasing returns on investments in residential properties has led to a substantial expansion of this type of activity. The growing complexity of business practices, particularly with respect to government regulation and taxation, also explains the increasing importance of this phase of residential real estate marketing.

### Trade-in Problems

Difficulties have been encountered in developing an effective system for trading in used houses. Although builders and brokers have made valiant efforts in this area, much remains to be done. Some business firms have made special efforts to facilitate the transfer of executive personnel from one part of the country to another. Financial institutions have experimented in this area as well. To date, however, there are few places where one can trade-in a house with anything approximating the ease with which one trades in a car.

One phase of the problem pertains to the local market. Those buying and selling houses or condominiums in the same city have a better chance of working out a trade-in arrangement than those moving from one city to another, which is the second phase of the problem.

Still another aspect of the problem is that of carrying an inventory of unsold houses that have been traded in. The financial commitments required soon exceed the resources of most house builders and brokers. Also, many homes need reconditioning and remodeling before being resold. This takes time and further financing. The buyer needs some sort of guarantee that the reconditioned or remodeled house will meet desired standards of performance.

Thus, the problem of developing an effective trade-in system for houses has been only partially solved; hence, this may be an area of significant future opportunity.

## USER PREFERENCES

Some of the users of housing prefer to own it, others to rent it. Some like single-family detached homes, other like town houses, either owned under a condominium arrangement or rented. Some like more than one house—second homes have gained rapidly in popularity. Some prefer to live in the suburbs, others near in, still others in new towns or the open countryside.

### Home Ownership

Preferences for owner-occupied homes are usually a reflection of higher incomes along with easy financing and some tax advantages. In 1920, owner-occupied homes represented 45.6 per cent of nonfarm dwellings. Prosperous conditions in the 1920's brought this to 47.8 per cent

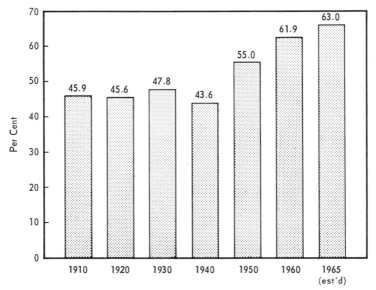

**Fig. 21–2.** Rise of home ownership. (Source: Bureau of the Census.)

by 1930. The depression reduced owner-occupied homes to 43.6 per cent of the nonfarm dwelling units by 1940, a slightly lower percentage than in 1920. The prosperity of the 1940's (and controlled rents, which limited access to rental properties), resulted in the most rapid gain of home ownership for any decade in our history, and, by 1950, 55 per cent of the nonfarm dwellings were occupied by owners. By 1960 this proportion had advanced to nearly 62 per cent and by 1970 to nearly 63 per cent (see Fig. 21–2). The number of owner-occupied units increased from 23.5 million in 1950 to 32.8 million in 1960 to 39.8 million in 1970.

A decline in incomes or in income prospects, tends to slow down the trend toward home ownership. When incomes move downward, consumers are reluctant to take on the long-range obligations that are involved in home ownership. Also, they may prefer not to be tied too closely to one area, since greater economic opportunities may develop elsewhere. During periods of recession most people attach great importance to the liquidity of their investments.

For most families, home ownership is advantageous when prices are rising since the investment involved is hedged against inflation and against rising costs of operation. Indeed, home ownership is one of the main ways by which a family of moderate means may protect itself against inflationary developments.

In a period of declining incomes the opposite is true; and consumers tend to favor rented rather than owned space, since rents tend to decline while the major costs of home ownership, such as taxes and mortgage payments, do not decline or do not move downward as rapidly as rents.

**TABLE 21–1.   Home Ownership by Decades**

| Year<br>Years | Occupied Units | Owner Occupied<br>Units | Percentage<br>Owned |
|---|---|---|---|
| 1930 | 29,905,000 | 14,280,000 | 47.8 |
| 1940 | 34,855,000 | 15,196,000 | 43.6 |
| 1950 | 42,826,000 | 23,560,000 | 55.0 |
| 1960 | 53,024,000 | 32,797,000 | 61.9 |
| 1970 | 63,417,000 | 39,862,000 | 62.9 |

SOURCES: Bureau of the Census, *1970 Census of Population;* United States Savings and Loan League, *Savings and Loan Fact Book* (Chicago: The League, 1971).

Home ownership tends to be more common in the smaller urban places than in large metropolitan communities. Less than half of the families own their homes in metropolitan communities, while over two-thirds are home owners in small towns and rural areas. There is some variation between large cities as well, however, with Detroit ranking much higher in terms of home ownership than New York. The lower percentage of home ownership in New York and Chicago than in other cities probably is due to the availability of a large number of apartments in these larger cities.

Home ownership tends to be higher among older than younger families. Only a small percentage of the families headed by persons 25 years of age or less are home owners, while over two-thirds of the families headed by persons 65 and over fall in this group. Frequency of home ownership increases most rapidly among families in the 40 to 44 age group, suggesting that strongest demand is found among families in this age range.

According to a study conducted by the U. S. Savings and Loan League, the average age of the buyer of the typical single-family house who uses savings and loan financing is about 41 years. Of the heads of households buying homes and using conventional mortgage financing provided by savings and loan associations, 14 per cent are under 30 years of age, 16 per cent between 30 and 35, 17 per cent between 35 and 40, 17 per cent between 40 and 45, 15 per cent between 45 and 50, and 10 per cent between 50 and 55. Thereafter, the percentages of buyers drops sharply, with only 11 per cent over 55 years of age.

Relative income affects home ownership, with more concentration in the higher brackets than in the lower-income levels. Home ownership varies somewhat with occupation; managerial and self-employed rank higher, and unskilled and service personnel lower than the average for all groups. Whether this is simply a reflection of incomes or whether occupation also has a bearing is not definite.

The bulk of owner-occupied homes are single-family, detached structures. In doubles, duplexes, and structures with three or four dwelling units, owners often occupy one unit and rent out the remaining space. Only a small percentage of the structures with five or more units are owner-occupied. Most of these are condominiums or cooperatively-owned apartment buildings. The trend toward the ownership of individual apartments has been rising, especially in the higher price ranges since the condominium arrangement has become more generally available.

### Rental Housing

The upsurge of rental housing represents one of the significant housing developments in recent years. In 1960, multi-family housing (much of which is intended for the rental market) comprised only 18.3 per cent of total housing starts; two-family housing accounted for 3.9 per cent, the remainder or 77.8 per cent being single-family homes. By 1970 these percentages were 55.6 for one-family homes, 3.3 for two-family and 41.2 for three or more family units.

The majority of the apartment house developments are of the garden type currently—one- to three-story buildings—but the volume of high-rise, elevator apartments has also been growing.

Factors that account for the rapid growth of interest in the apartment house field include rising costs of land, changes in consumer preferences, availability of equity funds, and shifts in the age distribution of the population especially the gains in the young adult and early middle age groups.

Home ownership has lost some of its appeal as the rental market for used houses has become more competitive in a number of localities. In addition, real estate taxes have tended to rise very rapidly in many places.

### Condominiums and Cooperatives

Garden apartments tend to employ the same general construction and materials as single-family dwellings. As in the case of town houses, garden-type apartments may be rented or sold directly or through a condominium arrangement. High-rise, elevator apartment buildings usually have concrete or steel-frame structures. Many are of the luxury type. They may be rented or sold through cooperative or condominium arrangements.

Cooperatives and condominiums are similar in that they both involve an ownership concept. In a cooperative the occupant acquires ownership by purchasing shares in a corporation that owns the building. Ownership of such shares gives him a preferred position as against non-share holders. He may be required to offer his shares to the corporation in case he wishes to sell, and he typically will need to get approval for improvements and changes he may wish to make.

The condominium provides for the individual ownership of a specific apartment together with ownership of an undivided interest in the land and other parts of the structure in common with other owners. Thus, an owner has the same general ownership rights in an apartment that he might have in a single-family home, except that he shares the ownership of land, hallways, lobbies, garages, swimming pools, and similar improvements. The buyer has a deed to his apartment; he can mortgage, sell, or bequeath it. This form of ownership has increased the attractiveness of apartments to a number of families. Previously, ground level occupancy had been much more attractive than other arrangements.

### Second Homes

Another development that appears to have long-term significance is the trend toward a "second home." More and more American families now own a second home, just as they own a second car; and the trend increases with rising incomes. In many families, especially large ones, a second home is an economical means of providing family vacations in favorite recreation spots. In some cases a vacation home is a "second" at the time of purchase but is intended eventually to serve as a retirement home.

The size and cost of a second home vary widely, but wealth is no requisite. Low-cost, do-it-yourself or premanufactured units are often chosen. In some cases, the cost of a land site in popular recreation areas may exceed construction costs.

While lake cottages, beach bungalows, and more elegant summer homes have been on the American scene for years, more and more vacation homes are built with the same year-round facilities that are found in permanent residences. The family can then spend extended periods out of the city, with the head of the family commuting into the city.

For some people second homes have proved to be sound investments. Arrangements are made to rent them to others when not being used. This not only provides added income but also depreciation can be offset against income. If located in rapidly expanding areas some second homes have gone up in value.

Much of the apartment building in resort areas definitely can be classed as for the second home market. Many of the new apartments are being rented on an annual basis, even though the tenants use them for only a few months of the year. Subleases frequently permit other families to have a second home at other seasons of the year.

### Growth Potential of Second Homes

The same factors that are encouraging the growing trend to second homes—improved highways, faster airplane schedules, increased leisure time and higher incomes as well as crime, pollution, unrest, and congestion in crowded cities—are also factors that should assure a vigorous resale market for second homes. In fact, families tend to "trade up" on second homes as they do with their permanent homes and their cars. With greater accessibility, marketability, and year-round construction, financing of vacation homes is becoming easier.

The number of vacation homes in the total housing stock of the United States is difficult to estimate. The 1960 Census reported 1.7 million "seasonal vacant" housing units, up about 600,000 from the 1950 Census. The 1970 Census reported 5.5 million units of this type. In addition, many vacation dwellings are mobile homes, travel trailers, house boats, or other accommodations that the Bureau of the Census does not count as housing units unless occupied as permanent residences.

Thus, the stock of homes in the United States used as a second place of residence seems to be rising continuously.

At least some of the demand for apartments in lieu of a house reflects the desire for a second home in a suburban or resort area. Weekend commuting and closing up the home for summer or winter vacation present fewer complications in the case of apartment living.

### Location Preferences

As we suggested in the introductory discussions in this chapter, people are likely to continue to move about in search of desirable locations. Past trends suggest further movement out from the center of cities and movement toward the South and West.

Modifications in such trends undoubtedly will occur. Some people will try suburban and outlying locations and move back to city centers. Others will be encouraged to continue to live near the center of cities rather than moving out.

The location of economic opportunities will be of major importance in location preferences. Some types of jobs, especially those in highly skilled and specialized occupations, undoubtedly will expand in or near city centers. Such opportunities will attract skilled workers and specialists. Less skilled jobs probably will continue to be decentralized and this may mean that the less skilled workers also will move outward. Thus, lower as well as middle and higher income groups are likely to move to outlying locations.

Movements of people to the South and West seem likely to continue, in part because of employment growth in such locations and also in response to the continuing search for a desirable climate. Fortunately, all do not like the same climate but there seems to be continuing interest in milder weather and in less congested locations. Retired people and others not tied to a specific locality for economic reasons are more likely to seek out such locations.

## SUMMARY

The housing needs and wants of our people will reflect population growth, changes in age distribution and movement of the people from place to place. Much will depend on the priorities people assign to housing, both for themselves and the general housing standards they believe should be established and enforced. Consumer wants may change over time especially as new housing services and products and new products and services in other areas are developed.

Major factors in potential housing demand will include income trends and expectations, the competition between new and used houses and the possibilities for greater filtering, the extent of doubling up, and the use of income and related subsidies. In addition housing demand will be influenced greatly by general economic policies and especially the impact of future tight money and credit policies. Financing will continue to play a major role in potential housing demand, reflecting inflationary or deflationary factors and money market conditions including the general availability of capital and the intensity of competition for funds.

The potential housing supply will reflect the repair and maintenance of the existing supply, demolitions and other reductions in supply, and the rate of house building. The increased popularity of mobile homes will be an important factor in future housing supply as will improved production and marketing methods.

The future housing of our people will reflect preferences for home ownership of various types including condominium and cooperative arrangements. Rental housing has tended to gain in popularity and may continue to do so if costs continue to advance and property taxes rise. Second homes seem likely to gain in popularity. Location preferences will also be important in determining future housing requirements.

## QUESTIONS FOR STUDY

1. What are the principal factors in determining housing needs and wants? Do you anticipate major changes in the 1970's relative to the 1960's?
2. Do you think a growing number of people will undertake to reduce their

living standards? Is housing more likely to be affected than other sectors by any such movement?

3. Do you think people will favor housing relative to other things in the expenditures of their future incomes? Why or why not?

4. Explain the filtering process. To what extent does it work or fail to work? Is it likely to be more effective in the future?

5. How important are income subsidies likely to be in future housing policies? Which types of subsidies do home owners enjoy?

6. Why will financing continue to be such an important factor in future housing demand? Would savings incentives be preferable to income subsidies as a way of assuring adequate funds for housing? Explain.

7. How important are specialized financial institutions in providing funds for housing finance?

8. In his excellent study of the savings and loan industry [6] Dr. Irwin Friend, who is Richard K. Mellon Professor of Finance at the University of Pennsylvania, points out that savings and loan associations have the most specialized asset structure of all the major groups of savings intermediaries; they are also the most important single supplier of mortgage credit for residential housing. Dr. Friend makes suggestions for improving the functioning of these institutions in order that they may operate more effectively as specialized financial intermediaries serving primarily the needs of housing finance.

There are others who believe that all financial institutions should have approximately the same powers and that none should have special inducements to serve the housing market or any other special needs. Any specialization under such arrangements would arise from other factors than special inducements.

a. Which of these positions do you favor? Why?

b. Which of these positions seems most likely to be followed in the years ahead? Explain.

9. How do you account for the wide diversity of housing in this country?

10. Why are dwelling units lost from the housing supply each year? How important are repair and modernization programs?

11. Will mobile homes be an important part of the future housing supply? Explain. Is house quality likely to improve if the number of housing starts annually is increased? Why or why not?

12. What is the outlook for improved production processes in housing? In which areas are advances most likely to be made?

13. Which improvements are needed in house marketing? Why are trade-in problems so important?

14. Is home ownership likely to be as popular in the future as in the past? Why or why not?

15. How important are condominiums and cooperatives likely to be in the future?

---

[6] Irwin Friend, *Study of the Savings and Loan Industry* (Washington, D.C.: U.S. Government Printing Office, 1970).

16. How do you account for the growing interest in second homes? Is the trend toward second homes likely to continue?

17. What are likely to be the preferences of people in regard to the location of their housing in the future? Explain.

## SUGGESTED READINGS

EDWARDS, EDWARD E., and ARTHUR M. WEIMER. *Cyclical Fluctuations in Residential Construction.* Bloomington, Inc.: Business and Real Estate Trends, Inc., 1968.

MUTH, RICHARD F. "Urban Residential Land and Housing Markets," in PERLOFF, HARVEY S., and LOWDEN WINGO, JR. (eds.), *Issues in Urban Economics.* Baltimore: The Johns Hopkins Press, 1968. Pp. 285–333.

NATIONAL COMMISSION ON URBAN PROBLEMS. *Building the American City* (The Douglas Report). Washington, D.C.: U.S. Government Printing Office, 1968. Pp. 1–40.

THE PRESIDENT'S COMMITTEE ON URBAN HOUSING, *A Decent Home* (The Kaiser Report). Washington, D.C.: U.S. Government Printing Office, 1968. Pp. 1–36, 39–53.

WEIMER, ARTHUR M. "Future Factors in Housing Demand: Some Comments," in Grebler, Leo, in honor of, *Essays in Urban Land Economics.* Los Angeles, Calif.: University of California Real Estate Research Program, 1966. Pp. 179–87.

## STUDY PROJECT 21–1

### Housing Myths and Realities *

In these trying and convulsive years, the attainment of the American dream by those who have "sat much too long below the salt" depends upon substantial improvements in housing, as well as in education and jobs.

With regard to housing, there are many myths abroad, despite the fact that for many years, housing has been high on the agenda of human concern.

What are these myths?

Let us look at a few concepts in our search for reality.

1. In 1949, Congress established a national housing policy of "a decent home and a suitable living environment for every American family." A generation later, this remains a myth for many of our people. The socially and economically disadvantaged have learned it is only rhetoric. More than 15 per cent of our population (about 30 million people) are in this category, They are commonly believed to be black, yet most are white.

The national housing goal is a reality only to those who can afford to pay the escalating price. Our actions shut out those who can not afford to buy or whose race counts them out. Though we failed to attain a just and fair objective for its own sake, now it is obvious, in the flame of dissent and growing violence, that our housing promise must be redeemed. Procrastination and excuse invites tragedy in our national life.

---

* By Philip M. Klutznick; reproduced by permission of Mortgage Guaranty Insurance Corporation, from the *MGIC Newsletter.*

This brings me to a second piece of mythology.

2. The act of 1949 contained two passages that are quoted: "Private enterprise shall be encouraged to serve as large a part of the total market as it can"; and "Governmental assistance shall be utilized where feasible to enable private enterprise to serve more of the total need."

Until quite recently, this meant the needs of those who could afford to pay. Our failure to help significantly the badly housed, combined with the disruptive events of the mid and late '60's, produced a whole series of new titles from 220 to 221-D-3's, D-4's, 234, 235 and 236. Belatedly we are trying to enable private enterprise to meet more of the total housing need. The below market interest rates, outright rental subsidies, and interest subsidies are pointed in the right direction.

As much as 25 per cent of 1970 housing starts involved direct federal subsidy to buyers and renters. It is a dramatic change from 1 to 4 per cent for public housing in the early days, to 10 per cent for public subsidies in 1969, and to 25 per cent in 1970.

Lest this percentage be considered a trend responsive to our national housing goal, it must be remembered that total production in 1969 and 1970 hovered around 1,500,000 or less, against a 1968 announced average goal of 2,600,000 units. So, even with this seemingly highly desirable percentage of government assistance to housing, which is encouraging, house building falls far short of needs proclaimed by the government.

Other questions should plague us. Are we really bringing about broader participation of the private enterprise system, or are we merely substituting subsidized programs for conventionally financed programs? Are we witnessing a housing financing revolution? Are institutional financing and conventional savings and loan programs being replaced by government subsidy and special inducements?

The new programs are helping private enterprise through government subsidy to help meet a part of the lower end of the scale of need. But unless further steps are taken, conventional programs meeting other needs could be adversely affected. Are we adding new money for housing? Some believe that we are creating a new disadvantaged class made up of families with incomes of $12,000 to $16,000. They do not qualify for subsidy, yet they are unable to meet charges for non-subsidized new or good used housing.

It does not make sense to meet the housing needs of lower income families at the expense of those who should be able to pay their own way and who also need housing. This is not increasing housing production. It is merely shifting the housing supply from one group to another.

3. There is another myth, that we are on the verge of dramatically reducing the capital cost of housing. Consider what goes into the production of a house. Typically, materials and onsite labor account for only 54 per cent of the cost, with land, financing, overhead and profit making up the remainder. Even if one could cut the cost of the house by 10 per cent, this would represent an overall savings of only 5 per cent. The present rate of inflation tends to offset such savings.

We are trying another great promotion called Breakthrough, a direct descendent of the major research programs initiated in 1946. If all or part of the Breakthrough projects succeed, about the best they can do is slow up cost increases. This is desirable, but hardly a major answer to the overall cost problem.

If we could find ways to reduce the peaks and valleys of inflation and deflation to a 2½ to 3 per cent rate, the industry could operate more evenly and could save the consumer as much or more than new fangled ideas, whether in construction, management or finance. When production rises to nearly 2,000,000 units and then drops to little more than half that annual number virtually overnight, additional costs creep in. The consumer gets the worst of it. He pays more as production is inflated; and pays the costs of slow marketing when deflation is in process.

4. Another myth has prevailed that the private housing industry is unlike typical private business and is selfishly concerned only with what it could do for itself.

We are not only engaged in business to make a profit, as we should be, but are also in a search for solutions to the gnawing failures to produce a decent house for every American family. The public concern with our business is vital and real. For many years, federal, state and local governments have interposed ideas, laws, subsidies, controls and the other products of the public world to help and sometimes to slow up the production of housing.

The most recent congressional enactments, coupled with a tight money market, have created a new mix of financing, with subsidies becoming increasingly utilized. The largest part of this government aided volume is calculated to encourage private enterprise to meet unmet needs.

Construction is the easiest aspect of the program. The management of subsidized housing for families with limited income suggests some of the same possibilities that have stigmatized public housing in many places. A few bad home owners or managers can cause a building or a neighborhood to decline. Those who upbraid public housing authorities for creating potential new slums must realize that some of the new, privately produced, subsidized programs carry the same potentials. The industry has social responsibilities. We must do as good a job or better than in self-supporting, non-subsidized housing. If we do not, we will be charged with creating the slums of the future. We will not have provided the environment that must go with a decent house.

5. Finally, there is a prevalent myth that as the world's richest nation, we have sufficient capital for everything our people want or need. The fact is, we are capital poor. The United States is affluent, but it carries burdens as the leader of the free world that dilute its resources. We must realize that we are not so capital rich as to be able to do everything at once.

**What Can Businessmen Do?** What constructive contribution can business managers make? We must discourage political promises of new worlds for everybody overnight. My greatest criticism of the 1965–1968 period in our national life is this: We businessmen slept while the political leadership tried to fight a major international engagement and combat a growing domestic struggle and social unrest at the same time. There just was not enough cash available to do both, even if one concedes that both are necessary.

Maybe the time has come to regulate the flow of private capital, within limits, to fill the economic-social need.  If the Treasury and large corporations issue debt instruments at relatively high interest rates, the savings institutions, long the mainstay of conventional financing for housing, will decline.  All of this talk of the free money market, with interest rates seeking their own level, is not supported by some of the regulations that are used.  The burning question is—are we willing to regulate to give priority to economic goals with a heavy social ingredient?

We cannot realize our economic-social goals if we continue up-and-down fluctuations or continue to offer new programs before existing ones are given a good test.  We will not realize standards of decency by making temporary trailers permanent homes or by reducing amenities below acceptance levels.  The tranquility of our society demands special efforts in the fields of housing, education and jobs.  We need to support that conviction by allocating public funds and even regulating private credit.

We must place a high priority on our national commitment to provide a decent house in a suitable environment for every American family.  That priority is lacking.  If we mean to achieve major social goals, the distribution of our limited capital demands the establishment of effective priorities.

There are times when only a well-known cliche can express the flavor of the hour: *We are living in revolutionary times.*  Neither the generation gap, which is traditional, nor the demand of the have-nots, which is historical, are of ordinary proportions.  The compelling peril of our predicament is that we may yield to hysterical solutions, ignore sound historical precedents or fail to assert positive and achievable objectives.

A free and democratic society can only persist if it supports a free enterprise system for those engaged in business and commerce and a free labor movement for those who man our production facilities.  The government and laws of such a society must do justice to all, including those who may be temporarily or permanently disadvantaged economically or socially.

**A Revolution in Housing.**    Recent events suggest the possibility that a revolution in housing production and financing is in the making.  To the extent that this encourages housing production for the economically and socially disadvantaged, it is a good; to the extent that conventional financing and production of housing for low middle income families is impeded, it is an ill; but, to the extent that new financing techniques open new sources of capital, it is a good; to the extent that new financing techniques shorten the supply of savings flowing into housing production, it is an ill.

Improvement in meeting subsidized housing needs is no cause for relaxation.  I urge the President to convene those who are vitally concerned with choices in the mix of capital use, both public and private, to prepare a meaningful and perhaps revolutionary program.  The task I have in mind demands a group deeply involved with day to day operations of the government and not a group of outsiders.  I believe the imperatives of the problem call for a governmental group consisting at least of the following:

The Director of the Office of Management and Budget.
The Secretary of the Treasury.
The Secretary of HUD.

## COMMENTARY

### by Edward E. Edwards *

Publicly declared goals for housing are very much like New Year's resolutions; they express more wish than determination. They also tend to be repeated year after year, and it is this repetition that has produced so much of the mythology that surrounds the housing problem.

My favorite myth is the one that housebuilding should be made a contra-cyclical industry, declining when everything else is expanding, and expanding when everything else is declining. Such a policy might make sense if there were no genuine need for more houses. On the other hand, the only reason why such a policy has a chance of working is that the need for housing is so great that demand cannot even be slowed down by a depression!

Why should we make a "yo-yo" of such an essential industry? Why should we adopt—and accept—stabilization policies that cut back housebuilding when everything else is expanding, then have to dream up a limitless number of new programs each time the economy slows down? And why do we listen to the arguments against credit controls in other sectors of the economy as being an interference with the free market?' Isn't it credit control that is used to cut back and then to stimulate housebuilding?

Our author's selection of myths, and his proof that that is what they are, should convince us that the housing problem is going to get worse unless business and government dedicate themselves to solving it. His doubts as to the availability of capital and as to the possibility of cutting costs are especially sobering. And so is his fear that programs to meet the housing needs of low income families may merely shift supply from one group to another, without increasing total production, which is the only real solution.

Philip Klutznick undoubtedly knows more about the myths and realities in housing than most of us know. His years of successful business entrepreneurship in this field are matched with equally distinguished public service. He was president of the company that developed Park Forest, winner of the American Institute of Architects post-war award for community development, and the National Association of Home Builders National Award of Merit. He headed the companies that developed Old Orchard, Oakbrook Center, and River Oaks, which are among the nation's 10 largest shopping centers.

Klutznick served as Commissioner of the Federal Public Housing Authority under both President Roosevelt and President Truman. He was appointed by President Kennedy as Representative of the United States to the Economic and Social Council of the United Nations with the rank of Ambassador in 1961–62.

Currently, Klutznick is a trustee and co-chairman of Research and Policy of the committee for Economic Development. A CED statement on Policy for Housing is now being researched under our author's chairmanship.

---

* As consulting editor in the MGIC Newsletter.

The Chairman of the Board of Governors of the Federal Reserve System.

The Chairman of the Federal Home Loan Bank Board.

The Chairman of the Council of Economic Advisors.

If we mean to produce new and effective adjustments in distributing or guiding the flow of the nation's capital, the job needs the minds and attention of those most knowledgeable and concerned with the process.

We are in the very eye of the storm. Revolutionary times demand revolutionary ideas, soundly based, arising out of firm but mutually developed divisions of labor between the public and the private sectors, with each trying to understand and help the other. The day of carefully guarding the gates against one another is at an end. Our tomorrow depends upon it.

### Questions

1. Do you agree or disagree with the author's list of myths? Explain.
2. Discuss the statement: "It does not make sense to meet the housing needs of lower income families at the expense of those who should be able to pay their own way and who also need housing. This is not increasing housing production. It is merely shifting the housing supply from one group to another."
3. What do you think of Professor Edwards suggestion that the myth that housing is a contra-cyclical industry should be a debt to the best? What other myths might be added to the list?
4. In your opinion, what is the best way to bring about a "revolution in housing?"

### STUDY PROJECT 21–2

#### Operation Breakthrough *

*Operation Breakthrough*, HUD Secretary George Romney's program for combining the potentials of modern industrial methods and large scale production to provide housing for a mass market, is easily the most exciting move yet made to bring residential construction into the technological age. More than this, in spite of the cynicism of those who have observed or participated in similar efforts in the past, it just might work.

The hope of "industrializing" house building is an ancient one. In its modern manifestation it goes back at least to the emergency housing of World War I and to the prototypes erected at the Chicago Exposition of 1933. Factory production of construction components made some advance following the research of the U. S. Forest Products Laboratory and the beginnings of practical prefabrication in the 1930's. Prefabricated methods made a significant contribution to the World War II housing program; and, in the immediate postwar years, a bold though ill-starred effort was made to reorganize residential building on an industrialized basis.

The results varied from modest success to dismal failure. The reasons for the repeated disappointment were generally the same.

* By Miles L. Colean; reproduced by permission of Mortgage Guaranty Insurance Corporation, from the *MGIC Newsletter*.

1. The innovations for the most part were limited to factory production of wall, floor, and roof components, which ordinarily represent no more than 25 per cent of total cost—thus leaving only a small margin for cost reduction.
2. Even these innovations were frequently blocked by crippling local building codes and restrictive union work rules, while the same obstacles made virtually impossible any innovation at all in mechanical and electrical elements, which otherwise would offer promising sources of cost reduction.
3. The above limitations kept housing a relatively small-scale industry subject to traditional small-scale financing for small-scale markets.

Secretary Romney came to his present job with a long and successful experience in large industrial operations out of which he could envisage the results that might follow the application of similar elements of scale to a tradition-bound industry. He saw that what was needed was indeed a breakthrough—a breakthrough of local legal and extra-legal restrictions, a breakthrough to wide markets, a breakthrough to large resources for technological development and capital.

Moreover, the Secretary had some reasons to believe that the time at last was ripe for his idea. During the decade in which housing was failing to come up to expectations, a number of significant developments had been taking place without attracting great public attention.

1. Home building organizations using more or less conventional methods, but applying organizational and managerial skill of a high order, were achieving unusually large annual production in large and growing metropolitan areas.
2. A number of these relatively large building firms were being acquired by industrial conglomerates in both unrelated as well as related fields of activity, thus making available to the builders greatly enlarged access to capital.
3. Mobile homes, true prototypes of modular dwelling units, were being produced in increasingly large volume each year, so far beyond official notice as not even to be included in the official count of new units. This extraordinary development proved that large numbers of people would accept these units as their settled abodes, notwithstanding unconventional appearance, cramped accommodations, frequently unattractive and inconvenient locations (often the result of hostile local ordinances), and exceedingly high money costs.
4. An inordinate housing demand, made up to considerable degree of small families in both the very young and the elderly age groups, created a market potential such as had not previously been experienced.

These developments provided a strong base from which to move forward. What was needed was to develop the "systems" approach, found in still rudimentary form in the mobile home, so as to take into account all elements of the dwelling and to give the systematized mass produced units freedom from hampering restrictions and access to markets and sources of capital. To these ends, HUD has endeavored to stimulate through *Breakthrough* the provision of complete housing packages, including design, production, assured markets, and adequate financing.

**The Breakthrough Idea.** To accomplish all this, governors, mayors and county officials were at the start asked to define housing needs and demands within their jurisdictions, to designate available sites, and to grant exemption from building and zoning provisions that would impede the erection of the proposed housing. Then industrial organizations—whether or not previously concerned directly or indirectly with housing construction—were asked to submit proposals for the design and production of dwelling units. A unique relationship between producers and local political officials was thus established. Labor organizations have been surprisingly cooperative in matters of factory employment and the elimination of cross-jurisdictional projects.

**Some Limitations.** At this stage, *Breakthrough* is still an exploratory and experimental project. Unless this is thoroughly understood, HUD faces the danger of deflated expectations, since the full potential of the program, however sound, will not be realized in the initial effort.

Although most of the construction systems proposed in the initial stage are suited only to single family houses or low-rise apartment buildings (in contrast to the high-rise structures called for in many central city locations), the technological side of the program is probably the most capable of successful achievement, especially if the already promising labor-management arrangements can be more broadly applied. The know-how is present and the resources are available to the new types of producers to assure not only large output and ultimate cost reduction but also savings in time (for both manufacture and erection) and dependability of quality.

**More Than Technology Needed.** As Secretary Romney has said, progress in building technology must be paralleled with access to a mass housing market and to the financing that market has to have. In these respects, most of the solutions offered in the first phase of *Breakthrough* are tentative at best.

The shortcomings of the financing arrangements have already been noted. Traditional methods of housing finance, like traditional methods of home building, will be inadequate for the mass housing needs of the future. Only one promising novelty—the GNMA guaranteed, mortgage-backed security—has been produced, but its success depends either upon better assurances of monetary stability than are yet at hand or some adaptations to an habitually inflationary economy that will permit future income adjustments. Unfortunately the financial community does not yet appear to be sufficiently imbued with a sense of urgency and opportunity to undertake the concerted kind of effort that is being made by the technological innovators.

Another problem barely touched upon in the first phase of *Breakthrough* is land. Plainly, local officials cannot be depended upon to supply sites indefinitely nor is surplus federal urban land in sufficient supply to be a long-term factor.

*Breakthrough* cannot be expected to solve these problems, most of which are beyond the jurisdiction of the federal government. HUD can point out their existence and may be of help in suggesting solutions. Final answers must come from the state, county and municipal governments, supported by the whole-hearted determination of their constituencies that cities must become better places to live in and that the supply of housing must be brought into closer relation with the need.

## COMMENTARY

### by Edward E. Edwards *

Miles Colean, one of our best known housing economists, was first an architect. He is thus exceptionally well qualified to review and appraise innovations that may be occurring in housebuilding.

Americans have long believed that houses are too expensive, and that they could be built at much lower cost if only technology and management know-how could be put to work on the problem. Secretary Romney, an obvious believer, has put the idea to the test in *Operation Breakthrough* and now everyone is waiting for the miraculous results. Unfortunately, production miracles do not happen overnight, and we should not expect any more from *Breakthrough* than proof that modern technology and business expertise can be applied successfully to the housing problem.

We should assume, as I believe Miles Colean does, that *Breakthrough* will produce some product improvement and cost reduction ideas, and also point the way toward further progress. But that does not mean that our housing problem will quickly be solved, or that its ultimate solution will require less new capital than otherwise. Millions of housing units today are obsolete by present standards. A real breakthrough in housing design and materials could easily make many more millions obsolete. Also, improved quality and lower costs very likely will not result in people spending less of their income for housing, but will cause them instead to buy (or rent) larger or better equipped houses, or perhaps to buy a second home.

If I am correct in assuming that families will demand housing in proportion to their ability to pay, rather than spend less and less for housing, the most important cost factors will be high interest rates, and rising dollar (as versus real) costs of labor and material as a result of inflation. What we need in addition to a technological breakthrough is a financial breakthrough, one that will bring an end to inflation and return interest rates to a lower and more reasonable level. While it is popular to blame inflation on a bad mix of monetary and fiscal policy, hence to put the burden on government, the ultimate solution undoubtedly requires a higher rate of personal savings. Getting people to save a little more, spend a little less, may be as difficult as building a better house at lower cost.

---

* As consulting editor in the MGIC Newsletter.

---

### Questions

1. What factors outside the construction and related technology (financing, developing, etc.) might limit the success of Operation Breakthrough?
2. What are the expected benefits of Operation Breakthrough?
3. What role may land play in the success or failure of Operation Breakthrough?
4. Is a financial breakthrough as important as a technological breakthrough? Why or why not?
5. How might Breakthrough be improved or supplemented?

# 22

# Business Real Estate: Commercial and Industrial Properties

## BUSINESS REAL ESTATE DECISIONS

The scope of the markets for commercial and industrial real estate varies; but in most instances it may be thought of as regional, and in some cases national and even international, in extent. Decisions related to these types of properties are affected by national, regional, and local factors.

### Scope of Markets

The leasing of a retail store is likely to involve virtually a national market if the tenant prospects are chain organizations. The extent of the interest of chain organizations in purchasing or leasing the store, however, will depend on local conditions, on the strength of the local market, and on the competitive position of the property under consideration in that market. Space in an office building may be leased by organizations operating on a regional or national basis, but their interest in a specific space will be influenced greatly by local market factors. Much the same thing is true of the market for industrial real estate.

## Owners and Users

Decisions to purchase or lease commercial and industrial real estate are generated by prospects for returns from the use of the properties that fit the needs of particular firms. The users of such real estate may own or rent. Investors may purchase for lease to users. Builders, promoters, and speculators may develop new properties for lease or sale to business firms. Decisions to buy or lease commercial and industrial real estate depend in part on the present level and future prospects of general business conditions, on the relative prosperity of the particular line of business activity involved, and on local real estate market conditions. As in the case of residential real estate, income and income prospects, plus the terms and availability of financing, play a major role in determining the strength of demand.

## Administration of Business Real Estate

In some business firms the decisions relating to real estate are made by one or another of the top officials. Only an occasional decision of importance is necessary. Between such decisions, real estate involves largely housekeeping activities that are parceled out to one of the operating divisions of the company.

For a growing number of business firms, however, real estate is of sufficient importance to call for full-time management direction and a specialized staff. This is notably true in chain store organizations, firms in the rubber industry and in petroleum, organic chemicals, and paper products. Of course, for firms in the construction field or in land development and subdividing, real estate is of basic importance to top management. Lumbering companies, public utilities, railroads, and various other transportation lines pay special attention to real estate functions.

In many cases the real estate manager of a company reports to the vice president and treasurer. In some cases the treasurer or assistant treasurer performs the required real estate functions in addition to his other duties. In a few instances there is a vice president for real estate because of its importance in the company's program.

## HISTORICAL CHANGES IN RETAILING

The department store originated in Paris and was introduced into the United States in the 1860's by Marshall Field in Chicago, Wanamaker in Philadelphia, and Stewart in New York. With the development of mass transportation beginning with horse-drawn streetcars in the 1860's, cable cars, elevated lines, and electric surface cars in the 1890's and subways in the early years of the twentieth century, downtown locations increased significantly in importance. All the various types of transportation converged in the central business district and created high land values at central locations such as State and Madison streets in Chicago, 34th Street and Sixth Avenue in New York, and Broad and Market streets in Philadephia. Department stores sought out such locations expanding both laterally and vertically. Macy's in New York, Hudson's in Detroit, and Marshall Field's in Chicago developed into huge establishments of 2 million square feet or more area and reached sales in peak shopping periods in excess of a million dollars a day.

### Decentralization

The department store continued to play a major role in retailing despite the decentralization of retail activity. They became the chief magnets for outlying shopping centers just as had been the case in downtown business districts.

The decentralization of retailing activities started after World War I. It was characterized at first by the rise of outlying centers at streetcar intersections or streetcar transfer corners, subway stations, and suburban railroad stations. The downtown area was not affected very much except in the larger cities.

### Automobiles and Highways

The automobile brought further decentralization, extending the process. This process of decentralization, however, proceeded at a leisurely rate. There were 27 million cars in the United States as early as 1929 but they had only little impact on the pattern of retail distribution. For example, the Country Club Plaza in Kansas City was built in 1920 and was the first large shopping center that did not depend on mass transportation but relied on private automobiles. Some other centers of this type began to make their appearance, but it was not until after World War II that the shopping center became a major force in the retailing pattern.

### Early Shopping Centers

Early centers of this type included Silver Spring in the Washington, D.C., area, Cameron Village in Raleigh, North Carolina, and Utica Square in Tulsa, Oklahoma. These were built on vacant tracts of land near the center of the city and at the edge of built-up areas.

As the highway network around cities expanded, opportunities for shopping centers, multiplied rapidly. Northland in Detroit, Old Orchard in Chicago, North Shore north of Boston, Southdale in Minneapolis, and many others were built on large tracts of land on or near expressways in trade areas with a large total population and income, but often there were relatively few families in the immediate vicinity.

### Mall Type Centers

The first of the mall-type centers with stores in the center of a large tract surrounded by parking was Northgate in Seattle. It was designed by John Graham and opened in 1950. The first types were open malls. The closed, heated and air-conditioned malls which have become very popular were first developed in the late 1950's and early 1960's. Examples include Ward Parkway in Kansas City (1958), Cherry Hill in New Jersey (1961), and Sharpstown in Houston (1961).

## CENTRAL BUSINESS DISTRICT

In the central retail district are located the largest department stores and the greatest concentration of stores selling women's and men's apparel, shoes, and jewelry, as well as variety stores. These stores are usually grouped together in a few blocks, within walking distance of each other in what is known as the "100 per cent" retail location.

The central business district often includes the central office building area or the financial district of a city, so that the office workers contribute to retail sales. It often serves also as the entertainment and cultural center. In the central business district there may also be located state, city, county, or federal office buildings and the courts. In the larger centers, international offices, both private and governmental, are often found as well.

### Location

This concentrated business district is usually at the converging point of mass transportation lines leading to all parts of the metropolitan area, such as State and Madison Streets in Chicago, 34th Street and Sixth Avenue in New York City, and 8th and Market Streets in Philadelphia. In smaller cities this center is often located at the intersection of the two principal traffic arteries.

This main business district has the highest pedestrian traffic count in the city. The store rentals and the land values are the highest in the metropolitan area. Although this business district frequently does not occupy more than 1 per cent of the area of the city, it may represent from 10 to 25 per cent of the total real estate value.

### Convenience and Competition

The basic reason for the concentration of all of these stores in fashion goods lines is the desire of shoppers to compare styles and fashions as to quality and price. It has been found that competing stores in apparel lines sell more merchandise per square foot when they are grouped together than when they are isolated. It is thus not merely the convenience and accessibility of the central business district to residents of the entire metropolitan area, but its ability to offer a complete range of styles and fashions that cause the volume of sales to reach the highest levels in these central areas. This is largely what prompts business decisions to locate there. Department stores cannot thrive on neighborhood trade because they cannot afford to offer a sufficiently large stock of merchandise to such a limited market. Such stores can operate successfully, however, in the larger outlying shopping centers.

### Volume

The store managers who bid for space in the central business district and pay the high rents for a position in the "100 per cent" location do so because of the opportunity to obtain a high volume of sales. They would locate on side streets or in outlying neighborhoods if their volume of business would be as great as on "Main Street." In fact, as we have said, some types of stores, like supermarkets, can do a record volume of business in neighborhood centers and do not need to pay the premium for central business locations. Other types of stores, like furniture stores, with a low volume of sales per square foot, are located on the fringe of the central business districts where rents are lower, or on the upper floors of buildings in central business districts.

### Department Stores

The greatest magnets in the central business district are the large department stores, which consist in effect of many stores under one roof. However, practically 60 per cent of their sales consist of apparel. These stores frequently occupy whole blocks, such as Macy's in New York, Marshall Field's in Chicago, and Hudson's in Detroit. The largest stores have 2 million square feet of floor area in a single building and have huge annual sales totals.

### Space Arrangements

Department stores usually own the land and building occupied by the store, or lease it on a long-term basis. The department store is a specialized building and can usually be used only by another department store. Chain department store organizations have grown in importance; for example, Allied Stores operate some ninety stores, each under an individual firm name, and have aggregate sales of around $1 billion. This organization has bought independent stores in many cities. Many department stores operate branches, which are usually located in the same metropolitan area; thus they can obtain the benefit of advertising in the local newspapers and use the same warehousing facilities. Other chain department stores include the May Company, Macy's, Federated Department Stores, Lord & Taylor, and others.

The sale or purchase of department stores as real estate does not occur frequently. The usual transaction is the purchase of the store with its land and buildings, fixtures, stock of goods, and good will by a national chain department store organization such as Allied or Federated Stores.

### Nearby Locations

Department stores typically generate demands for nearby space on the part of specialty apparel, shoe, and variety stores. Such firms often seek locations near a department store, which attracts customers from all over the metropolitan area by its advertising.

National chain organizations have discovered, from analyzing their own sales experience, the conditions under which they can thrive best. When they are selling merchandise in a certain price range, they seek locations where shoppers in that income group congregate. They know which types of stores complement each other. Many chain stores prefer to locate between two of the largest department stores.

## SHOPPING CENTERS

Whether there are too many or not enough shopping centers in any community depends in part upon the type established. We have classified them into the following types: [1]

### The Regional or Super-Regional Center

The regional centers typically include two to as many as four department stores of 100,000 square feet or more as the principal stores, supplemented by numerous women's and men's apparel stores, shoe stores, house-

---

[1] Hoyt, "Classification and Significant Characteristics of Shopping Centers," *The Appraisal Journal* (April, 1958), pp. 214–22. See also Hoyt's article "Appraisal of Shopping Centers," in *Encyclopedia of Real Estate Appraising* (Englewood Cliffs, N.J.: Prentice-Hall, Inc., 1959), pp. 281–95, and Homer Hoyt, *According to Hoyt* (2nd ed.; Washington, D.C.: Hoyt, 1970), Sec. XI, pp. 622–691; 813–828.

**Fig. 22–1.** Southgate Center, Cleveland, Ohio. (Courtesy Aerial Surveys, Inc.)

hold appliance stores, furniture stores, drugstores, and supermarkets with a total store area of 250,000 to 1,000,000 square feet on a 35- to 100-acre site. Around 200,000 people may be required to support this type of center.

### Community Center

The community center usually has a junior department store such as a J. C. Penney or W. T. Grant store as its principal tenant. This main store typically has 25,000 or more square feet, and the center has an over-all store area of 100,000 to 400,000 square feet on a 15- to 40-acre site. Super-markets, drugstores, variety stores, and some apparel stores are found in such a center.

## Neighborhood Convenience Center

The larger neighborhood center is one in which a variety store such as Woolworth or Kresge, with 10,000 to 20,000 square feet, is usually the principal unit, with a total store area of 50,000 to 100,000 square feet on a site of 10 to 20 acres. A supermarket, a drugstore, and local convenience stores are typical. Smaller neighborhood centers take a variety of forms.

## The Discount House

In recent years the discount house has played a growing role in the retailing field. Such stores as Korvette, Zayre's K-Mart (Kresge), Woolco (Woolworth), and others are important in this connection. They are self-service stores with the customer waiting on himself, paying cash, and taking his merchandise away in his own car, or paying a delivery charge. These stores are often large units with 100,000 square feet or more of store area on 10 or more acres and carry a number of lines of merchandise. Variety stores have moved into the discount area.

## Supermarkets

The recent trend toward the large supermarket of 20,000 to 40,000 square feet of store area, with a free parking lot, has caused hundreds of isolated locations to develop. Typically, 5,000 families will support a large supermarket. These stores seek locations with enough vacant land to afford free parking to their customers, and they may select an area where there are no other stores in order to secure such a tract. Such stores can do a record volume of business without supplementary establishments, since most families do not combine food purchasing with apparel or other shopping.

## Franchising

Although franchises have been used for a long time, the concept has been expanded, especially to retailing activities, in recent years. Examples include motels such as Howard Johnson's and Holiday Inns, drive-in eating places such as McDonald's and Denny's restaurants, auto and trailer rentals, building products and services and others. In general, franchising tries to combine a national effort with local ownership and initiative. Real estate brokers have been involved in franchising through the selection of desirable locations for various types of outlets and in some cases helping to arrange for construction and local financing.[2]

## Shopping Center Trends

The largest regional centers often duplicate the central business district, with several of the leading department stores represented in the location. However, rivalry between department stores has prevented such developments in a number of cases. In Philadelphia, Baltimore, Washington, New York City, and St. Louis, each principal department store has tended to develop its own location instead of joining with other department stores in the establishment of one large center. As a result a number of medium-size centers have evolved in such cases, each with a small following of other stores rather than one super center.

In Milwaukee, however, Marshall Field's and Gimbel's have occupied Mayfair center. In Westchester County in New York, Wanamaker's and Gimbel's have stores in the same center; in Evergreen Plaza, south of Chicago, there are The Fair, Montgomery Ward, and Carson Pirie Scott & Co.; North Shore of Boston, includes Jordan Marsh and Filene's; and in Lennox Square in Atlanta, Rich's and Davison & Paxon are located. Negotiations are under way in other cities to bring the leading department stores together in one center.

It is now the prevailing trend for the leading department stores to join together in one large center with a large department store at each end and one at the center or on a wing of an air-conditioned mall. As many as a hundred specialty shops may be located between them. Older centers that have two department stores have in some cases attracted a third by adding a wing or a parking deck. Office buildings have been built on the periphery of some regional centers.

## Parking

Free automobile parking for the shoppers is the indispensable requirement for the shopping center. The amount of land that should be set aside for parking varies according to the population of shoppers who come on mass transportation lines and the number who live within walking distance. For centers in which most of the shoppers come by private automobile, a 4-to-1 ratio between parking and mall areas and net selling area is considered sufficient. It is not necessary to take care of the peak load of Christmas shoppers, as parking areas used for this peak load would be idle eleven months of the year.

It is estimated that an average car space should produce an annual sales volume of $10,000 to $12,000 worth of general merchandise and

[2] See National Institute of Real Estate Brokers, Division Reports, *Franchising and the Realtor* (Chicago, Ill.: The Institute, 1968).

$15,000 to $18,000 worth of food.  The necessity of providing a large parking area means that even a small neighborhood center should have 5 acres of land, and a large regional shopping center 50 to 100 acres.  A developer planning a shopping center usually has to find this amount of land under one ownership or in a few ownerships, because he does not have the power of condemnation and may have to pay prohibitive prices in acquiring a number of separate parcels.  Since 80 per cent of the land must be made available for free parking, an extra-high land cost makes such projects unprofitable.

## Location

Some developers have followed the old-style retail pattern and located their centers at major highway intersections.  This creates a problem of traffic congestion, because the shoppers' traffic is added to that of the through traffic.  It is desirable that the shopping center location be on a major thoroughfare such as a radial highway and near a circumferential highway going around the periphery of the city.  It is not necessary or even desirable that a center be located at a cloverleaf intersection, if it is somewhere near the point of traffic interchange.  Frequently, the ideal location is not available because it is already filled in with houses, so the largest available tract under one ownership is selected.  Traffic volume on existing highways must be considered in planning a shopping center.  The problem of crossing any heavy streams of traffic must also be studied.

The location must have a sufficient number of families and buying power within a reasonable driving-time distance to support it, with allowances for competing centers of the same type.  The trade area cannot be measured entirely in terms of driving-time distance in all directions, however, because shoppers will often drive halfway across a state in rural areas to reach an outlying regional center, while they will not come from a downtown area only a few miles away.

The location of new shopping centers has been influenced considerably by the federal highway program, with its provision for limited-access roads between major cities and with belt highways around cities.  Instead of building shopping centers on the edge of the old cities, as in the case of the early postwar developments, new centers tend to be located at central points between a number of large and small cities.

## FUTURE RETAILING TRENDS

Population growth is likely to bring rising demands for single-family homes and for garden apartments in outlying locations.  Thus the urban area is likely to be extended farther, and probably a new group of shopping centers will rise to serve this outlying population belt.

**Fig. 22–2.** Northland Shopping Center, Southfield, Michigan. (Courtesy Urban Land Institute.)

Developments of this type will not eliminate retailing activities in the central cities. Improvements in mass transportation may revitalize many of the downtown areas and add growth potential to the retail establishments located there. New downtown developments that combine hotels, stores, offices and apartments in one aggregate like Bunker Hill in Los Angeles, Atwater Park Plaza in Montreal, the Church Street Redevelopment in New Haven, Penn Square in Philadelphia, and others will provide highly attractive centers. Many of these will include closed malls for shopping that will compete effectively with these types of developments in outlying regional centers.

### The Retail Brokerage Field

Emphasis has been placed upon shopping centers because this will undoubtedly be a major field for commercial brokerage and lending activity in the future. These centers are usually owned by one proprietor or developer. All the tenants are granted joint rights in the parking area and, as a result, a single store cannot readily be sold. However, the leasing of stores in these centers and the management of the centers has created a new field of real estate endeavor. These developments have required that adjustments in the older business districts be made. Tenants who move to outlying centers often are supplanted by others who find advantages in central locations.

### Lease Information

Prospective lessors or lessees of space often rely on brokers for information to guide their decisions. The broker who specializes in commercial leases hence must secure all the information available regarding the terms of leases in the area in which he is operating. These leases are usually recorded, but the rentals paid are not always revealed in the recorded instrument. Representatives of insurance companies and other brokers usually have knowledge of leases in which they have participated and can exchange information.

Retail store leases now are usually made on the basis of a percentage of sales, with a minimum guarantee. These percentages vary with the volume of sales per square foot and the type of store building required. The owner is of course primarily interested in the number of dollars per square foot he receives in rent. Supermarkets usually pay only 1 per cent of sales as rent, but they have sales volumes of from $150 to $350 a square foot, so that the rent per square foot would vary from $1.50 to $3.50.

Most apparel stores will pay 5 per cent of their gross sales as rent, and with sales volumes of from $50 to $100 per square foot, they would be paying $2.50 to $5 a square foot. Furniture stores have a lower volume per square foot because of the large area required to display davenports, tables, beds, and other bulky items. Their sales might not exceed $30 a square foot, so that on a 5 per cent basis they would not pay much over $1.50 a square foot in reñt.

Percentage leases in high-volume stores which yield $5 to $15 a square foot in rent, cover not only interest, depreciation, and real estate taxes on the building, but also a return on high land value. The land value is determined by capitalizing the amount that remains after deducting the annual charges on the building and real estate taxes on the land.

Retail store leases are usually executed for a term of ten years or more if a new building is being constructed for the tenant. Shorter terms may be employed for stores already in existence. These leases often provide for an option to renew on the part of the tenant.

### Guarantees and Percentages

In practically every lease in a shopping center, provision is made not only for a minimum guarantee but also a rental based on percentage of sales. Rents paid above the minimum guarantee are often referred to as overage rents. The minimum guarantees of strong tenants such as national chain organizations are the chief factor in providing security for mortgage loans. A high minimum, however, is often obtained at the sacrifice of a lower percentage of sales.

Percentage leases are sometimes on a sliding scale, with the percentage declining after a certain volume of sales is reached. In negotiating the leases the prospective tenant often asks for extras in the form of special store fronts, air conditioning, mezzanine floors, finished basements, and sometimes even the store fixtures. Consequently the real estate broker negotiating the lease must have a thorough knowledge of every element of construction and equipment costs.

National chain stores frequently offer the store owner a percentage which is fixed on a national basis. Extra percentages, however, may be obtained in centers which provide special features, such as special air conditioning, underground delivery facilities, or expensive store fronts. A regional shopping center with large department stores is often in a better bargaining position than a shopping center without a key tenant. For this reason the builders or developers often will give inducements in the form of a low minimum or low percentage lease to a key tenant such as a department store.

For certain types of stores, such as barbershops or small types of businesses that do not keep accurate books, the rental may be set on a fixed monthly basis plus a cost-of-living adjustment rather than on a percentage of sales. The Consumer's Price Index issued by the Bureau of Labor Statistics (Department of Commerce) is one of the more frequently used indices.

## OFFICE BUILDINGS

The modern office building evolved as a result of the need for bringing business executives, brokers, lawyers, investors, and others within walking distance of each other so that they could meet quickly in face-to-face contact.

### Early Development

The early office buildings prior to 1880 did not exceed six stories in height, except in a few rare instances.  Taller buildings were not practical because the walls of a solid masonry building would be so thick at the base that they would absorb most of the ground floor rentable area.  The invention of the steel-frame skyscraper in Chicago resulted in the construction of the Home Insurance Building in 1884.  The development of the hydraulic and then the electric elevator contributed further to the development of the modern skyscraper.  The early office buildings in Chicago, such as the Tacoma Building, the Capitol Building, and the Masonic Temple, built in 1889–90, did not exceed 16 to 22 stories in height.  After 1923, a revision of the zoning ordinance in Chicago permitted higher towers.  New York City has had the tallest office buildings, the Empire State Building having 102 stories, the Chrysler Building 73 stories, and the Woolworth Building 58 stories.  Chicago is challenging New York, however, with the John Hancock Building, The First National Bank Building, Marina City and the projected Sears Building which will be the tallest of all.  Many other cities have developed major office buildings in recent years.

### Supply of Office Space

Most of the larger office buildings that have ever been erected in this country are still in existence.  The office building supply is a result of an accretion to a large, existing stock of building space.  Office buildings have been built in a series of waves.  Periods of overbuilding in which more office building space was constructed than could be absorbed were followed by years of complete cessation of office building.  Office building in Chicago reached peaks in the early 1890's, from 1910 to 1914, and from 1923 to 1930.  Office building in New York City followed a cyclical pattern which was somewhat different from that in Chicago.  Recent years have witnessed another great period of expansion of office building construction.

### Overbuilding Problems

After periods of overbuilding of office space, office rents and net incomes tend to decline and may remain depressed for long periods, even if general business conditions are good. There was practically no office building construction in Chicago after the Field Building was completed in 1930 until the Prudential Insurance Building was constructed in 1953. It required a period of twenty-three years to absorb the excess supply of 8,500,000 square feet of vacant space that was created during the 1920's. In rapidly growing cities in Texas and California, the construction of office buildings has been an almost continuous process in recent years. Certain cities tend to develop as office building centers and there is no direct relationship between population and the amount of office building space.

## Office Rentals

The rent for modern office building space normally includes heat, cleaning service, janitor service, electricity, and water. Consequently the increasing cost of these services has compelled property managers to secure higher rents for space in new buildings. Because of the cost of these services, office building net income may decline rapidly when vacancies increase.

The office buildings in the United States erected prior to 1930 still constitute a significant proportion of the existing supply. A large number of these buildings were sold at foreclosure and refinanced with lower mortgages. Consequently these buildings have been able to carry the interest on the refinanced mortgages as well as operating costs and still rent for modest amounts. New buildings erected at current costs must in most cities secure much higher rentals. Consequently new office buildings must be able to compete with office buildings constructed at much lower cost levels. Their many attractive new features, however, often enable them to compete to advantage.

## Office Building Occupancy

Some office buildings are designed for use by a major corporation or government agency. Most office buildings, however, are erected for multiple-tenant occupancy. This means that a number of small offices are rented to a variety of tenants on every floor. In this type of occupancy the building manager must provide all services. Public hallways cannot be rented. When an entire floor is rented to a single company, however, all the floor area will produce an income.

Office buildings located in central business districts frequently contain retail stores on the ground floor. In financial districts, banks often occupy the ground floor of an office building which they own, and rent the space in the upper floors. In a few cases, such as the Terminal Building in Cleveland and the Carew Tower in Cincinnati, a hotel and department store are combined with the office building. In St. Louis, large department stores typically occupy the lower floors of office buildings, with offices on the upper floors. The Merchandise Mart of Chicago has offices on the five lower floors and manufacturers' representatives occupy the space on the upper floors. In office buildings on such main retail streets as State Street in Chicago there are numerous dentists' and doctors' offices. In other buildings, retail stores are found on upper floors, intermingled with offices. These office buildings with mixed types of uses involve special problems of management.

### Types of Office Building Locations

Office building districts may be concentrated, as in the Chicago Loop, or scattered in a number of sub-office building locations, as in New York. More recently offices have developed in suburban areas. In the course of time, office building districts tend to move. In Chicago the office building area of around 1890 was located at the south end of the Loop. Later new office buildings were developed on North Michigan Avenue. In New York there was a movement away from the downtown Wall Street areas to the uptown areas. Construction in the Wall Street financial district has revived in recent years.

Some office buildings have been developed in outlying locations, thus stimulating further the suburban trend. In some cases, office buildings are developed in conjunction with larger regional shopping centers, Northland in Detroit and Ward Parkway in Kansas City being cases in point. Of special importance in such locations are medical and dental clinics, real estate offices, and the home offices of various corporations. Parking is of growing importance. A one to-one ratio of parking space to office space is considered adequate and often necessary to get financing. Redevelopment programs have been important factors in office building development in such cities as Pittsburgh and Philadelphia. In nearly all cities new office buildings tend to be located in the direction of high-income areas; for example, to the northwest in Washington, D.C., to the north in New York City, to the south in Houston, and to the northwest in Los Angeles.

### Advantages of Various Office Building Locations

Tenants seek offices at points of maximum convenience from the standpoint of their own particular lines of business. Brokers typically want offices near the Stock Exchange, lawyers near the courts or title companies, insurance men near the insurance company offices, and the like. Specialized office building districts tend to develop, such as the financial district on LaSalle Street in Chicago, the fire and casualty insurance center in New York, and the advertising, radio, and television center in uptown New York. Convenient transportation to residential areas is also important. The midtown area of New York has the advantages of the major terminals with their suburban trains and the subways; the Loop in Chicago is at the point where suburban railroads, elevated lines, busses, and subways converge.

### Insurance Company Experience

Some organizations, for example insurance companies, maintain large office buildings for their own use. Here face-to-face contacts with other companies are not important and there is no need for them to be near other office buildings. The large insurance companies in New York—the Metropolitan Life Insurance Company, the New York Life, the Equitable, and the Mutual—probably maintain central offices because at the converging points of subway lines they can secure a large number of employees from all the boroughs of New York City. The Prudential and John Hancock office buildings in Chicago derive similar advantages from their central location.

In other cases, however, insurance companies, such as those in Hartford, Connecticut, have located their offices away from the central business district. In Houston, Texas, the Prudential Insurance Company developed a twenty-story office building that is located on a 26-acre tract opposite the Shamrock Hotel, five miles from downtown Houston. The large ground area permits ample free parking and a large outdoor swimming pool. Most of the workers live in the vicinity of the office building.

### Demand for Office Space

The amount of office space needed varies in different cities. On the average, about 2 square feet of office space per capita will serve the needs of the residents of an area. More is needed for regional, national, and international centers. New York's requirements may be over 15 feet per capita (excluding North Jersey), Chicago, 7 to 8 feet, and so on. The demand for office space reflects the general level of business activity and conditions in special lines of business.

### Ownership and Management of Office Buildings

Tall office buildings are the outstanding landmarks of most American cities. Because of the prestige attached to their ownership, banks, large insurance companies, and other financial institutions often own the buildings in which they occupy quarters. In the 1920's, office buildings were often financed by bond issues, with the equity retained by promoters. When these mortgages were foreclosed, new investment groups bought control, usually by acquiring the bonds far below par value. Recent office

**Fig. 22–3.**   Occupant-owned building—First National Bank of Chicago.

building construction has been financed largely by loans from insurance companies and not by sales of bonds to the public. The equity has often been retained by the builder or developer. In some cases, the lender takes an equity position or a "piece of the action."

The manager of an office building attempts to set rates for space that allow for differences in the desirability of various areas in the building.

The most desirable space is that with direct outside light on floors at elevator express stops. An ideal depth for most offices is 40 feet, which allows for a 20-foot reception area space and 20 feet for interior offices.

In selecting tenants, preference will usually be given to companies of outstanding prestige that may attract other desirable tenants to the building. It is necessary to consider the needs for expansion and, if possible, to have sufficient leeway to be able to meet the potential needs of desirable tenants.

The office building manager has the job not only of selecting tenants but also of employing service workers and supervising maintenance and repairs. Building managers' associations exchange information on operating experience, study relationships with building employee unions, and cooperate on other problems affecting the industry. The Building Owners and Managers Association plays a role of special importance.

## INDUSTRIAL REAL ESTATE

The market for industrial real estate is affected by factors substantially different from those which have a primary bearing on the markets for retail or office space. While the trend of demand for retail space has moved outward from the center of the city, and that for office space has moved outward to some extent, the demand for central locations for such uses remains stronger than in the case of industrial real estate. The most desirable sites for factories, in nearly all instances, are no longer found near the center of metropolitan areas but in outlying suburban or even in rural locations along railroad lines or highways, or near sources of raw materials.

### Central and Outlying Locations

At one time industrial uses also competed for central locations, since only in such areas could the combination of factors involving rail or water transportation, nearness to sources of power, and nearness to workers' homes be found. With the development of truck transportation and belt lines, power transmission over wider areas, and the general use of automobiles by workers, industry has moved outward from city centers.

In general, industries seek sites that are not congested and are easily accessible for materials and workers. Emphasis is placed on relatively low land costs and attempts are made to minimize tax burdens. The increasing use of single-story factory buildings, permitting continuity of operations on the same level, has emphasized the need for low-priced land. Industries engaged in heavy manufacturing or those with highly specialized requirements usually own the space they use. Others often lease or make use of the sale-leaseback device.

## Industrial Parks and Districts

Of special importance in the market for industrial real estate are industrial parks and districts. Such developments as the Central Manufacturing District and the Clearing Industrial District in Chicago, the Trinity Industrial District of Dallas, and the Bergen County Terminal in New Jersey are typical (see Fig. 22–4). Organizations of this type provide industrial facilities with rail service, financing arrangements, fire and police protection, heat, light, gas, water, and other services. Space is available for purchase or rent on varying bases. The Trinity Industrial District of Dallas is located within five minutes of the downtown area on property that was reclaimed from flood land. Levees were built and channels straightened so that industrial locations could be provided. Many industrial parks are located in suburban areas, however, where cheap land and low tax rates provide advantages. In many instances, industrial parks serve best the needs of the lighter industries, since heavy industry often requires special-purpose construction and equipment.

## Trends in Industrial Construction

With greater specialization, emphasis has been given to the development of facilities which serve the needs of specific industries. Some plants are referred to as "controlled conditions plants," providing ideal operating and working conditions with control of light, temperature, humidity, and noise.

Many plants are designed so that the interior arrangements may be as flexible as possible. Larger bays are being used, typically running up to 100 feet, in contrast to 50 to 60 feet in older plants. Building heights are being raised in order to allow for conveyor operations; greater emphasis is given to low-cost maintenance; and the exteriors of plants are being given greater attention, with carefully maintained grounds, landscaping, neat lawns, and recreational areas.

## Wholesale and Storage Warehouses

Wholesale and storage warehouses are often located near central-city areas. As a result of the direct delivery of merchandise from the manufacturer to the retailer, the wholesale function has declined. Large warehouses were once stored with merchandise near the Loop of Chicago and the downtown areas of other cities. Now frequent door-to-door deliveries are made by trucks from factories to stores. Cold storage warehouses still remain near central business districts, and department stores and other stores still maintain warehouses for distribution of goods within the metropolitan area.

**Fig. 22–4.** Sixty-fifth Street, Clearing Industrial District, Chicago, Illinois. (Courtesy Clearing Industrial District, Inc., Chicago, Illinois. Photo by Chicago Aerial Industries, Inc.)

The Merchandise Mart, in Chicago, once designed for wholesale use, is now highly successful as a headquarters for manufacturers' representatives. For example, one entire floor may be devoted to furniture, another to women's apparel, and so on. The Furniture Mart is the leading furniture wholesale market. Buyers come here—especially at certain seasons.

The supply of central warehouse and storage space probably is adequate for most future needs because many factories have moved away from the multi-story buildings to outlying one-story plants. Space in such multi-story buildings often is well designed for warehouse or storage use.

### Demand for Industrial Space

Decisions affecting real estate in the industrial field tend to reflect general company policies with respect to expansion programs, preferences in regard to adjoining or new locations in the same or in other cities, the use of branch operations, and the like. Tax burdens, freight rates, labor relations, local government attitudes, transportation facilities, power, water supply, pollution problems, and related factors all have a bearing. Typically, an industrial organization is not interested in local economic conditions to the same degree as a retail establishment. Indeed, some industries seek out locally depressed areas in order to take advantage of an available labor supply. The regional movement of industry to the South, for example, has been influenced to a degree by labor market conditions.

## SELECTION OF INDUSTRIAL LOCATIONS

As a general rule, processing plants which increase the bulk of products, or make a fragile or perishable product, prefer to be near their customers; plants which reduce the bulk of products, or make them less perishable, do not regard nearness to the consumer as particularly vital. Since a very large portion of all material going into factory production has already been processed by another factory, the supplier groups tend to locate near the industries which they serve. As a result there is a heavy concentration of industry on the New York–Chicago axis. There is more production of this type within 100 miles of New York than in the eight southeastern states, and within 100 miles of Chicago than in all of the western states excepting those on the Pacific Coast.

### Selection Factors

In selecting a factory location, business managers typically analyze (1) the general region in which the factory is to be built, (2) the particular city within the region, (3) the selected area within the metropolitan region, and (4) the specific site. The basic purpose of selecting the location is, of course, to find the site in which the industry can operate to maximum advantage, where production costs will be lowest, and the costs of marketing at a minimum.

## The Region

Most types of industries can operate economically only in definite regions. However, these regions may be rather broad in extent. Thus, the steel industry must be situated at the most economical meeting place of coal and iron ore. The steel industries in Chicago, Pittsburgh, and Cleveland are based on the accessibility to coal by rail or river and to the iron ore of the Mesabi Range, which is available by cheap water transportation on the Great Lakes. The increasing dependence on imported iron ore caused the building of the Fairless Steel Works on the Delaware River near Trenton and the doubling of the capacity of the Bethlehem Steel Plant at Baltimore.

Many steel-using industries find it necessary to locate near the primary steel plants. Industries refining bulky materials must also be located near the source of supply. Thus, the concentration plant of the Kennecott Copper Corporation's Utah mine is located at Bingham Canyon at the source of supply, because the copper-bearing rock has only 1 per cent copper and it would be uneconomical to transport this bulky material great distances.

Proximity to markets is also an important consideration in factory location. Many industries are located in the northeastern part of the United States because of the nearness to the great concentrations of urban population in that region.

The electronics industry and related activities have been less directly tied to raw materials and markets than some of the older industries. Also, research and development programs of various firms often are located in favorable environments such as university towns or in pleasant climates. We should note too that political factors may play a part in the location of various defense and similar types of installations.

## The Specific City Within the Region

It sometimes happens that the maximum advantages of location in a region can be obtained in only one specific city. Thus, industries depending upon ocean shipments must be located near ports, such as New York, Baltimore, New Orleans, or San Francisco. Where it is important to be at the center of the railroad network, the Chicago area is often preferred. In other cases, the specific industry must be located near others of the same type or near complementary industries. Women's ready-to-wear manufacturers find it desirable to be in the New York fashion center, because styles change quickly. Manufacturers of cameras prefer to be near Rochester, New York. The leading automobile firms obtain advantages by being close to the automobile-parts manufacturers in Detroit.

In many cases, however, an industry could be located to almost equal advantage in any of five, six, or more cities. The decision as to which city is selected is often governed by the availability of a site or factory building, by the preference of the factory manager for a certain city as a place of residence, by the promotional activities of the local chamber of commerce, by the tax situation, by the characteristics of the labor supply, or by the railroad, trucking, and other transportation facilities of a given city.

## The General Area Within the Metropolitan Region

As we have indicated, new plants are now more frequently located in outlying and suburban areas than in the central districts as was formerly the case. The chief cause of this move has been the growing preference for the one-story industrial building as compared with the multi-story type. The one-story plant requires extensive ground areas which usually cannot be found in central locations. It has been found in a number of cases that factory operations can be carried on in these single-story buildings at a saving of 25 per cent in cost compared with the same factory processes in factories with several floor levels. The advantages of one-story factory buildings located in suburban or rural areas include the following:

1. The factory process is continuous without the necessity of interrupting manufacturing operations at each floor level.
2. There is no waste space for elevators or ramps and no cost of elevator operation.
3. Heavy machinery can be installed in any part of the building.
4. Railroad freight cars and trucks can enter the plant directly, which results in a saving in handling costs.
5. Overhead cranes can be installed and the plant can be equipped with conveyor belts for moving goods in process through the building.
6. The one-story plant is far more flexible and can be more easily expanded to meet the growth of any particular department. If there is ample ground area and the building is constructed with curtain walls, any part of the building can be pushed out to meet the needs of growth.
7. The factory grounds usually include ample areas for the parking of the workers' cars.
8. There is more room for recreation areas on the ground and it is easier to provide cafeterias and restrooms within the buildings.
9. The cost of one-story buildings is often less per square foot than the multi-story type.

10. The land cost is lower in outlying locations than in central areas.
11. Real estate taxes are usually lower in suburban tracts.
12. The workers' homes, particularly those of the skilled workers, are often near these factories because of residential decentralization. Some factory sites have been selected because of their proximity to the homes of their workers, although this is not a factor of major consideration currently.
13. Because of widespread automobile ownership, workers prefer to work in pleasant modern factories with ample parking areas rather than in congested central-city areas. Workers can reach these locations more quickly on the highways encircling the metropolitan areas than they can the central districts with their heavy traffic.
14. Suburban and rural locations are more convenient for interstate trucks, which are widely used. Downtown traffic congestion can be avoided. Suburban plants also are more conveniently located with respect to outlying railroad belt lines.
15. Industrial districts in which a group of factories can obtain advantages by operating as neighbors also can be created more easily in suburban or rural locations than in downtown areas.

### The Specific Site

Having narrowed the choice down to one specific city and to a general area within the metropolitan area of that city, it is necessary to select the exact site. The following factors will be weighed by plant managers in this process:

1. In reviewing all the sites, it is necessary to find those that are zoned for industry and which will permit the location of the specific type of industrial plant proposed. If not actually zoned, opinions can be secured from zoning authorities as to what zoning is possible.
2. It is often desirable to have a location with direct access to a railroad from which a railroad siding could be constructed into the site at reasonable cost. It is often desirable also to be near a major highway for truck transportation.
3. Sites with bus transportation to the homes of the workers may be preferred, as some auxiliary transportation often is desirable even though most of the workers have cars.
4. The site should have sewer and water connections, particularly in the case of a small industry. Some large industries install their own sewage-disposal plants and develop their own water supply. In the case of such industries the availability of a source of water is important. It is also necessary to ascertain how sewage and factory wastes can be discharged without contributing to pollution problems.

5. Tracts of sufficient size for the type of operation under consideration must be selected. Consideration is often given to room for expansion. An area under one or at most two ownerships must usually be found.

6. When there are a number of different local municipalities or townships in the metropolitan area, the sites in the one which will do most to facilitate the location of the new industry usually are preferred.

7. The factory should be located on a site most convenient to the homes of the present workers or to the areas where most of the future labor supply may be located.

8. Access to power lines is necessary.

9. If all other advantages are equal, the site which can be obtained at the lowest price will usually be purchased.

## SUMMARY

The market for business real estate may be regional, national, or even international in scope.

Real estate administration may occupy various positions in the organization of a firm, depending upon the importance of real estate to the firm's operations. Major real estate decisions usually are made at top levels of management.

The highest land values for retail property are found in the central business district of a city, where pedestrian traffic density is greatest. Large department stores, central offices, and financial institutions usually form the nuclei of the district. Space in the central business district usually is leased for long periods, and percentage leases with a fixed minimum rent, or sometimes a sliding scale, are commonly used. Key tenants may be given special rent concessions because of their ability to attract other firms to the building or area.

The increased use of automobiles along with an expanding highway network has led to the development of outlying shopping centers, ranging from large regional centers to smaller neighbolhood outlets. Parking space is an essential feature of the larger centers, and a ratio of parking to store space of 4-to-1 is common. This greatly increases the amount of land needed by retail establishments. The location of new centers is influenced by the pattern of the developing highway system.

The modern skyscraper office building serves the desire of the executives of business firms to be located within easy access of each other. The skyscraper was made possible by the advent of steel-frame construction and the electric elevator. Office buildings historically have been built in waves; when overbuilding occurred, rents have been depressed for long periods, regardless of the trend of general business conditions. The supply of office space is relatively fixed in the short run. High occupancy rates typically are needed to make office buildings a financial success. Demand for office space depends to a considerable extent on the level of general business activity.

Improved transportation has allowed more decentralization of industry, and manufacturing firms now tend to seek uncongested sites readily accessible for suppliers and employees. Thus, they can make use of locations where land prices and tax burdens are lower. Some areas have seen the development of industrial parks or districts. Industrial location depends also on such important factors as the nature of the product, the location of raw materials and markets, and the supply of power and of labor. A growing preference for one-story buildings has increased the demand for land for industrial purposes.

## QUESTIONS FOR STUDY

1. How do the markets for commercial and industrial real estate differ from residential real estate markets?
2. Where do you think the real estate function should be placed in the firm's organization? Explain. To what extent will this depend on the nature of the firm's business?
3. Describe typical leasing agreements for each of the following: (a) supermarkets. (b) apparel stores. (c) furniture stores.
4. What is meant by a "100 per cent" retail location?
5. Why have fashion goods stores tended to concentrate in the central business district? Do you think they will continue to concentrate there? Explain.
6. Why has the large department store been an important inhabitant of the central business district? Will this be true in the future? Explain.
7. Do you think that the policy of national chain organizations in establishing percentages on a national basis is sound? Why or why not?
8. Define and describe each of the principal types of shopping centers.
9. How do you explain the popularity of large, centrally located office buildings?
10. Have office buildings tended to be decentralized in the manner that has characterized residential and retail developments? Why or why not?
11. Describe the major factors determining rentals of office space.
12. Explain the advantages and disadvantages of: (a) single-tenant versus multiple-tenant office buildings. (b) specialized-tenant versus generalized-tenant occupancy of office buildings.
13. What are the principal characteristics of the market for industrial real estate?
14. Describe the main characteristics of industrial parks and districts.
15. Indicate the main factors involved in selecting a site for an industrial location of: (a) The general region. (b) the choice among cities. (c) the site within a specific city.

## SUGGESTED READINGS

Hoover, Edgar M. *Location of Economic Activity*. New York: McGraw-Hill Book Co., Inc., 1948.

Hoyt, Homer. *According to Hoyt*. (2nd ed.). Washington, D.C.: Hoyt, 1970. Sec. XI.

Kinnard, William N., and Stephen D. Messner. *Industrial Real Estate* (2nd ed.). Washington, D.C.: Society of Industrial Realtors, 1971.

Wendt, Paul F., and Alan R. Cerf. *Real Estate Investment, Analysis and Taxation*. New York: McGraw-Hill Book Co., Inc., 1969. Chs. 7–9.

## CASE 22–1

## Western Federal Savings and Loan Association of Denver *

Since January 1962, Western Federal Savings and Loan Association of Denver has owned and occupied its modern, first class, 26 story home office building in the heart of downtown Denver's financial district (see Fig. 1). For many years now the Association has been the largest Savings and Loan Association in the Rocky Mountain West and currently the Association has assets of nearly $450,000,000.00.

The Association normally invests the greatest portion of its resources in high quality long-term mortgage loans on single and multi-family dwellings. In adidtion the Association regularly invests a portion of its resources in long-term mortgage loans on commercial real estate and is actively engaged in the short-term mortgage lending market through its construction loan activities.

Chartered as a United States Corporation, the Association is a mutual institution and, therefore, has no stock ownership. In addition the Association must operate within the regulations provided by the Federal Home Loan Bank System. Until recently, these regulations have permitted investment in real estate only when the real property was to be occupied fully or in part by the Association as home or branch office quarters. The Association, because of this limitation, has not speculated in real estate investments or other specialized land banking. However, since 1950 the Association has owned the real estate occupied by its home office and seven branch offices. These real estate investments have been very successful.

This success has encouraged management to consider additional real estate investment in the anticipation that their eventual sale will contribute to the surplus of the Association.

Some key statistics concerning the home office building are:

1. Original cost:
   a. Land        $1,000,000.00
   b. Building     $6,000,000.00    $7,000,000.00
2. Estimated Market Value:              $9,000,000.00

* Material used by permission of Western Savings and Loan Association.

**Fig. 1.** Western Savings Building.

    3. Estimated Loan Available:
       a. Amount                                    $6,300,000.00
       b. Term                                      25 yrs
       c. Interest Rate                             8½%

Some key operational statistics include:

1. Total Square Footage of Rental Space                       112,000 sq. ft.
2. Current Vacancy Ratio                                            −
3. Current Rent Schedule:
   a. Plaza Levels through 14th Floor                          6.50/sq. ft.
   b. 15th Floor through 19th Floor                            6.65/sq. ft.
   c. 20th Floor through 24th Floor                            6.90/sq. ft.
4. Current Return on Investment:
   $349,180 on $7,000,000 invested capital =                        4.99%
5. Rent Escalation Clause:
   1½¢/sq. ft. for every 1¢/hr of wage increase for Building
   Service Employees in the City of Denver

Because the Association owns its 26 store home office building free and clear, they have received numerous offers to either sell the building and lease it back or to mortgage the building. These offers present three interesting and challenging basic alternatives to the Association:

1. Should the building be sold and leased back?

   With long-term interest rates currently at a cyclical low, and a prime rate of 5½ per cent, this lower yield in the capital markets contributes to a higher market value for the building. This value could be seriously impared, however, by the flood of new office building now under construction in downtown Denver that will provide 4 million square feet of new space by the end of 1972 or approximately a 10-year supply at the current absorption rate of 300,000 square feet annually.

2. Should the building be mortgaged?

   Presuming that the Association could borrow at 8½ per cent and then either invest in fixed dollar investment with a return greater than 8½ per cent or invest in shorter-term Mobile Home loans or construction loans with even higher yields, such a move could provide the Association with reasonable long-term capital cost.

3. Should the Association leave the *Status Quo?*

   Recognizing that the Association has made a good real estate investment, that the return on invested capital is at a respectable 4.99 per cent, and that the benefits of future depreciation and/or cost appreciation would continue to accrue, the Association assumes little risk by leaving the status quo. (See Fig. 2.)

For reference and further information, please refer to the complete case study package provided by the Association.

## Questions

1. If Western Federal earns 8½ to 9 per cent on mortgage loans, how does its office building look as an investment?
2. What is a good capitalization rate for income on the building? Justify your answer.

Statement of Estimated Income and Expenses

Western Federal Savings Building
17th at California Street
Denver, Colorado

*Income:*

| | | |
|---|---|---:|
| Offices | 115,500 square feet | $649,560 |
| Western Federal Savings & Loan | | |
| 1, 2 and Mezzanine | 22,000 square feet | 132,000 |
| 5th floor | 6,000 square feet | 36,000 |
| Baur's, Barber, Steno (Basement) | 2,700 square feet | 20,000 |
| | 144,700 square feet | $837,560 |

*Expenses:*

| | |
|---|---:|
| Real Estate Taxes | 134,575 |
| Insurance—$5,000,000 | 10,200 |

*Utilities:*

| | |
|---|---:|
| Steam | 14,965 |
| Electricity | 86,635 |
| Water | 2,540 |

*Salaries and Labor:*

| | |
|---|---:|
| Chief Engineer and 3 Engineers | 42,910 |
| Guard Service | 19,040 |
| Janitorial (Contract) | 77,945 |
| Elevator Service (Contract) | 16,570 |

*Maintenance, Repair and Supplies:*

| | |
|---|---:|
| Restroom Supplies | 3,820 |
| Air conditioning | 10,750 |
| Plumbing | 45 |
| Electric | 4,540 |
| Painting, Decorating | 8,678 |
| General | 5,952 |

| | |
|---|---:|
| Administrative | 7,383 |
| Law Library | 8,550 |
| Management Fee | 25,000 |
| Tenant Alterations | 8,282 |
| | $488,380 |
| Cash Flow | $349,180 |

The above statement, while not guaranteed, is from sources which we believe to be reliable. Price, terms and information subject to change.
April, 197_

**Fig. 2.** Statement of estimated income and expense.

3. Using the capitalization rate from question 2, what is the value of the building?
4. How does that value compare to the estimated market value?
5. If you were a potential buyer, what rate of return would you want on your investment? What would you be willing to pay for the building?
6. Assume you are Western Federal's real estate officer. What is your recommendation to the board of directors?

## CASE 22–2

### A B Chemical Company

The A B Chemical Company manufactures a variety of pharmaceutical products at plants located at Maynard, Kansas, and Center City, Kansas. Early in 1966 a new product was being developed which would be marketed through a dual distribution system including direct sales to large customers and sales through distributors and warehouses to smaller customers. This product would be manufactured at a new location. A general statement of the requirements of the plant is described below.

The site cannot be chosen solely on the basis of meeting the requirements for the initial production. Company plans, while not specific in terms of precise products to be manufactured in the future, nevertheless contemplate growth and the introduction of new products into the new plant facility. Accordingly, the plant site selected must also contemplate the possibility of future substantial growth.

A decision was made to select the optimum location for the proposed new facility, bearing in mind the need not only of the immediate contemplated plant, but also possible future growth and development of the plant. It was decided to employ The Fantus Company of Chicago, location consultants, to conduct a search and study encompassing the entire United States. During the research the consulting company did not reveal the company name.

Some of the basic requirements for a suitable site were supplied to Fantus. These were as follows:

*Labor:* 150 people (start with 50). Community must have supply of high caliber trainable workers available. Company will train. Need a few skilled tradesmen.

*Freight:* Truck and rail. Rail potential 300 cars per year inbound plus part of outbound. Balance of shipments primarily full truckload throughout country. Require good truck service.

*Utilities:* Power: 6,000 KW, 90-95% P.F., 4,250,000 KWH per month. Loop feed or dual source desirable.

Fuel: 11,250 MCF per month of natural gas (peak load, 1 hour per day, 4 times average load, balance of load stable 24 hours per day). Oil can be used instead of gas.

Water: Sanitary use, maximum 500,000 gallons per month. Process uses 5,000 gallons per minute, continuous. Company will develop cooling water system, but water with a maximum summer temperature of 60° F must be available in this quantity.

Sewer: Company will treat effluent.

*Site:* 50–100 acres. Rail service available. Power and gas available (gas may be omitted). Water not exceeding 60° C maximum summer temperature available. Must be located on or near (with pipeline easement) a river with an average flow of at least 6,000 cubic feet per second. Prefer 2–5 miles from populated area.

**Defining the Area.** *Many factors operate to control the location of the proposed plant.* Among the most important cost factors are utility costs, transportation costs, labor costs, and taxes. Furthermore, many significant operating conditions had to be considered in the selection of the site and in the selection of a general area of location. Among these important operating conditions are labor attitude, productivity, quality of transportation service, accessibility of the area, living conditions, educational facilities, etc. The desire to construct certain proposed manufacturing buildings of open design would direct the search toward the south central states. Also, the desirability of TVA power was an important factor.

*Certain factors operate more restrictively than others in the proposed location project.* The factors which operate most restrictively to determine the area within which the plant may be located are the availability of streams with the required 6,000 cubic feet per second average flow and a minimum flow in excess of 300 cubic feet per second, the availability of 5,000 or more gallons per minute of water with a temperature never exceeding 60°F, and the cost of the very substantial quantity of electric power required. Another factor, which does not define the area as sharply, but which nevertheless indicates the general area of maximum interest, is that of transportation costs.

After completing their investigation, four sites were described:

1. Alderson, Alabama
2. Toptown, Tennessee
3. Warrentown, Kentucky
4. Travel City, Kentucky

For various reasons the consulting company selected the site at Alderson, Alabama, as the optimum location for the plant. Executive of the company examined the four sites but took no action.

Subsequently, the consulting company recommended a fifth site at Marchwood, Kentucky, which the company decided more closely satisfied their requirements; however, in inspecting other possible sites in surrounding counties, they found an area around Monterey, Kentucky, which they felt would best meet the requirements. After this decision was made, the Monterey Industrial Development Foundation obtained options on parcels of land selected by the company forming a tract of 188 acres about one mile north of Monterey. The options were assigned to the company and the purchase closed.

**Developments Within the Company During the Search for and Selection of a Site.** Successes of the research and development laboratories of the company during the time that the site search was being conducted resulted in increased production yields which deferred the decision to initiate construction and at the same time required the company to reappraise the site requirements. Because of increased complexity of products to be produced, it was decided that the site would have to be in a location providing for easy and quick communication between the proposed new plant and the research and development laboratories at Center City. The market estimates became more optimistic, and it was decided that the site would have to be considerably larger than originally determined. The revised specifications for the site called for a location within 1 or 1½ hours travel time from the research and development laboratories and in excess of 250 acres.

**Notification to Monterey Community of the New Requirements of the Company.** Representatives of the company visited the Monterey Industrial Development Foundation and explained to them the new requirements for a site and offered to grant the Foundation an option to purchase the Monterey site at its cost price without any of the costs which the company had incurred in investigating the site as well as offering to assist the Foundation in finding another industry that might be interested in locating on the Monterey site.

**Search for a New Site.** Action was initiated to immediately locate a satisfactory site in Kansas to meet the new specifications. The company conducted a study of all river areas with known ground water deposits within an approximate radius of 100 miles of Center City, and each possible site was thoroughly examined without revealing the company name. Extensive use was made of industrial development corporations, chambers of commerce, railroad companies, Realtors, and the director of industrial development of the State of Kansas. In addition, considerable "raw" searching was undertaken.

Early in the investigation it was determined that the Northtown, Kansas, Industrial Development Corporation, a small group of local businessmen, had acquired 46 acres five miles north of Northtown, Kansas, in the hope of attracting an industry. Upon examining this area it was found that the land surrounding this tract, if it could be assembled, would produce a tract of satisfactory size and upon further investigation was found that all other conditions prevailing in the area met reasonably well every specification for a site. The parcels for which purchase options were desired were outlined to the Northtown Industrial Development Corporation, and with their cooperation action was taken to obtain options as quickly as possible. This was accomplished, and when the parcels were assembled they created a tract of approximately 750 acres which has since been purchased by the company. The company name was not revealed to the Northtown Industrial Development Corporation until the last option was under negotiation.

While negotiations for options were under way, investigations were undertaken by the company to determine that all conditions pertaining to the site would satisfy the company needs. These investigations included:

1. Determination that the railroad company would agree to a spur track and would grant easements for culverts through the railroad right of way for effluent pipes.
2. Determined availability of electrical service.
3. Investigation of county zoning regulations.
4. Determination that access to the state highway would be granted.
5. Review of existing tenant leases.
6. Review of existing utility easements.
7. Determined the availability of natural gas.

8. Review of schooling and housing in general area.
9. Review of hospital facilities in the general area.
10. Determined the requirements by State Board of Health on discharge of treated effluent into river.
11. Official survey of all tracts of land.
12. Ground water pumping tests.
13. Soil resistance tests.
14. Procurement of aerial photographs from U.S. Department of Agriculture.
15. Review of history of flooding of Walnut River and effect of upstream flood reservoirs.

**Complications in Closing the Purchase.**    Some of the complications which developed as we approached the closing of the purchase transactions were:

1. Land swaps where the sellers requested us to purchase designated property and swap that property for the property we required.
2. Mineral rights leases previously granted by the seller had to be transferred to the purchaser.
3. One seller was granted a life residency in the farm house on the property we purchased.
4. One seller requested purchase payments to be made over a period of three years to spread taxes.

Ground-breaking took place on the site five months and nine days from the date the assignment was given to find a new site.

## Questions

1. Why was location close to Center City so important?
2. Which factors were of major importance in the final site selection?
3. Why were rural or semi-rural locations considered over urban locations?
4. Why would a place like Northtown, Kansas, be a better plant site than someplace in Center City, Kansas, where the problem of travel time would be virtually eliminated?

# 23

# Farms and Other Rural Real Estate

## TYPES OF RURAL REAL ESTATE

Classification is almost never easy and broad land use classifications present some special problems. The line between "rural" and "urban" becomes increasingly difficult to draw. If we consider as urban only the land in cities of 2,500 people or more, 21,400,000 acres were used in this way in 1969; estimated needs move up to 32 million acres in 1980 and to 45 million acres in the year 2000.[1] We should emphasize the land *withdrawn* from rural uses to serve urban purposes, since a third to a half of urban land is not in actual use but awaiting development.

### Rural Land Uses

The remainder of the land, nonurban land, includes farmland and ranch land such as crop land along with pasture and grazing land and nonproductive farmland; commercial forest land; land used for recreation, excluding reservoir areas and city parks; land used for transportation purposes; wildlife refuges; reservoirs; and finally, a residual classification. It is not our purpose here to consider each of these types of land use.

[1] Hans H. Landsberg, Leonard L. Fischman, and Joseph L. Fisher, *Resources in America's Future* (Baltimore: The Johns Hokpins Press, 1963), chap. xviii.

707

### Types Selected for Discussion

We center our attention on land uses that we believe to have special significance for real estate purposes and more or less arbitrarily have selected farms and ranches for primary consideration, plus presenting a summary discussion of land used for forestry and for rural, or rather, nonurban, recreation. Nonurban land that is used for residential purposes (rural nonfarm) is growing in importance and was considered in Chapter 21.

## THE MARKET FOR FARMS

Agriculture has been going through a revolution characterized in general by a shift toward a business and managerial type of operation with increasingly heavy investments per farm. Scientific and technological advances have been back of these changes including improved feeds and fertilizers, more effective plant and animal breeding, better agricultural implements and power, as well as improved roads and trucks, and related developments. There have been marketing as well as production changes; contract farming has increased in importance as have the efforts of various farm cooperatives. Government programs including various controls and supports have played an important role; in some cases, such programs have slowed down rates of change.

### Special Characteristics

Agriculture, with individual units varying through a wide range of productivity, size, and capital requirements, presents a real estate market with its own peculiar problems and characteristics. To lump all farms together in considering the characteristics of the farm real estate market is no more correct than to lump all factories or all retail stores together.

As in the case of other types of real estate, there is no organized market for farmland. Systems for grading and classifying farmland leave much to be desired. Furthermore, the principal buyers of farmland usually are found in the immediate locality. In some instances farms are purchased by outside investors.

Soil productivity, the condition of buildings and other improvements, accessibility to roads, schools, churches, electric power lines, and shopping centers, as well as community ties, family sentiment, and the like all have a bearing on the market for farms. Many of the factors are subjective in nature. Location plays a role of growing importance in determining farmland values.

Farmland is usually sold by the acre and is ordinarily priced in terms of so many dollars per acre with the value of farm buildings and other improvements included in such a price.

## Farm Brokers

Farm real estate brokers usually operate within a single community and seldom cover an area that extends much beyond several counties. Some real estate brokers specialize in farmland, and in some cases include professional farm appraisal and management as a part of their activities.

The practices followed by farm brokers differ little from those followed by the real estate brokers in urban communities. As in the case of urban real estate, income plus the terms and availability of financing are of major importance in determining the intensity of demand for farm real estate; during inflationary periods demand may rise from efforts to secure a hedge against inflation.

## Supply

Despite growing demands for agricultural products, the number of farms has declined from 3.9 million in 1960 to 2.9 million in 1970. At the same time, the average size of farms has increased. Farms with a thousand acres or more (less than 4 per cent of the total) account for approximately half of all farmland. The top 3 per cent of the farms account for more farm production than the bottom 78 per cent.[2]

About 10 million Americans lived on farms in 1970, a decline from around 15 million in 1960. Not all of the people who live on farms derive their main incomes from agriculture; many are industrial workers who farm part-time or retired persons or others not primarily dependent on agriculture.

## Size of Farms

The size of farms is usually measured in terms of acres of land. The acre is not an entirely satisfactory unit of measurement, since it includes the surface area only. It does not reflect the quality of farmland, and quality varies widely. Standards have been developed for grading the quality of agricultural land but additional progress is needed. In terms of acres the average size of farms in this country has been increasing, rising from slightly over 200 to around 300 acres in the past 10 years. The basic reason for this is the increased mechanization of agricultural pro-

[2] For a discussion of agricultural trends, see *An Adaptive Program for Agriculture* (New York: Committee for Economic Development, 1962); and Edward Higbee, *Farms and Farmers in an Urban Age* (New York: Twentieth Century Fund, 1963).

duction. In all probability, many farmers could utilize more acres than they do now. It appears that the farmers' ability to farm more acres has increased more rapidly than his ability to acquire land.

At the present time, however, it is not a simple matter to extend the acreage which a particular farmer has under cultivation. Farmland may usually be purchased in 40-, 80- or 160-acre multiples in the midwest and west. For example, a farmer may wish to add twenty-five acres of land to a farm. Such a block of land, however, is not likely to be available. He may have to buy an entire farm, including a set of farm buildings for which he would have little or no use. As a result of this situation, many farmers have expanded their scale of operations, not by adding more land, but by using more capital. Often the availability of improved and larger farm power and machinery virtually forces an expansion in the size of an operation. It is probable that the acreage of land in the average farm will continue to rise in future years.

### Demand for Farms

The demand for farm real estate in the case of commercial farms, just as is true of the demand for most other types of capital goods, is a derived demand. It is derived from the demand for the goods or services in the production of which the capital goods are used. Thus, an understanding of the demand for farm products is basic to understanding the demand for such farms themselves. In cases where farms are used primarily for residential rather than commercial purposes, demand would be similar to the demand for other residential real estate. It may be helpful to divide farms according to the purposes for which they are used, such as: (1) commercial, (2) residential, (3) part-time, or (4) subsistence.[3]

The income producing ability of farms depends on the production of crops and livestock and on the market for these products. Of course, farms are sometimes bought for essentially noneconomic reasons, such as the wish to pursue a rural way of life, sentimental attachments to a particular farm or locality, the desire to follow a hobby, such as the raising of a special strain of cattle or conducting special experiments, and for similar reasons. Thus, the demand for farms may arise from their ability to produce economic returns or from other motivations.

### Factors Affecting Demand

Although the supply of farm products varies with weather, technology and market conditions, the demand for them reflects income and population changes. The greatest fluctuations have occurred as a result of the

[3] Classification suggested by Prof. Robert C. Suter, Purdue University, whose assistance in reviewing this chapter is gratefully acknowledged.

shifting demands during war periods. In addition, however, the consumers of farm products adapt their purchases to their income situations. When incomes are high the demand for farm products is strong, particularly the demand for foods of higher quality. When incomes are low the demand for such foods as bread and potatoes does not tend to decline greatly, but the demands for foods of higher quality tend to move downward. Under high standards of living the demand for many types of food partakes of the nature of a luxury demand, with the result that substantial downward adjustments may be anticipated whenever incomes decline.

As a result of these conditions the prices which farmers have received for their products have sometimes fluctuated widely. Price changes for products tend to be reflected in the prices of farms although inflationary tendencies since World War II have given farm prices an upward bias.

### Investors in Farms

There are other areas of demand for farms that should be mentioned. One of these is the investor who is in the higher income tax brackets. People of this type may try to buy run-down farms, spend heavily for development purposes and may then sell the farms for a capital gain or continue to hold them.

In many cases investors buy farms as a long-term hedge against possible future inflation. Of course, there are always investors who buy land near settled areas in the hope of sale for urban rather than rural purposes. Whenever the yield on government bonds and similar investments moves downward, the interest of investors in farms tend to advance and vice versa.

### Farmland Tenure

A system of farmland tenure may be defined as the sum total of the various arrangements by which land is owned, rented, leased, used, controlled and transferred. All nations have struggled with the problem of devising satisfactory rules, laws, and other arrangements for controlling these matters. For example, feudalism was a system of agricultural land tenure. There have been many other systems as well. The land practices followed in this country from Revolutionary times have had the objective of widespread ownership of farms by those who operate them. By 1970 only about a quarter of all farm operators in the United States were tenants. About three-fifths of farm operators were full owners, and the remainder were part owners. The latter group owned part of the land they operated and rented some additional land.

The proportion of tenancy in the United States rose to 42 per cent in the early 1930's. By 1950 there were relatively fewer tenants on American farms than at any time since 1890. High prices for farm products enabled many farm tenants to become farm owners. The growing interest of investors in farms may make it easier for young men to get started in farming.

## FACTORS AFFECTING RURAL LAND VALUES

Like other real property, the value of rural real estate depends upon its ability to produce monetary or direct use income. The value of a producing farm is derived by capitalizing the anticipated future net income.

### Potential Urban Uses

Suburban land on the fringe of cities often derives its value from the anticipated urban use. Consequently, its present value is based on the value of urban land uses, discounted by the length of time it will take for such land to be utilized in that way. When sewer or water mains are extended into such areas, the price of land advances rapidly.

### Costs and Returns

The level of net farm earnings depends upon relationships between prices received by farmers and production costs, which will be affected by the quality of farm management, technological developments in production, changes in the efficiency of marketing agricultural products, real estate taxes, financing charges, government programs, and related factors.

The principal physical factors affecting the value of farmland are soil productivity, rainfall, and the length of the growing season. Other factors include buildings and other improvements available, location and accessibility to markets, schools, churches, shopping centers, and power lines. Buildings and other improvements are more important for some types of farming, such as dairying and poultry, than for other types, such as beef cow ranches.

### Low Yield Crops

The value of farmland depends also upon its suitability for different types of crops (see Fig. 23–1). The cheapest land is found in arid or semiarid regions. Its uses are limited to grazing. The value of such land may be related to the number of acres required to support one steer and the value added in the increased weight of the steer, minus labor and feeding costs. Other low-grade rural land includes that used for the production of pulpwood. Such a crop can be produced in around seven years where there is a long growing season. A slightly higher type of land is

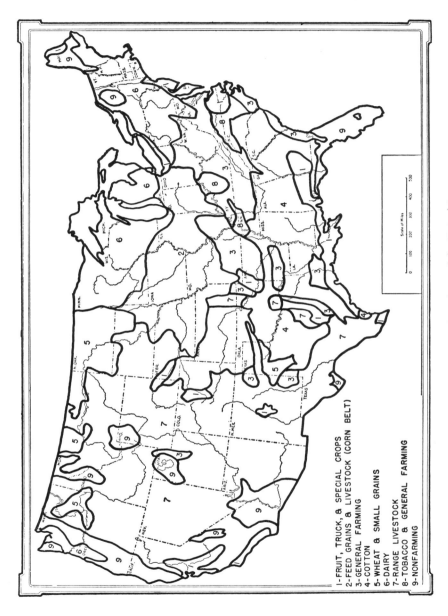

1-FRUIT, TRUCK, & SPECIAL CROPS
2-FEED GRAINS & LIVESTOCK (CORN BELT)
3-GENERAL FARMING
4-COTTON
5-WHEAT & SMALL GRAINS
6-DAIRY
7-RANGE LIVESTOCK
8-TOBACCO & GENERAL FARMING
9-NONFARMING

**Fig. 23–1.** Agricultural products of the United States.

permanent pasture in areas with abundant rainfall. In Florida, for example, there are areas of this type which will support one steer per acre.

## Higher Yields

Such rural land uses contrast with the rich farmland of the Middle West and California. The rich Midwest land, in an area provided with adequate summer rainfall and a growing season long enough to mature corn, produces high yields. Much of the land in this region is sufficiently level to permit the widespread use of tractors, harvesters, and similar mechanical equipment. Rainfall diminishes in the areas west of Iowa in the Dakotas, Nebraska, and Kansas. Wheat is the principal crop in these regions, as it is in Canada. The 20-inch rainfall line is an important one.

## Specialty Crops

The highest farmland values result from specialty crops, especially citrus fruits. Oranges and grapefruit can be raised only in a subtropical climate where the temperature does not fall below 25 degrees or if it falls below such levels does so only for short intervals. Some cool weather is required, however, for the production of the best quality of fruit. Consequently, commercial citrus fruits cannot be produced to any extent in the tropics. Citrus groves require eighteen to twenty years before they reach the full bearing stage. However, they have a bearing life of many years. Because of the long life and heavy capital investment required, extended periods of overproduction and low prices result when too many orchards are developed. Of special interest in connection with the growing of citrus fruits is the use of frozen concentrates, which permits the absorption of a much larger supply than formerly.

Apple orchards, peach orchards, grape vineyards, pecan groves, tung groves, and walnut groves share some of the characteristics of citrus farming, but each has its own peculiarities. Among these are greater annual fluctuations in yields and a shorter bearing life.

## Cotton

Cotton requires a longer growing season than corn, but a shorter one than various types of orchards. Cotton has long been one of the principal crops of the southern states, although its relative importance has diminished in more recent years.

## Tobacco

At the present time, tobacco acreage is limited by government control. Consequently the right to use specified acreage for tobacco production adds to the values of the land involved. The value of the allotment tends to be added to the value of the land in making appraisals. The inventory or cost approach and others may be used. Tobacco is raised in a number of states, largely in Kentucky, Virginia, and the Carolinas.

## Timberland

Timberland is valued on the basis of the estimated value of board feet of standing timber of saw-log size. Its value tends to fluctuate with the price of lumber. While scientific forestry has not been practiced extensively in the United States, there have been significant developments in more recent years. The adoption of sustained-yield management methods holds promise of adding to the value of timberlands.

## Valuation Factors

In summary, the valuation of an individual farm requires consideration of (1) the fertility of the soil; (2) climatic factors, especially rainfall and the length of the growing season; (3) topography; (4) the amount of land under cultivation and the amount used for woodland or grazing; (5) accessibility to hard roads; (6) character of the houses, barns, and other improvements; (7) quotas allowed for raising certain crops; and (8) specific location possibilities for conversion to urban uses.

## Appraising Farms

Although many rules of thumb are followed by farmers, real estate brokers, and investors in estimating the value of farms, more refined techniques of appraisal have been developed in recent years (see Fig. 23–2). The steps in a farm appraisal may be outlined as follows:

1. The legal descriptions are checked against the farm boundaries. Aerial photographs are being used to an increasing extent in this process. They are often available in the county offices of the U. S. Department of Agriculture.
2. An inventory of the soil and farm improvements is made. Soil tubes and augurs are used to estimate the soil's characteristics. Estimates are made of the remaining useful life of the buildings and their current condition.
3. An estimate is made of the land owner's income from the farm. Estimates are based on prices for the crops produced on the farm. A schedule of annual expenses is established, including building depreciation.
4. The estimated net income is capitalized at a rate which reflects the going rate for investments of this type.
5. Adjustments are made as required to fit the specific situation, giving

FLB 4-308
Rev. 2-71

BUREAU OF THE BUDGET
FORM NO. 108-RO19.1

## APPRAISER'S REPORT
### TO THE FEDERAL LAND BANK OF LOUISVILLE

Federal Land Bank Association of _____ Application No. _____

       (CITY OR TOWN)        (STATE)

I have made a personal examination of and identified the property described in above numbered application made

by _____ of _____

for a loan of $ _____ and report as follows:

### A. LOCATION, TYPE, AND QUALITY OF FARM

1. State _____ County _____ Civil District or Township _____ Section _____ Range _____ Total Acres _____

2. The farm is located _____ miles _____ from _____ miles _____ from _____
       (DIRECTION)      (NEAREST TOWN)      (DIRECTION)      (COUNTY SEAT)

3. Farm is on _____ miles _____ from nearest highway _____ Type of farming _____
    (KIND, NUMBER, AND CONDITION OF ROAD)    (DIRECTION)      (GIVE NUMBER AND TYPE)

4. in community is _____ Conveniences available are (✓) _____
       (RFD, SCHOOL BUS, MILK ROUTE, POWER LINE, TELEPHONE, ETC.)

5. This farm _____ in _____ drainage or levee district.
    (IS-IS NOT)      (NAME)

6. Adequacy of drainage _____ Overflow hazards _____

7. Adequacy of water supply (describe) _____

8. A comparison of this farm with the average in the community is: Location _____ ; General desirability and salability _____ ;

9. soils _____ ; Improvements _____

10. The general condition of farm is _____
       (EXCELLENT, GOOD, FAIR, POOR)

11. The farm is a class _____ farm. It is in a class _____ . area. Land _____ in a mineral area. (Discuss in Par. I)
    (A-B-C-D-E)     (1-2-3-4-5)     (IS-IS NOT)     (BEING MAINTAINED, IMPROVED, NO CHANGE, DEPRECIATING—DISCUSS)

### B. PURCHASE DATA OF FARM

1. Applicant acquired this farm _____ by _____
       (YEAR)        (PURCHASE OR INHERITANCE)

2. The purchase price was, without personal property, $ _____ ; with personal property _____ $ _____

3. Cash payment _____ $ _____ Changes since purchase (describe) _____

4. Contract _____ $ _____

5. Mortgage _____ $ _____

6. Trade _____ $ _____

7.       TOTAL _____ $ _____

8. Remarks _____ Purchase is a bona fide sale: Yes ☐ No ☐

### C. PLAT

1. The legal description given in the application _____ correct. Indicate corrections, if any, on plat and explain in remarks.
       (IS-IS NOT)

2. Extreme care should be used to ascertain location of corners if buildings are close to line. Indicate points of compass and show scale of map. Designate section number at section centers. Indicate roads and show direction and distance to nearest town.

**D. DESCRIPTION OF BUILDINGS**

| No. and Kind | Rooms | Size | Type of Construction | Type of Foundation | Type of Roof | Condition-Improvements and Adaptability to Probable Use for the Next Few Years. Also Any Other Features That Enhance or Reduce Salability, Including Conformity with Community Standards | *Value Insurable Buildings |
|---|---|---|---|---|---|---|---|
| | | | | | | | |
| | | | | | | | |
| | | | | | | | |
| | | | | | | | |
| | | | | | | | |
| | | | | | | | TOTAL $ |

* Present cost of replacement less depreciation, including obsolescence

**Fig. 23–2a.** Appraiser's report.

**E. DESCRIPTION OF LAND**

| Normal Use | Acres | Type and Quality of Soil; Topography; Crop Adaptability; Ease and Economy of Operation; Any Other Important Features. |
|---|---|---|
| | | |
| | | |
| | | |
| | | |
| **TOTAL** | | |

Number of acres irrigated: _____     Method Code No. _____

**F. EARNING POWER OF FARM (Typical Operator - - Usual Conditions)**

| Crop | Acres | Average Yield Per Acre | Average Total Production | Unit Value (Normal Price) | Average Gross Value | Average Normal Sales | Value Landlord's Share |
|---|---|---|---|---|---|---|---|
| | | | | $ | $ | $ | $ |
| | | | | | | | |
| | | | | | | | |
| | | | | | | | |
| | | | | | | | |
| Pasture | | | Units for _____ mos. @ $ _____ | | | | |
| **TOTALS** | | | | | $ | $ | $ |

Rentability of farm _____   Usual rental terms _____

Industrial employment $ _____. Normal net outside income of typical owner: _____; Professional employment $ _____;

Rented land $ _____ No. acres _____ Sources and dependability of outside income under usual conditions.

**G. INCOME AND EXPENSE**

| | Owner Operator | Rental |
|---|---|---|
| Sale of crops | $ | $ |
| Sale of livestock (pltry) | $ | $ |
| Sale of livestock products | $ | $ |
| Sale miscellaneous products | $ | $ |
| R: Cash $ _____ Share $ | $ | $ |
| Total Gross Income | $ | $ |
| Cash operating expenses | $ | $ |
| Feed | $ | $ |
| Real estate taxes | $ | $ |
| Personal property taxes | $ | $ |
| Drainage O&M costs | $ | $ |
| B. & I. pymts. for _____ yrs. | $ | $ |
| Building upkeep | $ | $ |
| Repair & replmt. equipmt. | $ | $ |
| Ins. on bldgs. & per. prop. | $ | $ |
| Int. on short term credit | $ | $ |
| Total Expenses | $ | $ |
| Net Return | $ | $ |

**H. VALUATIONS AND ACCEPTABILITY**

Normal value of farm $ _____          Present market value of farm $ _____

1. Consideration has been given to total taxes, O&M, and B&I charges of $ _____ per acre and project debt liability of $ _____ against this land.

2. Any shortage in the acreage of this farm that may be developed upon examination of the title and verification of the plat which does not exceed _____ percent of the total acreage shown in my report and which is not caused by the exclusion of a specified part of the property will not affect my estimate of the normal value.

3. This property _____ satisfactory security for a loan not to exceed _____ years subject to the following requirements
   (IS—IS NOT)

   being fulfilled: _____

4. Without the foregoing requirements being fulfilled the NV is $ _____

   it is a class _____ farm, and _____ satisfactory security for a loan not to exceed _____ years.
   (A-B-C-D-E)          (IS—IS NOT)

**I. REMARKS** (Explain any unusual features not sufficiently covered elsewhere. If security is not acceptable or if the term is limited, give reasons.)

_____
_____
_____
_____
_____
_____
_____
_____
_____

Compared to _____ Benchmark

Located in _____ County

BM Land Value P/Ac    $ _____

This Farm Land Value P/Ac    $ _____

Location _____
         (above)(equal)(below)

Quality-crop &
pasture land _____
         (above)(equal)(below)

Principal Commodity Produced - Code No. _____

Secondary Commodity Produced - Code No. _____

Part-time farm:  Yes [ ]  No [ ]

The above report is true and correct to the best of my knowledge and belief.

1. Date appraised _____ 19____
2. Date written _____ 19____
3. Date mailed _____ 19____
4. Date recieved by **FLBA** _____ 19____

_____          _____
                    Signature          Code No.

**Fig. 23-2b.** Apprasier's report—reverse.

added value to farms that are especially well located and deducting for improvements that need to be made immediately.

6. Sale prices of similar farms in the community are determined from county records, newspaper files, and real estate brokers and appraisers. Comparisons are made with the farm being appraised and an estimated value is derived by correlating the value as determined by the income, capitalization, sales comparison and inventory or cost methods.

## FARM FINANCING

### Capital Requirements

Total assets of American agriculture were estimated at $307.1 billion on January 1, 1970. About 77 per cent of this represented equity capital.

The value of all farm real estate in 1970 was estimated at $208.9 billion. This was about two-thirds of total farm assets. Outstanding against this was an estimated real estate debt of $28.4 billion. This means that farmers have close to a 90 per cent equity in their land.

The rate of capital turnover in agriculture is typically slow. Although at times farmers have a capital turnover (length of time required for receipts to equal total capital invested) of 3 to 4 years, the normal length of time is now more likely to be 6 to 8 years in the Midwest. Time required varies with type of farm, level of prices, and related factors. Dairy and poultry farmers turn their capital over more quickly than beef cattle farmers, for example.

**TABLE 23–1. Balance Sheet of American Agriculture, 1970**

| Item | January 1, 1960 (Billion Dollars) | Estimate January 1, 1970 |
|------|-----------------------------------|--------------------------|
| Assets | | |
| Physical assets: | | |
| Real Estate | 130.2 | 208.9 |
| Non-real estate | 54.7 | 79.7 |
| Financial assets | 18.2 | 23.8 |
| Total | 203.1 | 312.4 |
| Claims | | |
| Real estate debt | 12.1 | 28.4 |
| Non-real estate | 12.7 | 29.7 |
| Equities | 178.3 | 254.3 |
| Total | 203.1 | 312.4 |

SOURCE: Dept. of Agriculture, Economic Research Service, *The Balance Sheet of the Farming Sector.*

## Sources of Funds

As in the case of other real estate uses, the purchase of fee ownership with the use of both equity and debt funds, plus the leasing of properties, constitute the major methods of acquiring rights to use farm real estate. Funds for the financing of farms are made available by institutional lenders, such as commercial banks and insurance companies, by individuals (especially retired farmers), by cooperative credit agencies, and by the government. Much land is sold on contract with the seller financing the arrangement or at least the earlier stages of it.[4] During prosperous periods, banks and insurance companies are of major importance as sources of farm credit. During periods of depression and low farm incomes, the major burden of financing shifts to government agencies or to government guaranteed loans.

Of the $27.2 billion farm mortgage debt outstanding at the beginning of 1969, life insurance companies held about a fifth, banks a ninth, federal land banks a fifth, Farmers Home Administration about 6 per cent and individuals and others around a fourth. In recent years there have been no significant changes in the relative importance of these sources of funds.

## GOVERNMENT PROGRAMS

For many years we have had a system of government supports of the prices of farm products. Details of the system have varied from time to time, but the basic principles have remained much the same. Support programs of some type seem likely to continue. There are indications, however, that the interests of the consumer will be accorded increased attention. The political balance seems to be shifting away from the farmers.

### Basis of Support

Three basic questions are involved in a system of government support of farm prices: first, which prices shall be supported; second, on what level; and third, by what means. Government supports have tended to be on a selective rather than on a uniform basis. Originally, only the so-called basic products—wheat, corn, cotton, rice, and peanuts—were supported. From time to time others have been added to the list and some have been dropped.

---

[4] Robert C. Suter, Philip J. Scaletta, and C. J. Thomas, "The Installment Land Contract: Legal Provisions and Economic Implications," Lafayette, Ind.: Purdue University, *Economic and Marketing Information* (May 28, 1971).

**TABLE 23–2. Farm Mortgage Debt: Amount of Outstanding Loans Reported by Principal Lenders, Other Debt, and Total Debt, United States, Jan. 1, 1954–1969**

| Year | Federal Land Banks [2] | Federal Farm Mortgage Corporation | Farmers Home Administration | Life Insurance Companies | Commercial and Savings Banks | Other Farm-Mortgage Debt | Total Farm Mortgage Debt |
|---|---|---|---|---|---|---|---|
| | 1,000 dollars | 1,000 dollars | 1,000 dollars | 1,000 dollars | 1,000 dollars | 1,000 dollars | 1,000 dollars |
| 1954 | 1,169,418 | 17,628 | 282,098 | 1,892,773 | 1,131,214 | 3,246,800 | 7,739,931 |
| 1955 | 1,266,953 | 12,834 | 287,171 | 2,051,784 | 1,210,676 | 3,415,860 | 8,245,278 |
| 1956 | 1,480,204 | | 277,869 | 2,271,784 | 1,346,287 | 3,635,872 | 9,012,016 |
| 1957 | 1,722,381 | | 289,546 | 2,476,543 | 1,386,270 | 3,946,785 | 9,821,525 |
| 1958 | 1,897,187 | | 339,865 | 2,578,958 | 1,414,207 | 4,152,258 | 10,382,475 |
| 1959 | 2,065,372 | | 388,010 | 2,661,229 | 1,511,859 | 4,464,920 | 11,091,390 |
| 1960 | 2,335,124 | | 439,269 | 2,819,542 | 1,631,271 | 4,857,203 | 12,082,409 |
| 1961 | 2,539,044 | | 483,985 | 2,974,609 | 1,691,239 | 5,131,427 | 12,820,304 |
| 1962 | 2,803,103 | | 569,093 | 3,161,757 | 1,789,103 | 5,576,049 | 13,899,105 |
| 1963 | 3,024,013 | | 588,802 | 3,391,183 | 2,056,944 | 6,106,879 | 15,167,821 |
| 1964 | 3,281,797 | | 605,307 | 3,780,537 | 2,360,320 | 6,775,544 | 16,803,505 |
| 1965 | 3,686,755 | | 619,492 | 4,287,671 | 2,668,535 | 7,631,787 | 18,894,240 |
| 1966 | 4,240,227 | | 631,147 | 4,801,677 | 2,939,046 | 8,574,789 | 21,186,886 |
| 1967 | 4,914,522 | | 585,426 | 5,213,587 | 3,169,469 | 9,418,231 | 23,301,235 |
| 1968 | 5,563,204 | | 536,221 | 5,539,600 | 3,541,927 | 10,305,420 | 25,486,372 |
| 1969 | 6,081,229 | | 493,522 | 5,763,500 | 3,856,514 | 10,944,544 | 27,139,309 |

## Parity

The basic principle determining the level at which prices are supported has been the concept of "parity." Parity is defined as the ratio which prevailed between farm prices and nonfarm prices during the period 1909 to 1914. This period is considered to be one in which a "normal" ratio between these two sets of prices prevailed. Several methods have been used to maintain parity, the most important being the "loan and storage" system. For example, the farmer stores wheat at an approved storage facility and offers the stored wheat as collateral for a nonrecourse loan from the government on the basis of the support price. If the farmer sees fit, he may repay the loan, redeem his wheat, and sell it on the open market. If he does not, the government takes the wheat as payment for the loan and the transaction is concluded. In fact, such a loan is a sort of conditional sale to the government at a "pegged" minimum price. Other methods which the government has used to support prices include outright purchase in the open market, subsidized exports, market quotas, acreage restrictions, and the Soil Bank program.

## FARM TRENDS

In all probability, the trend toward larger and fewer farms will continue as farm management improves and as technology advances, thus making possible increased use of machinery and improved seeds and fertilizers. Farms are likely to take on to an increasing extent many of the characteristics of large-scale manufacturing operations. Although there has been discussion about a return to organic agriculture and some efforts have been made in this direction, present requirements for food could not even be approached with such methods.

### Declining Numbers

Fewer people will get their incomes from farming. As recently as a hundred years ago over half of our people made their living by farming. Now, about one in twenty derives his income from farms.

### Bigger Farms—More Machines

Larger farms and more machinery will require increasing capital investment per farm and for agriculture as a whole. Managerial requirements will increase.

Those who now attempt to operate marginal farms may move into other occupations although they shift slowly. Some farms of this type may be absorbed by larger commercial farms. Others may be used for reforestation and recreational purposes.

## Highways

The federal highway program is having significant effects on farming. Many farms are being brought closer to markets. More farm families may live in suburban homes and commute to farm operations. This is already true of much crop farming, as in the case of the wheatlands of Kansas.

## Ownership

The number of owner-operated farms may tend downward as farms grow in size. Because of the interest of investors, farm tenants may have increasing opportunities to become owners.

## Science and Technology

The long-term impact of scientific and technological research on farming may be very great. It may be that in the not-too-distant future many of our food requirements will be produced in the laboratory and factory.

**TABLE 23–3. Farm Ownership Transfers: Estimated Number by Various Methods, per 1,000 of All Farms, United States, Years Ending Mar. 15, 1954–70 (number per thousand)**

| Year | Voluntary Sales | Foreclosures | Tax Sales | All Other Sales | Total |
|------|------|------|------|------|------|
| 1954 | 29.9 | 1.7 | 0.4 | 12.1 | 44.1 |
| 1955 | 31.9 | 1.9 | .4 | 12.4 | 46.6 |
| 1956 | 32.3 | 2.9 | .6 | 14.4 | 50.2 |
| 1957 | 31.3 | 2.0 | .7 | 13.7 | 47.7 |
| 1958 | 31.2 | 1.7 | .7 | 14.5 | 48.1 |
| 1959 | 31.3 | 1.6 | .4 | 14.8 | 48.1 |
| 1960 | 30.7 | 1.6 | .6 | 14.2 | 47.1 |
| 1961 | 28.1 | 1.5 | .5 | 14.5 | 44.6 |
| 1962 | 28.5 | 1.6 | .6 | 15.2 | 45.9 |
| 1963 | 28.5 | 1.2 | .4 | 14.7 | 44.8 |
| 1964 | 28.5 | 1.6 | .4 | 14.6 | 45.1 |
| 1965 | 30.3 | 1.4 | .4 | 14.3 | 46.4 |
| 1966 | 31.1 | .9 | .6 | 13.7 | 46.3 |
| 1967 | 30.9 | .8 | .2 | 12.6 | 44.5 |
| 1968 | 30.4 | 1.1 | .2 | 12.5 | 44.2 |
| 1969 | 30.6 | 1.0 | .3 | 12.6 | 44.5 |
| 1970 | 27.8 | 1.1 |  | 12.0 | 40.9 |

## TIMBERLAND

A considerable portion of land in the United States is covered with timber. Not only is this a source of lumber, but also of a great many by-products, such as turpentine, resin, and camphor. Timberland produces both human and animal foods, such as nuts, acorns, and wild fruit. It acts as a watershed, helps to support wildlife, and also provides certain recreational resources.

### Types of Land

At least three different types of land may be used for forests: (1) that where forests now exist and which is well adapted to the continuation of such use, (2) land where forests previously existed and which is better adapted to the growing of trees than to any other use, and (3) land which was previously in cultivation and might have been kept in cultivation if proper protective measures had been taken in time, but which now can be best utilized for the growing of trees.

### Sustained Yield Management

Land which is now in timber and for which this is its proper use can best be kept in such use by sustained yield management. This means that the timber should be managed in such a way that it will yield a relatively uniform crop year after year, or at least at frequent intervals rather than only a single crop once every generation, half century, or longer. For many years most of our timberland has been "mined" rather than cropped. Sustained yield management involves selective cutting, taking only the mature trees for commercial lumber production. It also involves the cutting of malformed, diseased, and "weed" trees to give appropriate room, light, and plant food to the more desirable types. By this general process a forester can improve the quality of his timber in much the same manner that a livestock breeder improves the quality of his herd. Frequently the returns from the lower-grade products are sufficient to cover labor costs incurred in the process of sustained yield management. The trees that are cut, of course, must be replaced either by planting seedlings grown in nursery plots or by resetting certain trees which have been left standing for the purpose.

### Yield Management Problems

Adequate replacement can rarely be achieved if the woodland is grazed by domestic livestock. Cattle and hogs, especially the latter, destroy almost all young growth in a forest. In addiiton there is the need of protecting timber from fire, which is the ever-threatening enemy of woodland. Much progress in the field of fire prevention and protection has been made in recent decades, but highly destructive forest fires continue to occur.

There are those who believe it is better to cut larger tracts and reforest them rather than to follow sustained yield management programs. Much depends on the characteristics of the forest, the terrain and the location.

### Reforestation

In cases where cutover land has not proved to be suitable for agricultural use, programs for reforestation may be undertaken. In the northern parts of the country, unfortunately, a period of fifty to one hundred years is often required for the growing of trees from the seedling to the saw-log stage. Because of the long waiting period, interest on the investment, taxes, and risks from many sources, programs of this type are not always attractive to private persons or business firms. In the South, particularly along the lower Atlantic and Gulf coastal plains, where the growing season is long and the rainfall is heavier, the rate of tree growth is sufficiently rapid to be attractive to private developers and investors. In this area trees may grow to sufficient size for commercial lumber products in twenty to thirty years. There is also some possibility of income from turpentine and other naval stores in the meantime. Tax arrangements have been made somewhat more favorable to developments of this kind in recent years.

## RECREATIONAL LAND

Factors which impart recreational values to rural land include the following: (1) favorable climate, for example, cool summers, mild winters, large percentage of sunny days, snow for skiing, and the like; (2) scenic beauty; for example bodies of water, mountains, and forests; (3) a relative abundance of wildlife, with opportunities for hunting, fishing, nature study, and photography; (4) facilities for water sports, including swimming, boating, and related activities; (5) historic or antiquarian interests, such as battlefields, relics of pioneer settlements, and the like; if located near to large population centers the value of recreational land will tend to be well supported.

### Seasons

Obviously a tract of land does not need all of these characteristics to have recreational value; any one of them alone may be sufficient to merit some degree of recreational use of land. Rarely are all of the characteristics listed above found in combination, but it is not unusual to find several of them available at a given site. New England, the northern lake regions, and parts of the Rocky Mountains attract people because of their cool summers. Florida, the Gulf coast, and parts of Texas, New Mexico, Arizona, and California attract people because of their relatively warm winters. The Adirondacks, the White Mountains, and various regions in the Rockies appeal to smaller numbers of more active people for skiing and other winter sports.

## Hunting and Fishing

Traditionally, hunting and fishing have been the most common forms of recreational use of rural land. Private and public hunting preserves have been developed. Lakes and streams have been stocked with fish in recent years. It is estimated that more people go fishing than engage in any other form of recreation.

## Vacations

The attractiveness of lakes, streams, and ocean beaches for water sports is closely related to the almost universal search for favorable climates. More and more people have been taking regular vacations. To a large degree these are concentrated in the summer months, but winter vacations are growing more popular. As a result, the incomes of winter resorts have tended to expand. Interstate highways and jet aircraft are changing somewhat the pattern of preferences for various resort areas.

## Historic Interests

Almost all of us are to some extent interested in our history. Old battlegrounds, ghost towns, relics of early settlements, and similar points of historical interest have a wide appeal. While this country lacks the old castles and other romantic ruins of Europe, we do have a number of interesting relics of both Indian and early American culture.

## Parks

The use of rural land for parks has been growing in importance. Some of the large national parks and forests, such as Yellowstone and Glacier National parks, are famous throughout the world. In recent years a number of states have developed systems of state parks. Those of Indiana, such as Brown County, Turkey Run, and McCormicks's Creek, are cases in point. In addition the private development of parks has progressed. Usually such parks are located in accessible areas and tied in with such sports as hunting, fishing, horseback riding, and related activities.

## Growing Importance of Recreation

With the growth of population, higher incomes, and increased leisure time, the demands for recreational facilities of all types have tended to expand. Outdoor recreation has attracted great numbers of people in recent years. This is due in large part to the increased mobility of our people. Widespread ownership of automobiles; favorable airline, bus, and boat fares; improved highways; and more widespread and longer vacations have all contributed to the growing interest in outdoor recreation. Furthermore, there are more retired people who have both leisure and independent incomes.

In all probability such factors as growing population, rising incomes, greater leisure time, and increased mobility will continue to operate in the years ahead. Consequently, recreation activities in general and outdoor recreation activities in particular seem likely to grow in importance.

## SUMMARY

Rural real estate includes land in use for farms and ranches, forestry, recreation, nonfarm residences, and other uses. Of these, agriculture is the most important.

The income-producing ability of most rural real estate is influenced by natural resources and characteristics of the land as well as location, which is of growing importance. The market for rural real estate is largely localized, and not highly organized. In the Midwest and West rural real estate is sold by the acre, and prices are quoted in dollars per acre. Some brokers who deal in rural real estate also offer farm management services.

The demand for agricultural land for commercial purposes is a derived demand, depending upon the demand for and prices of farm products. Some demand reflects the interest of investors in the income tax advantages of farm ownership and development, and some reflects the speculative hope that the land may be required for urban expansion in the future. Some rural land is used for recreational purposes and for part-time farming.

The price support programs which have been in operation over the past four decades have been an important influence on product prices and therefore on rural real estate values.

A recent trend, reinforced by technological improvements, is toward fewer farms, and these of larger unit size. The higher capital requirements for modern farming tend to make entry into farming more difficult. The interest of large investors in agricultural properties, may be helpful to young farmers.

Timberland represents an important sector of rural real estate. Sustained yield management and tax advantages have tended to attract investors into timberland in recent years.

Recreation of all types appears to be a growing influence in American life. Demands for outdoor recreational facilities are growing; this indicates a substantial expansion in the use of various lands for recreational purposes.

## QUESTIONS FOR STUDY

1. Explain why agriculture has shifted toward managerial-type operations. What effect has this had on land uses and values?
2. How does the market for farms differ from the market for other types of real estate? Why?
3. Explain why the demand for commercial farms is a derived demand.
4. Do practices of farm real estate brokers differ from those in urban areas? Explain.
5. Explain the major factors that determine the value of rural land. Which of these is most important? Why?
6. Explain how farm operations can be expanded by using capital instead of additional land.
7. What factors explain the increasing average unit size of farms? What advantages do you see in this trend? If there are any disadvantages, explain why and for whom.
8. Why might investors not directly interested in farming desire to own farm property?
9. Compare and contrast the financing of farm and residential real estate. Identify and define the financing agencies that are most important in rural real estate.
10. What is your evaluation of farm price-support programs? How do these programs affect the income-producing ability of rural real estate? What is their effect on the values of rural real estate?
11. What are the major determinants of demand in the market for timberland? What are the major determinants of supply?
12. What is sustained yield management?
13. Is the amount of land devoted to recreational activities likely to increase or decrease in the years ahead? Why?

## SUGGESTED READINGS

BABCOCK, H. A. Appraisal Principles and Practice. Homewood, Ill.: Richard D. Irwin, Inc., 1968.

CLAWSON, MARION. Outdoor Recreation. Washington, D.C.: Resources for the Future, Inc., 1958.

————, et al. Land for the Future. Baltimore: The Johns Hopkins Press, 1960. Chaps. iii, vi.

Committee for Economic Development. *An Adaptive Program for Agriculture,* A Statement on National Policy, by the Research and Policy Committee. New York, July, 1962.

Economic Research Service, U. S. Department of Agriculture. *The Balance Sheet of the Farming Sector.* Washington, D.C.: U. S. Government Printing Office, 1970.

Higbee, Edward. *Farms and Farmers in an Urban Age.* New York: Twentieth Century Fund, 1963. Chap. iv.

Hoagland, Henry E., and Leo D. Stone. *Real Estate Finance* (4th ed.). Homewood, Ill.: Richard D. Irwin, Inc., 1969. Chap. 22.

Murray, W. G. *Farm Appraisal and Valuation* (4th ed.). Iowa State College, 1961.

## STUDY PROJECT 23–1

### Farm Management

Professor Robert C. Suter of Purdue University describes farm management in this way:

Farm Management is the science of the organization and operation of a farm for purposes of maximum efficiency and continuous profits. It is the business end of farming.

The functions of management are three:

1. To organize or coordinate the factors of production—land, labor and capital. This is essentially farm planning . . . enterprise selection, or farm organization.
2. To supervise the operation of the business after it has been set up or developed. This is essentially concerned with the factors affecting profits in farming, refinements in the farm plan, and selection of the most economical production practices.
3. To anticipate and, if possible, determine the future, especially the economics that may prevail with certain cost reducing technologies. This is essentially an economist's job . . . , one of prediction of technical innovation, and future prices and profits.

### Questions

1. How does this description of farm management compare with business management in general? With real property management? With the management of a real estate firm?
2. Are the functions of farm management likely to become more specialized or to grow increasingly similar to management in the urban real estate field? Explain.
3. Is farm management likely to become of greater or lesser importance in the field of agriculture? Explain your estimate.

# 24

# International Real Estate Trends

## WORLD URBANIZATION AND REAL ESTATE

The growth of cities at a more rapid rate than the surrounding rural areas is a worldwide phenomenon. London was the only metropolitan area approaching 1 million population in 1800; now there are around 150 metropolitan areas in the world with a million or more residents. The number of cities with a population of 100,000 or more increased from 36 in the year 1800 to 1,128 in 1960. The total urban population of the world increased from 45-to-50 million in 1800 to over a billion in a little over a century and a half. If the present population explosion continues, urban population may increase to around 3 billion by the year 2000.

This growth of cities is the consequence of a transition from a society dominated by agriculture to one with an increasing development of manufacturing, which began in England and then successively took hold in Germany, the United States, Japan and the Soviet Union and Red China. Industrialization is in its incipient stages in India, Brazil, Mexico and in many other countries.

### Relative Importance of Real Estate as an Investment

In many foreign nations real estate is a larger medium of investment than all other investments combined. More than $450 billion was invested in real estate mortgages in the United States in 1970 and nearly $420 billion in the non-farm area. Investment in commercial properties totaled over $80 billion, multi-family over $57 billion and single-family homes, $280 billion. In addiiton to these large investment opportunities, the U. S. offers many attractive stocks and bonds to those who prefer this type of investment. Similar opportunities do not always exist in undeveloped nations. In many nations, land has been the chief medium of investment because of the lack of industries offering their securities on the market.

## Investments by Nationals of Other Countries in American Real Estate

There is a recent trend toward investment by Europeans and other foreigners in income properties in the United States. These investments are prompted by a variety of motives: (1) vanity, or the prestige of owning property in Manhattan or some other American center; (2) fear of either confiscation in their home lands or discriminatory taxes on their own real estate; and (3) possibility of capital gains or tax advantage in investing outside their own nations. American brokers are becoming familiar with the problems involved in securing real estate investments from other nationals, such as getting authority from their governments to transfer funds, foreign exchange rates and practices, and financing and property management.

Foreign investors have recently made large investments in United States planned shopping centers, office buildings, and apartments. In addition to income property, thousands of lots in Florida resort developments have been sold to Europeans. Pan Am and General Motors Buildings in New York attracted British capital.

## The Multinational Corporation

The growing numbers of business firms that operate on an international basis have given added dimensions to the international nature of real estate markets and ownership. Many companies not only export goods and services or operate licensing arrangements but also establish branch offices and in many cases manufacturing and distribution facilities abroad. Indeed, some of the larger multinational companies rival governments in terms of their power and influence.[1]

The land and buildings required for operations may be leased or owned. In some cases partnership arrangements with the nationals of local countries are considered desirable rather than sole ownership by the multinational corporation. In some cases countries place limits on investments from abroad. Sometimes the ownership of real estate is limited to local people.

---

[1] See, for example, *U. S. News and World Report* of July 19, 1971.

As has been pointed out:

As American investments abroad have expanded, some countries have placed limits on them. This arises from a variety of causes such as nationalism, a fear of dominance by U. S. investments, the desire to maintain opportunities for local investment, and others. To an increasing extent American companies are sharing investment opportunities with the citizens of other countries.[2]

Investments abroad, including real estate, have been stimulated by such institutions as the International Monetary Fund, the International Bank for Reconstruction and Development, the North Atlantic Treaty Organization (NATO), The General Agreement on Tariffs and Trade (GATT), The European Common Market, The European Free Trade Association (EFTA) and the Organization of American States (OAS). The World Court at The Hague has helped to settle international problems. Other important institutions for U. S. business include The Export-Import Bank, Development Loan Fund, and The Agency for Industrial Development (AID).

Some countries offer tax concessions such as "tax holidays" to attract investments from abroad; some serve as tax havens. In some cases special market and investment protections are provided. Even so, the risks often are great.

### Ground Plans of Foreign and American Cities

Aerial views of foreign cities often disclose an irregular street pattern, with densely packed buildings, which gives the appearance of a giant organism. On the other hand, most American cities, excepting Boston, were built on a rectangular pattern. The newer suburbs of American cities built during the automobile age, reveal a pattern of curving streets, which distinguish them from the rigidly straight lines of the old cities based on streetcar transportation.

Latin American cities have followed the design laid down by the Spaniards and the Portuguese, in which the central plaza is bordered by square blocks. Washington, D.C., is an example of a city planned from its inception with radial streets intersecting the rectangular street pattern. In Brasilia, a planner's ideal has been realized by the creation of super blocks of 2,500 population with an elementary school at the center and with four super blocks constituting a community large enough for a high school. In Brasilia there is a rigid separation between government buildings and office areas and the residential areas, and there are no grade intersections at street crossings. Other planned capital cities are Canberra, in Australia, and Islambad, the new capital of West Pakistan.

---

[2] Arthur M. Weimer, *Introduction to Business: A Management Approach* (4th ed.; Homewood, Ill.: Richard D. Irwin, Inc., 1970), p. 535.

## TABLE 24–1. World Population—Countries with Populations of 1 Million or More

| COUNTRY | POPULATION (thousands) | GROWTH RATE (percent) | COUNTRY | POPULATION (thousands) | GROWTH RATE (percent) | COUNTRY | POPULATION (thousands) | GROWTH RATE (percent) |
|---|---|---|---|---|---|---|---|---|
| CHINA (Mainland) | 740,000 | | KOREA (North) | 13,300 | 2.6 | DOMINICAN REPUBLIC | 3,951 | 3.0 |
| INDIA | 526,043 | 1.5 | PERU | 13,172 | 3.1 | NIGER | 3,909 | 3.0 |
| USSR | 240,333 | 2.3 | NETHERLANDS | 12,873 | 1.3 | GUINEA | 3,890 | 2.7 |
| UNITED STATES | 203,213 | 1.3 | TANZANIA² | 12,557 | 2.6 | NORWAY | 3,851 | 0.8 |
| PAKISTAN | 126,740 | 2.7 | AUSTRALIA | 12,296 | 2.0 | SENEGAL | 3,790 | 2.2 |
| INDONESIA | 116,600 | 2.4 | CEYLON | 12,244 | 2.4 | RWANDA | 3,650 | 3.1 |
| JAPAN | 102,322 | 1.0 | KENYA | 10,890 | 3.1 | CHAD | 3,510 | 1.5 |
| BRAZIL | 92,282 | 3.2 | NEPAL | 10,845 | 1.8 | BURUNDI | 3,475 | 2.0 |
| NIGERIA | 64,560 | 2.6 | MALAYSIA | 10,600 | 3.0 | EL SALVADOR | 3,390 | 3.7 |
| GERMANY, FED. REP. OF | 60,842 | 1.0 | HUNGARY | 10,295 | 0.3 | IRELAND | 2,921 | 0.3 |
| UNITED KINGDOM | 55,534 | 0.7 | VENEZUELA | 10,035 | 3.5 | LAOS | 2,893 | 2.4 |
| ITALY | 53,170 | 0.8 | BELGIUM | 9,646 | 0.6 | URUGUAY | 2,852 | 1.3 |
| FRANCE | 50,330 | 1.1 | CHILE | 9,566 | 2.5 | ISRAEL | 2,822 | 3.3 |
| MEXICO | 48,933 | 3.5 | PORTUGAL | 9,560 | 0.9 | NEW ZEALAND | 2,777 | 1.8 |
| PHILIPPINES | 35,900 | 3.1 | UGANDA | 9,500 | 3.0 | PUERTO RICO | 2,739 | 1.7 |
| THAILAND | 35,128 | 3.1 | IRAQ | 9,350 | 3.5 | SOMALIA | 2,730 | 2.5 |
| TURKEY | 34,450 | 2.5 | GREECE | 8,835 | 0.7 | LEBANON | 2,645 | 2.5 |
| SPAIN | 32,949 | 0.9 | CUBA | 8,513 | 2.5 | DAHOMEY | 2,640 | 2.9 |
| POLAND | 32,555 | 1.0 | BULGARIA | 8,440 | 0.8 | SIERRA LEONE | 2,510 | 2.0 |
| EGYPT, ARAB REP. OF | 32,501 | 2.5 | GHANA | 8,341 | 2.5 | HONDURAS | 2,495 | 3.4 |
| KOREA, REP. OF | 31,139 | 2.6 | SWEDEN | 7,968 | 0.7 | PAPUA NEW GUINEA | 2,363 | 2.4 |
| IRAN | 28,475 | 3.0 | MOZAMBIQUE | 7,539 | 1.8 | PARAGUAY | 2,314 | 3.1 |
| BURMA | 26,980 | 2.1 | AUSTRIA | 7,371 | 0.5 | JORDAN | 2,242 | 3.2 |
| ETHIOPIA | 24,769 | 2.0 | KHMER REP. | 7,284 | 3.3 | ALBANIA | 2,075 | 2.9 |
| ARGENTINA | 23,983 | 1.6 | SAUDI ARABIA | 7,235 | 1.7 | SINGAPORE | 2,017 | 2.4 |
| VIET-NAM (North) | 21,340 | 3.2 | MALAGASY REPUBLIC | 6,656 | 2.4 | NICARAGUA | 1,915 | 3.5 |
| CANADA | 21,089 | 1.8 | SWITZERLAND | 6,230 | 1.7 | TOGO | 1,896 | 2.6 |
| COLOMBIA | 20,463 | 3.2 | ECUADOR | 5,890 | 3.4 | LIBYA, ARAB REP. OF | 1,869 | 3.7 |
| YUGOSLAVIA | 20,351 | 1.1 | SYRIA, ARAB REP. OF | 5,866 | 2.8 | JAMAICA | 1,863 | 1.5 |
| SOUTH AFRICA¹ | 20,218 | 2.3 | CAMEROON | 5,736 | 2.1 | COSTA RICA | 1,680 | 3.3 |
| ROMANIA | 20,010 | 0.9 | YEMEN, ARAB REP. OF | 5,556 | 2.1 | CENTRAL AFRICAN REPUBLIC | 1,518 | 2.4 |
| CONGO, DEM. REP. OF | 17,900 | 2.1 | ANGOLA | 5,430 | 1.3 | LIBERIA | 1,480 | 2.8 |
| VIET-NAM, REP. OF | 17,867 | 2.7 | UPPER VOLTA | 5,278 | 2.2 | PANAMA | 1,417 | 3.3 |
| GERMANY (Eastern) | 17,096 | -0.1 | RHODESIA | 5,090 | 3.2 | MONGOLIA | 1,251 | 3.1 |
| SUDAN | 15,186 | 2.9 | GUATEMALA | 5,014 | 3.1 | YEMEN, PEOPLE'S DEM. REP. OF | 1,220 | 2.2 |
| MOROCCO | 15,050 | 2.9 | IVORY COAST | 4,942 | 2.8 | MAURITANIA | 1,136 | 2.2 |
| CZECHOSLOVAKIA | 14,418 | 0.6 | TUNISIA | 4,919 | 3.0 | TRINIDAD AND TOBAGO | 1,040 | 2.5 |
| AFGHANISTAN | 13,975 | 2.0 | DENMARK | 4,891 | 0.7 | | | |
| CHINA, REP. OF | 13,800 | 3.0 | MALI | 4,881 | 2.1 | | | |
| ALGERIA | 13,349 | 2.4 | BOLIVIA | 4,804 | 2.6 | | | |
| | | | HAITI | 4,768 | 2.0 | | | |
| | | | FINLAND | 4,703 | 0.7 | | | |
| | | | MALAWI | 4,398 | 2.6 | | | |
| | | | ZAMBIA | 4,020 | 2.6 | | | |
| | | | HONG KONG | 3,990 | 2.9 | | | |

¹Including Namibia.
²Mainland Tanzania.

SOURCE: International Bank for Reconstruction and Development, 1968.

## OWNERSHIP

The discussions of real estate decisions set forth in this text have application chiefly to nations in which (1) real estate properties are privately owned, (2) there is no fear of total or partial confiscation of private property by the state, and (3) inflationary tendencies are limited.

### U. S. Ownership

The laws of property in the United States were first developed by the English common law, and the real estate principles observed in the United States are almost equally applicable in England and the British dominions of Canada and Australia, and in nations where English laws and principles were established as in South Africa and East Africa.

Of course, private real estate ownership in the United States is subject to public control of various types such as zoning, building regulations, financing arrangements, real estate taxes, and sometimes and in some places by rent control. Nevertheless, the United States is the outstanding example of a nation of private property ownership by millions of individuals, business firms, and independent institutions. The United States possesses the advantage, not only of a wide distribution of ownerships of all types of property, but also of a division of ownership into tolerably efficient economic units. There are few large tracts under one ownership except in grazing areas; on the other hand, there are few individually owned farms too small to be operated by machinery.

### Communist Ownership

At the opposite pole are Soviet Russia and Communist China, where the state owns practically all of the land, and where private ownership is limited to the right to use and occupy a single house or a small garden. It is obvious that the freedom to buy and sell buildings or vacant lands at prices determined by bargaining between a buyer and seller in an open market cannot exist where the right to buy or sell is denied. Movements of the buyer and seller are regulated; prices of all building materials are controlled by the state regardless of cost. The state, by its own fiat, determines where new industries, apartment developments, and new cities shall be located. In Russia rents bear no relationship to cost of construction. Consequently American principles of real estate value and real estate decision processes could not be applied to the Soviet Union without great modification.

## TABLE 24–2. Gross National Product Per Capita—Countries with Populations of 1 Million or More (U.S. dollars)

| COUNTRY | GNP per CAPITA (US dollars) | GROWTH RATE (percent) | COUNTRY | GNP per CAPITA (US dollars) | GROWTH RATE (percent) | COUNTRY | GNP per CAPITA (US dollars) | GROWTH RATE (percent) |
|---|---|---|---|---|---|---|---|---|
| UNITED STATES | 4,240 | 3.2 | URUGUAY | 560 | -0.8 | THAILAND | 160 | 4.7 |
| SWEDEN | 2,920 | 3.4 | JAMAICA² | 550 | 3.0 | CAMEROON | 150 | 2.0 |
| SWITZERLAND | 2,700 | 2.6 | CHILE | 510 | 1.7 | MAURITANIA* | 140 | 4.6 |
| CANADA | 2,650 | 2.8 | COSTA RICA | 510 | 2.9 | VIET-NAM, REP. OF | 140 | 1.8 |
| FRANCE | 2,460 | 4.8 | PORTUGAL | 510 | 4.9 | CENTRAL AFRICA REP. | 130 | 0.0 |
| DENMARK | 2,310 | 3.7 | MONGOLIA† | 460 | 1.0 | KENYA | 130 | 1.5 |
| AUSTRALIA | 2,300 | 2.9 | ALBANIA† | 430 | 4.9 | KHMER REP. | 130 | 0.5 |
| NEW ZEALAND | 2,230 | 2.0 | NICARAGUA | 380 | 2.8 | YEMEN, PEOPLE'S DEM. REP. OF | 120 | -4.6 |
| GERMANY, FED. REP. OF | 2,190 | 3.7 | SAUDI ARABIA | 380 | 7.1 | INDIA | 110 | 1.1 |
| NORWAY | 2,160 | 4.0 | GUATEMALA | 350 | 1.9 | LAOS* | 110 | 0.2 |
| BELGIUM | 2,010 | 3.5 | IRAN | 350 | 4.9 | MALAGASY REP. | 110 | 0.0 |
| FINLAND | 1,980 | 3.9 | TURKEY | 350 | 3.4 | PAKISTAN | 110 | 2.9 |
| UNITED KINGDOM | 1,890 | 1.8 | MALAYSIA | 340 | 3.8 | SUDAN | 110 | 0.6 |
| NETHERLANDS | 1,760 | 3.1 | PERU | 330 | 1.4 | UGANDA | 110 | 1.7 |
| GERMANY (Eastern)† | 1,570 | 4.1 | IRAQ | 310 | 3.0 | INDONESIA | 100 | 0.8 |
| ISRAEL | 1,570 | 5.3 | CHINA, REP. OF | 300 | 6.3 | TOGO | 100 | 0.0 |
| LIBYA, ARAB REP. OF | 1,510 | 21.7 | COLOMBIA | 290 | 1.5 | AFGHANISTAN | — | 0.3 |
| AUSTRIA | 1,470 | 3.9 | EL SALVADOR | 290 | 1.9 | BURMA | — | 1.8 |
| JAPAN | 1,430 | 10.0 | ZAMBIA | 290 | 5.4 | BURUNDI* | — | 0.0 |
| PUERTO RICO | 1,410 | 6.0 | CUBA† | 280 | -3.2 | CHAD | — | -1.3 |
| ITALY | 1,400 | 4.7 | DOMINICAN REPUBLIC | 280 | 0.4 | CHINA (Mainland)† | — | 0.8 |
| CZECHOSLOVAKIA† | 1,370 | 3.9 | JORDAN* | 280 | 4.7 | CONGO, DEM. REP. OF | — | 0.2 |
| USSR† | 1,200 | 5.6 | KOREA (North)† | 280 | 5.9 | DAHOMEY | — | 0.9 |
| IRELAND | 1,110 | 3.5 | BRAZIL | 270 | 1.4 | ETHIOPIA | — | 2.3 |
| HUNGARY† | 1,100 | 5.5 | ALGERIA | 260 |  | GUINEA | — | 2.6 |
| ARGENTINA | 1,060 | 2.6 | HONDURAS | 260 | 1.1 | HAITI | — | -1.0 |
| VENEZUELA | 1,000 | 2.5 | SYRIA, ARAB REP. OF | 260 | 4.7 | MALAWI | — | 1.0 |
| POLAND† | 940 | 5.1 | ECUADOR | 240 | 1.2 | MALI | — | 1.2 |
| TRINIDAD AND TOBAGO | 890 | 3.8 | IVORY COAST | 240 | 4.7 | NEPAL | — | 0.4 |
| BULGARIA† | 860 | 6.7 | PARAGUAY | 240 | 1.0 | NIGER | — | -0.9 |
| ROMANIA† | 860 | 7.5 | RHODESIA | 240 | 0.4 | NIGERIA | — | -0.3 |
| HONG KONG | 850 | 8.7 | TUNISIA | 230 | 2.1 | RWANDA | — | -0.8 |
| GREECE | 840 | 6.2 | ANGOLA | 210 | 1.4 | SOMALIA* | — | 1.5 |
| SPAIN | 820 | 6.5 | KOREA, REP. OF | 210 | 6.4 | TANZANIA³ | — | 1.6 |
| SINGAPORE | 800 | 4.5 | MOZAMBIQUE | 210 | 3.3 | UPPER VOLTA | — | 0.1 |
| SOUTH AFRICA¹ | 710 | 3.8 | PAPUA NEW GUINEA | 210 | 2.0 | VIET-NAM (North)† | — | 3.2 |
| PANAMA | 660 | 4.8 | PHILIPPINES | 210 | 1.9 | YEMEN, ARAB REP. OF* | — | 2.3 |
| LEBANON | 580 | 2.1 | LIBERIA | 200 | -0.1 |  |  |  |
| MEXICO | 580 | 3.4 | SENEGAL | 200 | -0.3 |  |  |  |
| YUGOSLAVIA | 580 | 4.6 | CEYLON | 190 | 2.1 |  |  |  |
|  |  |  | GHANA | 190 | 0.0 |  |  |  |
|  |  |  | MOROCCO | 190 | 3.4 |  |  |  |
|  |  |  | SIERRE LEONE | 170 | 1.2 |  |  |  |
|  |  |  | BOLIVIA | 160 | 2.4 |  |  |  |
|  |  |  | EGYPT, ARAB REP. OF | 160 | 1.2 |  |  |  |

Note: In view of the usual errors inherent in this type of data and to avoid a misleading impression of accuracy, the figures for GNP per capita have been rounded to the nearest $10.

¹Including Namibia.
²The estimate of rate of growth of GNP per capita of 0.8% in the 1970 Atlas was in error; the correct figure should have been 2.6%.
³Mainland Tanzania.
*Estimates of GNP per capita and its growth rate are tentative.
†Estimates of GNP per capita and its growth rate have a wide margin of error mainly because of the problems in deriving the GNP at factor cost from net material product and in converting the GNP estimate into US dollars.
—Estimated at less than 100 dollars.

## Mixed Types

Between the private ownership of the United States and the state ownership of Russia, there are numerous mixed types. In a number of countries there has been expropriation of large land holdings and redistribution among small farmers. In present-day Finland and in Sweden the state owns large tracts of land for control purposes.

## Surveys and Recording of Deeds

The transferability of real property and the ability to value parcels of real estate in the market depend upon accurate land surveys which identify each parcel, and help to assure protection for the title. As we pointed out in Chapter 4, in the United States, government land surveys established the base boundary lines for areas west of the Alleghenies, dividing most of this vast area into square mile tracts. Deeds to lands are recorded in the county courthouses, so that the names of titleholders are a matter of public record. Title guarantee companies, or lawyers examining the abstracts showing the chain of title, or the Torrens system, can assure the purchaser that he is securing a merchantable title to the land described in the deed or that title is faulty.

In contrast to this, in some of the new nations of Africa like Ghana, there are no accurate land surveys. The land, as in pre-Columbian North America, is owned by the tribe.

In many nations of Europe, land in small strips has been owned by the same family for generations and is constantly subdivided further by inheritance. In some village economies, as was the case in Czarist Russia, the village elders redistribute the land among the villagers at stated intervals.

## DANGERS TO OWNERSHIP

As we have suggested there are many dangers to private ownership including fear of confiscation and inflation.

## Fear of Confiscation

Any nation which has enjoyed protection of private property rights may fear that a change of government will reduce the value of real estate either by (1) outright confiscation, (2) condemnation at a low price, (3) rapid increase of real estate taxes, or (4) special advances in wages of building workers and operators. Activity in the real estate market will be virtually suspended in such cases.

### Inflation

A relatively stable currency has been important to the ownership and use of real estate in the United States. Although our dollar has lost value, long-term financing continues to be possible. Insurance companies, banks, and savings and loan institutions have been willing to make loans repayable thirty years or longer in the future in terms of fixed dollars. Whether this will continue to be true if inflationary tendencies continue is an open question.

In some countries inflation has discouraged long term financing and has brought interest rates to five per cent per month or higher. In such cases the desire to invest in real estate is strong in order to have an inflation hedge. Often it is necessary to pay cash, however, without the benefit of long term financing.

## REAL ESTATE MARKET DIFFERENCES

Among the major factors which help to account for differences between the real estate markets of the U. S. and other countries are: (1) income distribution, (2) transportation and especially differences in the ownership of automobiles, (3) land use patterns including operation of the sector theory, prevalence of shopping centers, high rise office buildings and soil qualities and (4) differences in real estate and appraisal practices. We will consider these topics briefly here. We should note, however, that there are trends in a number of countries that suggest movement in the direction of U. S. real estate market operations and practices.

### Income Distribution

The relatively high per capita incomes in the U. S. and the large middle class help to explain the differences between the scope and magnitude of the real estate market in this country and other parts of the world. Figures published by the International Bank for Reconstruction and Development compare per capita national product in a number of countries. (These figures, it should be noted, differ from per capita income or disposal income.) For example, GNP per capita in the U. S. is placed at $3520 for 1968; for the same year GNP per capita is reported as $2,240 in Canada, $1,840 in Australia, $1,730 in France, $1,700 in West Germany; $1,620 in the United Kingdom, $890 in the USSR, $860 in Japan, $780 in Argentina, $640 in Spain, $550 in South Africa, $510 in Yugoslavia, $470 in Mexico, $240 in Brazil, $90 in India and $90 in Pakistan. (See Table 24–2.)

The relatively high incomes in the U. S. make it possible for a large portion of the families to buy automobiles, single family homes, and a wide variety of equipment and conveniences. In 1970 there were almost 40 million owner-occupied dwelling units in the U. S. or 62.9 per cent of the total, as we have noted. The construction, financing and marketing of new housing units at an annual rate approximating 2 million units provides the basis for an active real estate market.

In countries where incomes are low and where there is a small middle class, the possibilities for an active real estate market are much more limited. Often there is a wide gulf between the relatively small number of wealthy families and the great majority of people, many of whom are very poor. With a small middle class, ownership concentrated in the wealthy, and many people living on small rural plots of land, market transfers of real estate tend to be quite limited. Most property is passed on through inheritance with few other types of transfers.

## Ownership of Automobiles

The relatively high incomes of families in the United States make possible the almost universal ownership of automobiles. In 1970, there were 87 million privately owned automobiles in the United States. The widespread ownership of a private means of transportation has had a far-reaching effect on the growth of suburbs, at a substantial distance from the central business district, and it has brought about the creation of shopping centers and a widespread dispersal of factories and office buildings to the periphery of cities.

In 1970, while the United States had 2.4 persons per automobile, Canada had 3.3 and the United Kingdom 4.9. (See Table 24–3.) In that year European nations had from 4.4 in France to 4.6 in West Germany and 5.9 in Italy; in Poland there were 82.2 persons per automobile, in East Germany 15.6 and in the USSR 186.6. Argentina had 19.1 persons per automobile, Japan 14.9, Mexico and Brazil 45.6. Most Asiatic, African and South American nations still have only a small number of automobiles in relation to the population. The number of automobiles has recently shown marked gains in Europe.

## Mass Transit Lines

Where only a small proportion of the population owns private automobiles, the predominant form of transportation is by bus or train. In some great cities like London, Paris, Berlin, Moscow, Tokyo, and Buenos Aires, there are subways in addition to buses and trains. Since mass transit lines cannot operate economically to thinly settled single-family housing areas, the majority of dwelling units in the great cities of Asia, Latin America, and Continental Europe are in apartment buildings, which are concentrated in bands along mass transit lines or bus lines, or in

**TABLE 24–3. World Automobile Registration, January 1, 1970**

|  | Total Autos | Average Persons per Auto |
| --- | --- | --- |
| World | 181,913,032 |  |
| United States | 87,153,381 | 2.4 |
| Canada | 6,460,000 | 3.3 |
| Mexico | 1,636,733 | 45.6 |
| Argentina | 2,041,000 | 19.1 |
| Brazil | 1,275,000 | 45.6 |
| United Kingdom | 11,365,020 | 4.9 |
| Italy | 9,054,205 | 5.9 |
| France | 13,770,000 | 4.4 |
| West Germany | 12,584,564 | 4.6 |
| East Germany | 1,039,229 | 15.6 |
| Poland | 401,764 | 82.2 |
| USSR | 1,300,000 | 186.6 |
| India | 545,500 | 1,106.6 |
| Japan | 6,933,739 | 14.9 |

SOURCE: "Motor Vehicle Registration in the World," *Automotive News* (1971 Almanac Edition; April 26, 1971), p. 10.

suburban clusters served by mass transit as in Moscow and Helsinki. Apartment units are also cheaper to build than single-family houses, and occupy far less ground area.

Mass transit lines leading to the center of the city also sustain the central business district. There has been less decentralization of cities abroad than in the U. S. although it is developing in Western Europe. In most cities outside the United States, the central areas contain the chief attractions of urban life—the parks, palaces, museums, ancient monuments, national capitols, as well as hotels, theatres, and restaurants. The Parthenon on the Acropolis is near the center of Athens; the Arche de Triomphe, the Louvre, and Notre Dame are at the center of Paris; Buckingham Palace, Westminster Abbey, the Houses of Parliament, and St. Paul's are in the center of London. The Ginza district of Tokyo—its shopping and amusement district—attracts throngs at night. The principal cathedrals, museums, the capitols, and monuments of Bogota, Lima, Buenos Aires, Rio de Janeiro, and Quito, as well as the tallest office buildings and the leading stores face or are located near the central plaza. In these foreign cities the central areas are continually rebuilt and renewed.

## Sector Theory

The rise of the middle class in many nations and the increased ownership of the automobile will make it possible for more and more families to live in single-family detached houses on the periphery of the city. This has already taken place in Latin America. Wealthy families have tended to move from patio type dwellings on the central plazas to homes or apartments on the outer fringe of one sector of the city, as in Bogotá, Lima, La Paz, Quito, Santiago, Buenos Aires, Montevideo, Rio de Janeiro, and Caracas.

### Shopping Centers

The increased ownership of automobiles will also lead to the establishment of outlying shopping centers with free automobile parking. Canada and Australia already have many shopping centers similar to those in the United States. There is a limited number of these shopping centers in other nations such as the Amstel Center in Amsterdam, Rosebank in Cape Town, South Africa, and others in Europe. Sears Roebuck has a number of stores in Latin America in midtown locations but most of these are solitary stores.

The practice of making leases, not only with minimum guaranteed rent, but also with rents based on a percentage of sales seems to be unknown in most countries. Difficulties may also be experienced in other countries in securing commercial zoning for a sufficient area of land to provide free parking areas.

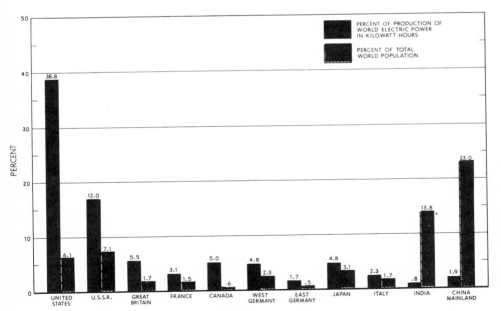

**Fig. 24–1.** Electric power production and population. (From United Nations data.)

### High-Rise Office Buildings

New tall office buildings have broken the old sky lines in London, Paris, and Milan, as well as in Rio de Janeiro and Mexico City. Thus, the uniform height of buildings, so long maintained, is giving way to the irregular skyline of American cities.

### Soil Qualities

In all parts of the world are found agricultural areas in which the composition of soils, rainfall, length of the growing season, and suitability for crops are similar to some areas in the United States, and they are measured and defined by soil scientists as in the United States. Differences in the values of crop lands or grazing lands in other nations compared to the United States would result from lower labor costs, lower selling prices if there is no price support of crops, and import restrictions or tariff duties of the other nations buying the crops.

### Appraisals and Real Estate Valuations

Where the titles to real estate are not jeopardized by confiscation, the value of real estate properties based on comparable sales, reproduction cost, and net income would be computed in a similar manner to that in the United States. The formula would be the same, but the figures in it would be different. Thus, in Johannesburg, South Africa, elevator office building costs of construction would be approximately $8 per square foot, due to partial use of native labor, compared with $22 to $30 per square foot in the United States, but office rents would be only $2.50 per square foot annually compared to $6 or $8 per square foot here.

Rent control in Brazil has the same depressing effect on values as in the United States. In Brazil, France, and other nations where rent control is applied to existing apartments, new apartments have been built and sold on a condominium basis.

## SUMMARY

World urbanization represents one of the significant developments of recent years. This reflects the increased industrialization of many parts of the world. With this has come a growing interest in real estate, notably in urban and urban-related areas. In recent years international investments in real estate have risen in importance. In many foreign countries real estate is a relatively more important medium of investment than in the United States because of the relatively greater importance of the securities market in this country. Investments of other nationals in the

United States have tended to rise and opposite trends are also to be noted. Differential yields on investments, differences in tax treatment, and the desire for a spreading of risks are all factors in these processes. The multinational corporation has been of growing importance.

The private ownership of real estate varies greatly as between countries around the world, as does the legal system which regulates such ownership. Fear of confiscation is an important factor in stimulating foreign investment on the part of many nationals. A closely related factor is the fear of inflation. The ownership of real property is influenced greatly by the distribution of income that prevails in particular countries. The large middle class in the United States is a significant factor in widespread real estate ownership.

Trends toward suburban developments are less extensive abroad, even in Western Europe, than in the United States, because of the lower per capita ownership of automobiles. This situation, however, is changing rapidly in Western Europe. As a result, there is likely to be an expansion of shopping centers in such countries.

## QUESTIONS FOR STUDY

1. Why does real estate tend to be a relatively more important form of investment in foreign countries than in the United States?
2. Contrast the typical ground plan of U. S. and foreign cities. What factors account for the principal differences?
3. Why are investors from other countries acquiring interests in income-producing property in the U. S.?
4. How does the expanding role of the multinational corporation affect the international real estate market?
5. How does the fear of confiscation affect the ownership of real estate? The trend of land values?
6. How is inflation likely to affect real estate ownership and investment? How important is a stable currency for real estate investors? Explain.
7. In which ways may income distribution affect real estate markets?
8. As mass automobile ownership extends to countries other than the U. S., what changes in city structure would you anticipate for those countries?
9. What types of real estate market changes are being created by automobiles in foreign countries? What effects will they have on real estate values?
10. Contrast real estate appraisals in the U. S. and abroad.
11. Assume you are going to Europe to promote investment in U. S. real estate. Outline a promotional approach, including the advantages of such investments.
12. Assume you are a foreign investor considering U. S. real estate. What disadvantages do you see in investing in U. S. real estate? Do they outweigh the advantages? Which factors do you think will be most significant in making your final decision.

13. It is reported that osffhore realty funds located in tax havens avoid U. S. taxation on their income and capital gains. They cannot sell shares to Americans, but they may invest substantially in U. S. property, mainly income-producing property in metropolitan areas. Shareholders have been mostly Latin Americans, but recently West Germans have also become important. These funds hope to sell many shares and to buy valuable U. S. realty.

  a. Would you want to invest in this type of arrangement if you were a citizen of another country? Why or why not?

  b. Would it be more desirable to invest directly in U. S. property? Explain.

## SUGGESTED READINGS

GINSBURG, NORTON. *Atlas of Economic Development.* Chicago: University of Chicago Press, 1961.

GOTTMAN, JEAN. *Economics, Esthetics and Ethics in Modern Urbanization.* New York: Twentieth Century Fund, 1962.

HOYT, HOMER. *According to Hoyt* (2nd ed.). Washington, D.C.: Hoyt, 1970. Pp. 306–58.

UNITED NATIONS. *Demographic Year Book.* New York: United Nations.

*The Worldmark Encyclopedia of the Nations.* New York: Worldmark Press and Harper & Row, Publishers, 1962.

## CASE 24–1

### The Edwards–Arthur Company

Edwards–Arthur, a U. S. manufacturer of pharmaceuticals and nutritional products has a pharmaceutical plant located in the Federal District of Mexico City (the equivalent of the District of Columbia in the U. S.). In addition, it has a contract manufacturer, Carrioca. for processing its powdered milk formulas for Latin American distribution.

In the past, company procedure for foreign distribution has been decided on a volume basis. First, the product is exported through a foreign distributor; as volume increases, the company establishes its own warehouse and distribution system; a further increase usually warrants a foreign contract manufacturer; and finally, more volume coupled with prosperous prospects for the future calls for the establishment of an Edwards–Arthur plant in the foreign country.

From the start, Edwards–Arthur has had its own equipment and process supervisors in the Carrioca powdered milk formula plant. Carrioca had always been a producer of butter and cheese and the quality control for these products has been far below that required for nutritional products. Recently, several problems with the Carrioca operation have become more pressing.

Raw milk is now coming from distances as far away as 300 miles. This means exceedingly higher transportation costs due to the large percentage of water in raw milk. Also, the Carrioca plant has become excessively crowded resulting in loss of efficiency of both operating personnel and management, and a lower quality products as well. Lastly, Jones Foods have been negotiating with Carrioca in an effort to gain control of the facility.

The above problems have forced Edwards–Arthur management to consider looking elsewhere. Actually there were two alternatives open to them: (1) locate a new plant in Mexico; (2) find another contract manufacturer.

A search for a new third party manufacturer revealed that there was only one possible contractor in Mexico who could do this type of work. This company was approached several times with the purpose of investigating possibilities for the manufacturing of Edwards–Arthur products but there appeared to be little interest in doing this type of work.

After careful consideration of all factors involved, the best alternative appeared to be the construction of a company-owned plant. This seemed to be the only permanent solution to the manufacturing of formula milk products. It would take care of long term requirements. Proper location of the plant would permit Edwards–Arthur to obtain good quality of milk at lower prices. Adequate designs and equipment would improve efficiency, lowering manufacturing costs and bettering quality of finished products. This would also place Edwards–Arthur in a better competitive position.

With a company owned plant, management would also have the necessary flexibility to produce products or formulas that might be required by market conditions. This would be difficult to attain with a third party manufacturing agreement.

Government sales, which are an important part of formula products sales (approximately 37 per cent, can be better protected if Edwards–Arthur manufactures its products in its own plant. Government institutions must follow the established policy of buying all their requirements directly from manufacturers, avoiding purchases from intermediaries or suppliers that do not manufacture their own products. In the past, Edwards–Arthur has been in serious danger of losing formula products sales to the Government for that particular reason. The company had been forced to exhibit proofs that it really had an investment in the former Carrioca plant and also that it was actually supervising the manufacturing processes and being responsible for them. The fact that Edwards–Arthur would manufacture the milk products in its own new plant, would undoubtedly represent a very strong promotional advantage over the present situation.

There have always been doubts in some physicians' and consumers' minds about the quality of the Edwards–Arthur milks, being made by a butter and cheese manufacturer whose products usually do not require the same careful processes. Quite naturally, competition has recognized this fact and has attempted to exploit it.

The present two milk formula products producers in Mexico are North and South; both have their own plants. North has three big modern plants spread around selected milk sheds in the country and South has only one plant but it is presently starting the construction of a new modern and efficient plant at the same location.

Actually, there were several additional factors which caused the decision to build the new facility to be made: (1) the return on investment was calculated to be 36 per cent, (2) projected sales for the market area served were favorable, (3) the Mexican Government's attitude toward the new plant was favorable since it penalized products produced in non-Mexican plants due to the fact it has been pushing for economic development, (4) there would be no problem of disposal of butter fat and other by-products, (5) the powdered milk sales contributed 60 per cent to the Mexican profits on only 30 per cent of gross sales (the gross Mexican sales were $5 million and net profits were $625,000).

**The Real Estate Decisions.** The real estate decision was divided into two parts:

1. Should the plant be located in the Federal District or outside?
2. If located outside, where?

A decision to locate outside of the Federal District was based on (1) the fact that transportation costs would be lower for powdered milk than liquid milk, and (2) the Mexican Government's attitude toward the outside location was more favorable.

Several areas, all within a 200 to 300-mile radius of Mexico City were considered for the site. Based on milk shed studies of the number and quality of the cattle, engineering studies, and the assistance of Mexican Agriculture Department official, loaned by the Mexican Government, three possible locations were found. These areas and their attributes are listed below. (Abbreviations have been used for simplicity's sake).

1. *D.C.*—320 miles from Federal District; good grazing and quality cattle but smaller supply than needed; high Government approval; equal construction costs of the other two; population of 150,000 with a small junior college; truck transportation but no rail service.
2. *T*—Good herds and co-ops; 1 other milk plant in area. Oversupply exists; 280 miles from Mexico City. Population of 90,000 with a higher education institution; Government only luke warm on approval; adequate rail service to Mexico City already exists.
3. *S.L.P.*—Good cattle, low labor supply, low educational level due to no higher educational institution in area. Population of 70,000, truck transportation, no rail service; high government approval; and nearest to Mexico City at 200 miles.

It was believed that the Mexican Government would guarantee the number and quality of cattle, give free land for the plant location, provide assurance of a substantially fixed price agreement for 3 years with the farmers, and develop rail service for the area within 3 years if sites 1 or 3 were chosen. Some assistance could also be expected if site 2 were chosen, but its form and extent were unknown.

**Costs and Financing.** The new plant is estimated to cost $1.5 million and the old equipment at the Carrioca plant would bring $250,000 in salvage price. The venture would be financed mostly from borrowed capital from local Mexican banks because (1) it provides a hedge against the possible devaluations of the peso, (2) the interest (11 per cent) is deductible against high Mexican tax levels and (3) progressive profit sharing laws in Mexico limit the amount of profits to be taken.

Edwards–Arthur's final decision was to build the plant at location 1.

### Questions

1. Is this the location you would have chosen? Why or why not?
2. Why was it decided to finance the plant through Mexican sources rather than using American sources or equity funds even though the interest rate is 11 per cent?

## STUDY PROJECT 24–1

### Urban Problems from an International Standpoint

There are important points of similarity and difference between the problems of cities in the United States and in other countries throughout the world. All face problems of congestion, unrest and pollution. Some of the more difficult urban problems in the United States, however, have developed out of racial tensions; race does not appear to be so significant a factor in most parts of the world. This is not true of the NATO (North Atlantic Treaty Organization) countries, for example. Crime and violence do not appear to be as widespread abroad as in U. S. cities. Drug problems are not as extensive in most cities in other parts of the world as they are in the United States.

1. How do you account for these differences?
2. Do you think U. S. cities are more "advanced" and that cities in other parts of the world soon will have similar problems? Why or why not?

Dr. Harold Finger of the Department of Housing and Urban Development has stressed the difficulty of comparing the housing problems of different countries. He says that the same kinds of people do not live in the same kinds of housing in one country as in another, hence, comparisons are difficult to make.

1. Do you agree with Dr. Finger's observation?
2. If you were going to try to compare the housing of two countries which points would you try to cover?

Mayor Lindsay of New York has suggested that large urban centers with population of a half million or more should be designated as "national cities," with some exemption from state government authority and with arrangements for dealing directly with the federal government in a number of areas. In many countries abroad major cities enjoy more of an independent status than they do in this country.

1. Do you agree or disagree with Mayor Lindsay's proposal?
2. Would it be possible to apply some of the experience of the more independent cities abroad to the problems of American cities?

Great Britain has established a program which provides a 50 per cent subsidy for modernization and repair efforts for housing units in designated areas provided these dwellings are certified as meriting such expenditures. In the U.S. relatively little has been done in the way of providing subsidies for the used house field; more attention has been centered on new housing.

1. Should the British program to subsidize modernization and repair efforts be tried in the United States? Why or why not?
2. Why has relatively less attention been given to used than to new housing in the United States?

Tokyo is the largest city in the world. Thus its experience may serve as an advance pattern of the experience of cities in other countries. Land in and around Tokyo has become so expensive that very few people can become home owners. More and more planning appears to be necessary as urban density increases. Commuting times of one and a half to two hours per day to work and an equal time from work have forced consideration of population dispersal efforts such as "new towns." Problems of air and water pollution grow increasingly difficult as urban density becomes greater.

1. Do you think Tokyo's problems may indicate what is ahead for other cities around the world?
2. How might some of Tokyo's problems be avoided?

# 25

# Toward Improved Real Estate Administration

## SOCIAL AND ECONOMIC PRIORITIES

The role of real estate resources in the American economy during the remaining years of the twentieth century will depend to a considerable extent on our general social and economic priorities. Our priorities have tended to change over time. How are they likely to change in the future? For example, how will such changes affect inflationary or deflationary tendencies? Domestic or international programs? Economic growth and stability? Environmental priorities? Saving or spending patterns? Public or private investment? Equality or excellence?

How will changes in our priorities affect real estate resources and investments? Housing? Urban life? The real estate business?

Not only will general priorities influence the role of real estate but so will the economic and social policies and arrangements that are set up to give effect to our priorities. Will we continue to rely as much as in the past on market competition as a form of social control? Will we rely to as great an extent as formerly on monetary and credit policies for economic stabilization purposes? Will fiscal policies and more direct forms of control be used to a greater extent than in the past? Which tax systems will be favored? Will our system of incentives be altered? For example, to what extent will profits be redefined?

The future role of real estate resources and the real estate business will depend to a considerable extent on the quality of administration both in general and in the real estate sector. Are the owners and users of real estate likely to be better administrators than in the past? Will the real

749

estate business be operated more efficiently? Will the administration of government agencies and especially those directly related to the real estate sector be improved?

We will undertake to consider these questions and others related to them in this final chapter of our discussions, which almost takes the form of a Study Project.

## Will General Priorities Change?

Extensive discussion and controversy suggest that changes in priorities are in the process of taking place. The extent and direction of changes, however, are less clear. For example, there is extensive debate as to the priorities that should be assigned to military and defense purposes on the one hand and nondefense programs on the other. The priorities that should be given to international and domestic programs are widely debated. Some appear to prefer a return to isolationism, others prefer that international programs be stressed.

Discussions of environmental priorities have been extensive. Questions have been raised as to whether economic growth should be slowed down in order to reduce environmental problems. Some have undertaken deliberately to reduce their living standards in the hope of reducing pressures on the environment. Bicycles have taken the place of motorbikes and small cars, for example. Special efforts have been made to conserve electricity, in some cases giving up air conditioning except under extreme conditions. Can we continue to enjoy economic growth and progress and at the same time solve our environmental problems?

Will people be willing to reduce rates of population growth? The Commission on Population Growth and The American Future has pointed out that if families have only two children on the average and if immigration continues at current rates, population will advance to about 265 million by the end of the century. If on the average families have three children, population will expand to 320 million in that time. Moreover, in a hundred years, that is by the 2070's, two children per family would lead to a population of 340 million; three per family would lead to a population of around a billion persons.[1] The implications of such different patterns of population growth are extensive.

## The Changing Social Contract

One of the more progressive of the various organizations largely sponsored by the business community is the Committee for Economic Develop-

---

[1] Commission on Population Growth and the American Future, *An Interim Report to the President and the Congress* (Washington, D.C., U. S. Government Printing Office, 1971).

ment, usually referred to as the CED. We referred to some of their work in our earlier discussions, especially in connection with the "Little Economies," the local economic regions and communities that are so important to real estate resources.

In a recent report the CED suggested that the relationships between business and our society as a whole are undergoing significant changes, that the "social contract" between business and society is being redefined. The report says:

Today it is clear that the terms of the contract between society and business are, in fact, changing in substantial and important ways. Business is being asked to assume broader responsibilities to society than ever before and to serve a wider range of human values. Business enterprises, in effect, are being asked to contribute more to the quality of American life than just supplying quantities of goods and services  Inasmuch as business exists to serve society, its future will depend on the quality of management's response to the changing expectations of the public.[2]

Is this an accurate description of the current relations between business and society? Is the "social contract" between business and society being redefined?

The goals which our society now seeks are outlined in the CED report as follows:

Elimination of poverty and provision of good health care.
Equal opportunity for each person to realize his or her full potential regardless of race, sex, or creed.
Education and training for a fully productive and rewarding participation in modern society.
Ample jobs and career opportunities in all parts of society.
Livable communities with decent housing, safe streets, a clean and pleasant environment, efficient transportation, good cultural and educational opportunities and a prevailing mood of civility among people.[3]

Does this adequately spell out our major goals at this time? More specifically, does it do so with respect to the last of the items which relate to our communities and housing? Does this mean that we are changing our priorities both generally and in the real estate sector? Are we likely to put higher priorities on improved urban life? On elimination of slums? On higher quality of housing?

If these questions are likely to be answered to some degree in the affirmative, what will this mean for real estate resources and real estate administration?

[2] Research and Policy Committee, CED, *Social Responsibilities of Business Corporations* (New York: Committee for Economic Development, 1971), p. 16.
[3] *Ibid.*, p. 13.

## POLICIES AND ARRANGEMENTS

As suggested above, the social and economic policies and arrangements that are set up to attain the objectives and priorities of our society will have an important bearing on the future of real estate resources and real estate administration. Such policies and arrangements will determine the extent to which we make use of competition as a form of social control or use more direct controls, the degree of reliance on monetary and credit policies for economic stabilization purposes, the use of fiscal policies for such ends, the use of selective and direct controls, changes in incentives and many others.

### Competition as a Form of Social Control

Since real estate markets do not function as effectively as markets in many other areas, there are questions as to whether the real estate sector would fare better under arrangements which would continue to rely heavily on competition as a form of social control or under direct types of controls. In general those in the real estate field have continued to prefer competitive arrangements and they are likely to continue to do so. At the same time they have welcomed modifications such as special subsidies and inducements which channeled greater support to the real estate sector. Examples include depreciation allowances, rent and interest rate subsidies, controls on rates paid on savings, tax exemption under certain conditions and others. Which directions are likely to be followed in the future? As our society grows more complex are we likely to rely to a greater or lesser extent on competition as a control device?

### Monetary vs. Fiscal or Other Controls

The heavy reliance on monetary and credit policies as major instruments in restraining inflation in recent years has worked a decided disadvantage on housing and has had unfavorable effects on the financing of real estate and other programs of smaller firms. Any shifts away from such policy would generally be beneficial to the real estate sector. It would appear to make relatively little difference whether this meant greater reliance on fiscal policy if this proved to be feasible or on more direct controls such as regulation of wages and prices.

Are such changes likely to occur? If they do will real estate benefit significantly?

## Stimulation of Housing, Savings, Other Real Estate Related Areas

Any programs which will help to stimulate housing directly would appear to be favorable to the housing sector relative to other areas of the economy. Subsidies, tax advantages, improvements of roads and other transportation facilities, better traffic controls and related developments would all be helpful. Past trends suggest the continuation of special aids to housing; are they as likely to be continued in the future as in the past? Or is housing going down relatively in our range of priorities?

Programs that will channel investments into public facilities will tend to favor real estate because of the great interdependence between public and private real property. Improvments in environmental conditions may help real estate relatively more than other sectors. The same is true for transportation systems, public parks, water systems, utilities and others. Similarly, improvements in public services contribute especially to the real estate sector.

Are we likely to see more public investment in the future? Which types of public investments would be most helpful to the real estate sector?

Programs which would stimulate saving undoubtedly would benefit housing and to some extent the real estate sector in general. This would be especially true if the increased savings were channeled into this sector. Any significant increase in the total capital available, however, would seem likely to aid the housing and real estate sector relative to others because of this sector's limited ability to compete for funds under tight money market conditions. Many small businesses and small municipalities also have limited ability in this area and improvement for them would seem likely to be beneficial to the real estate sector as well. Are we now a capital short economy? Are we likely to have special incentives to increase saving? What form might such incentives take?

## Incentives

Changes in incentives would have a greater or lesser impact in the real estate field depending on which incentives were changed or in what direction. We have already mentioned savings incentives. What about profits? Society defines profits. Income tax laws spell out what may be counted as costs, depreciation rates, losses that may be carried forward or back and other things. Real estate investments have been favored in the depreciation field; this has been notably true of housing. Modifications would change incentives. The 1969 income tax law changes, for example, had both favorable and unfavorable implications for the real estate sector relative to other sectors.[4]

Our tax laws have some responsibility for slum and other deteriorated areas since in most jurisdictions we tax improvements on the land more heavily than the land itself. Thus, there are fewer incentives for improving our stores, office buildings, factories and houses than would be the case if our property tax system were structured differently. Are we likely to change our tax laws? Will changes help or hinder the real estate area?

Because of the importance of incentives for all of us, any changes in our system of incentives could have widespread effects. Should our incentives be modified? Should we give greater incentives in the housing sector than in others? In the real estate field in general? Should small business be favored relative to big business? Should special tax incentives be given to small business to attract people into such enterprises? If so this would undoubtedly favor real estate since many of the enterprises in this field are relatively small operations.

### Equality of Economic Opportunity

The public school system has been one of the means we have relied upon to assure reasonable equality of economic opportunity in our system. Despite many efforts to assure all a reasonably equal change, however, discriminatory practices have persisted, especially in the areas of race, sex and creed. The impact of such practices may have been somewhat greater in the real estate field, especially in housing, than in others. Any arrangements that would help to break down barriers to opportunities would undoubtedly receive widespread support. What effect would this have on real estate resources? The effectiveness with which real estate resources are utilized? The real estate business? Local property values?

## FUTURE ROLE OF REAL ESTATE RESOURCES

What part will real estate resources play in the future of this country? Will their role be of greater or lesser importance than it has been in the past?

### Needs

Answers to these questions depend in part on our priorities and on the arrangements for carrying such priorities with effect, as we have pointed out. Answer will depend also on the number of people, their incomes,

---

[4] Emil M. Sunley, Jr., "Tax Incentive for The Rehabilitation of Housing," *The Appraisal Journal* (July, 1971).

their locations, and their changing standards; for example, how much of their incomes they wish to spend for real estate resources and services in relation to other things. Answers will reflect the relative cost of providing real estate resources and services in comparison to the costs of other goods and services. This will vary with the rate at which technological advances are made in the real estate field in comparison to advances in other areas and on the quality of the decisions determining the effectiveness with which resources are managed in the real estate field and in other fields. Changes in transportation that accelerate or retard new real estate developments will also have an effect.

In terms of the population pressures that have been generated, there is little doubt that space demands will increase in the years ahead. The main question is how much, as we have suggested. In view of the prospect for rising incomes, there may also be a demand for higher quality of real estate resources and resource services. The location of economic opportunities and, hence, the location of the homes of people will change. Thus, there may be a surplus of real properties in some places at the same time that there are shortages in others.

## Supplies

Because we add only a small percentage to the total supply of real estate resources each year, much depends on the efficiency with which existing resources are used. This in turn will vary with conservation and renewal programs. For a short period of time, real estate requirements could be met by more intensive use of existing properties. Over a longer period, the destruction and deterioration of a portion of the available supply would require the provision of some new facilities even with a static population with static incomes and standards. Every year some real estate resources are taken out of use as a result of demolition, fires, windstorms, or other causes. Also, some properties pass out of use through obsolescence.

We have been adding new housing facilities at a rate of about 3 per cent of the total supply per year. Even if we moved this rate up to 4 per cent per year or more we would add only at a slow rate to our present housing supply. Much the same thing may be said of the development of commercial and industrial real estate.

Decisions as to the rate of building or the conservation and renewal of older properties will be made in part by private individuals and the executives of business firms and in part by public officials reflecting the points of view of the electorate. As we have seen, if real estate resources are taxed on a more favorable basis than is now the case, for example, this will have an important effect on their future role; if people wish to add to or reduce various subsidies to real estate, it will affect the rate of development or redevelopment of these resources.

### Types of Properties

In a discussion of this type, distinctions need to be made between various types of properties. Changing technology and transportation patterns will undoubtedly alter the types of industrial real estate that will be most useful in the future. Recent rates of technological change suggest that industrial real estate resources will tend to grow obsolete rather rapidly in the years ahead. To a significant degree the same statement applies also to commercial real estate. The advent of regional and super regional shopping centers, supermarkets and discount houses, franchising and other arrangements has already brought rapid obsolescence to many ccommercial real estate resources. Obviously, new developments in the future will have similar effects.

The shopping habits and preferences of people in recent years have tended to favor outlying as against downtown locations. The continuation of this trend will have important effects in the future; a reversal of this trend, or a partial reversal, would affect the rate at which various types of commercial real estate would be required.

Residential real estate resources have undergone important changes in recent years, as we have seen in our previous discussions. The earlier preference for single-family suburban living has been modified to a degree by the rising demand for apartments. In some cases people are tending to prefer downtown or "near-in" locations for their regular residences, but are combining such living arrangements with nearby weekend cottages and other retreats.

Rural land uses have undergone rapid changes as we have seen in Chapter 23. Farmers are now living and working in what is essentially an urban society.

Power can be transmitted over wider areas than formerly. The new federal highway program is bringing a redistribution of both rural and urban land uses. Pipelines, new waterway developments, jet aircraft, and changes which we cannot as yet foresee will continue to bring shifts in land uses and in the intensity of land uses.

### Development Methods and Costs

As we suggested in our discussions of building, subdividing and land development, significant advances have been made in these fields in recent years. Still, costs have advanced substantially, and in general have risen more than in other fields. If the methods of land development can be improved, and if we can continue to come up with new products and processes, there undoubtedly will be rapid expansion of real estate resources. Except for historical buildings and sites, we are likely to continue our preference for new resources in contrast to the conservation, renewal, or redevelopment of older resources.

The quality of land planning methods and techniques will have an important bearing on the development of new real estate resources in the years ahead. While it is never possible to anticipate with great exactness the ways in which various areas should be developed, increased research and study undoubtedly will lead to the development of improved planning and better zoning in the years ahead. Expanded research and development programs may prove useful in the public policy areas as well as in the managerial and technological fields. Indeed, the invention of new social, political, and economic relationships would appear to be essential to enable various agencies of local and state government to function with sufficient effectiveness to meet future requirements.

### Conservation and Renewal

As we have pointed out, the real estate resources required in the future will be provided in part by the continued use of the resources now available. The effectiveness of such use will reflect the care with which these resources are used and managed, and on programs for redeveloping, rehabilitating, or renewing properties, neighborhoods, and districts—in short, programs that will lengthen the economic life of real properties.

Good housekeeping, both on a private and public basis, will be important in this connection. Programs which protect and improve the physical environment are likely to play a larger role. The development and enforcement of higher standards of land use and building occupancy will also play a part, as will the impact of tax burdens, land planning programs, and the like. In brief, the conservation of existing resources will affect the type and quality of the services they can provide and will influence the rate at which new resources are developed.

Historically it has been more expeditious to use up our forests, minerals, and similar resources as we needed them than to conserve them for future use. In part this resulted from the abundance of natural resources available and the continued discovery of new resources. In part this point of view represented a faith in the continuation of scientific and technological advances which provided substitutes for many natural resources. For example, weather control and the production of agricultural products in laboratories in future years, both distinct possibilities, would change greatly our interest in conserving the fertility of agricultural lands.

Even in the case of urban real estate resources it has often been more convenient and probably more economical to develop new areas on the periphery of cities or to establish new towns than to conserve, renew, or redevelop older areas. Also, the automobile and improved roads and streets reduced dependence on specific locations and increased greatly the amount of land area that could be used effectively for urban purposes.

The way in which a given piece of urban real estate is used, however, may have a considerable impact on other real properties as we have pointed out. This is especially true of adjacent or nearby properties. Thus, we often find it necessary to clear a slum in order to prevent the deterioration of properties in a nearby area.

The renewal problems of the downtown area are especially complex. The present functioning heart of the city can in some cases be supplanted by reliance on other downtown areas, particularly if larger interurbias emerge; in some cases, outlying business centers may absorb many of the functions typically performed by the downtown center. But in many cities it will be necessary to conserve, renew, and redevelop the downtown area.

As David L. Birch has aptly said:

Pulling all these interwoven threads together, the future course of the central cities is not totally uncertain. The cities are becoming and will continue to become specialized. Absolute declines in many types of jobs will be offset by substantial gains in communication-sensitive activities, such as banking, corporate headquarters, educational and health facilities, nonprofit membership organizations, and the specialized manufacturing and service firms that service these growth sectors.[5]

## IMPROVEMENTS IN ADMINISTRATION

How may real estate administration be improved in the years ahead and thus increase the efficiency with which our real estate resources are used? Direct answers to this question would be hard to present but some suggestions can be made as to areas of probable improvement.

One possibility is the improvement of management and administration in general. Real estate administration is not separated from other areas of administration. The same general concepts apply in real estate as in other fields. As our knowledge of decision making and implementing increases, real estate administration will benefit along with other fields. As we improve our capacity to do better planning, organizing and control processes, we may make use of such developments in real estate. Special adaptations may be required, of course, since decisions and programs for implementing decisions in the real estate field must be related to fixed sites, to long-

[5] David L. Birch, *The Economic Future of City and Suburb,* CED Supplementary Paper Number 30 (New York: Committee for Economic Development, 1970), p. 37.

term commitments, to large fixed investments, to special market conditions, and to other factors that pertain to the localized nature of real property income.

A second possibility for improved administration in the real estate field may arise from better administration of real estate by the owners and users of real estate—business firms, individuals and families, and various agencies and institutions. For example, many business firms are paying increased attention to the effective use of the real estate resources that are available to them. Private consumers of real estate and especially home buyers and owners are growing more sophisticated with respect to their use of real estate and their investments in it. At one time the objective of the home buyer appeared to be the achievement of debt-free home ownership. Today home owners tend to view their equity in a home as they do other types of investment. They borrow against their equity to finance a variety of family needs.

A third area from which improvements in administration may come is the real estate business itself. Business firms in the real estate field may be managed more effectively. Improvements may be made in the processes of land development and building, real estate marketing, or the financing of real estate ownership and use.

## R & D

Improvements in the various areas listed above may come about in part from research and development efforts. The real estate sector seems to make relatively less effort in this direction than most other fields. More efforts may be forthcoming. Government has helped with such programs as "Operation Breakthrough." Improvements may arise from new insights developed by businessmen or by students of business administration. Or improvements may come from sources that we cannot now foresee. The universities and independent research agencies may make important contributions. Business executives and private individual may point the way to improvements. Also, trade associations, and other organizations may contribute to improvements in a number of ways.

## Knowledge of Administration

Our knowledge of administrative theory, principles and practices has expanded greatly in recent years. The business firm has been viewed to an increasing extent as a key social institution and both the internal and external responsibilities of its management have been subjected to careful study. Management decision making has been given major attention by practicing managers and by students of business administration. Quantitative analyses have been used to improve decision making. Attempts have been made to draw on the social and behavioral sciences to find new insights into problems of management leadership and human relations.

University schools of business and various other areas of specialization in our universities, notably the behavioral sciences, have been giving increasing attention to the development of this type of framework as have various practicing business executives. As our knowledge of administrative theory expands, we may expect practices to improve, both in the real estate field and in others.

## Long-Range Planning

In connection with the implementation of managerial decisions, increasing emphasis has been given to long-range planning as one of the more important tools of management. Some managers have shied away from the term "planning" and prefer to think of "anticipations," "expectations," and "forecasts." Planning is of special importance in the administration of real estate resources because of their long economic life and the large investments that are represented.

New planning techniques have emerged. Model building and simulations have been used increasingly. The computer has contributed to such developments. The scenario technique, that is developing a scenario or a series of scenarios of anticipated future events, has come in for more widespread use. The Delphi technique, apparently named for the Delphic oracle of antiquity, provides for drawing on the opinions of a number of experts. The more frequently mentioned are then resubmitted to the same group for further analysis and response and the process is repeated until a consensus emerges.

Every business establishment, institution, and family is controlled to some degree by the real estate resources it uses. Thus, careful planning in order to anticipate future real estate requirements is highly important for business administration in general, but it acquires special significance in connection with real estate resources. For example, the growth of many business firms has been severely limited by the failure to anticipate space, equipment, and location needs.

Business managers and private individuals have tended to rely heavily on architects and engineers for assistance in planning the development or redevelopment of real estate resources. Such specialists, however, are able to do this type of planning effectively only as the owners and users of real property can outline realistically their potential needs for space and facilities. This is a planning responsibility of business management that is coming to be recognized to an increasing degree. Long-range planning for the development and use of real estate resources probably will be facilitated by improved projections of long-term economic trends as well as by better projections of the future potential of specific industries, localities, and areas.

Individuals and families are giving more attention to their real estate requirements over time. Typically, however, they do not have the degree of control over their locations nor can they translate future plans into action with the same degree of effectiveness as the owners and managers of business firms. To some extent this is true also of government agencies, since programs of government may change rapidly with shifts from one administration to another or with changes in the preferences of the electorate in regard to various programs.

### Organization of Resources

Marked improvement has been made in the ability of business managers to organize resources and operations. Managers have been giving real estate resources increasing attention, as we have seen. Many firms are establishing real estate departments or paying greater attention to allocating responsibility for real estate decisions. The proper mix of real estate and other resources in the organization of a business firm's operations is not always easy to determine. It appears that improvements are being made; and there is little question of the increasing concern of business firms about the role of real estate resources in influencing the effectiveness with which other types of resources may be utilized.

The relationship of real estate resources to others in the business firm depends to a considerable extent on whether the firm is primarily engaged in manufacturing, marketing, or service activities. It is probable that more changes will be forthcoming in the service lines than others, in part because greater advances have already been made in the manufacturing and marketing fields.

### Control of Operations

Significant improvements have been made in control processes in many lines of business. There has been more widespread use of budgeting in management planning and control operations. Cost accounting has contributed much to improved controls. High-speed computing equipment has broadened the types of records and controls that are feasible. Increased attention has been given to the establishment of realistic standards as a basis for measuring performance.

In the real estate field, rapidly changing values, have required that careful controls be imposed to adjust for insurance requirements, tax obligations, and refinancing possibilities. More careful controls of modernization and repair programs have also been stressed in order to preserve property values.

### Leadership and Entrepreneurial Ability

The magnitude of the potential requirements for real estate resources suggests that leadership of a high order will be essential to formulate and carry out the necessary programs. Such leadership will come in part from those now engaged in business administration or more particularly those engaged in one or another part of the real estate business. Such leadership will come also from younger people, many of whom are now preparing themselves for careers in the business world.

In the business world, leadership and entrepreneurial abilities often are combined. The distinction is far from easy to make. One may be a leader without being an entrepreneur if his leadership role requires him largely to execute programs and policies that are originated by others. But the more effective leaders often have "entrepreneurial minds." By this we mean that they have the capacity to think creatively, to innovate, to develop new ideas and concepts, and to apply them in the solution of problems. In this respect the entrepreneur and the artist may have much in common.

Traditionally, economists have also associated entrepreneurship with risk taking. Whether this is an essential requirement may be open to question. Also, risks may take a variety of forms; reputations may be risked as well as money. The entrepreneurial mind may be found among public officials as well as private businessmen. Indeed, the close relationship between public and private programs in the real estate field suggests that leadership and creative talents of a high order will be required in the public agencies related to real estate in the years ahead if substantial progress is to be achieved.

### Efficiency of Real Estate Firms

It is probable that those who develop, finance, and market real estate are as capable, work as hard, manage as carefully, and in general try to operate as efficiently as those in other fields of business. Although the numerous small organizations that are typical of this field may result in some inefficiencies and lack of coordination, there are many other fields in which enterprises are also small and not closely coordinated. Consider many of the service lines, for example.

It may be that such inefficiencies as exist are due to the nature of the commodity in which the real estate business deals and the institutional framework surrounding its operations. The long life of real properties, the fact that they represent relatively large economic units, and their fixity of location create special problems, as we have noted. Possibly, larger enterprises could deal with these problems more efficiently than those which now are typical of the field. Yet the mere fact of size is no guarantee of efficiency. We know from the experience of recent years that a large builder may be able to do more in the way of applying sound principles of land planning and reap some of the economies of large-scale operations from a project. There is always the danger, of course, that he may overexpand, interpret market demands incorrectly, or make other mistakes to which the smaller operator may be less susceptible. Even so, there is little doubt that larger-scale operations are paying off in the land development and building field.

With respect to real estate marketing, we might raise several questions suggested by the development of chain stores. Is there any basic difference between selling real properties or their services and selling groceries? Are the arguments against large-scale operations in the real estate brokerage field comparable to the arguments of the small, independent retailer against the chain stores?

Suppose we consider also the internal organization of our real estate enterprises. It has been suggested that the small brokerage offices, for example, cannot provide much for their employees in the way of training programs, opportunities for promotion, or provisions for retirement and the like. On the other hand, the independence of these smaller enterprises may offer great incentives through opportunities for achieving ownership of a small concern, and this may in large measure counterbalance the personnel programs of larger organizations. If the owners and operators of small business firms were accorded special tax treatment, the appeal of the small enterprise might be increased. For example, if the owners of small business firms could pay low taxes on, say, the first $50,000 of annual income, or if they were given tax advantages until they had accumulated capital of say, a half million dollars, managerial talent might move to small business firms rather than to the larger corporations.

There are also other advantages in the organization of a small establishment. The individual proprietorship or partnership form of organization may be used to a larger extent. Small organizations are more flexible, less cumbersome, and more easily adapted to changes in market requirements.

We should note that a number of techniques have improved in recent years. Appraising is an area in which real advances have been made; the same thing may be said of mortgage risk analysis.

The educational programs of a number of universities and colleges have contributed to improved practices. Special mention should be made of the institutes, short courses, and correspondence study programs sponsored by a number of the trade associations in this field.

Yet, much remains to be done. When we compare many real estate enterprises with those in other fields, the differences are not always in favor of the former.

## Users of Real Estate

As we have suggested business firms have been making significant improvements in their management of the real estate resources they own and use. Further improvements may be made. Governmental and institutional users of real estate may make further advances in the administration of their real estate resources.

The individuals and families owning and using real estate resources often are unable to bring to their management problems the degree of knowledge and experience that can be provided by business firms. There is little doubt, however, that home buyers and owners have become more knowledgable about real estate matters in recent years. In part this is due to a rather widespread improvement in the availability of economic and business information. In part it results from the rising incomes of individuals and families.

Despite these developments, the opportunities for improving the utilization of real properties are great. More information and a wider dissemination of knowledge about housing would undoubtedly improve our consumption of this commodity. More information about real properties and the problems related to their ownership and use probably would help those who buy and sell, own, manage, lease, and finance real properties.

## Government—Business Relationships

Do we need changes in our system of legal arrangements for the ownership, transfer of title, and mortgaging of real properties? A number of forms and processes that had their origin in medieval times are still in use, even though it is difficult in many instances to justify them by the requirements and standards of the modern market. If it is possible to buy the stocks or bonds of a corporation located in another part of the country by making a telephone call, why must we be burdened by the legal formalities and processes that are a part of every real property transfer? Could legislation improve these conditions? Is the real estate business carrying a part of the legal profession on its back because of these cumbersome legal formalities?

The processes of searching titles and of bringing abstracts up to date are difficult and time consuming. Would it not be possible, by the more widespread use either of private title insurance or of the Torrens system, to simplify these processes? Why should we not have a system of title insurance which insures against all defects in titles rather than against unknown defects only? Or is this more properly a government function?

Because many real estate enterprises are relatively small, should government undertake a greater amount of research for these establishments? Since larger corporations have their own research departments, is it proper for government to give special aid to small businesses in this manner?

While there is generally little question about the desirability of land planning and zoning regulations established by local governments, many of these laws need revision. In the process of making such revisions, would it be desirable to include provisions also for controlling the indiscriminate subdivision of lands? If such a step is considered desirable, how should new subdivisions be regulated?

While we recognize that taxation is always a point of friction between government and business establishments, do the facts of the situation call for a substantial revision of real property taxation? Should real estate taxes be frozen at current levels? Should taxes be used as a device for promoting developments which are considered to be in the public interest?

To what extent is government responsible for the improvement of business practices? Undoubtedly the activities of the Federal Home Loan Bank System and the FHA have made for such improvement. In the field of agriculture, government has assumed far-reaching responsibilities for the improvement of farm practices. Should it assume similar responsibilities in the real estate field? Do we need an extension service for real estate and other small businesses similar to the programs in the field of agriculture?

How should the Department of Housing and Urban Development help us cope with some of the rapidly expanding problems of the urban community and the impact of these problems on our real estate resources? Is private mortgage insurance likely to replace the FHA? Or are new types of mortgage insurance programs likely to emerge? Will we develop programs for insuring interest rate risk? Purchasing power risk? Is it desirable to have competing government systems of real estate finance? Despite some of the arguments for greater centralization of such agencies, there are real advantages in competition, even among government agencies.

## SUMMARY

In this final chapter of our discussions we have raised a series of questions about future trends of development and about the possibilities for future improvements in real estate administration. Changes in our general objectives and priorities, of course, will have major significance for the real estate sector. The policies and arrangements that are set up to give effect to the desired priorities will also have a profound influence on the future role of real estate resources. The needs of the people will reflect their general priorities; the resources provided will depend on the relative importance assigned to them, development methods and costs and on conservation and renewal programs.

Improvements in the administration of real estate resources and real estate firms will come from research and development efforts, from increased knowledge of administration, improvements in long-rang planning, better organization of resources and more effective control of operations. Leadership and entrepreneurial ability will play a major role in improved real estate administration. Much will depend on improved efficiency of real estate firms and on the care with which business, governmental and institutional users of real estate and individuals and families manage their real estate resources. Improvements in a number of government-business relationships may also prove to be helpful.

This final chapter has raised many questions, suggested only a few answers. Since it is largely in the form of a concluding study project, no study projects are included at the end of this chapter.

## QUESTIONS FOR STUDY

1. Outline the social and economic priorities that you believe will be most important in the next ten years. Do you believe these will be likely to change significantly in an additional ten years?
2. Which policies and arrangements for carrying priorities into effect seem most likely to be changed in the next five to ten years? How may such changes affect the real estate sector?
3. Do you think there will be significant changes in incentives?
4. Which major factors will determine the needs for real estate resources? The ability of our system to supply such needs?
5. How may research and development efforts contribute to the future supply and utilization of real estate resources? To improvements in the real estate business?
6. Outline recent developments in the field of long-range planning. Which of these will be of greatest importance in the real estate field?
7. How may improvement in the organization and control of real estate resources lead to advances in this area?
8. Outline the contributions that seem likely to come from entrepreneurship in the real estate sector.
9. Will real estate firms become more efficient? Why or why not?
10. List major improvements that may be developed in government-business relationships in the real estate sector. Are advances likely to be made in the administration of public agencies comparable to those in the private area?

## SUGGESTED READINGS

BIRCH, DAVID L. *The Economic Future of City and Suburb.* New York, CED, 1970; Committee for Economic Development. *Social Responsibilities of Business.* New York: CED, 1971.

GABOR, DENNIS. *Inventing the Future.* New York: Alfred A. Knopf, Inc., 1964. Chap. 1.

LANDSBERG, HANS H., LEONARD L. FISCHMAN, and JOSEPH L. FISHER. *Resources in America's Future.* Baltimore: The Johns Hopkins Press, 1963. Chaps. iv, xviii.

SCIENTIFIC AMERICAN. *Technology and Economic Development.* New York: Alfred A. Knopf, Inc., 1963. Pp. 3–19, 70–85.

TOFFLER, ALVIN. *Future Shock.* New York: Random House, 1970.

TOYNBEE, ARNOLD. *Cities on the Move.* New York: Oxford University Press, 1970. Chaps. 1 & 10.

# APPENDIXES

# A

# Glossary

**abstract of title.** A historical summary of the conveyances, transfers, and other facts relied on as evidence of title; a summary of the documents having a bearing on the history of the title to a property.

**acceleration clause.** A clause in a trust deed or mortgage giving the lender the right to call all sums owing him to be immediately due and payable upon the occurrence of a certain specified event, such as a sale, demolition, default, and so forth.

**accessibility.** Ease or difficulty of approach to real property via public land or private land maintained for public use.

**acre.** A unit of land measure containing 43,560 square feet.

**ad valorem.** According to value.

**ad valorem tax.** A tax varying with the value of the property.

**administration.** The superintending of the execution, use, or conduct of a business, activity, or resource.

**administration of real estate resources.** The efficient utilization of real estate resources in the achievement of desired results, usually in combination with other resources.

**advance.** In a construction loan, a periodic transfer of funds from the lender to the borrower during the process of construction.

**adverse possession.** The open and notorious possession of real property as a claim to title. Thus, a method of acquiring title.

**advertising real estate.** The act of informing the public with the intent to induce some desired impression, feeling, or action relative to real estate. Public announcements and messages, the purposes of which are to aid directly or indirectly in the sale of real properties or property services.

*institutional advertising.* Advertising that pertains to real estate in general and has for its purpose the creation of favorable public attitudes toward real estate, investments in real estate, or the people engaged in the real estate business.

For a more complete coverage of real estate terms, see the American Institute of Real Estate Appraisers, *Appraisal Terminology and Handbook* (5th ed. rev.; Chicago, Ill.: The Institute, 1965).

*name advertising.* Advertising that has for its main purpose the popularizing of the name, activities, and reputation of a specific real estate firm.

*specific advertising.* Advertising that pertains to individual properties and property services. Its purpose is to aid in the selling or renting of a specific property.

**agent.** One who acts for and has the authority to represent another who is known as a principal.

**air rights.** Rights in real property to use the space above the surface of the real estate without precluding the use of its surface area for some other purpose.

**allodial tenure.** A system of ownership of real property where ownership may be complete except for rights held by government. Allodial tenure is in contrast to feudal tenure.

**amenities, amenity return.** Pleasant satisfactions that are received through using rights in real property but that are not received in the form of money.

**American Bankers Association.** A trade association of commercial bankers.

**American Institute of Real Estate Appraisers.** A trade association of real estate appraisers. *See* **appraiser,** *MAI (Member Appraisal Institute).*

**amortization.** The process of payment of a debt or obligation by a series of payments over time. Generally the payments are in equal amounts that include principal and interest; and generally the payments are made at uniform intervals of time.

**amortized mortgage.** A mortgage in which repayment is made in accordance with a definite plan that requires the repayment of certain amounts at definite times so that all the debt is released by the end of the term. *See* **amortization.**

**appraisal, valuation.** An estimate of value. In real estate, an estimate of value of specific rights in a specific parcel of real estate as of a specific date for a specific purpose.

**appraisal report.** A report, usually written, of the appraised value, together with the pertinent information regarding the property appraised and the evidence and analysis leading to the reported value estimate.

**appraiser.** One who is in the business of making appraisals on the basis of a fee or salary or in conjunction with some other compensated service.

*MAI (Member Appraisal Institute).* A professional designation of an appraiser who is a member of the American Institute of Real Estate Appraisers, an association affiliated with the National Association of Real Estate Boards.

**appurtenance.** Property that is an accessory to or incidental to other property to which it is annexed.

**assessment.** The valuation of a property for the purpose of levying a tax. The tax so levied.

*special assessment.* An assessment levied for specific purposes such as providing streets, sewers, sidewalks, and the like. An assessment related to benefit derived by the taxed.

**assumption of a mortgage.** Agreement by the grantee of real property that is encumbered by a mortgage that he, the grantee, will pay such a mortgage; the assumption of a personal liability under an existing mortgage.

**axial growth.** City growth that takes the form of prongs or finger-like extensions moving out along main transportation routes.

**balloon mortgage payment.** *See* **mortgage,** *balloon mortgage payment.*
**base line.** *See* **legal description, land description.**

**basic employment, urban growth employment.** Employment in establishments that receive their income from outside the community. Basic employment is in contrast to nonbasic employment.

**basic income.** Income commanded from outside the community.

**bill of sale.** An executed written instrument given to pass title of personal property.

**blanket mortgage.** *See* **mortgage,** *blanket mortgage.*

**blight.** Decay; withering away, as of a neighborhood.

**broker.** An agent who negotiates for the sale, leasing, management, or financing of a property or of property rights on a commission basis that is contingent on success.

> *farm broker.* A broker who deals with farm properties. Farm brokers generally operate in localized areas.

**builder.** One who undertakes the improvement of land by erecting structures; one who undertakes the production of real estate resources by improving land through the erection of structures.

> *custom builder.* A builder who builds for a specific owner.
> *operative builder, speculative builder.* A builder who builds for sale to the public rather than for a specific owner.

**building codes.** Government regulations that specify minimum construction standards for the purpose of maintaining public health and safety.

**building permit.** Authorization or permission by local government for the erection, alteration, or remodeling of improvements within its jurisdiction.

**bundle of rights.** The assortment of rights in real property. *See* **estate; property.**

**business-government relations.** The collection of laws, codes, regulations, and contracts between business and government, within the framework of which business operates.

**buyer's market.** *See* **market,** *buyer's market.*

**CBD.** *See* **central business district.**

**CPM** *(Certified Property Manager).* *See* under **Institute of Real Estate Management.**

**capital gain.** Income that is a result of sale of an asset and not from the general course of business. Capital gains are taxed at a lower rate than ordinary income.

**capital market.** *See* **market,** *capital market.*

**capitalization.** The process of reflecting future income in present value; the discounting of the future income stream to arrive at a present value.

> *capitalization in perpetuity.* Capitalization without limit of time; perpetual.
> *capitalization rate.* The rate at which future income is discounted.
> *split rates.* Use of different capitalization rates for land and buildings in the income approach to value.

**cash flow.** The net income from a property before depreciation and other non-cash expenses.

**central business district.** The "downtown" section of a city where the downtown shopping area and office district are located.

**central city.** Sometimes used to refer to the "downtown" center; also a city that is the center of a larger geographic trade area for which it performs certain market and service functions.

**chattels.** Personal property; personalty.

**closing statement.** A listing of the debits and credits of the buyer and seller to a real estate transaction for the financial settlement of the transaction.

**cloudy title.** *See* title, *cloudy title.*

**cluster housing.** An arrangement of housing units which places them close together yet provides for large recreational areas, or "common areas" which are owned by all the neighbors.

**coercive regulations.** *See* **regulations,** *coercive regulations.*

**commercial properties.** Properties intended for use by all types of retail and wholesale stores, office buildings, hotels, and service establishments.

**commitment.** For a mortgage, a promise or statement by the lender of the terms and conditions under which he will lend.

    *conditional commitment.* A statement that mortgage funds will be provided or guaranteed if certain conditions are met which enables an owner or developer to finance construction or ownership.

    *firm commitment.* Written notification from a financial institution that it will lend money and the terms on which it will do so for each specific case.

**common law.** Rules based on usage; judge-made law in contrast to legislative or constitutional law.

**common property.** *See* **property,** *common property.*

**community property.** In certain states, the property jointly owned by husband and wife.

**condemnation.** The process of forcing a sale under eminent domain.

**conditional sales contract.** *See* **land contract.**

**condominium.** A form of property ownership providing for individual ownership of a specific apartment or other space not necessarily on ground level together with an undivided interest in the land or other parts of the structure in common with other owners.

**confiscation.** The seizing of property without compensation usually by unfriendly governments.

**conformity.** In real estate, the blending of an improvement with the surroundings or the essentially similar use of land in relation to its surroundings; the appearance and use of real estate that is harmonious with the surrounding real estate.

**construction loan.** A loan to finance the improvement of real estate.

**contract.** An agreement between two or more persons that is legally enforceable; a written evidence of such an agreement.

    *contract for deed.* *See* **land contract, contract for deed.**

**conservation.** The process of saving resources from use or of using them in such a way that they will not be depleted.

**consideration.** Anything of value given to induce one entering into a contract; money, trust deeds, services, etc. Consideration is essential to an enforceable contract.

**constant.** The percentage of the unpaid balance of a loan which is represented by the sum of the *principal and interest* payments for the following year, which is needed to fully amortize the loan. For example, a 6% loan amortized over 20 years has a constant of approximately 8½%. Annual payments necessary to amortize a $10,000 loan over 20 years would be about $850.

**contractor, general contractor.** One who supervises the improvement of land by erection of structures or other improvements; one who has the responsibility for such improvement but does not necessarily initiate the process as is done by a builder.

**conversion.** A change in the use of real estate without destruction of the improvements; a change in the use of real estate by altering improvements.

**conveyance.** Transfer of an interest in real property from one person to another person.

**cooperative ownership.** A form of apartment ownership. Occupant acquires ownership by purchasing shares in a corporation but typically must consult the corporation for such actions as sale or improvement.

**corner influence table.** A statistical table, sometimes used in real estate appraisal, that attempts to reflect the added value of a lot located on a corner.

**corporeal rights.** Possessory rights in real property.

**cost.** That which is, was, or would be given up to obtain property (or other things).

*replacement cost.* The cost of replacing real estate improvements with an alternative of like utility but that is not necessarily an exact replica.

*reproduction cost.* The cost of replacing real estate improvements with an exact replica.

**cost approach to value, summation approach.** Valuation approached by estimating the cost of providing a substitute for that which is being valued.

**covenant, restrictive covenant.** A contract between private persons usually to regulate land use or relating to land use.

**cul-de-sac.** A dead-end street that widens at the end to form a circular area sufficient to enable an auto to make a U turn.

**curtesy.** The life estate of the husband in the real estate owned by his wife.

**custom builder.** *See* **builder,** *custom builder.*

**cycle.** *See* **cyclical fluctuation.**

**cyclical fluctuation.** Variations around a trend in activity that recur from time to time; fluctuations remaining after removal of trend and seasonal factors.


**data plant.** A file of information on real properties maintained usually by an appraiser, mortgage lender, and the like.

**dealer-builder.** A builder who erects structures from prefabricated components, usually as a local representative of a prefabricated house manufacturer.

**deed.** An instrument conveying title to real property.

*deed of trust.* *See* **trust deed.**

*grant deed.* A deed in which the seller warrants that he has not previously passed title.

*quitclaim deed.* An instrument transferring only such title as the seller may possess.

*warranty deed.* A deed in which the seller warrants that title is "good and merchantable."

**deed restrictions.** Limitations placed upon the use of real property in the writing of a deed.

**default.** Failure to fulfill a duty or promise or to discharge an obligation.

**defective title.** *See* **title,** *defective title.*

**deficiency judgment.** A judgment for that part of a debt secured that was not liquidated by the proceeds from the sale of foreclosed real property.

**demand.** The set of conditions indicating how much of a good or service will be bought at various prices.

**demographic.** Pertaining to the structure of population; e.g., size, density, statistical characteristics.

**depletion.** *See* **depreciation,** *depletion.*

**deposit, earnest money.** A sum of money or other consideration tendered in conjunction with an offer to purchase rights in real property.

**depreciation.** Loss in property value due to any cause.

*accelerated depreciation.* Methods of reflecting depreciation (such as double declining balance and sum-of-the-year's-digits) that enable the owner of an asset to take more of his depreciation in the early years of the asset's life.

*contingent depreciation.* Loss in property value because of expectations of a decline in property services.

*depletion.* The exhaustion of a resource such as the removal of a mineral deposit.

*economic obsolescence.* Loss in property value from events outside the property that unfavorably affect income or income potentials.

*functional depreciation, functional obsolescence.* Loss in property value because of a loss in ability of the physical property to provide services as compared with alternatives.

*physical depreciation.* Loss in property value due to wearing away or deterioration.

**depth table.** A technique for real estate appraisal using statistical tables based on the theory that added depth increases the value of land.

**developer.** One who undertakes the preparation of land for income production, the construction of buildings and other improvements, and the making available of completed properties.

**direct subsidy.** *See* **subsidy,** *direct subsidy.*

**discount house.** Any of a number of stores whose function it is to sell in quantity at lower than usual retail prices.

**disposable income.** That portion of income that a household has to spend on personal consumption, i.e., after tax income.

**district.** A city area that has a land use different from adjacent land uses, e.g., commercial, industrial, and residential. *See* **neighborhood.**

**double, duplex.** Two dwelling units under one roof. A double usually means dwelling units side by side; a duplex, one dwelling unit above the other.

**double taxation.** *See* **taxation,** *double taxation.*

**doubling up.** The occupation of one dwelling unit by two or more families.

**dower.** The life estate of a wife in the real estate owned by her husband.

**drainage.** The running off of water from the surface of land.


**earnest money.** *See* **deposit.**

**easement.** The right to make limited use of real property owned by another; a right to use property without taking possession.

**economic base.** The major economic support of a community; economic activities that enable it to compete effectively with others.

**economic base analysis.** A technique for analyzing the major economic supports of a community; analysis as a means of predicting population, income, or other variables having an effect on real estate value or land utilization.

**economic goods.** Goods that have scarcity and utility; goods that provide desired services but that are not in sufficient abundance to be free.

**economics.** The branch of organized study dealing with the social organization for the utilization of resources in the attainment of objectives that the society or community sets for itself.

**economy.** Getting as much as possible of what one wants by the use of the means available.

**effective age.** A statement regarding the amount of depreciation that has occurred on a property. The amount is stated in terms of the number of years that would ordinarily be associated with the degree of depreciation.

**eminent domain.** The right of government to take private property for public use with just compensation.

**enabling act.** *See* **zoning,** *enabling act.*

**encroachment.** An improvement on a parcel of land that intrudes on or invades a contiguous parcel of land.

**encumbrance.** A claim against a property such as a debt secured by a mortgage.

**entrepreneur.** One who undertakes business activities, accepting all risks and responsibilities.

>*real estate entrepreneur.* One who undertakes real estate risks and responsibilities, i.e., builder, developer, broker, leasing agent, etc.

**equality of economic opportunity.** A state of affairs in which all people have equal chances for the same jobs at equal pay regardless of race, creed, color or sex.

**equity.** In finance, the value of the interest of an owner of property exclusive of the encumbrances on that property; also, justice.

**equity of redemption.** *See* **redemption,** *equity of redemption.*

**erosion.** The wearing of a ground surface.

**escheat.** The reversion of private property to the state.

**escrow.** An instrument in the hands of a third party that is held for delivery until certain acts are performed or conditions fulfilled; the arrangement for the handling of such instruments.

**estate.** The degree, quantity, nature, and extent of an interest in real property.

>*estates in expectancy.* A classification of estates by time of enjoyment when possession will be at some future time. *See* **remainder; reversion.**

>*estate in possession.* A classification of estates by time of enjoyment when possession is present. *See* **corporeal rights.**

>*estates in severalty.* Ownership in a single individual; a classification of estates by number of owners where the number is one.

>*freehold estate.* A nonleasehold estate such as a fee simple estate, fee tail estate, and life estate.

>>*fee simple estate.* The most complete form of estate ownership; the "totality of rights" in real property.

>>*fee tail estate.* An estate or a limited estate in which transfer of the property is restricted in that the property must pass to the descendants of the owner. Originally used to insure the passing of land in a direct ancestral line.

>>*life estate.* An estate that has a duration of the life of an individual. *See* **curtesy; dower.**

>*joint estates.* A classification of estates by number of owners where the number is two or more. *See* **tenancy,** *joint tenancy, tenancy in common.*

>*nonfreehold estate, leasehold estate.* The rights of tenants as distinguished from those of a freeholder. Includes estate for years, estate at will, and estate at sufferance.

>>*estate at sufferance.* Rights of a tenant in real property after the expiration of a lease if the tenant holds over without special permission.

*estate at will.* Rights of a tenant in real property that may be terminated by either landlord or tenant.

*estate for years.* Rights of a tenant in real property for a definite period of time.

**estate taxation.** *See* **taxation,** *estate taxation.*

**eviction.** The taking possession of real property from one in possession.

**exclusive agency listing.** *See* **listing,** *exclusive agency listing.*

**exclusive right-to-sell listing.** *See* **listing,** *exclusive right-to-sell listing.*

**execute.** To complete, to perform; e.g., to execute a deed.

**featherbedding rules.** Rules that preserve outmoded and inefficient work methods.

**Federal Deposit Insurance Corporation.** Agency of the federal government that insures deposits at commercial banks and savings banks.

**Federal Home Loan Bank.** A District bank of the Federal Home Loan Bank System that lends only to member financial institutions such as savings and loan associations.

**Federal Home Loan Bank Board.** The administrative agency that charters federal savings and loan associations and exercises regulatory authority over members of the Federal Home Loan Bank System.

**Federal Home Loan Bank System.** The Federal Home Loan Bank Board and the network of Federal Home Loan Banks and member financial institutions.

**Federal Housing Administration (FHA).** An agency of the federal government that insures mortgage loans.

**Federal National Mortgage Association.** An agency of the federal government that buys and sells FHA insured and VA guaranteed mortgage loans.

**federal savings and loan association.** A savings and loan association with a federal charter issued by the Federal Home Loan Bank Board. A federally chartered savings and loan association is in contrast to a state-chartered savings and loan association.

**Federal Savings and Loan Insurance Corporation.** An agency of the federal government that insures savers' accounts at savings and loan associations.

**farm broker.** *See* **broker,** *farm broker.*

**fee simple estate.** *See* **estate,** *fee simple estate.*

**fee tail estate.** *See* **estate,** *fee tail estate.*

**feudal tenure.** A system of ownership of real property where ownership rests with a sovereign but where lesser interests are granted in return for loyalty or service. Contrast to allodial tenure.

**feuds.** Grants of land.

**fidelity bond.** A bond posted as security for the discharge of an obligation of personal services.

**filtering down.** In housing, the process of passing the use of real estate to successively lower income groups as the real estate produces less income.

**financial institutions.** Organizations that deal in money or claims to money and serve the function of channeling money from those who wish to lend to those who wish to borrow. Such organizations include commercial banks, savings and loan associations, savings banks, and insurance companies.

**fiscal controls.** Efforts to control the level of economic activity by manipulation of the amount of federal tax and spending programs and the amount of surplus or deficit.

**fixity of location.** The characteristic of real estate that subjects it to the influence of its surroundings and prohibits it from escaping from such influence.

**flow of funds.** An accounting method (used primarily by the Federal Reserve) to describe the sources and uses of the nation's funds in a given period of time.

**Foreclosure.** The legal steps required by law to be taken by the mortgagee after the default of a debt before the property can be proceeded against for payment of the debt.

*foreclosure by sale.* Foreclosure either under court action resulting in a decree of sale or under power of sale contained in a mortgage or trust deed.

*strict foreclosure.* Action by a court that, after determination that sufficient time has elapsed for a mortgagor to pay a mortgage past due, terminates all rights and interest of the mortgagor in the real property.

**franchise.** A specific privilege conferred by government or, in the case of an exclusive dealership, conferred by a business firm.

**freehold estate.** *See* estate, freehold estate.

**functional plan.** The special arrangement of real estate improvements as it relates to property services.

**grant.** A transfer of real property by written instrument as in a deed.

*private grant.* The transfer of real property from one person to another.

*public grant.* A government grant of real property to a private party; a transfer of real property from government to a person.

**grantee.** One who receives a transfer of real property by deed.

**grantor.** One who transfers real property by deed.

**gridiron pattern, gridiron plan.** A layout of streets that resembles a gridiron; a system of subdivision with blocks of uniform length and width and streets that intersect at right angles.

**gross income multiplier.** A technique for estimating real estate value based on some factor (multiplier) times the gross income derived from the property in the past.

**gross national product (GNP).** The total value of all goods and services produced in the economy in any given period; also, the accounting method used to list the major income and expenditure (product) accounts of the nation.

**guaranteed mortgage.** A mortgage in which a party other than the borrower assures payment in the event of default by a mortgagor, e.g., Veterans' Administration guaranteed mortgages.

**heuristics.** The process of arriving at a decision through imagination or inspiration.

**highest and best use.** The utilization of real property to its greatest economic advantage; the use that provides the highest land value; the use of land that provides a net income stream to the land that when capitalized provides the highest land value.

**home associations.** *See* **property owners' association.**

**Home Owners Loan Corporation.** An agency of the federal government that refinanced mortgages in default in the early 1930's.

**homestead (right of), homestead exemption.** The interest of the head of a family in his owned residence that is exempt from the claims of creditors.


**improved value.** The difference between the income-producing ability of a property and the amount required to pay a return on the investment in the property.

**improvement.** That which is erected or constructed upon land to release the income-earning potential of the land; buildings or appurtenances on land.

*overimprovement.* An improvement of real estate in excess of that justifiable to release the earning power of land.

*underimprovement.* An improvement insufficient to release the earning power of land.

**incentive.** Spur, motive, special reward, such as extra payment for reaching or exceeding a standard of performance, or for performing in a certain way.

**incorporeal rights.** Nonpossessory rights in real estate.

**indirect subsidies.** *See* subsidy, *indirect subsidy.*

**inducive regulations.** *See* regulations, *inducive regulations.*

**industrial districts.** Areas in which the primary or major improvements to land are in the nature of factory, warehouse, or related property.

**industrial park.** An area in which the land is developed specifically for use for industrial purposes.

**inheritance taxation.** *See* taxation, *inheritance taxation.*

**input-output analysis.** A technique for analysis of an economy through description of the production and purchases of specific sectors of the economy.

**Institute of Real Estate Management.** A professional organization of property managers.

*CPM (Certified Property Manager).* Official designation for members.

**insured mortgage.** A mortgage in which a party other than the borrower, in return for the payment of a premium, assures payment in the event of default by a mortgagor, e.g., FHA insured mortgages.

**interest rate risk.** The risk of loss due to changes in the interest rate, earnings, or the value of a property may be affected as a result of changes in prevailing interest rates in the money market. When interest rates go up or down properties are generally capitalized at higher or lower rates.

**interurbia.** A contiguous urban development larger than a city or metropolitan area.

**intestate.** Legal designation of a person who has died without leaving a valid will.


**joint estates.** *See* estate, *joint estates.*

**joint tenancy.** A joint estate with the right of survivorship.

**joint venture.** An arrangement under which two or more individuals or businesses will go together on a single project as partners.

**judgment.** The acknowledgment or award of a claim through a court of law; an obligation or debt under a court decree; also, the decree.

**junior mortgage.** A mortgage having claim ranking below that of another mortgage.

**jurisdictional disputes.** As between two labor unions or trade unions, a disagreement as to which union's members shall perform certain services.

**land.** In a physical sense, the earth's surface; may include the minerals below the surface and the air above the surface.

**land contract, contract for deed.** A written agreement by which real property is sold to a buyer who agrees to pay in installments the established price, with interest, over a specified period of years, with title remaining with the seller until the purchase price or some portion of the purchase price is paid.

**land description.** *See* **legal description.**

**land economics.** The branch of general economics that deals with the social organization for the utilization of land resources in the attainment of the objectives that the society or community sets for itself.

**land planning.** The designing of land area uses, road networks, and layout for utilities to achieve efficient utilization of real estate resources.

**law.** A generalization from experience that applies almost universally. A demonstrated relationship between cause and effect. Also, in a legal sense, an established rule or standard of conduct or action that is enforceable by government.

*common law.* See **common law.**

*license law.* A law that regulates the practices of real estate brokers and salesmen.

*real estate law.* The body of laws relating to real estate; generally evolved from the English common law but now including regulations such as zoning, building codes, etc.

**leadership.** The vital motivating force that inspires and directs an organization toward the achievement of its objectives.

**lease.** A transfer of possession and the right to use property to a tenant for a stipulated period, during which the tenant pays rent to the owner; the contract containing the terms and conditions of such an agreement.

*graded or step-up lease.* A lease with a rental payment that increases to specified amounts at specified periods of time.

*ground lease.* A lease for vacant land upon which the tenant may erect improvements.

*index lease.* A lease in which the rental payment varies in accordance with variation of an agreed-upon index of prices or costs.

*lease with option to purchase.* A lease in which the lessee has the right to purchase the real property for a stipulated price at or within a stipulated time.

*leasehold, leasehold estate.* An estate held under a lease.

*net lease.* A lease in which the tenant pays certain agreed-upon property expenses such as taxes or maintenance.

*percentage lease.* A lease in which the rental is based on a percentage of the lessee's sales income.

*reappraisal lease.* A lease in which an arrangement is made for determination of the amount of rent at some future period by independent appraisers.

*tax participation clause (in a lease).* An agreement in a lease where the lessee agrees to pay all or a stated portion of any increase in real estate taxes.

**leasehold estate.** *See* **estate,** *nonfreehold estate.*

**legal description, land description.** A means of identifying the exact boundaries of land by metes and bounds, by a plat, or by township and range survey system.

*metes and bounds.* "Metes" refers to measures; "bounds," to direction. Metes and bounds descriptions are means of describing land by measurement and direction from a known point or marker on land.

*plat.* A recorded map of land that identifies a parcel by a number or other designation in a subdivision.

*township and range survey system.* A system of legal description of land with a township as the basic unit of measurement.

*base line.* A parallel that serves as a reference for other parallels.

*meridians.* North-south lines of survey 6 miles apart.

*parallel.* East-west lines of survey 6 miles apart.

*principal meridian.* A meridian that serves as a reference for other meridians.

*range.* A north-south row of townships; the 6-mile strip of land between meridian.

*section.* A 1-mile square in a township.

*tier.* An east-west row of townships; the 6-mile strip of land between parallels.

*township.* A 6-mile square of land bounded by parallels and meridians, and composed of 36 sections.

**lessee.** The tenant under a lease; one who receives possession and use of real estate for a period of time in return for the payment of rent.

**lessor.** The landlord under a lease; one who grants permission and use of real estate for a specified period for a specified rent.

**license law.** Law that regulates the practices of real estate brokers and salesmen.

**lien.** The right to have the property of another sold to satisfy a debt.

**lien theory of morgtage.** The mortgage arrangement whereby title to mortgaged property vests in the borrower, with the lender having a lien against the property.

**life estate.** *See* **estate,** *life estate.*

**listing.** An agreement or contract between a principal and an agent providing that the agent will receive a commission for finding a buyer who is ready, willing, and able to purchase a particular property under terms specified by the agreement.

*exclusive agency listing.* A listing contract providing that the agent shall receive a commission if the property is sold as a result of the efforts of that agent or any other agent, but not as a result of the efforts of the principal; the contract further provides that the agent will receive a commission if he secures a buyer under the terms of the contract.

*exclusive right-to-sell listing.* A listing contract providing that the agent shall receive a commission if the property is sold irrespective of whether as a result of the efforts of that agent or another agent or the principal; the contract also provides that the agent shall receive a commission if he produces a buyer under the terms of the contract.

*multiple listing.* A listing that in addition to employing the agent, provides for the services of other agents who have agreed among themselves that they will cooperate in finding a purchaser for the property.

*open listing.* A listing contract providing that the agent shall receive a commission if the property is sold as a result of the efforts of that agent or if the agent produces a buyer under the terms of the contract before the property is sold.

**localization of income.** Income production at fixed locations; i.e., from real estate, which has a fixed and unique location.

**location.** Position of land and improvements in relation to other land and improvements and to local or general economic activity.

**location quotient.** An analytic technique using proportionality comparisons as, for example, the comparison of the percentage of an activity in a city with the percentage of the same activity in the nation.

**lot.** A specific plot of land.

**MAI (Member Appraisal Institute).** *See under* **appraiser.**

**map.** A representation of some feature on the earth's surface such as physical features or boundary lines and the like. *See* **plat; plat map; Sanborn insurance maps; time interval maps; topographical map.**

**market.** A set of arrangements for bringing buyers and sellers together through the price mechanism.

*buyer's market.* A market in which buyers can fulfill their desires at lower prices and on more advantageous terms than those prevailing earlier; a market characterized by many properties available and few potential users demanding them at prevailing prices.

*capital market.* The activities of all lenders and borrowers of equity and long-term debt funds.

*market analysis.* A study of the supply, demand, and price forces at work in a particular market; also the process of studying supply, demand, and prices in a particular market, e.g., the real estate market.

*money market.* A market for borrowed funds, generally short-term.

*seller's market.* A market in which potential sellers can sell at prices higher than those prevailing in an immediately preceding period; a market characterized by very few properties available and a large number of users and potential users demanding them at prevailing prices.

**meridian.** *See* **legal description,** *township and range survey system.*

**metes and bounds.** A system of land description; "metes" refers to measures; "bounds," to direction. *See* **legal description,** *metes and bounds.*

**model house.** A house used for exhibition in order to sell other houses.

**modular construction.** Prefabrication in three dimensions; i.e. entire rooms of houses or apartments are built in the factory and shipped to their eventual location where very little on-site labor is required.

**modular planning.** The designing of structures using a designated size minimum dimension of length and width such as 4 feet.

**monetary controls.** Efforts by the Federal Reserve to influence the level of economic activity by regulating the availability of money and the rate of interest.

**money market.** *See* **market,** money market.

**mortgage.** The pledge of real property to secure a debt; the conveyance of real property as security for a debt; the instrument that is evidence of the pledge or conveyance.

*assumption of mortgage.* See **assumption of a mortgage.**

*balloon mortgage payment.* A large payment during the terms of a mortgage, often at the end.

*blanket mortgage.* A mortgage that has two or more properties pledged or conveyed as security for a debt, usually for subdividing and improvement purposes.

*junior mortgage.* A second or third mortgage; one that, in the event of liquidation, will not be paid off until after the senior mortgage.

*mortgage bonds.* Evidences of debt secured by a mortgage in favor of individual parties as a group, usually with the mortgage held by a third party in trust for the mortgage bond creditors.

*mortgage broker.* An agent who, for a commission, brings a mortgagor and mortgagee together.

*mortgage company.* A firm that, for a fee, brings mortgagor and mortgagee together or that acquires mortgages for the purpose of resale.

*open-end mortgage.* A mortgage with provisions for future advances to the borrower without the necessity of writing a new mortgage.

*package mortgage.* A mortgage in which the collateral is not limited to real property but includes personal property in the nature of household equipment.

*purchase money mortgage.* A mortgage that is given in part payment of the purchase price in contrast to a mortgage that is given as security for repayment of funds.

*subject to mortgage.* Grantee takes title but is not responsible for mortgage beyond the value of his equity in the property. No deficiency judgment.

**mortgagee.** The creditor or lender under a mortgage.

**mortgagor.** The debtor or borrower under a mortgage.

**motivation research.** Analysis of consumers in an attempt to determine why prospective buyers react as they do to products or services or to advertisements used in attempting to sell them.

**multifamily structure.** A dwelling for (usually) five or more household units.

**multiple listing.** *See* **listing,** *multiple listing.*

**mutual saving bank.** A financial institution in which the depositors are the owners. Mutual savings banks are a primary source of home mortgage funds.

**National Association of Home Builders.** A national trade association of house and apartment builders.

**National Association of Mutual Savings Banks.** A national trade association whose members are mutual savings banks.

**National Association of Real Estate Boards.** A national real estate trade association. Includes such trade associations as American Institute of Real Estate Appraisers, Institute of Farm Brokers, Institute of Real Estate Management, and others.

**national income accounting.** Statistical technique used in developing gross national product calculations; *see* **gross national product (GNP).**

**national wealth statistics.** Accounting technique for measuring the size and composition of wealth of the economic system and the changes in them.

**neighborhood.** A small area within a city that may be differentiated from adjacent areas, e.g., an area with homes of the same price range or people of the same income bracket. *See* **district.**

**neighborhood life cycle.** The succession of periods of growth, maturity and decline that most neighborhoods tend to go through.

**nonbasic employment, secondary employment, urban service employment.** Usually refers to employment in establishments that receive their income from within the community. Contrast to basic employment.

**nonbasic income.** Usually refers to income that comes from within the community.

**nonfreehold estate.** *See* **estate,** *nonfreehold estate.*

**obsolescence.** Loss in property value because of the existence of a less costly alternative that provides comparable or more desirable property services.

**open house.** A house that is available for inspection by potential purchasers without appointments.

**open listing.** *See* **listing,** *open listing.*

**operative builder.** *See* **builder,** *operative builder.*

**opinion of title.** *See* **title,** *opinion of title.*

**option (to purchase real estate).** The right to purchase property at a stipulated price and under stipulated terms within a period of time; the instrument that is evidence of such a right.

**ordinance.** A public regulation such as a law (usually local laws).

**orientation.** The position of a structure on a site and its general relationship to its surroundings.

**overbuilding.** The building of structures of a particular type more than can be absorbed by the market at prevailing prices.

**overimprovement.** *See* **improvement,** *overimprovement.*

**ownership of real property.** The holding of rights or interests in real estate. *See* **estate,** *fee simple estate.*

**PUD.** *See* **planned unit development.**

**package mortgage.** *See* **mortgage,** *package mortgage.*

**parallel.** *See* **legal description,** *township and range survey system.*

**parcel of real estate.** A particular piece of land and its improvements.

**parity.** Equality; often used to refer to an equivalence between farmers' current purchasing power and their purchasing power at a selected base period maintained by government support of commodity prices.

**parking lot.** A parcel of real estate used for the storage of automobiles. Usually about 300 square feet per auto is required for parking space and aisles.

**partially amortized mortgage.** A combination of an amortized mortgage and a term mortgage (straight-term mortgage).

**perpetuity.** Without limitation as to time, perpetual; as in capitalization in perpetuity.

**personal property.** The exclusive right to exercise control over personality; all property objects other than real estate.

**personality.** All property other realty; chattels.

**planned unit development.** A design for an area which provides for intensive use of land often through a combination of private and common areas with arrangements for sharing responsibilities for the common areas. Typically, zoning boards consider the entire development and allow its arrangements to be substituted for traditional mortgages. An example is a residential "cluster" development.

**planning.** The process of formulating a program in advance to achieve desired results.

*long-range planning.* Planning for a period of years in the future. This type of planning is used as a framework for shorter range planning.

**plat, plat map.** A map that shows boundary lines of parcels of real estate, usually of an area that has been subdivided into a number of lots. *See* **legal description,** *plat.*

**plat book.** A book containing a series of plat maps.

**plottage.** The extent to which value is increased when two or more lots are combined in a single ownership or use.

**police power.** The authority for governmental regulations necessary to safe-guard the public health, morals, and safety and to promote the general welfare.

**prefabrication.** The process of manufacturing component parts of a structure in a factory for later assembly on-site.

**present value.** *See* **capitalization.**

**price.** That amount of money at which property is offered for sale or is ex-changed for at a sale; value in terms of money.

**principal.** One who has another act for him; one who is represented by an agent. Also, the amount of a debt.

**priority.** A preferential rating; especially one that allocates scarce resources.

**private property.** *See* **property,** *private property.*

**probate.** The proof or act of proving at a court that a last will and testament is actually the last will and testament of a deceased person.

**property.** The exclusive right to exercise control over economic good. *See* **real property; personal property.**

*common property.* Ownership of a parcel of land by a number of people who hold their interests by virtue of ownership of adjoining parcels.

*private property.* Property held by individuals or by groups of individuals except when such a group constitutes a public organization.

*public property.* Property held by government.

**property brief.** A folder that presents pertinent information about a property.

**property management.** The operation of real property including the leasing of space, collection of rents, selection of tenants, and the repair and renova-tion of the buildings and grounds.

**property owners association, property owners maintenance association.** Or-ganizations with the purpose of administering private regulations affecting residential land uses.

**property services.** The benefits accruing from the use of property.

**property taxation.** *See* **taxation,** *property taxation.*

**proprietorship.** A business that is run by its owner as an individual rather than as a corporation; i.e., John Smith, Real Estate.

**public housing.** Housing owned by a governmental body.

**public property.** *See* **property,** *public property.*

**purchase on contract.** The purchase of property on installments with title re-maining with seller. *See* **land contract.**

**purchasing power risk.** Risk that the value of an investment will decline due to inflation (decline in the purchasing power of the dollar).

**quadrangular survey system.** *See* **legal description,** *township and range survey system.*

**R&D.** *See* **research and development.**

**range.** *See* **legal description,** *township and range survey system.*

**real estate.** In a physical sense, land with or without buildings or improvements; in a legal sense, the rights in such physical objects.

**real estate administration.** *See* **administration of real estate resources.**

**real estate appraisal.** *See* **appraisal.**

**real estate broker.** An agent who negotiates the sale of real property or real property services for a commission that is contingent on success.

**real estate business.** The business that deals in rights to income or income potentials at fixed locations. It is concerned with production, marketing, and financing of these rights.

**real estate developing.** The process of preparing land for use, constructing buildings and other improvements, and making the completed properties available.

**real estate financing.** The channeling of savings into the production and use of real estate; facilitating the production and use of real estate through borrowed or equity funds. Also, the area of study dealing with the foregoing.

**real estate investment corporation.** A corporation that sells its securities to the public and has a special interest in real estate or is a builder or developer of real estate.

**real estate investment trusts.** A trust established in a form similar to that of an investment or mutual fund for the purpose of allowing investors to channel funds into the real estate market.

**real estate marketing.** The process or putting real properties and their services into the hands of consumers. Brokerage and property management are the two main subdivisions of real estate marketing.

**real estate operator.** An individual engaged in the real estate business acting for himself rather than as an agent.

**real estate syndicate.** A partnership organized for participation in a real estate venture. Partners may be limited or unlimited in their liability.

**real property.** The exclusive right to exercise control over real estate; a parcel of real estate.

**real property taxation.** *See* **taxation,** *real property taxation.*

**Realtor.** A broker who is a member of a local real estate board that is affiliated with the National Association of Real Estate Boards.

**realty.** The property objects of land and all things permanently attached to it.

**recapture.** Usually a provision for assuring return of investment. It may be accomplished by inclusion in the capitalization rate in the income approach to valuation.

**recorder.** *See* **registrar of deeds.**

**recording acts, registry laws.** Laws providing for the recording of instruments affecting title as a matter of public record and that preserve such evidence and give notice of their existence and content; laws providing that the recording of an instrument informs all who deal in real property of the transaction and that unless the instrument is recorded, a prospective purchaser without actual notice of its existence is protected against it.

**redemption.** The regaining of title to real property after a foreclosure sale.

*equity of redemption.* The interest of the mortgagor in real property prior to foreclosure.

*statutory right of redemption.* The right under law of the mortgagor to redeem title to real property after a foreclosure sale.

**redevelopment.** Typically the processes of clearance and reconstruction of blighted areas.

**regional analysis.** When applied to real estate, pertaining mainly to local economies and the surrounding area; for other purposes, the area of a "region" may be defined more broadly.

**registrar of deeds, recorder.** Officer in charge of a land records office.

**registry laws.** *See* **recording acts.**

**regulations.** Rules for controlling activities or procedures.
   *coercive regulations.* Regulations which provide penalties for noncompliance.
   *inducive regulations.* Regulations which provide incentive for compliance.

**rehabilitation.** The removal of blight by repair and renovation rather than by destruction of improvements.

**remainder.** The right of a person to interests that mature at the end of another estate; a classification of estates by time of enjoyment.
   *contingent remainder.* An interest that will become a remainder only if some condition is fulfilled.

**renewal.** The process of redevelopment or rehabilitation in cities; often used in relation to rebuilding or restoration of blighted areas.

**rent.** The return on land or real property.

**rent controls.** The legal provision for a maximum rental payment for the use of real property.

**rent multiplier.** A factor or number used to estimate value by multiplying the rent. A rent multiplier may be either a gross rent multiplier or a net rent multiplier.

**research and development.** The process of developing new products or new methods.

**reversion.** The residue of an estate left with the grantor that entitles him to possession after the end of another estate; a classification of estates by time of enjoyment.

**rod.** A unit of linear measure representing a length of 5½ yards.

**SMSA.** *See* **standard metropolitan statistical area.**

**sale-leaseback.** An arrangement that provides for a simultaneous transfer of ownership and execution of lease—the grantor becomes the lessee and the grantee the lessor.

**sales kit.** A file of information about the properties a broker has for sale.

**Sanborn insurance maps.** Maps showing locations of individual structures in many cities. Developed for underwriting insurance.

**search of title.** *See* **title,** *search of title.*

**seasonal fluctuations.** Variations in economic activity that recur at about the same time each year.

**seasoned mortgage.** A mortgage in which the principal has been reduced through amortization.

**secondary employment.** *See* **nonbasic employment.**

**secondary income.** *See* **nonbasic income.**

**section.** *See* **legal description,** *township and range survey system.*

**sector theory.** A theory of city growth that considers the city as a circle with wedge-shaped sectors pointing to the center.

**secular trend.** *See* **trend.**

**seller's market.** *See* **market,** seller's market.

**senior mortgage.** A mortgage having a claim ranking above that of another mortgage.

**shopping center.** A planned shopping area usually in outlying locations. Typically stores are surrounded by parking area.

*mall-type shopping center.* A shopping center in which the stores face inward an enclosed walkway rather than fronting on the parking lot, so that the shoppers can stay inside one building while they visit various stores.

*super regional shopping center.* A large shopping center with 250,000 to 1,000,000 square feet of store area, serving 200,000 or more people.

**single-family home.** A dwelling intended for occupancy by one household only.

**site.** A parcel of real estate that is improved or suitable for improvement.

**situs.** Location.

**slum clearance.** The removal of blighted improvements by destruction of the improvements. *See* **redevelopment; rehabilitation; renewal.**

**Society of Real Estate Appraisers.** A trade association of residential real estate appraisers.

**"snob zoning."** *See* **zoning.**

**social contract.** (business) A broad term relating to the laws and customs that have evolved to regulate relationships between business and society, indicating the rights and duties of each.

**special assessment.** *See* **assessment,** *special assessment.*

**specific performance, specifically enforceable.** The requirement that a party must perform as agreed under a contract in contrast to compensation or damages in lieu of performance; the arrangement whereby courts may force either party to a real estate contract to carry out an agreement exactly.

**spot zoning.** *See* **zoning,** *spot zoning.*

**standard metropolitan statistical area.** A city or cities and their suburbs that constitute a single metropolitan area for statistical purposes. SMSA's must have a minimum population of 50,000.

**Statute of Frauds.** Legislation providing that all agreements affecting title to real estate must be in writing to be enforceable.

**statutory right of redemption.** *See* **redemption,** *statutory right of redemption.*

**straight-term morgage.** A mortgage in which repayment of principal is in one lump sum at maturity.

**subcontractor.** A contractor who contracts from another, usually a general contractor. A subcontractor usually is concerned only with one particular part of the improvement of real estate such as plumbing, masonry, carpentry, and the like.

**subdivision.** An area of land divided into parcels or lots generally of a size suitable for residential use.

**subsidy.** In real estate, a grant by government that eases the financial burden of holding, using, or improving real property.

*direct subsidy.* A subsidy which is of direct, visible benefit to the recipient, such as a cash grant.

*indirect subsidy.* A subsidy whose benefit is felt indirectly; such as tariffs or farm price supports may affect the land values in a particular area.

**suburb.** A development of real estate in areas peripheral to the central area of a city.

**supermarket.** A 20,000 to 40,000 square foot grocery store that is often free-standing.

**supersession costs.** Costs incurred in scrapping existing improvements in order to make possible new land uses.

**supply.** Amount available for sale.

**survey.** A measurement of land to determine boundaries or points of location on land; the process of determining, or the map that shows, the exact dimension and location of a site and possibly such things as levels of the land by contour lines, boundaries and their relationship to natural formations, and the location of streets, sewers, water, and gas and electric lines.

**sustained yield management.** Selective harvesting of slow-growing crops such as trees to provide for a relatively stable yield every year rather than one large yield or at irregular times.


**tax lien.** A claim against property arising out of nonpayment of taxes; the claim may be sold by the taxing authority.

**tax participation clause.** *See* **lease.**

**tax title.** *See* **title,** *tax title.*

**taxation.** The right of government to payment for the support of activities in which it engages.

  *double taxation.* In real estate, the taxation of the property as an asset and the taxation of the property income the owner receives.

  *estate taxation.* Taxation imposed by government on property passed by will or descent.

  *inheritance taxation.* Taxation imposed on property received through inheritance.

  *property taxation.* Taxation imposed upon owners of property.

  *real property taxation.* Taxation imposed upon the owners of real property.

**taxing district.** The geographical area over which a taxing authority levies taxes.

**tenancy.** An interest in real property; the right to possession and use of real property.

  *at will.* By agreement of the parties, with no specified termination date.

  *joint tenancy.* A joint estate that provides for the right of survivorship; a joint estate in which the interest of joint tenants passes to the surviving joint tenant or tenants.

  *periodic tenancy.* The rights to use and occupancy under a lease that is renewed from period to period.

  *tenancy by entirety.* An estate held by husband and wife where both are viewed as one person under common law, which thus provides for the right of survivorship.

  *tenancy in common.* A joint estate in which each tenant in common (co-owner) may dispose of his interest by devise or descent.

**tenure.** The act, right, manner or term of holding something.

  *farmland tenure.* The sum total of the various agreements by which land is owned, rented, leased, used, controlled and transferred.

**term mortgage.** *See* **straight-term mortgage.**

**tier.** *See* **legal description,** *township and range survey system.*

**time interval maps.** A series of maps that show land use or some other feature as of different dates.

**title.** Proof or evidence of ownership or ownership rights.

*abstract of title, abstract.* A historical summary of the conveyances, transfers, and other facts relied on as evidence of title; a summary of the documents having a bearing on the history of the title to a property.

*cloudy title.* A title that would be impaired if an outstanding claim proved to be valid.

*defective title.* A title that would be impaired if an outstanding claim proved to be valid and where such a claim could be shown to be valid.

*opinion of title.* The statement, usually of an attorney, as to whether he believes a title to be clear or defective.

*search of title.* A study of the history of the title to a property.

*tax title.* The title to real property acquired through a forced sale for taxes; an interest in real property that will become ownership if the defaulting taxpayer does not redeem the property.

*title by descent.* Title acquired by the laws of succession; title acquired by an heir in the absence of a will.

*title by devise.* Title received through a will.

**title insurance.** Insurance that a title is clear or clear except for defects noted; a policy of insurance that indemnifies the insured for loss occasioned by unknown defects of title.

**title theory of mortgage.** The mortgage arrangement whereby title to mortgaged real property vests in the lender.

**topographical map.** A map that shows the slope and contour of land; a map of the physical features of a parcel of real estate or an area of land.

**topography.** Contour and slope of land and such things as gullies, streams, knolls, and ravines.

**Torrens system.** A system of land title registration in which the state guarantees title.

**township.** *See* **legal description,** *township and range survey system.*

**trade area.** That geographical area from which purchasers of particular goods and services will ordinarily be drawn.

**trade association.** A voluntary organization of individuals or firms in a common area of economic activity; the organization has for its purpose the promotion of certain aspects of the common area of activity.

**trade-up.** *See* **filtering down.**

**trend.** A prevailing tendency of behavior of some observable phenomenon such as economic activity over time; a tendency that is exhibited over a long period of time despite intermittent fluctuations.

**trust deed.** An instrument that is evidence of the pledge of real property as security for a debt where the title to the real property is held by a third party in trust while the debtor repays the debt to the lender; the debtor is known as the *trustor;* the lender is known as the *beneficiary,* the third party is known as the *trustee.*

**United States Savings and Loan League.** A trade association of savings and loan associations.

**urban growth employment.** *See* **basic employment.**

**urban plan.** The community facilities that enable the community to function as a unit; e.g., the system of streets, sewers, water mains, parks, playgrounds, and the like.

urban renewal. *See* renewal.

urban service employment. *See* nonbasic employment.

urban size ratchet. The theory that once a town reaches a certain size, it will continue to grow of its own accord.

user of real estate. One who has the use of property rights whether it be through ownership, lease, easement, or license.


valuation. *See* appraisal.

value of property. The usefulness of the property relative to its scarcity.

Veterans' Administration (VA). An agency of the federal government that, among other activities, guarantees loans made to veterans.


zoning. Government regulation of land use; regulation by local government under police power of such matters as height, bulk, and use of buildings and use of land.

 *enabling act.* A state statute necessary to provide a legal base for zoning codes.

 *"snob zoning."* Zoning regulations that require large lots, etc., as a method of excluding those in 10w-income groups.

 *spot zoning.* A case in which the zoning code allows pockets of nonconforming uses or where such pockets are allowed by variances.

 *zoning variance.* A legal exception to the zoning generally obtained through the zoning board or city council.

# B

# Real Estate License Laws*

The regulatory body of each state and the year in which the license law was effective or approved.

**Alabama.** Alabama Real Estate Commission (1927).

**Alaska.** Alaska Real Estate Commission (1957).

**Arizona.** State of Arizona Real Estate Department (1928).

**Arkansas.** Arkansas Real Estate Commission (1929).

**California.** California Real Estate Commission (1919).

**Colorado.** Real Estate Brokers Board (1925).

**Connecticut.** Insurance Department (1953).

**Delaware.** Delaware Real Estate Commission (1927).

**District of Columbia.** Real Estate Commission of District of Columbia (1937).

**Florida.** Florida Real Estate Commission (1927).

**Georgia.** Georgia Real Estate Commission (1925).

**Hawaii.** Real Estate License Commission (1933).

**Idaho.** Idaho Real Estate Brokers Board (1921).

**Illinois.** The Department of Registration and Education (1921).

**Indiana.** Indiana Real Estate Commission (1949).

**Iowa.** Iowa Real Estate Commission (1930)

**Kansas.** Kansas Real Estate Commission (1947).

**Kentucky.** Kentucky Real Estate Commission (1938).

**Louisiana.** Louisiana Real Estate Board (1920).

**Maine.** Maine Real Estate Commission (1937).

**Maryland.** Maryland Real Estate Commission (1939).

**Massachusetts.** Board of Registration of Real Estate Brokers and Salesmen (1957).

**Michigan.** Michigan Corporation and Security Commission (1919).

**Minnesota.** Securities Division (1955).

**Mississippi.** Mississippi Real Estate Commission (1954).

* Information on license laws provided by Mr. Robert W. Semenow, Executive Vice President, National Association of Real Estate License Law Officials (NARELLO), and from Mr. Semenow's book, *Questions and Answers on Real Estate.* Sixth Edition. Englewood Cliffs, N.J.: Prentice-Hall, Inc., 1969.

**Missouri.** Missouri Real Estate Commission (1943).

**Montana.** Montana Real Estate Commission (1921).

**Nebraska.** Nebraska Real Estate Commission (1935).

**Nevada.** Real Estate Division (1923).

**New Hampshire.** Insurance Commission (1959).

**New Jersey.** Division of New Jersey Real Estate Commission in the Department of Banking and Insurance (1921).

**New Mexico.** New Mexico Real Estate Commission (1951).

**New York.** Department of State, Division of Licenses (1922).

**North Carolina.** North Carolina Real Estate Licensing Board (1957).

**North Dakota.** North Dakota Real Estate Commission (1957).

**Ohio.** Ohio Real Estate Commission (1925).

**Oklahoma.** Oklahoma Real Estate Commission (1949).

**Oregon.** Real Estate Division of Department of Commerce (1919).

**Pennsylvania.** State Real Estate Commission (1929).

**Rhode Island.** Rhode Island Real Estate Commission (1959).

**South Carolina.** South Carolina Real Estate Commission (1956).

**South Dakota.** Real Estate Commission (1955).

**Tennessee.** Tennessee Real Estate Commission (1951).

**Texas.** Texas Real Estate Commission (1939).

**Utah.** State Securities Commission (1921).

**Vermont.** Vermont Real Estate Commission (1930).

**Virginia.** Virginia Real Estate Commission (1924).

**Washington.** Department of Licenses, Real Estate Division (1925).

**West Virginia.** West Virginia Real Estate Commission (1937).

**Wisconsin.** Wisconsin Real Estate Brokers Board (1920).

**Wyoming.** Wyoming Real Estate Board (1921).

# C

# Code of Ethics *

### Preamble

Under all is the land. Upon its wise utilization and widely allocated ownership depend the survival and growth of free institutions and of our civilization. The Realtor is the instrumentality through which the land resource of the nation reaches its highest use and through which land ownership attains its widest distribution. He is a creator of homes, a builder of cities, a developer of industries and productive farms.

Such functions impose obligations beyond those of ordinary commerce. They impose grave social responsibility and a patriotic duty to which the Realtor should dedicate himself, and for which he should be diligent in preparing himself. The Realtor, therefore, is zealous to maintain and improve the standards of his calling and shares with his fellow-Realtors a common responsibility for its integrity and honor.

In the interpretation of his obligations, he can take no safer guide than that which has been handed down through twenty centuries, embodied in the Golden Rule:

"Whatsoever ye would that men should do to you, do ye even so to them."

Accepting this standard as his own, every Realtor pledges himself to observe its spirit in all his activities and to conduct his business in accordance with the following Code of Ethics:

### Part I. Relations to the Public

**Article 1.** The Realtor should keep himself informed as to movements affecting real estate in his community, state, and the nation, so that he may be able to contribute to public thinking on matters of taxation, legislation, land use, city planning, and other questions affecting property interests.

* National Association of Real Estate Boards.

**Article 2.** It is the duty of the Realtor to be well informed on current market conditions in order to be in a position to advise his clients as to the fair market price.

**Article 3.** It is the duty of the Realtor to protect the public against fraud, misrepresentation or unethical practices in the real estate field.

He should endeavor to eliminate in his community any practices which could be damaging to the public or to the dignity and integrity of the real estate profession. The Realtor should assist the board or commission charged with regulating the practices of brokers and salesmen in his state.

**Article 4.** The Realtor should ascertain all pertinent facts concerning every property for which he accepts the agency, so that he may fulfill his obligation to avoid error, exaggeration, misrepresentation, or concealment of pertinent facts.

**Article 5.** The Realtor should not be instrumental in introducing into a neighborhood a character of property or use which will clearly be detrimental to property values in that neighborhood.

**Article 6.** The Realtor should not be a party to the naming of a false consideration in any document, unless it be the naming of an obviously nominal consideration.

**Article 7.** The Realtor should not engage in activities that constitute the practice of law and should recommend that title be examined and legal counsel be obtained when the interest of either party requires it.

**Article 8.** The Realtor should keep in a special bank account, separated from his own funds, monies coming into his possession in trust for other persons, such as escrows, trust funds, client's monies and other like items.

**Article 9.** The Realtor in his advertising should be especially careful to present a true picture and should neither advertise without disclosing his name, nor permit his salesmen to use individual names or telephone numbers, unless the salesmen's connection with the Realtor is obvious in the advertisement.

**Article 10.** The Realtor, for the protection of all parties with whom he deals, should see that financial obligations and commitments regarding real estate transactions are in writing, expressing the exact agreement of the parties; and that copies of such agreements, at the time they are executed, are placed in the hands of all parties involved.

### Part II.  Relations to the Client

**Article 11.** In accepting employment as an agent, the Realtor pledges himself to protect and promote the interests of the client. This obligation of absolute fidelity to the client's interest is primary, but it does not relieve the Realtor from the obligation of dealing fairly with all parties to the transaction.

**Article 12.** In justice to those who place their interests in his care, the Realtor should endeavor always to be informed regarding laws, proposed legislation, governmental orders, and other essential information and public policies which affect those interests.

**Article 13.** Since the Realtor is representing one or another party to a transaction, he should not accept compensation from more than one party without the full knowledge of all parties to the transaction.

**Article 14.** The Realtor should not acquire an interest in or buy for himself, any member of his immediate family, his firm or any member thereof, or any entity in which he has a substantial ownership interest, property listed with him, or his firm, without making the true position known to the listing owner, and in selling property owned by him, or in which he has such interest, the facts should be revealed to the purchaser.

**Article 15.** The exclusive listing of property should be urged and practiced by the Realtor as a means of preventing dissension and misunderstanding and of assuring better service to the owner.

**Article 16.** When acting as agent in the management of property, the Realtor should not accept any commission, rebate or profit on expenditures made for an owner, without the owner's knowledge and consent.

**Article 17.** The Realtor should not undertake to make an appraisal that is outside the field of his experience unless he obtains the assistance of an authority on such types of property, or unless the facts are fully disclosed to the client. In such circumstances the authority so engaged should be so identified and his contribution to the assignment should be clearly set forth.

**Article 18.** When asked to make a formal appraisal of real property, the Realtor should not render an opinion without careful and thorough analysis and interpretation of all factors affecting the value of the property. His counsel constitutes a professional service.

The Realtor should not undertake to make an appraisal or render an opinion of value on any property where he has a present or contemplated interest unless such interest is specifically disclosed in the appraisal report. Under no circumstances should he undertake to make a formal appraisal when his employment or fee is contingent upon the amount of his appraisal.

**Article 19.** The Realtor should not submit or advertise property without authority and in any offering, the price quoted should not be other than that agreed upon with the owners as the offering price.

**Article 20.** In the event that more than one formal written offer on a specific property is made before the owner has accepted an offer, any other formal written offer presented to the Realtor, whether by a prospective purchaser or another broker, should be transmitted to the owner for his decision.

### Part III. Relations to His Fellow-Realtor

**Article 21.** The Realtor should seek no unfair advantage over his fellow-Realtors and should willingly share with them the lessons of his experience and study.

**Article 22.** The Realtor should so conduct his business as to avoid controversies with his fellow-Realtors. In the event of a controversy between Realtors who are members of the same local board, such controversy should be arbitrated in accordance with regulations of their board rather than litigated.

**Article 23.** Controversies between Realtors who are not members of the same local board should be submitted to an arbitration board consisting of one arbitrator chosen by each Realtor from the real estate board to which he belongs or chosen in accordance with the regulations of the respective boards. One other member, or a sufficient number of members to make an odd number, should be selected by the arbitrators thus chosen.

**Article 24.**  When the Realtor is charged with unethical practice, he should place all pertinent facts before the proper tribunal of the member board of which he is a member, for investigation and judgment.

**Article 25.**  The Realtor should not voluntarily disparage the business practice of a competitor, nor volunteer an opinion of a competitor's transaction. If his opinion is sought it should be rendered with strict professional integrity and courtesy.

**Article 26.**  The agency of a Realtor who holds an exclusive listing should be respected. A Realtor cooperating with a listing broker should not invite the cooperation of a third broker without the consent of the listing broker.

**Article 27.**  The Realtor should cooperate with other brokers on property listed by him exclusively whenever it is in the interest of the client, sharing commissions on a previously agreed basis. Negotiations concerning property listed exclusively with one broker should be carried on with the listing broker, not with the owner, except with the consent of the listing broker.

**Article 28.**  The Realtor should not solicit the services of an employee or salesman in the organization of a fellow-Realtor without the knowledge of the employer.

**Article 29.**  Signs giving notice of property for sale, rent, lease or exchange should not be placed on any property by more than one Realtor, and then only if authorized by the owner, except as the property is listed with and authorization given to more than one Realtor.

**Article 30.**  In the best interest of society, of his associates and of his own business, the Realtor should be loyal to the real estate board of his community and active in its work.

### Conclusion

The term *Realtor* has come to connote competence, fair dealing and high integrity resulting from adherence to a lofty ideal of moral conduct in business relations. No inducement of profit and no instructions from clients ever can justify departure from this ideal, or from the injunctions of this Code.

*The Code of Ethics was adopted in 1913. Amended at the Annual Convention in 1924, 1928, 1950, 1951, 1952, 1955, 1956, 1961, and 1962.*

# D

# Interest and Annuity Tables for the Real Estate Appraiser

Pages 800 to 818.

Used with permission of American Institute of Real Estate Appraisers, Chicago.

## TABLE 1.  Present Worth of One; What $1 Due in the Future is Worth Today

| Years | 3% | 4% | 4½% | 5% | 5½% | 6% | 6½% | 7% | 7½% |
|---|---|---|---|---|---|---|---|---|---|
| 1 | .9709 | .9615 | .9569 | .9524 | .9479 | .9434 | .9390 | .9346 | .9302 |
| 2 | .9426 | .9246 | .9157 | .9070 | .8985 | .8900 | .8817 | .8734 | .8653 |
| 3 | .9151 | .8890 | .8763 | .8638 | .8516 | .8396 | .8278 | .8163 | .8050 |
| 4 | .8885 | .8548 | .8386 | .8227 | .8072 | .7921 | .7773 | .7629 | .7488 |
| 5 | .8626 | .8219 | .8025 | .7835 | .7651 | .7473 | .7299 | .7130 | .6966 |
| 6 | .8375 | .7903 | .7679 | .7462 | .7252 | .7050 | .6853 | .6663 | .6480 |
| 7 | .8131 | .7599 | .7348 | .7107 | .6874 | .6651 | .6435 | .6227 | .6027 |
| 8 | .7894 | .7307 | .7032 | .6768 | .6516 | .6274 | .6042 | .5820 | .5607 |
| 9 | .7664 | .7026 | .6729 | .6446 | .6176 | .5919 | .5673 | .5439 | .5216 |
| 10 | .7441 | .6756 | .6439 | .6139 | .5854 | .5584 | .5327 | .5083 | .4852 |
| 11 | .7224 | .6496 | .6162 | .5847 | .5549 | .5268 | .5002 | .4751 | .4514 |
| 12 | .7014 | .6246 | .5897 | .5568 | .5260 | .4970 | .4697 | .4440 | .4199 |
| 13 | .6810 | .6006 | .5643 | .5303 | .4986 | .4688 | .4410 | .4150 | .3906 |
| 14 | .6611 | .5775 | .5400 | .5051 | .4726 | .4423 | .4141 | .3878 | .3633 |
| 15 | .6419 | .5553 | .5167 | .4810 | .4479 | .4173 | .3888 | .3624 | .3380 |
| 16 | .6232 | .5339 | .4945 | .4581 | .4246 | .3936 | .3651 | .3387 | .3144 |
| 17 | .6050 | .5134 | .4732 | .4363 | .4024 | .3714 | .3428 | .3166 | .2924 |
| 18 | .5874 | .4936 | .4528 | .4155 | .3815 | .3503 | .3219 | .2959 | .2720 |
| 19 | .5703 | .4746 | .4333 | .3957 | .3616 | .3305 | .3022 | .2765 | .2531 |
| 20 | .5537 | .4564 | .4146 | .3769 | .3427 | .3118 | .2838 | .2584 | .2354 |
| 21 | .5375 | .4388 | .3968 | .3589 | .3249 | .2942 | .2665 | .2415 | .2190 |
| 22 | .5219 | .4220 | .3797 | .3418 | .3079 | .2775 | .2502 | .2257 | .2037 |
| 23 | .5067 | .4057 | .3633 | .3256 | .2919 | .2618 | .2349 | .2109 | .1895 |
| 24 | .4919 | .3901 | .3477 | .3101 | .2766 | .2470 | .2206 | .1971 | .1763 |
| 25 | .4776 | .3751 | .3327 | .2953 | .2622 | .2330 | .2071 | .1842 | .1640 |
| 26 | .4637 | .3607 | .3184 | .2812 | .2486 | .2198 | .1945 | .1722 | .1525 |
| 27 | .4502 | .3468 | .3047 | .2678 | .2356 | .2074 | .1826 | .1609 | .1419 |
| 28 | .4371 | .3335 | .2916 | .2551 | .2233 | .1956 | .1715 | .1504 | .1320 |
| 29 | .4243 | .3207 | .2790 | .2429 | .2117 | .1846 | .1610 | .1406 | .1228 |
| 30 | .4120 | .3083 | .2670 | .2314 | .2006 | .1741 | .1512 | .1314 | .1142 |
| 31 | .4000 | .2965 | .2555 | .2204 | .1902 | .1643 | .1420 | .1228 | .1063 |
| 32 | .3883 | .2851 | .2445 | .2099 | .1803 | .1550 | .1333 | .1147 | .0988 |
| 33 | .3770 | .2741 | .2340 | .1999 | .1709 | .1462 | .1251 | .1072 | .0919 |
| 34 | .3660 | .2636 | .2239 | .1904 | .1620 | .1379 | .1175 | .1002 | .0855 |
| 35 | .3554 | .2534 | .2142 | .1813 | .1535 | .1301 | .1103 | .0937 | .0796 |
| 36 | .3450 | .2437 | .2050 | .1727 | .1455 | .1227 | .1036 | .0875 | .0740 |
| 37 | .3350 | .2343 | .1962 | .1644 | .1379 | .1158 | .0973 | .0818 | .0688 |
| 38 | .3252 | .2253 | .1878 | .1566 | .1307 | .1092 | .0914 | .0765 | .0640 |
| 39 | .3158 | .2166 | .1797 | .1491 | .1239 | .1031 | .0858 | .0715 | .0596 |
| 40 | .3066 | .2083 | .1719 | .1420 | .1175 | .0972 | .0805 | .0668 | .0554 |
| 41 | .2976 | .2003 | .1645 | .1353 | .1113 | .0917 | .0756 | .0624 | .0515 |
| 42 | .2890 | .1926 | .1574 | .1288 | .1055 | .0865 | .0710 | .0583 | .0480 |
| 43 | .2805 | .1852 | .1507 | .1227 | .1000 | .0816 | .0667 | .0545 | .0446 |
| 44 | .2724 | .1780 | .1442 | .1169 | .0948 | .0770 | .0626 | .0509 | .0415 |
| 45 | .2644 | .1712 | .1380 | .1113 | .0899 | .0726 | .0588 | .0476 | .0386 |
| 46 | .2567 | .1646 | .1320 | .1060 | .0852 | .0685 | .0552 | .0445 | .0359 |
| 47 | .2493 | .1583 | .1263 | .1009 | .0807 | .0647 | .0518 | .0416 | .0334 |
| 48 | .2420 | .1522 | .1209 | .0961 | .0765 | .0610 | .0487 | .0389 | .0311 |
| 49 | .2350 | .1463 | .1157 | .0916 | .0725 | .0575 | .0457 | .0363 | .0289 |
| 50 | .2281 | .1407 | .1107 | .0872 | .0688 | .0543 | .0429 | .0339 | .0269 |

This is a single deposit today which, with interest, will amount to 1 in a given time; or, the present or discounted value of 1 due at a given future time.

## TABLE 1—Continued

| Years | 8% | 9% | 10% | 11% | 12% | 13% | 14% | 15% |
|---|---|---|---|---|---|---|---|---|
| 1 | .9259 | .9174 | .9091 | .9009 | .8929 | .8850 | .8772 | .8696 |
| 2 | .8573 | .8417 | .8264 | .8116 | .7972 | .7831 | .7695 | .7561 |
| 3 | .7938 | .7722 | .7513 | .7312 | .7118 | .6930 | .6750 | .6575 |
| 4 | .7350 | .7084 | .6830 | .6587 | .6355 | .6133 | .5921 | .5718 |
| 5 | .6806 | .6499 | .6209 | .5935 | .5674 | .5428 | .5194 | .4972 |
| 6 | .6302 | .5963 | .5645 | .5346 | .5066 | .4803 | .4556 | .4323 |
| 7 | .5835 | .5470 | .5132 | .4816 | .4523 | .4250 | .3996 | .3759 |
| 8 | .5403 | .5019 | .4665 | .4339 | .4039 | .3762 | .3506 | .3269 |
| 9 | .5002 | .4604 | .4241 | .3909 | .3606 | .3329 | .3075 | .2843 |
| 10 | .4632 | .4224 | .3855 | .3522 | .3220 | .2946 | .2697 | .2472 |
| 11 | .4289 | .3875 | .3505 | .3173 | .2875 | .2607 | .2366 | .2149 |
| 12 | .3971 | .3555 | .3186 | .2858 | .2567 | .2307 | .2075 | .1869 |
| 13 | .3677 | .3262 | .2897 | .2575 | .2292 | .2042 | .1821 | .1625 |
| 14 | .3405 | .2992 | .2633 | .2320 | .2046 | .1807 | .1597 | .1413 |
| 15 | .3152 | .2745 | .2394 | .2090 | .1827 | .1599 | .1401 | .1229 |
| 16 | .2919 | .2519 | .2176 | .1883 | .1631 | .1415 | .1229 | .1069 |
| 17 | .2703 | .2311 | .1978 | .1696 | .1456 | .1252 | .1078 | .0929 |
| 18 | .2502 | .2120 | .1799 | .1528 | .1300 | .1108 | .0946 | .0808 |
| 19 | .2317 | .1945 | .1635 | .1377 | .1161 | .0981 | .0829 | .0703 |
| 20 | .2145 | .1784 | .1486 | .1240 | .1037 | .0868 | .0728 | .0611 |
| 21 | .1987 | .1637 | .1351 | .1117 | .0925 | .0768 | .0638 | .0531 |
| 22 | .1839 | .1502 | .1228 | .1007 | .0826 | .0680 | .0560 | .0462 |
| 23 | .1703 | .1378 | .1117 | .0907 | .0738 | .0601 | .0491 | .0402 |
| 24 | .1577 | .1264 | .1015 | .0817 | .0659 | .0532 | .0431 | .0349 |
| 25 | .1460 | .1160 | .0923 | .0736 | .0588 | .0471 | .0378 | .0304 |
| 26 | .1352 | .1064 | .0839 | .0663 | .0525 | .0417 | .0331 | .0264 |
| 27 | .1252 | .0976 | .0763 | .0597 | .0469 | .0369 | .0291 | .0230 |
| 28 | .1159 | .0895 | .0693 | .0538 | .0419 | .0326 | .0255 | .0200 |
| 29 | .1073 | .0822 | .0630 | .0485 | .0374 | .0289 | .0224 | .0174 |
| 30 | .0994 | .0754 | .0573 | .0437 | .0334 | .0256 | .0196 | .0151 |
| 31 | .0920 | .0691 | .0521 | .0394 | .0298 | .0226 | .0172 | .0131 |
| 32 | .0852 | .0634 | .0474 | .0354 | .0266 | .0200 | .0151 | .0114 |
| 33 | .0789 | .0582 | .0431 | .0319 | .0238 | .0177 | .0132 | .0099 |
| 34 | .0730 | .0534 | .0391 | .0288 | .0212 | .0157 | .0116 | .0086 |
| 35 | .0676 | .0490 | .0356 | .0259 | .0189 | .0139 | .0102 | .0075 |
| 36 | .0626 | .0449 | .0323 | .0234 | .0169 | .0123 | .0089 | .0065 |
| 37 | .0580 | .0412 | .0294 | .0210 | .0151 | .0109 | .0078 | .0057 |
| 38 | .0537 | .0378 | .0267 | .0189 | .0135 | .0096 | .0069 | .0049 |
| 39 | .0497 | .0347 | .0243 | .0171 | .0120 | .0085 | .0060 | .0043 |
| 40 | .0460 | .0318 | .0221 | .0154 | .0107 | .0075 | .0053 | .0037 |
| 41 | .0426 | .0292 | .0201 | .0139 | .0096 | .0067 | .0046 | .0032 |
| 42 | .0395 | .0268 | .0183 | .0125 | .0086 | .0059 | .0041 | .0028 |
| 43 | .0365 | .0246 | .0166 | .0112 | .0076 | .0052 | .0036 | .0025 |
| 44 | .0338 | .0225 | .0151 | .0101 | .0068 | .0046 | .0031 | .0021 |
| 45 | .0313 | .0207 | .0137 | .0091 | .0061 | .0041 | .0027 | .0019 |
| 46 | .0290 | .0190 | .0125 | .0082 | .0054 | .0036 | .0024 | .0016 |
| 47 | .0269 | .0174 | .0113 | .0074 | .0049 | .0032 | .0021 | .0014 |
| 48 | .0249 | .0160 | .0103 | .0067 | .0043 | .0028 | .0019 | .0012 |
| 49 | .0230 | .0147 | .0094 | .0060 | .0039 | .0025 | .0016 | .0011 |
| 50 | .0213 | .0134 | .0085 | .0054 | .0035 | .0022 | .0014 | .0009 |

This is a single deposit today which, with interest, will amount to 1 in a given time; or, the present or discounted value of 1 due at a given future time.

## TABLE 1—Continued

| Years | 3% | 4% | 4½% | 5% | 5½% | 6% | 6½% | 7% | 7½% |
|---|---|---|---|---|---|---|---|---|---|
| 51 | .2215 | .1353 | .1059 | .0831 | .0652 | .0512 | .0403 | .0317 | .0250 |
| 52 | .2150 | .1301 | .1014 | .0791 | .0618 | .0483 | .0378 | .0297 | .0233 |
| 53 | .2087 | .1251 | .0970 | .0753 | .0586 | .0456 | .0355 | .0277 | .0216 |
| 54 | .2027 | .1203 | .0928 | .0717 | .0555 | .0430 | .0333 | .0259 | .0201 |
| 55 | .1968 | .1157 | .0888 | .0683 | .0526 | .0406 | .0313 | .0242 | .0187 |
| 56 | .1910 | .1112 | .0850 | .0651 | .0499 | .0383 | .0294 | .0226 | .0174 |
| 57 | .1855 | .1069 | .0814 | .0620 | .0473 | .0361 | .0276 | .0211 | .0162 |
| 58 | .1801 | .1028 | .0778 | .0590 | .0448 | .0341 | .0259 | .0198 | .0151 |
| 59 | .1748 | .0989 | .0745 | .0562 | .0425 | .0321 | .0243 | .0185 | .0140 |
| 60 | .1697 | .0951 | .0713 | .0535 | .0403 | .0303 | .0229 | .0173 | .0130 |
| 61 | .1648 | .0914 | .0682 | .0510 | .0381 | .0286 | .0215 | .0161 | .0121 |
| 62 | .1600 | .0879 | .0653 | .0486 | .0362 | .0270 | .0201 | .0151 | .0113 |
| 63 | .1553 | .0845 | .0625 | .0462 | .0343 | .0255 | .0189 | .0141 | .0105 |
| 64 | .1508 | .0813 | .0598 | .0440 | .0325 | .0240 | .0178 | .0132 | .0098 |
| 65 | .1464 | .0781 | .0572 | .0419 | .0308 | .0227 | .0167 | .0123 | .0091 |
| 66 | .1421 | .0751 | .0547 | .0399 | .0292 | .0214 | .0157 | .0115 | .0084 |
| 67 | .1380 | .0722 | .0524 | .0380 | .0277 | .0202 | .0147 | .0107 | .0079 |
| 68 | .1340 | .0695 | .0501 | .0362 | .0262 | .0190 | .0138 | .0100 | .0073 |
| 69 | .1301 | .0668 | .0480 | .0345 | .0249 | .0179 | .0130 | .0094 | .0068 |
| 70 | .1263 | .0642 | .0459 | .0329 | .0236 | .0169 | .0122 | .0088 | .0063 |
| 71 | .1226 | .0617 | .0439 | .0313 | .0223 | .0160 | .0114 | .0082 | .0059 |
| 72 | .1190 | .0594 | .0420 | .0298 | .0212 | .0151 | .0107 | .0077 | .0055 |
| 73 | .1156 | .0571 | .0402 | .0284 | .0201 | .0142 | .0101 | .0072 | .0051 |
| 74 | .1122 | .0549 | .0385 | .0270 | .0190 | .0134 | .0095 | .0067 | .0047 |
| 75 | .1089 | .0528 | .0368 | .0258 | .0180 | .0126 | .0089 | .0063 | .0044 |
| 76 | .1058 | .0508 | .0352 | .0245 | .0171 | .0119 | .0083 | .0058 | .0041 |
| 77 | .1027 | .0488 | .0337 | .0234 | .0162 | .0113 | .0078 | .0055 | .0038 |
| 78 | .0997 | .0469 | .0323 | .0222 | .0154 | .0106 | .0074 | .0051 | .0035 |
| 79 | .0968 | .0451 | .0309 | .0212 | .0146 | .0100 | .0069 | .0048 | .0033 |
| 80 | .0940 | .0434 | .0295 | .0202 | .0138 | .0095 | .0065 | .0045 | .0031 |
| 81 | .0912 | .0417 | .0283 | .0192 | .0131 | .0089 | .0061 | .0042 | .0029 |
| 82 | .0886 | .0401 | .0271 | .0183 | .0124 | .0084 | .0057 | .0039 | .0026 |
| 83 | .0860 | .0386 | .0259 | .0174 | .0117 | .0079 | .0054 | .0036 | .0025 |
| 84 | .0835 | .0371 | .0248 | .0166 | .0111 | .0075 | .0050 | .0034 | .0023 |
| 85 | .0811 | .0357 | .0237 | .0158 | .0106 | .0071 | .0047 | .0032 | .0021 |
| 86 | .0787 | .0343 | .0227 | .0151 | .0100 | .0067 | .0044 | .0030 | .0020 |
| 87 | .0764 | .0330 | .0217 | .0143 | .0095 | .0063 | .0042 | .0028 | .0019 |
| 88 | .0742 | .0317 | .0208 | .0137 | .0090 | .0059 | .0039 | .0026 | .0017 |
| 89 | .0720 | .0305 | .0199 | .0130 | .0085 | .0056 | .0037 | .0024 | .0016 |
| 90 | .0699 | .0293 | .0190 | .0124 | .0081 | .0053 | .0034 | .0023 | .0015 |
| 91 | .0679 | .0282 | .0182 | .0118 | .0076 | .0050 | .0032 | .0021 | .0014 |
| 92 | .0659 | .0271 | .0174 | .0112 | .0073 | .0047 | .0030 | .0020 | .0013 |
| 93 | .0640 | .0261 | .0167 | .0107 | .0069 | .0044 | .0029 | .0019 | .0012 |
| 94 | .0621 | .0251 | .0160 | .0102 | .0065 | .0042 | .0027 | .0017 | .0011 |
| 95 | .0603 | .0241 | .0153 | .0097 | .0062 | .0039 | .0025 | .0016 | .0010 |
| 96 | .0586 | .0232 | .0146 | .0092 | .0059 | .0037 | .0024 | .0015 | .0010 |
| 97 | .0569 | .0223 | .0140 | .0088 | .0055 | .0035 | .0022 | .0014 | .0009 |
| 98 | .0552 | .0214 | .0134 | .0084 | .0053 | .0033 | .0021 | .0013 | .0008 |
| 99 | .0536 | .0206 | .0128 | .0080 | .0050 | .0031 | .0020 | .0013 | .0008 |
| 100 | .0520 | .0198 | .0123 | .0076 | .0047 | .0029 | .0018 | .0012 | .0007 |

This is the single deposit today which, with interest, will amount to 1 in a given time; or, the present or discounted value of 1 due at a given future time.

## TABLE 1—Continued

| Years | 8% | 9% | 10% | 11% | 12% | 13% | 14% | 15% |
|---|---|---|---|---|---|---|---|---|
| 51 | .0197 | .0123 | .0077 | .00488 | .00309 | .00196 | .001252 | .000802 |
| 52 | .0183 | .0113 | .0070 | .00440 | .00276 | .00174 | .001098 | .000697 |
| 53 | .0169 | .0104 | .0064 | .00396 | .00246 | .00154 | .000963 | .000606 |
| 54 | .0157 | .0095 | .0058 | .00357 | .00220 | .00136 | .000845 | .000527 |
| 55 | .0145 | .0087 | .0053 | .00322 | .00196 | .00120 | .000741 | .000458 |
| 56 | .0134 | .0080 | .0048 | .00290 | .00175 | .00107 | .000650 | .000398 |
| 57 | .0124 | .0073 | .0044 | .00261 | .00157 | .00094 | .000570 | .000346 |
| 58 | .0115 | .0067 | .0040 | .00235 | .00140 | .00083 | .000500 | .000301 |
| 59 | .0107 | .0062 | .0036 | .00212 | .00125 | .00074 | .000439 | .000262 |
| 60 | .0099 | .0057 | .0033 | .00191 | .00111 | .00065 | .000385 | .000228 |
| 61 | .0091 | .0052 | .0030 | .00172 | .00099 | .00058 | .000337 | .000198 |
| 62 | .0085 | .0048 | .0027 | .00155 | .00089 | .00051 | .000296 | .000172 |
| 63 | .0078 | .0044 | .0025 | .00139 | .00079 | .00045 | .000260 | .000149 |
| 64 | .0073 | .0040 | .0022 | .00126 | .00071 | .00040 | .000228 | .000130 |
| 65 | .0067 | .0037 | .0020 | .00113 | .00063 | .00035 | .000200 | .000113 |
| 66 | .0062 | .0034 | .0019 | .00102 | .00056 | .00031 | .000175 | .000098 |
| 67 | .0058 | .0031 | .0017 | .00092 | .00050 | .00028 | .000153 | .000085 |
| 68 | .0053 | .0029 | .0015 | .00083 | .00045 | .00024 | .000135 | .000074 |
| 69 | .0049 | .0026 | .0014 | .00075 | .00040 | .00022 | .000118 | .000064 |
| 70 | .0046 | .0024 | .0013 | .00067 | .00036 | .00019 | .000103 | .000056 |
| 71 | .0042 | .0022 | .0012 | .00061 | .00032 | .00017 | .000091 | .000049 |
| 72 | .0039 | .0020 | .0010 | .00054 | .00029 | .00015 | .000079 | .000042 |
| 73 | .0036 | .0018 | .0010 | .00049 | .00025 | .00013 | .000070 | .000037 |
| 74 | .0034 | .0017 | .0009 | .00044 | .00023 | .00012 | .000061 | .000032 |
| 75 | .0031 | .0016 | .0008 | .00040 | .00020 | .00010 | .000053 | .000028 |
| 76 | .0029 | .0014 | .0007 | .00036 | .00018 | .00009 | .000047 | .000024 |
| 77 | .0027 | .0013 | .0006 | .00032 | .00016 | .00008 | .000041 | .000021 |
| 78 | .0025 | .0012 | .0006 | .00029 | .00014 | .00007 | .000036 | .000018 |
| 79 | .0023 | .0011 | .0005 | .00026 | .00013 | .00006 | .000031 | .000016 |
| 80 | .0021 | .0010 | .0005 | .00024 | .00012 | .00006 | .000028 | .000013 |
| 81 | .0020 | .0009 | .0004 | .00021 | .00010 | .00005 | .000024 | .000012 |
| 82 | .0018 | .0008 | .0004 | .00019 | .00009 | .00004 | .000021 | .000010 |
| 83 | .0017 | .0008 | .0004 | .00017 | .00008 | .00004 | .000018 | .000009 |
| 84 | .0016 | .0007 | .0003 | .00016 | .00007 | .00003 | .000016 | .000007 |
| 85 | .0014 | .0007 | .0003 | .00014 | .00006 | .00003 | .000014 | .000006 |
| 86 | .0013 | .0006 | .0003 | .00013 | .00006 | .00003 | .000012 | .000006 |
| 87 | .0012 | .0005 | .0003 | .00011 | .00005 | .00002 | .000011 | .000005 |
| 88 | .0011 | .0005 | .0002 | .00010 | .00005 | .00002 | .000009 | .000004 |
| 89 | .0011 | .0005 | .0002 | .00009 | .00004 | .00002 | .000008 | .000003 |
| 90 | .0010 | .0004 | .0002 | .00008 | .00004 | .00002 | .000007 | .000003 |
| 91 | .0009 | .0004 | .0002 | .00007 | .00003 | .00001 | .000006 | .000003 |
| 92 | .0008 | .0004 | .0002 | .00007 | .00003 | .00001 | .000005 | .000002 |
| 93 | .0008 | .0003 | .0001 | .00006 | .00003 | .00001 | .000005 | .000002 |
| 94 | .0007 | .0003 | .0001 | .00005 | .00002 | .00001 | .000004 | .000001 |
| 95 | .0007 | .0003 | .0001 | .00005 | .00002 | .00001 | .000003 | .000001 |
| 96 | .0006 | .0003 | .0001 | .00004 | .00002 | .00001 | .000003 | .000001 |
| 97 | .0006 | .0002 | .0001 | .00004 | .00002 | .00001 | .000003 | .000001 |
| 98 | .0005 | .0002 | .0001 | .00004 | .00002 | .00001 | .000002 | .000001 |
| 99 | .0005 | .0002 | .0001 | .00003 | .00001 | .00001 | .000002 | .000001 |
| 100 | .0005 | .0002 | .0001 | .00003 | .00001 | .00001 | .000002 | .000001 |

This is the single deposit today which, with interest, will amount to 1 in a given time; or, the present or discounted value of 1 due at a given future time.

## TABLE 2.    Present Worth of One per Period—What $1 Payable Periodically is Worth Today

| Years | Speculative Interest Rates | | | | | | | |
|---|---|---|---|---|---|---|---|---|
| | 3% | 4% | 4½% | 5% | 5½% | 6% | 6½% | 7% |
| 1 | 0.971 | 0.961 | 0.957 | 0.952 | 0.948 | 0.943 | 0.939 | 0.935 |
| 2 | 1.913 | 1.886 | 1.873 | 1.859 | 1.846 | 1.833 | 1.821 | 1.808 |
| 3 | 2.829 | 2.775 | 2.749 | 2.723 | 2.698 | 2.673 | 2.648 | 2.624 |
| 4 | 3.717 | 3.630 | 3.587 | 3.546 | 3.505 | 3.465 | 3.426 | 3.387 |
| 5 | 4.580 | 4.452 | 4.390 | 4.329 | 4.270 | 4.212 | 4.156 | 4.100 |
| 6 | 5.417 | 5.242 | 5.158 | 5.076 | 4.996 | 4.917 | 4.841 | 4.766 |
| 7 | 6.230 | 6.002 | 5.893 | 5.786 | 5.683 | 5.582 | 5.485 | 5.389 |
| 8 | 7.020 | 6.733 | 6.596 | 6.463 | 6.334 | 6.210 | 6.089 | 5.971 |
| 9 | 7.786 | 7.435 | 7.269 | 7.108 | 6.952 | 6.802 | 6.656 | 6.515 |
| 10 | 8.530 | 8.111 | 7.913 | 7.722 | 7.538 | 7.360 | 7.189 | 7.024 |
| 11 | 9.253 | 8.760 | 8.529 | 8.306 | 8.093 | 7.887 | 7.689 | 7.499 |
| 12 | 9.954 | 9.385 | 9.118 | 8.863 | 8.618 | 8.384 | 8.159 | 7.943 |
| 13 | 10.635 | 9.986 | 9.683 | 9.394 | 9.117 | 8.853 | 8.600 | 8.358 |
| 14 | 11.296 | 10.563 | 10.223 | 9.899 | 9.590 | 9.295 | 9.014 | 8.745 |
| 15 | 11.938 | 11.118 | 10.739 | 10.380 | 10.038 | 9.712 | 9.403 | 9.108 |
| 16 | 12.561 | 11.652 | 11.234 | 10.838 | 10.462 | 10.106 | 9.768 | 9.447 |
| 17 | 13.166 | 12.166 | 11.707 | 11.274 | 10.865 | 10.477 | 10.110 | 9.763 |
| 18 | 13.753 | 12.659 | 12.160 | 11.690 | 11.246 | 10.828 | 10.432 | 10.059 |
| 19 | 14.324 | 13.134 | 12.593 | 12.085 | 11.608 | 11.158 | 10.735 | 10.336 |
| 20 | 14.877 | 13.590 | 13.008 | 12.462 | 11.950 | 11.470 | 11.019 | 10.594 |
| 21 | 15.415 | 14.029 | 13.405 | 12.821 | 12.275 | 11.764 | 11.285 | 10.835 |
| 22 | 15.937 | 14.451 | 13.784 | 13.163 | 12.583 | 12.042 | 11.535 | 11.061 |
| 23 | 16.444 | 14.857 | 14.148 | 13.489 | 12.875 | 12.303 | 11.770 | 11.272 |
| 24 | 16.935 | 15.247 | 14.495 | 13.799 | 13.152 | 12.550 | 11.991 | 11.469 |
| 25 | 17.413 | 15.622 | 14.828 | 14.094 | 13.414 | 12.783 | 12.198 | 11.654 |
| 26 | 17.877 | 15.983 | 15.147 | 14.375 | 13.662 | 13.003 | 12.392 | 11.826 |
| 27 | 18.327 | 16.330 | 15.451 | 14.643 | 13.898 | 13.210 | 12.575 | 11.987 |
| 28 | 18.764 | 16.663 | 15.743 | 14.898 | 14.121 | 13.406 | 12.746 | 12.137 |
| 29 | 19.188 | 16.984 | 16.022 | 15.141 | 14.333 | 13.591 | 12.907 | 12.278 |
| 30 | 19.600 | 17.292 | 16.289 | 15.372 | 14.534 | 13.765 | 13.059 | 12.409 |
| 31 | 20.000 | 17.588 | 16.544 | 15.593 | 14.724 | 13.929 | 13.201 | 12.532 |
| 32 | 20.389 | 17.874 | 16.789 | 15.803 | 14.904 | 14.084 | 13.334 | 12.647 |
| 33 | 20.766 | 18.148 | 17.023 | 16.002 | 15.075 | 14.230 | 13.459 | 12.754 |
| 34 | 21.132 | 18.411 | 17.247 | 16.193 | 15.237 | 14.368 | 13.577 | 12.854 |
| 35 | 21.487 | 18.665 | 17.461 | 16.374 | 15.390 | 14.498 | 13.687 | 12.948 |
| 36 | 21.832 | 18.908 | 17.666 | 16.547 | 15.536 | 14.621 | 13.791 | 13.035 |
| 37 | 22.167 | 19.143 | 17.862 | 16.711 | 15.674 | 14.737 | 13.888 | 13.117 |
| 38 | 22.492 | 19.368 | 18.050 | 16.868 | 15.805 | 14.846 | 13.979 | 13.193 |
| 39 | 22.808 | 19.584 | 18.230 | 17.017 | 15.929 | 14.949 | 14.065 | 13.265 |
| 40 | 23.115 | 19.793 | 18.401 | 17.159 | 16.046 | 15.046 | 14.145 | 13.332 |
| 41 | 23.412 | 19.993 | 18.566 | 17.294 | 16.157 | 15.138 | 14.221 | 13.394 |
| 42 | 23.701 | 20.186 | 18.724 | 17.423 | 16.263 | 15.224 | 14.292 | 13.452 |
| 43 | 23.982 | 20.371 | 18.874 | 17.546 | 16.363 | 15.306 | 14.359 | 13.507 |
| 44 | 24.254 | 20.549 | 19.018 | 17.663 | 16.458 | 15.383 | 14.421 | 13.558 |
| 45 | 24.519 | 20.720 | 19.156 | 17.774 | 16.548 | 15.456 | 14.480 | 13.605 |
| 46 | 24.775 | 20.885 | 19.288 | 17.880 | 16.633 | 15.524 | 14.535 | 13.650 |
| 47 | 25.025 | 21.043 | 19.415 | 17.981 | 16.714 | 15.589 | 14.587 | 13.692 |
| 48 | 25.267 | 21.195 | 19.536 | 18.077 | 16.790 | 15.650 | 14.636 | 13.730 |
| 49 | 25.502 | 21.341 | 19.651 | 18.169 | 16.863 | 15.708 | 14.682 | 13.767 |
| 50 | 25.730 | 21.482 | 19.762 | 18.256 | 16.931 | 15.762 | 14.724 | 13.801 |

Equal annual amounts; payable at *end of year*.

## Table 2—Continued

| Years | Speculative Interest Rates | | | | | | | |
|---|---|---|---|---|---|---|---|---|
| | 7½% | 8% | 9% | 10% | 11% | 12% | 13% | 14% |
| 1 | 0.930 | 0.926 | 0.917 | 0.909 | 0.901 | 0.893 | 0.885 | 0.877 |
| 2 | 1.796 | 1.783 | 1.759 | 1.736 | 1.713 | 1.690 | 1.668 | 1.647 |
| 3 | 2.600 | 2.577 | 2.531 | 2.487 | 2.444 | 2.402 | 2.361 | 2.322 |
| 4 | 3.349 | 3.312 | 3.240 | 3.170 | 3.102 | 3.037 | 2.974 | 2.914 |
| 5 | 4.046 | 3.993 | 3.890 | 3.791 | 3.696 | 3.605 | 3.517 | 3.433 |
| 6 | 4.694 | 4.623 | 4.486 | 4.355 | 4.231 | 4.111 | 3.998 | 3.889 |
| 7 | 5.297 | 5.206 | 5.033 | 4.868 | 4.712 | 4.564 | 4.423 | 4.288 |
| 8 | 5.857 | 5.747 | 5.535 | 5.335 | 5.146 | 4.968 | 4.799 | 4.639 |
| 9 | 6.379 | 6.247 | 5.995 | 5.759 | 5.537 | 5.328 | 5.132 | 4.946 |
| 10 | 6.864 | 6.710 | 6.418 | 6.145 | 5.889 | 5.650 | 5.426 | 5.216 |
| 11 | 7.315 | 7.139 | 6.805 | 6.495 | 6.206 | 5.938 | 5.687 | 5.453 |
| 12 | 7.735 | 7.536 | 7.161 | 6.814 | 6.492 | 6.194 | 5.918 | 5.660 |
| 13 | 8.126 | 7.904 | 7.487 | 7.103 | 6.750 | 6.424 | 6.122 | 5.842 |
| 14 | 8.489 | 8.244 | 7.786 | 7.367 | 6.982 | 6.628 | 6.302 | 6.002 |
| 15 | 8.827 | 8.559 | 8.061 | 7.606 | 7.191 | 6.811 | 6.462 | 6.142 |
| 16 | 9.142 | 8.851 | 8.313 | 7.824 | 7.379 | 6.974 | 6.604 | 6.265 |
| 17 | 9.434 | 9.122 | 8.544 | 8.022 | 7.549 | 7.120 | 6.729 | 6.373 |
| 18 | 9.706 | 9.372 | 8.756 | 8.201 | 7.702 | 7.250 | 6.840 | 6.467 |
| 19 | 9.959 | 9.604 | 8.950 | 8.365 | 7.839 | 7.366 | 6.938 | 6.550 |
| 20 | 10.194 | 9.818 | 9.128 | 8.514 | 7.963 | 7.469 | 7.025 | 6.623 |
| 21 | 10.413 | 10.017 | 9.292 | 8.649 | 8.075 | 7.562 | 7.102 | 6.687 |
| 22 | 10.617 | 10.201 | 9.442 | 8.772 | 8.176 | 7.645 | 7.170 | 6.743 |
| 23 | 10.807 | 10.371 | 9.580 | 8.883 | 8.266 | 7.718 | 7.230 | 6.792 |
| 24 | 10.983 | 10.529 | 9.707 | 8.985 | 8.348 | 7.784 | 7.283 | 6.835 |
| 25 | 11.147 | 10.675 | 9.823 | 9.077 | 8.422 | 7.843 | 7.330 | 6.873 |
| 26 | 11.299 | 10.810 | 9.929 | 9.161 | 8.488 | 7.896 | 7.372 | 6.906 |
| 27 | 11.441 | 10.935 | 10.026 | 9.237 | 8.548 | 7.943 | 7.409 | 6.935 |
| 28 | 11.573 | 11.051 | 10.116 | 9.307 | 8.602 | 7.984 | 7.441 | 6.961 |
| 29 | 11.696 | 11.158 | 10.198 | 9.370 | 8.650 | 8.022 | 7.470 | 6.983 |
| 30 | 11.810 | 11.258 | 10.274 | 9.427 | 8.694 | 8.055 | 7.496 | 7.003 |
| 31 | 11.917 | 11.350 | 10.343 | 9.479 | 8.733 | 8.085 | 7.518 | 7.020 |
| 32 | 12.015 | 11.435 | 10.406 | 9.526 | 8.769 | 8.112 | 7.538 | 7.035 |
| 33 | 12.107 | 11.514 | 10.464 | 9.569 | 8.801 | 8.135 | 7.556 | 7.048 |
| 34 | 12.193 | 11.587 | 10.518 | 9.609 | 8.829 | 8.157 | 7.572 | 7.060 |
| 35 | 12.272 | 11.655 | 10.567 | 9.644 | 8.855 | 8.176 | 7.586 | 7.070 |
| 36 | 12.347 | 11.717 | 10.612 | 9.676 | 8.879 | 8.193 | 7.598 | 7.079 |
| 37 | 12.415 | 11.775 | 10.653 | 9.706 | 8.900 | 8.207 | 7.609 | 7.087 |
| 38 | 12.479 | 11.829 | 10.691 | 9.733 | 8.919 | 8.221 | 7.618 | 7.094 |
| 39 | 12.539 | 11.879 | 10.726 | 9.757 | 8.936 | 8.233 | 7.627 | 7.100 |
| 40 | 12.594 | 11.925 | 10.757 | 9.779 | 8.951 | 8.244 | 7.634 | 7.105 |
| 41 | 12.646 | 11.967 | 10.786 | 9.799 | 8.965 | 8.253 | 7.641 | 7.110 |
| 42 | 12.694 | 12.007 | 10.813 | 9.817 | 8.977 | 8.262 | 7.647 | 7.114 |
| 43 | 12.738 | 12.043 | 10.838 | 9.834 | 8.989 | 8.270 | 7.652 | 7.117 |
| 44 | 12.780 | 12.077 | 10.861 | 9.849 | 8.999 | 8.276 | 7.657 | 7.120 |
| 45 | 12.819 | 12.108 | 10.881 | 9.863 | 9.008 | 8.283 | 7.661 | 7.123 |
| 46 | 12.855 | 12.137 | 10.900 | 9.875 | 9.016 | 8.288 | 7.664 | 7.126 |
| 47 | 12.888 | 12.164 | 10.918 | 9.887 | 9.024 | 8.293 | 7.668 | 7.128 |
| 48 | 12.919 | 12.189 | 10.933 | 9.897 | 9.030 | 8.297 | 7.670 | 7.130 |
| 49 | 12.948 | 12.212 | 10.948 | 9.906 | 9.036 | 8.301 | 7.673 | 7.131 |
| 50 | 12.975 | 12.233 | 10.962 | 9.915 | 9.042 | 8.305 | 7.675 | 7.133 |

Equal annual amounts; payable at *end of year*.

## Table 2—Continued

| Years | Speculative Interest Rates | | | | | |
|---|---|---|---|---|---|---|
| | 15% | 16% | 17% | 18% | 19% | 20% |
| 1 | 0.870 | 0.862 | 0.854 | 0.847 | 0.840 | 0.833 |
| 2 | 1.626 | 1.605 | 1.585 | 1.565 | 1.546 | 1.527 |
| 3 | 2.283 | 2.245 | 2.209 | 2.174 | 2.139 | 2.106 |
| 4 | 2.855 | 2.798 | 2.743 | 2.690 | 2.638 | 2.588 |
| 5 | 3.352 | 3.274 | 3.199 | 3.127 | 3.057 | 2.990 |
| 6 | 3.785 | 3.684 | 3.589 | 3.497 | 3.409 | 3.325 |
| 7 | 4.160 | 4.038 | 3.922 | 3.811 | 3.705 | 3.604 |
| 8 | 4.487 | 4.343 | 4.207 | 4.077 | 3.954 | 3.837 |
| 9 | 4.772 | 4.606 | 4.450 | 4.303 | 4.163 | 4.030 |
| 10 | 5.019 | 4.833 | 4.658 | 4.494 | 4.338 | 4.192 |
| 11 | 5.234 | 5.028 | 4.836 | 4.656 | 4.486 | 4.327 |
| 12 | 5.421 | 5.197 | 4.988 | 4.793 | 4.610 | 4.439 |
| 13 | 5.583 | 5.342 | 5.118 | 4.909 | 4.714 | 4.532 |
| 14 | 5.724 | 5.467 | 5.229 | 5.008 | 4.802 | 4.610 |
| 15 | 5.847 | 5.575 | 5.324 | 5.091 | 4.875 | 4.675 |
| 16 | 5.594 | 5.668 | 5.405 | 5.162 | 4.937 | 4.729 |
| 17 | 6.047 | 5.748 | 5.474 | 5.222 | 4.989 | 4.774 |
| 18 | 6.128 | 5.817 | 5.533 | 5.273 | 5.033 | 4.812 |
| 19 | 6.198 | 5.877 | 5.584 | 5.316 | 5.070 | 4.843 |
| 20 | 6.259 | 5.928 | 5.627 | 5.352 | 5.100 | 4.869 |
| 21 | 6.312 | 5.973 | 5.664 | 5.383 | 5.126 | 4.891 |
| 22 | 6.359 | 6.011 | 5.696 | 5.409 | 5.148 | 4.909 |
| 23 | 6.399 | 6.044 | 5.723 | 5.432 | 5.166 | 4.924 |
| 24 | 6.434 | 6.072 | 5.746 | 5.450 | 5.182 | 4.937 |
| 25 | 6.464 | 6.097 | 5.766 | 5.466 | 5.195 | 4.947 |
| 26 | 6.491 | 6.118 | 5.783 | 5.480 | 5.206 | 4.956 |
| 27 | 6.513 | 6.136 | 5.797 | 5.491 | 5.215 | 4.963 |
| 28 | 6.534 | 6.152 | 5.809 | 5.501 | 5.222 | 4.969 |
| 29 | 6.551 | 6.165 | 5.820 | 5.509 | 5.229 | 4.974 |
| 30 | 6.566 | 6.177 | 5.829 | 5.516 | 5.234 | 4.978 |
| 31 | 6.579 | 6.187 | 5.837 | 5.522 | 5.239 | 4.982 |
| 32 | 6.590 | 6.195 | 5.843 | 5.527 | 5.243 | 4.985 |
| 33 | 6.600 | 6.203 | 5.849 | 5.531 | 5.246 | 4.987 |
| 34 | 6.609 | 6.209 | 5.854 | 5.535 | 5.248 | 4.989 |
| 35 | 6.617 | 6.215 | 5.858 | 5.538 | 5.251 | 4.991 |
| 36 | 6.623 | 6.220 | 5.861 | 5.541 | 5.253 | 4.992 |
| 37 | 6.629 | 6.224 | 5.864 | 5.543 | 5.254 | 4.994 |
| 38 | 6.634 | 6.227 | 5.867 | 5.545 | 5.256 | 4.995 |
| 39 | 6.638 | 6.230 | 5.869 | 5.546 | 5.257 | 4.995 |
| 40 | 6.642 | 6.233 | 5.871 | 5.548 | 5.258 | 4.996 |
| 41 | 6.645 | 6.235 | 5.872 | 5.549 | 5.258 | 4.997 |
| 42 | 6.648 | 6.237 | 5.874 | 5.550 | 5.259 | 4.997 |
| 43 | 6.650 | 6.239 | 5.875 | 5.551 | 5.260 | 4.998 |
| 44 | 6.652 | 6.240 | 5.876 | 5.551 | 5.260 | 4.998 |
| 45 | 6.654 | 6.242 | 5.877 | 5.552 | 5.261 | 4.998 |
| 46 | 6.656 | 6.243 | 5.878 | 5.552 | 5.261 | 4.998 |
| 47 | 6.657 | 6.244 | 5.878 | 5.553 | 5.261 | 4.999 |
| 48 | 6.659 | 6.244 | 5.879 | 5.553 | 5.261 | 4.999 |
| 49 | 6.660 | 6.245 | 5.879 | 5.553 | 5.262 | 4.999 |
| 50 | 6.661 | 6.246 | 5.880 | 5.554 | 5.262 | 4.999 |

Equal annual amounts; payable at *end of year*.

## Table 2—Continued

| Years | Speculative Interest Rates | | | | | | | |
|---|---|---|---|---|---|---|---|---|
| | 3% | 4% | 4½% | 5% | 5½% | 6% | 6½% | 7% |
| 51 | 25.951 | 21.617 | 19.867 | 18.338 | 16.996 | 15.813 | 14.765 | 13.832 |
| 52 | 26.166 | 21.747 | 19.969 | 18.418 | 17.058 | 15.861 | 14.803 | 13.862 |
| 53 | 26.374 | 21.872 | 20.066 | 18.493 | 17.117 | 15.906 | 14.838 | 13.890 |
| 54 | 26.577 | 21.992 | 20.159 | 18.565 | 17.172 | 15.949 | 14.872 | 13.916 |
| 55 | 26.774 | 22.108 | 20.248 | 18.633 | 17.225 | 15.990 | 14.903 | 13.940 |
| 56 | 26.965 | 22.219 | 20.333 | 18.698 | 17.275 | 16.028 | 14.932 | 13.963 |
| 57 | 27.150 | 22.326 | 20.414 | 18.760 | 17.322 | 16.064 | 14.960 | 13.984 |
| 58 | 27.331 | 22.429 | 20.492 | 18.819 | 17.367 | 16.098 | 14.986 | 14.003 |
| 59 | 27.505 | 22.528 | 20.566 | 18.875 | 17.409 | 16.131 | 15.010 | 14.022 |
| 60 | 27.675 | 22.623 | 20.638 | 18.929 | 17.449 | 16.161 | 15.033 | 14.039 |
| 61 | 27.840 | 22.714 | 20.706 | 18.980 | 17.488 | 16.190 | 15.054 | 14.055 |
| 62 | 28.000 | 22.802 | 20.771 | 19.028 | 17.524 | 16.217 | 15.075 | 14.070 |
| 63 | 28.155 | 22.887 | 20.833 | 19.075 | 17.558 | 16.242 | 15.093 | 14.084 |
| 64 | 28.306 | 22.968 | 20.893 | 19.119 | 17.590 | 16.266 | 15.111 | 14.098 |
| 65 | 28.452 | 23.046 | 20.950 | 19.161 | 17.621 | 16.289 | 15.128 | 14.110 |
| 66 | 28.595 | 23.121 | 21.005 | 19.201 | 17.650 | 16.310 | 15.144 | 14.121 |
| 67 | 28.733 | 23.194 | 21.058 | 19.239 | 17.678 | 16.330 | 15.158 | 14.132 |
| 68 | 28.867 | 23.263 | 21.108 | 19.275 | 17.704 | 16.349 | 15.172 | 14.142 |
| 69 | 28.997 | 23.330 | 21.156 | 19.309 | 17.729 | 16.367 | 15.185 | 14.152 |
| 70 | 29.123 | 23.394 | 21.202 | 19.342 | 17.753 | 16.384 | 15.197 | 14.160 |
| 71 | 29.246 | 23.456 | 21.246 | 19.373 | 17.775 | 16.400 | 15.209 | 14.169 |
| 72 | 29.365 | 23.515 | 21.288 | 19.403 | 17.796 | 16.415 | 15.219 | 14.176 |
| 73 | 29.480 | 23.572 | 21.328 | 19.432 | 17.816 | 16.429 | 15.230 | 14.183 |
| 74 | 29.592 | 23.627 | 21.366 | 19.459 | 17.835 | 16.443 | 15.239 | 14.190 |
| 75 | 29.701 | 23.680 | 21.403 | 19.484 | 17.853 | 16.455 | 15.248 | 14.196 |
| 76 | 29.807 | 23.731 | 21.438 | 19.509 | 17.871 | 16.467 | 15.256 | 14.202 |
| 77 | 29.910 | 23.779 | 21.472 | 19.532 | 17.887 | 16.479 | 15.264 | 14.208 |
| 78 | 30.009 | 23.826 | 21.504 | 19.555 | 17.902 | 16.489 | 15.271 | 14.213 |
| 79 | 30.106 | 23.872 | 21.535 | 19.576 | 17.917 | 16.499 | 15.278 | 14.217 |
| 80 | 30.200 | 23.915 | 21.565 | 19.596 | 17.930 | 16.509 | 15.285 | 14.222 |
| 81 | 30.292 | 23.957 | 21.593 | 19.615 | 17.944 | 16.518 | 15.291 | 14.226 |
| 82 | 30.380 | 23.997 | 21.620 | 19.633 | 17.956 | 16.526 | 15.297 | 14.230 |
| 83 | 30.466 | 24.035 | 21.646 | 19.651 | 17.968 | 16.534 | 15.302 | 14.234 |
| 84 | 30.550 | 24.072 | 21.671 | 19.668 | 17.979 | 16.541 | 15.307 | 14.237 |
| 85 | 30.631 | 24.108 | 21.695 | 19.683 | 17.989 | 16.548 | 15.312 | 14.240 |
| 86 | 30.709 | 24.142 | 21.717 | 19.698 | 17.999 | 16.555 | 15.316 | 14.243 |
| 87 | 30.786 | 24.175 | 21.739 | 19.713 | 18.009 | 16.561 | 15.320 | 14.246 |
| 88 | 30.860 | 24.207 | 21.760 | 19.726 | 18.018 | 16.567 | 15.324 | 14.249 |
| 89 | 30.932 | 24.237 | 21.780 | 19.739 | 18.026 | 16.573 | 15.328 | 14.251 |
| 90 | 31.002 | 24.267 | 21.799 | 19.752 | 18.034 | 16.578 | 15.331 | 14.253 |
| 91 | 31.070 | 24.295 | 21.817 | 19.764 | 18.042 | 16.583 | 15.335 | 14.255 |
| 92 | 31.136 | 24.322 | 21.834 | 19.775 | 18.049 | 16.588 | 15.338 | 14.257 |
| 93 | 31.200 | 24.348 | 21.851 | 19.785 | 18.056 | 16.592 | 15.341 | 14.259 |
| 94 | 31.262 | 24.373 | 21.867 | 19.796 | 18.063 | 16.596 | 15.343 | 14.261 |
| 95 | 31.322 | 24.397 | 21.882 | 19.805 | 18.069 | 16.600 | 15.346 | 14.263 |
| 96 | 31.381 | 24.420 | 21.897 | 19.815 | 18.075 | 16.604 | 15.348 | 14.264 |
| 97 | 31.438 | 24.443 | 21.911 | 19.823 | 18.080 | 16.608 | 15.350 | 14.265 |
| 98 | 31.493 | 24.464 | 21.924 | 19.832 | 18.086 | 16.611 | 15.352 | 14.267 |
| 99 | 31.546 | 24.485 | 21.937 | 19.840 | 18.091 | 16.614 | 15.354 | 14.268 |
| 100 | 31.598 | 24.504 | 21.949 | 19.847 | 18.095 | 16.617 | 15.356 | 14.269 |

Equal annual amounts; payable at *end of year*.

## Table 2—Continued

| Years | Speculative Interest Rates | | | | | | | | |
|---|---|---|---|---|---|---|---|---|---|
| | 7½% | 8% | 9% | 10% | 11% | 12% | 13% | 14% | 15% |
| 51 | 13.000 | 12.253 | 10.974 | 9.923 | 9.047 | 8.308 | 7.677 | 7.134 | 6.661 |
| 52 | 13.023 | 12.271 | 10.985 | 9.930 | 9.051 | 8.310 | 7.679 | 7.135 | 6.662 |
| 53 | 13.045 | 12.288 | 10.996 | 9.936 | 9.055 | 8.313 | 7.680 | 7.136 | 6.663 |
| 54 | 13.065 | 12.304 | 11.005 | 9.942 | 9.058 | 8.315 | 7.682 | 7.137 | 6.663 |
| 55 | 13.084 | 12.319 | 11.014 | 9.947 | 9.062 | 8.317 | 7.683 | 7.137 | 6.664 |
| 56 | 13.101 | 12.332 | 11.022 | 9.952 | 9.065 | 8.319 | 7.684 | 7.138 | 6.664 |
| 57 | 13.117 | 12.344 | 11.029 | 9.956 | 9.067 | 8.320 | 7.685 | 7.139 | 6.664 |
| 58 | 13.132 | 12.356 | 11.036 | 9.960 | 9.070 | 8.322 | 7.686 | 7.139 | 6.665 |
| 59 | 13.146 | 12.367 | 11.042 | 9.964 | 9.072 | 8.323 | 7.687 | 7.140 | 6.665 |
| 60 | 13.159 | 12.377 | 11.048 | 9.967 | 9.074 | 8.324 | 7.687 | 7.140 | 6.665 |
| 61 | 13.172 | 12.386 | 11.053 | 9.970 | 9.075 | 8.325 | 7.688 | 7.140 | 6.665 |
| 62 | 13.183 | 12.394 | 11.058 | 9.973 | 9.077 | 8.326 | 7.688 | 7.141 | 6.666 |
| 63 | 13.193 | 12.402 | 11.062 | 9.975 | 9.078 | 8.327 | 7.689 | 7.141 | 6.666 |
| 64 | 13.203 | 12.409 | 11.066 | 9.978 | 9.079 | 8.327 | 7.689 | 7.141 | 6.666 |
| 65 | 13.212 | 12.416 | 11.070 | 9.980 | 9.081 | 8.328 | 7.690 | 7.141 | 6.666 |
| 66 | 13.221 | 12.422 | 11.073 | 9.981 | 9.082 | 8.329 | 7.690 | 7.142 | 6.666 |
| 67 | 13.228 | 12.428 | 11.077 | 9.983 | 9.083 | 8.329 | 7.690 | 7.142 | 6.666 |
| 68 | 13.236 | 12.433 | 11.079 | 9.985 | 9.083 | 8.329 | 7.690 | 7.142 | 6.666 |
| 69 | 13.243 | 12.438 | 11.082 | 9.986 | 9.084 | 8.330 | 7.691 | 7.142 | 6.666 |
| 70 | 13.249 | 12.443 | 11.084 | 9.987 | 9.085 | 8.330 | 7.691 | 7.142 | 6.666 |
| 71 | 13.255 | 12.447 | 11.087 | 9.988 | 9.085 | 8.331 | 7.691 | 7.142 | 6.666 |
| 72 | 13.260 | 12.451 | 11.089 | 9.990 | 9.086 | 8.331 | 7.691 | 7.142 | 6.666 |
| 73 | 13.265 | 12.455 | 11.090 | 9.990 | 9.086 | 8.331 | 7.691 | 7.142 | 6.666 |
| 74 | 13.270 | 12.458 | 11.092 | 9.991 | 9.087 | 8.331 | 7.691 | 7.142 | 6.666 |
| 75 | 13.274 | 12.461 | 11.094 | 9.992 | 9.087 | 8.332 | 7.692 | 7.142 | 6.666 |
| 76 | 13.279 | 12.464 | 11.095 | 9.993 | 9.088 | 8.332 | 7.692 | 7.143 | 6.667 |
| 77 | 13.282 | 12.467 | 11.097 | 9.994 | 9.088 | 8.332 | 7.692 | 7.143 | 6.667 |
| 78 | 13.286 | 12.469 | 11.098 | 9.994 | 9.088 | 8.332 | 7.692 | 7.143 | 6.667 |
| 79 | 13.289 | 12.471 | 11.099 | 9.995 | 9.089 | 8.332 | 7.692 | 7.143 | 6.667 |
| 80 | 13.292 | 12.473 | 11.100 | 9.995 | 9.089 | 8.332 | 7.692 | 7.143 | 6.667 |
| 81 | 13.295 | 12.475 | 11.101 | 9.996 | 9.089 | 8.332 | 7.692 | 7.143 | 6.667 |
| 82 | 13.298 | 12.477 | 11.102 | 9.996 | 9.089 | 8.333 | 7.692 | 7.143 | 6.667 |
| 83 | 13.300 | 12.479 | 11.102 | 9.996 | 9.089 | 8.333 | 7.692 | 7.143 | 6.667 |
| 84 | 13.303 | 12.480 | 11.103 | 9.997 | 9.089 | 8.333 | 7.692 | 7.143 | 6.667 |
| 85 | 13.305 | 12.482 | 11.104 | 9.997 | 9.090 | 8.333 | 7.692 | 7.143 | 6.667 |
| 86 | 13.307 | 12.483 | 11.104 | 9.997 | 9.090 | 8.333 | 7.692 | 7.143 | 6.667 |
| 87 | 13.309 | 12.484 | 11.105 | 9.997 | 9.090 | 8.333 | 7.692 | 7.143 | 6.667 |
| 88 | 13.310 | 12.486 | 11.105 | 9.998 | 9.090 | 8.333 | 7.692 | 7.143 | 6.667 |
| 89 | 13.312 | 12.487 | 11.106 | 9.998 | 9.090 | 8.333 | 7.692 | 7.143 | 6.667 |
| 90 | 13.313 | 12.488 | 11.106 | 9.998 | 9.090 | 8.333 | 7.692 | 7.143 | 6.667 |
| 91 | 13.315 | 12.489 | 11.107 | 9.998 | 9.090 | 8.333 | 7.692 | 7.143 | 6.667 |
| 92 | 13.316 | 12.489 | 11.107 | 9.998 | 9.090 | 8.333 | 7.692 | 7.143 | 6.667 |
| 93 | 13.317 | 12.490 | 11.107 | 9.999 | 9.090 | 8.333 | 7.692 | 7.143 | 6.667 |
| 94 | 13.318 | 12.491 | 11.108 | 9.999 | 9.090 | 8.333 | 7.692 | 7.143 | 6.667 |
| 95 | 13.319 | 12.492 | 11.108 | 9.999 | 9.090 | 8.333 | 7.692 | 7.143 | 6.667 |
| 96 | 13.320 | 12.492 | 11.108 | 9.999 | 9.091 | 8.333 | 7.692 | 7.143 | 6.667 |
| 97 | 13.321 | 12.493 | 11.109 | 9.999 | 9.091 | 8.333 | 7.692 | 7.143 | 6.667 |
| 98 | 13.322 | 12.493 | 11.109 | 9.999 | 9.091 | 8.333 | 7.692 | 7.143 | 6.667 |
| 99 | 13.323 | 12.494 | 11.109 | 9.999 | 9.091 | 8.333 | 7.692 | 7.143 | 6.667 |
| 100 | 13.324 | 12.494 | 11.109 | 9.999 | 9.091 | 8.333 | 7.692 | 7.143 | 6.667 |

Equal annual amounts; payable at *end of year*.

## Table 2—Continued

| Years | Speculative Interest Rates | | | | | |
|-------|--------|--------|--------|--------|--------|--------|
|       | 3%     | 4%     | 4½%    | 5%     | 5½%    | 6%     |
| 101 | 31.649 | 24.524 | 21.961 | 19.855 | 18.100 | 16.620 |
| 102 | 31.698 | 24.542 | 21.972 | 19.862 | 18.104 | 16.622 |
| 103 | 31.746 | 24.559 | 21.983 | 19.868 | 18.108 | 16.625 |
| 104 | 31.792 | 24.576 | 21.993 | 19.874 | 18.112 | 16.627 |
| 105 | 31.837 | 24.593 | 22.003 | 19.880 | 18.116 | 16.629 |
| 106 | 31.880 | 24.608 | 22.013 | 19.886 | 18.119 | 16.632 |
| 107 | 31.923 | 24.623 | 22.022 | 19.891 | 18.122 | 16.633 |
| 108 | 31.964 | 24.638 | 22.030 | 19.897 | 18.125 | 16.635 |
| 109 | 32.004 | 24.652 | 22.038 | 19.901 | 18.128 | 16.637 |
| 110 | 32.042 | 24.665 | 22.046 | 19.906 | 18.131 | 16.639 |
| 111 | 32.080 | 24.678 | 22.054 | 19.911 | 18.134 | 16.640 |
| 112 | 32.116 | 24.690 | 22.061 | 19.915 | 18.136 | 16.642 |
| 113 | 32.152 | 24.702 | 22.068 | 19.919 | 18.138 | 16.643 |
| 114 | 32.186 | 24.714 | 22.075 | 19.923 | 18.141 | 16.644 |
| 115 | 32.220 | 24.725 | 22.081 | 19.926 | 18.143 | 16.646 |
| 116 | 32.252 | 24.735 | 22.087 | 19.930 | 18.145 | 16.647 |
| 117 | 32.283 | 24.745 | 22.093 | 19.933 | 18.147 | 16.648 |
| 118 | 32.314 | 24.755 | 22.098 | 19.936 | 18.149 | 16.649 |
| 119 | 32.344 | 24.765 | 22.104 | 19.939 | 18.150 | 16.650 |
| 120 | 32.373 | 24.774 | 22.109 | 19.942 | 18.152 | 16.651 |
| 121 | 32.400 | 24.782 | 22.114 | 19.945 | 18.153 | 16.652 |
| 122 | 32.428 | 24.791 | 22.118 | 19.948 | 18.155 | 16.653 |
| 123 | 32.454 | 24.799 | 22.123 | 19.950 | 18.156 | 16.653 |
| 124 | 32.480 | 24.806 | 22.127 | 19.952 | 18.158 | 16.654 |
| 125 | 32.504 | 24.814 | 22.131 | 19.955 | 18.159 | 16.655 |
| 126 | 32.529 | 24.821 | 22.135 | 19.957 | 18.160 | 16.655 |
| 127 | 32.552 | 24.828 | 22.139 | 19.959 | 18.161 | 16.656 |
| 128 | 32.575 | 24.834 | 22.142 | 19.961 | 18.162 | 16.657 |
| 129 | 32.597 | 24.841 | 22.146 | 19.963 | 18.163 | 16.657 |
| 130 | 32.618 | 24.847 | 22.149 | 19.964 | 18.164 | 16.658 |
| 131 | 32.639 | 24.853 | 22.152 | 19.966 | 18.165 | 16.658 |
| 132 | 32.659 | 24.858 | 22.155 | 19.968 | 18.166 | 16.659 |
| 133 | 32.679 | 24.864 | 22.158 | 19.969 | 18.167 | 16.659 |
| 134 | 32.698 | 24.869 | 22.161 | 19.971 | 18.167 | 16.659 |
| 135 | 32.716 | 24.874 | 22.163 | 19.972 | 18.168 | 16.660 |
| 136 | 32.734 | 24.879 | 22.166 | 19.973 | 18.169 | 16.660 |
| 137 | 32.752 | 24.884 | 22.168 | 19.974 | 18.169 | 16.660 |
| 138 | 32.769 | 24.888 | 22.171 | 19.976 | 18.170 | 16.661 |
| 139 | 32.785 | 24.892 | 22.173 | 19.977 | 18.171 | 16.661 |
| 140 | 32.801 | 24.896 | 22.175 | 19.978 | 18.171 | 16.661 |
| 141 | 32.817 | 24.900 | 22.177 | 19.979 | 18.172 | 16.662 |
| 142 | 32.832 | 24.904 | 22.179 | 19.980 | 18.172 | 16.662 |
| 143 | 32.846 | 24.908 | 22.181 | 19.981 | 18.173 | 16.662 |
| 144 | 32.860 | 24.911 | 22.182 | 19.982 | 18.173 | 16.662 |
| 145 | 32.874 | 24.915 | 22.184 | 19.983 | 18.174 | 16.663 |
| 146 | 32.888 | 24.918 | 22.186 | 19.983 | 18.174 | 16.663 |
| 147 | 32.901 | 24.921 | 22.187 | 19.984 | 18.174 | 16.663 |
| 148 | 32.913 | 24.924 | 22.189 | 19.985 | 18.175 | 16.663 |
| 149 | 32.925 | 24.927 | 22.190 | 19.986 | 18.175 | 16.663 |
| 150 | 32.937 | 24.930 | 22.192 | 19.986 | 18.175 | 16.663 |

Equal annual amounts; payable at *end of year*.

# APPENDIX D

## Table 2—*Continued*

| Years | Speculative Interest Rates | | | | | |
|---|---|---|---|---|---|---|
| | 3% | 4% | 4½% | 5% | 5½% | 6% |
| 151 | 32.949 | 24.933 | 22.193 | 19.987 | 18.176 | 16.664 |
| 152 | 32.960 | 24.935 | 22.194 | 19.987 | 18.176 | 16.664 |
| 153 | 32.971 | 24.938 | 22.195 | 19.988 | 18.176 | 16.664 |
| 154 | 32.981 | 24.940 | 22.196 | 19.989 | 18.177 | 16.664 |
| 155 | 32.992 | 24.942 | 22.198 | 19.989 | 18.177 | 16.664 |
| 156 | 33.001 | 24.944 | 22.199 | 19.990 | 18.177 | 16.664 |
| 157 | 33.011 | 24.947 | 22.200 | 19.990 | 18.177 | 16.664 |
| 158 | 33.021 | 24.949 | 22.201 | 19.991 | 18.177 | 16.664 |
| 159 | 33.030 | 24.951 | 22.201 | 19.991 | 18.178 | 16.665 |
| 160 | 33.038 | 24.952 | 22.202 | 19.991 | 18.178 | 16.665 |
| 161 | 33.047 | 24.954 | 22.203 | 19.992 | 18.178 | 16.665 |
| 162 | 33.055 | 24.956 | 22.204 | 19.992 | 18.178 | 16.665 |
| 163 | 33.063 | 24.958 | 22.205 | 19.992 | 18.178 | 16.665 |
| 164 | 33.071 | 24.959 | 22.205 | 19.993 | 18.179 | 16.665 |
| 165 | 33.079 | 24.961 | 22.206 | 19.993 | 18.179 | 16.665 |
| 166 | 33.086 | 24.962 | 22.207 | 19.993 | 18.179 | 16.665 |
| 167 | 33.093 | 24.964 | 22.207 | 19.994 | 18.179 | 16.665 |
| 168 | 33.100 | 24.965 | 22.208 | 19.994 | 18.179 | 16.665 |
| 169 | 33.107 | 24.966 | 22.209 | 19.994 | 18.179 | 16.665 |
| 170 | 33.114 | 24.968 | 22.209 | 19.995 | 18.179 | 16.665 |
| 171 | 33.120 | 24.969 | 22.210 | 19.995 | 18.179 | 16.665 |
| 172 | 33.126 | 24.970 | 22.210 | 19.995 | 18.179 | 16.665 |
| 173 | 33.132 | 24.971 | 22.211 | 19.995 | 18.180 | 16.665 |
| 174 | 33.138 | 24.972 | 22.211 | 19.995 | 18.180 | 16.666 |
| 175 | 33.144 | 24.973 | 22.212 | 19.996 | 18.180 | 16.666 |
| 176 | 33.149 | 24.974 | 22.212 | 19.996 | 18.180 | 16.666 |
| 177 | 33.155 | 24.975 | 22.213 | 19.996 | 18.180 | 16.666 |
| 178 | 33.160 | 24.976 | 22.213 | 19.996 | 18.180 | 16.666 |
| 179 | 33.165 | 24.977 | 22.213 | 19.996 | 18.180 | 16.666 |
| 180 | 33.170 | 24.978 | 22.214 | 19.996 | 18.180 | 16.666 |
| 181 | 33.175 | 24.979 | 22.214 | 19.997 | 18.180 | 16.666 |
| 182 | 33.179 | 24.980 | 22.214 | 19.997 | 18.180 | 16.666 |
| 183 | 33.184 | 24.980 | 22.215 | 19.997 | 18.180 | 16.666 |
| 184 | 33.188 | 24.981 | 22.215 | 19.997 | 18.180 | 16.666 |
| 185 | 33.192 | 24.982 | 22.215 | 19.997 | 18.180 | 16.666 |
| 186 | 33.196 | 24.983 | 22.216 | 19.997 | 18.180 | 16.666 |
| 187 | 33.200 | 24.983 | 22.216 | 19.997 | 18.181 | 16.666 |
| 188 | 33.204 | 24.984 | 22.216 | 19.997 | 18.181 | 16.666 |
| 189 | 33.208 | 24.984 | 22.216 | 19.998 | 18.181 | 16.666 |
| 190 | 33.212 | 24.985 | 22.217 | 19.998 | 18.181 | 16.666 |
| 191 | 33.215 | 24.986 | 22.217 | 19.998 | 18.181 | 16.666 |
| 192 | 33.219 | 24.986 | 22.217 | 19.998 | 18.181 | 16.666 |
| 193 | 33.222 | 24.987 | 22.217 | 19.998 | 18.181 | 16.666 |
| 194 | 33.225 | 24.987 | 22.217 | 19.998 | 18.181 | 16.666 |
| 195 | 33.228 | 24.988 | 22.218 | 19.998 | 18.181 | 16.666 |
| 196 | 33.231 | 24.988 | 22.218 | 19.998 | 18.181 | 16.666 |
| 197 | 33.234 | 24.988 | 22.218 | 19.998 | 18.181 | 16.666 |
| 198 | 33.237 | 24.989 | 22.218 | 19.998 | 18.181 | 16.666 |
| 199 | 33.240 | 24.989 | 22.218 | 19.998 | 18.181 | 16.666 |
| 200 | 33.243 | 24.990 | 22.218 | 19.998 | 18.181 | 16.666 |

Equal annual amounts; payable at *end of year*.

## TABLE 3. Amortization Rates, Sinking Fund—Periodic Deposit That Will Grow to $1 at Future Date

| Years | ⅓% | 1% | 1½% | 1¾% | 2% | 2½% | 3% | 3½% | 4% | 4½% | 5% | 5½% | 6% | 7% |
|---|---|---|---|---|---|---|---|---|---|---|---|---|---|---|
| 1 | 1.00000 | 1.00000 | 1.00000 | 1.00000 | 1.00000 | 1.00000 | 1.00000 | 1.00000 | 1.00000 | 1.00000 | 1.00000 | 1.00000 | 1.00000 | 1.0000 |
| 2 | .49917 | .49751 | .49628 | .49566 | .49505 | .49383 | .49261 | .49140 | .49020 | .48900 | .48780 | .48662 | .48544 | .48309 |
| 3 | .33222 | .33002 | .32838 | .32757 | .32675 | .32514 | .32353 | .32193 | .32035 | .31877 | .31721 | .31565 | .31411 | .31105 |
| 4 | .24875 | .24628 | .24444 | .24353 | .24262 | .24082 | .23903 | .23725 | .23549 | .23374 | .23201 | .23029 | .22859 | .22523 |
| 5 | .19867 | .19604 | .19409 | .19312 | .19216 | .19025 | .18835 | .18648 | .18463 | .18279 | .18097 | .17918 | .17740 | .17389 |
| 6 | .16528 | .16255 | .16053 | .15952 | .15853 | .15655 | .15460 | .15267 | .15076 | .14888 | .14702 | .14518 | .14336 | .13980 |
| 7 | .14143 | .13863 | .13656 | .13553 | .13451 | .13250 | .13051 | .12854 | .12661 | .12470 | .12282 | .12096 | .11913 | .11555 |
| 8 | .12355 | .12069 | .11858 | .11754 | .11651 | .11447 | .11246 | .11048 | .10853 | .10661 | .10472 | .10286 | .10104 | .09747 |
| 9 | .10964 | .10674 | .10461 | .10356 | .10252 | .10046 | .09843 | .09645 | .09449 | .09257 | .09069 | .08884 | .08702 | .08349 |
| 10 | .09851 | .09558 | .09343 | .09238 | .09133 | .08926 | .08723 | .08524 | .08329 | .08138 | .07950 | .07767 | .07587 | .07238 |
| 11 | .08940 | .08645 | .08429 | .08323 | .08218 | .08011 | .07808 | .07609 | .07415 | .07225 | .07039 | .06857 | .06679 | .06336 |
| 12 | .08182 | .07885 | .07668 | .07561 | .07456 | .07249 | .07046 | .06848 | .06655 | .06467 | .06283 | .06103 | .05928 | .05590 |
| 13 | .07539 | .07241 | .07024 | .06917 | .06812 | .06605 | .06403 | .06206 | .06014 | .05828 | .05646 | .05468 | .05296 | .04965 |
| 14 | .06989 | .06690 | .06472 | .06366 | .06260 | .06054 | .05853 | .05657 | .05467 | .05282 | .05102 | .04928 | .04758 | .04434 |
| 15 | .06512 | .06212 | .05994 | .05888 | .05783 | .05577 | .05377 | .05183 | .04994 | .04811 | .04634 | .04463 | .04296 | .03979 |
| 16 | .06095 | .05794 | .05577 | .05470 | .05365 | .05160 | .04961 | .04768 | .04582 | .04402 | .04227 | .04058 | .03895 | .03586 |
| 17 | .05727 | .05426 | .05208 | .05102 | .04997 | .04793 | .04595 | .04404 | .04220 | .04042 | .03870 | .03704 | .03544 | .03243 |
| 18 | .05400 | .05098 | .04881 | .04774 | .04670 | .04467 | .04271 | .04082 | .03899 | .03724 | .03555 | .03392 | .03236 | .02941 |
| 19 | .05107 | .04805 | .04588 | .04482 | .04378 | .04176 | .03981 | .03794 | .03614 | .03441 | .03275 | .03115 | .02962 | .02675 |
| 20 | .04843 | .04541 | .04325 | .04219 | .04116 | .03915 | .03722 | .03536 | .03358 | .03188 | .03024 | .02868 | .02718 | .02439 |
| 21 | .04605 | .04303 | .04087 | .03981 | .03878 | .03679 | .03487 | .03304 | .03128 | .02960 | .02800 | .02646 | .02500 | .02229 |
| 22 | .04388 | .04086 | .03870 | .03766 | .03663 | .03465 | .03275 | .03093 | .02920 | .02755 | .02597 | .02447 | .02305 | .02041 |
| 23 | .04190 | .03888 | .03673 | .03569 | .03467 | .03270 | .03081 | .02902 | .02731 | .02568 | .02414 | .02267 | .02128 | .01871 |
| 24 | .04009 | .03707 | .03492 | .03389 | .03287 | .03091 | .02905 | .02727 | .02559 | .02399 | .02247 | .02104 | .01968 | .01719 |
| 25 | .03842 | .03541 | .03326 | .03223 | .03122 | .02928 | .02743 | .02567 | .02401 | .02244 | .02095 | .01955 | .01823 | .01581 |
| 26 | .03688 | .03387 | .03173 | .03070 | .02970 | .02777 | .02594 | .02421 | .02257 | .02102 | .01956 | .01819 | .01690 | .01456 |
| 27 | .03546 | .03244 | .03032 | .02929 | .02829 | .02638 | .02456 | .02285 | .02124 | .01972 | .01829 | .01695 | .01570 | .01343 |
| 28 | .03413 | .03112 | .02900 | .02798 | .02699 | .02509 | .02329 | .02160 | .02001 | .01852 | .01712 | .01581 | .01459 | .01239 |
| 29 | .03290 | .02989 | .02778 | .02676 | .02578 | .02389 | .02211 | .02045 | .01888 | .01741 | .01605 | .01477 | .01358 | .01145 |
| 30 | .03175 | .02875 | .02664 | .02563 | .02465 | .02278 | .02102 | .01937 | .01783 | .01639 | .01505 | .01381 | .01265 | .01059 |

This is the annual amount which, deposited at the *end of each year*, with interest will amount to 1 at the end of a given time.

## TABLE  3—Continued

| Years | ½% | 1% | 1½% | 1¾% | 2% | 2¾% | 3% | 3½% | 4% | 4½% | 5% | 5½% | 6% | 7% |
|---|---|---|---|---|---|---|---|---|---|---|---|---|---|---|
| 31 | .03067 | .02767 | .02557 | .02457 | .02360 | .02174 | .02000 | .01837 | .01686 | .01544 | .01413 | .01292 | .01179 | .00980 |
| 32 | .02966 | .02667 | .02458 | .02358 | .02261 | .02077 | .01905 | .01744 | .01595 | .01456 | .01328 | .01210 | .01100 | .00907 |
| 33 | .02872 | .02573 | .02364 | .02265 | .02169 | .01986 | .01816 | .01657 | .01510 | .01374 | .01249 | .01133 | .01027 | .00841 |
| 34 | .02782 | .02484 | .02276 | .02177 | .02082 | .01901 | .01732 | .01576 | .01431 | .01298 | .01176 | .01063 | .00960 | .00789 |
| 35 | .02698 | .02400 | .02193 | .02095 | .02000 | .01821 | .01654 | .01500 | .01358 | .01227 | .01107 | .00997 | .00897 | .00723 |
| 36 | .02619 | .02321 | .02115 | .02017 | .01923 | .01745 | .01580 | .01428 | .01289 | .01161 | .01043 | .00937 | .00839 | .00672 |
| 37 | .02544 | .02247 | .02041 | .01944 | .01851 | .01674 | .01511 | .01361 | .01224 | .01098 | .00984 | .00880 | .00786 | .00624 |
| 38 | .02473 | .02176 | .01972 | .01875 | .01782 | .01607 | .01446 | .01298 | .01163 | .01040 | .00928 | .00827 | .00736 | .00580 |
| 39 | .02405 | .02109 | .01905 | .01809 | .01717 | .01544 | .01384 | .01239 | .01106 | .00986 | .00876 | .00778 | .00689 | .00539 |
| 40 | .02341 | .02045 | .01843 | .01747 | .01656 | .01484 | .01326 | .01183 | .01052 | .00934 | .00828 | .00732 | .00646 | .00501 |
| 41 | .02280 | .01985 | .01783 | .01688 | .01597 | .01427 | .01271 | .01130 | .01002 | .00886 | .00782 | .00689 | .00606 | .00466 |
| 42 | .02222 | .01927 | .01726 | .01632 | .01542 | .01373 | .01219 | .01080 | .00954 | .00841 | .00739 | .00649 | .00568 | .00434 |
| 43 | .02167 | .01873 | .01672 | .01579 | .01489 | .01322 | .01170 | .01033 | .00909 | .00798 | .00699 | .00611 | .00533 | .00404 |
| 44 | .02114 | .01820 | .01621 | .01528 | .01439 | .01273 | .01123 | .00988 | .00866 | .00758 | .00662 | .00576 | .00501 | .00376 |
| 45 | .02063 | .01770 | .01572 | .01479 | .01391 | .01227 | .01079 | .00945 | .00826 | .00720 | .00626 | .00543 | .00470 | .00350 |
| 46 | .02015 | .01723 | .01525 | .01433 | .01345 | .01183 | .01036 | .00905 | .00788 | .00684 | .00593 | .00512 | .00441 | .00326 |
| 47 | .01969 | .01677 | .01480 | .01389 | .01302 | .01141 | .00996 | .00867 | .00752 | .00651 | .00561 | .00483 | .00415 | .00304 |
| 48 | .01924 | .01633 | .01437 | .01347 | .01260 | .01101 | .00958 | .00831 | .00718 | .00619 | .00532 | .00456 | .00390 | .00283 |
| 49 | .01882 | .01591 | .01396 | .01306 | .01220 | .01062 | .00921 | .00796 | .00686 | .00589 | .00504 | .00430 | .00366 | .00264 |
| 50 | .01841 | .01551 | .01357 | .01267 | .01182 | .01026 | .00887 | .00763 | .00655 | .00560 | .00478 | .00406 | .00344 | .00246 |
| 55 | .01660 | .01373 | .01183 | .01096 | .01014 | .00865 | .00735 | .00621 | .00523 | .00439 | .00367 | .00305 | .00254 | .00174 |
| 60 | .01509 | .01224 | .01039 | .00955 | .00877 | .00735 | .00613 | .00509 | .00420 | .00345 | .00283 | .00231 | .00188 | .00123 |
| 65 | .01380 | .01100 | .00919 | .00838 | .00763 | .00628 | .00515 | .00419 | .00339 | .00273 | .00219 | .00175 | .00139 | .00087 |
| 70 | .01271 | .00993 | .00817 | .00739 | .00667 | .00540 | .00434 | .00346 | .00275 | .00217 | .00179 | .00133 | .00103 | .00062 |
| 75 | .01176 | .00902 | .00730 | .00655 | .00586 | .00465 | .00367 | .00287 | .00223 | .00172 | .00132 | .00101 | .00077 | .00044 |
| 80 | .01093 | .00822 | .00655 | .00582 | .00516 | .00403 | .00311 | .00238 | .00181 | .00137 | .00103 | .00077 | .00057 | .00031 |
| 85 | .01019 | .00752 | .00589 | .00519 | .00456 | .00349 | .00265 | .00199 | .00148 | .00109 | .00080 | .00059 | .00043 | .00022 |
| 90 | .00955 | .00690 | .00532 | .00465 | .00405 | .00304 | .00226 | .00166 | .00121 | .00087 | .00063 | .00045 | .00032 | .00016 |
| 95 | .00896 | .00635 | .00482 | .00417 | .00360 | .00265 | .00193 | .00139 | .00099 | .00070 | .00049 | .00034 | .00024 | .00011 |
| 99 | .00854 | .00596 | .00446 | .00383 | .00328 | .00238 | .00170 | .00120 | .00084 | .00058 | .00040 | .00028 | .00019 | .00009 |
| 100 | .00844 | .00586 | .00437 | .00375 | .00320 | .00231 | .00165 | .00116 | .00081 | .00056 | .00038 | .00026 | .00018 | .00008 |

This is the annual amount which, deposited at the *end of each year*, with interest will amount to 1 at the end of a given time.

## TABLE 4. Amount of One—How $1 Left at Compound Interest Will Grow

| Years | 3% | 4% | 4½% | 5% | 5½% | 6% |
|---|---|---|---|---|---|---|
| 1 | 1.0300 | 1.0400 | 1.0450 | 1.0500 | 1.0550 | 1.0600 |
| 2 | 1.0609 | 1.0816 | 1.0920 | 1.1025 | 1.1130 | 1.1236 |
| 3 | 1.0927 | 1.1249 | 1.1412 | 1.1576 | 1.1742 | 1.1910 |
| 4 | 1.1255 | 1.1699 | 1.1925 | 1.2155 | 1.2388 | 1.2625 |
| 5 | 1.1593 | 1.2167 | 1.2462 | 1.2763 | 1.3069 | 1.3382 |
| 6 | 1.1941 | 1.2653 | 1.3023 | 1.3401 | 1.3788 | 1.4185 |
| 7 | 1.2299 | 1.3159 | 1.3609 | 1.4071 | 1.4546 | 1.5036 |
| 8 | 1.2668 | 1.3686 | 1.4221 | 1.4775 | 1.5346 | 1.5938 |
| 9 | 1.3048 | 1.4233 | 1.4861 | 1.5513 | 1.6190 | 1.6895 |
| 10 | 1.3439 | 1.4802 | 1.5530 | 1.6289 | 1.7081 | 1.7908 |
| 11 | 1.3842 | 1.5395 | 1.6229 | 1.7103 | 1.8020 | 1.8983 |
| 12 | 1.4258 | 1.6010 | 1.6959 | 1.7959 | 1.9012 | 2.0122 |
| 13 | 1.4685 | 1.6651 | 1.7722 | 1.8856 | 2.0057 | 2.1329 |
| 14 | 1.5126 | 1.7317 | 1.8519 | 1.9799 | 2.1160 | 2.2609 |
| 15 | 1.5580 | 1.8009 | 1.9353 | 2.0789 | 2.2324 | 2.3966 |
| 16 | 1.6047 | 1.8730 | 2.0224 | 2.1829 | 2.3552 | 2.5404 |
| 17 | 1.6528 | 1.9479 | 2.1134 | 2.2920 | 2.4848 | 2.6928 |
| 18 | 1.7024 | 2.0258 | 2.2085 | 2.4066 | 2.6214 | 2.8543 |
| 19 | 1.7535 | 2.1068 | 2.3079 | 2.5269 | 2.7656 | 3.0256 |
| 20 | 1.8061 | 2.1911 | 2.4117 | 2.6533 | 2.9177 | 3.2071 |
| 21 | 1.8603 | 2.2788 | 2.5202 | 2.7860 | 3.0782 | 3.3996 |
| 22 | 1.9161 | 2.3699 | 2.6337 | 2.9253 | 3.2475 | 3.6035 |
| 23 | 1.9736 | 2.4647 | 2.7522 | 3.0715 | 3.4261 | 3.8197 |
| 24 | 2.0328 | 2.5633 | 2.8760 | 3.2251 | 3.6145 | 4.0489 |
| 25 | 2.0938 | 2.6658 | 3.0054 | 3.3864 | 3.8133 | 4.2919 |
| 26 | 2.1566 | 2.7725 | 3.1407 | 3.5557 | 4.0231 | 4.5494 |
| 27 | 2.2213 | 2.8834 | 3.2820 | 3.7335 | 4.2444 | 4.8223 |
| 28 | 2.2879 | 2.9987 | 3.4297 | 3.9201 | 4.4778 | 5.1117 |
| 29 | 2.3566 | 3.1187 | 3.5840 | 4.1161 | 4.7241 | 5.4184 |
| 30 | 2.4273 | 3.2434 | 3.7453 | 4.3219 | 4.9839 | 5.7435 |
| 31 | 2.5001 | 3.3731 | 3.9139 | 4.5380 | 5.2580 | 6.0881 |
| 32 | 2.5751 | 3.5081 | 4.0900 | 4.7649 | 5.5472 | 6.4534 |
| 33 | 2.6523 | 3.6484 | 4.2740 | 5.0032 | 5.8523 | 6.8406 |
| 34 | 2.7319 | 3.7943 | 4.4664 | 5.2533 | 6.1742 | 7.2510 |
| 35 | 2.8139 | 3.9461 | 4.6673 | 5.5160 | 6.5138 | 7.6861 |
| 36 | 2.8983 | 4.1039 | 4.8774 | 5.7918 | 6.8720 | 8.1473 |
| 37 | 2.9852 | 4.2681 | 5.0969 | 6.0814 | 7.2500 | 8.6361 |
| 38 | 3.0748 | 4.4388 | 5.3262 | 6.3855 | 7.6488 | 9.1543 |
| 39 | 3.1670 | 4.6164 | 5.5659 | 6.7048 | 8.0694 | 9.7035 |
| 40 | 3.2620 | 4.8010 | 5.8164 | 7.0400 | 8.5133 | 10.2857 |
| 41 | 3.3599 | 4.9931 | 6.0781 | 7.3920 | 8.9815 | 10.9029 |
| 42 | 3.4607 | 5.1928 | 6.3516 | 7.7616 | 9.4755 | 11.5570 |
| 43 | 3.5645 | 5.4005 | 6.6374 | 8.1497 | 9.9966 | 12.2505 |
| 44 | 3.6715 | 5.6165 | 6.9361 | 8.5571 | 10.5464 | 12.9855 |
| 45 | 3.7816 | 5.8412 | 7.2484 | 8.9850 | 11.1265 | 13.7646 |
| 46 | 3.8950 | 6.0748 | 7.5744 | 9.4343 | 11.7385 | 14.5905 |
| 47 | 4.0119 | 6.3178 | 7.9153 | 9.9060 | 12.3841 | 15.4659 |
| 48 | 4.1323 | 6.5705 | 8.2715 | 10.4013 | 13.0652 | 16.3939 |
| 49 | 4.2562 | 6.8333 | 8.6437 | 10.9213 | 13.7838 | 17.3775 |
| 50 | 4.3839 | 7.1067 | 9.0326 | 11.4674 | 14.5419 | 18.4202 |

Factors shown are for deposits made at *beginning of year;* interest compounded annually. The factor for twice any period is the square of the factor for that period.

## TABLE 4—Continued

| Years | 6½% | 7% | 7½% | 8% | 9% | 10% |
|---|---|---|---|---|---|---|
| 1 | 1.0650 | 1.0700 | 1.0750 | 1.0800 | 1.0900 | 1.1000 |
| 2 | 1.1342 | 1.1449 | 1.1556 | 1.1664 | 1.1881 | 1.2100 |
| 3 | 1.2079 | 1.2250 | 1.2422 | 1.2597 | 1.2950 | 1.3310 |
| 4 | 1.2864 | 1.3107 | 1.3354 | 1.3604 | 1.4115 | 1.4641 |
| 5 | 1.3700 | 1.4025 | 1.4356 | 1.4693 | 1.5386 | 1.6105 |
| 6 | 1.4591 | 1.5007 | 1.5433 | 1.5868 | 1.6771 | 1.7715 |
| 7 | 1.5539 | 1.6057 | 1.6590 | 1.7138 | 1.8280 | 1.9487 |
| 8 | 1.6549 | 1.7181 | 1.7834 | 1.8509 | 1.9925 | 2.1435 |
| 9 | 1.7625 | 1.8384 | 1.9172 | 1.9990 | 2.1718 | 2.3579 |
| 10 | 1.8771 | 1.9671 | 2.0610 | 2.1589 | 2.3673 | 2.5937 |
| 11 | 1.9991 | 2.1048 | 2.2156 | 2.3316 | 2.5804 | 2.8531 |
| 12 | 2.1290 | 2.2521 | 2.3817 | 2.5181 | 2.8126 | 3.1384 |
| 13 | 2.2674 | 2.4098 | 2.5604 | 2.7196 | 3.0658 | 3.4522 |
| 14 | 2.4148 | 2.5785 | 2.7524 | 2.9371 | 3.3417 | 3.7974 |
| 15 | 2.5718 | 2.7590 | 2.9588 | 3.1721 | 3.6424 | 4.1772 |
| 16 | 2.7390 | 2.9521 | 3.1807 | 3.4259 | 3.9703 | 4.5949 |
| 17 | 2.9170 | 3.1588 | 3.4193 | 3.7000 | 4.3276 | 5.0544 |
| 18 | 3.1066 | 3.3799 | 3.6758 | 3.9960 | 4.7171 | 5.5599 |
| 19 | 3.3085 | 3.6165 | 3.9514 | 4.3157 | 5.1416 | 6.1159 |
| 20 | 3.5236 | 3.8696 | 4.2478 | 4.6609 | 5.6044 | 6.7274 |
| 21 | 3.7526 | 4.1405 | 4.5664 | 5.0338 | 6.1088 | 7.4002 |
| 22 | 3.9966 | 4.4304 | 4.9089 | 5.4365 | 6.6586 | 8.1402 |
| 23 | 4.2563 | 4.7405 | 5.2770 | 5.8714 | 7.2578 | 8.9543 |
| 24 | 4.5330 | 5.0723 | 5.6728 | 6.3411 | 7.9110 | 9.8497 |
| 25 | 4.8276 | 5.4274 | 6.0983 | 6.8484 | 8.6230 | 10.8347 |
| 26 | 5.1414 | 5.8073 | 6.5557 | 7.3963 | 9.3991 | 11.9181 |
| 27 | 5.4756 | 6.2138 | 7.0473 | 7.9880 | 10.2450 | 13.1099 |
| 28 | 5.8316 | 6.6488 | 7.5759 | 8.6271 | 11.1671 | 14.4209 |
| 29 | 6.2106 | 7.1142 | 8.1441 | 9.3172 | 12.1721 | 15.8630 |
| 30 | 6.6143 | 7.6122 | 8.7549 | 10.0626 | 13.2676 | 17.4494 |
| 31 | 7.0442 | 8.1451 | 9.4115 | 10.8676 | 14.4617 | 19.1943 |
| 32 | 7.5021 | 8.7152 | 10.1174 | 11.7370 | 15.7633 | 21.1137 |
| 33 | 7.9898 | 9.3253 | 10.8762 | 12.6760 | 17.1820 | 23.2251 |
| 34 | 8.5091 | 9.9781 | 11.6919 | 13.6901 | 18.7284 | 25.5476 |
| 35 | 9.0622 | 10.6765 | 12.5688 | 14.7853 | 20.4139 | 28.1024 |
| 36 | 9.6513 | 11.4239 | 13.5115 | 15.9681 | 22.2512 | 30.9126 |
| 37 | 10.2786 | 12.2236 | 14.5249 | 17.2456 | 24.2538 | 34.0039 |
| 38 | 10.9467 | 13.0792 | 15.6142 | 18.6252 | 26.4366 | 37.4043 |
| 39 | 11.6582 | 13.9948 | 16.7853 | 20.1152 | 28.8159 | 41.1447 |
| 40 | 12.4160 | 14.9744 | 18.0442 | 21.7245 | 31.4094 | 45.2592 |
| 41 | 13.2231 | 16.0226 | 19.3975 | 23.4624 | 34.2362 | 49.7851 |
| 42 | 14.0826 | 17.1442 | 20.8523 | 25.3394 | 37.3175 | 54.7636 |
| 43 | 14.9979 | 18.3443 | 22.4163 | 27.3666 | 40.6761 | 60.2400 |
| 44 | 15.9728 | 19.6284 | 24.0975 | 29.5559 | 44.3369 | 66.2640 |
| 45 | 17.0110 | 21.0024 | 25.9048 | 31.9204 | 48.3272 | 72.8904 |
| 46 | 18.1168 | 22.4726 | 27.8477 | 34.4740 | 52.6767 | 80.1795 |
| 47 | 19.2944 | 24.0457 | 29.9362 | 37.2320 | 57.4176 | 88.1974 |
| 48 | 20.5485 | 25.7289 | 32.1815 | 40.2105 | 62.5852 | 97.0172 |
| 49 | 21.8842 | 27.5299 | 34.5951 | 43.4274 | 68.2179 | 106.7189 |
| 50 | 23.3066 | 29.4570 | 37.1897 | 46.9016 | 74.3575 | 117.3908 |

Factors shown are for deposits made at *beginning of year;* interest compounded annually. The factor for twice any period is the square of the factor for that period.

## TABLE 4—Continued

| Years | 11% | 12% | 13% | 14% | 15% |
|---|---|---|---|---|---|
| 1 | 1.1100 | 1.1200 | 1.1300 | 1.1400 | 1.1500 |
| 2 | 1.2321 | 1.2544 | 1.2769 | 1.2996 | 1.3225 |
| 3 | 1.3676 | 1.4049 | 1.4428 | 1.4815 | 1.5208 |
| 4 | 1.5180 | 1.5735 | 1.6304 | 1.6889 | 1.7490 |
| 5 | 1.6850 | 1.7623 | 1.8424 | 1.9254 | 2.0113 |
| 6 | 1.8704 | 1.9738 | 2.0819 | 2.1949 | 2.3130 |
| 7 | 2.0761 | 2.2106 | 2.3526 | 2.5022 | 2.6600 |
| 8 | 2.3045 | 2.4759 | 2.6584 | 2.8525 | 3.0590 |
| 9 | 2.5580 | 2.7730 | 3.0040 | 3.2519 | 3.5178 |
| 10 | 2.8394 | 3.1058 | 3.3945 | 3.7072 | 4.0455 |
| 11 | 3.1517 | 3.4785 | 3.8358 | 4.2262 | 4.6523 |
| 12 | 3.4984 | 3.8959 | 4.3345 | 4.8179 | 5.3502 |
| 13 | 3.8832 | 4.3634 | 4.8980 | 5.4924 | 6.1527 |
| 14 | 4.3104 | 4.8871 | 5.5347 | 6.2613 | 7.0757 |
| 15 | 4.7845 | 5.4735 | 6.2542 | 7.1379 | 8.1370 |
| 16 | 5.3108 | 6.1303 | 7.0673 | 8.1372 | 9.3576 |
| 17 | 5.8950 | 6.8660 | 7.9860 | 9.2764 | 10.7612 |
| 18 | 6.5435 | 7.6899 | 9.0242 | 10.5751 | 12.3754 |
| 19 | 7.2633 | 8.6127 | 10.1974 | 12.0556 | 14.2317 |
| 20 | 8.0623 | 9.6462 | 11.5230 | 13.7434 | 16.3665 |
| 21 | 8.9491 | 10.8038 | 13.0210 | 15.6675 | 18.8215 |
| 22 | 9.9335 | 12.1003 | 14.7138 | 17.8610 | 21.6447 |
| 23 | 11.0262 | 13.5523 | 16.6266 | 20.3615 | 24.8914 |
| 24 | 12.2391 | 15.1786 | 18.7880 | 23.2122 | 28.6251 |
| 25 | 13.5854 | 17.0000 | 21.2305 | 26.4619 | 32.9189 |
| 26 | 15.0798 | 19.0400 | 23.9905 | 30.1665 | 37.8567 |
| 27 | 16.7386 | 21.3248 | 27.1092 | 34.3899 | 43.5353 |
| 28 | 18.5799 | 23.8838 | 30.6334 | 39.2044 | 50.0656 |
| 29 | 20.6236 | 26.7499 | 34.6158 | 44.6931 | 57.5754 |
| 30 | 22.8922 | 29.9599 | 39.1158 | 50.9501 | 66.2117 |
| 31 | 25.4104 | 33.5551 | 44.2009 | 58.0831 | 76.1435 |
| 32 | 28.2055 | 37.5817 | 49.9470 | 66.2148 | 87.5650 |
| 33 | 31.3082 | 42.0915 | 56.4402 | 75.4849 | 100.6998 |
| 34 | 34.7521 | 47.1425 | 63.7774 | 86.0527 | 115.8048 |
| 35 | 38.5748 | 52.7996 | 72.0685 | 98.1001 | 133.1755 |
| 36 | 42.8180 | 59.1355 | 81.4374 | 111.8342 | 153.1518 |
| 37 | 47.5280 | 66.2318 | 92.0242 | 127.4909 | 176.1246 |
| 38 | 52.7561 | 74.1796 | 103.9874 | 145.3397 | 202.5433 |
| 39 | 58.5593 | 83.0812 | 117.5057 | 165.6872 | 232.9248 |
| 40 | 65.0008 | 93.0509 | 132.7815 | 188.8835 | 267.8635 |
| 41 | 72.1509 | 104.2170 | 150.0431 | 215.3272 | 308.0430 |
| 42 | 80.0875 | 116.7231 | 169.5487 | 245.4730 | 354.2495 |
| 43 | 88.8972 | 130.7299 | 191.5901 | 279.8392 | 407.3869 |
| 44 | 98.6758 | 146.4175 | 216.4968 | 319.0167 | 468.4950 |
| 45 | 109.5302 | 163.9876 | 244.6414 | 363.6790 | 538.7692 |
| 46 | 121.5785 | 183.6661 | 276.4447 | 414.5941 | 619.5846 |
| 47 | 134.9522 | 205.7060 | 312.3826 | 472.6373 | 712.5223 |
| 48 | 149.7969 | 230.3907 | 352.9923 | 538.8065 | 819.4007 |
| 49 | 166.2746 | 258.0376 | 398.8813 | 614.2394 | 942.3108 |
| 50 | 184.5648 | 289.0021 | 450.7359 | 700.2329 | 1083.6574 |

Factors shown are for deposits made at *beginning of year;* interest compounded annually. The factor for twice any period is the square of the factor for that period.

## TABLE 5.  Amount of One per Period—How $1 Deposited Periodically Will Grow

| Years | 3% | 4% | 4½% | 5% | 5½% | 6% |
|---|---|---|---|---|---|---|
| 1 | 1.0000 | 1.0000 | 1.0000 | 1.0000 | 1.0000 | 1.0000 |
| 2 | 2.0300 | 2.0400 | 2.0450 | 2.0500 | 2.0550 | 2.0600 |
| 3 | 3.0909 | 3.1216 | 3.1370 | 3.1525 | 3.1680 | 3.1836 |
| 4 | 4.1836 | 4.2464 | 4.2781 | 4.3101 | 4.3422 | 4.3746 |
| 5 | 5.3091 | 5.4163 | 5.4707 | 5.5256 | 5.5810 | 5.6370 |
| 6 | 6.4684 | 6.6329 | 6.7168 | 6.8019 | 6.8880 | 6.9753 |
| 7 | 7.6624 | 7.8982 | 8.0191 | 8.1420 | 8.2668 | 8.3938 |
| 8 | 8.8923 | 9.2142 | 9.3800 | 9.5491 | 9.7215 | 9.8974 |
| 9 | 10.1591 | 10.5827 | 10.8021 | 11.0265 | 11.2562 | 11.4913 |
| 10 | 11.4638 | 12.0061 | 12.2882 | 12.5778 | 12.8753 | 13.1807 |
| 11 | 12.8077 | 13.4863 | 13.8411 | 14.2067 | 14.5834 | 14.9716 |
| 12 | 14.1920 | 15.0258 | 15.4640 | 15.9171 | 16.3855 | 16.8699 |
| 13 | 15.6177 | 16.6268 | 17.1599 | 17.7129 | 18.2867 | 18.8821 |
| 14 | 17.0863 | 18.2919 | 18.9321 | 19.5986 | 20.2925 | 21.0150 |
| 15 | 18.5989 | 20.0235 | 20.7840 | 21.5785 | 22.4086 | 23.2759 |
| 16 | 20.1568 | 21.8245 | 22.7193 | 23.6574 | 24.6411 | 25.6725 |
| 17 | 21.7615 | 23.6975 | 24.7417 | 25.8403 | 26.9964 | 28.2128 |
| 18 | 23.4144 | 25.6454 | 26.8550 | 28.1323 | 29.4812 | 30.9056 |
| 19 | 25.1168 | 27.6712 | 29.0635 | 30.5390 | 32.1026 | 33.7599 |
| 20 | 26.8703 | 29.7780 | 31.3714 | 33.0659 | 34.8683 | 36.7855 |
| 21 | 28.6764 | 31.9692 | 33.7831 | 35.7192 | 37.7860 | 39.9927 |
| 22 | 30.5367 | 34.2479 | 36.3033 | 38.5052 | 40.8643 | 43.3922 |
| 23 | 32.4528 | 36.6178 | 38.9370 | 41.4304 | 44.1118 | 46.9958 |
| 24 | 34.4264 | 39.0826 | 41.6891 | 44.5019 | 47.5379 | 50.8155 |
| 25 | 36.4592 | 41.6459 | 44.5652 | 47.7270 | 51.1525 | 54.8645 |
| 26 | 38.5530 | 44.3117 | 47.5706 | 51.1134 | 54.9659 | 59.1563 |
| 27 | 40.7096 | 47.0842 | 50.7113 | 54.6691 | 58.9891 | 63.7057 |
| 28 | 42.9309 | 49.9675 | 53.9933 | 58.4025 | 63.2335 | 68.5281 |
| 29 | 45.2188 | 52.9662 | 57.4230 | 62.3227 | 67.7113 | 73.6397 |
| 30 | 47.5754 | 56.0849 | 61.0070 | 66.4388 | 72.4354 | 79.0581 |
| 31 | 50.0026 | 59.3283 | 64.7523 | 70.7607 | 77.4194 | 84.8016 |
| 32 | 52.5027 | 62.7014 | 68.6662 | 75.2988 | 82.6774 | 90.8897 |
| 33 | 55.0778 | 66.2095 | 72.7562 | 80.0637 | 88.2247 | 97.3431 |
| 34 | 57.7301 | 69.8579 | 77.0302 | 85.0669 | 94.0771 | 104.1837 |
| 35 | 60.4620 | 73.6522 | 81.4966 | 90.3203 | 100.2513 | 111.4347 |
| 36 | 63.2759 | 77.5983 | 86.1639 | 95.8363 | 106.7651 | 119.1208 |
| 37 | 66.1742 | 81.7022 | 91.0413 | 101.6281 | 113.6372 | 127.2681 |
| 38 | 69.1594 | 85.9703 | 96.1382 | 107.7095 | 120.8873 | 135.9042 |
| 39 | 72.2342 | 90.4091 | 101.4644 | 114.0950 | 128.5361 | 145.0584 |
| 40 | 75.4012 | 95.0255 | 107.0303 | 120.7997 | 136.6056 | 154.7619 |
| 41 | 78.6632 | 99.8265 | 112.8466 | 127.8397 | 145.1189 | 165.0476 |
| 42 | 82.0231 | 104.8195 | 118.9247 | 135.2317 | 154.1004 | 175.9505 |
| 43 | 85.4838 | 110.0123 | 125.2764 | 142.9933 | 163.5759 | 187.5075 |
| 44 | 89.0484 | 115.4128 | 131.9138 | 151.1430 | 173.5726 | 199.7580 |
| 45 | 92.7198 | 121.0293 | 138.8499 | 159.7001 | 184.1191 | 212.7435 |
| 46 | 96.5014 | 126.8705 | 146.0982 | 168.6851 | 195.2457 | 226.5081 |
| 47 | 100.3965 | 132.9453 | 153.6726 | 178.1194 | 206.9842 | 241.0986 |
| 48 | 104.4083 | 139.2632 | 161.5879 | 188.0253 | 219.3683 | 256.5645 |
| 49 | 108.5406 | 145.8337 | 169.8593 | 198.4266 | 232.4336 | 272.9584 |
| 50 | 112.7968 | 152.6670 | 178.5030 | 209.3479 | 246.2174 | 290.3359 |

Factors shown are for deposits made at the *end of the year;* interest compounded annually. If deposits are made at the beginning of the year, subtract 1 from the factor for the next succeeding year.

## TABLE 5—Continued

| Years | 6½% | 7% | 7½% | 8% | 9% |
|-------|------|------|------|------|------|
| 1  | 1.0000  | 1.0000  | 1.0000  | 1.0000  | 1.0000  |
| 2  | 2.0650  | 2.0700  | 2.0750  | 2.0800  | 2.0900  |
| 3  | 3.1992  | 3.2149  | 3.2306  | 3.2464  | 3.2781  |
| 4  | 4.4071  | 4.4399  | 4.4729  | 4.5061  | 4.5731  |
| 5  | 5.6936  | 5.7507  | 5.8083  | 5.8666  | 5.9847  |
| 6  | 7.0637  | 7.1532  | 7.2440  | 7.3359  | 7.5233  |
| 7  | 8.5228  | 8.6540  | 8.7873  | 8.9228  | 9.2004  |
| 8  | 10.0768 | 10.2598 | 10.4463 | 10.6366 | 11.0284 |
| 9  | 11.7318 | 11.9779 | 12.2298 | 12.4875 | 13.0210 |
| 10 | 13.4944 | 13.8164 | 14.1470 | 14.4865 | 15.1929 |
| 11 | 15.3715 | 15.7835 | 16.2081 | 16.6454 | 17.5602 |
| 12 | 17.3707 | 17.8884 | 18.4237 | 18.9771 | 20.1407 |
| 13 | 19.4998 | 20.1406 | 20.8055 | 21.4952 | 22.9533 |
| 14 | 21.7672 | 22.5504 | 23.3659 | 24.2149 | 26.0191 |
| 15 | 24.1821 | 25.1290 | 26.1183 | 27.1521 | 29.3609 |
| 16 | 26.7540 | 27.8880 | 29.0772 | 30.3242 | 33.0033 |
| 17 | 29.4930 | 30.8402 | 32.2580 | 33.7502 | 36.9737 |
| 18 | 32.4100 | 33.9990 | 35.6773 | 37.4502 | 41.3013 |
| 19 | 35.5167 | 37.3789 | 39.3531 | 41.4462 | 46.0184 |
| 20 | 38.8253 | 40.9954 | 43.3046 | 45.7619 | 51.1601 |
| 21 | 42.3489 | 44.8651 | 47.5525 | 50.4229 | 56.7645 |
| 22 | 46.1016 | 49.0057 | 52.1189 | 55.4567 | 62.8733 |
| 23 | 50.0982 | 53.4361 | 57.0278 | 60.8932 | 69.5319 |
| 24 | 54.3546 | 58.1766 | 62.3049 | 66.7647 | 76.7898 |
| 25 | 58.8876 | 63.2490 | 67.9778 | 73.1059 | 84.7008 |
| 26 | 63.7153 | 68.6764 | 74.0762 | 79.9544 | 93.3239 |
| 27 | 68.8568 | 74.4838 | 80.6319 | 87.3507 | 102.7231 |
| 28 | 74.3325 | 80.6976 | 87.6793 | 95.3388 | 112.9682 |
| 29 | 80.1641 | 87.3465 | 95.2552 | 103.9659 | 124.1353 |
| 30 | 86.3748 | 94.4607 | 103.3994 | 113.2832 | 136.3075 |
| 31 | 92.9892 | 102.0730 | 112.1543 | 123.3458 | 149.5752 |
| 32 | 100.0335 | 110.2181 | 121.5659 | 134.2135 | 164.0369 |
| 33 | 107.5357 | 118.9334 | 131.6833 | 145.9506 | 179.8003 |
| 34 | 115.5255 | 128.2587 | 142.5596 | 158.6266 | 196.9823 |
| 35 | 124.0346 | 138.2368 | 154.2516 | 172.3168 | 215.7107 |
| 36 | 133.0969 | 148.9134 | 166.8204 | 187.1021 | 236.1247 |
| 37 | 142.7482 | 160.3374 | 180.3320 | 203.0703 | 258.3759 |
| 38 | 153.0268 | 172.5610 | 194.8569 | 220.3159 | 282.6297 |
| 39 | 163.9736 | 185.6402 | 210.4711 | 238.9412 | 309.0664 |
| 40 | 175.6319 | 199.6351 | 227.2565 | 259.0565 | 337.8824 |
| 41 | 188.0479 | 214.6095 | 245.3007 | 280.7810 | 369.2918 |
| 42 | 201.2711 | 230.6322 | 264.6983 | 304.2435 | 403.5281 |
| 43 | 215.3537 | 247.7764 | 285.5506 | 329.5830 | 440.8456 |
| 44 | 230.3517 | 266.1208 | 307.9669 | 356.9496 | 481.5217 |
| 45 | 246.3245 | 285.7493 | 332.0645 | 386.5056 | 525.8587 |
| 46 | 263.3356 | 306.7517 | 357.9693 | 418.4260 | 574.1860 |
| 47 | 281.4525 | 329.2243 | 385.8170 | 452.9001 | 626.8627 |
| 48 | 300.7469 | 353.2700 | 415.7533 | 490.1321 | 684.2804 |
| 49 | 321.2954 | 378.9989 | 447.9348 | 530.3427 | 746.8656 |
| 50 | 343.1796 | 406.5289 | 482.5299 | 573.7701 | 815.0835 |

Factors shown are for deposits made at the *end of the year;* interest compounded annually. If deposits are made at the beginning of the year, subtract 1 from the factor for the next succeeding year.

## TABLE 5—Continued

| Years | 10% | 11% | 12% | 13% | 14% | 15% |
|---|---|---|---|---|---|---|
| 1 | 1.0000 | 1.0000 | 1.0000 | 1.0000 | 1.0000 | 1.0000 |
| 2 | 2.1000 | 2.1100 | 2.1200 | 2.1300 | 2.1400 | 2.1500 |
| 3 | 3.3100 | 3.3421 | 3.3744 | 3.4069 | 3.4396 | 3.4725 |
| 4 | 4.6410 | 4.7097 | 4.7793 | 4.8497 | 4.9211 | 4.9933 |
| 5 | 6.1051 | 6.2278 | 6.3528 | 6.4802 | 6.6101 | 6.7423 |
| 6 | 7.7156 | 7.9128 | 8.1151 | 8.3227 | 8.5355 | 8.7537 |
| 7 | 9.4871 | 9.7832 | 10.0890 | 10.4046 | 10.7304 | 11.0667 |
| 8 | 11.4358 | 11.8594 | 12.2996 | 12.7572 | 13.2327 | 13.7268 |
| 9 | 13.5794 | 14.1639 | 14.7756 | 15.4157 | 16.0853 | 16.7858 |
| 10 | 15.9374 | 16.7220 | 17.5487 | 18.4197 | 19.3372 | 20.3037 |
| 11 | 18.5311 | 19.5614 | 20.6545 | 21.8143 | 23.0445 | 24.3492 |
| 12 | 21.3842 | 22.7131 | 24.1331 | 25.6501 | 27.2707 | 29.0016 |
| 13 | 24.5227 | 26.2116 | 28.0291 | 29.9847 | 32.0886 | 34.3519 |
| 14 | 27.9749 | 30.0949 | 32.3926 | 34.8827 | 37.5810 | 40.5047 |
| 15 | 31.7724 | 34.4053 | 37.2797 | 40.4174 | 43.8424 | 47.5804 |
| 16 | 35.9497 | 39.1899 | 42.7532 | 46.6717 | 50.9803 | 55.7174 |
| 17 | 40.5447 | 44.5008 | 48.8836 | 53.7390 | 59.1176 | 65.0750 |
| 18 | 45.5991 | 50.3959 | 55.7497 | 61.7251 | 68.3940 | 75.8363 |
| 19 | 51.1590 | 56.9394 | 63.4396 | 70.7494 | 78.9692 | 88.2118 |
| 20 | 57.2749 | 64.2028 | 72.0524 | 80.9468 | 91.0249 | 102.4435 |
| 21 | 64.0024 | 72.2651 | 81.6987 | 92.4699 | 104.7684 | 118.8101 |
| 22 | 71.4027 | 81.2143 | 92.5025 | 105.4910 | 120.4359 | 137.6316 |
| 23 | 79.5430 | 91.1478 | 104.6028 | 120.2048 | 138.2970 | 159.2763 |
| 24 | 88.4973 | 102.1741 | 118.1552 | 136.8314 | 158.6586 | 184.1678 |
| 25 | 98.3470 | 114.4133 | 133.3338 | 155.6195 | 181.8708 | 212.7930 |
| 26 | 109.1817 | 127.9987 | 150.3339 | 176.8500 | 208.3327 | 245.7119 |
| 27 | 121.0999 | 143.0786 | 169.3740 | 200.8406 | 238.4993 | 283.5687 |
| 28 | 134.2099 | 159.8172 | 190.6988 | 227.9498 | 272.8892 | 327.1040 |
| 29 | 148.6309 | 178.3971 | 214.5827 | 258.5833 | 312.0937 | 377.1696 |
| 30 | 164.4940 | 199.0208 | 241.3326 | 293.1992 | 356.7868 | 434.7451 |
| 31 | 181.9434 | 221.9131 | 271.2926 | 332.3151 | 407.7370 | 500.9569 |
| 32 | 201.1377 | 247.3236 | 304.8477 | 376.5160 | 465.8201 | 577.1004 |
| 33 | 222.2515 | 275.5292 | 342.4294 | 426.4631 | 532.0350 | 664.6655 |
| 34 | 245.4766 | 306.8374 | 384.5209 | 482.9033 | 607.5199 | 765.3653 |
| 35 | 271.0243 | 341.5895 | 431.6634 | 546.6808 | 693.5727 | 881.1701 |
| 36 | 299.1268 | 380.1644 | 484.4631 | 618.7493 | 791.6728 | 1014.3456 |
| 37 | 330.0394 | 422.9824 | 543.5986 | 700.1867 | 903.5070 | 1167.4975 |
| 38 | 364.0434 | 470.5105 | 609.8305 | 792.2110 | 1030.9980 | 1343.6221 |
| 39 | 401.4477 | 523.2667 | 684.0101 | 896.1984 | 1176.3378 | 1546.1654 |
| 40 | 442.5925 | 581.8260 | 767.0914 | 1013.7042 | 1342.0250 | 1779.0903 |
| 41 | 487.8518 | 646.8269 | 860.1423 | 1146.4857 | 1530.9086 | 2046.9538 |
| 42 | 537.6369 | 718.9778 | 964.3594 | 1296.5289 | 1746.2358 | 2354.9969 |
| 43 | 592.4006 | 799.0654 | 1081.0826 | 1466.0777 | 1991.7088 | 2709.2464 |
| 44 | 652.6407 | 887.9626 | 1211.8125 | 1657.6678 | 2271.5480 | 3116.6334 |
| 45 | 718.9048 | 986.6385 | 1358.2300 | 1874.1646 | 2590.5647 | 3585.1284 |
| 46 | 791.7953 | 1096.1688 | 1522.2176 | 2118.8060 | 2954.2438 | 4123.8977 |
| 47 | 871.9748 | 1217.7473 | 1705.8837 | 2395.2508 | 3368.8380 | 4743.4823 |
| 48 | 960.1723 | 1352.6995 | 1911.5898 | 2707.6334 | 3841.4753 | 5456.0047 |
| 49 | 1057.1895 | 1502.4965 | 2141.9805 | 3060.6257 | 4380.2818 | 6275.4054 |
| 50 | 1163.9085 | 1668.7711 | 2400.0182 | 3459.5071 | 4994.5213 | 7217.7162 |

Factors shown are for deposits made at the *end of the year;* interest compounded annually. If deposits are made at the beginning of the year, subtract 1 from the factor for the next succeeding year.

# Index